GLOBAL 1968

To our friends

Robert and Elizabeth Nanovic

and

Sharon Konopka

CONTENTS

PART 4. THEN AND NOW

ILLUSTRATIONS AND TABLES

FIGURES

TABLES

PREFACE

This book is the result of a unique international collaboration that began in early 2017. At that time, we decided to take advantage of the impending fiftieth anniversary of the revolutionary events of the year 1968 by bringing experts from around the world to the University of Notre Dame to explore a period that continues to stir the imagination of those who study the topic. Rather than wait to meet for the first time at a conference, we spent more than a year engaging in extended conversations with potential participants from Europe, Latin America, and the United States about how to make a distinctive contribution to the scholarship on this tumultuous time in world history. We discussed many questions: What did we mean by "1968"? When did "1968" begin and end? What topics, cases, and periods should we include? Could one meaningfully speak of a shared "1968 experience" from one country to the next? Or were there multiple 1968s?

These conversations paid off immensely, inspiring us to narrow our project's scope in two ways. First, rather than concentrate on well-traveled approaches to 1968, such as those emphasizing politics and social movements, we decided to concentrate on the issue of cultural revolution. Because we defined the word "culture" in a generous way, this approach had the advantage of encouraging us to include often neglected fields in our planning, such as musicology, film, and photography. Second, we deliberately chose to decenter our approach from the conventional scholarly focus on events in the United States. Instead, we emphasized the experience of 1968 in two other world regions, Latin America and Europe.

Thanks to these early conversations, the participants in our project were already thinking about these themes when they began to write their papers.

We circulated drafts of their papers well before the conference began. As a result, when we finally met as a group at Notre Dame on April 26–28, 2018, for our conference titled "1968 in Europe and Latin America," we had no need for paper presentations or other formalities. We were already prepared to discuss our different approaches to a common subject. By the end of our meeting, our collaboration had paid off. Each of us was prepared to write the chapters in this book in response to a question that came up in all of our conversations: Was 1968 a cultural revolution?

This volume would not have come to fruition without the generous support of many people in the Notre Dame community. The conference was organized by a committee of faculty fellows from the Nanovic Institute for European Studies and the Kellogg Institute for International Studies, the two institutional sponsors of the conference. Aside from the editors, the committee members were William C. Donahue, Jaime M. Pensado, and Carmen-Helena Téllez. The conference also benefited from the cooperation of the DeBartolo Performing Arts Center, the Snite Museum of Art, and the Hesburgh Libraries. Angela Fritz at Notre Dame Archives and our faculty colleague Susan Ohmer worked generously with a team of undergraduate students to create a permanent online exhibition about Notre Dame in 1968. Notre Dame faculty members served as panel chairs and commentators, including Michel Hockx, Peter Casarella, and María Rosa Olivera-Williams. Victoria Langland, Stephen Wrinn, and Ohmer made important contributions to the conference's concluding panel. Above all, the staffs of the Nanovic Institute and the Kellogg Institute did the organizational work required to make this ambitious international event a success. Melanie Webb played a heroic role in arranging all aspects of our participants' visit to Notre Dame and the conference proceedings. She was assisted by many other staff members from the Nanovic and Kellogg Institutes, including Sharon Konopka, Jenn Lechtanski, Monica Caro, and Therese Hanlon. To all of these individuals, we express our deepest gratitude.

We also express our sincere thanks to everyone involved in producing this volume. Cathy Bruckbauer played an instrumental role in organizing all of the chapter submissions. Elaine Yanlin Chen collated the images and illustrations. We are especially grateful to Stephen Wrinn and Rachel Kindler at the University of Notre Dame Press for their enthusiastic support and expert guidance. Rachel worked far beyond the call of duty to help us address all of the technical and organizational issues involved in producing this volume.

We are honored to dedicate this volume to three individuals whose devotion to Notre Dame's students and faculty members has made the Nanovic Institute for European Studies a special place for posing enduring questions about the European past, present, and future: Robert Nanovic, Elizabeth Nanovic, and Sharon Konopka.

A. J. M.

A. P. M.

ONE

Revolutionary 1968

Contending Approaches to an Elusive Concept

A. JAMES McADAMS

Why should we study the revolutions of 1968 today? At first glance, the answer to this question seems self-evident. Looking back on the tumultuous events that transpired more than a half century ago, one can hardly avoid raising the topic of revolution. Over the extended period that we associate with this year—roughly the mid-1960s to the early 1970s—this was a time of intense confrontation between the new and the old. During these years, societies were engulfed by conflicts over every seemingly incontestable convention and practice. Students and workers protested against what they viewed as the unjust and corrupt institutions that held sway over their lives. Intellectuals and activists demanded that the ruling classes address systematic discrimination against marginalized social and political groups. Writers and filmmakers experimented with controversial themes and innovative forms of artistic expression. Remarkably, this explosive assault on the perspectives and practices that preceding generations had taken for granted was not limited to specific political systems, countries, or continents. It was a global phenomenon. In the words of Paul Berman, a student radical at Columbia University in 1968, "the weird quality of 1968 was the way that, for the first time since 1848, things took place nearly simultaneously all over the world."[1]

Because of this striking conjunction of events, scholars across a wide range of disciplines, from the social sciences to literature and the arts, have sought to capture the manifold dimensions of this period by speaking of the "Long '60s."[2] In fact, some observers contend that these years marked the transition to a new age. Historian Arthur Marwick concluded his landmark study *The Sixties* with the following pronouncement. These years, he remarked, were "no transient time of ecstasy and excess, fit only for nostalgia or contempt." In Marwick's judgment, "there has been nothing like it." And, he added, "Nothing [will] ever be quite the same again."[3] Other scholars have come to similar conclusions. For a group of German and American historians writing in the late 1990s, these events were evidence of "a world transformed."[4] Even onlookers who view these developments negatively have not disputed their influence. For the political theorist Harvey C. Mansfield Jr., "the late sixties were a comprehensive disaster," an epoch, it seems, that is best expunged from liberal democratic society "like a powerful toxic waste."[5] In a campaign speech on April 29, 2007, the center-right French politician Nicolas Sarkozy declared that the memory of 1968 should be "liquidated" for having imposed "intellectual and moral relativism" on his country.[6] Two weeks later, Sarkozy was elected France's president.

Nevertheless, however contemporary scholars assess the events of the 1960s, positively or negatively, they must all confront an unavoidable question. Given the vast body of scholarship that already exists on the topic, are there issues on which there remains significant room for disagreement? The most fruitful way of responding to this challenge is to treat it as three separate questions: Can a given event or activity legitimately be called "revolutionary"? Has the event had the transformative effect that we typically associate with revolutions? Was this event a manifestation of a unitary set of developments, that is, evidence of a *universal* 1968?

The first question requires us to set the parameters of the term "revolution." In the tradition of social theorists from Max Weber to Émile Durkheim, a revolutionary act is necessarily destructive. Unlike most challenges to authority, its instigators seek to overturn entrenched institutions, roles, and ideas and replace them with new ways of thinking and acting. In line with this approach, revolutionary events have been, if not frequent, at least recurrent features of the modern era. All of the best-known cases between the late eighteenth and early twentieth centuries, including the North American, French, and Bolshevik revolutions, took the form of full-scale assaults on the status quo. Their proponents reveled in the opportunity to overthrow long-standing aristocratic regimes, upend seemingly impregnable class and social structures, and introduce new conceptions of justice and human worth.

In 1848, Karl Marx captured the cataclysmic nature of revolutions in a vivid passage in the *Communist Manifesto*. "All fixed, fast-frozen relations," he wrote, "with their train of ancient and venerable prejudices and opinions are swept away, all new-formed ones become antiquated before they can ossify. All that is solid melts into air."[7] Writing 170 years later, the American sociologist Todd Gitlin made virtually the same observation about 1968. The "sheer number, pace, volume, and intensity of the shocks, delivered worldwide to living room screens," he noted, "made the world look and feel as though it was falling apart. It's fair to say that if you weren't destabilized, you weren't paying attention."[8]

In this spirit, many of the first generation of scholars working on the upheavals of the 1960s focused their attention on the high-visibility events and themes involving political conflict and the exercise of political power.[9] By itself, the year 1968 was a time of direct and often violent confrontation between governments and citizens. Students at the Sorbonne in Paris seized control of the university and the stock exchange and engaged in fierce street battles with the police. Millions of workers joined these protests, conducting both organized and wildcat strikes and occupying factories, and they eventually declared a general strike. In June, a less violent, but equally consequential, assault on established authority took place in a different part of the continent, Eastern Europe. Under much more difficult political conditions, sixty-one writers, artists, intellectuals, and scientists published a bold manifesto, "Two Thousand Words to Workers, Farmers, Scientists, Artists, and Everyone," that effectively questioned the legitimacy of Communist Party rule. The manifesto's signatories demanded rights and freedoms that extended significantly beyond the cautious political reforms then underway under Communist Party leader Alexander Dubček in Czechoslovakia.[10]

On the other side of the Atlantic, protests swept across Latin America throughout the summer months of 1968. Brazilian students, artists, and Roman Catholic clergy took to the streets, demanding an end to the restrictions and human rights violations of the military dictatorship. In Venezuela, the Movement for the Reform of the University campaigned for progressive forms of academic governance and for freedom of the press. In Argentina, an unlikely alliance of students, workers, and local business owners shut down a section of the country's second largest city, Córdoba, in protest against the Onganía military dictatorship. Tragically, on the eve of the 1968 Olympic Games in October, the Mexican army and police forces violently responded to a massive antigovernment rally in the Tlatelolco section of Mexico City, killing hundreds of university students and arresting thousands of others.

It is one thing to argue that these events bore revolutionary traits, but in addressing them it is more difficult to provide satisfactory answers to the second question about 1968. Did these instances of political and social defiance have a lasting effect on established institutions and ways of thinking? To answer this question, we need to begin by keeping these events in historical perspective. Arguably, the consequences of these challenges to the status quo pale in comparison with the revolutions in North America and France at the end of the eighteenth century and in Russia at the beginning of the twentieth. The grand revolutions of these eras precipitated decades of sustained violence and social disorientation. During these tumultuous periods, American and European revolutionaries went far beyond the overthrow of the rulers of the old regimes. They laid the groundwork for thoroughgoing changes in elite attitudes about the nature of the just society. At the same time, they emboldened their populations to think in new ways about the state's responsibility to its citizens.

In contrast, the challenge of assessing the political influence of 1968 in Europe and the Americas is more elusive. For example, students occupied university administration buildings across the United States, attempting to use these institutions as platforms to call for the withdrawal of U.S. troops from Vietnam and to support the civil rights movement. However, their actions were short-lived and ineffective. University leaders often responded with punitive measures. Moreover, in these and many other cases of political protest, the activists inadvertently generated greater public support for the politicians and policymakers they opposed. "What haunted America," Gitlin observed about the years that followed, "was not the misty specter of revolution but the solidifying specter of reaction."[11]

In Latin America, widespread protest and rebellion caught the world's attention, but they failed to produce an opening of the political arena. In many countries, they had the opposite effect. They provided authoritarian leaders with the ammunition they needed to defend the status quo. In 1968, Mexico's ruling party, the Institutional Revolutionary Party (Partido Revolucionario Institucional, PRI) was rocked by the strikes and protests of nearly every segment of the population, including workers, students, merchants, and peasants. Yet the regime successfully held on to power for another thirty-two years. Elsewhere in Latin America, the consequences were devastating. Across the continent, military *juntas* came to power, using the supposed threat from left-wing groups and communist sympathizers as a pretext for mass repression. Both actively and tacitly, the rulers of these dictatorships were complicit in the killing of tens of thousands of people. To be sure, democracy returned to these states in the 1980s and 1990s, but this transition took place under circumstances—gradual reform and negotiated transitions—that had little to do with the revolutionary spirit of the late 1960s. In many cases, the victory of democracy was only possible because the rising elites reached an understanding with their predecessors that they would not hold accountable those who were responsible for past crimes and abuses.

In the Soviet Bloc, the effect of independent political activity was even less evident. After the collapse of Dubček's experiment with socialist reform following the Soviet invasion of Czechoslovakia in August 1968, more than a decade passed before the possibility of systemic reform took hold in a single Eastern Bloc country, Poland. The prospect of more sweeping changes became conceivable only after Soviet leader Mikhail Gorbachev endorsed the idea of socialist transformation in the second half of the 1980s. In the interim, a small number of Eastern European and Soviet dissidents demanded that their governments adhere to the human rights guarantees and legal protections that were formally included in their countries' constitutions. With the exception of opposition elements in Poland, however, their influence on their governments was negligible. In this respect, when these regimes fell during the revolutions of 1989–91 and a new generation of postcommunist leaders actively committed themselves to democratic principles and the protection of basic freedoms, the dissidents' protests were largely no more than antecedents to these changes, rather than their causes.[12]

In fact, if one uses the political behavior of the aging American and European '68 generation of the 2010s and 2020s as a measure, one might reasonably conclude that there has been a regression in the era's vociferously democratic ideals. More than fifty years on, segments of the same demographic stratum that once demanded that its leaders adhere to liberal democratic norms, respect diverse political views, and treat all people as equals cast their votes for neo-authoritarian populist parties in Western Europe, the formerly communist Eastern Europe, Latin America, and the United States. One does not need to look hard to find antidemocratic elected officials in nearly every advanced democracy. Interestingly, the repudiation of "1968" has become an explicit component of the platforms of many of these groups.[13] Additionally, it is a striking indication of how much the political climate has changed since the late 1960s and 1970s that even some of the era's most visible personalities have expressed doubt about their achievements. In an interview in 2003, Daniel Cohn-Bendit, the charismatic symbol of the French student rebellion, conceded as much. The man once known as "Dany le Rouge" acknowledged that the period had become less relevant to current times. "In the late '60s," Cohn-Bendit observed, "the world began to change, and we have a completely different world today. The legacy of 1968 is very difficult, because if you say, 'Do you think you can do politics like you did in the '60s?,' I'd say no. If you say, 'Do you think that '68 had an influence on the world of today?,' I'd say no, except that it changed the world so that we have another world today."[14]

In light of the ambiguous political influence of these developments, a second generation of scholars has gravitated toward a broader treatment of 1968 as a possible "cultural revolution."[15] The contributors to this volume take this approach. Admittedly, the term "culture" is notoriously difficult to pin down. In the foundational study of the subject, Alfred Kroeber and Clyde Kluckhohn provided a definition of the term that covers an enormous range of subjects related to the human experience. "Culture," they argue, "consists of patterns, explicit and implicit, of and for behavior acquired and transmitted by symbols, constituting the distinctive achievements of human groups."[16] Nonetheless, there is a major advantage to the concept's breadth. The focus on cultural change allows us to look beyond the themes of political power and domination to explore potentially enduring shifts in values, beliefs, life styles, and artistic sensibilities. By taking this approach, we are also free to examine topics that are frequently neglected in studies of revolutionary change, such as in educational policy, musical composition, work and family life, sexuality, and religious practice. Moreover, this focus alerts us to the possibility that cultural change, when it occurs, may have a deeper and longer-lasting effect than political change. One can readily imagine cases where the fall of political institutions is not accompanied by a fundamental shift in values. Conversely, when people's ways of viewing the world are transformed, their political perspectives will almost certainly be affected. Demands for institutional change may follow shortly thereafter.

The second advantage of the focus on culture is that it, too, provides opportunities for ongoing scholarly research. Arguably, the search for alternatives to the status quo in the 1960s was not a passing phenomenon. Its enthusiasts raised questions about the human experience that are as salient in the contemporary world as they were a half century ago. Importantly, there also remains ample room for disagreement about the influence of their activities. To appreciate these differences, let us consider three of the most prominent examples of cultural change in the era: the reinterpretation of religious practices, the reassessment of gender roles, and the rejection of established norms of social behavior.

One of the most profound changes in the Long '60s was in the public profile of the Roman Catholic Church. Beginning with Vatican II (1962–65) and spreading quickly throughout the Catholic world, religious officials, parish clergy, and laypersons posed searching questions about the relationship between the institutional Church and its followers. In Latin America and Europe, liberation theologians, such as Hélder Câmara in Brazil, Gustavo Gutiérrez in Peru, and Jon Sabrino in Spain, championed radical ideas (e.g., the "preferential option for the poor") and underscored the spiritual obligation of religious leaders to be responsive to the struggles of the downtrodden. The historical significance of the ensuing conflict between the traditional and radical wings of the Church over these theological innovations is incontestable.

Just the same, the influence of liberation theology remains open to debate. From one perspective, the verdict is sobering. For decades, critics regarded the failure of Church authorities on the European and American continents to condemn their countries' military dictatorships in the 1970s as proof that the institutional Church was impervious to change. From a contemporary standpoint, however, one can come to a more sanguine judgment. The ideas of the leftist theologians of the 1960s have become an established feature of Catholic thinking about the Church's role and mission throughout Latin America. The election of a sympathetic Argentine cardinal, Jorge Mario Bergoglio, to the papacy in 2013 lends substance to the argument that the revolutionary thinking of the 1960s has had an enduring importance.[17]

In the same way, the depiction of this period as a cultural revolution calls attention to changing perceptions of gender roles. Student movements in West Germany and the United States provided the context in which activists could address the practical implications of controversial perspectives in the works of writers such as Betty Friedan and Simone de Beauvoir about gender equality, sexual discrimination, and the treatment of mothers. Ultimately, these were questions about the meaning of human identity and its openness to redefinition. Yet here, too, there is room for debate over the influence of these ideas. Observers looking for evidence of the long-term effects of this reassessment of traditional roles might find it in the proliferation of women's organizations in later years and increased participation by women in politics and public life in the 2000s. Of all of the attempts to transform social structures, Jeremy Rabkin has provocatively argued, "feminism alone has maintained the fires of sixties radicalism."[18] In contrast, skeptics can argue that continuing wage inequality and the scarcity of women in corporate leadership positions is an indication of the uneven influence of an earlier generation's ideals. Nonetheless, there do seem to have been significant changes in attitudes about gender relations. The efficacy of the global #MeToo movement of the late 2010s against sexual assault and harassment demonstrates that issues that appeared radical one half century ago have become an accepted feature of mainstream discourse.

Finally, the Long '60s were marked by the unabashed desire to expose the arbitrary foundations of all forms of authority and, to borrow Marx's words again, to overturn "all fixed, fast-frozen relations with their train of ancient and venerable prejudices and opinions." In particular, activists extended the principle of freedom of thought and action beyond the realm of politics to the cultivation of alternative lifestyles, habits of speech and dress, and experimentation in literature, music, and the arts. From one perspective, this openness to countercultural attitudes and behavior has had an enduring effect on the sentiments and dispositions of later generations. To cite a mundane, but revealing, example, we would like to think that we no longer live in a world in which the proprietor of a restaurant would throw a young woman out of a window for wearing a miniskirt. When this event occurred in Zurich in 1967, it was a sign of the rigid conventions of the times that public officials agreed to condemn the owner only after university students staged angry demonstrations.[19] Still, even if this particular event would be less likely today, the desirability of overturning established cultural norms remains less than straightforward. The French government's ban on the wearing of face-covering veils in public places in the 2000s is an instructive example of the potentially paradoxical application of the principle of social tolerance. In the eyes of human rights activists, the clothing rule is necessary to combat the denial of basic freedoms to women. In contrast, many Muslims, including women, regard the ban as an act of religious intolerance.

Beyond the debates over how one defines and then assesses the importance of the events of 1968, one must also wrestle with a third question about the era: Were the revolutionary events of the 1960s a unitary phenomenon? On one level, this is a simple matter of periodization. Marwick defines the 1960s as roughly the years 1958 to 1974.[20] George Will suggests that the era extended from November 1963 (the assassination of JFK) until October 1973 (the Yom Kippur War and the global energy crisis).[21] Yet, the more challenging task behind this question is to identify commonalities in the lived experiences of individuals who were active during these tumultuous times. One possibility is that the radical thinkers and countercultural activists in the Americas and Europe shared enough in common to allow one to speak of a "1968 experience," or even a "universal 1968." Conversely, another possibility is that their differences were so significant from one continent, country, or locale to the next that one should speak instead of multiple 1968s. Depending on the issue, one can make convincing arguments to support each perspective.

On the one hand, one can make a strong case for the shared quality of these experiences by emphasizing the theme of generational conflict. From West Berlin to Berkeley, Paris, and Mexico City, a transnational cohort of young people declared itself at odds with the traditions of its parents and grandparents. In the spirit of the rallying cry of the protesting

Parisian students in 1968, *il est interdit d'interdire* ("it is forbidden to forbid"), these new social actors asserted their right as freethinking persons to make autonomous decisions about their lives. The French novelist and cultural theorist André Malraux may have set the threshold too high when he attributed this rebellious spirit to a single factor: the death of God.[22] But at least two of the causes of protest and cultural experimentation were the same across the continents. Western Europe, the United States, and Latin America had in common the first relatively affluent and educated generation to come out of the post–World War II era. Sharing both the rising expectations of a burgeoning middle class and adolescent anxieties about an uncertain future, students in rapidly expanding and overcrowded universities were presented—much like Marx's proletariat in the factories of nineteenth-century England—with plentiful opportunities to exchange countercultural ideas and militant objectives that were distinctly at odds with their upbringings. When their universities' leaders refused to give in to their demands and their governments responded with hostility and repression, they took their grievances into the streets.[23]

In addition, spectacular advances in communications technology in the 1960s had an indisputable unifying effect. The revolution of 1968 was literally televised. In the comfort of their living rooms, middle-class viewers took part vicariously in the latest developments in the space race, reveled in musical performances by the Beatles and the Rolling Stones, and developed personal impressions of the most prominent figures of the age, among them Charles de Gaulle, Pope Paul VI, and Che Guevara. At the same time, they were front-row witnesses to the brutal suppression of street demonstrations in Berlin, Chicago, Rio de Janeiro, and especially Mexico City. They were horrified by the loss of life on all sides in the Vietnam War. The broadcast of Eddie Adams's photograph of the execution of a Vietcong prisoner by Saigon's police chief was truly "a shot heard round the world."[24]

On the other hand, one can make an equally strong case that the spirit of 1968 was not a unitary experience. From one country to the next, the challenge to the status quo took significantly different forms. In Western Europe, generational conflict took place in the context of agonizing debates about the character of postwar liberal democracy, which by this point had taken hold in every country on the continent, with the exception of the three countries still under dictatorial rule (Greece, Portugal, and Spain). In West Germany in particular, students condemned their parents' failure to live up to the duty to address the barbarous crimes of National Socialism. In their eyes, their leaders' inaction proved that German democracy was a sham. For many young militants, only a defiant "long march through the institutions," the activist Rudi Dutschke's cryptic reference to Mao Zedong's armed struggle for survival in the 1930s, would suffice to force the German people to come to terms with their sordid past. In the 1970s, some of these radicals expressed their indignation through senseless acts of violence and terrorism.[25]

In Eastern Europe, dissent took a very different form. Because of the sobering lessons of the Soviet invasion of Czechoslovakia, would-be challengers to the socialist establishment, such as Václav Havel, the playwright and future president of postcommunist Czechoslovakia, pragmatically chose to voice their discontent in unconventional and less explicitly provocative ways. They used theatrical performances to spread antiestablishment ideas, played in nonconformist rock and roll bands, and fostered a subtly subversive film culture. Likewise, dissident groups throughout the Soviet Bloc engaged in their own creative efforts to "live within the truth" (Havel) by engaging in similarly unorthodox forms of protest and artistic ingenuity.[26] By the end of the 1980s, these contrarian ideas had become so ingrained in popular culture that they were vividly represented in the protests surrounding the fall of East European communism.

In Latin America, the expression of discontent took different forms than in both parts of Europe. In particular, the continent's traditions of protest had much deeper historical roots, reaching back to the era of colonial exploitation, the existence of unjust economic institutions, such as the hacienda system, the experience of decades of dictatorial rule, and repeated U.S. military interventions. As a result, more than in Europe, critics focused their demands for change directly on issues of class, race, poverty, and imperialism. In creative ways, novelists such as Mario Vargas Llosa (Peru), Gabriel García Márquez (Colombia), and Carlos Fuentes (Mexico) called their readers' attention to the profound inequalities and ingrained injustices of their societies and warned about the creeping hand of authoritarianism. They and other writers attacked their governments for courting U.S. corporate and military interests; some looked to the Cuban Revolution for fresh ideas about social equality and community engagement, and to the Non-Aligned Movement.

Despite the differences among these cases, it would be a mistake to assume that these manifestations of nonconformist behavior and social dissent were necessarily isolated events. In the twenty-first century, an impressive body of scholarship has emerged that focuses on the events of the 1960s from the perspective of global history. Eric Zolov, a scholar of Latin American history, has provided a succinct description of this approach. The study of the global 1960s, he writes, "reflects a new conceptual approach to understanding local change within a transnational framework, one constituted by multiple crosscurrents of geopolitical, ideological, cultural, and economic forces. Such forces produced a 'simultaneity,' of 'like' responses across disparate geographical contexts, suggesting interlocking causes."[27]

This global historical approach has many advantages. Unlike earlier scholarly approaches, it encourages us to step outside the conventional frames of reference of Cold War studies and neoliberal economics and consider forms of behavior, such as the activities of nonstate actors and local communities. It also calls our attention to the international networks that brought together the lives of discontented individuals on multiple continents. During the Long '60s, idealistic Latin American students in universities in Europe and the United States experimented with remarkably similar types of living arrangements and musical and fashion styles. Much like scholars attending international conferences abroad, many of these young radicals traveled to other countries to meet their peers. In the process, they acquired organizational skills that they brought back home. Similarly, international organizations, such as the Non-Aligned Movement and the Catholic Church, provided transcontinental forums for politicians, activist priests, and intellectuals to exchange perspectives on contending ideologies and strategies for effecting social change. In these fecund times, the most fruitful interactions were frequently the result of the initiatives of single persons. In Medellín, Colombia, in 1968, an innovative gallerist, Leonel Estrada, generated electric debates over the latest trends in conceptual art, abstractionism, and pop art by exhibiting the works of contemporary artists from all over Latin America, among them Sarah Grilo, Santiago Cárdenas, Bernardo Salcedo, and Fernando Szyszlo. In 1970, he expanded these international exchanges to include European artists.[28]

In addition, the focus on the global '60s encourages scholars to study the indirect ways in which new ideas and attitudes transected the continents. Historian Victoria Langland has coined the term "aspirational connections" to capture the extent to which students, artists, and intellectuals in one part of the world were inspired simply by learning about the contemporaneous activities of radicals in countries they had never visited. Under different circumstances and without having the specific ideologies, approaches, or techniques, they sought to apply the example of their peers' fortitude and creativity to their own movements.[29] In this spirit, they shared a mutual, if tacitly felt, sense of mission. They had both the opportunity and the obligation to contribute to the betterment of humanity.

In these respects, the idea of a global 1968 has many advantages. Nonetheless, whenever one broadens the scope of a topic, one must also be careful not to burden it with more weight than it can bear. It is indisputable that the second half of the 1960s was a disruptive and tumultuous time for countries and peoples around the world. However, this does not mean that one can use a concept such as the global '60s to account for all of these events effectively. To take an illustrative example, the title Mao Zedong gave to China's Great Proletarian Cultural Revolution (GPCR) contained all of the words one could find in a typical student demonstration in Berlin or Mexico City in 1968. Nevertheless, although many youthful protesters found the colorful language and images of the GPCR attractive, this does not mean that Mao's objectives in launching a wave of recrimination and violence against millions of his fellow citizens over these years will yield particularly fruitful comparisons. Indeed, if not undertaken with sufficient care, such broad-brush comparisons can lead to highly misleading conclusions.

For the same reason, conceptual stretching can inadvertently make comparative scholarship more difficult. For example, in an important work, one expert suggests that "1968 in the global imagination was about many different things. The most one may generalize is that it was not primarily about revolution, or class struggle, or even feminism. It was about autonomy, very often personal and individual rather than collective."[30] As sensible as this claim may seem at first glance, however, the substitution of a nearly all-encompassing concept such as "autonomy" for a narrower concept such as "revolution" may lead to less useful generalizations than one desires.

1968 IN LATIN AMERICA AND EUROPE

This volume seeks to make a fresh contribution to our understanding of the Long '60s by "bringing the revolution back in." It aims to accomplish this by approaching the topic of cultural revolution in two distinctive ways. First, the contributors focus primarily on the experience of 1968 on two continents, Europe and Latin America, in contrast to most studies of the period that use the United States as their principal point of reference. Of course, no one will deny the importance of the revolutionary events of the era in Berkeley, New York, and other U.S. cities and their substantial influence on world politics, social relations, and cultural attitudes. One could legitimately argue that the events of 1968 would not have had the same transnational significance without the hegemonic influence of these ideas and events. Still, the shortcoming of studies that concentrate on the United States and, in some cases, a limited number of Western European countries—primarily France, Britain, and Germany—is that they make it more difficult to acquire a comprehensive understanding of the period.[31] For example, one of the consequences of this approach has been the relative neglect of themes that do not relate directly to U.S.-centric topics such as superpower tensions, the civil rights movement, and the war in Vietnam. The neglected topics include the transnational influence of the Catholic Church, the Non-Aligned Movement, the allure of guerrilla warfare, and class conflict. Moreover, the emphasis on the U.S. experience undoubtedly accounts for the comparatively few studies of the experience of the Long '60s in the former Soviet Bloc, southern Europe, and Latin America. In these respects, this volume seeks to be a needed corrective.

Second, this volume is deliberately interdisciplinary. In contrast to the many books about the Long '60s that emphasize political and social change, our contributors give greater standing to often neglected disciplinary approaches to this dynamic era. These include revolutionary developments in photography, musicology, film, and literature.[32] We also include understudied subjects, such as educational reform and the refusal to work. Making this interdisciplinary approach even richer, we begin and end with the personal reflections of two individuals whose lives were shaped by the events of 1968. One, film director Volker Schlöndorff, was directly involved in the revolutionary events of the period. The other, politician and social scientist Ignacio Walker, is a representative of the generation that inherited the memory of this time and the opportunity to act on its lessons.

The reader will discover that this volume's contributors do not always agree about how to assess the topic of cultural revolution in the 1960s. In many cases, they have opposing views, both subtle and significant, about the issues I have raised here: the proper definition of a revolutionary event, the challenge of assessing its influence, and the meaning of 1968 in its respective domestic and international contexts. To return to the question with which I began this chapter—Why should we study the revolutions of 1968 today?—these differences are welcome news. They mean that for years to come, we will still find many good reasons for continuing to wrestle with the remarkable events and ideas of the Long '60s.

NOTES

I am grateful to Patrice McSherry, Michael Seidman, Carmen-Helena Téllez, Anthony Monta, Monica Caro, and Eric Zolov for their helpful comments on this chapter.

1. Paul Berman, *A Tale of Two Utopias: The Political Journey of the Generation of 1968* (New York: W. W. Norton, 1997), cited in *Independent*, April 23, 2008.

2. For example, Christopher B. Strain, *The Long Sixties: America, 1955–1973* (Hoboken, NJ: Wiley-Blackwell, 2016).

3. Arthur Marwick, *The Sixties: Cultural Revolution in Britain, France, Italy and the United States, c. 1958–c. 1974* (London: Bloomsbury Reader, 1998), 730.

4. Carole Fink, Philipp Gassert, and Detlef Junker, *1968: The World Transformed* (New York: Cambridge University Press, 1998).

5. Harvey C. Mansfield Jr., "The Legacy of the Late Sixties," in *Reassessing the Sixties*, ed. Stephen Macedo (New York: W. W. Norton, 1997), 21, 45. Mansfield's chapter focuses on the United States, but this also seems to be his judgment about these events in the rest of the world.

6. *The Telegraph*, April 29, 2008.

7. Karl Marx and Friedrich Engels, "Manifesto of the Communist Party," in *The Marx-Engels Reader*, ed. Robert Tucker (New York: W. W. Norton, 1978), 476.

8. Todd Gitlin, "1968: Year of Counter-Revolution," *New York Review of Books*, May 8, 2018, https://www.nybooks.com/daily/2018/05/08/1968-year-of-counter-revolution/.

9. For example, Samuel Huntington, *American Politics: The Promise of Disharmony* (Cambridge, MA: Harvard University Press, 1983), chap. 7; Todd Gitlin, *The Whole World Is Watching* (Berkeley: University of California Press, 1980); Ronald Fraser, *1968: A Student Generation in Revolt* (London: Chatto

and Windus, 1988); Robert V. Daniels, *Year of the Heroic Guerrilla: World Revolution and Counterrevolution in 1968* (New York: Basic Books, 1989).

10. See A. James McAdams, *Vanguard of the Revolution: The Global Idea of the Communist Party* (Princeton, NJ: Princeton University Press, 2017), 393.

11. Gitlin, "1968: Year of Counter-Revolution."

12. I address the causes in McAdams, *Vanguard of the Revolution*, chap. 22.

13. On this theme, see Thomas Wagner, *Die Angstmacher: 1968 und die Neuen Rechten* (Berlin: Aufbau Verlag, 2017).

14. Caleb Daniloff, "'Dany the Red' on Student Revolutions, Then and Now: 1968 European Agitator Speaks at SMG Tonight," *BU Today*, March 18, 2008, http://www.bu.edu/today/2008/%E2%80%9Cdany-the-red%E2%80%9D-on-student-revolutions-then-and-now/.

15. Marwick, *The Sixties*, 3–19.

16. A. L. Kroeber and C. Kluckhohn, *Culture: A Critical Review of Concepts and Definitions* (Cambridge, MA: Peabody Museum, 1952), 181.

17. For evidence that this struggle over the Catholic Church's identity in the 1960s has extended into the twenty-first century, compare Ross Douthat, *To Change the Church: Pope Francis and the Future of Catholicism* (New York: Simon & Schuster, 2018), with James Chappel, *Catholic Modern: The Challenge of Totalitarianism and the Remaking of the Church* (Cambridge, MA: Harvard University Press, 2018).

18. Jeremy Rabkin, "Feminism: Where the Spirit of the Sixties Lives on," in Macedo, ed., *Reassessing the Sixties*, 47. Notwithstanding this seemingly positive assertion about the feminist movement, Rabkin's overall assessment is decidedly negative. "Feminism finally seems to have carried on for too long for the awe and respect it received for decades." "It still faces no solemn patriarchs in its path," he declares, "but it is having difficulty responding to the mirthful mockery of [its critics]" (74).

19. Ironically, this event took place at the Café Odeon in Zurich, the countercultural haunt of such iconoclastic figures as James Joyce, Lenin, and various Dadaist artists; see David Eugster and Lena Rentsch, "When Zurich's New Left Rode the Pop Culture Revolution," swissinfo.ch, April 16, 2018, https://www.swissinfo.ch/eng/business/social-upheavals_when-the-new-left-tried-to-ride-the-miniskirt-revolution/44017600.

20. Marwick, *The Sixties*, 7.

21. George Will, "Foreword," in Macedo, ed., *Reassessing the Sixties*, 4.

22. Cited in Peter Steinfels, "Paris 1968: The Revolution That Never Was," *New York Times*, May 11, 2008.

23. Michael Seidman, *The Imaginary Revolution: Parisian Students and Workers* (New York: Berghahn Books, 2004), 19–20.

24. On the effect of such iconic images, see Willem Melching's analysis in chapter 13 of this volume.

25. On this topic, see Volker Schlöndorff's reflections about the influence of 1968 in chapter 2.

26. On the challenge of "living within the truth," see Václav Havel, "The Power of the Powerless," in *The Power of the Powerless: Citizens against the State in Central Eastern Europe*, ed. John Keane (Armonk, NY: M. E. Sharpe, 1985), 23–96.

27. Eric Zolov, "Latin America in the Global Sixties," *The Americas* 70, no. 3 (2014): 354. Among the many important works that are representative of this historiography, see Wolfgang Kraushaar, "Die erste globale Rebellion," in *1968 als Mythos, Chiffre und Zäsur* (Hamburg: Hamburger Edition, 2000), 19; Jeremy Suri, *Power and Protest: Global Revolution and the Rise of Détente* (Cambridge, MA: Harvard University Press, 2005); and Jian Chen et al., eds., *The Routledge Handbook of the Global Sixties: Between Protest and Nation-Building* (New York: Routledge, 2018).

28. Alexa Halaby, "The 1968, 1970, and 1972 Coltejer Art Biennials: Six Years of Cultural Revolution in Medellín, Colombia," https://www.guggenheim.org/blogs/map/the-1968-1970-and-1972-coltejer-art-biennials-six-years-of-cultural-revolution-in-medellin-colombia.

29. Victoria Langland, "Transnational Connections of the Global Sixties as seen by an Historian of Brazil," in Jian et al., eds., *The Routledge Handbook of the Global Sixties*, 20.

30. Odd Arne Westad, "Preface: Was There a 'Global 1968?,'" in Jian et al., eds. *The Routledge Handbook of the Global Sixties*, xxii.

31. For example, Marwick only considers four countries in his massive 800-page volume: France, the United States, Great Britain, and Italy. He has nothing to say about the Southern Hemisphere or the communist world. Only one chapter of *1968: The World Transformed* addresses the countries of the global South; this short chapter, "The Third World" by the eminent China scholar Arif Dirlik, is devoted to multiple, manifestly different cases, including the People's Republic of China, India, Turkey, and Mexico. See *1968*, 295–317. *The Routledge Handbook* is an exception. Its contributors cover literally every region in the world. A potential—though not inevitable—pitfall of this all-inclusive approach is that although anything can be compared, not all comparisons are equally useful.

32. A similar, interdisciplinary approach is taken by the contributors in Daniel J. Sherman, Ruud van Dijk, Jasmine Alinder, and A. Aneesh, eds., *The Long 1968: Revisions and New Perspectives* (Bloomington: Indiana University Press, 2013).

BIBLIOGRAPHY

Barr-Melej, Patrick. *Psychedelic Chile: Youth, Counterculture, and Politics on the Road to Socialism and Dictatorship*. Chapel Hill: University of North Carolina Press, 2017.

Berman, Paul. *A Tale of Two Utopias: The Political Journey of the Generation of 1968*. New York: W. W. Norton, 1997.

Cueto, Alonso. *The Blue Hour*. London: Random House, 2014.

Daniels, Robert V. *Year of the Heroic Guerrilla: World Revolution and Counterrevolution in 1968*. New York: Basic Books, 1989.

Davis, Belinda, W. Mausbach, M. Klimke, and C. MacDougall, eds. *Changing the World, Changing Oneself: Political Protest and Collective Identities in the 1960s/70s West Germany and U.S.* New York: Berghahn Books, 2010, 2012.

De Giuseppe, Massimo. *L'altra America: I cattolici italiani e l'America latina. Da Medellín a Francesco*. Brescia: Morcelliana, 2017.

Donahue, William C. *Holocaust as Fiction: Bernhard Schlink's "Nazi" Novels and Their Films*. New York: Palgrave/Macmillan, 2010.

Drott, Eric. *Music and the Elusive Revolution: Cultural Politics and Political Culture in France, 1968–1981*. Berkeley: University of California Press, 2011.

Fink, Carole, Philipp Gassert, and Detlef Junker. *1968: The World Transformed*. New York: Cambridge University Press, 1998.

Fraser, Ronald. *1968: A Student Generation in Revolt*. London: Chatto and Windus, 1988.

Gitlin, Todd. *The Whole World Is Watching*. Berkeley: University of California Press, 1980.

Huntington, Samuel. *American Politics: The Promise of Disharmony*. Cambridge, MA: Harvard University Press, 1983.

Jian, Chen, Martin Klimke, Masha Kirasirova, Mary Nolan, Marilyn Young, and Joanna Waley-Cohen, eds. *The Routledge Handbook of the Global Sixties: Between Protest and Nation-Building*. New York: Routledge, 2018.

Kurlansky, Mark. *1968: The Year That Rocked the World*. New York: Random House, 2005.

McAdams, A. James. *Vanguard of the Revolution: The Global Idea of the Communist Party*. Princeton, NJ: Princeton University Press, 2017.

McSherry, J. Patrice. *Chilean New Song: The Political Power of Music, 1960s–1973*. Philadelphia: Temple University Press, 2015.

Macedo, Stephan, ed. *Reassessing the Sixties*. New York: W. W. Norton, 1997.

Manzano, Valeria. *The Age of Youth in Argentina: Culture, Politics, and Sexuality from Perón to Videla*. Chapel Hill: University of North Carolina Press, 2014.

Markarian, Vania. *Uruguay, 1968: Student Activism from Global Counterculture to Molotov Cocktails*. Berkeley: University of California Press, 2016.

Marwick, Arthur. *The Sixties: Cultural Revolution in Britain, France, Italy and the United States, c. 1958–c. 1974*. London: Bloomsbury Reader, 1998.

Melching, Willem. *Main Trends in Cultural History: Ten Essays*. Vienna: Met Wyger, 1994.

Pensado, Jaime, and Enrique C. Ochoa, eds. *México Beyond 1968: Revolutionaries, Radicals, and Repression during the Global Sixties and Subversive Seventies*. Tucson: University of Arizona Press, 2018.

Ryback, Timothy. *Rock around the Bloc: A History of Rock Music in Eastern Europe and the Soviet Union, 1954–1988*. Oxford: Oxford University Press, 1990.

Schlöndorff, Volker. *Licht, Schatten und Bewegung: Mein Leben und meine Filme*. Munich: Carl Hanser Verlag, 2008.

Seidman, Michael. *The Imaginary Revolution: Parisian Students and Workers*. New York: Berghahn Books, 2004.

Sherman, Daniel J., Ruud van Dijk, Jasmine Alinder, and A. Aneesh, eds. *The Long 1968: Revisions and New Perspectives*. Bloomington: Indiana University Press, 2013.

Slobodian, Quinn. *Foreign Front: Third World Politics in Sixties West Germany*. Durham, NC: Duke University Press, 2012.

Suri, Jeremy. *Power and Protest: Global Revolution and the Rise of Détente*. Cambridge, MA: Harvard University Press, 2005.

Wagner, Thomas. *Die Angstmacher: 1968 und die Neuen Rechten*. Berlin: Aufbau Verlag, 2017.

Walker, Ignacio. *Chile and Latin America in a Globalized World*. Singapore: ISEAS, 2006.

Zolov, Eric. *The Last Good Neighbor: Mexico in the Global Sixties*. Durham, NC: Duke University Press, 2020.

Performance

Carmen-Helena Téllez, performance of Arvo Pärt's *Which Was the Son of*... with the Indiana University Contemporary Vocal Ensemble, https://www.youtube.com/watch?v=gGOPckF3iS8.

PART ONE

Foundations

TWO

The Slow but Long Coming of a Cultural Revolution

VOLKER SCHLÖNDORFF

The events of the year 1968 shaped my life and my view of the world to a degree I could not foresee at the time. During the Prague Spring I was shooting a film in Czechoslovakia's capital,[1] a story set in the sixteenth century. What was happening around us, and the echo from simultaneous uprisings in Berlin (the shooting of Rudi Dutschke) and Paris (Daniel Cohn-Bendit's activities at the Sorbonne), was so overwhelming that I introduced newsreel footage of these events into Kleist's novella. Later I followed up with films about similarly tumultuous times: *The Lost Honor of Katharina Blum* (1975), *Knife in the Head* (1978), and *Leaden Times* (1981) (*Marianne and Julianne*, being the U.S. distributor's title), all of which I produced.

Please allow me to set all modesty aside and let me take my own biography as a case study leading up not only to '68 but to the violent period of the Baader–Meinhof gang and the Red Army Faction (RAF) terrorists, with which I was accused at the time of being a "sympathizer," if not, as

Heinrich Böll, "the spiritual father" of the violence—all ending in 1979 with a number of murders, among them Hanns Martin Schleyer's (the head of the German Entrepreneurs' Association), and the multiple suicides of some of the protagonists, as depicted in our collective movie *Germany in Autumn* (1978).

There was no doubt in our minds that we were living in revolutionary times, even though we did not follow enough the American protests, which were less theoretical and more focused on specific social realities, such as racism and the war in Vietnam. Today I would say ours was more a cultural than a political or social revolution. By culture I mean above all our way of life, our way of communicating and relating to each other, within our generation and toward the generation of our parents. Fundamental changes occurred in the way people thought about the past, present, and future.

Today what I find most remarkable is the almost simultaneous explosion of 1968 all over the world, a truly global event, even though at the time of its happening most people were not aware of this simultaneity. It must have been caused by quite different forces in all these different countries, from France to Chile, from Prague to Berkeley, from Berlin to Turin. I can only speak of Germany—and myself as one of the participants, not causes, of course. For me '68, defined as an antiauthoritarian movement, started right at the end of World War II with the collapse of the old German middle class. It was fueled by the 1950s, the Adenauer years in the Federal Republic, and finally by the influence of my French education in the late 1950s and early 1960s in Paris.

THE END OF THE GROWN-UPS' WORLD

My father came from Oldenburg in the north of Germany and was born a few years before 1900, just like his siblings and most of his friends, as a subject of the kaiser, Emperor Wilhelm II. Even their external appearance made that generation look as if they came from another world. In the late 1940s and the 1950s our father, a medical doctor, always wore a three-piece suit with a waistcoat, white shirt, and tie, sometimes an overcoat and certainly a hat, and he also carried a stick that he vigorously employed when taking a walk. Known as "the Doctor" and addressed by all with the respectful "Herr Doktor," he transferred this honor automatically to me and my brothers, who were known as "the Doctor's kids."

Somehow, in the last days of World War II we must have sensed that the grown-ups were abdicating, and that soon the children's hour would strike. A couple of weeks after my sixth birthday, white bed sheets were hurriedly hung out the windows. My older brother, Georg, was allowed to climb up the still leafless beech tree to raise the sign of capitulation from a high branch. As a precaution, the house was blocked up and abandoned. When we finally got the word, "They're coming!," we hid in the forest.

The Americans moved in on the bumpy path through the forest into our small location, by its suffix "Bad" a spa, but in fact rather a village. They sat on Jeeps, heavy trucks, and tanks. A burnt-out Wehrmacht vehicle blocked the road in the curve at the entrance to Schlangenbad.

The GIs were setting off explosions to clear the way, and in doing so they also blew up the old entertainment hall. It was a little casino in which Russian aristocrats, supposedly even Dostoyevsky, used to gamble away their money and the souls of their serfs. The ivory chips were left for us to play with in the ruins; the roulette wheel had been broken.

What impressed us children were the drivers of the U.S. Army trucks. They were Black, though they looked much different from the picture of the little "Moor" in our children books. Tall, and equipped with fearsomely white teeth, they seemed to us like supermen. Only men this big and strong could drive such monster trucks, we thought. Decades later I learned from Arthur Miller, while working with him in New York on *Death of a Salesman*, that the U.S. Army was only integrated beginning with the Korean War. Under Eisenhower in World War II, white and Black troops were still strictly segregated. Maybe they made friends with us, the children of the defeated, more quickly because of their underprivileged position. It didn't take long for each of us to take on "his own Yankee" from among the very young GIs from Indiana, the Dakotas, and Nebraska. Since these young men had beaten our parents, they were our natural allies.

Authority was no longer a privilege of the elders. A true clash of civilizations ensued from this reversed order. We liked the style of these GIs; they didn't act like victors, and they were so different from the bitter, tattered figures of the last German soldiers whose retreat we had witnessed during the last days, still hoping for a final victory. Chewing gum, Coca-Cola, Hershey bars, and Butterfingers were the convincing *Wunderwaffen*[2] of these young soldiers. We were interested in their guns and vehicles; they were interested in our bicycles and sisters. The first words we learned to ignore were "off limits" and "no fraternization." We simply defected to the enemy, who cruised around the lawns and flower beds with one leg dangling out of their Jeeps, ignoring all the "keep off the grass" signs—which so far had stopped even German revolutions.

For us, new times began; the adults, however, lived in great fear of the occupiers. All kinds of Nazi publications, knives and daggers, countless editions of *Mein Kampf*, soup bowls with swastikas stamped underneath, large flags and small, even sports badges and canoe club membership cards were buried in the forest by night.

The world of the youth and that of the adults would drift apart in the next years. I was six and wore *Lederhosen*. In amazement, we discovered the new world. One day at the height of summer, word of the first atom bomb went around. A Jeep drove through the upper main street, honking wildly, and we children ran yelling alongside. "The war is over, the war is over," we chanted, to the rhythm of "The witch is dead, the witch is dead."

DISCOVERING MY OWN WORLD

Way into my teens my "artistic" education was shaped by illustrated magazines in the waiting room of my father's surgery. Although culture was prized by society, in daily life it was limited to the request hour on the radio and a few quotations from Faust. For my father there were only two categories of art—pleasant and unpleasant. Since in life he experienced enough of the latter, art had to provide him with the former. He tried to undermine my first film, *Young Törless* (1966), based on Robert Musil's *The Confusions of Young Törless*, resorting to intrigue, and he held that *The Tin Drum* (1979) was, in a word, "dreadful!" Coming from the world of the kaiser, having rejected the Weimar Republic, it was as hard for him to accept the new, postwar society as it had been to accept the Weimar Republic.

I first rebelled against his world by sneaking off after school to the Roxy, the Rio, the Apollo, or the Valhalla—the biggest cinemas in the nearby town of Wiesbaden—to watch American Westerns and gangster movies, which we did not yet call "film noir." They appealed to me and my friends because they were shunned as "filth and trash," the opposite of the bourgeois high culture of concerts and opera. Besides, these movies came from the United States, which made it even worse for the adults and all the more attractive for us.

Film became an ever-greater part of my life. In the mid-1950s, the German Film Industry Self-Censorship Commission (FSK), established by the Allies and conveniently located in my home town of Wiesbaden, classified films according to the values of the Allies. A friend of my older brother, Franz Rath, worked there as projectionist, and by climbing a small iron ladder I was able to enter the screening booth. I watched films during the afternoons caught between two rattling projectors and the heat of their arc lights. For the first time film was not just the light, shadows, and movement on the screen, but something tangible. I pestered my father, wanting to quit school and to become a camera man, which he refused outright. "First graduate and get some university degree."

UNDER THE (FRENCH) INFLUENCE

In 1956, our school organized three-month sojourns in a French boarding school for the purpose of learning the language and for bringing European youth together. This was exactly what my father wished for, so he agreed to let me go.

It was a Jesuit school where I enrolled; it became the model for the faraway Austrian military academy in *Young Törless*, and it's where I saw my first silent film, Dreyer's *La Passion de Jeanne d'Arc* (1928). *The Ninth Day* (2005) is my belated tribute to my Jesuit priests, who from then on were to educate me. A master–student relationship grew out of the many afternoons I spent in one of the priests' cells, and that led to a friendship spanning over thirty years. When RP de Solages died, I had the honor of being a pallbearer carrying his coffin down into the Jesuits' vault in Tours.

One day the entire school was invited to the local cinema to see a film by one of the former students, Alain Resnais. The film was *Nuit et Brouillard* (*Night And Fog*) (1955), the documentary about the concentration camps.

Of course I had heard about the camps, mostly through jokes about the use of gas and the making of glue from bones. I cannot recall a genuine description of the Holocaust, nor had I seen images or statistics during our history lessons in Wiesbaden. It was a taboo subject in Adenauer's Germany, practically willed out of existence by the collective silence on the matter in schools as much as at home. Therefore I was neither mentally nor physically prepared for the horror of the images that unfolded before me.

As the lights went up in the auditorium I—the sole German among a few hundred French kids who now looked at me—found it extremely hard to get up. I still see my friends whose silent faces begged the same question that, half a century later, we are still asking ourselves: How was it possible?

I was forced to adopt my own view and not collapse in contriteness whenever the topic was raised. Deep down I have never been able to surmount it, and most of my films, beginning with *Törless* and up to *The Ninth Day*, still seek an answer to the question unleashed on that day. When a few years later in Frankfurt the first so-called Auschwitz trials started, this question started to get a few timid answers, and the 1968 students' revolt resulted from them.

COLONIAL POLITICS

Instead of the three months planned at the boarding school, I stayed in France for about ten years. In 1956, the Budapest uprising against the Soviets was the first political event we discussed vividly with our teachers, the priests. The French defeat in Vietnam and the Algerian war for independence were the next steps of my own independence. We read Sartre and Camus, we wore black turtlenecks and smoked Gauloises. I smuggled the forbidden pamphlet against torture in Algeria, "La Question," by Henri Alleg, into our school.

French society as a whole was divided by this last colonial war. Graduating in Paris, partly at the Sorbonne, partly at the film school, soon working as an assistant director, I became politically involved, and as a film technician was a member of the communist Union. In 1958 a small cultural revolution started, the French New Wave, and by chance or choice I was there, as the assistant to the very same Alain Resnais of *Night and Fog*, to Melville, and foremost to Louis Malle, who took me to Algeria for reportage on the last days of the war in that country. We met the young soldiers, the torturers Sartre and others had denounced. My first short, in the summer of 1960, dealt with Algerian freedom fighters. Both French and German censorship prohibited the innocent eleven-minute film. Like the generation around me, I felt that only a revolution could end such a cowardly materialistic republic as Adenauer's, and such an unjust regime as the colonial power France was at the time. And indeed, after the failed putsch of the generals, de Gaulle did just that. A new République started, Brigitte Bardot was the official Marianne, and I assisted Louis Malle in Mexico during the joyous celebration of anarchy his picture *Viva Maria!* was meant to be. None of us expected the bloody price the students of Mexico's national university, UNAM, had to pay a few years later for their anti-imperialist engagement.

The longer I stayed in France, and the more assimilated I felt, the more my friends treated me like a German, often addressing me with, "You as a German, . . ." Even Malle advised me not to mix with the large crowd of New Wave filmmakers, to "return to where I came from," and to become a German filmmaker.

THE YOUNG GERMAN CINEMA

I had read Musil's *Young Törless*, describing an authoritarian world of boarding schools, and the lofty nature of the novel and detached connection to life was quite close to my own.

First films usually possess a quality that can be reached again only years later with the wealth of experience. It is possible that one eventually makes better and more successful films, but the urgency and innocence of the first one never returns. Everything in life that has welled up inside until that moment now sought to escape.

Young Törless certainly represents my experience of boarding school life. But today I believe it was not just an individual impulse of mine, but that society at large was fueling my creativity. I felt a "historical mission," to give it a pathetic name, asking for a break with the generation of our parents, and excited by the challenge to bridge the gap with German cinema before 1933.

Young Törless turned out to be the proper vehicle to speak of my own experiences, growing up in an almost imperial German society first, rebelling against it, formed by French socialist-leaning teachers and comrades, finally affirming a new identity—part of a cultural revolution that would soon lead to '68. To start with, the picture was invited to the festival in Cannes.

Cannes was indisputably the mecca of film art in the '60s. The greater honors were bestowed there, not in Hollywood at the Oscars. The moment

Figure 2.1 *Young Törless* (1966).

I entered the theater following the press screening to take questions from journalists, I was overwhelmed: there was sustained applause.

The "New German Film" was born. I don't know where the expression came from, but it was appropriate. I missed the true incident during the screening in the large theater. My friend, master, and coproducer Louis Malle had taken me off to the Blue Bar as soon as the theater lights went out. He was of the opinion that the public should see the film without the director. It was a question of propriety, and, anyway, it seemed more elegant. After I'd served as his assistant in Paris for years, he had encouraged me to go back to Germany and make films there.

Louis and I were a bit tipsy as we sneaked back to our seats in the dark, shortly before the end of the film. There was excited whispering. Where had I been? There'd been a scandal! The German cultural *attaché* had left the theater, protesting loudly. This was not a German film! The students' torments in the film seemed to confirm foreign prejudices regarding Teutonic sadism, and the scene where a white mouse was slapped against a wall was simply too much. But his outrage hadn't just been faked in order to grab headlines for my film. The *attaché* later wrote to the foreign office, "One is not obliged to tolerate absolutely everything. This sequence could have led the foreign audience to lower its opinion of Germans."

This was 1966, and his opinion fit in nicely with that of the middle-class audience on the Croisette. Cannes was a strange place at the time. Here the most talented people on earth screened their films for an audience that consisted mainly of widows dripping with diamonds, aging playboys, hotel workers, and theater owners on tax-deductible vacations.

But this was also the place where I met Glauber Rocha and Carlos Diegues, this is where we young Germans were inspired by the Brazilian *cine novo* and their call for *tropicalismo* films, inspiring us to do "barbaric" films, which was our definition of being German. This is where I first met directors from the Arab world, from Argentina, Mexico, Cuba, and Japan, all united in various colors of anti-imperialism. We spent days and nights on the steps of the festival palace. This was how cinema should be: speaking directly about our lives and society, each filmmaker about his own people, his city, his landscape, his music. The author's voice was meant to be heard in every film, just like in literature and painting.

REVOLT IN THE AIR

Back in Munich I was surrounded by young people in revolt. They let their hair grow, refused consumerism by wearing parkas, listened to the Beatles, the Stones, and Bob Dylan—but without much political consciousness. I tried to portray them, with the Stones' muse Anita Pallenberg in the lead of a road movie, *A Degree of Murder* (1967), with a score by Brian Jones. German society shunned these dirty young people, the Auschwitz trials in Frankfurt once and for all terminated the dialogue among generations, and around the same time students started to articulate their protest in a more political way. In Berlin in April 1968 shots were fired at Rudi Dutschke; Angela Davis was there, amplifying the message from Berkeley; a few weeks later Daniel Cohn-Bendit called for revolution from the steps of the Sorbonne.

In Cannes the directors of the French New Wave, among them Jean-Luc Godard and Louis Malle, drew the curtain in front of the bourgeois audience with their tuxedoes and evening gowns. It was the eventful May 1968.

But I was not there. I was caught up in another revolution, shooting a picture on location in Czechoslovakia, not for political but for budget reasons, just at Dubček's moment during the uprising of the Prague Spring.

Today, in retrospect, I can say I felt it coming from the distant past of World War II, and was overcome with joy when our movement finally reached present times. Nothing would ever be the same as we had inherited it from our fathers. All authority was going to be questioned from now on.

The picture I was working on, *Michael Kohlhaas—Der Rebell*, was based, as was Doctorow's *Ragtime* (1975), on a novella by Kleist. Under the influence of events, I soon neglected the original story and tried to integrate the events of May 1968 into the historical narrative—with the result that neither the events of the sixteenth nor those of the twentieth century could be understood.

Soon the Soviets moved in, and it was the end of the Prague Spring. It had lasted one season only, from spring to August. "Why is it poor mankind has to be on earth?," our Czech wardrobe assistant asked me every morning, posing a question I am still pondering today.

A UTOPIA ENDED BY VIOLENCE

However, for us in the West nothing was over yet. Looking for role models of revolution, we could not find much in the German past, except some Spartacists and Rosa Luxemburg. Students turned to Lenin's, Mao's, and Trotsky's theories, while we artists chose the aesthetics of the 1920s, Expressionist painting, writing, and filmmaking, and Bauhaus architecture. I found inspiration in Brecht's first play, *Baal*, written during the failed revolution of 1919. I remembered Glauber Rocha's advice that we Germans, instead of imitating the French, should look for our own, "barbarian" aesthetics. The anarchic early Brecht seemed to be just the right vehicle. My film, *Baal*, turned out to be a wonderful work, with the very young, still unknown Rainer Werner Fassbinder and Margarethe von Trotta in the leads, celebrating the freedom the cultural revolution of '68 had given us. The film led to a storm of indignation. The viewers (who didn't read Brecht and mistook the film for a documentary) saw parallels to the anarchy they sensed behind the '68 revolt and demanded that Fassbinder should be "hanged," "beaten," and "thrown into a vat of boiling oil."

Figure 2.2 *Die Stille nach dem Schuss* (D 1999/2000).

Indeed, some of the students had taken a violent turn, no doubt because of the shots fired at Rudi Dutschke, but also because of the general climate in the country. The Springer media, the police, and the politics helped to create a climate of true hysteria and witch-hunt, which I depicted in *The Lost Honor of Katharina Blum* and also in *The Legend of Rita* (*Die Stille nach dem Schuss*). Indeed, Heinrich Böll asked matter-of-factly how six people from the small Baader–Meinhof gang could pose such a threat to a nation of 60 million. Why had the state to arm itself, the police to mobilize, and the media to stoke up mass hysteria? Shouldn't the leader of the group be given a sort of safe passage and a dialogue to halt the escalation of violence?

There was an uproar in the media, and the Springer press in particular stirred up the issue. They called Böll himself "the spiritual father of violence." Those who knew him could only imagine how the charge of violence must have hurt this man—he was a pacifist of the first rank, who wrote in his novels and short stories about soldiers in World War II who fled home wounded and defeated by the Nazis; he gently chided the rich and powerful, displayed sympathy for their victims, and felt for all disinherited ones; he was a Rhineland Catholic for whom the Church had become too fat and complacent.

Figure 2.3 *Die verlorene Ehre der Katharina Blum* (BRD 1975).

Böll launched a court case to restore his reputation. He lost all appeals and a great deal of money too, but in his view the loss of honor mattered most of all. He defended himself by writing a pamphlet, the manuscript of which he sent me—we knew each other by then through numerous demonstrations. It was "The Lost Honor of Katharina Blum," and the subtitle was "How Violence Develops and Where It Can Lead." Through this pamphlet, Böll restored his honor, and the movie, *Die verlorene Ehre der Katharina Blum*, co-written and directed by Margarethe von Trotta, was extremely popular with the younger generations who distanced themselves more and more from the so-called establishment. By the same token the escalation between a quite militarized state and the more and more violent RAF terrorists continued until the shocking kidnappings, killings, and final suicides of the main leaders in the autumn of 1979.

A group of filmmakers—Alexander Kluge, Fassbinder, and I—got together to document these events. So much has been said and written recently about Baader–Meinhof and *Germany in Autumn* that I don't want to dwell on it, except to say that this was truly the moment I felt the beginning of the end of the socialist utopia I had believed in since my years in France.

If from the 1960s student movement for a more open, more liberal, more enlightened society, all that was left was senseless violence, Mafia-style murders, and the suicides of former idealists, then indeed there was not much hope for a socialist society.

CONCLUSION

I do not know why, but by fate, hazard, or simple curiosity I came to witness all over the world what a tectonic shift 1968 had been. Whether visiting peasant cooperatives in Alentejo, Portugal, after Salazar's downfall, or documenting other peasants' fight against the airport in Narita, Japan, or visiting young filmmakers in Quebec, or in Argentina, whether in Poland during the Solidarity period, or in countries in and around Palestine, again and again I felt what a global event '68 had been, even though at the time of its happening most people were not aware of the simultaneity of the movement and its aspirations. Claude Lévi-Strauss speaks of long-term movements, unbeknownst to most of us but fueling our engagements, producing almost inevitable political waves from authoritarian leanings to liberation movements—and the other way around. I hope we are not entering a phase of such a backlash right now, as elections in Central Europe, Germany, Israel, Turkey, Russia, and maybe even in the United States seem to suggest.

As far as my country is concerned, we had the incredible luck of the fall of the Berlin Wall and German reunification, eclipsing 1968 almost entirely.

But it would be most unfair to forget it, and even more unfair to reduce it to some violent, indeed terrorist aspects. It was truly a cultural revolution, long overdue in our history. It had been attempted in 1848, in 1918/19, in 1949—and it finally happened. Within our society, whether in politics or in the justice system, in schools or universities, at the workplace, within kindergartens or families, between men and women, nothing would ever be the same, nothing would be as it had been during too long a past.

NOTES

1. The film, *Michael Kohlhaas—Der Rebell* (1969), was based on a novella written by Heinrich von Kleist in 1810.

2. "Miracle weapons."

BIBLIOGRAPHY

Books

Schlöndorff, Volker. *Licht, Schatten und Bewegung: Mein Leben und meine Filme*. Munich: Carl Hanser Verlag, 2008.
Schneider, Peter. *Rebellion und Wahn*. Cologne: Kiepenheuer und Witsch, 2010.

Audio Book

Cohn-Bendit, Daniel, and Georges-Marc Benamou. *Liquider 68?* Paris: Frémeaux & Associés, 2008.

Films

Bellocchio, Marco. *I Pugni in Tasca* (1966).
Bertolucci, Bernardo. *Before the Revolution* (1964).
Brustellin, Alf, Hans Peter Cloos, Rainer Werner Fassbinder, Alexander Kluge, Beate Mainka-Jellinghaus, Maximiliane Mainka, Edgar Reitz, Katja Rupé, Volker Schlöndorff, Peter Schubert, and Bernhard Sinkel. *Germany in Autumn* (1978).
Forman, Miloš. *Taking Off* (1971).
Godard, Jean-Luc. *La chinoise* (1967).
———. *Masculin Féminin* (1966).
Hopper, Dennis. *Easy Rider* (1969).
Lester, Richard. *Help*! (1965).
Penn, Arthur. *Bonnie and Clyde* (1967).
Schlöndorff, Volker. *Young Törless* (1966).
Schlöndorff, Volker, and Margarethe von Trotta. *The Lost Honor of Katharina Blum* (1975).
von Trotte, Margarethe. *Marianne and Juliane* (1981).

THREE

Italian Catholics and Latin America during the "Long '68"

MASSIMO DE GIUSEPPE

INTRODUCTION: ITALIAN CATHOLICS AND THE "LONG '68"

Was there a long '68? Was this symbolic year—a year that forced itself into the collective imagination because of its global repercussions and revolutionary breaks from history—a decisive turning point? Or was it simply the gradual amplification, globalization, and, in a certain sense, trivialization of the trials, tribulations, and changes that had been building up since the second half of the 1950s?[1]

In particular, I think back to the changes that swept over Italian society during the years of the economic miracle,[2] a creative mix of both domestic transformation (on the social, cultural, and generational fronts) and international transformation. This corresponded with a period of crisis for the Christian Democrats and their centrist governments, leading to the slow and difficult birth of the first center-left governments starting in 1963–64.[3] Meanwhile, international relations were being disrupted by Cold War polarization, what with the birth of Third Worldist–inspired liberation movements[4] and the Non-Aligned Movement, not to mention the escalation of the Vietnam War in the mid-1960s.[5] The historian Paolo Pombeni recently noted the interesting parallels between the revolutions of 1848 (in Italy and in the West in general) and the 1968 uprisings: "It was not an unexpected phenomenon because there had been several signs of unrest among the new generations. . . . [It could be seen in] their reactions to the social changes that had led to modernization and the disruption of their sociocultural norms—a phenomenon that would come to be known as 'secularization.' What was unexpected was the ease with which these youth protests would take off."[6]

Almost simultaneously, in that season also Latin America, the great mysterious subcontinent with a strong Catholic majority, underwent a series of disruptive and challenging mutations and ruptures at the demographic, social, political, cultural, and ecclesial level. This articulated process offered the basis for the construction of new relationships and internationalist dynamics, in which the religious dimension played a far from secondary role. Here we will try to present, in fact, a peculiar meeting between Italian and Latin American Catholicism, matured in the Long '68 season.

But returning to Pombeni's sentence, just how easily did those protests take off? What rules did they change? And above all, did they really turn into a cultural revolution? It goes without saying that on the Catholic front, this revolutionary dichotomy between a long buildup and a sudden cultural shock was connected to a complex series of "enabling conditions." First of all, various balancing acts that for years had seemed stable were upended by the appearance of never before seen international scenarios and religious, social, political, and cultural transformations.[7]

There was the influence of Vatican II, inaugurated on October 11, 1962, which formed the impetus for Pope John XXIII's Vatican diplomatic actions during the Cuban missile crisis (seen as a dangerous East/West, North/South clash), and his encyclical *Pacem in terris* (April 11, 1963), which the pope had addressed "to all men of good will."[8] At the same time, Catholic missionary work was undergoing a profound transformation as the economic miracle of the period had led to the secularization of families, the results of which were being seen for the first time. Efforts on the part of Italy's National Hydrocarbons Authority (Ente Nazionale Idrocarburi, or ENI) had led to a measure of energy independence, resulting in talk of an Italian "third way" in the Mediterranean, albeit within the framework of NATO. And those years—described by the UN as the "decade of development"—saw issues such as world hunger push new generations of young Catholics towards new forms of association, especially in the wake of the media's extensive coverage of the Biafra famine.[9]

As all of this unfolded, Latin America, facing a new and an ancient horizon at the same time, ended up playing an increasingly important role for the Church and for Italian Catholics in general (laity and clergy, men and women). This concern for Latin America stirred up old emotions, but it also lit a spark in the new generations come of age during the economic miracle. There was a new sense of closeness with "the other America," in contrast with the United States, a nation of modernizers and Protestants. And to some Catholics—namely, those who were more open to dialogue with the newly formed left-wing groups that had broken away from the Italian Communist Party (PCI)—U.S. policy in the region represented a new form of imperialism. Renewed interest in Latin America's state of tumult was a natural consequence of the rapidly changing 1960s, what with the Cuban Revolution, President Kennedy's Alliance for Progress, the development of "dependency theory" by Argentinian economist Raúl Prebisch and CEPAL/ECLAC, and the wave of dictatorships that followed the Brazilian coup. But it also had roots that went far back into history. Indeed, ever since its "discovery," "conquest," and "evangelization," Latin America had become an integral part of the Italian consciousness. It had had a profound religious, philosophical, and cultural effect, and it had even changed Italian dietary habits (the presence of tomatoes, corn, chocolate, and more in the Mediterranean diet can be traced back to Columbus).

Subsequently, a new wave of Italian emigration to the Americas (United States, Argentina, Uruguay, Brazil, Venezuela, Colombia, Cuba) in the early 1900s saw these past influences resurface in a new form and with new meaning. Later, when Che Guevara was killed in the Bolivian Andes in October 1967, it was not seen as a failure of focalism (*foquismo*); on the contrary, it inspired many young Catholics to view the Argentinian revolutionary as a sort of Christian martyr, ignoring the fact that he had been a self-professed atheist and proponent of armed revolution. Thus, the legend of Che (and for Marxist sympathizers, Mao's Little Red Book) found its way to the very heart of European student protests.[10]

Here I try to reconstruct, through research among archival documents and publications, an idea of that attempted bridge between Italian and Latin American Catholics across the Atlantic. The goal is to understand what Italians were looking for in those distant lands and what Italy, the country that housed the Vatican city-state and the Chair of St. Peter, could represent for Latin American Catholics in a season of turbulence and effervescence that connotes the Long '68. This path will help us, I hope, to understand the terms, and also the prospects, of that cultural revolution then in place.

TWO WORLDS AND THE INFLUENCE OF VATICAN II

The novelty of Vatican II and its maturation through four sessions and two pontificates proved crucial in marking a "spirit of time."[11] The choice to leave a rigidly dogmatic-doctrinal position to open up to new experiments in the theological, liturgical, pastoral, and synodal fields, as evoked by the pope in the inaugural speech,[12] would have found fertile ground both in Italy and Latin America. Beyond controversy and historiographical interpretations, this line would have found a counterpoint also in the action of John XXIII's successor, the archbishop of Milan, Giovanni Battista Montini, who ascended the papal throne as Paul VI on June 21, 1963, five days before John Kennedy's famous Berlin speech.

In the following autumn, at the resumption of the council—only one month after the signing of the Limited Test Ban Treaty in Moscow, which laid the first rules for the nuclear race—Paul VI identified four strong guidelines: (1) redefinition of the concept of the Church, (2) ecclesial renewal, (3) unity of Christians, and (4) dialogue with the contemporary world.[13] The council closed after four working sessions on December 8, 1965, while the war in Vietnam was raging (a few weeks after the battle of Ia Drang).

In that scenario, even between resistances and difficulties, the innovative drive would have enervated in particular those that have been defined as the "implementing decrees" of the council and that would have marked, during the following years, the redefinition of the Church–world relationship. These were the constitutions *Sacrosanctum concilium* (December 4, 1963), which redefined the times and methods of the liturgy, opening the celebration of the sacraments to the "vulgar" languages, and *Gaudium et spes* (December 7, 1965), which imagined a new "Christian humanism," open to the revision of personal relations inside the family, social bodies, labor unions, politics, and parties, but also cultural systems and international networks. Additionally, the decree *Apostolicam actuositatem* (November 18, 1965) opened up unprecedented avenues for freedom of maneuver for the apostolate of the laity; the declaration *Nostra aetate* (October 28, 1965) invited dialogue with non-Christian religions; and, finally, the *Ad gentes* decree (December 7, 1965) called for missionary activity directed to the deep principles of enculturation and respect for "the other" and his or her different historical experiences.

If Vatican II had a powerful effect on the ecclesial world, especially from a pastoral point of view, its reception had a detonating effect on young lay Catholics of both sexes: in terms of re-elaborating cultural proposals, educational formulas (the lesson of the "open school" of Don Lorenzo Milani after the success of his essay *Lettera a una professoressa*),[14] and through the construction of actions of social commitment "from below." Spontaneity, resourcefulness, and community youth activism seemed to be endowed and recognized by the new spirit of the council.

At the political level, in Italy the historical centrality of Christian Democracy was questioned as the only party horizon, generating those formulas of Catholic dissent that would have animated the years of maturation of '68. The experience of very different characters appears paradigmatic: the journalist Ettore Masina, founder already in 1964 of the pacifist/Third Worldist/internationalist and ecumenical network Rete Radiè Resch; or Giovanni Bianchi, at the time a high school professor of philosophy and a Catholic trade unionist, open to dialogue with the leftist movements conceived as a political translation of the spirit of the council.[15] Bianchi published in December 1968 an essay on the concept of Catholic dissent in Italy, introduced by an emblematic slogan: "Through the impatience and general frustration of the repressive society of consumption, politics and churches, the forces of dissent and protest are finally delineated."[16]

From Bologna's group of Giuseppe Dossetti and Giuseppe Alberigo, to the Milan activism of "resistant priests" such as David Maria Turoldo, Camillo de Piaz and the world of the Corsia dei Servi, to the Tuscany of Father Ernesto Balducci and the Lapirian circles, different formulas of political, social, and cultural mobilization of young Catholics took place.[17]

In the years of the Vietnamese conflict and the birth of a political Third World perspective, and on the basis of a growing antiauthoritarianism, this turmoil generated new utopias and at the same time sharpened the first forms of protest, putting the Curia and Paul VI himself in difficulty.[18]

The historian Guido Formigoni has well summarized the change of Italian Catholics, placing them within a framework of profound social and cultural changes that marked the country in a transversal way. He wrote: "It also accelerated the cultural transformation, subjectivism and will of emancipation of individuals . . . also the positive echo of the liberation struggles spread in the Third World contributed to undermining old deeds. In the Italian Church, the ferments consequent to Vatican II seemed to unfreeze traditional rigidity, without immediate political implications but causing changes in the widespread mentality weakening the consensus of the Christian Democratic synthesis."[19]

A crucial role in this process of transformation was played by Catholic publishing houses, such as Cittadella (Assisi), Cultura (Firenze), Queriniana (Brescia),[20] and magazines such as *Questitalia*, directed by the Venetian historian Wladimiro Dorigo, *Il Regno*, the progressive newsletter of the Dehonian Missionaries from Bologna, and the weekly *Settegiorni in Italia e nel mondo*, directed by Ruggero Orfei and which boasted among its collaborators intellectuals such as Piero Pratesi, Valerio Onida, Franco Rodano, Emanuele Severino, Umberto Segre, Mario Gozzini, and Adriana Zarri, to name a few.[21] Again the Florentine *Note di cultura* and *Testimonianze*, a magazine directed by the innovative priest Ernesto Balducci, one of the most dynamic postcouncil interpreters, created space for a radical change of paradigms.[22]

Above all, however, the growing fascination with the forms of renewal that animated many young activists, religious, and lay people, inside and outside the ecclesial structures, was imbued with a new type of internationalism[23] and motivated the search for a universal Church dimension, offering new perspectives towards the extra-European world.

New experiments in international solidarity quickly brought about innovation, but also tensions and clashes. As a result, there was a sort of gradual but constant acceleration leading up to the explosion of '68, when the "glocalization" process seemed to reach a point of no return.

It is precisely here that Latin America comes into play, an area of the world marked in turn, at that time, by profound social, cultural, and political changes that on the one hand included it in the dynamics of the Cold War and the changing Third Worldism,[24] while others called into question a transformation underway in the ecclesial dynamics and perspectives; all this against the backdrop of a new significance of youth, as clearly described for the Argentinian case by Valeria Manzano.[25] The theme of social and political mobilization, that of the liberation of man, as a pastoral and theological horizon but also economic, together with the rediscovery of the Other (starting from the dimension of the "option for the poor"),[26] would become the guidelines of what we can define as a real cultural revolution.

FROM BUILDUP TO ACCELERATION: A PERIOD OF EXPERIMENTS (1965–1967)

The period leading up to the Medellín Conference in 1968 was characterized by an increasing number of reforms, proposals, and experiments, all of which helped bring Italian Catholicism and Latin America much closer. They also shed light on the gradual buildup that preceded a once-in-a-lifetime cultural revolution that exploded in '68.[27] This process played out on three main levels: in ecclesiastical/missionary work, in lay organizations, and within Christian Democrat–inspired political groups. Generational turnover played a key role in all three cases, bringing a "new" group of young people into the fold and involving the student world in a way that had never been seen before.

On an ecclesiastical level, as the postconciliar process gained momentum, four new pillars of reform became the focus of Paul VI's papacy: the redefinition of the idea of the Church; the renewal of Catholicism; Christian unity; and dialogue with the contemporary world.[28] On November 8, 1964, just one month before going to India (a key moment in the globalization of the papacy),[29] Paul VI opened the new home of the "pro–Latin America" seminary in Verona (originally established in 1959). In so doing, he renewed the call for a joint effort in favor of the subcontinent.[30] The Italian Episcopal Council for Latin America (Comitato Episcopale Italiano per l'America Latina, or CEIAL) had been formed around that same time, tasked not only with assisting missionaries but also with training young volunteers from the laity. The goal was to develop an "awareness of solidarity" that would encompass parishes, youth centers, and Catholic organizations in order to make "the faithful increasingly aware of their membership in the universal Church." CEIAL organized 26 training courses between 1963 and 1977, sending 1,648 missionaries, 409 diocesan priests, 292 clergymen, 687 clergywomen, and 292 lay volunteers to Latin America. The growing presence of Catholic organizations in Latin America really started to be felt in 1965–66, when efforts on the part of the Latin American Episcopal Council (CELAM) led to the development of basic ecclesial communities. At the same time, innovative bishops were becoming increasingly famous around the world, such as the Brazilian Dom Hélder Câmara, the Chilean Manuel Larraín, the Ecuadorian Leonidas Proaño, and the Mexicans Sergio Méndez Arceo and Samuel Ruiz. Young priests such as the Chilean Segundo Galilea were reinvigorating the pastoral ministry, and theologians such as the Peruvian Gustavo Gutiérrez were breaking from past traditions.[31]

Meanwhile, Third Worldism was gaining steam (strengthened by the birth of the UN Group of 77 and the Algerian and Cuban revolutions) and the first movements were being organized against the war in Vietnam. This brings us to the second aspect of the buildup in the '60s: the involvement of lay movements and associations. Driven by a predominantly young membership, these groups were increasingly experimenting with new methods, leading them to break from traditional organizations such as Catholic Action (Azione cattolica italiana, ACI) and the Italian Catholic Federation of University Students (Federazione degli Universitari Cattolici, FUCI). In other cases, they modernized the tactics of "white" workers' movements, as was seen with the Italian Confederation of Workers (Confederazione Italiana Sindacati Lavoratori, CISL), which established a committee for an International Solidarity Fund in 1966,[32] or the Italian Christian Workers' Associations (Associazioni Cristiane Lavoratori Italiani, ACLI), first under Livio Labor and later under Giovanni Bianchi.[33]

The *Ad gentes* decree on missionary activity was to have a transformative effect along these lines. The decree's influence was quickly felt in Italy with the establishment in January 1966 of the Lay Movement for Latin America (Movimento laici per l'America latina, MLAL). In those same days in Havana, there was held in a very different spirit the Tricontinental Conference of the revolutionary movements of Africa, Asia, and Latin America (Primera Conferencia de Solidaridad de Los Pueblos de Africa,

Asia, Latin America) that tried to present Cuban *foquismo* (focalism) as a formula of exportation of armed revolution in the Third World movements.[34] The line of MLAL, on the other hand, was inspired, according with the reception of the spirit of Vatican II, by an explicit rejection of violence, opposed to an ideal and concrete revolution in peace, as a form of social promotion, a Christian commitment to development and a new form of discernment starting from the lesson of local churches.

MLAL's first president was Armando Oberti, one of the leading proponents among the laity of postconciliar cultural reform. The members of the association consisted almost entirely of young people between the ages of eighteen and twenty-five, and in its first three years of existence, 119 volunteers were trained and sent to Latin America (the first volunteer to be sent over was a woman, Annamaria Mellini, who went to Brazil). MLAL launched a newsletter, *Lettera agli amici*, and starting in 1967 it began publishing a book series entitled Quaderni ASAL, which was to play a crucial role in spreading liberation theology in Italy.[35] The first was the translation of a critical essay against Brazilian landowners, written by Pedro Casaldáliga, the Spanish Claretian bishop of São Feliz in Mato Grosso, followed by a liberationist dossier *Liberare gli oppressi* (*Freeing the Oppressed*), with a preface by the bishop of Crateus, Antônio Batista Fragoso.[36]

Furthermore, MLAL became a key player in the development of Italian–Latin American relations, organizing training courses and trips while also inviting guests (intellectuals, theologians, experts in social ministry, but also peasants and activists of basic ecclesial communities) to Italy to speak about their experiences. One of the group's first major interlocutors was the Brazilian educator Paulo Freire, former director of the Department of Cultural Extension at the University of Recife, who had been persecuted by Brazil's military government after the coup of 1964 and forced into exile in Chile. MLAL's trailblazing cultural exchanges with Freire represented a new form of internationalism, providing an opportunity to raise critical consciousness among Christians, share in the experiences of the first basic ecclesial communities in Brazil, and mobilize against "networks of structural injustice."

There was another lay association that began to open up to the needs of Latin America during these formative years: Mani Tese. This organization was made up of small groups spread throughout Italy, with mostly young volunteers as members (university students, but also high school students and workers). It was founded in 1964 by four missionary groups (Comboni, PIME, Xaverian, and Consolata), with its main office in Milan and an important branch in Florence. It was originally meant to be a social movement to raise awareness among Italians about the fight against world hunger. However, Mani Tese was soon able to free itself from missionary control, becoming advocates of conscientious objection and the rights of indigenous peoples (in addition to continuing the fight against hunger). As protest movements heated up and Catholic dissent grew, the role of political, social, and religious affiliations in the construction of national and global identities came to be redefined. A new frame of reference was needed, not to mention new forms of mobilization. The association made a big leap forward in 1967 when it saw its ranks grow to 1,000-plus members (and 3,500-plus sympathizers), divided into more than 120 local groups. Even though the headquarters were in Milan and Lombardy had the largest number of groups, the presence of Mani Tese spread throughout the whole peninsula, with important bases in "red" regions such as Tuscany (Florence) and Emilia Romagna (Faenza) but also in southern areas such as Naples or Catania in Sicily.[37]

Mani Tese's mission resonated with many of its youngest members, who were fed up with social injustice and attracted by the "liberationist" spirit coming out of South America. In any case, Mani Tese's growth continued to be driven by broader issues: poverty (which was related to social injustice) and that of freedom as an expression of personal and community development, both within and beyond a nation's borders.

Gioventù Studentesca (GS) also began its own Brazilian experience in that period. This Catholic Action–inspired movement was founded in Milan by Don Luigi Giussani, who by the early '60s was already working with the auxiliary bishop of Belo Horizonte on a project to train young lay missionaries and send them to Brazil. Financial backing was provided by the entrepreneur Marcello Candia, while local support came from Juventude estudiantil católica (JEC) and Juventude operária católica (JOC), whose international president was the Italian-Canadian Romeo Maione.[38] This was the start of an exchange program between young university students in Brazil and Italy. Some GS members—including its vice president, Lidia Acerboni—ended up doing social work in the *favelas*, becoming important contributors to local ecclesial communities. Another key figure in

Figure 3.1 Father Arturo Paoli (left) in Fortín Olmos, Argentina, with coalmen and migrants, late 1960s. Fondo Documentazione Arturo Paoli, Lucca, Christeller cards, Photographies 1961–1969 (donation of Gabriella and Giorgio Christeller).

these relations was Alberto Antoniazzi, former president of Gioventù di Azione Cattolica (Catholic Action Youth, or GIAC). He later recalled the reaction of young people to the military dictatorship in Brazil: "The Maritain-influenced Catholics were already heavily politicized, so much so that some of them would become Marxist-Leninists and form a movement called *Azione Popolare*. Politicized too were the Jesuits, who at the time were very conservative here. We did not exactly embrace the 'revolution,' as the military coup defined itself, in part because there was a group of politicized seminarians with us who came from various areas of Brazil."[39] This growing ferment was also echoed in the experiences of other Italian missionaries, such as that of the Little Brother Arturo Paoli,[40] who settled in the rural community of Fortín Olmos, Argentina, in the early '60s; or that of the Florentine priest Renzo Rossi, whose reports from Bahia struck the same hard, militant tone as Fanon's *The Wretched of the Earth*.[41] These experiences also help us understand how political issues gradually worked their way into relations with Latin America.

Indeed, a third form of mobilization seen in this buildup phase was political in nature, with many Catholic dissidents pursuing solutions that were not necessarily within the realm of the Christian Democrats. In that sense, Latin America presented itself as a unique sort of laboratory in which Catholics could experiment with both Marxism and liberation theology. This was encouraged in part by the message in *Populorum progressio*, Paul VI's encyclical on "man's complete development," released on March 26, 1967. The pope seemed to single out those with political responsibility (among others), exhorting them to reflect on the tasks of younger generations. He wrote of equity in trade relations, dialogue between cultures, and becoming more aware of the common good; he even touched on the subject of revolution (albeit with extreme caution). He launched an appeal to youth and made special reference to Latin America, where Christians were fighting on all fronts of the widening gap between rich and poor.[42]

Another influential group of that time was the International Union of Young Christian Democrats (IUYCD). The formation of the IUYCD had been inspired by the Christian Democrat World Union (CDWU), which was the Christian Democrat international created in Santiago de Chile in 1961 (its first leader was the Venezuelan Rafael Caldera). From very early on, several key exponents of Italy's youth movement were also members of IUYCD's Italian delegation, such as Angelo Bernassola, president of the Christian Democrats' European section; Tina Anselmi, leader of its feminist movement; Giuseppe Zamberletti, who represented the Association of Young Administrators; and others, including Carlo Fuscagni and Gilberto Bonalumi. Against this backdrop, and in keeping with the Alliance for Progress, a relationship had developed between the Italian Christian Democracy and the initially progressive Partido Demócrata Cristiano (PDC) in Chile, led by Eduardo Frei Montalva.[43] In general, relationships with Latin American Christian Democrats (in Chile, Venezuela, Bolivia, El Salvador, and Guatemala) could rely on a network of financial, cultural, and media support, and also the backing of the Italian party itself. Look no further than the ways in which the two worlds stayed connected and informed—one such example was Inter Press Service (IPS), a "Third Worldist" press agency founded by the journalist Roberto Savio while he was writing for *Il Popolo*. The IPS archives contain a vast amount of material that dates back to the years in question, including press clippings and correspondence. They even contain letters that were exchanged with former

Prime Minister Amintore Fanfani, who had founded the Italo-Latin American Institute (Istituto Italo-latinoamericano, IILA) in 1966 to promote scientific, cultural, economic, and technical cooperation between Italy and twenty-one Latin American countries.

Lastly, it is important to remember the role played by universities and research centers, which were extremely active in the lead-up to '68. American studies was a well-established discipline in Italy by that point,[44] while the country (and the world) was witnessing a Latin American literary boom. Between 1963 and 1967, "new" authors were published in Italy for the first time, hailing from such countries as Mexico (Carlos Fuentes), Cuba (Alejo Carpentier), Colombia (Gabriel García Márquez), Guatemala (Miguel Ángel Asturias), Peru (Mario Vargas Llosa), Argentina (Julio Cortazar), and Brazil (Jorge Amado). The Italian publisher Giangiacomo Feltrinelli played a decisive role in the promotion of Latin American new leftist (and potentially revolutionary) literature. Breaking into those years with the Communist Party and gradually moving towards increasingly radical ultra-leftist and pro-Cuban positions, Feltrinelli started publishing the Italian version of the *Tricontinental Bulletin*, becoming one of the main cultural agents in Europe of the myth of Che Guevara. After '68, the path of clandestine armed struggle led to Feltrinelli's death in a suburb of Milan during a failed bomb attack in 1972.[45]

Under a veneer of the fantastical, the stories told by these authors were a profound mix of crude realism, social commentary, political criticism of dictatorships, and revolutionary utopias.[46] One of the key figures behind the Documentation Center in Bologna, the historian Paolo Prodi, tried to establish a direct partnership with the Centro Intercultural de Documentación (CIDOC), founded by Ivan Illich in Cuernavaca, Mexico.[47] Illich's works aimed for a "complete renewal," eventually leading him to reflect upon the deinstitutionalization of society and the "de-Yankeefication" of Latin America. He would end up turning accepted logic on its head when it came to development/underdevelopment, institutionalization/deinstitutionalization, and even schooling/deschooling. In so doing, Illich was actually incorporating the lesson learned from Don Lorenzo Milani's pedagogy of freedom; he exercised a heavy influence on many exponents of the Italian protest movement.[48] On the way back from a trip to Cuernavaca, where he had been working on a documentary for RAI (Italy's public broadcaster) called *Cristo Libertador*, Prodi wrote the following in his journal: "It is in the passage from a static society to an increasingly dynamic society that one begins to see this crisis as a historical emergency."[49] But he also warned against "rampant sociologism." Both groups had agreed to conduct research on alternatives to armed revolt. This was especially relevant in light of the growing fascination with Guevara-inspired *foquismo*, which seemed to be attracting many Latin American Catholics in the wake of the Primera Conferencia de solidaridad de los pueblos de Africa, Asia, America latina—better known as the Tricontinental Conference—held in Havana on January 3–15, 1966, to "fight against imperialism, colonialism and neocolonialism."[50] The tragic death of Camilo Torres Restrepo—the Colombian priest and sociologist who was killed in guerrilla combat—had also resonated with the Italian public. After all, he had started out in Catholic Action, only to join political militants in the Marxist group Frente Popular Unido (FPU) before eventually crossing over to the guerrilla organization Ejercito de Liberación Nacional (ELN). In 1967, while Fidel Castro was opening the Policlínico Camilo Torres in Santiago de Cuba, the Uruguayan singer-songwriter Daniel Viglietti wrote a song that the Chilean Victor Jara eventually turned into an anthem of sorts for militant groups. Its very first verse included the words "donde cayó Camilo, nació una cruz, pero no de madera sino de luz."[51]

1968: A REVOLUTIONARY TURNING POINT?

Student protests were spreading like wildfire in Italy in April 1968. Just a few days had passed since the assassination of Martin Luther King Jr. in Memphis, and there were still three weeks to go before that fateful May in France. Demonstrators were occupying public universities (in Trento, Turin, Bologna, Padua, Pavia, Naples, Milan, Modena, Palermo), and they eventually reached private universities (the Catholic University of the Sacred Heart in Milan, starting on May 24).

Meanwhile, a relatively new publishing house in Milan called Jaca Book, founded by a group of students (including Sante Bagnoli and Maretta Campi, who were both involved with GS), had just launched the seventh volume in a series entitled Chiesa e società.[52] The title was militant in itself: *America latina: Parole come armi* (*Latin America: Words as Weapons*). It was a selection of texts that had previously been published by

CIDOC, including works by such authors as Carlos Fuentes (*Our Societies Do Not Want Witnesses* and *Every Act of True Language Is in Itself Revolutionary*), the Jesuit Joseph Fitzpatrick (*Strange Church in a Strange Land*), Antonio Quarracino (*Against an Immoral Economy*), Segundo Galilea (*New Structures for the Pastoral Ministry in Latin America*), and Juan Lefevbre (*New Dimensions of Poverty*). The appearance of this publication was emblematic of the political climate at the time: liberation theory was gaining ground, non-Christians were becoming part of the dialogue, and there were growing calls for a reaction to social injustices. The Church was becoming more and more involved in all of these issues, both in America and in Europe.[53] At the Mutualité in Paris the previous March 22, Father Jean Cardonelle, who openly sympathized with Marxism, had launched an appeal to "break all the shackles of injustice."[54]

It is worth mentioning the introduction to the Italian edition, wherein the editors (Luciano Di Pietro, Ugo Maggioli, and Monique Pellegrini) explained the reason behind the project. First of all, they wanted to relaunch the publishing house itself, which that very same year had published such groundbreaking texts as *The Pillage of the Third World* by Pierre Jalee and *Voice and Phenomenon* by the philosopher Jacques Derrida (part of a series entitled Essays for an Awareness of Transition). The introduction to *America latina: Parole come armi* contained the following words: "The idea for this book came from exchanges we had with our readers about the problem of Latin America. Too often in these exchanges the word 'Christians' was used to indicate a monolithic category: a political party characterized by rigid discipline. 'The Christians are constantly behind when it comes to social development' or 'The Christians are the true masters of the word *revolution*.' To us it is clear that such statements represent a limitation."[55] They reaffirmed their vision of the Church, namely, that it was not simply a spiritual institution detached from the rest of the world. In so doing, they brought up the much debated topic of revolution, while at the same time laying claim to their own freedom through the power of words. And they were convinced of the Church's multifaceted role—that indeed it was urgent for the Church to get involved in politics.

In general, the transition from 1967 to 1968 was key to understanding the irruption of Latin America into the Catholic consciousness. The Italian Catholic world had been shaken by student unrest, and the electoral campaign had been upended by news of a plot for an Italian coup (the so-called *Piano Solo*), leading to fears of potential "South American" scenarios that threatened the democratic stability of the republic.[56] As Moro's third government was drawing to a close (its term would end on June 24), the effects could still be felt from the clashes between students and police during the "Battle of Valle Giulia" in Rome on March 1 (which resulted in injuries to 478 protesters and 150 police officers, and 228 arrests). That incident even led a defiant Pier Paolo Pasolini to sympathize with the police, calling them "sons of the poor."[57]

In his recent memoirs on the Long '68, left-wing Catholic Marco Boato—among the protagonists of the mobilization in the new faculty of sociology of the University of Trento (together with the future ideologue of the terrorist movement Red Brigade, Renato Curcio, and the member of Lotta continua, Mauro Rostagno)[58]—recalled the effect of student rebellion as an attempt to update a culture of antifascist resistance intertwined with the experiments of free university and the reactions to the turmoil occurring outside Europe.[59] Francesca Socrate highlighted, in her recent study on '68, the tendency to a "possessive" storytelling of that season by the main players.[60] On the fiftieth anniversary, by the way, we were finally assisting in a process of confrontation and dialogue between historians and witnesses, which is offering new interpretations.

In general, the idea of an actualization of the resistance experience, together with the influence of Marcuse's theses and the fascination with a social, religious, and institutional renewal, animated the cultural centers and spontaneous groups that proliferated throughout the country. But in the Catholic case this approach dealt with the postconciliar openings to the external world, fused with a deep intraecclesial renewal, especially through the Latin American experiences. A census carried out by the cultural association Presenza at the end of 1968 estimated 300-plus centers with a Catholic heritage or explicit affiliation, including the Isolotto Group in Florence, the Christian Students Movement of Cinisello Balsamo (Milan), the J. F. Kennedy of Correggio (Reggio Emilia), the Cenacolo of Modena, the Social Christian Movement of Livorno, and the Committee for International Solidarity in Rome. Some clubs brought explicit Latin American references in their own heading, such as the Camilo Torres Group of Altopascio (Lucca) or the Guevara Group in Imola.[61]

Nevertheless, although the dissatisfied youth of the Italian Communist Party and the Italian Socialist Party were taken with Mao's Little Red

Book and the working-class struggle, and the new generation of right-wing militants were energized by neofascism, the Catholic protest movement came to be defined by Latin American issues. And it led to the development of new concepts such as "liberation," "option for the poor," and "pedagogy of the oppressed." Again in March of '68, the missionary publisher EMI released Dom Hélder Câmara's best seller *Terzo mondo defraudato* (*The Defrauded Third World*; there were five reprints in little over a year), which was followed shortly thereafter by *Rivoluzione nella pace* (*Revolution through Peace*), published by Jaca Book. As both a devout pacifist and ardent supporter of emerging Latin American liberationist demands, Câmara had a strong influence on Catholic grassroots movements, helping to break down barriers between religious and political activists. Through networks, initiatives, translations of books, and the influence of strong witnesses of political or social injustice experiences, a real bridge between European and Latin American movements was consolidated. Meanwhile, the flow of information was probably asymmetric and locally articulated. While Latin America (also in its mythical dimension) was beginning to occupy completely unprecedented spaces in the collective imagination of young Italian Catholics, the voluntary push of groups and movements began to experiment with new formulas of solidarity, crossing the ocean or within movements, groups, or basic ecclesial communities. Although impregnated with an increasingly categorized discourse (the saving myth of the Church in movement opposed to the reactionary one), the developing Latin American base communities offered Italians another plural experience with which to confront each other.[62] At the same time they granted a precious element of experimentation of networks and contacts, launching signals and images from a scenario increasingly marked by the violence of dictatorships (explicit and latent). Also their being suspended between postconciliar suggestions (the return to a primitive Ecclesia, the return to the reading of the Bible) and idealizations of the sense of community—which in the indigenous areas of Central America or the Andes assumed very different traits compared to the Brazilian rural experiences or to the urban emergencies in the endless suburbs of megalopolises such as Mexico City or Buenos Aires—became a central element of Catholic mobilization for Latin America.

In the spring of 1968, for example, Father Giulio Girardello, the vice rector of the seminary for Latin America in Verona, decided to leave Italy for Brazil to carry out an experimental mission (destined to last ten years), but he continued to maintain a very close relationship with his Italian reference groups, thanks to bulletins, open letters, and informative documents.[63]

The movements of 1968, as the drivers of the base communities experiences, were accelerated even further by a series of events that occurred during the preparations for and eventual launch of the Second General Conference of CELAM, held between August 25 and September 7 in Medellín, Colombia. First of all, these dates corresponded with the first-ever papal visit to Latin America (August 22 to 25). What's more, this revolutionary pastoral assembly could be symbolically bookended by two historical events, both of which received heavy media attention, and both of which would have far-reaching effects across cultures. The first was the death of Ernesto "Che" Guevara in the Bolivian Andes (October 9, 1967). His image would soon be forever immortalized in Alberto Korda's iconic photograph *Guerrillero heróico*, which was reproduced throughout Italy by Giangiacomo Feltrinelli. The image was able to transfigure Che into a sort of intergenerational liberationist legend, increasingly separating him from any connotation of institutional communism.[64] The other event—the tragic culmination of this brief yet intense period of ferment—was the massacre of university students in Plaza de Las Tres Culturas in the Tlatelolco section of Mexico City (October 2, 1968), just a few days before the start of the 1968 Summer Olympics (famous for John Carlos's and Tommie Smith's Black Power salutes).[65] The tragedy in Mexico City only served to demonstrate the profound nature of the "other" '68—the one outside of Europe. It would also cause a considerable stir in Italy, especially because the journalist Oriana Fallaci, a famous war reporter working for the magazine *L'Europeo*, was wounded in the clash.[66]

Returning to Che's influence on Italy's 1968, the archives at Fondazione La Pira provide an interesting perspective. Even before his death, Italian eyes were on the case of the French intellectual and Castro sympathizer Régis Debray, author of *Revolución en la Revolución?* (translated and published in Italy by Feltrinelli). He had been arrested in Bolivia, charged with being part of pro-Cuba guerrilla activity.[67] The case would soon shine a spotlight on the presence of Guevara himself in the *foquista* cell (he had entered the country under a false name in November 1966). The Debray affair was being closely followed by Giorgio La Pira, former mayor of Florence and president (since 1967) of the World Federation of United

Cities (UTO). Once a member of the Italian Constituent Assembly, La Pira was one of those Christian Democrats willing to dialogue with younger generations and open to the idea of reforming political structures. He personally wrote to the Bolivian president, Barrientos, in the hope of starting talks on Debray's behalf.[68] That led to mediation efforts carried out by the Florentine journal *Note di cultura*, with the support of both the UTO and Lelio Basso's International League for the Rights and Liberation of Peoples.[69] One of the participants in the talks was Corrado Corghi, member of the Foreign Affairs Commission for the DC National Committee, and also the young mathematician Mario Primicerio (who had already been with La Pira in Hanoi). Corghi eventually wrote a report on the experience, which shed light on both the intentions and the difficulties of their unique mission.[70] Indeed, just as the three Italians were about to leave Peru and enter Bolivia, news arrived that the revolutionaries were surrounded, and that the special forces had determined that Che was among them. Thus, La Pira launched a second appeal to Barrientos, writing, "A grain of wheat buried underground does not die; it becomes an irresistible historical and political attraction for younger generations and sprouts liberation and justice for oppressed peoples."[71] Nonetheless, Guevara was captured on October 8 and killed shortly thereafter. Corghi made it to La Paz where, on behalf of a group of Italian and French Catholic intellectuals, he met with the president of the Bolivian Christian Democratic Party, Luis Ossio. Ossio provided him with an overview of the political repression in Bolivia; there would be further meetings, such as that with Antonio Aranibar, president of the young Christian Democrats, along with religious and political leaders, intellectuals, and students (all of whom belonged to "Catholic Marxist-Castroist groups"). Corghi then separated from his travel companions and made a stop in Buenos Aires, where he reported a climate of strong "political confusion," before moving on to Montevideo, which was still reeling after a wave of arrests of workers' rights activists and opposition deputies, including several Catholics. There he attended a student rally in commemoration of Che, which left an impression on him by its vehement tone and incitement to violence.

The trip lasted more than a month, and it provided a very interesting, in-depth survey of the political situation in Latin America, of the systems and structures in place, of the repressive nature of the military regimes, and of the widespread fascination among young people with Castroism, even in Catholic movements. At the same time, Corghi's report helps us understand how Guevara's legend spread throughout protest groups in '68, becoming a common source of inspiration around the world. The *Note di cultura* group, for example, became more and more convinced that action needed to be taken in order to favor peaceful development, without isolating the Christian Democrats—or Catholics in general—from the reforms that were taking place. Indeed, they believed in a nonviolent resistance movement, in keeping with the ideas of the archbishop of Recife, who claimed that armed rebellion would only lead to counterinsurgency warfare. Indeed, youth protest movements were meant to pursue other courses of action, such as social criticism and civic engagement, and to be actively nonviolent in doing so. In any case, whereas La Pira placed his trust in the maturity of young Catholics, Corghi seemed more open to accepting armed struggle, albeit as the last possible solution. He reportedly broached the subject with some Tupamaros and Montoneros militants, and it would come up again much later in his exchanges with the Red Brigade.[72] In Corghi's view, armed struggle was only valid if the resistance was justified. This remained an unresolved (and uncertain) topic for him even during his second visit to Latin America as a young Christian Democrat in January 1968,[73] during which he was able to meet the French philosopher in prison in Camiri. Shortly thereafter, a committee was formed for the liberation of Debray; twenty-five different groups pledged their support for the initiative. The committee was coordinated by a group of people with wide-ranging political leanings, including several important figures from that period of dissent, such as Giorgio Giovannoni and Saverio Tutino. Its headquarters was at a new bookstore in Rome called Paesi nuovi, founded by Marcella Glisenti; the bookstore would go on to become an important hub of Third Worldist culture in the 1970s, a place where Catholics, left-wingers, and radicals could have political exchanges, and where an original form of Catholic feminism and environmentalism could flourish.[74] Once freed, Debray would recognize the role played by the Italian mediators, paying a visit to Corghi in Reggio Emilia and to Cardinal Lercaro in Bologna.

From a more general point of view, interest in Latin America during the spring of 1968—a time during which Leone's "transitional" government was taking office—brought people together from a variety of political backgrounds: from "pure" Catholic pacifists and human rights activists to hardliners and supporters of armed liberation. And though their paths did not always overlap and their relationships were at times quite complex, they all saw Latin America as a sort of extreme proving ground that was actually more and more comparable to an Italy in which the center-left appeared to be losing its grip. Indeed, by that point Latin America seemed to attract Italy's attention on many levels, increasingly becoming the ideal triangulation point between "North–South and America–Europe"—a place where, ideally, international relations were not dictated by party politics or religious affiliation but rather the result of progressively deinstitutionalized forms of cooperation that had value in and of themselves. This issue also concerned the West's general responsibility for the events in Latin America, as the Servite friar David Maria Turoldo explained years later by writing: "I am now more interested in the West than in the other, as that is the part of the world where my Church is most responsible."[75] This concept was reminiscent of Bertrand Russell's "appeal" to the people of the United States, not to mention Arturo Paoli's reflections on humanitarianism from 1968,[76] but it also echoed the concerns of the Atlanticists among the Italian Christian Democrats. Such appeared evident in a dossier contained in the Moro papers in Italy's National Archives (Archivio centrale dello Stato, ACS), entitled "Brief Summary of Communist Penetration in Latin America and in Underdeveloped Areas Marked by Land Hunger, Poverty and Illiteracy."[77] In the heart of '68, the basic idea driving many socially committed Catholics—those active in clubs, research centers, editorial boards, and universities—was not just to fight against the war in Vietnam; they also wanted to study the specific nature of the social, political, and religious issues in Latin America. By doing so, they hoped to build a bridge between two different yet increasingly interconnected worlds—a bridge that the majority of Italian Catholics would then be able to cross. It was an explosion following a period of acceleration, though some issues were also standardized and oversimplified in the process.

Further impetus came from the debate surrounding the pope's trip to Latin America and the Medellín Conference at the end of the summer. Indeed, it was becoming evident that the old model of Italian Catholic solidarity with Latin America was showing significant cracks. The conference proceedings overlapped with the descent of the Red Army upon Prague as the international climate continued to heat up. In describing the conference, the historian Silvia Scatena highlighted the "organizational spirit" and "creative disorder" that pervaded the event,[78] in keeping with the times. But in any case, the strong effect of the conference's conclusions could not be denied. The bishops produced a set of documents on *Justice, Peace,* and *Education* (among other topics), which represented the assimilation of Freire's bottom-up pedagogy, opening up new horizons for Christian school systems.[79] From *Il Regno* (a journal run by the Dehonians, which also edited the first Italian edition of the conference's concluding documents)[80] to *Mondo e missione*, the Catholic press at the time was closely following the developments in Medellín, and the topic of reform was consistently brought up. The Salesian Dario Viganò wrote: "When the Latin American bishops assure us that the continent is on the verge of a new historical era, they speak of a cultural change that will influence at least the entire Western world. Thus, involvement in Latin American issues means listening more closely to a voice of the future."[81]

Having ushered in a series of innovative changes (on the strength of slogans such as "A continent in motion" and "it's time to take action"), the Medellín Conference garnered much attention. It also overlapped perfectly with the unrest of the summer of '68. In that same period, the Venice Biennale had opened to scuffles between police and protesters, with Cesare Zavattini organizing his own counterfestival. That was immediately followed by a group of young Catholic dissenters who occupied the cathedral in Parma on September 14; Bishop Amilcare Pasini ended up calling the police, who cleared out the protesters a few hours later. The Parma protesters had made their requests known by distributing a leaflet in which they urged the diocese to have the "courage to make choices in favor of the poor and against capitalism"; they also demanded the reinstatement of a young priest—Don Pino Setti, the parish priest of Santa Maria della Pace—who was a promoter of "Beat-style Mass" and pro–Latin America movements. However, this swing to the left did have some immediate consequences: for example, the editor of the journal *Il Regno*, Comelli, was replaced after the publication of a series of articles—deemed too radical—on the legitimacy of Latin American resistance movements and the dialogue between Christianity and Marxism.[82] Various other Catholic journals stood out in that period because of their dissenting voices, such as *I-doc* in Rome, *Note di Cultura*, and *Testimonianze*, the latter of which was edited by Father Ernesto Balducci, the priest of Fiesole. Balducci reexamined Guevara's concept of the making of a "new man" through Catholic eyes (eventually interpreting it as a "planetary man").[83]

In the second half of '68, however, this climate of mounting protest pushed the Church beyond its limits. Rifts opened up within the ecclesiastical world, both in Italy and in the Latin American episcopate. Ivan Illich and CIDOC were even put on "trial" at the Vatican during those same months of '68, leading to a ban on the research center and Illich's eventual leaving of the priesthood.[84] At the same time, a number of ecclesiastical groups on the social and political front lines were facing increasing political pressure; this was true for Golconda, Sacerdotes para el pueblo, and Sacerdotes para el Tercer mundo,[85] not to mention the Jesuits at UCA El Salvador under Ignacio Ellacuría, female congregations, and the laity involved in social research centers, cooperatives, humanitarian groups, grassroots organizations, and basic ecclesial communities.

An emblematic case was that of Linda Bimbi, who transformed into an ardent supporter of Catholic Third Worldism in 1968.[86] Originally from Lucca, Bimbi joined the Canossians in 1952 after obtaining a degree in linguistics. She went to Brazil as a missionary, where for years she would work in education in the state of Minas Gerais. It was there that she began to cultivate her critical consciousness and become politicized. She experimented with basic ecclesial communities, a solution founded on group solidarity; she recognized how important it was to share experiences and to read scripture together; and she established contact with liberationist groups, student movements, and farmers who were open to a Christian–Marxist dialogue. Fitting, then, that in the fall of 1968, Linda Bimbi found herself at the height of a serious crisis—both on a personal level and in terms of the community she was serving—leading her to give up her vows. She was expelled from Brazil because of her show of sociopolitical engagement, returning to Italy with thirty-two fellow sisters in order to work with Basso on the establishment of a Peoples' Tribunal for Latin America (the future Russell Tribunal II). Pro–Latin America slogans could also be heard at a meeting in Rimini on November 2, 1968, between Catholic dissenters and representatives of the "spontaneous groups" of the New Left. This was a turbulent time of unrest that saw Italian Catholics become more independent in a certain sense; indeed, there used to be little difference between the Italian Catholic Church on a local level and the universal mission of the Holy See, but rising dissent now gave Italian Catholics the courage—both within and outside ecclesial forms of association—to refuse the contradiction between a "false church and a true church." Criticism was directed towards both the Holy See and Western governments, in what amounted to an assimilation of Fanon's condemnation of neocolonialism. The famous *Rockefeller Report on the Americas* appeared shortly thereafter.[87] Third Worldist *foquismo* also had a profound influence on future Italian liberation theologians, starting with Giulio Girardi, who at the time was a philosophy professor at the Salesian universities in Turin and Rome (he was eventually expelled from the latter). Girardi was the theorist behind "active nonviolence," but he was also a devout believer in the "revolutionary legend" of Che and Camilo Torres.[88]

Was this a sort of "cultural short-circuit" intensified by the unrest of that period, or was it a generational change of perspective on a crucial issue in contemporary Catholicism? After all, it was a Catholicism ostensibly divided between demands for justice and demands for liberation—demands naturally sublimated into the values of the Italian resistance movement (which still exerted a strong influence on the collective consciousness in late '60s Italy) while maintaining the Church's ethical and moral principles of nonviolence and total refusal of death as a means for progress. Even conservative Catholics—who were against such revolutionary movements—were concerned about this issue. Such emerged at a roundtable in Rome on March 12, 1968, entitled The Socioreligious Situation in Latin America, organized by the Institute of Latin American Studies at Father Morlion's Pro Deo University (a pro-Atlanticism institution). In the words of the Institute's president, Attilio Napoleone, the goal of the meeting (which saw the participation of 700 people, encompassing the clergy, the laity, and students) was to take stock of "that noble Christian continent which now sees itself in history's limelight," in order to "avoid great mistakes in judgment, careless prejudice, or inappropriate reactions."[89] However, the real specter hanging over this event was the fear that Latin American Catholics would fall into the grip of revolutionaries, and that this would then influence young European Catholics. Silvano Burgalassi warned that armed revolutions might "wantonly misappropriate" the gospel and *Populorum progressio*.[90] Indeed, what with the widespread occupation of universities and factories, 1968 drew to a close in the midst of rampant unrest—and this unrest seemed to be changing the terms of the protest movement, further cementing liberation theology in the collective consciousness.[91] What was highlighted in the eyes of Italian readers were three elements considered crucial in the postconciliar age: a new style of thinking in the Church, a different way of being in the Church, and the emergence of a new Church. If the first point legitimated in full a methodology of research, already destined to be consecrated by the theology of liberation, and the second highlighted a Church that "learns to learn," the insistence on the popular dimension was therefore the true interpretative code that helped to reread, also in political terms, the idea of liberation and of the option for the poor. As stated some years later by Carlos Mesteres, the ecclesial base communities experience would have demonstrated "that the ideas of the suffering people are not necessarily clear, beautiful and well-arranged."[92]

In this climate of reflection, engagement, and breaks from the norm, the relationship between Catholicism and Latin America reached a fever pitch. Even many young Christian Democrats seemed open to turning this ongoing cultural revolution into political action. To alleviate tensions, the Moro and Rumor governments began to push for public policies that would favor development cooperation in a world that was moving from bipolarity to multipolarity, thereby supporting the work of nascent Italian NGOs. As minister of foreign affairs in October of 1969, Moro referred to "Italy's interest in a coherent Community policy on Latin America," inviting his European colleagues to take inspiration from that period's "open and imaginative" political climate. Thus, it seemed that the Italian government was cautiously receptive to the demands of the '68 protest movement.[93]

CONCLUSIONS

Let us then return to the original question, namely, whether '68 was really a cultural revolution, and add a rather challenging second question: What was its legacy? From the Catholic point of view, that period was characterized by the networks, relationships, and social imaginaries built between Italy and Latin America. Thus, I believe we can look at how things played out in '68 as the culmination of a process of "buildup, acceleration, and explosion," keeping in mind the complex nature of such a model. Even when it standardized or oversimplified certain issues, the explosion had an undeniable influence on culture, society, and politics. First, '68 was a year in which Europe was brought closer to realities outside of its borders. This was made possible thanks to the birth of a creative dialogue (with its fair share of clashes and divisions) between different cultures and generations, each with their own needs and proposals, and each contributing to the creation of new ideals and new expectations. These were worlds that up to that point had been completely separated by the impenetrable wall of the Cold War, but now they were mixing on many different levels, giving rise to new experiences that not even the radicalization and political polarization of the 1960s would be able to undo.

This led to a combination of influences the likes of which had never been seen in the Catholic world. Indeed, in the buildup phase during the years of Vatican II, and even in the acceleration phase between 1965 and 1967, there was still a certain degree of separation between the ecclesiastical world, lay associations, and political actors (a state of affairs with roots in the crisis of the 1930s); in 1968, however, there was a multilevel fusion of sociopolitical needs that brought the political into the religious and the religious into the political (including the politics of bipolarity and North–South relations), with the social at the center of it all. In an era of rapidly growing consumerism, the Italianization of concepts such as the "option for the poor" and a "commitment to liberation" was indicative of this mixed approach—an approach that characterized the years to come, albeit with new divergences, divisions, and technical specializations. As evidenced by documents such as the encyclical *Laudato si'* (May 2015),[94] the papacy of Pope Francis seems to draw much inspiration from this cultural revolution, itself the result of an intense dialogue between the teachings of the Church, on one hand, and the world, the economy, and society, on the other.

There was another delicate issue that came to characterize the long 1970s: it was a period that marked the height of military dictatorships in Latin America and the *Anni di piombo* ("Years of Lead") in Italy. Indeed, this era felt the enormous effect of technological modernization, but also that of political and economic crisis (the end of the "Golden Age of Western Capitalism"). The decade was further weakened by a resurgence in—and sophistication of—the Mafia, and also a number of brutal terrorist attacks perpetrated by both the Far Right (from the Piazza Fontana bombing on December 12, 1969, to the Bologna train station massacre on August 2, 1980) and the Far Left (culminating on May 9, 1978, with the kidnapping and killing of Aldo Moro, president of the Christian Demo-

Figure 3.2 Special issue of *L'Italiano democratico*, supplement of *Il Popolo*, edited by the Young Democratic Christian of Milan, June 1969.

crats and supporter of dialogue with the communists).[95] It must be noted, however, that although some activists had their doubts, the concept of "revolution through peace" remained the predominant characteristic of Catholic protest movements in Italy. And although Catholic dissenters revealed themselves to be the most genuine of Third Worldists, they stayed out of the terrorist spiral that swept up Far Left and Far Right opposition groups. In the end, radical neo-Marxist groups such as Potere Operaio and Lotta continua had a much more Eurocentric, Fordist vision than even the most radical of Catholic activists. At a convention of young Christian Democrats held in Milan in May 1969, participants not only lodged their opposition to the Soviet invasion of Czechoslovakia and the war in Vietnam, they also discussed the prospects for peace and development in Latin America. One of the posters on display during the event read: "Che, King, Torres; different paths, one goal: peace."[96]

In the years to come, the cultural revolution of '68 was to be entwined with the important issue of liberation theology, a concept that would become a profound part of the Italian consciousness (often in oversimplified terms) thanks to the great success of Gutiérrez's book on the subject (published in Italy in 1972). Nonetheless, although interest in "the oppressed" of Latin America was certainly able to move Italian Catholics to sympathize with and even support liberationist struggles (as demonstrated by the case of Chile, and even more so by the Sandinista revolution in Nicaragua and the mobilization in favor of El Salvador following the murder of Archbishop Oscar Romero), there was still not the same "shift" towards more militant tactics seen with many groups active in Latin America. In other words, Italian Catholic activists were not moved to carry out domestic terrorist acts in the name of revolution. If anything, the influence of the cultural revolution of '68 was felt on two fronts in the Catholic world: first, after that fateful year of 1973 (oil crisis and Chilean coup), when there was a shift towards solidarity, condemnation of injustice, and the defense of human rights (the politically transcendent Permanent Peoples' Tribunal was an example); and second, after the "night of the Republic" in 1978 (the Moro assassination and the new Cold War), when Catholic activism shifted towards development cooperation, becoming less political in nature but also opening itself up to new issues (gender equality, environmental protection, criticism of the international financial system) and new methods.

What were Italian Catholics looking for in Latin America in the Long '68? A different and distant way, a magic mirror? It seems clear they felt a sense of belonging with Latin Americans as they wrestled with issues sinking into the deepest dimension of their Christian identities and with their relationship to a world perceived as brutal and unjust. These efforts forced them to question themselves in a new way around the relationship between faith and society, faith and economy, faith and politics. The year 1968 and the Medellín Conference's option for the poor opened a dialogue on the idea of liberation, which called into question a biblical, theological, ecclesial dimension, on the one hand, and social, economic, and political projects, on the other. Solidarity with the Latin American peoples, beyond mythical or idealized representations, controversies, and contradictions, showed the possible search for a liberating practice inspired by Christian values.

Yet, Rome continued to represent a symbolic center of gravity for the increasingly heterogeneous Latin American Catholicism, while Italian Catholics seemed in this sense to be ideal intermediaries, suspended between the Vatican world and the pushes of modernity. And on this ground, bridges, fractures, dreams, and utopias were built.

NOTES

1. M. Flores and G. Gozzini, *1968: Un anno spartiacque* (Bologna: Il Mulino, 2018); G. Orsina and G. Quagliariello, eds., *La crisi del sistema politico italiano e il Sessantotto* (Rubbettino: Soveria Manelli, 2005); M. Flores and A. De Bernardi, *Il Sessantotto* (Bologna: Il Mulino, 2003); M. Tolomelli, *Il Sessantotto: Una breve storia* (Rome: Carocci, 2008); M. Boato, *Il lungo '68 in Italia e nel mondo* (Brescia: La Scuola, 2018).

2. G. Crainz, *Il paese mancato: Dal miracolo economico agli anni Ottanta* (Rome: Donzelli, 2003).

3. The first two legislatures of the Italian Republic (1948–58) were based on the "centrist" formula that placed the Christian Democrats (DC) at the center of the government structures, supported by a series of minor allies. After a long genesis, DC came to an agreement with the Italian Socialist Party (PSI), which from the fourth legislature, from December 1963, entered the first Aldo Moro cabinet, inaugurating the "center-left" formula. See G. Vecchio and P. Trionfini, *Storia dell'Italia repubblicana (1946–2014)* (Milan: Monduzzi, 2014); L. Baldissara, ed., *Le radici della crisi: L'Italia fra gli anni Sessanta e Settanta* (Rome: Carocci, 2001); Y. Voulgaris, *L'Italia del centro-sinistra 1960–1968* (Rome: Carocci, 1998).

4. M. De Giuseppe, "Il 'terzo mondo' in Italia: Trasformazioni di un concetto tra opinione pubblica, azione politica e mobilitazione civile (1955–1980)," *Ricerche di storia politica* 1 (2011): 29–52.

5. G. Formigoni, *Storia d'Italia nella guerra fredda (1943–1978)* (Bologna: Il Mulino, 2016); U. Gentiloni Silveri, *L'Italia e la nuova frontiera: Stati Uniti e centro-sinistra (1958–1965)* (Bologna: Il Mulino, 1998); A. Giovagnoli and G. Del Zanna, eds., *Il mondo visto dall'Italia* (Milan: Guerini, 2005).

6. P. Pombeni, *Che cosa resta del '68?* (Bologna: Il Mulino, 2018), 11.

7. S. Inaudi and M. Margotti, *La rivoluzione del Concilio: La contestazione cattolica negli anni Sessanta e Settanta* (Rome: Studium, 2017); D. Saresella, *Dal Concilio alla contestazione: Riviste cattoliche negli anni del cambiamento (1958–1968)* (Brescia: Morcelliana, 2005); M. Forno, *La cultura degli altri: Il mondo delle missioni e la decolonizzazione* (Rome: Carocci, 2017).

8. *Pacem in terris*, April 11, 1963, http://w2.vatican.va/content/john-xxiii/it/encyclicals/documents/hf_j-xxiii_enc_11041963_pacem.html.

9. A. Melloni, *Il Concilio e la grazia: Saggi di storia sul Vaticano II* (Milan: Jaca Book, 2016); A. Giovagnoli, ed., *"Pacem in terris" tra azione diplomatica e guerra globale* (Milan: Guerini, 2003); A. Canavero and D. Saresella, eds., *Cattolicesimo e laicità: Politica, cultura e fede nel secondo Novecento* (Brescia: Morcelliana, 2016); A. Benci, *Il prossimo lontano: Alle origini della solidarietà internazionale in Italia* (Milan: Unicopli, 2016).

10. G. Girardi, *Che Guevara visto da un Cristiano: Il significato etico della sua scelta revoluzionaria* (Milan: Sperling & Kupfer, 2005).

11. G. R. Horn, *The Spirit of Vatican II: Western European Progressive Catholicism in the Long Sixties* (Oxford: Oxford University Press, 2015).

12. John XXIII, "Gaudet Mater Ecclesia," October, 11, 1962, http://w2.vatican.va/content/john-xxiii/it/speeches/1962/documents/hf_j-xxiii_spe_19621011_opening-council.html. In general, see G. Alberigo (director) and Alberto Melloni, ed., *Storia del Concilio Vaticano II*, 5 vols. (Bologna: Peeters/Il Mulino, 1995–2001).

13. Paolo VI, "Allocuzione per il solenne inizio della Seconda sessione del Concilio ecumenico Vaticano II," September, 29, 1963, https://w2.vatican.va/content/paul-vi/it/speeches/1963/documents/hf_p-vi_spe_19630929_concilio-vaticano-ii.html.

14. L. Milani, *Lettera a una professoressa, come Scuola di Barbiana* (Florence: Libreria Editrice Fiorentina, 1967); now see L. Milani, *Tutte le opere*, Vol. 1, edizione diretta da A. Melloni, ed. F. Ruozzi, A. Carfora, V. Oldano, and S. Tanzarella (Milan: Mondadori, 2017).

15. M. Cuminetti, *Il dissenso cattolico in Italia: L'avventura politica di un riformatore cristiano* (Milan: Rizzoli, 1983); L. Labor, *Scritti e discorsi*, ed. C. F. Casula (Milan: M&B Publishing, 2003); M. Margotti, *Cattolici del sessantotto: Protesta politica e rivolta religiosa nella contestazione tra gli anni Sessanta e Settanta* (Rome: Studium, 2019).

16. G. Bianchi, *L'Italia del dissenso* (Brescia: Queriniana, 1968).

17. P. Pombeni, *Giuseppe Dossetti: L'avventura politica di un riformatore Cristiano* (Bologna: Il Mulino, 2013); D. Saresella, *David M. Turoldo, Camillo de Piaz e la Corsia dei Servi di Milano (1943–1963)* (Brescia: Morcelliana, 2008).

18. A. Santagata, *La contestazione cattolica: Movimenti, cultura e politica dal Vaticano II al '68* (Rome: Viella, 2016).

19. G. Formigoni, *Storia d'Italia nella guerra fredda (1943–1978)* (Bologna: Il Mulino, 2016), 371.

20. A. Zambarbieri, ed., *Linee per una storia dell'editoria cattolica in Italia* (Brescia: Morcelliana, 2013).

21. D. Saresella, *Dal Concilio alla Contestazione: Riviste cattoliche negli anni del cambiamento (1958–1968)* (Brescia: Morcelliana, 2005).

22. G. Verucci, "Il post-concilio, la crisi del 1968 e il dissenso in Italia," in *Ernesto Balducci: La Chiesa, la società, la pace*, ed. B. Bocchini Camaiani (Brescia: Morcelliana, 2005), 35–44.

23. J. Cellini, *Universalism and Liberation: Italian Catholic Culture and the Idea of International Community* (Leuven: Leuven University Press, 2017).

24. R. Holden and E. Zolov, *Latin America and the United States: A Documentary History* (Oxford: Oxford University Press, 2010); H. Brands, *Latin America's Cold War* (Cambridge, MA: Harvard University Press, 2012); D. Spenser, ed., *Espejos de la guerra fría: México, América Central y el Caribe* (México, D.F.: Porrúa/Ciesas, 2006).

25. V. Manzano, *The Age of Youth in Argentina: Culture, Politics, and Sexuality from Perón to Videla* (Chapel Hill: University of North Carolina Press, 2014).

26. D. G. Groody and G. Gutiérrez, *The Preferential Option for the Poor beyond Theology* (Notre Dame, IN: University of Notre Dame Press, 2013).

27. S. Scatena, *In populo pauperum: La Chiesa latinoamericana dal Concilio a Medellín (1962–1968)* (Bologna: Il Mulino, 2007).

28. F. De Giorgi, *Paolo VI: Il Papa del moderno* (Brescia: Morcelliana, 2015), 359.

29. G. La Bella, *L'umanesimo di Paolo VI* (Soveria Mannelli: Rubbettino, 2015).

30. Paul VI, "Radiomessaggio al Seminario Nuestra Señora de Guadalupe in Verona," November 8, 1964, https://w2.vatican.va/content/paul-vi/it/speeches/1964/documents/hf_p-vi_spe_19641108_seminario-verona.html.

31. L. Ceci, *La teologia della liberazione in America latina: L'opera di Gustavo Gutiérrez* (Milan: Franco Angeli, 1999).

32. P. Trionfini, *La laicità della CISL: Autonomia e unità sindacale negli anni Sessanta* (Brescia: Morcelliana, 2014); A. Ciampiani, *La CISL tra integrazione europea e mondializzazione: Profilo storico del sindacato nuovo nelle relazioni internazionali* (Rome: Edizioni Lavoro, 2000).

33. C. F. Casula, *Le Acli: Una bella storia italiana* (Rome: Anicia, 2008); S. Sandri, *La donna nella storia delle Acli: I luoghi, i tempi, le persone* (Trento: EAC, 2010).

34. Tricontinental, *Tricontinental Bulletin*, Executive Secretariat of the Organization of Solidarity with the Peoples of Africa, Asia and Latin America, OSPAAL, l'Havana, 1966. See also M. Randall, *Exporting Revolution: Cuba's Global Solidarity* (Durham, NC: Duke University Press, 2017).

35. S. Scatena, *La teologia della liberazione in America latina* (Rome: Carocci, 2008).

36. P. Casaldáliga, *Una Chiesa dell'Amazzonia in conflitto con il latifondo e l'emarginazione sociale* (Rome: Asal, 1972).

37. A. Benci, *Il prossimo lontano: Alle origini della solidarietà internazione in Italia* (Milan: Unicopli, 2016).

38. M. Busani, *Gioventù studentesca: Storia di un movimento cattolico dalla ricostruzione alla contestazione* (Rome: Studium, 2016).

39. A. Antoniazzi, "La mia esperienza di vita e di fede, tra Milano e il Brasile," *Appunti di cultura e politica* 6 (2006): 32–38.

40. A. Paoli, *"Vivo sotto la tenda": Lettere ad Adele Toscano* (Cinisello Balsamo: San Paolo, 2006), 7–21. An important amount of documents is available at the archive of the Fondo di Documentazione Arturo Paoli, in Lucca, Tuscany.

41. F. Fanon, *I dannati della terra* (Torino, 1962); original French ed., *Les damnés de la terre* (Paris: Maspero, 1962).

42. Paul VI, *Populorum progressio*, March 26, 1967, http://w2.vatican.va/content/paul-vi/it/encyclicals/documents/hf_p-vi_enc_26031967_populorum.html.

43. R. Nocera, *Acuerdos y desacuerdos: La Dc italiana y el Pdc chileno, 1962–1973* (Santiago: Fondo de cultura económica, 2015), 23.

44. L. Guarnieri and M. R. Stabili, "Il mito politico dell'America latina negli anni Sessanta e Settanta in Italia," in Giovagnoli and Del Zanna, eds., *Il mondo visto dall'Italia*, 228–44.

45. See the documented biography written by his son Carlo, C. Feltrinelli, *Senior Service* (Milan: Feltrinelli, 1999).

46. H. Cerutti Guldberg and J. Pakkasvirta, eds., *Utopía en marcha* (Quito/Helsinki: Abya Yala-Renvall Institute/Helsinki University, 2009).

47. M. Kaller-Dietrich, *Vita di Ivan Illich* (Rome: Edizioni dell'Asino, 2011; original ed., 2007).

48. A. Gaudio, ed., *Ivan Illich: Un profeta postmoderno* (Brescia: La Scuola, 2012).

49. P. Prodi, *Giuseppe Dossetti e le Officine bolognesi* (Bologna: Il Mulino, 2016), 177.

50. Among others at the conference, participants included the socialist Chilean Salvador Allende, as chairman of the works, the Cape Verdean Amílcar Cabral, the Guatemalan Luis Augusto Turcios, the Argentine Jorge Moreno of Joventud Peronista Revolucionaria, and the Vietnamese Nguyen Van Tien. A tribute was paid to the Moroccan el Mehdi Ben Barka, just killed in Paris. See S. Christiansen and Z. Scarlet, eds., *The Third World in the Global 1960s* (New York: Berghahn, 2013).

51. In Italy two books about Torres were published in 1968: Norberto Habegger, *Camilo Torres prete e guerrigliero* (Florence: Cultura, 1968); and Germán Guzmán Campos, *Cattolicesimo e rivoluzione in America Latina: Vita di Camilo Torres* (Bari-Rome: Laterza, 1968).

52. This series of books was part of a larger collection entitled Cronache alla prova (described as "a collection in which the reader can act as the co-author").

53. G. R. Horn, *The Spirit of '68: Rebellion in Western Europe and North America, 1956–1976* (Oxford: Oxford University Press, 2007).

54. G. Barrau, *Le mai 68 des catholiques* (Paris: Les Editions de l'Atelier, 1998).

55. CIDOC informa, *America latina: Parole come armi* (Milan: Jaca Book, 1968), 7–8.

56. In 1967 an investigation of the magazine *L'Espresso* brought to light a coup plan prepared three years earlier by the then commander of the Carabinieri, General Giovanni De Lorenzo. The story, not yet fully clarified, caused a trial of the journalists involved and landed in parliament where, in January 1968, the independent deputy Luigi Anderlini denounced omissions in the investigation. In the legislative elections of May 19–20, DC received 39.1% of the votes, pressed by the unified list of PCI-PSIUP-independents with 30%, while the united front of the socialists, PSU, stopped at 14.5%. See M. Franzinelli, *Il piano Solo: I servizi segreti, il centro-sinistra e il "golpe" del 1964* (Milan: Mondadori, 2010).

57. The Pasolini poem, "Il PCI ai giovani," published in *L'Espresso*, June 16, 1968, raised strong controversy inside and outside the communist front and among intellectuals interested in the new youth movement. See http://temi.repubblica.it/espresso-il68/1968/06/16/il-pci-ai-giovani/?h=0.

58. M. Tolomelli, *Terrorismo e società: Il pubblico dibattito in Italia e in Germania negli anni Settanta* (Bologna: Il Mulino, 2007). Rostagno created the Milanese leftist cultural center Macondo (inspired by García Márquez), and, after a period spent in India, he founded the Samaden community to help young people with drug addiction, near Trapani, Sicily, where he was killed in a Mafia attack in 1988.

59. M. Boato, *Il lungo '68 in Italia e nel mondo* (Brescia: La Scuola, 2018).

60. F. Socrate, *Sessantotto. Due generazioni* (Rome-Bari: Laterza, 2018), 7–8.

61. "Per un'anagrafe dei gruppi e circoli spontanei," *ACLI Bulletin* 12 (1968). Also in Bianchi, *L'Italia del dissenso*, 201–16.

62. A. Puente Lutteroth, *Innovaciones y tensiones en los procesos socio-eclesiales: De la acción católica a las comunidades eclesiales de base* (Cuernavaca: Uaem-Cehila, 2002).

63. G. Girardello, ed., *Preti e laici veronesi raccontano la missione* (Verona: Centro missionario diocesano, 2011).

64. Korda, born Alberto Díaz Gutiérrez, already a fashion photographer, had taken that image on the edge of a public funeral. Giangiacomo Feltrinelli used it at the death of Che for a poster and as the cover of the Italian version of the book by E. Guevara, *Diario in Bolivia* (Milan: Feltrinelli, 1968). See T. Ziff, *Che Guevara: Revolutionary and Icon* (London: Abrams Image, V&A, 2006); C. Feltrinelli, *Senior Service*. In general, see V. Oikión Solano, M. López Ávalos, and E. Rey Tristán, eds., *El estudio de las luchas revolucionarias en América Latina, 1959–1996: Estado de la cuestión* (Morelia: El Colegio de Michoacán, Universidad de Santiago de Compostela, 2014).

65. J. Pensado, *Rebel Mexico: Student Unrest and Authoritarian Political Culture during the Long Sixties* (Stanford, CA: Stanford University Press, 2013).

66. The testimony-reportage of the journalist is in O. Fallaci, "La notte di sangue in cui sono stata ferita," *L'Europeo* 42, October 17, 1968. G. Flaherty, *Hotel Mexico: Dwelling on the '68 Movement* (Berkeley: University of California Press, 2016). See also O. Fallaci, *1968: Dal Vietnam al Messico: Diario di un anno cruciale* (Milan: Rizzoli, 2017).

67. R. Debray, *Rivoluzione nella rivoluzione?* (Milan: Feltrinelli, 1967). On the arrest and the trial, see R. Debray, *Processo a chi?* (Milan: Jaca Book, 1968), and Debray, *Autodifesa davanti al tribunale militare di Camiri* (Milan: Feltrinelli, 1968).

68. Telegram, September 27, 1967, in Afglp, busta XIX, fasc. 9, doc. 1.

69. A few months later an editorial of the magazine reported: "The trip was intended to document the situation of Latin American political movements, to investigate the possibility of obtaining the release of Debray . . . in exchange for the release of some opponents to the Castro regime detained in Cuba. We had indeed noted in some of Fidel Castro's speeches the general provision for an operation of this type and we hoped to contribute to its realization. To increase the effectiveness of the action, we have also sought international partnerships: the International League of Human Rights and the World Federation of United Cities (of which Prof. La Pira is president)" ("Giro d'orizzonte," *Note di cultura* 35 (1968): 3).

70. C. Corghi, *Resoconto del viaggio in America Latina*, in Afglp, busta XIX, fasc. 9, doc. 4.

71. Telegram, October 7, 1967, in Afglp, busta XIX, fasc. 9, doc. 2.

72. G. Panvini, *Cattolici e violenza politica: L'altro album di famiglia del terrorismo italiano* (Venice: Marsilio, 2014). As highlighted by the author, the relationship between Corghi and some Red Brigadists such as Franceschini with whom he would discuss the experience of Latin American revolutionary groups, remains to be clarified; even his distance from the group has been proved. Furthermore, see G. Panvini, *Ordine nero, guerriglia rossa: La violenza politica nell'Italia degli anni Sessanta e Settanta, 1966–1975* (Turin: Einaudi, 2009).

73. C. Corghi, "Diario di due viaggi in America Latina," *Note di cultura* 35 (1968): 16–46. He thus concluded his article: "In front of the rich Parisian shops I always have the image of the military Casinò of Camiri, of the barriadas, of the poor Indios, of the miners. The contrast is violent. Terribly violent."

74. The appeal for the release of Regis Debray was later published in *Note di cultura* 6 (1969): 422–23, n52.

75. David Maria Turoldo, "La morte come rivoluzione," afterword to O. A. Romero, *Diario* (Molfetta: La Meridiana, 1990), 559. See also M. De Giuseppe, *L'altra America: I cattolici italiani e l'America latina. Da Medellín a Francesco* (Brescia: Morcelliana, 2017).

76. P. Gauthier, A. Paoli, and P. Mazzolari, *La collera dei poveri: Testi e documenti sulla povertà*, ed. A. Barbero and P. Barbero (Turin: Gribaudo, 1967).

77. *Breve sintesi sulla penetrazione comunista nell'America latina e nelle aree sottosviluppate segnate da fame di terra, povertà e analfabetismo*, in ACS, Aldo Moro, s.3, ss.2, b. 58.

78. Scatena, *In Populo pauperum*, 338.

79. The Italian translation is *Seconda Conferenza generale dell'Episcopato latinoamericano* (Medellín, 1968), in *Enchiridion: Documenti della Chiesa latinoamericana* (Bologna: Emi, 1995), 139–59.

80. *Il Regno, Medellín: Documenti: La Chiesa nell'attuale trasformazione dell'America latina alla luce del Concilio Vaticano II* (Bologna: Edizioni Dehoniane Bologna, 1969).

81. D. Viganò, "L'ora dell'America latina," in *Enchiridion: Documenti della Chiesa latinoamericana*, 159.

82. M. M. Benzoni, "Attualità e profezia: I cattolici italiani e l'America latina negli anni del Post-concilio (1967–1974). Appunti su una ricerca in corso," in *Al di là dei confini. Cattolici italiani e vita internazionale*, ed. A. Canavero (Milan: Guerini, 2004), 91–124.

83. E. Balducci, *L'uomo planetario* (Milan: Camunia, 1985).

84. The CIDOC Collection, which contains about 7,000 documents on Church and society, ecclesiastical history, movements, sanctuaries, popular piety, is kept in the Daniel Cosío Villegas Library of El Colegio de México.

85. Movimiento de Sacerdotes para el Tercer Mundo, *Los sacerdotes para el Tercer Mundo y la actualidad nacional* (Buenos Aires: La Rosa Blindada, 1973).

86. C. Bonifazi, *Linda Bimbi: Una vita, tante storie* (Torino: Edizioni Gruppo Abele, 2015).

87. In 1969, Nelson Rockefeller presented his famous report to the Nixon administration at the end of a long journey to Latin America. The document highlighted the risk of a revolutionary turning point in a part of the Church. See "Quality of Life in the Americas: Statement by President Nixon and Text of the Rockfeller Mission Report," *The Department of State Bulletin* 61, no. 1589, December 8, 1969, 493–540, https://archive.org/details/departmentofstat6169unit/page/n233/mode/2up. *The Rockefeller Report on the Americas* (New York: Quadrangle, 1969).

88. G. Girardi, *Cristianesimo, liberazione umana, lotta di classe* (Assisi: Cittadella, 1971). The large personal archive of the activist is now deposited at the Basso Foundation, AFLLB/ISSOCO, G. Girardi Fund.

89. *La situazione socioreligiosa in America latina*, Istituto di studi latinoamericano (Rome: Pro Deo, 1968), 2.

90. Ibid., 6.

91. A. Agosti, L. Passerini, and N. Tranfaglia, *La cultura e i luoghi del '68* (Milan: FrancoAngeli, 1991); A. Mangano, *Le culture del '68: Gli anni Sessanta, le riviste, il movimento* (Pistoia: CDS, 1989).

92. "Una Chiesa che nasce dal popolo," *Quaderni Asal* 21-22 (1975): 14.

93. In *Comunicazione alla Commissione esteri della Camera dei deputati*, January 21, 1971, ACS, AM, s.1, ss.14, b. 23.

94. Pope Francis, *Laudato si'*, May 24, 2015, http://w2.vatican.va/content/francesco/it/encyclicals/documents/papa-francesco_20150524_enciclica-laudato-si.html. See also the interview by Eugenio Scalfari with Pope Francis, "E' un onore essere chiamato rivoluzionario," *La Repubblica*, March 29, 2018.

95. G. Formigoni, *Aldo Moro: Lo statista e il suo dramma* (Bologna: Il Mulino, 2016); L. Baldissara, ed., *Le radici della crisi: L'Italia fra gli anni Sessanta e Settanta* (Rome: Carocci, 2001); G. M. Ceci, *Il terrorismo italiano: Storia di un dibattito* (Rome: Carocci, 2013); L. Cominelli, *L'Italia sotto tutela: Stati Uniti, Europa e crisi italiana degli anni Settanta* (Florence: Le Monnier, 2014); M. Dondi, *L'eco del boato: Storia della strategia della tensione (1965–1974)* (Rome-Bari: Laterza, 2015).

96. See the private archive of Gilberto Bonalumi and *L'Italiano democratico*, supplement of *Il Popolo lombardo*, June 21, 1969.

FOUR

Revolutionary Time and the Belatedness of Music in May '68

ERIC DROTT

Writing in the wake of 1968, critic Louis-Jean Calvet observed that during periods of revolutionary upheaval people seldom sing songs born of the moment. "One always sings the previous revolution," he declared,[1] observing that the two songs most indelibly linked to moments of revolutionary upheaval in the French social imagination—"La Marseillaise," in connection with the French Revolution, and "L'Internationale," in connection with the Paris Commune—in fact both postdated the events they were associated with:

> "La Marseillaise" evokes for us the bourgeois revolution of 1789 . . . and "L'Internationale" evokes for us, through the intermediary of Pottier [the poet who composed the song's text], the Paris Commune. . . . Yet neither of these two songs played a role in the events they were supposed to "represent." "La Marseillaise," composed in Strasbourg by Claude-Joseph Rouget de Lisle in 1792, of course played no role in

> the events of 1789. . . . Clearly we find ourselves confronted with a song that was only considered *afterwards* [*après coup*] as a sign of '89. As for "L'Internationale," which was indeed written in 1871, just after the suppression of the Commune, it was set to music in 1888 by Pierre Degeyter, well after the fact.[2]

More recent events seemed to confirm Calvet's thesis. It may have been the case that "a good part of the songs inspired by the May '68 events were written and performed in the course of these events," but these were not the songs most often sung by militants during protests, sit-down strikes, and other actions: "On the barricades, however, and in the various demonstrations, one sang something altogether different: 'La jeune garde,' 'L'Internationale,' etc., that is to say once again, the *previous* revolution."[3] Newspaper accounts and oral histories of the uprising bear out Calvet's anecdotal observations.[4] Far from representing a radical break, far from unleashing the pent-up creative energies of the masses, watershed events like May '68 tend to be characterized instead by a return to the familiar, to learned repertoires of political and artistic action. In formulating this thesis, Calvet drew inspiration from none other than Marx himself, echoing the latter's claim (from the *Eighteenth Brumaire of Louis Bonaparte*) that in "periods of revolutionary crisis [the living] anxiously conjure up the spirits of the past to their service."[5] The difference is that for Calvet such moments conjure up not just the spirits of the past, but also their songs. It is for this reason that the music of May '68 did not coincide with May '68, its place having been usurped by that of revolutions prior.

In this chapter I explore the question of music's perceived belatedness vis-à-vis May/June 1968, and some of the responses this perception generated on the part of musicians. Music was hardly the only form of creative expression to grapple with the sense that the May events had been for it something of a "missed encounter."[6] James Williams, for instance, has described the "regret" felt by filmmakers as a result of cinema's having "somehow 'missed' the events and 'arrived' too late for its moment of destiny with revolutionary history."[7] He cites in this connection an exclamation made by Jean-Luc Godard at that year's Cannes Film Festival, before it was brought to a premature end by the protests roiling the country: "There's not a single film showing the problems of workers and students today—we're late!"[8] Curiously, the media that Godard bemoaned for having failed to keep up with the crush of political history, film, and magnetic tape, were central to the strategies certain musicians developed to mitigate the troubling sense that the time of musical production was out of step with that of revolutionary action—what Peter Schmelz has described as the sentiment that music in general and art music in particular "tends to lag behind history."[9] Revealing in this regard are songs and compositions that incorporated field recordings made during the uprising of May/June '68.

Two such works are the focus of the second part of the chapter. Both were created in the months immediately following May '68: *Rumeurs*, a mixed media piece featuring tape, instrumentalists, and a massive chorus of more than 3,500 singers, jointly written by electronic music composers Guy Reibel and François Bayle; and "Nous sommes le pouvoir," the opening track of singer-songwriter Colette Magny's album *Magny 1968*. Of note is how both *Rumeurs* and "Nous sommes le pouvoir" make use of what Andrea Bohlman has dubbed "sound documents" as a means of conferring sociopolitical authority upon music and musician alike. Equally of note is how such sound documents were used to collapse the distance that was seen to separate musical action from political action.[10]

That musical action should have been perceived as standing at a remove from political action is implicit in Calvet's thesis regarding the belatedness of music vis-à-vis revolutionary events. Yet it would seem to fly in the face of received wisdom about what transpired in 1968, in France and elsewhere. Didn't '68 mark a cultural revolution, a radical change in customs and creative practice, one whose legacies still haunt us today? Aren't the French May events renowned for being an all-too-brief parenthesis during which "poetry ruled the streets," when the separation of art and everyday life was momentarily held in suspense?[11] Perhaps music was a case apart, which, by virtue of historical accident or some internal necessity, was unable to intervene as forcefully in the uprising as, say, poetry or the visual arts? Or perhaps the issue was more specifically a French one, given that in the run-up to the May events there was scant evidence in the country of the sort of vibrant counterculture that had developed in the United States and the UK over the course of the 1960s?

This last possibility is worth dwelling on, if only because music's situation in France does seem to stand out relative to other countries during the same historical moment. Elsewhere, under different political conditions, in response to different historical legacies, the relation between culture—above all music—and politics appeared far less troubled. In Soviet Bloc countries such as Czechoslovakia, Poland, or East Germany, restrictions on political expression both before and especially after 1968 made musical expression all the more important as an outlet for dissent, as Timothy Ryback makes clear in his contribution in this volume.[12] In Chile, as J. Patrice McSherry points out, the reclamation of hitherto marginalized traditions during the 1960s helped make the *nueva canción* and its offshoots in other Latin American countries into important means of not only representing but also mobilizing working-class and peasant populations.[13] And in the United States, the counterculture's rejection of prevailing social norms suggested that it stood in a symbiotic relation to the more explicitly politicized New Left and antiwar movements, with rock and folk music in particular serving as important pathways into political activism for many young people.

Yet even in this last instance, in the United States, where the rock counterculture and the New Left are often portrayed as two sides of the same coin, interactions between political and cultural revolutionaries were not always as smooth, as frictionless, or as lacking in conflict as the subsequent mythologization of the '60s might lead one to believe. As Patrick Burke has noted in connection with Jefferson Airplane's flirtation with radical politics in the late 1960s, the band's "ambiguous view of revolution" found an echo within the broader rock community, where there was no clear "consensus about rock's role in revolution or even about the value of revolution itself."[14] On the other side of the culture/politics divide, attitudes were equally mixed with regard to the counterculture. It wasn't just that different ideological factions held different views of rock and the hippie lifestyle; even individual activists found themselves torn on the subject. "Pop music has become a financial staple of US internal imperialism," a form of "totalitarian leisure," according to one author writing in the underground paper *The Old Mole* in August 1969.[15] But the same author also had to concede that for many young people, "the music is real and crucial. Like drugs, rock music is a component of cross-class rebel youth culture."[16] Rock may have been revolutionary, but not necessarily in the way militants construed the term. For the author of the article in question, Bonny Cohen, this made it imperative to bring political and cultural revolution into closer alignment, if the energies of the latter were to be harnessed on behalf of the former: "We must pick up on the energy and the image:

create an underground of music, hard-core revolutionary rock. Groups should, will, spring directly out of the movement, ending the cultural-political schizophrenia of the new left."[17] Musical and political revolution by this reading could be brought into alignment, but this was something that had to be achieved rather than simply assumed.

That such "cultural/political schizophrenia" was manifest even somewhere like the United States suggests that France was perhaps less of an outlier than might first appear. And though there may indeed have been peculiarities about music's standing in French society circa 1968 that led to the less prominent role it played in the events of May '68, especially compared to other forms of creative expression, I would contend that Calvet's remarks nonetheless bear witness to an important aspect of the ambiguous place that culture in general—and music in particular—occupied during the particular moment of global crisis that was 1968. What it attests to is a certain ambivalence regarding the role art in general and music, in particular, played in the antisystemic movements of this period, which in turn reflected an ambivalence that coursed through these movements themselves. As Giovanni Arrighi, Terence Hopkins, and Immanuel Wallerstein have noted, 1968 "was born of hopes at least as much as discontents," its protests targeting not just the capitalist world system and the United States as global hegemon, but just as importantly the Old Left, whose "original goals" it sought to fulfill through "an effort to overcome [its] limitations."[18] That is to say, 1968 can be understood as having been animated by a desire to realize the promise left unfulfilled by the Old Left, the promise that exploitation would at last be made a thing of the past. Yet precisely because the Old Left had left this promise unfulfilled—or worse still, had betrayed it, a charge that student activists Daniel and Gabriel Cohn-Bendit leveled at what they derided as the "senile malady of communism"[19]—it became one of the movement's principal targets. Similarly, 1968 was animated at least in certain quarters by a desire to realize the promise left unfulfilled by art, the promise of a world freed of alienation. Yet precisely because art had left this promise unfulfilled—or worse still, functioned as a kind of escape valve that *ensured* this promise would go unfulfilled—it too became one of the movement's principal targets.[20] In both cases, a dialectic of desire and repudiation was at work. Certain inherited forms of political and artistic conduct served at once as models whose ideals were to guide the way forward and historical legacies whose burden was to be cast off.

MUSICAL TIME AND REVOLUTIONARY TIME

Ironically, one of the most important legacies informing the actions of artists and militants alike during May/June 1968 was the very separation of art and politics that many among them endeavored to surmount. The enduring influence of their perceived estrangement can be seen in the sentiment, expressed by no small number of cultural producers, that political exigencies demanded they set aside their creative activities, that they leave behind the atelier and the concert hall in order to join students on the barricades and workers in the factories. Gérard Fromanger, a participant in the Atelier populaire des beaux-arts, noted that in May "artists [were] no longer in their studios, they no longer work, they can't work anymore because the real is more powerful than their inventions. Naturally, they become militants, me among them."[21] Similar attitudes were expressed by the musicians whose work is the focus of the second part of this paper. In an account of *Rumeurs*, Reibel (writing with Michel Chion) noted how during the month of May "the public, soon imitated by composers themselves, progressively deserted cultural 'enclosures' in order to go to other places, where a game of much greater importance was being played. Professional activities ground to a halt for about two months: current events [*l'actualité*] and life unfolded elsewhere than in the studios and auditoriums."[22] More pointedly still, Colette Magny wryly remarks at one point in the course of the opening track of her album *Magny 68* that during the May events "singing had become ridiculous [*dérisoire*]" (an aside whose significance I will expand upon in what follows). Nor was the notion that music had receded in importance in the face of other, more pressing demands restricted to artists working in France during the May/June uprising. One need only think of one of the more famous songs of 1968—the Rolling Stones' "Street Fighting Man," notably inspired by the May events in France—to see how widely shared was the belief that making music had become a poor substitute for the more serious business of making history. Particularly revealing is the song's refrain, with its complaint that in "sleepy London town" the only way to voice one's dissent was by singing in a "rock 'n' roll band," not having any other viable outlet. Across the English Channel, away from the epicenter of revolutionary ferment, Mick Jagger and his bandmates were reduced to lamenting the way political fervor had been sublimated into music.

The sense that there were more urgent matters to attend to during the upheavals of 1968 goes some way towards explicating music's belatedness in relation to these upheavals. The perceived disjunction of musical action and revolutionary action suggested that pursuit of the former precluded pursuit of the latter. To this disjunction one might add another: that which placed revolutionary time at odds with the time of artistic and musical creation. Quite a few participants have attested to the way their experience of time shifted during the course of *les événements*, at once compressed and dilated during the few short weeks the uprising lasted. "Very early on . . . we were caught up in a sort of whirlwind" was how Jean-Franklin Narot characterized the experience, describing the "unheard of acceleration of time" that resulted from the realization that "the effects of our actions . . . infinitely surpassed their anticipated results."[23] His comments resonate with those of others. A participant in a roundtable discussion organized by the sociologist Alfred Willener at the Nanterre campus of the Université de Paris in November 1968 recounted how "there was a difference in the rhythm of time, even in the meaning of time. For example, decisions were made in the morning to be implemented that same evening. . . . 'Where are we going?' Nobody told us, nothing was written down, we had to decide what to do together, then to do it straight away. . . . So there was a change in real historical time. What happened could not be encompassed in the old conception of time."[24] This "change in real historical time," along with the heightened tempo at which events seemed to unfold, placed tremendous pressure on the habitual rhythms of artistic production. As Kristin Ross notes, "only the most 'immediate of artistic techniques' . . . could keep up with the speed of events."[25] At the Atelier populaire des beaux-arts, the struggle to keep pace with a movement that consistently outstripped any and every effort to capture it, both in terms of political and artistic representation, impressed itself on the posters that artist-activists fabricated. In terms of the posters' content, this can be seen in the stress placed on the need to do nothing other than keep the movement moving. "The 'message' of the majority of the posters," Ross writes, "was the certification, and at times the imperative, that whatever it was that was happening . . . simply *continue*: 'Continuons le combat.' 'La grève continue.' 'Contre offensive: la grève continue.' 'Chauffeurs de taxi: la lutte continue.' 'Maine Montparnasse: la lutte continue.'"[26] At the level of technique, this imperative led artists to replace lithography with serigraphy as the preferred means of producing posters, on account of the latter's increased speed and flexibility. The more quickly images could be turned out, the closer one came to attaining "the absolute interpenetration of art and event," the receding target where revolutionary time and artistic time coincide.[27]

The foregoing suggests one very practical reason why, despite having been "written and performed in the course of these events," as Calvet reports, "a good part of the songs inspired by the May '68 events" nevertheless had such a limited presence during the uprising itself. Namely, technologies permitting the large-scale mechanical reproduction of sound recordings were much more expensive and much less accessible to activists at the time than were serigraphs, mimeographs, and other cheap methods of reproducing images and prints: "During the insurrection of May '68," wrote one observer, "collective imagination was more often written than it was sung."[28] The development of magnetic tape and the subsequent mass marketing of portable tape recorders (most notably the Nagra III) in the decades after World War II may have made it easier for people to make their own amateur recordings, whether of music, speech, or the sounds of everyday life, but facilities for engraving records and pressing them in significant quantities were for the most part still industrial concerns, and as such out of the reach of most ordinary people. Even when artist-activists did manage to gain access to such facilities, the logistics involved in doing so all but guaranteed a delay between the moment of music's inspiration, composition, and/or performance, and that of its public circulation. Such was the case with a 45-rpm EP produced by singer-songwriter Dominique Grange. Containing four songs she had composed both during and shortly after *les événements*, the disc did not come out until the fall of 1968, well after the revolutionary moment had passed.[29] For the most part, however, music created during May '68, in response to May '68, did not enjoy the posthumous existence that Grange's songs did, having never been captured on tape or vinyl for posterity. Rather, they were doomed to the sort of ephemeral existence that is the fate of any music performed live. "Certainly there were . . . songs improvised in situ, according to the needs or the pleasures of the moment," observed critic Jacques Vassal in summing up music's place within the movement. But the fact that such songs "went unrecorded" was for him "only logical." "In moments like these," he mused, "one is hardly worried about fixing events on paper, on magnetic tape, or on film; one thinks above all about living them!"[30]

Speed alone was not the only salient feature of revolutionary time, such as it was experienced during May '68. It was also characterized by its radical indeterminacy, by the sense of pure possibility that permeated each moment, as the future was called into question. Elsewhere in his remarks on the different "historical time" to which May '68 gave rise, the same anonymous participant in Willener's Nanterre roundtable contrasted this "new, very special, purely synchronic time" with that of everyday life in capitalist modernity: "Before, society reproduced itself at an increasing, progressive rate. Then suddenly there is a break, and instead of finding themselves in the rhythm in which they normally live, morning, evening, holidays, . . . people find themselves in a rhythm in which they have to decide what they're going to do from one minute to the next."[31] In this analysis, the empty time of everyday life, structured according to routines that predetermine the unfolding of events, is set in stark contrast to moments in a revolutionary crisis like that of May '68, where such normative and normalizing patterns of action are thrown out of joint. One can hear reverberating in this commentary the writings of contemporary figures such as Henri Lefebvre or Guy Debord. Indeed, the anonymous roundtable informant's remark calls to mind the opposition Debord draws between the abstract historical time, which under capitalism is estranged from the very masses whose labor produces it, versus the "pseudo-cyclical time" of everyday life, an ideological image of changelessness that masks real historical change and impedes its reappropriation by those responsible for it. The resulting rediscovery of the openness immanent within the moment, its indeterminacy vis-à-vis a future whose contours could no longer be clearly foreseen, would seem connected to the Debordian ideal wherein the proletariat would at last be able to "*live* the historical time that it creates."[32] But it also seems connected to the broader crisis of representation that May '68 is often said to have effected. Boris Gobille, for one, has remarked on how the uprising constituted a "critical event" par excellence, in the sense of "break[ing] with the ordinary regimes of intelligibility within the social world," forcing actors to "confront the uncertain meaning of what is happening."[33] As the movement spread from one sector to another, as the familiar, compartmentalized identities to which people were assigned (student, worker, intellectual, artist) began to destabilize, the habitual frameworks by means of which they might make sense of events and act upon them also began to destabilize. And since the way in which people "interpret what happens" shapes "their expectations, their calculations and their actions,"[34] the pervasive sense of uncertainty as to what exactly was taking place as the crisis unfolded only served to heighten uncertainty as to what could or should happen next.

For Willener's anonymous interlocutor, such uncertainty was clearly experienced as a form of liberation, as the habits, customs, and laws that normally govern social life were momentarily suspended, giving individuals greater license to actively intervene in events as they unfolded. No longer alienated from time's unfolding, the revolutionary subject was suddenly empowered to reappropriate it, as reified social forces (e.g., capital) ceased to determine in advance "what [one is] going to do from one moment to the next." This points to another cause—and another effect—of culture's ambivalent position within the May events. Unlike the humdrum routines of everyday life, shaped as they are by the dictates of material necessity, art has long been figured within post-Romantic discourse as a space where the free play of the imagination may be pursued. Within this discursive tradition, art is cast as a privileged, exceptional domain in which social norms may be safely relaxed (within limits) and creativity granted free rein (also within limits). But it was precisely this privileged, exceptional status that many "cultural agitators" took aim at during the May events, in an effort to emancipate creativity from the circumscribed sites and occasions where it was bottled up (an endeavor that likewise reverberated with the theses of Debord and other situationists). The most visible representatives of this tendency were the Comité révolutionnaire d'agitation culturelle (CRAC) in the Sorbonne and the Comité d'action révolutionnaire (CAR) in the occupied Odéon theater, but myriad other groups active during the May/June events took up the call to radically democratize creative practice, thus realizing the powers of invention that were latent in all. One might cite in this regard the Mouvement international révolutionnaire des arts (in the "ex-École des beaux-arts"), Art et Révolution (in Lyon), the Comité d'Agitation Culturelle Autonome (in Strasbourg), the commission Université et Culture (part of the Université critique at the Faculté de droit), and the commission Culture et Contestation (at Nanterre), among others. "There mustn't be people who are artists and people who are non-artists," declared the group Université et Culture in one tract. "All of us are capable of doing something, of bringing more than the reactions of bleating sheep to each of the acts that comprises everyday life."[35] For the group Art et Révolution the main goal was likewise to "REVEAL

THE CREATOR IN EACH PERSON."[36] Even more succinctly, the Comité d'agitation culturelle announced in one handwritten bulletin that "culture has fallen to pieces: CREATE."[37] It is tempting to read this last, lapidary pronouncement as a syllogism: once the monopoly that culture exercised over people's creative energies had come to an end, it became not just possible but imperative that these same energies be redirected to the more vital task of reinventing society.

Once the revolutionary moment had passed, culture's ambivalent relation to politics persisted, even as the changed environment of *l'après-mai* period reconfigured how art, creativity, and the everyday related to one another. On the one hand, the resumption of work within the cultural sector was viewed with a jaundiced eye by a number of militants, a turn of events that in their estimation threatened to rein in the creative impulses that the uprising had loosed. The danger was that revolutionary energies might be subverted by being rerouted into the cul-de-sac of culture. In a tract published by the militants of CRAC in late July 1968, they denounced the rush among publishers to churn out books recounting, analyzing, and/or commemorating the revolt that had just taken place: "YOU TRANSFORM REVOLUTION INTO A COMMERCIAL AND 'CULTURAL' EXCREMENT."[38] On the other hand, as critiques of Art (with a capital A) subsided in the months and years following May '68, various forms of cultural practice were reconceived as offering a space where revolutionary impulses awakened during May might live on. Henri Lefebvre, for instance, saw in music "a counter-space, a counter-regard, a lived contradiction, the rebound of revolt, the ultimate recourse."[39] How music was understood to discharge such functions varied from one genre community to another. Within the nascent rock scene, it was the collective effervescence to which concerts and festivals gave rise that held out the promise of rekindling the still fresh embers of revolutionary fervor. "Since May '68," rock critic Paul Alessandrini wrote, "the youth movement has been severely repressed, militants jailed, political actions smashed or by necessity cloaked in secrecy. Outside the factory or workplace, youth has but one shared place of its own where it can gather: the rock concert."[40] Within the world of experimental music, it was through works and practices that elicited the active co-participation of audiences that the creative potential of people might be realized and put to work in transforming society. The music-activists Jean-Claude Lartigot and Eric Sprogis put it this way in a representative post-'68 text:

> For us, it is clear that a veritable musical action, one which will ensure at the same time that the language of music doesn't remain frozen at the level of form or at the level of technique, is an action that will lead music to be more closely linked to everyday life than ever before, to express or simply to take into consideration the multiple and at times contradictory aspirations of the people of today in their totality. . . . Under capitalism, only a tiny fraction of the population can express . . . the musical potential of an era. It will therefore be necessary for us to try to orient our action toward the realization of a music that is created by all.[41]

A different model for democratizing creative practice was to be found in connection with *chanson révolutionnaire*, where it was less a question of ensuring that one and all might partake of "the musical potential of an era" than of giving voice to the lived experience of social struggle: "Revolutionary song is necessary, even if it is but a 'a little cog and screw within the general mechanism of revolution.' . . . The new partisans who rise up each day will know how to seize hold of this arm that the bourgeoisie has stolen from them. Tomorrow hundreds of revolutionary songs will flourish, written by calloused hands, in the fires of struggle, in the factory, in the slums, in demonstrations."[42]

Anxieties engendered by music's perceived belatedness vis-à-vis May '68 only increased the obligation felt by engaged artists and musicians to produce work that would continue the struggle by other means. Yet if music was to provide a "counter-space" along the lines described by Lefebvre, if it were to serve as a repository where the revolutionary impulses and ideals of *les événements* might be sustained, it was necessary for it to avoid falling back into well-worn patterns and familiar social functions. That is, if music and other cultural practices were not simply to serve as buffers absorbing the friction generated by mounting social contradictions, if they were to preserve if not advance May's unfinished project, then some sort of break was seen to be necessary. In the case of *chanson révolutionnaire*, the break was with the processes of commodification that had transformed song from the common property of the people into something "the bourgeoisie has stolen from them." In the case of experimental music, the break was with the customary division of artistic labor and concomitant passivity of audiences within the art music tradition.

And in the case of rock, the break was inscribed in the genre's own self-understanding, as simultaneously youth culture and popular culture, positioned in opposition to the broader parent culture on the one hand and elite culture on the other.

A particularly vivid example of this line of thinking can be seen in an account of free jazz developed by Willener in conjunction with his efforts to make sense of the uprising. Its significance for him resided not in any substantial presence experimental jazz might have enjoyed during the events of May '68; on the contrary, the only instance of "jazz in May" he cites is dismissed as having no more in common with the jazz avant-garde than "the need to express something and the absence of all arrangement, even of the oral kind," what he sums up as "the 'happening' element."[43] Rather, the significance of free jazz for Willener was to be found in the "general kinship" it had with the student protests and general strike, specifically the role that "collective improvisation" played in both. What they shared, in other words, was a tendency to take leave of existing conventions and models for action, preferring to invent these on the fly. In this regard, Willener describes how free jazz musicians gradually abandoned the various frameworks by which the flow of music had hitherto been ordered—metric schemes, harmonic patterns, timbral and sonic norms, and so on—in order to create a music that "aims to awaken rather than intoxicate."[44] With the free-form style of improvisation that figures such as Ornette Coleman and Albert Ayler had pioneered, Willener writes, "we are as far removed as possible from pre-established *structures*—they are constantly being developed." Rather, "if there are any norms, they are worked out in the course of the action—they are ephemeral—both rhythmically and melodically."[45]

Compounding the sense that musicians had an obligation not just to respond to the May events, but to do so in a way that disrupted norms and expectations, was another facet of 1968's complex temporality. Even as the uprising and general strike was experienced as a brief, tantalizing hiatus in the flow of empty time under monopoly capitalism, an event in the strong sense of the term, the end of this hiatus was not perceived purely and simply as an end. Rather, the field of possibility that the May events opened up remained open to the extent these events were perceived as a harbinger, a promissory note for a revolution that would make good on their unfulfilled potential. A survey of some of the texts published by militants in the aftermath of May '68 attests to the notion that the unrest had been but a foretaste of greater things yet to come. Philippe Labro and his collaborators, for instance, recycled one of the more popular slogans chanted during May for the title of their account of the protests: *Ce n'est qu'un début* ("This is only a beginning"). For Trotskyites Daniel Bensaïd and Henri Weber, the events were cast instead as a "dress rehearsal," per the title of their book *Mai 68: Une répétition générale*. Observers outside France echoed this line of interpretation. Telling in this regard is the title of Tom Nairn and Angelo Quattrocchi's analysis of the May movement: *The Beginning of the End*. Of course, with fifty years' hindsight, their title appears telling in a way they could not have anticipated. From the perspective of 2018, 1968 appears not as the beginning of the end of capitalism, as so many *soixante-huitards* believed. Rather, it appears as the beginning of the end of both a certain kind of capitalism, along with the institutions and tactical repertoires that had been developed over the course of the previous century in struggle against it. At the time, however, such a turn of events was, if not unthinkable, then at least not the direction in which history appeared to be moving. From this angle, the return to work in June and July 1968 did not mark the revolution's failure, so much as a momentary delay in its realization. And from this same angle, musicians and other artists might not have been "too late," as Godard lamented, but arriving just in time for the revolution's imminent, inevitable return.

RECORDING AND THE RECOVERY OF LOST TIME

What, then, were some of the ways musicians responded to this sense of belatedness in the wake of 1968? How did they seek to close the distance that seemed to separate their activities as artists from the moment of revolutionary crisis and prepare the way for its potential return? As with many others, a number of musicians were so profoundly affected by the uprising that in the months and years after May '68 they radically reoriented their creative activities in response. Some forsook commercial careers to devote themselves more fully to militancy (as was the case with Dominique Grange); others sought to break down the barriers separating different musics and, by extension, the barriers separating the social groups to which these musics were indexed (as did François Tusques with his Intercommunal Free Dance Music Orchestra);[46] others pursued grassroots efforts at democratizing musical creativity (as was the case with the Mouvement d'action musicale);[47] and still others engaged in what might best be described as a form of rhetorical overcompensation, loudly proclaiming their commitment to revolutionary ideals (as when composer and conductor Pierre Boulez declared himself to be "300% Marxist-Leninist").[48] One particularly noteworthy strategy that certain musicians adopted in the immediate aftermath of May '68 was to incorporate documentary recordings made during the protest and general strike into their compositions. Juxtaposing fragments of the acoustic reality in this fashion served to puncture music's artificiality and abstraction, at the same time as the presence of such recordings served to extend the recent past into the present, collapsing the gap between the two.

In the case of Bayle's and Reibel's *Rumeurs*, the incorporation of "found sound" into their music was hardly without precedent. By 1968, both composers had worked for a number of years at the Groupe de recherches musicales (GRM), a research center housed within the French radio and television services. Though officially founded in 1958 by Pierre Schaeffer, the GRM was a continuation of work he had pursued over the course of the preceding decade following his invention of *musique concrète*, a species of electroacoustic music whose main source material is recorded sound. Unlike the earlier Groupe de recherche de musique concrète that it replaced, the newly rechristened GRM expanded its purview under Schaeffer's leadership to include research into the perception of sound, using recording technologies as a means of isolating and abstracting sounds from their sources.[49] For Schaeffer, it was by means of this technologically mediated separation that something along the lines of the *époché*, or bracketing, of Husserlian phenomenology could be performed; that is, by suspending knowledge of the object or event that gave rise to a sound, one could thereby better attend to its shape, development, texture, and other morphological features (Schaeffer likened this use of recording technology to the acousmatic veil of Pythagoras, by means of which the master was hidden from his students so they might focus all the more intently on his voice—a fact that led Bayle to dub music composed according to these Schaefferian precepts as "acousmatic music").[50] Schaeffer's ultimate goal was to develop a universal *solfège*, not limited to any particular musical tradition (as was the case with traditional *solfège*), but that was capable of describing any sound whatsoever. Yet as resources were increasingly directed to this project—which culminated in the 1966 publication of Schaeffer's magnum opus, the *Traité des objets musicaux*[51]—a number of composers began to chafe at the limits being placed on their compositional activities, both practically and aesthetically. Space does not allow for a full accounting of the disagreements to which Schaeffer's prioritization of research over composition gave rise, but suffice it to say that many of those active within the GRM began to lose patience with the demand that sounds be abstracted from the familiar, recognizable contexts from which they had been drawn. Beginning with Luc Ferrari's *Hétérozygote* (1963–64), tape pieces produced by composers associated with the GRM increasingly exploited referential sounds, along with the symbolic, narrative, and political possibilities that such sounds afforded.[52]

Both Bayle and Reibel found themselves right in the middle of these heated aesthetic debates. Both had been heavily involved in the *Traité des objets musicaux*, Reibel in particular having produced the examples for the four-disc set of recordings that accompanied the text. Yet with *Rumeurs*, both composers departed from acousmatic orthodoxy, creating a piece in which recorded sounds were not to be distanced from their real-world sources, but were instead to provide direct access to these sources. As later described by Reibel, their initial plans for a piece blending massed choral voices and tape had been thrown into disarray by the events of May '68. Not only did they set aside work on the composition during the course of *les événements*, there being "better things to do, to experience" at that particular moment in time, but when they did return to work in July, their conception of the composition had changed significantly. "We started over from scratch," he noted. "Change of project, it now being adapted to the events that we just lived through, and that we wished to be in 'resonance,' after a fashion, with these events." Elsewhere in the same account he reiterates this point: the piece, he notes, was to "echo . . . the upheavals that we had recently experienced."[53] Reibel's choice of words is significant. It is not just that he uses the language of acoustics to describe the relation that *Rumeurs* had to the uprising that inspired it, which is perhaps to be expected for a musician. No less important are the particular acoustic phenomena his account invokes. What his use of terms such as "resonance" and "echo" highlights is the degree to which *Rumeurs* as a whole and the documentary recordings of *les événements* that it utilized were conceived as a means of prolonging, rather than representing, May '68. Much as echoes, resonances, and reverberations all describe effects produced when the waves propagated as a result of some event come into contact with an object that either reflects them or begins vibrating in turn, so too may *Rumeurs* be read as a result of the waves given off by an event coming into contact with an object—in this case the aftershocks of the event that was May '68 coming into contact with a particular tradition of experimental music. And much as sound waves continue to propagate after such a collision, albeit in the transformed guise of an echo or reverberation, so too would the repercussions of May ideally continue to agitate through the medium of *Rumeurs*.

Taking leave of the dominant, quasi-institutional aesthetic of the GRM was not the only transgression that Reibel and Bayle effected in *Rumeurs*. Significant in this regard is the occasion for which the piece had been composed: the sixth Choralies festival, an event held every three years in Vaison-la-Romaine that brought together amateur choral groups from across France and the rest of the world. The Choralies festival and the piece that Reibel and Bayle were commissioned to compose for it were both initiatives of À Cœur Joie ("To one's heart's content"), an organization dedicated to promoting amateur singing as a form of social and cultural uplift. À Cœur Joie has long declared its "openness to all contemporary vocal repertoires and practices,"[54] but for the most part the music that member groups performed was fairly traditional in character; in the words of one ethnologist, choirs associated with À Cœur Joie tended to prefer "a legible repertoire, simple but of high quality, derived equally from classical music and European folk traditions."[55] Given such aesthetic proclivities, the decision to commission a work from two composers associated with a center dedicated to experimental music represented something of a risk, despite Reibel's background in writing vocal and choral music. And by all accounts, the organizers of the 1968 Choralies festival got much more than they had bargained for. In addition to making ample use of electroacoustic music, at times superimposed on choral parts, at other times alternating with them, the piece as it was reconceived in the wake of May '68 interspersed quasi-theatrical interludes between musical sections, performed by a troupe of actors led by singer Jacques Higelin (who would subsequently rise to prominence as a *chanson* artist in the mid-1970s). As for the material that the amateur choral singers were asked to perform, not only did it make use of forms of vocalization that went well beyond conventional singing, but it also demanded that they recite slogans that Bayle and Reibel had transcribed from the graffiti that had covered the walls of Paris during May '68. One otherwise sympathetic reviewer remarked on the chance that the two composers were taking in asking amateur singers and a "narrow-minded public" (*un public bien pensant*) to indulge in such extravagances: "When one asks habitués of Baroque music to whisper, to yell, to scream viscerally, when one has four thousand people sing to a thunderous applause that has been orchestrated, when one places the show in the audience and remains silent on the stage, when one provokes individual dread and unleashes collective panic, when one has decided to pass beyond the patience and resistance of the most even-tempered listener, then one can expect for the worst."[56]

The discomfort *Rumeurs* aroused in certain participants was not wholly a function of the slogans or unconventional sounds singers were asked to produce. The work's transgressions were as much social as sonic. During a section of the work entitled "Paroles" (Words), Bayle and Reibel endeavored to replicate the experience of the *Tribune Libre* that had taken place in the occupied Odéon theater following its seizure by protesters. Having commandeered a symbol of state-sanctioned culture the evening of May 15, 1968, members of the Comité d'action révolutionnaire proceeded to invert the customary relation between stage and seats. To facilitate free expression, they placed a microphone in the middle of the auditorium, so that people otherwise lacking opportunities to have their voices heard might be able to speak their minds about issues of concern to them.[57] As the exemplary site of the much vaunted "prise de parole" that took place during May '68—despite criticisms that such speechifying represented a hedonistic distraction from more pressing forms of political action—the *Tribune Libre* of the Odéon was an obvious point of reference for Reibel and Bayle, given their aspiration to rouse all those in attendance to action. During the section of the piece in question, Higelin and his actors, armed with microphones, scattered themselves among the crowd, posing questions to audience members, provoking them, and otherwise inciting them to speak.[58] Documentary recordings provided a different sort of incitement, as Bayle and Reibel not only enjoined those present to emulate the *Tribune Libre*, but included recordings made at the Odéon as part of the sonic *mise-en-scène*. In one particularly striking passage, a montage juxtaposing sounds of street protests with excerpts taken from Frank Zappa's "Are You Hung Up" is cut short by shouts of people in the occupied Odéon demanding silence. The din subsiding, one hears the voice of a woman who begins her intervention at the *Tribune Libre* with an acknowledgment of her class position that was equal parts self-aware and self-abasing: "In my capacity as a bourgeois woman, I thank you. . . . I thank you for your understanding" (En tant que bourgeoise, je vous remercie. . . . Je vous remercie pour votre compréhension). Of all the recordings, of all the utterances spoken during the weeks-long open discussion held at the Odéon, the choice of this one in particular cannot help but appear as a provocation, particularly given the largely middle-class composition of the Choralies festival. It was as if the two composers were daring those in attendance to hear themselves in this woman's voice, to adopt the same self-consciousness regarding their class position as she exhibited.

If documentary recordings made at the Odéon during May '68 offered an example that those taking part in the performance of *Rumeurs* could follow, other sounds captured during the uprising played a rather different role within Bayle's and Reibel's piece. A high point of *Rumeurs* occurred when the more than 3,000 singers assembled were brought to a state of sonic frenzy (a "racket," in Reibel's own words), at which point their bellowing voices were joined by those of protesters whose shouts and chants had been recorded in the Latin Quarter during May. These sound documents were soon followed by others: the beating feet of a police charge, the report made by tear gas canisters detonating, the blare of police and ambulance sirens, among others. Reibel later singled out this moment for special attention. "For a moment," he recalled, "the crowds of Paris and of Vaison intermingled their voices: cries, yells, slogans, vociferations."[59] Whereas other uses of sound documents within *Rumeurs* seemed to strive after a form of naïve verisimilitude—as when an ambulance whose passage had been recorded in stereo was panned across the amphitheater, creating the auditory illusion that it was traversing the space—what is notable in this instance was the fusion of recorded sounds and those produced in performance. Less a question of making those in attendance feel as if they were there in the Latin Quarter, in the midst of police and students as they skirmished during the Night of the Barricades, the blurring of sonic distinctions allowed for a certain blurring of the distance separating revolutionary past from musical present, political action from artistic action. It was for this reason that Bayle and Reibel declined to call their creation a work in the conventional sense of the term, opting to describe it as a demonstration (*une manifestation*). And it is perhaps for the same reason that *Rumeurs* was only ever performed once, in August 1968, the conditions that had made it possible being as irretrievable as the event upon which it was modeled.

A similar merging of past and present, documentary recording and music, political action and artistic action can be witnessed in Colette Magny's "Nous sommes le pouvoir," despite the very different tradition in which both she and her music were rooted. Magny arrived rather late to the music profession. She had long sung and played the guitar as a pastime, but it was not until 1962 when, at the age of thirty-six, she quit her job as a secretary in order to pursue music full-time.[60] During the early years of her career, up until 1967 or so, she was renowned first and foremost for the power of her voice, which led a number of critics to liken her (not unproblematically) to American blues singers such as Bessie Smith.[61] But her voice was not the only distinctive quality of Magny's music. Already in her earliest recordings, she exhibited a proclivity for formal experimentation that set her apart from the stereotypical Left Bank singer-songwriter of the period. Exemplary in this regard is her approach to lyrics. Even as she adhered to the by-then well-established practice among *chanson* artists of setting texts by consecrated poets to music, in line with the literary aspirations of the genre, the way in which she did so was often quite innovative. In such early songs as "Frappe ton cœur" (1963), for instance, she created collages from excerpts derived from a number of different sources (including Alfred de Musset, from whose poem "A mon ami Edouard B." the title of the song derives).[62] This was a practice she would return to again on *Magny 68*, whose second track, "Le fin de tout," combined excerpts from a pair of poems by Max Jacob. This interest in breaking with the conventions of the *chanson* genre also led her to collaborate with artists from very different musical backgrounds over the course of her career, most notably free jazz musicians during and after 1968: besides the participation of bassist Beb Guérin on the *Magny 68* album, one might cite her 1972 collaboration with pianist François Tusques, *Repression*, or her 1975 album with the Free Jazz Workshop, *Transit*. But even prior to 1968, Magny was pushing well beyond the confines of the *chanson* tradition. Such was the case with the 1966 album *Avec*, in which texts written and performed by Magny were set against an electroacoustic accompaniment created by André Almuro, at that time one of Bayle's and Reibel's colleagues at the GRM.

Developing in tandem with Magny's musical and poetic innovations was the political character of her music. Already in her first few albums she addressed various forms of social and economic injustice, both past and present; her song "Monangamba," from her second album, *Les Tuileries*, for instance, put to music a poem by the Angolan poet and anticolonial militant António Jacinto, whose text depicted the brutalities of plantation slavery. As political commentary and critique assumed an increasing prominence in Magny's music from the mid-1960s onward, their expression simultaneously shaped and was shaped by her penchant for formal experimentation. Such was evident from the outset of *Magny 68*. The first sounds heard on the opening track, "Nous sommes le pouvoir," are not those of her voice or her guitar. Rather, what one hears is a recording of a young man shouting, "Pas de panique! Pas de panique, camarades! Pas de panique, s'il vous plaît!" (Don't panic! Don't panic, comrades! Please don't panic!). His voice is soon joined by others, one of whom yells out a word, "lacrymogène" (tear gas), a warning to fellow protesters that also serves to clarify for listeners the exact nature of the event preserved in this documentary recording: it is none other than one of the many confrontations between students and police that took place during the course of May '68. Other sounds drift in and out of the auditory scene: tear gas canisters exploding, people coughing, followed by the noise of objects being shifted around, piled on top of one another, perhaps to build a barricade. Or perhaps not: it is of course impossible to know for sure what these noises index, given the separation of sound from sight that is a defining feature of acousmatic media, most notably sound recording. Likewise, it is difficult to know for sure when Magny's music begins to encroach on the protest soundscape. As the clatter of objects continues, the sound of a beating drum emerges from amidst the din. Is this an overdub added after the fact, during the recording of *Magny 68*? Or is it just another of the ambient sounds that the indiscriminate ear of the microphone happened to capture in the heat of the protest?

Even when the unmistakable sound of Magny's guitar finally does arrive, heralding the beginning of the song proper, care is taken to smooth the transition from documentary to musical sound. As the voices of student protesters chanting "CRS-SS" fade out around the 1'15" mark, one hears the wail of a siren in the distance, whose oscillating high-low contour is mimicked by a pair of dissonant chords Magny quietly strums on her guitar. Initially the chords double this particular feature of the protest soundscape, creating a bridge between political past and musical present. Like any sort of mediation, however, the link provided by this sort of sonic similarity both separates and connects. This irreducible difference is reinforced as Magny's chords gradually go out of phase with the siren from which they derive. What is more, she continues to play them well after the siren has disappeared into the distance, transforming this discordant progression into an accompaniment for the spoken-word interlude that follows: "One evening I came back from singing. Somebody telephoned me. There had been injuries, kids who had been clubbed. I was afraid; I didn't even go to help gather the wounded" (Un soir je revenais de chanter. On m'a téléphoné. Il y avait des blessés, des gosses matraqués. J'ai eu peur, je ne suis même pas allée ramasser les blessés). The remainder of the roughly seven-minute-long song follows the same pattern: passages during which recordings of the May events dominate the audio field alternate with those in which they recede into the background, giving way before Magny's largely (but not exclusively) spoken recollections of the uprising.

This alternation distinguishes the two types of recording out of which the piece is composed: those made in the field, capturing a political act, versus those made in the studio, capturing a musico-poetic act. Yet these two types of recording echo one another throughout "Nous sommes le pouvoir." At times this echoing is quite literal, established on the basis of some sonic resemblance between the two, what Peirceans would refer to as an iconic relation between sign and referent; such is the case when Magny emulates the sound of sirens with her guitar, or when drums are added to the percussive sounds of street fighting (if that is indeed what occurs here). At other times, however, the connection is less direct, more symbolic than iconic. It is as if Magny's words conjure up the sounds of the things that they reference, and vice versa. But like the more straightforward iconic relations that bind together documentary recording and studio recording, symbolic ones also serve to close the gap between the two.

Perhaps the most striking instance of the latter occurs at 2'29", when for the first time in "Nous sommes le pouvoir" one hears the sound of singing. But it is not the voice of Magny that we hear; instead, it is a recording of protesters singing "L'Internationale," audible evidence in support of Calvet's claim that during May '68 what militants sang was "the *previous* revolution."[63] The moment is notable for a number of other reasons besides. At a basic level, the emergence of this "song within the song" throws into stark relief the fact that, at least up to this point, Magny has opted to speak rather than sing about May. It is tempting to see in this refusal of song the outlines of an opposition that sets the truth of the spoken word against the artifice of song, much as the truth of documentary sound is set against the artifice of music throughout much of "Nous sommes le pouvoir."[64] But this fragment of "L'Internationale" is notable also because it troubles such straightforward oppositions, simply by virtue that what we hear here is a *documentary recording of song*. In a way, this can be seen as another strategy for narrowing the gap between music and political event: if embedding documentary recordings within Magny's song functions as a way of piercing the artifice of music with a shard of the real, the embedding of song within documentary recording imbues music-making with some of the authenticity that is seen to accrue to the historical event preserved on tape. It is as if this context lends the act of singing a facticity—and hence a truth-value—it otherwise lacked, making it more than just "mere" singing.

Further complicating how one might interpret this moment is what Magny says immediately afterwards. As "L'Internationale" recedes from the acoustic foreground, Magny makes her (self-)deprecating comment that in May "singing had become ridiculous." I have already noted the way in which this remark can be read as a symptom of the sort of anxieties artists felt about their position vis-à-vis the student-worker movement. But coming right on the heels of this recording in particular, her comment might be construed as a critique not of singing in general, but of a specific kind of singing, one exemplified by the sort of ritualized performance of "L'Internationale" by student protesters that we have just heard.[65] In this connection, a theme that runs through "Nous sommes le pouvoir" is the indifference bordering on disdain with which Magny treats the more ludic aspects of the student protests. "I didn't see anything, I wasn't in the street," Magny remarks as "L'Internationale" begins to filter in behind her voice, a short time after a clip of students chanting "in the streets" (*dans la rue*) over and over again. "I missed everything that was gay," she remarks, just prior to the point when "L'Internationale" fills the audio field. In later interviews, she explicated further on her disinterest in what was taking place in the Latin Quarter. "Ridiculous" (*dérisoire*) was the way she described her impressions of the occupied Sorbonne, where she had been invited to perform on the night of May 13, using the same word she used to describe singing more broadly in "Nous sommes le pouvoir."[66] As for groups advocating cultural agitation, they were in her opinion "the worst of all." In the interview, conducted a few years after '68, she reiterated her sense that making music was futile under the circumstances: "What could artists invent, if it weren't the cries that could have frightened the CRS without frightening demonstrators at the same time?"[67] In her estimation, the true epicenter of the movement was to be found in the occupied factories, with the striking workers, where she spent much of May and June. This is reflected in the other songs on *Magny 68*, many of which concern the brutalizing conditions of factory work ("the machine embraces us like a boa constrictor / in the heat, the noise, the hours / I can't breathe," she sings in the song "Le Boa"). But it is also reflected in the original cover art for the album, which reproduced the timetable for shifts at a plant running at full tilt, twenty-four hours a day.

Regardless of whether Magny's dismissal of singing is directed at this particular performance or music-making in general, her comment further serves to bind song and sound document more closely together, at the same time as the critical attitude it adopts drives them apart. A similar ambivalence plays out the one other time we hear singing in "Nous sommes le pouvoir." Towards the end of Magny's final spoken-word intervention, she finally breaks out in song, albeit briefly. There are a couple of things to be noted about this moment. One concerns the words she sings, which celebrate the oft-cited fact that during May people who under different circumstances might never have said a word to one another began to converse: "In the month of May, out of hope, everybody began to speak to each other."[68] Earlier in the track Magny had spoken about singing; here, she sings instead about speech. And, perhaps unsurprisingly by this point in the song, her paean to dialogue segues into a recording of people talking (specifically, a student at Censier who reassures a distressed mother over the phone that her son, who is taking part in the protests, is safe). Another notable feature of this moment is that it represents something of a belated vindication for song, earlier derided by Magny as useless, "ridiculous" even. Her comments just before this exceptional moment set the stage for this turn. Having cast doubt on song's efficacy within revolutionary action, Magny ponders what else she might be able to contribute to the movement: "I know how to type," she muses, looking back to her earlier life as a pink-collar clerical worker. And yet this recollection forces an admission on her part: "Perhaps I sing better than I type." Music may be "ridiculous." It may be a poor substitute for direct political action, as the lyrics to "Street Fighting Man" would suggest. But it is better than nothing—or at least this is what Magny would seem to imply. Even "a little cog and screw within the general mechanism of revolution" may be just what is needed to keep this mechanism running.

CONCLUSION

To conclude, let us return to Calvet's observations about the belatedness of music with regard to 1968, my point of departure. As we have seen, the perception that music had missed its rendezvous with history was a source of anxiety for no small number of musicians. And such anxieties generated no small number of responses in turn, among them the use of sound documents as a means of minimizing the perceived distance between music and politics. But if one reads Calvet further, what stands out is how decidedly unconcerned he is about such perceptions of music's belatedness, or the anxieties to which these gave rise. For Calvet, this was simply a "fact," and as such something about which "one is neither to bemoan or, to be sure, rejoice."[69] On the contrary, the gap separating art from event was in his estimation a condition of possibility for revolutionary culture. What forged a link between the political event and the cultural expressions to which it gave rise was not the immediacy of their temporal coincidence, which Calvet dismissed as a "thesis falsified by an excess of spontaneism."[70] Rather, it was only through the mediation of history that music might become bound to the revolutionary act, albeit in a very specific way: as a symbol of the latter. Commenting on the fact that "L'Internationale" and other songs of the Paris Commune were revived during May '68, Calvet thus noted that "what is most striking in these songs of protest is that *they are above all signs*. Signs springing from an ideological context and therefore bearers of ideology themselves: to sing in a demonstration such and such a song amounts to a profession of such and such an ideology."

Needless to say, the relation between music and politics that Calvet is describing here is of a very different kind than that which *Rumeurs* or "Nous sommes le pouvoir" endeavored to forge with May '68. Whereas these two pieces sought, each in its own way, to bridge the social and historical gap that separated musical and political event, song's transformation into a symbol of some revolution past demands by contrast that a degree of detachment or distance be established—that the past be understood as well and truly past. This may seem something of a dispiriting conclusion to draw, with its insistence that music will always be in some respect "too late." But even though Calvet's analysis is modest in its assessment of the degree to which music and revolution can coincide, his modesty should not be mistaken for pessimism. For the historical mediation that retrospectively links music and revolution is one in which history is not just something that simply occurs, but something actively made. "This somewhat vague qualification 'revolutionary' is affirmed through usage," Calvet observes, noting that "from this point of view, revolutionary would be the song sung in revolutionary practice."[71] It is through its use in political action at present—and in the future—that assures music's connection to the revolution of which it sings. What matters is whether or not a song is put to work in ensuing moments of crisis, in the name of unfulfilled promise of revolutions past.

Perhaps the same might be said of 1968 more generally. From this perspective, what matters is less the question of whether 1968 was a cultural revolution—which it most certainly was. What matters is the question of whether it remains so today, and whether it will continue to be one in the future. As with revolutionary song, what matters is how the legacy of 1968 is put to work in ensuing moments of crisis. Will it serve merely as a source of nostalgia or left-wing melancholia? Or will it instead serve as a resource that political and cultural activists can draw on, in their ongoing struggles against class domination, neo-imperialism, racial and gender discrimination, and the environmental degradation wrought by unrestrained global capitalism? The year 1968 may well have been a cultural revolution. But it will only remain one so long as its unrealized claims continue to be advanced, in the service of political and cultural revolutions still to come.

NOTES

1. Louis-Jean Calvet, *La production révolutionnaire* (Paris: Payot, 1976), 136.

2. Ibid., 135.

3. Ibid., 136.

4. See Eric Drott, *Music and the Elusive Revolution: Cultural Politics and Political Culture in France, 1968–1981* (Berkeley: University of California Press, 2011), chap. 1.

5. Karl Marx, *The Eighteenth Brumaire of Louis Bonaparte*, ed. C. P. Dutt (New York: International Publishers, 1957), 13.

6. My use of the figure of the "missed encounter" is indebted to Seth Brodsky's discussion of musical modernism and the very different "revolution" that occurred in 1989. Brodsky describes a "missed encounter between modernism and revolution" that consisted of "modernism's 'failure' to execute a temporal revolution it is always auguring, and its correspondent 'success' as a repeated turning in place, a constant coming back to where it started"; see Brodsky, *From 1989, or European Music and the Modernist Unconscious* (Berkeley: University of California Press, 2017), 13.

7. James S. Williams, "Performing the Revolution," in *May 68: Rethinking France's Last Revolution*, ed. Julian Jackson, Anna-Louise Milne, and James S. Williams (London: Palgrave, 2011), 281.

8. Ibid.

9. Peter Schmelz, "Valentin Silvestrov on the Maidan," in *The Oxford Handbook of Protest Music*, ed. Noriko Manabe and Eric Drott (Oxford: Oxford University Press, forthcoming).

10. Andrea Bohlman, "Solidarity, Song, and the Sound Document," *Journal of Musicology* 33, no. 2 (2016): 232–69.

11. Andrew Feenberg and Jim Freedman, *When Poetry Ruled the Streets: The French May Events of 1968* (Albany: SUNY Press, 2001).

12. See Timothy Ryback, chapter 8 in this volume.

13. See J. Patrice McSherry, chapter 11 in this volume.

14. Patrick Burke, "Tear Down the Walls: Jefferson Airplane, Race, and Revolutionary Rhetoric in 1960s Rock," *Popular Music* 29, no. 1 (2010): 70 and 72.

15. Bonny Cohen, "Stop, Look, What's That Sound, Everybody Look What's Goin' Down," *The Old Mole* 19 (August 1, 1969): 23.

16. Ibid.

17. Ibid., 19.

18. Giovanni Arrighi, Terence K. Hopkins, and Immanuel Wallerstein, *Antisystemic Movements* (London: Verso, 1989), 98. See also Immanuel Wallerstein,

"1968, Revolution in the World-System: Theses and Queries," in *The Essential Wallerstein* (New York: New Press, 2000), 355–73.

19. Daniel Cohn-Bendit and Gabriel Cohn-Bendit, *Le Gauchisme, remède à la maladie sénile du communisme* (Paris: Seuil, 1968).

20. Such sentiments were most evident among groups engaged in "cultural agitation," which are discussed below. For a lengthier discussion, see Drott, *Music and the Elusive Revolution*, 40–49.

21. Gérard Fromanger, cited in Kristin Ross, *May '68 and Its Afterlives* (Chicago: University of Chicago Press, 2002), 16.

22. "Le public, bientôt imité par les compositeurs eux-mêmes, déserts peu à peu les enceintes 'culturelles' pour se rendre sur d'autres lieux où se jouait une partie d'une plus grande importance. Les activités professionnelles cessèrent pendant deux mois environ: l'actualité et la vie se déroulaient ailleurs que dans les studios et les salles de concerts"; Michel Chion and Guy Reibel, *Les musiques électroacoustiques* (Aix-en-Provence: Edisud, 1976), 71.

23. "Très tôt . . . nous fûmes pris par une sorte de tourbillon où l'accélération inouïe du temps nous confrontait jour après jour à la stupéfaction de découvrir que les effets de nos actes, aussi divers qu'instantanés, dépassaient infiniment leurs résultats escomptés. Tout craquait, comme par réaction en chaîne"; Jean-Franklin Narot, "Mai 68 raconté aux enfants: Contribution à la critique de l'inintelligence organisée," *Le Débat* 4, no. 51 (1988): 188.

24. R. Linbaum, cited in Alfred Willener, *The Action-Image of Society: On Cultural Politicization*, trans. A. M. Sheridan Smith (New York: Pantheon, 1970), 74–75.

25. Ross, *May '68 and Its Afterlives*, 15.

26. Ibid.

27. Ibid., 16.

28. Jacques Vassal, *Français, si vous chantiez* (Paris: Albin Michel, 1976), 31. This observation applies just as well to music's distribution. In the absence of technologies that allowed the rapid production and dissemination of recordings, activists in some cases turned to "contrafacta," that is, versions of familiar songs whose lyrics had been parodied, altered, or replaced. This musico-political practice had the advantage of cheap and easy transmission; all that was necessary was to print a lyric sheet indicating the tune (or *timbre*, as it is often referred to in France) to which it is to be sung. For more on this topic, see Drott, "Music and May 1968 in France: Practices, Roles, Representations," in *Music and Protest in 1968*, ed. Beate Kutschke and Barley Norton (Cambridge: Cambridge University Press, 2013), 258–61.

29. For more on Grange's *soixante-huitard* songs, see Drott, *Music and the Elusive Revolution*, 72–73.

30. Vassal, *Français, si vous chantiez*, 14.

31. Linbaum, cited in Willener, *The Action-Image of Society*, 75.

32. Guy Debord, *The Society of the Spectacle*, trans. Donald Nicholson-Smith (New York: Zone Books, 1995), 106.

33. Boris Gobille, "L'événement Mai 68: Pour une sociohistoire du temps court," *Annales* 63, no. 2 (2008): 325.

34. Ibid., 325–26.

35. "Université et Culture." Maupéou-Abboud Archives, Bibliothèque de documentation internationale contemporaine, carton F delta 1061 (10).

36. *Tracts de mai 1968*, fiche no. 375, documents nos. 9898–99.

37. *Tracts de mai 1968*, fiche no. 57, document no. 1410.

38. "Une dernière contestation: Celle des éditeurs," in *La Sorbonne par elle-même*, ed. Jean-Claude Perrot, Michelle Perrot, Madeleine Rebérioux, and Jean Maitron (Paris: Les éditions ouvrières, 1968), 405.

39. Henri Lefebvre, "Musique et sémiologie," *Musique en jeu* 4 (1971): 60.

40. Paul Alessandrini, "Free, Pop, et Politique," *Actuel* 6, March 1971, 6.

41. Jean-Claude Lartigot and Eric Sprogis, *Libérer la musique* (Paris: Editions Universitaires, 1975), 138–39.

42. "Les Nouveaux Partisans," *La Cause du people*, no. 21, May 8, 1970, 2.

43. Willener, *The Action-Image of Society*, 232.

44. Ibid., 244.

45. Ibid., 239.

46. Philippe Carles, "Tusques: D'où viennent les sons justes?" *Jazz Magazine*, no. 202, July 1972, 22; Sylvain Guérino, "Le Temps des cerises," *Jazz Magazine*, no. 228, December 1974, 10; "Concert de l'Intercommunal Free Dance Music Orchestra," *L'Humanité rouge* (December 20, 1976): 7.

47. "Texte d'orientation," *Action musicale*, no. 1 (1977): 28–31.

48. Pierre Boulez, cited in Dominique Jameux, *Pierre Boulez* (Cambridge, MA: Harvard University Press, 1991), 158.

49. On the history of *musique concrète* and the development of the GRM, see Chion and Reibel, *Les musiques électroacoustiques*; and Evelyne Gayou, *Le GRM: Groupe de Recherches Musicales: Cinquante ans d'histoire* (Paris: Fayard, 2007).

50. On the phenomenological inspirations for Schaeffer's theory of acousmatic listening, see Brian Kane, *Sound Unseen: Acousmatic Sound in Theory and Practice* (Oxford: Oxford University Press, 2014).

51. Pierre Schaeffer, *Traité des objets musicaux* (Paris: Seuil, 1966).

52. On Ferrari's "anecdotal music," see Drott, "The Politics of *Presque Rien*," in *Sound Commitments: Avant-Garde Music and the Sixties*, ed. Robert Adlington (Oxford: Oxford University Press, 2009), 145–68.

53. Guy Reibel, *L'Homme musicien: Musique fondamentale et création musicale* (Aix-en-Provence: Edisud, 2000), 371.

54. *Choralies: Une initiative À Cœur Joie* (Lyon: À Cœur Joie, 2017), 6.

55. "Un répertoire lisible, simple mais de qualité, emprunté à la fois à la musique classique et au folklore européen"; in Paul Gerbod, "La musique populaire en France dans la deuxième moitié du XXe siècle," *Ethnologie française* 18, no. 1 (1988): 17.

56. Maurice Fleuret, "Un météor fou," *Le Nouvel Observateur* 197, August 19, 1968, 31.

57. On the occupation of the Odéon, see Christian Brouyer, *Odéon est ouvert: Tribune libre* (Paris: Nouvelles Editions Debresse, 1968); and Patrick Ravignant, *L'Odéon est ouvert* (Paris: Stock, 1968).

58. Reibel, *L'Homme musicien.*

59. Ibid., 370.

60. Vassal, *Français si vous chantiez*, 19.

61. In an interview from 1972, Magny notes that it was "la 'grande presse' qui m'a collé l'etiquette 'chanteuse de blues,'" adding that "je n'en suis pas responsable. . . . Et ça n'était pas vrai: je chantais des chansons américaines qui se trouvaient être des blues, mais je n'étais pas une chanteuse de blues"; Colette Magny, cited in Francis Marmande, "Le free parler de magny," *Jazz Magazine*, no. 201, June 1972, 22.

62. "Colette Magny," *Le Hall* (September 29, 2010), http://www.lehall.com/consultez-l-histoire/artistes/magny-colette.

63. Calvet, *La production révolutionnaire*, 136.

64. In this regard Magny's work is of a piece with the broader tendency towards "factualism" in avant-garde art circa 1968, what Joshua Shannon has described as "a common fascination with fact as a predominant form of talking, thinking, and knowing." As he goes on to note, this "fascination with fact" was bound up with a fascination with recording devices that could capture and inscribe facts, most notably cameras. But moving beyond the visual domain that is the focus of Shannon's study, one sees a parallel interest in the powers of magnetic tape within the sonic register; see Joshua Shannon, *The Recording Machine: Art and Fact during the Cold War* (New Haven, CT: Yale University Press, 2017), 5.

65. On controversies over which groups had the "right" to lay claim to symbols of the revolutionary tradition, such as "L'Internationale," and the critiques leveled at students for having appropriated elements of working-class culture, see Drott, *Music and the Elusive Revolution*, 39–40.

66. "Colette Magny chante: Interview pour *Tout*," *Tout*, no. 8 (February1, 1971): 11.

67. Ibid.

68. Compare Magny's line to Michel de Certeau's reflection on the emancipation of speech that 1968 effected: "On s'est mis à discuter enfin de choses essentielles, de la société, du bonheur, du savoir, de l'art, de la politique. Une palabre permanente se répandait comme le feu, immense thérapeutique nourrie de ce qu'elle délivrait, contagieuse avec toute ordonnance et tout diagnostic; elle ouvrait à chacun ces débats qui surmontaient à la fois la barrière des spécialités et celle des milieux sociaux, et qui changeaient les spectateurs en acteurs"; Michel de Certeau, "Prendre la parole" (1968), in *La prise de parole et autres écrits politiques* (Paris: Seuil, 1994), 42–43.

69. Calvet, *La production révolutionnaire*, 136.

70. Ibid., 134.

71. Ibid., 136.

BIBLIOGRAPHY

Alessandrini, Paul. "Free, Pop, et Politique." *Actuel* 6 (March 1971): 6–7.

Arrighi, Giovanni, Terence K. Hopkins, and Immanuel Wallerstein. *Antisystemic Movements*. London: Verso, 1989.

Bohlman, Andrea. "Solidarity, Song, and the Sound Document." *Journal of Musicology* 33, no. 2 (2016): 232–69.

Brodsky, Seth. *From 1989, or European Music and the Modernist Unconscious*. Berkeley: University of California Press, 2017.

Brouyer, Christian. *Odéon est ouvert: Tribune libre*. Paris: Nouvelles Editions Debresse, 1968.

Burke, Patrick. "Tear Down the Walls: Jefferson Airplane, Race, and Revolutionary Rhetoric in 1960s Rock." *Popular Music* 29, no. 1 (2010): 61–79.

Calvet, Louis-Jean. *La production révolutionnaire*. Paris: Payot, 1976.

Carles, Philippe. "Tusques: D'où viennent les sons justes?" *Jazz Magazine*, no. 202, July 1972, 22–23, 60.

Certeau, Michel de. *La prise de parole et autres écrits politiques*. Paris: Seuil, 1994.

Chion, Michel, and Guy Reibel. *Les musiques électroacoustiques*. Aix-en-Provence: Edisud, 1976.

Choralies: Une initiative À Cœur Joie. Lyon: À Cœur Joie, 2017.

Cohen, Bonnie. "Stop, Look, What's That Sound, Everybody Look What's Goin' Down." *The Old Mole* 19 (August 1, 1969): 19, 23.

Cohn-Bendit, Daniel, and Gabriel Cohn-Bendit. *Le Gauchisme, remède à la maladie sénile du communism*. Paris: Seuil, 1968.

"Colette Magny." *Le Hall* (September 29, 2010). http://www.lehall.com/consultez-l-histoire/artistes/magny-colette.

"Colette Magny chante: Interview pour *Tout*." *Tout*, no. 8, February 1, 1971, 11.

"Concert de l'Intercommunal Free Dance Music Orchestra." *L'Humanité rouge*, December 20, 1976, 7.

Debord, Guy. *The Society of the Spectacle*. Translated by Donald Nicholson-Smith. New York: Zone Books, 1995.

Drott, Eric. "Music and May 1968 in France: Practices, Roles, Representations." In *Music and Protest in 1968*, edited by Beate Kutschke and Barley Norton, 255–72. Cambridge: Cambridge University Press, 2013.

———. *Music and the Elusive Revolution: Cultural Politics and Political Culture in France, 1968–1981*. Berkeley: University of California Press, 2011.

———. "The Politics of *Presque Rien*." In *Sound Commitments: Avant-Garde Music and the Sixties*, edited by Robert Adlington, 145–68. Oxford: Oxford University Press, 2009.

Feenberg, Andrew, and Jim Freedman. *When Poetry Ruled the Streets: The French May Events of 1968*. Albany: SUNY Press, 2001.

Fleuret, Maurice. "Un météor fou." *Le Nouvel Observateur* 197, August 19, 1968, 30–31.

Gayou, Evelyne. *Le GRM: Groupe de Recherches Musicales: Cinquante ans d'histoire*. Paris: Fayard, 2007.

Gerbod, Paul. "La musique populaire en France dans la deuxième moitié du XXe siècle." *Ethnologie française* 18, no. 1 (1988): 15–26.

Gobille, Boris. "L'événement Mai 68: Pour une sociohistoire du temps court." *Annales* 63, no. 2 (2008): 321–49.

Guérino, Sylvain. "Le Temps des cerises." *Jazz Magazine*, no. 228, December 1974, 10.

Jameux, Dominique. *Pierre Boulez*. Cambridge, MA: Harvard University Press, 1991.

Kane, Brian. *Sound Unseen: Acousmatic Sound in Theory and Practice*. Oxford: Oxford University Press, 2014.

Lartigot, Jean-Claude, and Eric Sprogis. *Libérer la musique*. Paris: Editions Universitaires, 1975.

Lefebvre, Henri. "Musique et sémiologie." *Musique en jeu* 4 (1971): 52–62.

"Les Nouveaux Partisans." *La Cause du people*, no. 21, May 8, 1970, 2.

Marmande, Francis. "Le free parler de Magny." *Jazz Magazine*, no. 201, June 1972, 22–23.

Marx, Karl. *The Eighteenth Brumaire of Louis Bonaparte*. Edited by C. P. Dutt. New York: International Publishers, 1957.

Narot, Jean-Franklin. "Mai 68 raconté aux enfants: Contribution à la critique de l'intelligence organisée." *Le Débat* 4, no. 51 (1988): 179–92.

Perrot, Jean-Claude, Michelle Perrot, Madeleine Rebérioux, and Jean Maitron, eds. *La Sorbonne par elle-même*. Paris: Les éditions ouvrières, 1968.

Ravignant, Patrick. *L'Odéon est ouvert*. Paris: Stock, 1968.

Reibel, Guy. *L'Homme musicien: Musique fondamentale et création musicale*. Aix-en-Provence: Edisud, 2000.

Ross, Kristin. *May '68 and Its Afterlives*. Chicago: University of Chicago Press, 2002.

Schaeffer, Pierre. *Traité des objets musicaux*. Paris: Seuil, 1966.

Schmelz, Peter. "Valentin Silvestrov on the Maidan." In *The Oxford Handbook of Protest Music*, edited by Noriko Manabe and Eric Drott. Oxford: Oxford University Press (forthcoming).

Shannon, Joshua. *The Recording Machine: Art and Fact during the Cold War*. New Haven, CT: Yale University Press, 2017.

"Texte d'orientation." *Action musicale*, no. 1 (1977): 28–31.

Vassal, Jacques. *Français, si vous chantiez*. Paris: Albin Michel, 1976.

Wallerstein, Immanuel. "1968, Revolution in the World-System: Theses and Queries." In *The Essential Wallerstein*, 355–73. New York: New Press, 2000.

Willener, Alfred. *The Action-Image of Society: On Cultural Politicization*. Translated by A. M. Sheridan Smith. New York: Pantheon, 1970.

Williams, James S. "Performing the Revolution." In *May 68: Rethinking France's Last Revolution*, edited by Julian Jackson, Anna-Louise Milne, and James S. Williams, 281–98. London: Palgrave, 2011.

FIVE

Non-Alignment and Student Protest in 1968 Mexico

ERIC ZOLOV

Alongside France, Czechoslovakia, and the United States, Mexico is rightfully incorporated in the pantheon of nations dramatically affected by the revolutionary ferment of 1968. From late July until the start of October, tens of thousands of students joined a National Strike Committee (Comité Nacional de Huelga), shutting down the major universities and high schools, while transforming the usage—and perception—of public space across the nation's capital. Unlike in other countries where student-led protests erupted, however, the Mexican authorities faced a pressing deadline by which the demonstrations needed to end. Mexico had been awarded the 1968 Summer Olympics, the first time a "developing nation" had been so honored. The opening ceremonies were slated to begin on October 12, and Avery Brundage, chairman of the International Olympic Committee, was engaged in frantic conversations with Mexican officials regarding the cycle of protest and increasingly bloody response that characterized Mexico City. Frustrated by the students' irreverent taunts, anxious that Brundage might declare the Olympics postponed or relocated, and fearful that the protests constituted part of a broader conspiracy aimed at toppling his government, on October 2, President Díaz Ordaz decided to put a definitive end to the demonstrations. Using tanks and high-caliber weapons, the police and army massacred more than a hundred people (the actual number has never been established) at the Plaza of the Three Cultures. To this day, the "Massacre at Tlatelolco"—named after the public housing complex in which the events transpired—remains an unhealed wound that continues to influence public discourse and protest politics.[1]

Yet Mexico occupies a unique place in the global history of 1968. Within Latin America, by the late 1960s Mexico was one of a diminishing number of countries still under civilian rule. When student-led protests erupted in the summer of 1968, these were directed not against an oppressive military-run state, as in Brazil or Argentina, but rather toward a president who had been democratically elected, albeit in an election backed by the resources of a ruling party that monopolized the political process. Moreover, unlike student-led protests in France and Germany, not to mention elsewhere in Latin America, Mexican students sought not to overthrow the state, but rather to push the government to uphold its revolutionary obligations, ones derived directly from the nation's 1917 constitution. The Mexican student movement, in other words, was fundamentally reformist despite the fact that the emblems and symbolic language used by the students invoked revolutionary objectives. Finally, among countries outside the Soviet Bloc that experienced antigovernment student revolt during 1968, Mexico arguably stood apart in one key respect: the nation had cemented a reputation as a progressive force in the international arena, in particular by defending Cuban sovereignty and openly identifying with (while not formally endorsing) the movement of non-aligned nations.

In the early 1960s, the Mexican Left had been unified around three central tenets. First, support for the Cuban Revolution, which, having been launched from the shores of Mexico and especially after facing U.S. intervention, was based on deep bonds of solidarity. Second, loyalty to the leadership of former president Lázaro Cárdenas, whose defense of the Cuban Revolution and criticism of the conservative direction of the country's ruling party (which he had helped found) thrust the former president back into the political limelight. And third, broad-based support for President López Mateos's (1958–64) efforts to establish what I label a "global pivot," a strategy of geopolitical diversification that included meaningful diplomatic engagement with the major actors of the Non-Aligned Movement (NAM). By late 1966, however, the Left in Mexico had become ideologically fragmented, leaderless, and politically untethered from the patronage of the ruling party for the first time ever in the postrevolutionary system. In 1968, as the antigovernment youth revolt spread globally, a new epistemology of protest linked to the global counterculture provided the tools of irreverence and antipatriarchal rebellion that fueled an attack on the Mexican presidency. This attack—a cultural revolutionary uprising—extended, moreover, to the sacrosanct emblems of "revolutionary nationalism" that had previously formed the basis for national unity. It was an uprising that happened precisely at a moment when the world system faced unprecedented threats from an insurgent Third World.[2]

Why at the pinnacle of the nation's international prestige did Mexican students turn against their president, accusing him of having failed to uphold Mexico's progressive traditions, including that of solidarity with other Third World nations? In what respect did the students' protest tactics (overwhelmingly cultural in nature) embody revolutionary *acts*, even while their stated aims never encompassed revolutionary *goals* (with the exception of a far smaller, more militant handful of protesters)? Might a more internationally oriented president have successfully channeled student demands toward support for the regime, as Mexico's previous president had done in the wake of the Cuban Revolution? Or did an intensified Cold War dynamic—propelled by U.S. intervention in Vietnam and the Sino–Soviet split—limit Mexican options to assert its "solidarity" with progressive forces internationally and thus eliminate an essential political tool necessary for co-opting student protesters? How, in short, were domestic and global factors interrelated?

I ask that we think through the linkages between geopolitics, Mexican foreign policy, and the crisis of legitimacy that confronted President Gustavo Díaz Ordaz during the summer and early fall of 1968. As such, this chapter represents part of a growing effort to move beyond a narrow interpretation of the Mexican student movement by placing the events of 1968 into a wider conceptual framework.[3] By seeking to link domestic protest to geopolitical shifts, I also aim to further our analytical understanding and narrative perspective on the historiographical field of the global 1960s.[4] Recently, the centrality of NAM to historical discussion of the

1960s has received renewed scholarly attention.[5] Yet there is still little detailed investigation available for Latin American engagement with this movement and the broader "Third World Project," as Vijay Prashad terms it, from a Latin American perspective.[6] The global solidarity movement, of which NAM was one key strand, had significant resonance within Latin America, at the grassroots and at the state level. Still our understanding of this resonance, much less an acknowledgment of how government engagement with NAM shaped domestic politics, remains limited.

ORIGINS AND TRAJECTORY OF NAM

The Non-Aligned Movement was launched in Belgrade, Yugoslavia, in September 1961 and reflected the vision in particular of Josip Tito (Yugoslavia), Sukarno (Indonesia), and Jawaharlal Nehru (India).[7] The movement's central tenets were anticolonialism, denuclearization, a halt to Cold War geopolitical rivalry, and the demand that the capitalist order meet the development needs of countries in Africa, Asia, and Latin America. In the context of the time, these were not especially "revolutionary" objectives. After all, anticolonialism and "development" were already squarely on the agenda of the United Nations. But by the end of the 1960s, political frustration with the failure to block U.S. intervention in Vietnam coupled with a stagnation in progress toward more equitable distribution of global trade helped to reconstitute NAM as part of a Third World revolutionary vanguard.

NAM's original organizing logic was to marshal a large enough bloc of nations pledged to a "neutral" stance in the Cold War and thereby break through the hardening of geopolitics that resulted from the Soviet–U.S. rivalry. This stance was never envisioned as a "passive neutralism" but rather one of "active neutrality," that is, to use the power of individual and collective member states to bring about structural change at the international level—militarily, diplomatically, and economically. The Kennedy administration recognized the underlying motives of NAM and in fact sought to encourage a true position of "non-alignment" as a strategy of keeping the newly decolonized nations in Africa and Asia out of the Soviet camp. Still, the ideological stance of the decolonizing nations ("anti-imperialism") matched more with that of the Communist Bloc, and from the start the United States thus found itself on the defensive, fearful that NAM would undermine U.S. global leverage and influence. This was especially the case with regard to Latin America, where the notion of a "Pan-American" alliance—one bound by diplomatic and military agreements, and by a presumption of shared objectives—was considered by the United States as nonnegotiable.[8]

It is important, moreover, to understand that NAM was one of two offshoots of the earlier conference of Asian and African nations that met in Bandung, Indonesia, in 1955, a gathering that effectively launched the concept of a "Third World."[9] NAM sought to transform the Cold War order by enlarging participation at the state level by working directly through membership at the UN, but a second offshoot of the Bandung Conference, the Afro-Asian Peoples' Solidarity Organization (AAPSO), adopted a different organizational strategy. AAPSO was formed in 1958 and headquartered in Cairo. Its solidarity politics was built around a notion of shared geographical and racial attributes, rather than geopolitical interests. Although membership in NAM and AAPSO overlapped and the two organizations initially pursued a set of shared objectives, by 1964 their collective vision of a "Third World Project" was rapidly fragmenting along lines that were simultaneously ideological, economic, and geopolitical. The notion, born at Bandung, that the "Third World" was intrinsically united around a set of common goals and principles, turned out to be increasingly illusory. China's brief border war with India in the fall of 1962 reflected a larger reality: despite calls for solidarity, whether around questions of "race" (AAPSO) or "geopolitics" (NAM), there were competing development needs as well as competing aspirations for regional influence. These divergencies appeared within a rapidly mutating ideological global environment, one that conspired against the goals of collective action. By 1965 the prestige and potential of NAM to have a practical effect on alleviating if not transforming Cold War politics was very much in doubt.

The second meeting of NAM in Cairo in October 1964 marked the movement's climax and simultaneous denouement. The Cairo meeting attracted a far greater number of participants than the initial gathering in Belgrade three years earlier, yet the diversity of participants also signaled the challenges in holding together a collective sense of mission. This challenge became especially fraught in the context of the Sino–Soviet split, a dramatic fissure that cut through the global politics of solidarity by generating an ideological and geopolitical cold war within the Cold War. The central rhetorical weapon utilized by the Chinese (and their allies) against the Soviet Union was a critique of the Soviet leitmotif of "Peaceful Coexistence." This foreign policy stance, though belied in certain aspects (such as the delivery of missiles to Cuba), nevertheless reflected the fundamental Soviet belief, at once both ideological and practical, that the Communist Bloc could win the political struggle with the capitalist West through "competition" rather than armed conflict. "Peaceful coexistence," however, was also a founding statement espoused at Bandung in 1955 and incorporated into the set of principles that came to define NAM. A semantic overlap between the non-aligned version of this concept and the Soviet version—each implicitly positioned the United States as the *source* of global conflict—therefore provided a ready basis from which to attack NAM as a pro-Soviet movement. (The participation of Cuba in NAM directly contributed to this elision.) The Chinese attack on "peaceful coexistence" thus struck at the Soviet Union but also at the essentially reformist stance of NAM and worked to drive a wedge between NAM's leadership, while elevating the more revolutionary elements.

In part, the Chinese position was a reflection of the Communist mainland's lack of geopolitical standing within the world community. (Communist China [PRC] would not gain formal entry into the UN until 1971.) Wrecking, rather than reforming, the global order had far less cost for the Chinese than for the Soviets. This ideological radicalization, however, was compounded by regional geopolitical conflicts that directly challenged the premise of "global solidarity" and that came to pit key players such as Indonesia, Pakistan, China, and India against one another, despite a veneer of like-minded interests. Finally, with the entry of the United States into Vietnam following the Gulf of Tonkin Resolution in August 1964 (on the eve of the second meeting of NAM in Cairo), the space for "neutralism" and "coexistence" quickly evaporated. Vietnam became the central battleground and litmus test of Third World solidarity. Ultimately, the war in Vietnam would pull NAM in a more radical direction, which in turn influenced NAM's rhetoric and its organizing strategy.

The effect of these forces on NAM was revealed in the wake of the 1964 conference. Despite the appearances of rising success, the movement was quickly overshadowed by efforts taking place within AAPSO to convene a "Second Bandung" conference in the summer of 1965 in Algeria. Bandung-II, as it was being called, had openly revolutionary goals with respect to overturning the capitalist world system. Yet the conference fell apart in the face of fierce ideological divisions between pro-Soviet and pro-Chinese positions, divisions that were exacerbated by a series of military coups against key (and mostly, pro-Chinese) political actors.[10] The first of these coups occurred on the eve of a preparatory conference when the military overthrew the left-wing government of Algerian president Ahmed Ben Bella. Although this did not immediately doom Bandung-II, it was a significant blow, one compounded by military intervention against President Sukarno in Indonesia, who by then had turned on his more moderate cofounders of NAM and adopted an openly pro-Chinese line.

The sudden turn in fortunes both for NAM and the prospect of a Bandung-II (organized under the auspices of AAPSO) created a window of opportunity for the celebration of a "Tricontinental Conference" in Havana, Cuba, in January 1966. This event had been in the planning stages for years within AAPSO and was also subject to the fierce ideological disputes that were dividing that body among itself. In spite of these internal divisions, the Tricontinental made a significant mark on the conception of global solidarity. This was largely because Cuba now claimed direct ownership over the new organization. (The Tricontinental emerged severed from AAPSO.) But it was also because the Tricontinental filled an important vacuum as NAM and AAPSO both struggled to stay relevant in an era of fractious ideological politics and conflicts of interest within the developing world.[11]

MEXICO AND THE NON-ALIGNMENT MOVEMENT

Several Latin American countries, Mexico included, sought to bandwagon with NAM during this initial period (1961–64). None, however, with the exception of Cuba, formally joined the movement. Fearful that Latin American involvement with NAM would directly undermine the Pan-American alliance, the United States exerted varying degrees of diplomatic and economic pressure in an effort to ward off any official involvement. Still, this did not prevent various Latin American countries from pursuing contacts with NAM, and throughout the early to mid-1960s several of the most significant nations in the region—including Brazil, Chile, and Mexico—hosted visits by leading NAM actors. In 1964, many of these same Latin American countries sent "observers" to the second conference held in Cairo. "Flirting" with NAM in this way became a visible means of enacting an "independent" foreign policy vis-à-vis the United States. This had important domestic and foreign policy implications, both in helping to shore up (or further destabilize) internal political coalitions and in enhancing Latin American bargaining power vis-à-vis the United States.[12] But many in Latin America also regarded NAM—and the broader "spirit of Bandung"—as the pathway toward a more equitable basis of international relations. In Bolivia, for instance, President Paz Estenssoro championed the leadership of Tito, Sukarno, Nasser, and Nehru as role models for an alternative vision of global politics.[13]

Mexico's political and economic dependencies on the United States tempered the possibility of open affiliation, but President López Mateos arguably identified the country with NAM and the broader post-Bandung solidarity movement more than any other Latin American country, with the exception of Cuba. Although Mexico bowed to U.S. pressure and did not send a representative to NAM's founding conference in Belgrade (1961), López Mateos nevertheless warmly welcomed Sukarno, Nehru, and Tito during official state visits, and he used these visits as an opportunity to highlight Mexico's alignment with NAM's guiding principles. Furthermore, López Mateos reciprocated these visits during two extended trips in 1961–62, when he undertook elaborate tours of Indonesia, India, and Yugoslavia (among other countries). In speeches abroad, he celebrated Mexico's shared pursuit of NAM goals, such as the creation of a Latin American "nuclear-free zone" and the convening of a UN Conference on Trade and Development (UNCTAD), and spoke openly of how Mexico's revolutionary principles were in fundamental accord with those of NAM. In an address in Belgrade, for instance, he spoke of the need for "a new order for international relations" in order to "guarantee the peace." "On these questions," he underscored, Mexicans and Yugoslavians shared a "position that is the same or quite similar."[14]

López Mateos openly pursued an alignment of interests with NAM as part of a broader strategy aimed at elevating Mexico's international stature and diversifying the country's diplomatic and economic interests. This strategy directly intersected with programmatic (and ideological) aspects of Mexico's organized Left, and it forces us to reconsider the axiomatic argument that foreign policy in this moment was primarily aimed at "domestic consumption."[15] Part of the problem with this assessment is that Mexico's foreign policy has been seen as synonymous with support for the Cuban Revolution. But we need to view Mexican internationalism within a much wider scope. Moreover, by doing so we find that the regime sought to harness (and not simply to placate) the energies of the Left in support of a strategy of geopolitical diversification, one that included engagement with NAM at its center. To cite one telling example, Carlos Fuentes, who positioned himself as a vocal critic of the regime, nevertheless lauded the government's principled stance on Cuba and engagement with NAM's leaders. Indeed, despite persistent criticisms from the Left that the ruling party (Partido Revolucionario Institucional, PRI) was repressive and undemocratic—that the PRI had abandoned its revolutionary trajectory—by the end of his presidency, López Mateos had nevertheless succeeded in establishing bonds of political camaraderie with key individuals of the nation's intelligentsia. Thus even Manuel Marcué Pardiñas, editor of the country's most truculent left-wing newsmagazine, *Política*, later referred to López Mateos as "a refined man, a bohemian, someone who showed an interest in Cuba and understood what that nation aspired to achieve."[16]

TITO'S INVITATION

In the spring of 1968, just months before the eruption of Mexico's student movement, President Díaz Ordaz (1964–68) received a letter from Tito urging Mexico's participation in a preparatory conference for a third meeting of NAM, tentatively scheduled for Ethiopia that fall. Tito hoped to coax Díaz Ordaz into lending Mexico's new-found international prestige—a prestige directly reflected in Mexico serving as host for the forthcoming Summer Olympics—to provide a needed dose of legitimacy to a movement that had fallen precipitously in stature since its founding in 1961. Nehru, a founding leader, was dead. Sukarno and Nkrumah, two other key figures of the movement, had been overthrown in military coups. The fourth founding leader, Nasser, had been weakened politically and militarily by the Six-Day War the previous summer, a war that further divided NAM and contributed to an intensified politicization around the status of

Israel. The movement had also proved utterly incapable of reining in U.S. intervention in Vietnam. The global animus generated by that war continued to exert a radicalizing influence on non-aligned member states and affiliates. UNCTAD, the one tangible result of NAM organizing, existed in fact but had failed to produce concrete results.[17] As one author assessed it, non-alignment needed to "undergo a revitalization that [was] nowhere in sight."[18]

Tito's invitation to Mexico was directly part of that revitalization. Over a four-month period at the start of the year, he had traveled to India, Pakistan, Cambodia, Ethiopia, Egypt, Japan, Iran, and other NAM-affiliated countries in Asia and Africa in an all-out effort to drum up support for another conference. Nearly four years had passed since the second meeting of NAM in Cairo, and without a third meeting there was concern that NAM had become, as Tito heard leaders on his recent journey lament, "a lost cause."[19] Thus when Tito reached out to Díaz Ordaz in the spring of 1968, he was operating under the assumption that Mexico's internationalist trajectory, initiated under former president López Mateos, was still in force.

There were certainly good reasons to believe this was the case. For one, there was Mexico's rousing defense of non-alignment given by López Mateos's delegate to the meeting in Cairo four years earlier. Second, Mexico continued to maintain diplomatic relations with Cuba in defiance of the embargo sanctioned by the United States and the Organization of American States (OAS). Third, a treaty that transformed Latin America into the world's first nuclear-free zone, an idea championed by López Mateos, had recently been ratified in Mexico City in the country's gleaming new Ministry of Foreign Relations building. Fourth, Mexico remained a member of the G-77 bloc, a group constituted by (mostly) developing nations that had positioned itself as a lobbying force within UNCTAD to push for agreements on commodity price stabilization and greater access to markets for industrialized goods produced in the developing world. Finally, Mexico was gearing up to welcome the world for the Olympics. This, perhaps more than anything else, was a clear indication of the nation's rising international stature and potential for leadership. At a moment when NAM was in danger of losing its direction and international legitimacy, and when various nations across Latin America had succumbed to military rule or were wracked by a destabilizing political polarization, Tito's appeal to Mexico was loaded with geopolitical significance.

But Tito's assumptions about Mexican internationalism, though not entirely mistaken, were in fact misplaced. Díaz Ordaz had little interest in following through on the foreign policy activism of his predecessor, and even less desire to expend any of Mexico's newfound political capital propping up the faltering NAM.

Díaz Ordaz's rejection of Tito's plea to join forces reflected the Mexican president's disinclination to follow the trajectory of his predecessor. His response, however, was in the form of a six-page letter, one in which the Mexican president underscored how his country's special standing with Tito gave him license to write to him "with loyal frankness." He began by establishing a tone of moderation in response to Tito's evidently passionate reflections concerning the state of anticolonialism and postcolonialist reconstruction in Africa and Asia. Although the situation in those countries "merited active sympathy," the Mexican president wrote, it nevertheless required "most careful study." Goals and methods needed to be established that were "the most effective permitted by circumstance." He regarded Tito's proposal to bring together heads of state as "an exceptional remedy," one that had little point if "positive outcomes" could not be guaranteed in advance. Most pointedly, he dismissed the utility of such international meetings since they tended to "awaken great expectations" among a nation's populace and thus would likely be "transformed into bitter frustration if the results did not correspond with the hopes that had been aroused." There was no doubt truth to this point, but it nevertheless represented a reversal of the logic employed under López Mateos, who had used high-profile meetings as a means of mobilizing the populace from above and thus harnessing an otherwise dissident, left-wing alliance to the regime. For Díaz Ordaz, however, the rhetoric and raised expectations generated by large international gatherings had little to offer. Such meetings, he argued somewhat scornfully in his response to Tito, produced "a media circus" while failing to resolve "the complex problems facing our world today." In the end, the prospect of an additional conference would likely generate more conflict than resolution and establish an impossible bar for leaders to meet without facing domestic criticism. "At times, it is simply not possible to reconcile multiple domestic and international perspectives, even when one acts with utmost sincerity," Díaz Ordaz added.[20]

The larger concern, however, was that NAM rhetoric and objectives had veered too far from the movement's original reformist positions. The number of member and affiliate states had multiplied exponentially since the founding meeting in 1961. New members had increasingly more radical stances, shaped in large part by the deepening conflict in Vietnam. Tito hoped to attenuate this radicalization—which threatened to undermine the credibility and influence of NAM with the West—by proposing to broaden the invitation to include "pro-peace nations" (*paises amantes de la paz*), a gambit aimed in particular at bringing more Latin American states on board. Yet Díaz Ordaz feared this might send a message to those not invited—and here, the implication was clearly the United States and other Western-allied nations—"who may in turn be regarded as less pro-peace."[21] Díaz Ordaz had scant reason to jeopardize bilateral relations with the United States for a cause that had by then earned the ire of Washington on account of NAM's increasingly vitriolic stance on Vietnam.

Latin American participation in NAM had long been a central objective of Tito. In part, this was to balance out the membership of Cuba, whose open alliance with the Soviet Union had steadily undermined the credibility of NAM principles. But enticing Latin American affiliation was also key to a broader strategy of diversifying NAM membership to include more mid-level nations that could serve as regional leaders and provide political moderation to counterbalance the younger, more ideologically inclined nation-states from Africa and Asia—those increasingly influenced by the radical rhetoric emanating, in particular, from AAPSO. In mid-June, Joaquín Bernal, Mexico's ambassador to Ethiopia, relayed the message that Ethiopia's foreign minister and India's ambassador to Ethiopia had assured him that "a key objective of the three organizers [Yugoslavia, Ethiopia, India] is to obtain substantial Latin American participation, not as observers but as active participants."[22] In late June 1968, Bernal conveyed yet another message that Tito "begged him to consult" with Díaz Ordaz regarding the possibility of Mexican participation as part of a larger Latin American contingent, one that was sure to include Chile, Uruguay, Brazil, Colombia, Peru, Ecuador, and "maybe" Argentina.[23] Shortly after, Mexico's ambassador to Yugoslavia wrote that a high-level Yugoslavian trade delegation would arrive in Mexico to discuss increased trade opportunities and other aspects of technological exchange. Heading the delegation was a member of the Yugoslavian State Council of Ministers, who was "clearly authorized to speak about current international concerns" and sought a meeting directly with Díaz Ordaz.[24] A memorandum prepared for the president by Mexico's Foreign Ministry spelled out what was obvious: "It is likely that this high level Yugoslavian official is the bearer of a personal message from President Tito . . . related to the project of convening a new conference of 'non-aligned' nations."[25]

At that point, Mexico's Foreign Ministry seemed inclined to participate in the meeting. This may have simply reflected a certain momentum generated within the Foreign Ministry from an earlier policy of engagement under López Mateos. Or it may have indicated a desire to remain visible in global conversations so that Mexico could retain a leadership role. Significantly, the Foreign Ministry also chose to interpret Díaz Ordaz's letter to Tito as a conditional rather than absolute rejection. In a detailed memorandum prepared for Díaz Ordaz in advance of the president's meeting with the Yugoslav economic delegation—a meeting that the Foreign Ministry correctly anticipated contained a further appeal from Tito—Mexico's foreign minister made the case for participation. The memorandum began by noting that Díaz Ordaz's response to Tito had concluded that Mexico "in principle" supported the goals of the conference and went on to recapitulate the extent of messages conveyed by Mexico's ambassadors to Yugoslavia and Ethiopia regarding Mexican participation. These messages had contained reassurances that the preparatory meeting would concern "only those themes of a general character that will be of interest to all participants," themes such as nuclear disarmament and economic development, to which Mexico was already committed. There was a pledge to avoid issues "related to particular regional interests, and disputes that were primarily bilateral or that dealt with positions pertaining to particular countries." The clear implication here was that Vietnam and the Middle East would not be broached, but how these issues could in fact be kept from the agenda seemed unclear. Significantly, the memorandum recommended that Mexico "could participate . . . but it might be wise for such participation to be limited to that of observer status." Clearly, despite a change in leadership at the head of the ministry, the history of Mexico's direct diplomatic engagement with NAM leaders and, perhaps especially, Mexican participation in the second meeting of NAM in Cairo (1964) remained influential. Here was a chance to shape the final conference agenda, the memorandum concluded: "It would be wise to be able to participate actively [in the preparatory meeting], although without needing to commit ourselves before knowing the full scope" of the conference agenda.[26] Three days later, however, Díaz Ordaz confirmed that Mexico would not participate in the preparatory conference in any capacity, citing the "various and important qualifications" he had already expressed in his letter to Tito.[27]

Díaz Ordaz's decision made perfect sense in terms of geopolitical realities, but it also encapsulated his retreat from an activist foreign policy agenda that had direct implications for political support domestically. From early on in his presidency, Díaz Ordaz had evinced none of the international showmanship and spirit of globe-trotting diplomacy that characterized his predecessor. In fact, throughout the entirety of his time in office, Díaz Ordaz left the country only twice, to travel to Guatemala and the United States. He never left the hemisphere. Even the UK ambassador was shocked to learn that an invitation to pay a state visit to England was rejected by Díaz Ordaz.[28] In a global context that had become increasingly perilous and was rapidly fracturing along ideological lines, Díaz Ordaz's strategy of more closely aligning Mexico with the United States while seeking to repair regional relations with Central America made sense. But the cost in domestic political terms was high. Mexico's internationalism had played a key role in tethering the left-wing intelligentsia to the regime during 1959–63, a period that was otherwise rife with domestic political dissent. His failure to follow through on that internationalism would cost Díaz Ordaz the allegiance of the intelligentsia at another moment of domestic political upheaval, this time heralded by the student movement that broke out barely two weeks after his definitive rejection of Tito's invitation.

To be certain, the Left was already predisposed to be antagonistic toward the president. As former minister of the interior and a hardline anticommunist, Díaz Ordaz had been widely viewed as President López Mateos's political henchman. When his nomination to become the presidential candidate became public—in Mexican politics, the nominee was virtually guaranteed the election—the Left let out a collective wail of frustration and disillusionment with the progressivism of López Mateos. As a letter to the editor of the left-wing magazine *Política* articulated, López Mateos "deceived us all" (*engañó a todo el mundo*).[29] This early antagonism was exacerbated by a series of conflicts between Díaz Ordaz and the cultural intelligentsia early on in his administration. In contrast to his predecessor, who had carefully cultivated key cultural and intellectual figures by offering support for their activities and undertaking an ambitious expansion of cultural institutions (epitomized by the opening of the Museum of Modern Art and Museum of Anthropology toward the end of Lopez Mateos's term in office), Díaz Ordaz embittered the intelligentsia. Notably, he fired the progressive head of the state-sponsored publisher, Fondo de Cultura Económica, and sought to clamp down on cultural experimentation at the national university. By late 1967, feelings of mistrust, cynicism, and open hostility characterized the relationship between the intelligentsia and the regime. Carlos Fuentes, a bellwether intellectual whose earlier defense of López Mateos's progressive internationalism played a key role in sheltering the president from domestic critics at the time, severed all ties to the Mexican establishment during the period of Díaz Ordaz. When the new regime launched a "Cultural Olympiad" leading up to the start of the sporting events meant, in part, to mend this divide, it was too little, too late. Certain intellectuals' participation in these cultural events ultimately did not translate into support for the regime in any broader sense.[30]

A REVOLUTIONARY 1968

Two weeks after Díaz Ordaz rejected Tito's invitation, a series of skirmishes in downtown Mexico City between student protesters and the country's riot police set in motion the largest-scale, student-led protests ever witnessed in Mexico. The protests and government repression continued throughout August and September before being put to a definitive end when the military brutally repressed scores of students and other bystanders in the Plaza of Three Cultures in the Nonoalco-Tlatelolco housing complex on October 2, ten days before the opening ceremony of the Olympics. To be certain, this dynamic of protest and response had nothing to do per se with Mexico's decision to disengage from NAM. The young students marching in the street were barely teenagers when Tito had visited the country in the fall of 1963, at the peak of NAM's popularity and influence. Moreover, the optimistic support for an alternative project of "non-alliance," one in which Mexican leadership had staked out a singular role, was gone and, for the most part, largely forgotten. Ex-president López Mateos had fallen gravely ill, and the central intellectual and political figures who had earlier been cheerleaders of the administration's dalliance with NAM were no longer relevant.[31] The rupture in a long-standing alliance between the government and the intelligentsia that had served to mediate dissent had opened a vacuum in intellectual leadership on the Left, one that had been filled by other, far less reverent figures. A "New Left" had risen, one that was less ideologically tolerant yet also less conformist.[32]

Still, the rejection of Tito's invitation signified a broader retreat from an internationalist, outward-looking foreign policy and defense of post-colonial sovereignty that was palpable to the student marchers. When Mexican students marched behind the banner of Che Guevara and renamed one of the National University's central auditoriums after the iconic revolutionary, they did so less to signal their support of Che's call to arms against their own state (although some, later on, would certainly come to embrace this call) but rather in support of Che as an emblem of Tricontinentalism. Che stood for Third World solidarity, the same political sentiment and call to action born at the conference of newly decolonized nations held at Bandung in 1955 and that had coursed its way through the formation of AAPSO in 1958, NAM in 1961, and most recently climaxed in the convening of a "Tricontinental Conference" in Cuba in 1966. In their embrace of Che, Mexican youth were thus rejecting the government's implicit claim that the Olympics heralded Mexico's official exit from the Third World.

Díaz Ordaz became the personalized target of their collective loathing, a concrete symbol not only of the regime's domestic authoritarianism but of the failure to wield Mexico's diplomatic clout in defense of Vietnam and Third World issues more generally. In response, the government quickly sought to use the students' celebration of Che to make the case that "foreign ideologies" were influencing the movement, which in turn led student leaders to urge marchers to drop references to the Argentine-born revolutionary and embrace instead emblems of their own nation's struggle, such as Emiliano Zapata, Pancho Villa, Rubén Jaramillo, Demetrio Vallejo, and others. But the government could not suppress the larger ethos of a movement that saw itself as upholding Mexico's true spirit of internationalism—not the gloss of internationalism reflected in the world coming to Mexico for the Olympics, but of Mexico's call to be a leader in a world transformed.

Ironically, student protesters bore identities that were very much shaped by the modernist forces that had brought the Olympics to Mexico.

This was revealed in their consumption of foreign rock music, the introduction of transliterated English-language slang, and an embrace of new styles in clothing, such as the miniskirt and blue jeans. Youth's embrace of this other set of "foreign ideologies"—consumer values that were directly encouraged by the regime's capitalist development strategy—helped to channel a repertoire of protest that was truly revolutionary within the context of Mexican politics. Youth were now openly defying the patriarchal values—*las buenas costumbres*—that organized social life within the family, and that between citizens and the government.[33] But unlike in France or Germany, where utopian proposals to "abolish work" shaped protest imaginaries (see chapter 12 in this volume by Michael Seidman), or the United States where drugs played an important role in the forging of communal bonds of protest, or Argentina where student-worker alliances had larger revolutionary objectives (see chapter 7 in this volume by Valeria Manzano), in Mexico revolutionary protest stances were comparatively mild. For most students, the extent of rebellion involved staying out until all hours, and for women it meant going around unchaperoned. Yet in the Mexican context, this lack of obedience to one's parents (especially, one's father) became in itself a revolutionary act, one that had wider societal reverberations.

An even greater revolutionary act was the open contempt shown by students toward Díaz Ordaz, the father figure writ large. Posters appeared of the president with his visage distorted by caricature. Protest chants and the rewriting of popular *corridos* (folk ballads) mocking Díaz Ordaz revealed an unprecedented lack of respect for presidential authority.[34] Such displays of irreverence were fundamentally revolutionary in their implications. To borrow from Jeremy Suri's term, a new "language of dissent" was in circulation, one that revealed the possibilities for a democratization of political values and, beyond that, the demystification of national culture.[35] But revolutionary acts were not the same as revolutionary ends, and the government retained a monopoly on violence—one that it soon chose to employ.

A month after the massacre at Tlatelolco, Joaquín Bernal, Mexico's ambassador to Ethiopia, sent an update to Mexican foreign minister Antonio Carrillo Flores about preparations for the third summit of NAM leaders. Progress had been slow. Ethiopia "has done nothing up to this point, absolutely nothing" to lay the groundwork for the preparatory meeting. It was likely, Bernal surmised, that Ethiopia was holding out for a guarantee the country would also serve as host for the conference itself, though "it will not be an easy job." The country's resources were paltry and its infrastructure weak. Moreover, both Algeria (which had initially hoped to host the failed "Second Bandung" conference in June 1965) and the Congo were also now angling for the spotlight.[36] Non-alignment was transforming as new countries, mostly in postcolonial Africa, were vying to become integral to the movement and fill the gaps in leadership created by the demise of leaders such as Sukarno and Nasser. Meanwhile, the date for the preparatory meeting itself was pushed back further. Originally slated for February 1969, it was now set for the following July.

In the end, forty-eight countries accepted Tito's invitation to participate in the preparatory meeting. Eight countries from Latin America sent delegates as observers: Chile, Bolivia, Brazil, Uruguay, Trinidad and Tobago, Jamaica, Argentina, and Peru.[37] When the conference eventually convened in Lusaka, Zambia, in September 1970, the tone and stance of the movement had changed dramatically from its origins nearly a decade earlier. Opposition to the United States and support for the struggle in Vietnam predominated. NAM, which had begun in the early 1960s as a movement that sought to forge an independent geopolitical space for developing nations outside of the Cold War framework, had morphed into an anti-U.S. alliance determined to push through a developmentalist agenda that would radically upend the global capitalist order. Díaz Ordaz wanted no part in this, but his successor did.

In 1970, when Díaz Ordaz nominated *his* minister of the interior, Luis Echeverría, to succeed him as president, the latter was also widely scorned as an agent of repression. Yet under Echeverría, the intelligentsia quickly returned to the fold of the ruling party and proved willing to play, once again, the coveted role of interlocutor between the PRI and the country's left-wing social forces. Echeverría enacted numerous policies that aimed to court the intelligentsia, including massive new increases to subsidize the film industry and other areas of the arts. The key element that accounts for the embrace of his presidency by the Left, however, was an activist foreign policy that again positioned Mexico squarely within the Third World. Indeed, as president, Echeverría assumed the most internationalist posture taken by any Mexican president to date (or since). He resumed (and surpassed) the global travels initiated by López Mateos, fully backed the formation of a "New International Economic Order" (the central goal of the fourth meeting of NAM held in Algeria in September

1973), convened a global conference on women, and sought to become secretary-general of the UN. He also welcomed political refugees from repressive military regimes across South America and established an unprecedented trade pact with the Soviet Union.[38] This ethos of internationalism had been established earlier under López Mateos, yet it was left to wither under Díaz Ordaz.

The symbolic acts of defiance expressed by students in 1968 toward Díaz Ordaz and against the nationalist mythologies that undergirded the regime's ideological hegemony, and parental authority in general, were indeed revolutionary. They forged new spaces for political dissent, ones defined as much by a cultural politics of irreverence as that of a more traditional politics characterized by mass organizing. In time, after 1968, it was no longer regarded as an act of political or cultural treason to openly mock the president. These acts of defiance—whether conveyed through political protest or in more modest, quotidian ways—had profound implications for the long-term democratization of Mexican political culture. The societal cleavage opened up by the protest movement of 1968 produced new ways of thinking and acting politically. At the same time, paradoxically, the return to an activist position that openly aligned Mexico with Third World causes and boasted of a pivot away from the United States on foreign policy became a key factor in sustaining the legitimacy of an authoritarian, ruling party for nearly thirty more years.

NOTES

1. The literature on the Mexico student movement is vast. Among the more significant works in English are George Flaherty, *Hotel Mexico: Dwelling on the '68 Movement* (Berkeley: University of California Press, 2016); Kevin Witherspoon, *Before the Eyes of the World: Mexico and the 1968 Olympic Games* (DeKalb: Northern Illinois University Press, 2014); Elaine Carey, *Plaza of Sacrifices: Gender, Power, and Terror in 1968 Mexico* (Albuquerque: University of New Mexico Press, 2005); Paco Ignacio Taibo II, *'68*, trans. Donald Nicholson-Smith (New York: Seven Stories Press, 2004).

2. Eric Zolov, *The Last Good Neighbor: Mexico in the Global Sixties* (Durham, NC: Duke University Press, 2020).

3. See Jaime Pensado and Enrique Ochoa, eds., *México Beyond 1968: Revolutionaries, Radicals and State Repression during the 1960s and 1970s* (Albu-

querque: University of New Mexico Press, 2018). Earlier interpretations include Jaime Pensado, *Rebel Mexico: Student Unrest and Authoritarian Political Culture during the Long Sixties* (Stanford, CA: Stanford University Press, 2013); Eric Zolov, *Refried Elvis: The Rise of the Mexican Counterculture* (Berkeley: University of California Press, 1999).

4. For an excellent perspective on the state of the field, see Chen Jian et al., eds., *The Routledge Handbook of the Global Sixties: Between Protest and Nation-Building* (New York: Routledge, 2018).

5. Robert Rakove, *Kennedy, Johnson and the Nonaligned World* (New York: Cambridge University Press, 2014).

6. Vijay Prashad, *The Darker Nations: A People's History of the Third World* (New York: New Press, 2008). Important exceptions include the recently published collection by Thomas Field Jr., Stella Krepp, and Vanni Pettinà, eds., *Latin America and the Global Cold War* (Chapel Hill: University of North Carolina Press, 2020); Vanni Pettinà, "Global Horizons: Mexico, the Third World, and the Non-Aligned Movement at the Time of the 1961 Belgrade Conference," *The International History Review* (December 2015): 1–24; J. G. Hershberg, "'High-Spirited Confusion': Brazil, the 1961 Belgrade Non-Aligned Conference, and the Limits of an 'Independent' Foreign Policy during the High Cold War," *Cold War History* 7 (2007): 373–88. Tanya Harmer's excellent work on the Allende period in Chile is also an exception, though she focuses mostly on the early 1970s period; see Harmer, *Allende's Chile and the Inter-American Cold War* (Chapel Hill: University of North Carolina Press, 2014). For some discussion regarding Bolivia and NAM, see Thomas C. Field Jr., *From Development to Dictatorship: Bolivia and the Alliance for Progress in the Kennedy Era* (Ithaca, NY: Cornell University Press, 2014).

7. Gamal Nasser (UAR/Egypt) also assumed a leadership role, but the fact that Cairo was the headquarters of a second offshoot of the Bandung Conference, the Afro-Asian Peoples' Solidarity Organization (AAPSO), placed Nasser in a more tenuous position in his effort to guide NAM apart from AAPSO (see below).

8. Rakove, *Kennedy, Johnson*, offers the most detailed discussion of this strategy dynamic.

9. Christopher Lee, ed., *Making a World after Empire: The Bandung Moment and Its Political Afterlives* (Athens: Ohio University Press, 2010); Prashad, *Darker Nations.*

10. For an excellent discussion, see Eric Gettig, "'Trouble Ahead in Afro-Asia': The United States, the Second Bandung Conference, and the Struggle for the Third World, 1964–1965," *Diplomatic History* 39, no. 1 (2015): 126–56.

11. Robert Young, "Disseminating the Tricontinental," in Jian et al., eds., *Routledge Handbook of the Global Sixties*, 517–47; Gettig, "Trouble Ahead in Afro-Asia"; Zolov, *Last Good Neighbor*, chap. 8.

12. Pettinà, "Global Horizons"; Zolov, *Last Good Neighbor*, chap. 4.

13. Field, *From Development to Dictatorship*, 11.

14. *Documentos para la historia de un gobierno, no. 102. Nueva Dimension Internacional de México: Gira de trabajo en Francia, Yugoslavia, Polonia, Holanda y Alemania*, intro. By Antonio Luna Arroyo (Mexico: Editorial La Justicia, n.d.), 103–4. For further discussion, see Zolov, *Last Good Neighbor*, chap. 7.

15. Renata Keller, "A Foreign Policy for Domestic Consumption: Mexico's Lukewarm Defense of Castro, 1959–1969," *Latin American Research Review* 47, no. 2 (2012): 100–119.

16. Interview with Manuel Marcué Pardiñas, quoted in Carlos Perzabal, *De las Memorias de Manuel Marcué Pardiñas* (Mexico: Editorial Rino, 1997), 65.

17. In early 1968, the second UNCTAD conference had met in India. Mexico's delegation was notably stripped down and the outcome of the meeting produced more frustration than optimism with respect to global trade fairness for developing nations. See Rene Arteaga, *México y la UNCTAD* (Mexico: Fondo de Cultura Económica, 1973); Edgar Dosman, *The Life and Times of Raúl Prebisch, 1901–1986* (Montreal: McGill-Queen's University Press, 2010), 424–27.

18. Alvin Rubinstein, *Yugoslavia and the Nonaligned World* (Princeton, NJ: Princeton University Press, 1970), 331.

19. Ibid., 330.

20. Gustavo Díaz Ordaz to Josip Broz Tito [undated], "Conferencia de Paises No Alineados (1968)," III-5900-13, Secretaría de Relaciones Exteriores (SRE). Unfortunately, Tito's original letter is missing from the archives. However, the context of the invitation is readily gleaned from other sources.

21. Ibid.

22. Ambassador Joaquín Bernal (Ethiopia) to SRE, June 18, 1968, SRE, "Conferencia de Paises No Alineados (1968)," III-5900-13, SRE.

23. Ambassador Joaquín Bernal (Ethiopia) to SRE, June 25, 1968.

24. Mexican Embassy (Yugoslavia) to SRE, July 2, 1968, SRE, "Conferencia de Paises No Alineados (1968)," III-5900-13, SRE.

25. "Memorandum Para Acuerdo del Señor Presidente," July 3, 1968, SRE, "Conferencia de Paises No Alineados (1968)."

26. "Memorandum Para Acuerdo del Señor Presidente," July 8, 1968, SRE, "Conferencia de Paises No Alineados (1968)."

27. Carlos González Parrodi to Alfonso García Robles (Subsecretaría de

Asuntos Multilaterales y Culturales, SRE), July 11, 1968, "Conferencia de Paises No Alineados (1968)." Significantly, a handwritten note at the bottom of the document indicated, "Según resultados revisaremos pos. participar en Conf" (Depending on the outcome we will revisit the possibility of participating in the Conf.).

28. Sir Nicholas Cheetham to Foreign Office (London), January 17, 1966, FO 371/184919, The National Archives, Kew Gardens, UK.

29. Letter to Editor ("ALM y la Izquierda"), *Política*, January 1, 1964, 2.

30. For discussion and analysis of the Cultural Olympiad, see Eric Zolov, "Showcasing the 'Land of Tomorrow': Mexico and the 1968 Olympics," *The Americas* 61, no. 2 (2004): 159–88.

31. He would die from a brain aneurism in September 1969. Former president Lázaro Cárdenas, the figure around whom the Left gravitated in the earlier part of the decade, had thrown his political support behind Díaz Ordaz.

32. See Zolov, *Last Good Neighbor*, chap. 8.

33. See Zolov, *Refried Elvis*.

34. Ibid.; Jaime Pensado, *Rebel Mexico*.

35. Jeremy Suri, *Power and Protest: Global Revolution and the Rise of Détente* (Cambridge, MA: Harvard University Press, 2005).

36. Ambassador Joaquín Bernal (Ethiopia) to Carrillo Flores, November 4, 1968, SRE, "Conferencia de Paises No Alineados (1968)."

37. Ambassador Ramón Ruiz Vasconcelos (Yugoslavia) to Carrillo Flores, July 1, 1969, "Conferencia de Paises No Alineados (1968)." A fascinating aspect and one that merits further research is that Argentina, Brazil, and Bolivia were all under right-wing military rule at the time.

38. A. S. Dillingham, "Mexico's Turn toward the Third World: Rural Development under President Luis Echeverría," in Pensado and Ochoa, eds., *México Beyond 1968*, 113–33.

PART TWO

Images of Change

SIX

Pressure-Release Valve or Cultural Catalyst?

The Revolutionary Potential of The Legend of Paul and Paula *in the German Democratic Republic*

WILLIAM COLLINS DONAHUE

A TURN TO THE EAST

To what extent may we think of Eastern Europe as having participated in the '68 cultural revolution? Much, of course, depends on how we define that notoriously protean event that continues to signify radically different (and sometimes contradictory) things. With the exception of Czechoslovakia, I think it is fair to say that we mostly think of Western Europe (rather than Europe more broadly) when we invoke '68. This chapter gives us a chance to look eastward to a less considered region in this context and to define operationally what is by all accounts an otherwise famously elusive and amorphous assortment of events, aspirations, and movements. In the manner of Neil McGregor's *A History of the World in 100 Objects* (2010) and *Germany: Memories of a Nation* (2015), I will take Heiner Carow's film *Die Legende von Paul und Paula* (1972) as a cultural artifact that is intrinsically and metonymically interesting. That is, as an object that calls for an interpretation in its own right while simultaneously serving to illuminate larger social and political trends related to the cultural upheavals associated with '68. Can the cultural revolution associated with '68 be coded as part and parcel of the socialist transformation already long underway in the East, or is it more properly seen as a Western force that would ultimately upend that very order? It has—understandably—been claimed by both sides.

In the following, I will seek to situate this epoch-making film within the "force field" (*Kraftfeld*) that encompasses the instruments of state control, on the one hand, and the emancipatory possibilities attributed to various "honeycombed" social formations, on the other.[1] At times, it may seem that I am favoring one pole over the other, but that is only to clarify the respective point. I expressly do not want to present a foregone conclusion by favoring a single theoretical point of departure. Thus—and to exemplify the foregoing—although I will make initial use of the Frankfurt School's notion of "dominant cinema," I will do so provisionally, in order to elucidate one notable potential within the force field of East German society. *The Legend of Paul and Paula* surely entered the German Democratic Republic's (GDR) cultural discourse by way of a high-level political calculation, but what it did there during its extraordinary run from the time of its release until long after the *Wende* (the fall of communism) cannot be fully appreciated exclusively from the perspective of social control and media manipulation by government elites. In fact, it calls for interpretation precisely because it is the stuff of both repression and revolution.[2]

A "CULTURAL" '68: SEX, DRUGS, AND ROCK 'N' ROLL

Arguably the most frequently screened film in the history of the Deutsche Film Aktien-Gesellschaft (DEFA) (the East German official film company), *The Legend of Paul and Paula* almost did not see the light of day. A local Communist Party official by the name of Harry Tisch demanded it be banned, but Erich Honecker himself intervened at the last minute to ensure its release.[3] The story, a melodrama of mutual but frustrated attraction, is fairly quickly told. Paul and Paula are both unhappy in their current relationships: Paul, a mid-level bureaucrat in the Ministry of Foreign Trade, is married to a misogynistically drawn shrew named

Ines, who is beautiful but materialistic and spectacularly unfaithful. Paula is unmarried and currently in a relationship with a man who is father to the child she has just borne; she returns home from the hospital with the new baby in her arms only to find him in bed with another, younger woman. Left with two young children from two failed relationships, Paula is sorely tempted by the economic security that would come with marriage to the much older suitor nicknamed "Reifen-Saft" (the small-scale but relatively wealthy tire dealer who gently pursues her throughout the film). Paula nevertheless sets her sights on the already married Paul, the love of her life. The problem is—and again here Carow indulges a cultural stereotype with a grain of truth—Paul seems happy to have an affair with her, but is not at first ready to divorce Ines in order to commit to Paula. By the time he is (following the tragic traffic death of one of Paula's children), Paula is no longer willing to have him. So the plot is one of mutual but asymmetrical pursuit. It concludes with a happy/unhappy ending: they are ultimately united, have a child together, but Paula (who has been repeatedly warned not to have another pregnancy) dies in childbirth. The concluding voiceover and the consoling image of Paul parenting all three of Paula's children—they are all snuggled together into one big bed—leaves us with a warm and upbeat feeling.

In the case of *Paul and Paula*, figuring out what is meant by the sprawling notion of '68 becomes a manageable task. The film itself delimits the phenomenon to the cultural side. Thus, the volatile "political" side—protests affiliated with the Vietnam War and civil rights—makes no appearance here, not to mention, of course, the Soviet military suppression of Czech reformers during the infamous *Prager Frühling*, or Prague Spring. The separation of the "political" from the "cultural" (if we may, in defiance of the movement itself, use such crude markers for the time being) was by no means incidental, nor was it without an intrinsic logic. The Prague Spring was off the table; that we can simply stipulate. But as for Vietnam and civil rights, here the GDR was already "on the right side," as it were. As Knut Lennartz (former GDR dramaturge and official in the East Berlin Ministry of Culture) puts it: "The student revolts from Paris to West Berlin seemed to confirm that socialism is the only conceivable social model that could bring about the dream of social justice. All the recognizable betrayals of socialism by the GDR were accepted by critical intellectuals as almost unavoidable childhood illnesses."[4] The GDR was surely not without its flaws, its peccadillos, but it was further along the road to the protesters' goals than was the West.

We see this both in the GDR's self-representation and in the view of many Western protesters, who often idealized the Eastern Bloc as a place that had already come to a clearer understanding of the war in Vietnam as a consequence of Western imperialism, and of the subjugation of Blacks as a manifestation of objectification (*Verdinglichung*) symptomatic of late capitalism's crisis, quite possibly betokening its death throes. As a "socialist brother" state, East Germany stood on the "right side" of virtually all the overtly political questions that were, let us recall, united by a Marxist-inspired critique of Western society.[5] In real socioeconomic terms also, the GDR of the mid- to late 1960s appears to have lacked the specific tensions that fueled protest within West Germany.[6] It comes as no surprise, then, to learn that the GDR provided not only refuge but also material support to student protesters in the Federal Republic and to certain notorious members of the Rote Armee Fraktion (Red Army Faction).[7] What may seem to some observers a mere Machiavellian move to exploit dissent within Western societies (and that it surely *also* was) was viewed by many within the movement as an instance of socialist solidarity, which to some extent explains the positive view of the GDR among left-leaning critics within many Western countries, whereby the GDR was widely viewed as "das bessere Deutschland" (the better Germany) in part because it realized or at least expressed the aspirations of so many in the student movement.[8]

Paul and Paula thematizes its progressive stance vis-à-vis race relations and the so-called Third World in a compelling scene that shows us Paul at work. Ostensibly this scene—rarely considered in the secondary literature—serves the purpose merely of complicating the melodramatic love triangle. Paula, who is in hot pursuit of her man, appears incognito in order to gain access to a fancy party being held in honor of some guests from East Africa, who, we surmise, have just concluded some lucrative contracts with the GDR. Paul makes clear that these East African business associates—their precise country of origin is never specified—are true partners, and not mere recipients of development aid. Though Paula keeps bringing the topic back to their personal love life, Paul insists upon the importance of *Devisen* (hard foreign currency) to the GDR, and divulges that he has been hard at work learning Swahili in order to better manage this economic relationship. Without losing the pacing of the ro-

Figure 6.1 Heidemarie Wenzel, playing the role of Paul's wife, Ines, dances expressively and sensually with one of his business associates. In the film script she is known only as "die Schöne" (the beauty), which suits the principal role she is given here of entertaining men. ©DEFA-Stiftung/Manfred Damm, Herbert Kroiss.

mantic plot line—Paula will ultimately be rebuffed at the conclusion of this segment, and then it will be Paul's turn to entreat her to take him back—we are given two powerful images. One is of Ines, Paul's wife, dancing rather intimately with a dark-skinned African; the other is a sequence of approving, appreciative glances from male East German and African colleagues alike.

Ines touches and holds the African in a free and natural way, and then dances not only with but for him in an openly flirtatious manner. Even if somewhat at odds with GDR social reality, the message seems clearly to be that race is no barrier. Second, we see the GDR in a cooperative, respectful relationship with the developing world. Unlike so many other cases treated in this volume tracing the connections between Europe and Latin America, representatives of postcolonial countries are here treated as equals, rather than with suspicion or condescension. These may constitute ideal and rather self-congratulatory self-images. The point is not to critically assess the images against social reality, but rather to identify the socially progressive images encoded in this film. By that measure, the GDR is clearly presented as both racially tolerant and innocent of nefarious colonial legacies. In short, the better Germany.

But to say this is not to say that the East—or the GDR in particular—"owned" '68, or presented an image to Western activists of a fully achieved revolution. It was the "cultural" side that was indeed its Achilles' heel. That which we (in the United States) would come to associate with Woodstock—openness about sex and the erotics of personal relationships; the recreational use of consciousness-altering drugs; and the enjoyment of rock 'n' roll as a form of social (and, yes, political) bonding—was utterly lacking in the GDR.[9] So when all of this made an unexpected appearance in *Paul and Paula*, it resonated profoundly and lastingly. The famous "flower child" scene of lovemaking, in which a scantily clad Paula "liberates" Paul from his military uniform (he has just returned from reserve duty) is perhaps the most memorable, and "edgy" in terms of contemporaneous imagery.[10] Reminiscent of Woodstock, and visually affiliated with the "make love not war" slogans of the Western student movement, this sequence cautiously moves within GDR orthodoxy. For it is marked first as a kind of drug-induced fantasy (Paul's work colleagues show up as band members to accompany their lovemaking); second, and perhaps most importantly, Paul's identity as a soldier/bureaucrat is never seriously called into question, or pitted against the sensuality Paula exudes. It is really about him learning to have it both ways. He needs to loosen up, not abandon his socialist commitments.

The film introduced many East Germans to the rock music of the Puhdys, a home-grown band that drew heavily (and recognizably) on Western models, such as Deep Purple and Uriah Heep. Their first concert was in the fall of 1969, but it was Carow's 1973 film that really established their fame within the GDR and later in West Germany. Like the film, the band was permitted to play in the West, and found favor there. Their songs, especially those written for the film, were memorable and often overtly sexual, such as the hit "Lass deinen Drachen steigen" (Let your dragon rise, or Let your kite fly), which accompanied the famous lovemaking scene staged on the barge floating down the River Spree.[11]

The hallucinogenic drugs (that seem to affect Paul but not Paula) and the fairly explicit lovemaking were at once revolutionary within GDR culture and reminiscent of recent cultural developments in the West. "No

Figure 6.2 Appearing unnanounced, Paul surprises his wife, Ines, in bed with her lover. ©DEFA-Stiftung/Manfred Damm, Herbert Kroiss.

film before this one," observes film scholar Wolfgang Gersch, "had indulged to this degree in individual concerns or presented a plot so grounded in the erotic. Shocked, the Party immediately responded by setting certain parameters for criticism."[12]

The blatant portrayal of sex and drugs—noted sometimes only indirectly in the GDR press[13]—shocked some, to be sure. And for this very reason, I would argue, they are accompanied by traditional-looking vintage photos and images of older couples and family members meant, I would argue, to frame and stabilize the narrative—to serve, in other words, as "shock absorbers." The message appears to be that no matter how radical a break this may be in terms of cultural practice, the desires themselves are simply "human," and thus safely embeddable within time-honored family genealogies. The film's obsession with old family photos—particularly with those that appear at these sexually explicit junctures—can thus be read as a way of domesticating the potentially aberrant content. It becomes in this way more universally "human" and less, perhaps, a radical break with prior GDR film conventions and cultural habits.[14] Moreover, if these grandmotherly figures are indeed knitting baby clothes, as they seem

Figure 6.3 A virtually naked Paula on her fantasy wedding day, with elderly women looking on approvingly as they knit baby clothes. ©DEFA-Stiftung/Manfred Damm, Herbert Kroiss.

to be, these visuals would appear to yoke rogue erotic energies to child-bearing and child-rearing—a message fully in line with Paula's insistence on having Paul's child as a sign of her love for him, and with Paul's iconic final scene in bed with all three children.

To put this in the context of contemporaneous cultural theory—which was then just breaking on the scene as part of the '68 revolution—we could view the film's studied juxtaposition of the old (for example, daguerreotype family photos) with the shockingly new (overt sexuality and drug use) in view of Roland Barthes's then revolutionary study, *Mythologies*, which appeared in English for the first time the year before the film debuted (1972). Barthes, it will be remembered, had argued that modern capitalist culture tends to conceal its own historicity by creating a veneer of timelessness and naturalness. Myth, in other words, supplants history—and in the process, we lose an appreciation of the contingency of social arrangements. This, in turn, undermines our ability to advocate for social change, let alone mount the great revolution. It is a neo-Marxist critique reminiscent of Brecht and broadly in line with the Frankfurt School notion of "affirmative culture."

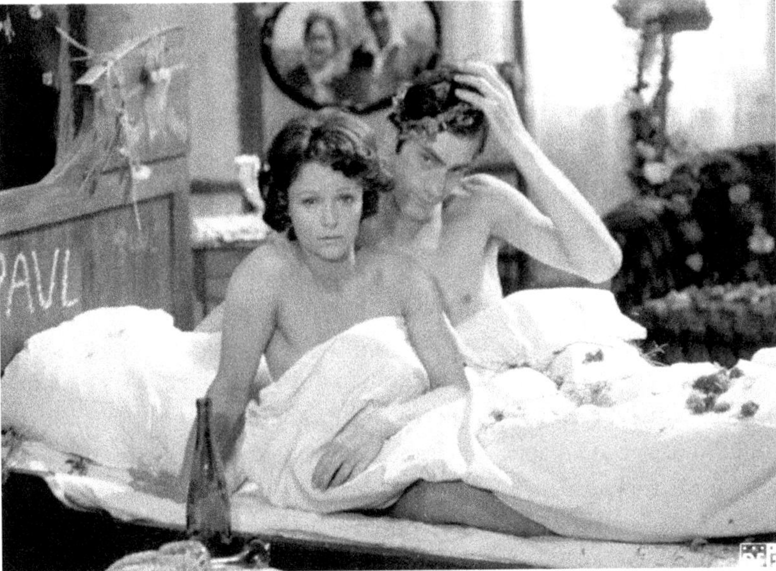

Figure 6.4 Paul and Paula awake from their "wedding night" of sex, drugs, and rock 'n' roll. ©DEFA-Stiftung/Manfred Damm, Herbert Kroiss.

What I am proposing here is that Barthes's celebrated notion of cultural mythologies can productively be recruited—despite the fact that it was designed for the analysis of Western capitalist cultures—to understand a central strategy of *Paul and Paula*: Carow's pairing of the old with the new strongly suggests a narrative of continuity and naturalness. He mythologizes the cultural rupture. When the older generations "step out" of the stills in the famous lovemaking scene in order to observe, comment upon, and even playfully ogle the young couple, they do so explicitly to endorse and approve their exploits. Contrary to a dominant narrative in Western culture at this time, this celebration of sex, drugs, and rock 'n' roll is enacted *within* an irenic intergenerational discourse. The generational strife that is elsewhere absolutely constitutive of "'68"—remember that Peter Schneider names the attack on the fathers as an integral part of the student protest movement—is utterly lacking here.[15] Along these same lines of tempering potentially revolutionary content with traditional form is that, as Volker Schlöndorff put it, the film is "not daring aesthetically. If it had been, it would have been banned."[16] Its familiar, melodramatic format made it both accessible to the masses and less of a threat politically.

But this is only part of the story. At root, *Paul und Paula* does not merely absorb, but fundamentally rewrites '68 as it was experienced in the West. By means of these scenes of intergenerational benediction, Carow appropriates the so-called sexual revolution of the West and redirects us to its "source" within the socialist, antibourgeois cultural revolution. It is, after all, *bourgeois* sexual norms—including the view of matrimony as sacrosanct that Paula openly flouts—that are fundamentally at issue here.[17] Hence, the romance can be viewed within a securely socialist framework—that, at least, is the film's gambit—without risking the appearance that DEFA has adopted Western models. Paula's resolutely antibourgeois behavior can elsewhere be seen not only in her rejection of the middle-class petit entrepreneur Saft, but perhaps most poignantly in her failure to applaud at the "right" juncture at an open-air classical concert. Overcome with the emotion of the moment—a moment that intermingles her love of Paul with her response to the music of Beethoven—she spontaneously erupts with applause at the conclusion of a movement, rather than waiting for the completion of the entire piece. Paul is momentarily embarrassed, but Paula wins the hearts not only of the intradiegetic auditors, but presumably also those of the film's viewers. Precisely as an antibourgeois icon, Paula manages to give "'68" a specifically socialist genealogy.[18]

As we consider these various attempts to provide a properly socialist pedigree to what might well seem like an importation of Western decadence,[19] it is worth reminding ourselves of the film's relatively safe starting point. Carow is making his film at a time of stability and relative relaxation in the GDR. The Berlin Wall had long since been erected and reinforced, such that the remarkable hemorrhage of labor to the West had ceased and the regime could turn its attention to consolidation. Erich Honecker had replaced Walter Ulbricht, and the infamous 11th Party Plenum (1965), which harshly denounced "bourgeois" art that failed to toe the socialist-realist line, was a thing of the past. Hard-liners had had their day, and perhaps precisely because they had, there seemed to be room for a cultural opening.

This is reflected in the film's stunning opening shot, which reveals a remarkably confident GDR. Long before we meet the principal actors in the love story for which the film is perhaps best remembered, we encounter a city that is boldly in the process of reconstruction, an obvious image for the bourgeoning socialist order. What Gerd Gemünden says about

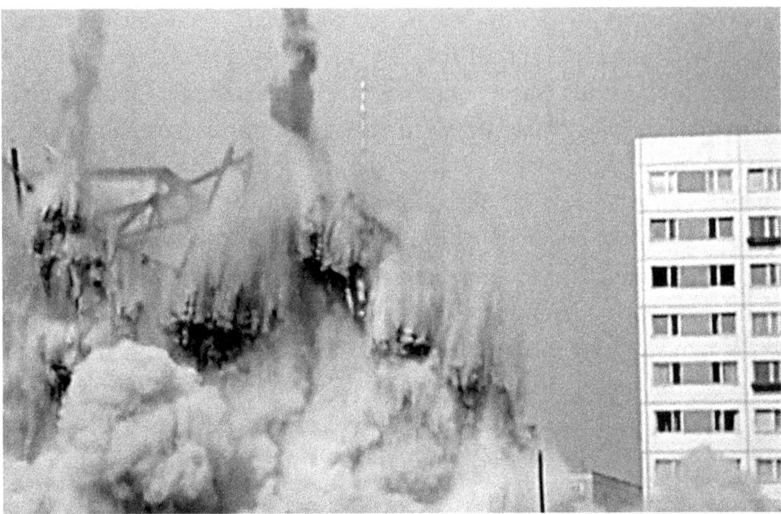

Figure 6.5 The optimism of East Germany in the early 1970s is expressed in its ambitious building campaign. *The Legend of Paul und Paula* features a series of scenes such as this one, in which the demolished building makes way for a new socialist order, here represented by the iconic Fernsehturm antenna (red and white, looming in the distance), and the smart, new apartment house to the right. ©DEFA-Stiftung/Manfred Damm, Herbert Kroiss.

Billy Wilder's Berlin (in *A Foreign Affair*) is no less true here: the city is the film's central protagonist.[20] In a dramatic long shot, Carow shows us the detonation of older, war-damaged buildings. The site is the Singerstraße in Berlin-Friedrichshain, the locale, as GDR viewers would know, most closely associated with major reconstruction projects, including above all the Stalin-Allee, renamed in 1961 the Karl-Marx-Allee. As the dust settles, the red and white antenna of the sleek, new TV tower (*Fernsehturm*), pride of the young GDR, gradually comes into view in the distance. From our sight line, the old has literally made way for the new. Here, to speak metaphorically, we can say that the GDR is visually laying claim to the mantle of an achieved revolution.[21]

The post-1968 message may be richer yet. The visual suggestion in this scene, at a site metonymically bound to the erstwhile Stalin-Allee (where the workers' uprising of 1953 began), may be this: the Soviet intervention that put down that revolt is now also a thing of the settled and relatively distant past. In this way, Czechoslovakia is made incommensurate, if not quite irrelevant.[22] The GDR has, it is suggested, "mastered" this past too (not just the Nazi one) principally via an ambitious building program that is bringing social justice to workers where it is most immediately felt: housing. Taking this as the film's starting point means that the subsequent love story—no matter how unorthodox with regard to East German letters and mores—occurs on the basis and within the setting of this already "established" revolution. And this is not merely an opening shot: similar scenes of demolition and reconstruction punctuate and frame the entire film such that the optimistic construction of the socialist state is the film's central motif.[23] There is a good deal more to do, the images themselves suggest, but the fundamental reversal has been set in motion. Neither is this a mere framing device: Paul's modern apartment is pointedly contrasted throughout with Paula's *Altbau*, which, according to the film's logic, seems destined for demolition. Given this firm socialist foundation, one needn't fear being understood as "appropriating" a Western revolution, even if the film's adaption of "Western" themes would suggest precisely this.

A TRUE GDR HIT

Before proceeding with our analysis, it will be useful to establish the place this film occupied in GDR culture. For a long time, the prominence of *Paul and Paula* in the GDR was not well understood. The standard line, still to be found in the classic reference works on GDR film, and still propagated by the German Wikipedia site about this film, is that *Paul and Paula* was an initial success, but then virtually disappeared from the scene because of the defection to the West of its two leading actors.[24] It is asserted—all too authoritatively—that the film rather abruptly went out of circulation as a matter of course, for all such incidents of *Republikflucht* (fleeing the republic) were treated in this way.[25] The respective artist's work was simply "disappeared." The German Wikipedia entry picks up the film's reception story after Unification, noting that *Paul and Paula* became a beloved subject of *Ostalgie*, the post-*Wende* nostalgia of former GDR citizens for their erstwhile socialist paradise. This narrative could well leave one wondering whether the alleged resonance of the film is perhaps in the end fundamentally a post-GDR phenomenon that has been read back into the Honecker era. The other suspicion one might entertain—equally misleading, it turns out—is that the excitement about *Paul and Paula* is primarily a West German phenomenon projected back upon the East, owing to the fact that the film succeeded in the Federal Republic.

To learn more about the reception, and with the help of the "Zeitungsportal DDR-Presse" at the Staatsbibliothek zu Berlin, I tracked East Germany's three leading newspapers, the *Berliner Zeitung*, *Neue Zeit*, and *Neues Deutschland* from 1971 through the early 1990s.[26] In fact, there was a buzz about *Paul and Paula* even before the film's release. Rumors of the film potentially being banned may have increased its appeal: within the first year alone, it drew almost 2 million viewers.[27] Since its premier on April 29, 1973, not a single week went by (through 1989 and beyond) when the film was not screened in one or more of Berlin's movie houses, and presumably elsewhere. Surprisingly (to me, at least), even after it was first broadcast on television in 1975, *Paul and Paula* continued to be screened regularly in cinemas, and is to be found again and again in the newspaper listings for "Neues auf der Leinwand" (New Screen Attractions)—decades after its debut.[28] Contrary to the claims of F.-B. Habel and Wikipedia, it continued to play on GDR television. The film is mentioned almost 800 times in these papers during this period. And even though one finds relatively few substantive reviews, the evidence for its ongoing prominence is clear. There is absolutely no retraction of the film as a result of the defection of its star, Angelica Domröse. On the contrary, as time goes on, there is gathering evidence that *Paul and Paula* has become a proud classic within the GDR, and not just in retrospect.[29]

THE GDR GOES HOLLYWOOD

In the street where Paula lives, we see an old cinema playing what appears to be a popular melodrama. The movie house, the Elektra-Lichtspiele (see fig. 6.6) appears several times—often enough to make us ask about the role of film and cinema in Paula's troubled life. Paula's winsome and unstoppable search for personal fulfillment can be said to be mirrored in the melodrama currently playing: *Wedding Night in Rainfall* (*Hochzeitsnacht im Regen*), the 1967 DEFA musical about an unlikely female jockey who ultimately manages to find both fame and romance.[30]

Figure 6.6 This run-down prewar cinema, the Elektra-Lichtspiele, forms the portal to Paula's apartment building, and appears to proffer romantic escapism (or fulfillment) in a manner similar to Carow's own film. ©DEFA-Stiftung/ Manfred Damm, Herbert Kroiss.

The prominence of this old-fashioned movie house may also raise the question at another level about the role of cinema more generally. The standard East German response—to which we will turn our attention below—is the doctrine of socialist realism, the official GDR policy that seeks to yoke art to the purposes of building the socialist society. But this agenda fails to capture the role of cinema in either sense—within the film (that is, intradiegetically) or in our meta-reflections about *Paul and Paula* as a (de-)stabilizing factor within East German society. Both seem to fall clearly outside that prescription for aesthetic orthodoxy. What I would suggest instead is the simple notion that at this optimistic time in GDR history, the very shrewd Honecker felt he could afford a little Hollywood, in particular a sort that generously exploits salient motifs from the "Western" cultural revolution. He was not willing to cede the "revolution"—already successfully underway in the GDR, after all—to the West. He would instead "triangulate" those energies by approving the release of Carow's film.

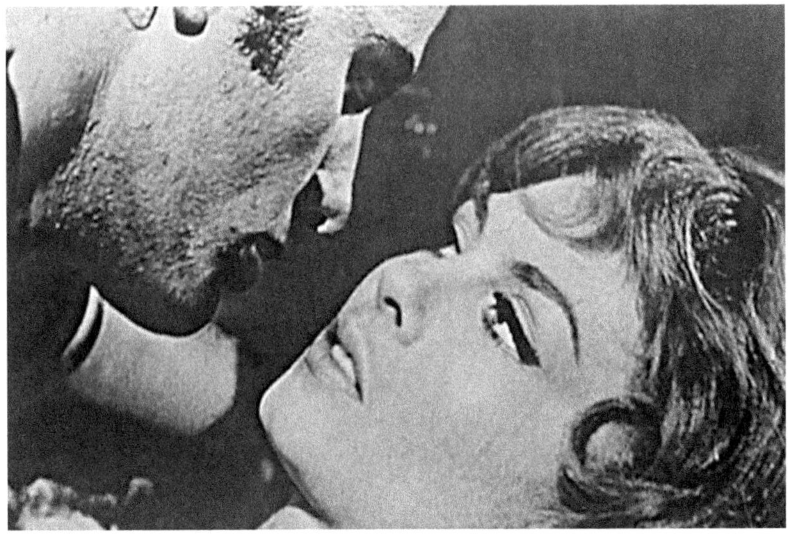

Figure 6.7 This scene from *Hochzeitsnacht im Regen* is intercut as Paula passes by the movie theater on the way to her apartment. As she laboriously drags bucket after bucket of coal up the stairs, she seems to become a viewer (along with us) of this romantic comedy. The contrast of quotidian East German reality with high romance could hardly be starker. ©DEFA-Stiftung/Manfred Damm, Herbert Kroiss.

But if it was a concession made on the basis of achieved socialist goals, it was also one designed to promote further stabilization. Not merely largesse, in other words, but also an effort to defuse building pressures for personal fulfilment via "Hollywood." Let us assume that with *Paul and Paula*, Honecker was importing a bit of the Hollywood dream factory—when Volker Schlöndorff took on the post-*Wende* reorganization of DEFA-Babelsberg, he in fact called it a "zerrüttete Traumfabrik" (a dilapidated dream factory)[31]—thereby partially supplanting official notions of socialist realism. Honecker may have felt that he could risk a bit of the Western "poison" with the reasonable hope that it would lead not to Western decadence, but rather prove an adroit instrument of social control.

To understand this counterintuitive claim, we need to turn our attention briefly to Marxists one would not readily associate with the name Erich Honecker. It was Max Horkheimer and Theodor Adorno who made the claim that popular art in a capitalist society does not—indeed cannot—serve as protest. In the famous article "Commitment," Adorno argued that even art which fancies itself politically progressive typically fails to deliver any meaningful intervention. On the contrary, art of this nature—and melodrama falls squarely into this category—only affirms regnant capitalist power relations. By deflecting our attention via escapism it conceals the real social determinants, contributing to "false consciousness." In the realm of cinema, this line of thinking produced the Frankfurt School's notion of "dominant cinema," a form of mass entertainment that affirms rather than critiques the status quo (despite any apparent or nominal critique). In film studies, the term is frequently used simply to indicate any Hollywood commercial formula film. But without foregrounding the elements of social control and surface-level social critique (which is ultimately neutralized by a deeper-level affirmation of the status quo) the term loses its essential contribution.

For Paula, who inhabits this cinema both psychically and literally (the theater is located prominently on the ground floor of her building), the effect might indeed be "regime-stabilizing" in that the world of romance and fantasy seems to help get her through the daily challenges of GDR life. But if Carow intended this palimpsestic technique (of placing a film within a film) as a warning about his own film's regime-stabilizing potential, this would have to have constituted an irony that utterly evaded the censors. Nor do I claim that Honecker was an Adorno crypto-acolyte, or that he consciously adopted Frankfurt School theory, let alone adapted it to the circumstances of real-existing GDR socialism. I make this point, rather, because it illuminates how "going Hollywood" can in some ways dovetail with efforts at social control.

For Honecker, this dalliance with Hollywood may have been intuitive, perhaps even a bit egotistical. But at some level it will have been clear to him, as it was in other contexts, that by indulging carefully administered doses of dissidence, he might stabilize the Communist Party's monopoly on power. This was precisely the explanation observers applied to Ulrich Plenzdorf's great success, *Die neuen Leiden des Jungen W.*, which famously features a socially maladjusted hero "am Rande des FDJ-Lebens."[32] As Peter Jelavich attests, the GDR was adept at precisely this.[33] For example, "critical" poetry could be tolerated, but only because it provided a safe outlet for activism: very few people read such poetry to begin with, it was assumed. The critique is in any case elaborately coded, and with carefully controlled publication runs (justified by a real or feigned shortage of paper), not to mention Stasi follow-up, the effect could in any case be handily managed.

More interesting is Jelavich's treatment of the East German cabaret: here we learn that regime-critical theater was not simply tolerated, but actively encouraged because of its capacity to bleed critique away from meaningful subversive political activity, thus dissipating critical energies in the ephemeral heat of audience entertainment.[34] Could this same, cynical *Ventilfunktion* (pressure-release function) be at play in Honecker's somewhat surprising decision to allow Carow's film—contrary to the expectation of many—to see the light of day?[35] The point is not to speculate on motives, but rather to consider the full range of the film's functionality as a tool (unwitting, from the perspective of Carow, to be sure) of social control. One can conceive of it as a power broker's pure manipulation or, from a more compassionate point of view, as a way of compensating the GDR population via film for experiences it was not otherwise very likely to have. At any rate, I think we need to remain open to this counterrevolutionary possibility even as we move forward to consider the film's revolutionary potential.

THE OSTENSIBLE CLASH WITH SOCIALIST REALISM

Paula doesn't overtly exhibit any solidly socialist virtues. On the contrary, she is out for personal fulfillment, and does not see the current marriage of her lover as an acceptable obstacle to their future happiness. In the end, Paul, always the more conventional of the two (though a romantic at heart), leaves his shrew of a wife, a misogynistic stereotype identified in the film script only as "die Schöne" (the beauty), for Paula. Against the advice of her doctors (Paula simply doesn't accept a world that fails to accord with her dreams), she gives birth to Paul's child—her third—and promptly dies in childbirth. The film ends in a mix of emotions: tears for Paula's demise, but joy because her family, her dream, will live on. And like all popular music, the Puhdys are there not only to provide the backdrop to her particular story, but to supply the soundtrack to our own. With the Puhdys, we live out (and relive) Paula's story, so to speak. So even though hers is a narrative of individual (un)happiness, it becomes by way of its eminently portable desires and emotions a *social* one. In short, Plenzdorf's plot (which he wrote in collaboration with Carow) is indeed the stuff of bourgeois melodrama rather than that of socialist realism.

But there is a difference, one that echoes the opening destruction/construction scene discussed above. Unlike so much officially sanctioned GDR fiction—and unlike so much of the critical discourse that imposed socialist-realist criteria on literature of all kinds—the Plenzdorf story does not pit the individual *against* the social.[36] This is not, in other words, the paradigmatic story of *Der geteilte Himmel*, in which Rita's choice to leave her lover, Manfred, in West Berlin is fundamentally a rejection of egotistical, hedonistic capitalist society, and an embrace of socialism. Paula is never presented with this trumped-up dilemma. On the contrary, when we see her at work as a grocery store cashier—one of the few "socialist" settings not dedicated to the pursuit of personal happiness—she is cooperative, cheerful, and utterly supportive of the collective enterprise. She doesn't want happiness at the expense of the collective; she simply wants both. This is underscored by the perhaps flat-footed plot segment that involves her suitor, the tire salesman (Reifen-Saft) (played by Paul Delmare). Paula's gentle rejection of his persistent overtures is not freighted with canned metaphorical meaning; it frankly has nothing to do with the frequent demonization of individual happiness bought at the expense of social (and socialist) commitments. On the contrary, her ultimate union with Paul is if anything a short-lived communion of the personal and the social, the terms so often at loggerheads in socialist realism, as Paul is a Party member openly committed to "die gute Sache" (the good, i.e., socialist, cause). The film thus goes out of its way to deconstruct one of the GDR's most tired tropes, and in doing so lays the groundwork for its acceptance across the spectrum. Censors did not feel compelled to condemn it (though some did), critics were free to praise it (many did), and viewers got the message that they might just have it both ways.

One such supportive critic, writing for the *Neue Zeit* just prior to the film's release, notes the tendency to indulge in "große Gefühle" (great emotions) only when they are sufficiently packaged as a legitimate "gesellschaftliche Fragestellung" (social concern).[37] The critic correctly perceives a departure from the expected didacticism of socialist realism—and is expressly grateful for it—but argues that in this film the personal *is* the political. This is, as I've said, a significant shift for the GDR, where a standard joke (the humor of which frankly has always escaped me, but I think one simply had to be there) ran something like this:

Genosse, Du kommst mir verstimmt vor; hast du Probleme?
Ja, habe ich.
Welche, wenn ich fragen darf?
Ach, persönliche
Also denn, keine!

———

Buddy, you seem upset. What's wrong?
Oh, I've got problems.
What kind?
Well, personal ones.
Oh, then none at all!

Against this typical denigration of the personal in favor of the social, the *Neue Zeit* critic sees Carow's film as linking the two in a relationship of consonance. No love story could be more "intimate and private," and yet in this very intimacy *Paul and Paula* engages the larger "times and society that have set as their goal the emancipation and development of individual personality."[38] The author asserts this conflation of the personal and social twice more in this article, firmly linking the love story to the permissible priorities of social analysis. Appearing just before the film's premier, this review smooths the way for a film that could quite easily run afoul of official aesthetic doctrine—which, as we will now see, it also did.

We should not think of GDR officialdom as a well-oiled, single-minded monolith. Academics, such as a certain Prof. Dr. Hans Koch, who in June 1973 wrote an article called "Der einzelne und die Gesellschaft" (The Individual and Society) for *Neues Deutschland*, cut their teeth on decades of state-enforced socialist realism.[39] Not all that long before the debut of *Paul and Paula* they had witnessed the rigors and denunciations of the infamous 11th Party Plenum (1965). So they could perhaps be forgiven for not understanding that Honecker had recently changed course or, more likely, had simply made a tactical decision to "vent" certain pent-up yearnings for personal fulfillment that may indeed have been fueled by the '68 activists in the West. Koch, at any rate, writes a perfectly conformist column, condemning works of contemporary literature and film that stray from Marxist orthodoxy by indulging "Individualismus" (individualism) at the expense of society. In this pedantically overwritten article, he disparages among other things the artists' "verkannte soziale

Werte und Prinzipien" (misjudged social values and principles). About Carow's film in particular, he had this to say:

> Paula is preoccupied with personal happiness, friendliness, and human warmth. Her claim to happiness (also in its personal and intimate dimensions) appears here as a *goal unto itself*, whereby personal happiness is segregated from the social well-being. The moral perseverance with which Paula follows *her own* star becomes a non-negotiable moral ideal in itself. In making her purely personal desires absolute—in the face of all social contradictions, demands, codes of conduct and conventions—she constitutes her so-called act of "self actualization."[40]

Even in free societies, with only market restrictions on the press and other publication venues, reception criticism is at best a fraught and an imprecise undertaking; in authoritarian societies such as the GDR, it becomes more complicated yet.[41] The two fundamental views I've documented above—one arguing, with second-wave feminism, that the personal is the political; the other (Koch) stubbornly dismissing "individualism" as intrinsically antisocial (and antisocialist)—should be seen as diverging types of contemporary viewer reactions that give us only a rough sense of the range of response. But given these limitations, they nevertheless reveal two things. The former suggests that the GDR, with its own modest *Wirtschaftswunder* (economic miracle) in progress, can now more confidently stage dramas of personal happiness.[42] The latter is perhaps counterintuitive, because precisely in his party-line rigidity, Prof. Koch articulates the case for the contestatory nature of the film. If he is right, *Paul and Paula* really does give voice to destabilizing desires that are incompatible with the socialist status quo. His very warning—and others like it—enhance the film's aura as dangerously dissident.[43]

CONSERVATION OR DISSIPATION OF REVOLUTIONARY ENERGIES?

Only the Janus-faced nature of *Paul and Paula* can explain both its official endorsement and promotion and the pervasive perception that it was simultaneously subversive. This bimodal quality goes to the heart of the *fab-*

ula itself: Paula is the undoubted locus of a bundle of sympathetically drawn energies focusing on personal happiness in spite of social strictures. But she is ultimately "killed off." One way of making this point is to attend to the film's self-designation as "legend," which to a number of critics places the film in the land of fantasy and the imaginary, rather than in the context of contemporary socialism. In his review for the *Berliner Zeitung*, for example, Günter Sobe declares: "*The Legend of Paul and Paula* is, to be precise, the story of Paula's love. Fancifully [*phantasiereich*] she emerges into view, and this rich fantasy takes us captive."[44] Paul pales in comparison to her remarkable vitality, Sobe says. But despite Paula's heralded halo of joy—"cheerful, tragic, entertaining, colorful" (*heiter, tragisch, unterhaltsam, bunt*)—she must die: "Paula is essentially ejected from the game; she dies giving birth to her third child, the symbol of her commitment to Paul."[45] This affiliation of Paula with the realm of the "legendary" (read: ultimately fantastical and unworldly) core of the film highlights its potential for defusing rather than stoking dissident and possibly anarchic energies. In this view, she embodies escapist fantasies fit for ephemeral entertainment but not for the real world. Or worse: a pleasurable fantasy that metamorphoses into a cautionary tale.

For despite Paula's remarkable cultural currency (she is referred to in the press not only as an icon but occasionally as a real person), what lurks behind this figure, from this point of view, is the misogynist trope of the "punished woman."[46] We may vicariously savor her pursuit of pleasure, but we, no less than she, are in the end "disciplined"—taught to reject these ambitions as unreal, or, rather, fit for the cinema, but not for society.[47] Further, there is no liberation of sex from childbearing to be found here; on the contrary, in a very traditional way of demonstrating their love, Paula insists on bearing Paul a child, despite the options available to her, given the GDR's relatively more liberal policies on contraception and abortion. On this reading—the dismissal of Paula as "legendary"—the film seems to evoke female power only to quash it or to restrict it to tradition and/or fantasy.[48] Staging precisely what Brecht abhorred about "culinary" theater, *Paul and Paula*, seen from this perspective, would hardly qualify for its retrospective classification as one of the great DEFA films of women's liberation.[49] This defeatist view may explain Max Frisch's reaction to the film, recorded in his Berlin journals, where he writes, "The film is lousy—sad as a symptom of frustration whose dream of fulfillment just produces more stench."[50]

But the case is by no means closed. If Paula dies in the film, she lives a remarkable afterlife in GDR cultural discourse and beyond. It is not just that the film played continuously since its first screening, as we noted above. Paula was in a sense reincarnated through a number of works that reprised or alluded to her character. Plenzdorf wrote a sequel in 1979 called *Legende vom Glück ohne Ende* (*The Legend of Happiness without End*) in which a certain Laura fills the gap left by Paula. Reviewers did not really warm to that book, but were grateful for the opportunity to relive the film and to state their preference for Paula over Laura.[51] Undeterred, Plenzdorf made a play out of that book, which again proved an occasion for reviving Paula in public discourse.[52] When years later Plenzdorf adapted Günter de Bruyn's novella "Freiheitsberaubung" for the stage (1988), a reviewer couldn't help comparing the heroine, Anita Paschke, to Paula: "Looking at her [Anita], one is reminded of Paula from the Heiner Carow film . . . similar social circumstances, similar life challenges, and a similar demand for love and happiness."[53] "Similarities," it seems, are everywhere you look.

In 1992—after the *Wende*—Carow made a film called *Verfehlung*, in which he cast Angelica Domröse (who played Paula in 1973) as the female lead, now as a middle-aged cleaning woman. Though the plot similarities are slim indeed, a critic nevertheless reads this figure as an aging Paula: "Paula mit fünfzig, alt geworden in der DDR."[54] This latter remark is particularly telling, because for this critic, as for many in the GDR, I suspect, Paula never really died. (A later opera by Ludger Vollmer, based on the sequel, *Paul und Paula, oder die Legende von Glück ohne Ende*, manages to "resurrect" Paula by having the same actor sing both roles—that of Paula and Laura.) And the Puhdys—the most famous band in the history of the GDR—kept her alive by incessantly reprising hits from the movie ("Geh zu ihr," "Lass deinen Drachen steigen," and "Wenn ein Mensch lebt") that first established their fame.[55] Thus, although the "punished woman" thesis may at the level of plot possess some cogency, it does not adequately explain the Paula phenomenon in the GDR. There is good reason to believe that *Paul and Paula* functioned less like a cautionary tale than one of inspiration and yearning. "Audiences in the GDR recognized Paula's role as a thorn in the side of modernizing East Germany," Reimer and Zachau affirm, going so far as to make the rather outsized claim that "*Die Legende von Paul und Paula* in 1973 and the Biermann crisis in 1976 are considered the trigger for the collapse of the GDR fifteen years later."[56]

There is yet another cultural feature of the GDR that may encourage the "subversive" reading. In discussing the English title he approved for one of his own films (namely, *The Legend of Rita* for the 2000 German film *Stille nach dem Schuß*), Volker Schlöndorff draws our attention to the double meaning of the word "Legende" in Germany, and in the GDR in particular. A "legend," he explains, is a code word, a new identity given to an agent or witness who is going undercover. It allows someone to continue operating without being easily discovered or targeted. A legend, in this sense, is a kind of "slave language," Schlöndorff insists, used by those who need to conceal potentially subversive behavior from the authorities. In this sense, then, we may imagine that East Germans really saw Paula as a kind of "legend"—killed off at the plot level, but quite "alive" in their cultural lives. And while we are fully savoring the semantic valence of the word "legend," we might note that it also connotes the way in which narrative is deployed in subsequent iterations and historical contexts, quite apart from the original "constative" or factual claims of the respective plot. It is, in other words, very much about the social function and evolution of narrative as it plays out over time.

In retrospect, at any rate, the film was generally assumed to be regime-critical. Of course, this is not a view one could have easily encountered in the GDR press. But after Unification, when Carow was nominated for a position in the Medienrat Berlin-Brandenburg (a media-cultural board for the state of Berlin-Brandenburg), he was credited precisely with having created "a series of critical films like *The Legend of Paul and Paula*" (eine Reihe kritischer DEFA-Filme wie "Die Legende von Paul und Paula").[57] And in 2005, the New York Museum of Modern Art mounted a retrospective called "Rebel with a Cause: The Cinema of East Germany," featuring *Paul and Paula*. The fact that it also became a prime target of *Ostalgie*, however, does make one wonder whether this retrospective view is perhaps not a bit too self-congratulatory, or simply a case of writing history from the perspective of the victor. Honecker can only have approved the film, I have argued, because he saw it as a bit of escapism that might defuse the widespread sense of frustration. Shedding the explicitly political edge of Western '68, *Paul and Paula* imports only those cultural elements—sex, drugs, and rock 'n' roll—that can be used to "inoculate" the GDR against a true cultural revolution. But Honecker miscalculated, I believe, and this "vaccination effort" seems to have communicated a bit of the disease itself. Responding to a similar phenomenon in the area of literature, Peter Jelavich observes, "Writers like Christa Wolf could legitimately argue that they were acting in a subversive manner by making claims for subjectivity and individuality; such issues are subversive almost by definition in a society whose government strives to control all means of socialization." But he tempers that claim with this caveat: "By arguing for interiority, such works fashioned citizens who did not conform to the state's norms, but who did not actively oppose them either."[58] I think something similar can be said of *Paul and Paula*: it is the kind of art that keeps hope and desire alive, reminding people of what is really important, nourishing their souls for the time when a political revolution is possible. But it is not identical with the revolution itself. Movie theaters—like churches—may have served as one of these treasured "honeycombed" niches that nourished a modicum of revolutionary potential that so unexpectedly came to fruition in 1989.

NOTES

I wish to thank Heidi Madden of Duke University Libraries for her generous assistance with source material.

1. The *Kraftfeld* metaphor comes from Walter Benjamin and Theodor Adorno and is deployed to promote nuance and eschew mono-causality in historical and cultural investigations. Martin Jay remarks on "the suggestive use of the force field metaphor by Theodor Adorno, who frequently employed it, along with the related Benjaminian image of a constellation, to suggest a nontotalized juxtaposition of changing elements, a dynamic interplay of attractions and aversions, without a generative first principle, common denominator, or inherent essence"; see Martin Jay, *Force Fields: Between Intellectual History and Cultural Critique* (New York: Routledge, 1993), 2. The reference to the "honeycombed" social formations of East Germany is attributable to Mary Fulbrook (see below), and draws upon Günter Gaus's famous description of the GDR as a "*Nischengesellschaft*" (niche society) that provided certain kinds of "free space" within the dictatorship. For further reflection on this key concept, see Mary Fulbrook, "The State and the Transformation of Political Legitimacy in East and West Germany Since 1945," *Comparative Studies in Society and History* 29, no. 2 (April 1987): 211–44, here 231–35.

2. A helpful introduction to the film can be found in Stephen Brockmann, "*Die Legende von Paul und Paula* (1973) or East Germany in the 1970s,"

in *A Critical History of German Film* (Rochester, NY: Camden House, 2010), 259–74. The "Filmbuch" itself is indispensable: Ulrich Plenzdorf, *Die Legende von Paul & Paula: Filmerzählung*, 20th ed. (Berlin: Suhrkamp, 2017).

3. The Communist Party in the GDR is, more precisely, the Sozialistische Einheitspartie, known colloquially as the SED. See F.-B. Habel, *Das große Lexikon der DEFA-Spielfilme: Die vollständige Dokumentation aller DEFA-Spielfilme von 1946 bis 1993* (Berlin: Schwarzkopf & Schwarzkopf, 2000), 349–50.

4. "Die Studentenrevolten von Paris bis Westberlin [schienen] zu bestätigen, daß der Sozialismus das einzig denkbare Sozialmodell ist, um den Traum von sozialer Gerechtigkeit zu verwirklichen. Alle erkennbaren Gebrechen am Sozialismus à la DDR waren von kritischen Intellektuellen als kaum vermeidbare Kinderkrankheiten hingenommen"; see Knut Lennartz, "Hinter den Kulissen des DDR-Theaters. Das Etikett der optimistischen Heiterkeit. Sozialistisch-realistisches Volkstheater in Halle und Rostock," *Neue Zeit*, August 19, 1991, 13.

5. "Typischer für die Atmosphäre der endsechziger Jahre aber war eine kaum getrübte Zukunftsgewißheit und Fortschrittsgläubigkeit, die auch von den Theatermachern getragen und propagiert wurde. *Prognose* war das Zauberwort, *EDV* die Zauberformel. Und politisch profitierte die DDR von den Nöten des Westens"; Knut Lennartz, "Hinter den Kulissen des DDR-Theaters. Das Etikett der optimistischen Heiterkeit. Sozialistisch-realistisches Volkstheater in Halle und Rostock," *Neue Zeit*, August 19, 1991, 13.

6. Speaking of the GDR's "New Economic System" of 1963, Mary Fulbrook observes: "Many [in the GDR] had also experienced remarkable social mobility, as a result of educational and social policies and new opportunities. In West Germany, on the other hand, the 1960s saw the rise of movements highly critical of West German materialism, affluence, and unwillingness to confront the past"; Fulbrook, *A Concise History of Germany*, 2nd ed. (Cambridge: Cambridge University Press, 1991), 217. Fulbrook touts the relative success of the East German economy, but she notes that its comparative strength vis-à-vis other East European economies was not sufficient to keep its citizens from fleeing as soon as the border between Hungary and Austria was opened (239).

7. This is a topic unto itself, of course, but one thinks first of Karl-Heinz Kurras, the Berlin police officer who shot and killed Benno Ohnesorg on June 2, 1967—the event that is often thought to have inaugurated the West German student movement. Kurras turned out to be a Stasi agent and SED member. The GDR support of West German terrorists was of course the subject of Volker Schlöndorff's great 2000 film, *Die Stille nach dem Schuß*, known in English as *The Legend of Rita* (released 2001). For an insightful analysis of this film, see Molly Knight, "Smoking Guns: Gender, Terror, and the German Story in Volker Schlöndorff's *Die Stille nach dem Schuss*," *Germanic Notes and Reviews* 40, no. 1

(2009): 22–30. See also Jeremy Varon, *Bringing the War Home: The Weather Underground, the Red Army Faction, and Revolutionary Violence in the Sixties and Seventies* (Oakland: University of California Press, 2004).

8. This tendency is richly satirized in Walter Kempowski's hilarious 2003 novel, *Letzte Grüße* (New York: Random House, 2005).

9. Barbara Honigmann, who came of age at this time in the GDR, recalls this period (beginning with the 1963 Kafka Conference) as one of relative cultural openness, if not quite the "Kulturrevolution" she associates with the Beatles and the Rolling Stones. The cultural "Lockerung" to which she refers, however, ends with the 11th Party Congress (December 1965) and definitively with the brutal repression of the Prague Spring uprising; see her latest memoir, Honigmann, *Georg* (Munich: Hanser, 2019), 144–46. But "Lockerung" came in waves, often made possible precisely by a prior series of rigorous measures that made the state feel secure enough to be able to afford some cultural flexibility.

10. Martin Mund, *Weltbühne* 25 (1993), lists this as one of the scenes that will have bothered GDR officials; quoted in Habel, *Das große Lexikon der DEFA-Spielfilme*, 349.

11. "Drachen" is also translated as "kite," but either way, the image is clearly phallic and sexually explicit.

12. "Keiner der Filme zuvor hatte sich so konsequent ins Individuelle begeben und eine im Erotischen begründete Handlung vorgestellt. Erschrocken regelte die Partei sogleich die Sprache der Kritik"; Wolfgang Gersch, "Film in der DDR: Die besten Jahre," in *Geschichte des deutschen Films*, ed. Wolfgang Jacobsen, Anton Kaes, and Hans Helmut Prinzler (Stuttgart: Metzler, 1993), 347. I don't wish to overplay this point, however. For nudity itself was much less of a taboo in East Germany. As Volker Schlöndorff put it, with only some exaggeration, "It is not the nudity that was the problem; the whole country was a nudist colony" (University of Notre Dame conference discussion, "1968 in Europe and Latin America," April 26–28, 2018).

13. It is understandable, I think, that the sex-and-drugs aspect of the film is glossed over in the GDR press. Nevertheless, one does occasionally find it noted there. See, for example: "Die Puhdys auf Abschiedstour," *Berliner Zeitung*, May 11, 1989, 7, where the band in an interview refers to all the mail they received about the music they wrote for the "bed scene" (Bettszene), some of which was pretty critical. See also the short piece by Reiner Kunze, which directly addresses the allegedly "pornographic" nature of the film; Kunze, "Kamasutra," *Neue Zeit*, August 4, 1990, 10.

14. I am grateful to John Davidson (Ohio State University) for challenging me to make sense of the family photos. We seem to agree that some kind of staged genealogy and ideological contextualization are at play here.

15. Schneider's other two essential ingredients, with respect to the West German student movement, are (1) the protest of the Vietnam War, and (2) the rejection of the traditional German Ordinarius-university; see Peter Schneider, *The German Comedy: Scenes of Life after the Wall* (London: I. B. Tauris, 1992).

16. Volker Schlöndorff, University of Notre Dame conference, April 2018.

17. For a fuller view of sexuality in everyday East Germany and in East German art, see Wolfgang Engler, *Die Ostdeutschen: Kunde von einem verlorenen Land* (Berlin: Aufbau, 1999), 257–76. I am grateful to Hannes Krauss for his counsel on this and on all things East German.

18. For the specifically antibourgeois nature of Paula's rebellious behavior, I am grateful to the discussants in the Literaturwissenschaftliches Kolloquium at the Universität Duisburg-Essen, where I presented a version of this chapter on June13, 2018. I am particularly indebted to my host, Rolf Parr.

19. Reimer, Zachau, and Sinka assert this flow of cultural influence rather baldly: "The *Aufbruchstimmung* (mood of new beginning) was copied from West Germany, where anti-Vietnam protests had changed a stale country into a new and exciting one that had elected a left-liberal government for the first time" (152); Robert C. Reimer, Reinhard Zachau, and Margit Sinka, *German Culture through Film* (Newburyport, MA: Focus/Pullins, 2005), 152.

20. "The real protagonist is clearly the city of Berlin"; quoted in Gerd Gemünden, *A Foreign Affair: Billy Wilder's American Films* (New York: Berghahn Books), 58.

21. Heinz Kerstin, one of very few West Germans who regularly reviewed East German cinema, argued in his 1973 review for the importance of the reconstruction scenes in this film: "[Der Film] zeigt, daß in Ost-Berlin auch noch alte, abbruchreife Häuser stehen, die allerdings immer neuen, modernen Wohnblocks weichen müssen, und durch den Kontrast erscheint die Aufbauleistung imponierender als in den Filmen, die den Eindruck erwecken wollen, das Neue habe das Alte schon überall völlig verdrängt"; Kerstin, *So viele Träume* (Berlin: VISTAS, 1996), quoted in Habel, *Das große Lexikon der DEFA-Spielfilme*, 349.

22. Obviously, for critical socialists in the GDR (and elsewhere) the 1968 invasion of Czechoslovakia remained a caesura, *the* break for many. And no bit of filmic propaganda could salve that still fairly recent wound. Nevertheless, the film's powerful opening gambit does attempt to portray the events of 1953 as a settled matter put to rest, as it were, by the ambitious and successful construction program in the present of the early 1970s. I'm grateful to Cathy Gelbin for emphasizing '68 as a turning point (and to some extent a point of no return) for a number of GDR critical socialists of the founders' generation.

23. Two prominent scenes of similar demolition are to be found twenty-three minutes into the film, and at 1:40:00, which is the penultimate scene

(voiceover: "Paula hat die Geburt ihres Kindes nicht überlebt"). Thus we can speak of an overt framing device here, underscored by the reprise of the opening song, "Wenn ein Mensch." But there is more: Paula is frequently portrayed with iconography reminiscent of the "Trümmerfrau," especially as she gathers coal amidst the detritus in the vicinity of her war-era, dilapidated tenement. The fact that the air-raid siren sounds to announce the demolition (and its conclusion) only brings us closer, semiotically, to postwar Germany. The message seems to be this: the GDR may still find itself in the phase of postwar reconstruction, but it is nonetheless firmly engaged in the process and moving in the right direction.

24. Habel asserts: "*Die Legende von Paul und Paula* wurde . . . zu einem der wenigen wirklichen 'Kult-Filme' der DEFA, ein Ruf, den er auch in den Jahren behielt, in denen er nicht gezeigt werden durfte, weil die Protagonisten die DDR verlassen hatten" (*Das große Lexikon der DEFA-Spielfilme*, 349). This is correct except that there was virtually no time when the film did not play in one form or another (cinema or television) in the GDR. Though he updates his entry in other ways, Habel repeats this misleading claim verbatim in the new edition: Habel, *Das große Filmlexikon der DEFA-Spielfilme: Die vollständige Dokumentation aller DEFA-Spielfilme von 1946–1993. Neuasgabe in zwei Bänden*, Band 1: A–L (Berlin: Schwarzkopf & Schwarzkopf, 2017), 518.

25. "Nachdem die beiden Hauptdarsteller Anfang der 1980er Jahre in den Westen gegangen waren, wurde der Film im DDR-Fernsehen nicht mehr gezeigt. Es war üblich, prominente Republikflüchtige auf diese Weise aus dem öffentlichen Bewusstsein zu verbannen. Gelegentlich war der Film aber noch in Programmkinos zu sehen"; https://de.wikipedia.org/wiki/Die_Legende_von_Paul_und_Paula. Similarly misleading claims about the film are made on the IMDb website: https://www.imdb.com/title/tt0070299/trivia.

26. For more information and archival access, see http://zefys.staatsbibliothek-berlin.de/ddr-presse/?confirm_open_id=06062f9c152525e54203e171bfe95c34euhanodcw&n=euhanoD+snilloC+mailliW. The search produced almost 800 references to the film, many of which were, of course, simply listings of screenings or broadcasts.

27. Gersch, "Film in der DDR," 348.

28. Just one example to illustrate this continuity: "Neues auf der Leinwand," *Neue Zeit*, July 13, 1990, 16. It was also rebroadcast on DDR television multiple times from 1975 through to the end of the GDR.

29. One sees this, for example, in articles celebrating Carow's sixtieth birthday, e.g., Klaus Klingbeil, "Räume für Phantasie," *Berliner Zeitung*, September 19, 1989, 7; and Horst Knietzsch, "Mit der Filmkunst Leute in Bewegung bringen," *Neues Deutschland*, September 19, 1989, 4. At the end of the GDR, to be sure, *Paul and Paula* is celebrated as a DEFA classic ("Bilder und Botschaften, die

Spuren hinterlassen," *Neue Zeit*, May 13, 1989, 9) and as "an unusually big DEFA hit of the 1970s" ("Wesentliche Einblicke in das Lichtspiel," *Neue Zeit*, January 16, 1989, 4). But much earlier also, and long after Domröse's defection, it is lauded as a "successful film of the recent past" in W. H. Kr. [author not otherwise identified], "Dreidimensionaler Humor aus Dresden: Unterhaltsames Programm zum Kinosommer," *Neue Zeit*, May 16, 1984, 8.

30. *Hochzeitsnacht im Regen*, dir. Horst Seemann, is a 1967 DEFA confection that features the young woman jockey Gabi, who against all odds manages to succeed in a male-dominated sport and in her romance with Freddy. Interestingly, the film thematizes the shortage of Berlin apartments in its exposition, but culminates in a Hollywood happy ending.

31. Peter Claus, "Babelsberger Reinigung," *Berliner Zeitung*, December 31, 1992, 45. Here Schlöndorff credits Babelsberg with a few distinctive achievements of "Weltformat," including *Paul and Paula*, as rising above the ideologically tainted pablum more typical of DEFA productions.

32. See Lennartz, "Das Etikett," 13.

33. Peter Jelavich, "Metamorphoses of Censorship in Modern Germany," *German Politics and Society* 27 (Fall 1992): 25–35. (Special Issue "Getting over the Wall: Recent Reflections on German Art and Politics since the Third Reich," guest editors William Donahue, Rachel Freudenburg, and Daniel Reynolds.)

34. Ibid., 34.

35. Fulbrook's term of choice is "safety valve," which she uses to describe the role of the Church in East Germany. For Fulbrook, however, this function does not preclude the Church's ability to curate, even foment dissent. The same entity can at various times perform both functions (Fulbrook, *Concise History*, 228–29). The same, I will argue, can be said of *Paul and Paula*.

36. In the scene discussed above, at the party where Paul is hosting some East African business associates, Paul desperately accuses Paula precisely of seeking personal happiness "auf Kosten anderer" (at others' expense), and Paula too quickly assents: "So what if I am!" But she is not in fact doing so, as the subsequent plot bears out.

37. "Li" [author not otherwise identified], "Legende von einer ungewöhnlichen Liebe: Bei den Dreharbeiten zu dem DEFA-Film 'Paul und Paula' notiert," *Neue Zeit*, January 17, 1973, 6.

38. Ibid.

39. Prof. Dr. Hans Koch, "Der einzelne und die Gesellschaft: Einige geistige Probleme unserer Gegenwartsliteratur," *Neues Deutschland*, June 16, 1973, 4.

40. Koch, "Der einzelne"; emphasis in original. The German—which I have slightly modified here for readability—is even more turgid: "Die Aktivität der Paula . . . ist auf die Verwirklichung von persönlichem Glück, Freundlichkeit,

menschlicher Wärme gerichtet. Glücksanspruch *auch* im persönlich-intimen Leben . . . erscheint hier als das *Ganze* selbst, persönliches Glück von gesellschaftlichem Wohl isoliert. Die moralische Unbedingtheit, mit der Paula *ihrem* Stern folgt, wird zum unbedingten moralischen Ideal. Die Unbedingtheit rein persönlichen Wollens, die allen gesellschaftlichen Widersprüchen, Widerständen, 'Verhaltensvorschriften,' Konventionen trotzt, wird zum Akt der sogenannten 'Selbstverwirklichung' Paulas."

41. The newspaper portal I have used is extremely valuable in making accessible the three main organs of East German journalism, but it fails to include precisely those sources (smaller newspapers) that, according to Jacobsen, Kaes, and Prinzler, may have yielded views somewhat less dogmatically in line with official party doctrine. See Wolfgang Jacobsen, Anton Kaes, Hans Helmut Prinzler, eds., *Geschichte des deutschen Films* (Stuttgart: Metzler, 1993), 347–49. There is, in other words, a presumably richer GDR reception story to be told about this film.

42. Knut Lennartz, for example, writes: "Und, nicht vergessen, es ging den Leuten leidlich gut, mehr noch, auch wenn es im Alltag noch immer die üblichen Mangelerscheinungen gab, es vermittelte sich ein Gefühl, daß es aufwärtsgeht" ("Hinter den Kulissen," 13).

43. Habel assures us that the film's popularity worried Party officials such that similar films could not be made in the aftermath of *Paul und Paula*: "Der riesige Publikumsandrang machte die Staatsführung jedoch nervös, so daß thematisch ähnlich gelagerte Filme nicht mehr produziert werden konnten"; Habel, *Das große Lexikon der DEFA-Spielfilme* (2000), 350.

44. "'Die Legende von Paul und Paula' . . . ist, genau genommen, die Geschichte von Paulas Liebe. Phantasiereich kommt sie ins Bild, und dieser Phantasiereichtum nimmt gefangen"; Günter Sobe, "Paula oder die Legende von der Liebe," *Berliner Zeitung*, April 11, 1973, 6.

45. "Paula nämlich ist (dramaturgisch) aus dem Spiel genommen; sie kommt um bei der Geburt ihres dritten Kindes, ihrem Bekenntnis zu Paul" (Sobe, "Paula oder die Legende," 6).

46. For a feminist reading of the film, see Irene Dölling, "We All Love Paula but Paul Is More Important to US," *New German Critique* 82 (Winter 2001): 77–90.

47. These options were not necessarily clearly drawn as mutually exclusive. One finds a mix of claims regarding the film's social rootedness (some of which strike me as ritual or obligatory in nature) alongside assertions regarding the unattainability of individual happiness. See, for example, Helmut Ulrich, "Filme mit dem Mut zu großen Gefühlen," *Neue Zeit*, September 19, 1989, 4.

48. Carow would later deny that the two—individual happiness and socialism—were incompatible. See Sibylle Licht, "Anfang und Ende: Konrad-Wolf-Preis für Heiner Carow und Wolfram Witt," *Neue Zeit*, October 19, 1990, 10. Here Carow is celebrated as central both to DEFA and GDR culture more generally. A word of caution regarding Carow's views: during the GDR he enjoys his DEFA success without protest; after Unification, he develops a far more critical attitude to the entire DEFA mission of "producing the socialist human being" in film. See Dieter Nürnberger, "Wie die DDR mit ihren Künstlern umsprang: Ausstellung beleuchtet 45 Jahre DEFA-Geschichte," *Berliner Zeitung*, December 6, 1991, 12.

49. On this, see "Porträt einer jungen Frau: 'Christine,' Slatan Dudows letzter Film, im 'Studio Camera' aufgeführt," *Neue Zeit*, November 7, 1974, 8. There are other reasons for caution here. For example, Paul's wife is drawn stereotypically as a shrew. Even our beloved Paula urges her daughter to sleep so that she can be healthy and beautiful. "Why is it important to be beautiful?" the child asks. "In order to get a man," Paula explains. Reimer and Zachau also affiliate *Paul und Paula* with what they call "the category of women movies" exhibiting "feminist emancipation" in various ways (*German Culture through Film*, 152–53).

50. "Der Film ist lausig; traurig als Symptom einer Frustration, deren Wunschtraum noch Mief produziert"; Max Frisch, *Aus dem Berliner Journal* (Berlin: Suhrkamp, 2015), 128.

51. Gloria Zimmermann, "Liebesgeschichte zwischen Traum und Wirklichkeit," *Neues Deutschland*, March 29, 1980, 14; Bernd Heimberger, "Legenden mit und ohne Ende. Zu einem neuen Buch von Ulrich Plenzdorf im Hinstorff Verlag," *Neue Zeit*, March 3, 1980, 4; H. U., "Vom Glück ohne Ende: Marion van de Kamp las aus Plenzdorfs Erzählung," *Neue Zeit*, October 21, 1981, 4.

52. K.-P. Gerhardt, "Fröhliches Hausfest: 'Legende vom Glück ohne Ende' in Schwedt," *Neue Zeit*, November 3, 1983, 4; "Schnell reagiert. 75. Vorstellung in der Volksbühne," *Berliner Zeitung*, November 2, 1984, 7.

53. "Man kann sich bei ihr an die Paula aus dem nach einem Plenzdorf-Szenarium entstandenen Heiner-Carow-Film 'Die Legende von Paul und Paula' erinnern—ähnliche soziale Umstände und ähnliche Lebensschwierigkeiten und ein ähnliches Glücks- und Liebesverlangen"; Helmut Ullrich, "Resolute Berliner Type [sic] aus dem 'Milljöh': Neues Plenzdorf-Stück im Theater im Palast," *Neue Zeit*, June 15, 1988, 4.

54. Michael Hanisch, "Die Putzfrau und der Westfreund. Im Kino: Die neue Defa-Produktion 'Verfehlung' von Heiner Carow," *Neue Zeit*, March 19, 1992, 13.

55. Volker Blech, "Die Puhdys auf Abschieds-Tour," *Berliner Zeitung*, May 11, 1989, 7. See also Birgit Walter, "Die Puhdys: nach drei Jahren wieder ein Konzert," *Berliner Zeitung*, April 18, 1992, 3.

56. Reimer, Zachau, and Sinka, *German Culture through Film*, 149. Elsewhere, they insist that "Paula is subversive or anarchist," and that Paula's behavior constitutes "a protest against the establishment" (150). They later retract some of that enthusiasm, conceding that she assumes a more conventional role when it comes to gender (152).

57. "Heiner Carow für Medienrat vorgeschlagen," *Neue Zeit*, October 7, 1992, 17. The identical notice appeared the next day under the title "Heiner Carow soll in den Medienrat," *Berliner Zeitung*, October 8, 1992, 32.

58. Jelavich, "Metamorphoses," 33.

SEVEN

Out of Place

Students, Workers, and the Politics of Encounter in Argentina

VALERIA MANZANO

In his memoirs, Alejandro Ferreyra, a former militant with the People's Revolutionary Party (Partido Revolucionario del Pueblo, PRT), depicts his process of growing up in Argentina during the 1960s as propelled by seemingly incontrollable "winds of change." However, looking at the turning points in his memoirs, these winds can be interpreted as the myriad decisions Alejandro made over his life. He grew up in a well-to-do family in Córdoba province and recalls that, until he was a secondary school student, he used to spend the weekdays and most of his time in the company of his social equals—playing rugby, attending parties, or simply hanging out. It was only in the last year of his secondary school that he began to develop a social consciousness. Despite not being Catholic, he decided that upon graduation (in the summer of 1967) he would go with a priest to do social work in a little town in Misiones. There, as part of a group of thirty young women and men, he helped the impoverished woodcutters (*hacheros*) with their daily chores. During the nights, the young people had long conversations with the priest, who, like many others in Latin America, was embroiled in the debates and concerns triggered by Vatican II (1962–65). Alejandro recalls that the priest said, "Empty yourself out, leave all you know behind, and learn from the poor." Those words—and the experience among the *hacheros*—resonated deeply, and ultimately guided his future decisions. Although he had wanted to major in English literature, Alejandro chose instead to do something more socially useful and enrolled in the School of Medicine at the University of Córdoba. There, in a highly politicized atmosphere, he interacted with many groups that covered all the possible variants within the Left. He joined the PRT student group and was among the tens of thousands of students who, in May 1969, participated in the coordinated revolts in Corrientes, Rosario, and Córdoba. After that May, Alejandro and the PRT fully embarked on what they interpreted as the "two best possible ways" to fight in the revolution they saw coming, by armed struggle and proletarianization. Alejandro did not become a combatant, but went to live in a working-class neighborhood in the greater Buenos Aires area where he got a job as a metalworker. He focused on organizing a chapter of his party and, also, at remaking his *self* along the lines of what the PRT deemed "proletariat morals."[1]

Rather than merely being "blown by the wind," Alejandro joined the multitude of young women and men in 1960s and 1970s Argentina—and Latin America at large—who participated in, and eventually were creators of, new ways of conceptualizing and making politics. In surprisingly short time spans (in Alejandro's case, just three years) young people from middle- and even upper-class origins made decisions that implied a refusal to follow their expected path. In many respects, they literally interpreted what Ernesto Che Guevara mandated vis-à-vis the building of a "new man." Willing to learn from and lead "the people" and eager to shed the hedonism of bourgeois societies, in his effort to build a socialist society the self-sacrificing "new man" would remake himself.[2] Scores of middle-class, educated youth experimented with ethical and political displacements. Like many of their European and North American counterparts, they coupled their desire to achieve social and political change with their efforts to change themselves, which many times involved "seeing other worlds."[3] The worlds that young people like Alejandro saw and experienced were those showing socially oppressed populations, which helped them mobilize new feelings and a belief in the need for urgent action.

In this chapter, I will focus on experiences such as Alejandro's to ask what those dynamics of displacement implied for a new conceptualization of politics, which in my view marked one of the crucial novelties of the 1960s in general and of the "'68 moment" in particular. Following Jacques Rancière, I understand those dynamics as part of a "political subjectivation [that was] primarily the result of disidentification."[4] In their political socialization, middle-class youth, especially students, expressed a profound willingness to disidentify themselves in terms of class origins and cultural backgrounds. In doing so, they questioned the narratives of social modernization, which in 1960s Latin America focused on the processes of upward social mobility made possible by transformations in the industrializing labor markets and the exponential expansion of enrollments in secondary schools and universities. Although they likely benefited themselves from those socioeconomic changes, for the scores of middle-class students who came of age politically during the 1960s and 1970s, the dynamics involved in the social modernization narratives reinforced social inequality. In that dual movement of criticism and disidentification, middle-class youth aligned themselves with the socially oppressed. Unlike what Rancière and Kristin Ross argue for the French middle classes in the 1960s, their "Other" was not geographically distant—namely, the peoples of Algeria first, or the fighting Vietnamese afterwards.[5] For young middle-class Latin Americans, the social "others" to encounter were closer: the Guatemalan and Salvadoran peasants, or the Argentine blue-collar workers.[6] Like their French counterparts, though, thousands of middle-class youth in Latin America formed the basis of a new politics when—through a series of practical decisions, both individual and collective—they moved away from their legitimate, established "place" to forge ties and identify with their social and cultural "others." Through their willingness to carve out a revolutionary political project—either in its classless, Marxist sense, or its national variant—that cohort of young people became, first and foremost, protagonists of a cultural revolution that entailed questioning their sociocultural "place" or "role" in society. This questioning was part of a political culture composed of shared beliefs, values, vocabulary, and representations of the past and the future, which broke through a broad spectrum of political groups.[7]

I divide my presentation into three parts. First, I explore some of the initial traces of the "movement towards the people" in 1960s Argentina, showing that it had multiple roots (Catholic, Marxist, Peronist) and crystallized in countless initiatives, which nevertheless converged on a key point: the practical questioning of the narratives of sociocultural modernization that swept across the intellectual and political elites. Beginning in 1955, those elites illegalized the most popular political movement (Peronism) and, starting in 1966, agreed on the imposition of a military coup (the so-called *Revolución Argentina*) that promised both national security and economic development. Second, I briefly reconstruct the sequence of popular revolts that made the Argentine May 1969 by paying special attention to the types of encounters they entailed, chiefly between university students and workers. I argue that those encounters were instrumental in the process of disidentification: many student activists attempted to erase the markers of their student—and even youth—condition, to completely merge within "the people." In this context, students and intellectuals engaged in debates on the necessity of dissolving what they called a "corporatist" position in order to move into a deeply different form of political involvement. Finally, I follow some of the embodiments of the "movement towards the people" by accounting for experiences of proletarianization and day-to-day encounters with the socially oppressed. In the immediate aftermath of the Argentine May 1969, an intense process of politicization and radicalization unfolded, one in which droves of young people understood that they were participating in a social revolution tout court. Alejandro and many others of his age and class origins aimed at completing their disidentification to approach—and become—the blue-collar workers. Others, notably those associated with Peronism, although not fully endorsing proletarianization, participated in a cluster of social and political activities that also entailed encounters with the socially oppressed. Those encounters were both transformative and deeply problematic. In the concluding section I focus on the uncertainties of being "out of place."

SOUTHERN NARODNIKI

As almost everywhere in the world, the yearning for and the anxiety about change in both its collective and individual senses pervaded the Latin American "long '60s." From the entry of Fidel Castro's troops into Havana in 1959 until the U.S.-backed coup d'état that overthrew the socialist experiment led by Salvador Allende in Chile in 1973, the Latin American "long '60s" transpired in projects aimed at social transformation, either in the form of accelerated economic development and modernization (key words for the era) or in all-encompassing revolutions that ideally would revamp Latin American societies completely. Young people, chiefly in their role as students, were the tip of the iceberg of the dynamics of sociocultural modernization and, importantly, of the reactions against them. Those dynamics were entwined with the enforcement of political authoritarianism and the prevalence of deep social inequalities. They had multiple predecessors. In 1860s Russia, in the context of social and political transformations that substantially changed property relations and the links between the state and society, groups of well-to-do young men, known as the Narodnikis (populists), engaged in a "movement towards the people" by abandoning their comfortable homes and setting up encounters with impoverished peasants, whom they tried to mobilize.[8] As did their Russian predecessors, in the 1960s these "Southern Narodnikis" also produced geographical and cultural displacements. More fundamentally, they attempted to build an ethical and political movement out of their place in society, one that entailed questioning their role as students along with the social and cultural expectations attached to that role.

In the 1960s and 1970s, the enrollment in higher education exponentially expanded, an occurrence that generated pride among the "developmentalist" elites and many citizens, young and adult alike. In the early 1960s, Argentina ranked third in the world with regard to the number of university students per total population (there were 756 university students for each 100,000 inhabitants).[9] Although a minority, the percentage of university students among the twenty to twenty-four age group steadily grew: in 1950, 5 percent of that age group was enrolled; in 1960, the figure jumped to 11 percent; and, in 1972, it rose to 20 percent. In Argentina, the university penetrated deep into the middle class and gradually incorporated children of small traders, clerks, teachers, and highly qualified manual workers. In the late 1960s, 70 percent of the college students were first-generation.[10] The elites and broad societal segments projected onto the first-generation students their hopes for achieving collective and individual betterment. One of the prime examples of the "developmentalist" politicians, President Arturo Frondizi (1958–62), for example, referred to the young students as the fuel that might help push the "takeoff" that the country needed to develop economically and socially. Similarly, in one key manifesto of the 1960s modernizing elites, "The Charter of Punta del

Este" that launched the Alliance for Progress, Frondizi and his peers from all over the Americas agreed on prioritizing the enhancement of funding to secondary and higher-level education in order to "provide the competent personnel required for rapidly-growing societies."[11] Those expectations were partially fulfilled. Census data for 1970 show that, in Argentina, women and men alike joined the labor market later and were better prepared than their parents, and their first jobs were in the ever-expanding tertiary sector of the economy.[12] Perhaps a majority of young women and men who gained access to secondary and higher education were as proud as the developmentalist elites and many anonymous Argentines for their opportunities, in a country where the educational ladder was regarded as the most respectable venue for gaining upward social mobility. However, one key novelty of the 1960s and early 1970s was that an increasingly visible cohort of students, coming from the heterogeneous middle classes and from the upper classes, plainly rejected the cultural and political meaning of the opportunities and expectations attached to being a student. In doing so, they leaned more toward other social groups, peasants and blue-collar workers.

Albeit with different intensities and modalities, three "political families" acted as venues for this movement towards the poor in 1960s Argentina: Catholicism, Peronism, and a "New" Marxism. As it happened in all Latin American countries, the Argentine Catholic community felt deeply the effects of Vatican II.[13] The discussions set in motion over the council provided the framework for the emergence of new ways of action, which coincided with, and were reinforced by, the imposition of a military regime in 1966 that closed the political scenario by making illegal all the political parties and student federations. At the same time, the regime mandated military intervention in the thus far autonomous public universities. In that context, the organizational networks of the Catholic Church afforded young women and men with both safe places to gather (parishes) and written materials to discuss (initially, the council's documents).[14] In this respect, the journal *Cristianismo y Revolución* played a paramount role, as it appealed to and helped politicize scores of Catholic youth. Launched in 1966 by the former seminarian Juan García Elorrio, its first editorial noted that the journal would reflect "the feeling, the urgency, the forms, and the moments of Christians' commitment to the revolution."[15] The journal—whose readership soon mounted to 40,000—promoted materials authored by local clerics, who, in 1967, founded the Movement of Priests for the Third World and by those who, in 1968, fully endorsed the conclusions of the conference of archbishops in Medellín, which set the scene for the spread of liberation theology. The journal likewise served as the nexus for two dozen young activists who founded the Camilo Torres Commando—and who later on would create the Peronist Montoneros guerrilla group. The Commando was named for the Colombian priest turned guerrilla (assassinated in 1966), who represented an inspirational figure for the journal's staff and followers. *Cristianismo y Revolución* published a letter addressed to university students wherein Torres reminded them that in "underdeveloped societies," they were privileged. If they wanted to become revolutionary, Torres asked them to "ascend to the masses, share their poverty."[16]

Catholic networks were crucial to the organization of groups that literally "moved to the people." The members of the Camilo Torres Commando, for example, spent time in a small town in northern Santa Fe conducting literary campaigns, teaching the gospel to children, and helping workers with their daily chores.[17] In the same region, a university student group named Movimiento Ateneísta not only performed similar tasks but also produced a sociological report recounting their experiences with their province's woodcutters (*hacheros*). This report posited that those crossing the threshold of the forest gained access to a world dominated by the crudest social exploitation and collected data on the *hacheros'* malnutrition, illiteracy, and peonage. For these students, sharing the *hacheros'* daily life constituted "an accelerated class on the nature of dependency and neocolonialism." As with other student groups who carried out social work with cotton and cane cutters, the Movimiento Ateneísta took the most impoverished workers in the country as the people's synecdoche and viewed in their "reality" as the most significant proof that the "real" country rested far from university life.[18] The cohorts of students who participated in the University Students' Working Camps (Campamentos Universitarios de Trabajo), led by a priest and a sociology professor from 1964 to 1970, reached similar conclusions. After spending two months in the outskirts of a sugar plantation in Jujuy, a university student from Buenos Aires concluded that "living among those who suffer the most" had led him to a "personal transformation" that included "the rise of a social and political consciousness."[19] In his account, the transformation of his *self* went hand in hand with that "social and political consciousness" that aspired to change.

As the members of the Movimiento Ateneísta and the Camilo Torres Commando did, beginning in the second half of the 1960s, many Catholic youth engaged with the Peronist movement, which they interpreted as the most suitable route to politically encounter "the people." I will discuss more prominently the transformations in this "political family" in the last section. Meanwhile, I am interested in the shifts within a third political family, namely, the varied Marxist groups that made up a "New Left," often by splitting from the Socialist and Communist parties. As other scholars have shown, the concept of New Left in 1960s Argentina related not only to the embracing of armed struggle—as it happened in other Latin American countries—but also to the reevaluation of Peronism and the attempts to connect with workers and, eventually, peasants.[20]

Two examples illustrate how New Leftist groups appealed to university students through offering them means to "move towards the People." On the one hand, at the beginning of the 1960s, the Guerrilla Army of the People (Ejército Guerrillero del Pueblo, EGP), a group led by journalist Jorge Masetti and supported by Che Guevara, developed a rural cell (*foco*) in Salta province. Inspired by the Cuban experience, the EGP attracted university students as urban liaisons—in Córdoba, Tucumán, and Buenos Aires—and fundamentally as organizers and combatants. At least thirty young men had left behind their experiences as militants in the student movement to engage in what one of them later depicted as a "total immersion in the poorest people's ways of life, in their suffering" prior to developing the cell.[21] The experience proved a disaster: some of the thirty guerrillas died of hunger, while soldiers killed other comrades who tried to leave the project. Still others were killed or imprisoned by the gendarmerie, including two former students at the School of Humanities and Social Sciences, University of Buenos Aires. In a publicized announcement, the school's dean, social historian José Luis Romero, stated, "They were youths who, wrong or right, have adopted a dramatic solution in response to well-known situations of our country that require urgent solutions."[22] In Romero's words, those "well-known situations" of poverty and exclusion, which the former students saw directly, required urgent solutions—guerrilla warfare was probably the most dramatic way of facing them. On the other hand, while plainly rejecting guerrilla insurgency as a method, a group of students and intellectuals that split with the Socialist Party in 1965 to create a tiny group called Communist Vanguard (Vanguardia Comunista,

VC) also emphasized its difference vis-à-vis the "Old Left" by urging its members to "go to the people." Self-identified as Maoists, VC members initially aimed at mobilizing the admittedly limited peasant population in the country, a strategy they soon changed to target blue-collar workers. In 1968, VC had 400 members, mostly coming from (banned) student activism, who initiated a process of proletarianization of the privileged to workers, and tried to organize chapters in the largest cities, including Rosario and Córdoba.[23]

Throughout the 1960s, when developmentalist elites and thousands of anonymous Argentines vindicated the seemingly all-encompassing social modernization, many of those who benefited the most from the rising educational opportunities it entailed started to question it. In doing so, they initiated a "movement towards the People." Engaged in Catholic or Marxist groups, middle-class university students aligned themselves with the most impoverished workers in the country in a dynamic that implied disidentification. The process entailed a rejection of their "student role" as a legitimate place in society, and a rather romantic attempt to merge with the most impoverished peasants and workers. This dynamic was full-fledged in the Argentine May 1969.

THE ARGENTINE MAY

In July 1969, Juan Domingo Perón compared the events of May 1968 in Paris with the revolt in Córdoba province in May 1969. He quoted graffiti that appeared on Parisian walls, chiefly one that read, "We are the guerrillas against the air-conditioned death they want to sell us with the name of future." Perón believed that the spirit of struggle against cultural and political conformism was rampant among Córdoba rebels. He foresaw, too, the beginning of a global revolution in which Argentine youth were destined to take the lead (*tomar el rabo*).[24] For rising numbers of youth, mostly students, Perón's message was growing in significance. After presiding over the country between 1946 and 1955, when he led a political project that implemented a local version of a "welfare state" and gained the support of the working classes (and the hatred of the upper and middle classes), a civic-military coup d'état banned his political movement and sent him into exile. Over the 1960s, though formally banned, Peronism kept attracting increasing numbers of working-class supporters and underwent a process of ideological transformation, to the point that Perón himself tried to conceptualize his movement as one of "national liberation"—akin to others in Africa and Asia. In their process of political socialization, middle-class students interacted with the persistent Peronist identity among the workers and the ideological shifts within that movement. Many of them also interacted with strong anti-Peronist sentiments among their own middle- and upper-class families.[25] Ironically, although Perón's messages had an enthusiastic audience among many students, only a few of them would have agreed with his comparison between Paris 1968 and Argentina 1969. As protagonists of the interwoven popular revolts in Corrientes, Rosario, and Córdoba, many youths saw theirs as incomparable to what they, then, represented as the French events. In the Argentine May 1969, young people tried to erase markers of youthfulness, chiefly their student condition, in order to merge with "the people."

The articulation between the new student groups, whether Catholic, Marxist, or Peronist, and "the people" crystallized, in particular, in the experience of the General Labor Confederation of Argentina (Confederación General de Trabajadores de la Argentina, CGTA). Founded in March 1968, the CGTA was the outcome of rifts within the labor movement caused by the differing positions vis-à-vis the Onganía regime. The unions that coalesced into the CGTA represented those workers most affected by the regime's economic policies and those who had long opposed the bureaucratic tendency of the labor movement.[26] Led by Raimundo Ongaro—a fervent Catholic and Peronist representative of the print workers—the CGTA called for the creation of a worker-based, democratic, and anticapitalist alliance to oppose Onganía. Although short-lived, this experience served as a point of encounter between the working class and radicalized artists, intellectuals, professionals, and students, who used the CGTA headquarters in Córdoba, Buenos Aires, and Rosario to hold meetings and helped with administrative and press tasks, while they participated in the permanent "worker-student" committee.[27]

In 1968, when the global revolts were unleashed, the Argentine student activists questioned their status and university politics alike. Only a few Argentine student groups (mostly those identified with Maoism) took heed of the notion that their European counterparts also tried to bridge the gap with the working classes, as was evident in the Paris demonstrations and in the joint occupations of university and factory buildings in Turin.[28] Even though from today's vantage point former young people tie the Argentine May to a global wave of rebellion in which most protagonists were young, in 1968 and 1969 that scope was denied and oftentimes the commonalities rejected. In 1968, for example, a popular magazine surveyed Argentine youth about their opinions of the "youth revolt" in Europe, and many responded that they did not agree with demands "centered on their problems." Another survey, seeking to elucidate the circulation of Herbert Marcuse's ideas, showed that "his influence is minimal." In fact, the interviewees disagreed with Marcuse's statement regarding the student revolutionary status in societies where the working class had presumably lost its vanguard role. "If that thesis works for Europe, it does not for us," one student argued. A Catholic student leader was more emphatic: "Marcuse can go to hell."[29] A Peronist student clarified that, in Argentina, "those who think that the workers would follow the students are dreaming of Paris, when the revolution is taking place in [the working-class suburb] Avellaneda or in Tucumán."[30] "Our" rebellion would sharply differ from what those student activists represented as European: "here" students would always go behind the workers.[31]

In May 1969, however, when a series of popular revolts erupted in Corrientes, Rosario, and Córdoba, students were in fact the leading force alongside workers and broad segments of the local populations. The unifying thread of the Argentine May was political, although articulated around economic and social demands. The beginning of the Argentine May occurred in Corrientes province, at the University of the Northeast (UNNE). Created in 1959, the UNNE was one of the smallest national universities (it had 7,000 students in 1969), and it had been one of only three whose authorities had not opposed the military intervention in 1966. Opposition to the Onganía regime escalated among the students. In mid-1968, some groups had begun to mobilize against *limitacionismo*, the attempts to set limits to the enrollments according to student test scores. In April 1969, diverse student groups joined to oppose a more localized problem: the university administrators had increased the price for meals in the student canteen. The students improvised canteens and meeting places at the CGTA headquarters and in local parishes. In early May, students carried out silent marches after the rector refused to receive them. On May 15 the police imprisoned dozens of students, raided their houses, and shot to death Juan José Cabral, age nineteen. The popular anger incited by Cabral's death was heightened by the untimely response of the minister of the interior, who accused the students of "working for international extremists."[32]

The events initiated in Corrientes made visible the fact that repression was the only way the regime coped with dissent, which was rampant among broad segments of Argentines, and that the students could effectively forge alliances with the "people." The student-"people" alliance was particularly successful in Rosario, which was the epicenter of popular revolts between May 17 and May 22. On May 17, around 400 students met at the canteen of the local university and then marched to the city center, where the police shot to death Alfredo Bello, a twenty-two-year-old law student. Students and workers affiliated with the CGTA agreed to organize a rally on May 21, and they received support from the local chapters of most unions, professional groups, and business associations. On that day, at a sit-in, the police shot to death a metalworker named Luis Blanco, who was only fifteen. When news about his death spread, the revolt generalized. "At every corner," a reporter wrote, "homemakers, children, all helped keep bonfires burning."[33] The city was already paralyzed when, on May 23, a general strike was declared.

The regime's peace (*pax*), which had thus far constituted its main source of legitimacy since it represented itself as a guarantor of social order, had been unequivocally broken, and the students had been the main force initially fueling that crisis. However, most student leaders noted that their participation and leadership had been insufficient. A representative of a Maoist group stated that the students should insert themselves into a "process of liberation led by the workers" if they did not want to be protagonists of "isolated episodes." A Peronist spokesperson, meanwhile, stated that the students should become involved with the "only national movement that allows for the people's liberation."[34] Consistent with the motto guiding student activism over the 1960s, the leaders downplayed the significance of any student-led revolt, as many students, in their "movement towards the people," also downplayed their student role. For them, as for most observers then and now, the popular revolt in Córdoba, known as the *Cordobazo*, was the turning point.

The *Cordobazo* was distinct in that the labor movement was the force leading the popular revolt. As scholars have shown, the most immediate complaints driving the workers' massive involvement were related to working conditions, which created an opening for airing the most diverse grievances within the labor movement.[35] After several partial strikes, the workers called for a general strike in the city on May 29. Gathered in massive meetings of about 8,000 people, the students at the University of Córdoba discussed whether to participate and if so, how, and on May 29 most took to the streets. The usual chronology of the *Cordobazo* divides the day into three moments. The first moment (until noon) was marked by the presence of unionized workers accompanied by students. Coming largely from the automobile plants in the suburban areas, the workers marched toward the city center in columns. Their leaders were at the front—notably Augusto Tosco, from the Power Workers Union. The police tried to prevent the columns from arriving at the central plaza, and in doing so they shot to death a worker named Máximo Mena. The second moment (the afternoon) was a time of generalized rebellion, which involved not only the strike spreading throughout the city but also the active incorporation of larger segments of the local population. At 5:00 p.m. when the government decided to militarize Córdoba, the third moment began. Most workers abandoned the streets, some of them hiding from the military. The epicenter thus shifted to the student neighborhoods, which the police raided house by house. At the end of the day, 14 people were dead (10 of them students), and 500 went to jail.[36]

The *Cordobazo* was the core event of the Argentine May, a synecdoche for the entire uprising. As scholar Carlos Altamirano has pointed out, it rapidly became mythic in that it encoded both the promises and drawbacks that insurrection represented for a revolution that to many seemed imminent.[37] At the level of institutional politics, the month of May prompted the beginning of the end of the military regime: everyone in the president's cabinet resigned, although Onganía did not do so until June 1970 when the Montoneros guerrillas, in their baptism of fire, kidnapped and executed former president Pedro Eugenio Aramburu (responsible for the 1955 coup against Perón). That event was significant because it succinctly represents the dynamics of Argentine politics by 1970. These new actors, the guerrilla groups, in part legitimated their raison d'être in the conditions that prevailed in May 1969, namely, the popular readiness to struggle against the regime, the limits of "popular insurrection" to fight back against the army, and the violence "from above" that they wanted to respond to "from below."[38] Unlike the experience of "'68" in Mexico and

Brazil, which ended with tragic repression (such as the massacre of Tlatelolco) and repressive legislation (such as the infamous Acta Institucional 5, or AI-5), the Argentine May paved the way for a dynamics of societal mobilization dominated by the emergence of new political actors: the guerrillas, certainly, but also a cohort of politicized young activists. A significant portion of the students who participated in the Argentine May, associated with both Peronism and Marxism, decided to abandon their militancy in the student movement altogether in an effort to reinforce the organization in popular neighborhoods in the main Argentine cities.[39] The "children of the *Cordobazo*" reinforced the "movement towards the People" initiated in the 1960s, now convinced that the time was ripe for a social revolution.

TOWARDS THE PEOPLE

In 1970, a major Mexican-based publishing house organized an essay contest on youth and politics. The main prize went to the Argentinean Antonio Brailovsky, twenty-two, who, in both his essay and his acceptance address argued that young people "have two options: either following the *caminito* (little road) that an unjust system has traced for us, or following the *camino* (road) towards a different, new society."[40] The belittled *caminito* implied pursuing a university career and the possibility of upward mobility and integration into a bourgeois life. The *camino*, in contrast, was the promise of a different and allegedly better future society. "I felt confused," wrote Viviana, age sixteen, "but I learned that the Revolution is the only possible *camino*."[41] For many young men and women, following the *camino* implied adopting—in theory, though not necessarily in practice—the images of the heroic guerrilla as a figure and armed struggle as a method for achieving the dramatic solutions that many interpreted as urgent. The emergence of five guerrilla groups (including the Peronist Montoneros and the Marxist People's Revolutionary [Ejército Revolucionario del Pueblo, ERP], which was the armed branch of the PRT) was coupled with a seemingly unstoppable process of politicization, which had young people as protagonists. That process reached its peak between 1971 and 1974. In that period, the military negotiated the transition to elections with the exiled Juan Perón; this resulted in the victory of Perón's delegate,

Héctor Cámpora, in March 1973. Soon after that triumph, Perón came back to Argentina, and in October 1973 became president until his death.[42] In that politically convoluted triennium, the pro-Montoneros Peronist Youth (Juventud Peronista, JP) and the PRT-ERP promoted initiatives that strengthened the collective "movement towards the People."

The PRT-ERP drew upon and amplified previous leftist traditions, particularly Trotskyism, to forge a distinctive militant style that centered on the vindication of patience, humility, tenacity, and self-sacrifice, all of them in stark opposition to the supposed hedonism and individualism that swept across the petit-bourgeoisie.[43] In practical terms, this entailed the requirement of proletarianization for those who had been raised in middle- and upper-class families (who represented a majority, yet by no means all the Party members). That was Alejandro's case, and it was also José Polti's experience. José was the son of a landowning family from Córdoba. Like Alejandro, he went on to study medicine at the University of Córdoba and, during the Argentine May, he joined the PRT. In 1971, he was shot to death in a skirmish with the police. Written by a cadre from the Party, an obituary for José stated that "all his militancy was characterized by a continuous proletarianization of his habits, of his life style." The obituary concluded that "the students have understood that the revolution is the only career that will transform them into authentic human beings."[44] Rather than a fact taken for granted, the PRT-ERP insisted on prioritizing that understanding among the students: only those who abandoned the "illusion of a career"—a "petit-bourgeois illusion"—would become truly human beings.[45] As in Alejandro's and José's cases, the dynamics of transformation had a first step: upon joining the Party, they were destined to live in working-class neighborhoods in the largest cities and to take jobs in factory plants. As an oft-quoted document crafted by a PRT-ERP leader in 1972, titled precisely *Moral y proletarización*, suggested, it was only in the daily and complete interaction with the working classes that a "new moral" would replace the old, "petit-bourgeois" one. That new moral would ideally cover all aspects of human life, from work ethics to family and sexual relations, in a pedagogical process that militants were called to engage in if they wished to become revolutionary.[46]

As it happened with experiences of proletarianization in other settings, such as post-'68 Mexico and France, the memoirs of former militants point not only to the encounters but also, perhaps fundamentally, to the many disencounters with "the people."[47] Thus, for example, a former PRT-ERP militant remembers how difficult it was for him and his wife to be trusted by their working-class neighbors when they moved from the city to the greater Buenos Aires area: they were not merely *the* newcomers but also the only blonde-haired couple on the whole street. They could not get rid of one of the bodily markers of class, and their attempts to disguise their way of speaking "intellectually" were also a failure. In his memoirs, however, those misunderstandings are narrated humorously: the couple could not pass as working-class, yet they actually lived as workers, sharing their housing conditions and learning how to "stand every day on the assembly line."[48] All in all, the couple went on to learn practically what they knew theoretically and, in doing so, attempted to build new selves in line with "proletariat morals." Other accounts are far more critical vis-à-vis those morals. Rolo Diez, a former militant, recalls the story of three female comrades from middle-class origins whom the PRT-ERP assigned to Rosario, where they got jobs in a meat-packing plant. The Party cadre in charge of their team was a male worker, an authentic proletarian. The young women soon accused him of sexual harassment, yet the Party leadership never acknowledged their complaint or sanctioned him. As Rolo concludes, the Party leadership and "many proletarian men were truly machista"—and that was part and parcel of the "proletariat morals" that the PRT-ERP aimed at instilling among its militants.[49] Class, cultural, and sexual codes separated many middle-class, mostly young, militants from "the people," and were at the core of profound disencounters. However profound they were—as former militants now recall—they did not prevent the "movement towards the people" that marked the Argentine political scenario in the early 1970s, and that left traces in the making of new political identities in those who embarked upon that movement.

Although many so-called revolutionary Peronist groups also endorsed initiatives of proletarianization, these were not as crucial as for the PRT-ERP members. In fact, those engaging with Peronism shared the belief that they would connect with, even become, "the people" within the frontiers of that movement that already had the support of most workers. Thus, for example, when recalling his political experiences, a former middle-class schoolboy noted that he circulated among different groups, including Marxist groups, before settling on the Peronist Secondary School Students' Union (*Unión de Estudiantes Secundarios*). "The other groups were alien to the people and, if the revolution was to happen, it would happen through Peronism: it was natural," he said.[50] Rather than natural, the engagement of young people with revolutionary Peronist trends was at the junction of at least three interrelated phenomena. In the first place, Peronism represented itself as the most suitable venue to connect with and mobilize "the people." Second, Perón and many of his younger followers learned to position that movement within new ideological and cultural coordinates, notably a Third World framework. Thus, many of those who joined Peronism in the late 1960s and early 1970s believed that it represented a national liberation movement, and eventually a road to construct a national variant of socialism. Third, Peronism indeed benefited from, and helped intensify, the whole dynamics of youth politicization that covered the entire political spectrum (though certainly more on the Left). In any case, it was within the Peronist movement where youth, and even student, became legitimate categories, signaling also an ideological and cultural positioning.[51]

In 1973, when a Peronist ticket won 50 percent of the electorate, the JP and Montoneros asserted that they would "support, defend, and control the popular government," while they embarked upon an organization of mass fronts soon to be known as the "Revolutionary Tendency."[52] Notably, the Tendency strove to organize the "people" by appropriating a youthful framework, perhaps because they viewed their place within Peronism as coded generationally. Aside from the JP, the most important fronts were the Working Peronist Youth (Juventud Trabajadora Peronista, JTP), the UES, and the Peronist University Youth (Juventud Universitaria Peronista, JUP). Their actions were determined by their willingness to belong to a movement that soon after the elections turned to the right. They were, though, the largest youth organizations ever in Argentina, both affirming and neglecting youth, and even student, as legitimate political categories and actors.

Launched in April of 1973, the JUP helped amplify the Peronization of university students initiated in the late 1960s. Unlike previous Peronist student groups, the JUP valued the university as a legitimate site to battle "cultural and economic dependency" and, also, the students per se, providing they could undergo significant changes and reinforce the "movement towards the People." First, the JUP suggested that all students, no matter their majors, should conduct both manual and intellectual work in an effort to acclimatize themselves to a future society in which the divide would no longer exist. Second, the JUP proposed to reinforce the funding for, and the enrollment into, "priority" schools or careers like engineering and veterinary medicine that would ideally help overcome economic dependency.[53] Third, the endeavors to connect the university to the people were the ones that both generated further student engagement and allowed for larger recruitment for the JUP. In the School of Humanities and Social Sciences at the University of Buenos Aires, for example, the sociology students worked in government agencies and as consultants for unions; the educational science students conducted literacy campaigns and contributed materials to adult schooling; and the psychology students did practical outreach in the greater Buenos Aires area.[54] Many of them alternated their student- and university-based militancy with political work at the locales the JP opened in working-class neighborhoods. In Lanús, medical students staffed first-aid clinics and psychology students conducted psychological advising and family counseling. The students at the University of Córdoba pursued analogous initiatives, with a focus on vaccinations and literacy campaigns.[55]

Similar drives for connecting with the people inspired the creation of the second student-based organization of the Tendency: the UES, which also embarked upon a series of social works. Among the tasks developed by the UES, those related to vaccination campaigns, literacy campaigns, and children's recreation prevailed. In the city of Santa Rosa in La Pampa province, for example, the UES students ran seventeen literacy circles to improve adult education, and they also ran twelve day care centers. Moreover, the students with the UES were proud to help paint and do maintenance work at schools and hospitals in their respective districts.[56] These activities coalesced into what was the UES's largest venture, the "Operativo Güemes." In January 1974, 500 students from all over the country went to Salta province to help build roads, canals, and schools. These activities resembled the eye-opening travel practices of Catholic youths: as one student argued, he was encountering an impoverished Argentina that he "could not believe existed." Unlike the youth in the 1960s, they were nonetheless confident: they were helping fulfill the "national reconstruction mandated by the popular government."[57]

Although the Peronist JP and Montoneros and the Marxist PRT-ERP shared the "movement towards the people" and confidence in the pedagogical process of approaching the poor to raise a new consciousness, their tactics of disidentification differed. For the PRT-ERP militants, the requirements of proletarianization involved a practical, day-to-day effort to undo class-based habits and expectations. The PRT-ERP members who survived Argentina's most dramatic dictatorship (1976–83) and revisited their past recalled these experiences with a mix of humor, self-criticism, and nostalgia, especially as it related to the apparent determination to re-create themselves through their encounters with romanticized blue-collar workers. The middle-class young people who joined the JP and Montoneros, in contrast, thought that they were already crossing the "bridge to the People" by subscribing to the Peronist movement. In so doing, most did not abandon their youth and student identity; rather, the opposite was true. They thus continued well-entrenched Catholic practices dating from the 1960s: the Peronist students "went to the people in their spare time"—as contemporary critics would say—without questioning their student (and middle-class) status. The myriad social work that many of them did also channeled significant doses of "extreme willingness" (*voluntarismo*) and a romanticized view of the people. However, the initiatives did not imply the same relationship with identity and identification.

CONCLUSION

The cultural critic Diana Sorensen has argued that the Latin American '60s were "pervaded by a feeling of imminence, of change about to happen or to be voluntaristically ushered in."[58] Droves of middle-class students, who were likely the privileged "face" of the Argentine 1960s, endorsed that feeling and participated "voluntaristically" in projects of change, which included both the self and the collective. I have argued here that one key novelty of the 1960s culture and politics in Argentina—and probably elsewhere—was the dynamics that, following Rancière, I termed "disidentification." In their process of political socialization, droves of middle- and upper-class youth refused to accept what the developmentalist elites (and many unaffiliated Argentines) interpreted as the main achievement of modernization, namely, access to higher education and eventually to better career and job opportunities than their parents had had. Equipped with the debates triggered by Vatican II, the discussions amidst the international Left (with the rising star of Maoism), and the struggles in what was being called the Third World, a cohort of Argentine university students started through the 1960s a literal "movement towards the people." As their Russian predecessors did, they also sometimes geographically moved to actually encounter, "see," the world of the more socially oppressed. In that process, they questioned the legitimacy of their roles as student and even youth. Those questions were prevalent during the Argentine May 1969, which on the one hand showed the dynamism of the student movement and its ability to initiate and delineate alliances with "the people" and, on the other hand, attested to the student dissatisfaction with a supposed vanguard role in the concatenated popular revolts. For the students who participated in the Argentine May, as it had happened with many student groups from the organized Left in Mexico and France in 1968, what mattered was the encounter—in organizational, political, and ideological ways—with one segment of the labor movement, which they viewed as hegemonizing any popular alliance.[59] The willingness to generate those encounters and connections was prevalent in other geographical settings in the "moment of 1968," both in Europe and Latin America.

To learn from the workers, or "the people"—depending on the ideological inflexion of each group—became pivotal in the early 1970s, when scores of youth and adults alike saw a social and/or national revolution as an ongoing phenomenon. In that pedagogical process of learning from the more socially oppressed, some groups, chiefly those of Marxist origins, went a step further and required a complete proletarianization, which entailed—as I have tried to show—a profound reworking of the militants' *selves*: through acts of complete disidentification. In contrast, the most successful initiatives (at least in numeric terms) were those associated with Peronism, through which middle-class students had a chance to value and legitimate their student and youth roles, while becoming themselves part of the bridge that Peronism allegedly represented for different social classes. Those middle-class Peronist students did go "towards the People," yet their initiatives were mediated through the prism of a populist movement that claimed the representation of a cross-class alliance hegemonized by the workers (and surely by Perón himself).

Viewed from today's vantage point, the expectations of producing a dynamics of disidentification in the process of creating alternative political communities read as extemporaneous—even lunatic. However, those expectations, rooted in myriad collective and individual decisions, formed the core of an era and configured (with all their romanticizing of the socially oppressed) an alternative way of conceiving politics and the political. This was revolutionary not only because of the intent, but also because it implied that social and cultural actors did not keep their "usual places." Not randomly, Jorge Rafael Videla, the first president of the military junta that started the systematic application of state terrorism in 1976, stated in a well-publicized interview what the military described as "order." In his interpretation, "order" entailed "remaining in one's place: as son and daughter, at home; as workers, in the factory; as students, in the schools and universities."[60] The young women and men who came of age politically in the aftermath of the Argentine May had done the opposite: they went "out of their places." They could not foresee that, in the years that followed, in Argentina and all over Latin America, being "out of place" would mean being "subversive."

NOTES

1. Alejandro Ferreyra, *Memoria del viento* (Córdoba: Babel, 2008).

2. Ernesto Che Guevara, "Socialism and Man in Cuba [1965]," in *Che Guevara Reader: Writings on Guerrilla Strategy, Politics, and Revolution*, ed. David Deutschmann (Melbourne: Ocean Press, 1997), 196–98.

3. Belinda Davis, "A Whole World Opening Up: Transcultural Contact, Difference, and the Politicization of New Left Activists," in *Changing the World, Changing Oneself: Political Protest and Collective Identities in West Germany and the US in the 1960s and 1970s*, ed. Belinda Davis et al. (New York: Berghahn, 2010), 255–73.

4. Jacques Rancière, "The Cause of the Other," *Parallax* 4, no. 2 (1998): 25–33, my quotes on 29.

5. See Kristin Ross, *May '68 and Its Afterlives* (Chicago: University of Chicago Press, 2002).

6. See Joaquín Chávez, *Poets and Prophets of the Resistance: Intellectuals and the Origins of Salvador's Civil War* (New York: Oxford University Press, 2017); Heather Vrana, *The City Belongs to You: Student Activism in Guatemala, 1944–1996* (Oakland: University of California Press, 2017).

7. On the concept of political culture, see Jean-François Sirinelli, "Éloge de la complexité," in *Pour une histoire culturelle*, ed. Jean-Pierre Rioux and Jean-François Sirinelli (Paris: Pluriel, 1997), 430–44.

8. For a recent study, see Ben Eklof, *A Generation of Revolutionaries: Nikolai Charushin and Russian Populism from the Great Reforms to Perestroika* (Bloomington: Indiana University Press, 2017).

9. Gino Germani and Ruth Sautu, *Regularidad y origen social de los estudiantes universitarios* (Buenos Aires: Instituto de Sociología, 1965), 14.

10. Daniel Cano, *La educación superior en la Argentina* (Buenos Aires: Grupo Editor Latinoamericano, 1985), 46; Doris Kublitshko, *El origen social de los estudiantes de la Universidad de Buenos Aires* (Washington, DC: PNUD–CEPAL, 1980), 19.

11. Arturo Frondizi, *Mensajes presidenciales* (Buenos Aires: Centro de Estudios Nacionales, 1978), 1:18; "Charter of Punta del Este," *The Department of State Bulletin* 45, no. 1159 (1961): 468.

12. *Censo Nacional de Población, Familias y Viviendas, 1970* (Buenos Aires: Ministerio de Economía, 1974), 2:38–39.

13. See chapter 3 in this volume by Massimo De Giuseppe.

14. On this context, see José Zanca, "Más allá de la espada y el hisopo: Religión, política y sociedad durante el Onganiato," in *Política y cultura durante el Onganiato: Nuevas perspectivas para la investigación de la presidencia de Juan Carlos Onganía (1966–1970)*, ed. Valeria Galván and Florencia Osuna, 45–65 (Rosario: Prohistoria, 2014); for the military intervention in the public universities, see Valeria Manzano, *The Age of Youth in Argentina: Culture, Politics, and Sexuality from Perón to Videla* (Chapel Hill: University of North Carolina Press, 2014).

15. Juan García Elorrio, "El signo revolucionario," *Cristianismo y Revolución*, no. 1, September 1966, 2. For a recent analysis of this journal, see Esteban Campos, *Cristianismo y Revolución: El origen de Montoneros* (Buenos Aires: Edhasa, 2016).

16. Camilo Torres, "Carta a los estudiantes," *Cristianismo y Revolución*, no. 2/3, November 1966, 19.

17. See Graciela Daleo's testimony in Eduardo Anguita and Martín Caparrós, *La voluntad: Historia de la militancia revolucionaria en la Argentina* (Buenos Aires: Norma, 1997), 1:26–29.

18. "Informe especial: Los hacheros," *Cristianismo y Revolución*, no. 8, July 1968, 5–13; "Corrientes," ibid., no. 9, September 1968, 9–11; "Tucumán: Informe de la Asociación de Estudios Sociales de Córdoba," ibid., no. 10, October 1968, 7–11; Mauricio Fontan, "Informe sobre el noroeste argentino," *Antropología 3er Mundo* 1, no. 1, May 1969, 14–26.

19. "Asomarse a las provincias," *Vivir en familia*, no. 62, November 1968, n.p. On the Catholic working camps, see José María Llorens, *Opción fuera de la ley* (Buenos Aires: Lumen, 2000), 96–100.

20. As regards the uses of "New Left" in Argentina, one of its first appearances in public discussions occurred before the echoes of the Cuban Revolution spread, in a book of interviews with intellectuals and militants who evaluated how to integrate the Left with the apparent persistence—and radicalization—of a Peronist identity among the working classes; see Carlos Strasser, *Las izquierdas en el proceso politico argentino* (Buenos Aires: Pallestra, 1959). For recent historiographical uses, see María Cristina Tortti, *El viejo Partido Socialista y los orígenes de la Nueva Izquierda* (Buenos Aires: Prometeo, 2010).

21. Cf. Gabriel Rot, *Los orígenes perdidos de la guerrilla en la Argentina* (Buenos Aires: Waldhuter, 2010), 116.

22. "Episodios del 9 de junio," *Gaceta de Filosofía y Letras* 2, no. 5 (1964): 8.

23. Brenda Rupar, "El partido Vanguardia Comunista: Elementos para avanzar en una caracterización del maoísmo en la Argentina, 1965–1971," *Izquierdas*, no. 36 (2017): 105–25.

24. "Carta del General Perón," *Cristianismo y Revolución*, no. 19, August 1969, back cover.

25. Daniel James, *Resistance and Integration: Peronism and the Argentine Working Class, 1946–1976* (New York: Cambridge University Press, 1993), and Carlos Altamirano, *Peronismo y cultura de izquierda* (Buenos Aires: Temas, 2001).

26. See especially James Brennan, *The Labor Wars in Córdoba, 1955–1976: Ideology, Work, and Labor Politics in an Argentine Industrial City* (Cambridge, MA: Harvard University Press, 1994), 123–34.

27. "Junio, movilización popular," *Semanario CGT*, no. 6, June 6, 1968, 1; "La CGT de los estudiantes," *Siete Días*, no. 61, July 7, 1968, 18–19.

28. "Solidaridad con los trabajadores y los estudiantes de Francia," *Vocero de la FUA*, no. 2, May-June 1968, 5. For worker–student alliances in France and Italy, see especially Ross, *May '68*, and Robert Lumley, *States of Emergency: Cultures of Revolt in Italy, 1968–1978* (London: Verso, 1998).

29. "Made in France," *Gente*, no. 152, June 20, 1968, 5–7; "Marcuse, el nuevo profeta de la izquierda," *Panorama*, no. 73, September 17, 1968, 82; "Estudiantes, los fantasmas tienen nombre," *Panorama*, no. 110, June 3, 1969, 14.

30. "Hablan los dirigentes estudiantiles," *Semanario CGT*, no. 33, December 12, 1968, 3.

31. For the reception of the European events in Argentina and Latin America, see Horacio Tarcus, "El Mayo Argentino," *Observatorio Social de América Latina*, no. 24, October 2008, 161–80, and Jeff Gould, "Solidarity under Siege: The Latin American Left, 1968," *American Historical Review* 112, no. 2 (2009): 348–75.

32. "Borda habló de Corrientes," *Clarín*, May 16, 1969, 21.

33. Andrés Zavala, "La sublevación de los rosarinos," *Primera Plana*, no. 335, May 27, 1969, 18–19.

34. "Dirigentes universitarios, después del desborde," *Panorama*, no. 109, May 27, 1969, 16–17.

35. See Brennan, *Labor Wars in Cordoba*, chap. 5; and Mónica Gordillo, *Córdoba en los 60's: La experiencia del sindicalismo combativo* (Córdoba: Universidad Nacional de Córdoba, 1996), chap. 6.

36. For a complete reconstruction, see Manzano, *The Age of Youth in Argentina*.

37. Altamirano, *Peronismo y cultura de izquierda*.

38. See, for instance, "Hablan los Montoneros," *Cristianismo y Revolución*, no. 26, November-December 1970, 10–14; "A dos años del Cordobazo," *Estrella Roja*, no. 3, June 1971, 3.

39. See Valeria Manzano, "La Reforna (no) ha caducado, 1968–1974," in *La Reforma Universitaria cuestionada*, ed. Alejandro Eujanian (Rosario: Prohistoria, 2018), 227–55.

40. "Crítico pájaro de juventud," *Análisis*, no. 458, December 23, 1969, 42; see also Antonio Brailovsky, "Cuestionamiento de la Argentina contemporánea," in *México y Argentina visto por sus jóvenes* (México: Siglo XXI, 1970), 21.

41. "Cartas," *Nuevo Hombre*, no. 25, March of 1972, 12.

42. The literature on this process of political radicalization is abundant. For general overviews, see Alfredo Pucciareli, ed., *La primacía de la política: Lanusse, Perón y la Nueva Izquierda en tiempos del GAN* (Buenos Aires: EUdeBA, 1999), and Liliana de Riz, *La política en suspenso, 1966–1976* (Buenos Aires: Paidós, 2000).

43. See especially Pablo Pozzi, *Por las sendas argentinas: El PRT-ERP, la guerrilla marxista* (Buenos Aires: EUdeBA, 2001), 130–43, and Vera Carnovale, *Los combatientes: Historia del PRT-ERP* (Buenos Aires: Siglo XXI, 2009).

44. "Tres héroes del pueblo," *Estrella Roja*, no. 2, May 1971, 4.

45. See also the pamphlets "Por qué luchamos" (1972), and "La burguesía muestra su cara" (1972), both signed by the Línea de Acción Revolucionaria, PRT, Student Movement Collection, SJMP/CMS R4/5-1, CEDINCI.

46. Luis Ortolani (signing as Julio Parra), "Moral y proletarización," *Políticas de la Memoria*, no. 5, 2004–5, 99–100. It first appeared in a clandestine publication of the PRT-ERP militants who, like Ortolani, were imprisoned in 1972. Its reading was mandatory for the incoming PRT-ERP militants until 1974.

47. For different accounts of other experiences of proletarianization in France and Mexico, see Robert Linhart, *De cadenas y de hombres* (Mexico City: Siglo XXI, 1979), and Paco Taibo II, *El regreso de la verdadera araña y otras historias que pasaron en algunas fábricas* (Mexico City: Joaquín Mortiz, 1988).

48. Cacho Narzole, *Nada a cambio: Una historia militante* (Buenos Aires: Imago Mundi, 2009), 42–43. The focus on hair color is also at the center of Albertina Carri's movie *Los rubios* (*The Blondes*, 2003), which narrates her family's experience of proletarianization. Her parents were not PRT-ERP members, but Peronist.

49. Rolo Diez, *El mejor y el peor de los tiempos: Cómo destruyeron al PRT-ERP* (Buenos Aires: Nuestra América, 2010), 48–50.

50. Interview with Daniel Burak, File 0139, Memoria Abierta Archive.

51. See Manzano, *The Age of Youth*, chap. 6; and also Richard Gillespie, *Soldiers of Perón: Argentina's Montoneros* (Oxford: Clarendon, 1982).

52. "Comunicado de FAR y Montoneros: Apoyar, defender y controlar," *El Descamisado*, no. 2, May 29, 1973, 3–4.

53. "Declaración del Congreso General de Estudiantes Peronistas," *Envido*, no. 7, October 1972, 78–80; "Juventud Universitaria Peronista," *Envido*, no. 9, May 1973, 54–61; "Estudiantes de ingeniería," *Cuestionario*, no. 2, June 1973, 13; "Ejemplo de colonización," *Cuestionario*, no. 2, June 1973, 19.

54. *Filosofía y Letras en la Reconstrucción Nacional: Boletín Informativo*, October 1973, Student Movement Collection, SMJP/CMS C5/5-1, CEDINCI.

55. Interview with Elena A. (b. in 1940 in Buenos Aires), August 24, 2007; Mesa "Referencia," File 15.979, vol. 2, DIPPBA Archive.

56. Oscar Gatica, *Tiempos de liberación: Memorias de un militante de la JP, 1973–1976* (Buenos Aires: Pitanguá, 2008), 53–58; "Van a Salta y hacen falta," *El Descamisado*, no. 34, January 1974.

57. "El día en que la UES hizo vibrar a toda Salta," *El Descamisado*, no. 37, January 29, 1974. For similar processes among the Chilean youth that joined the parties with the Unidad Popular, see Patrick Barr-Melej, *Psychedelic Chile: Youth, Counterculture, and Politics on the Road to Socialism and Dictatorship* (Chapel Hill: University of North Carolina Press, 2017), 232–46.

58. Diana Sorensen, *A Turbulent Decade Remembered: Scenes from the Latin American Sixties* (Stanford, CA: Stanford University Press, 2007), 7.

59. See Jaime Pensado, *Rebel Mexico: Student Unrest and Authoritarian Political Culture during the Long Sixties* (Stanford, CA: Stanford University Press, 2013), esp. chap 8; Ross, *May '68*.

60. "El primer mano a mano con el president," *Gente*, no. 560, April 15, 1976, 4.

BIBLIOGRAPHY

Primary sources

Books

Anguita, Eduardo, and Martín Caparrós. *La voluntad: Historia de la militancia revolucionaria en la Argentina*. Vol. 1. Buenos Aires: Norma, 1997.

Brailovsky, Antonio, et al. *México y Argentina visto por sus jóvenes*. México City: Siglo XXI, 1970.

Censo Nacional de Población, Familias y Viviendas, 1970. Vol. 2. Buenos Aires: Ministerio de Economía, 1974.

Diez Rolo. *El mejor y el peor de los tiempos: Cómo destruyeron al PRT-ERP.* Buenos Aires: Nuestra América, 2010.

Ferreyra, Alejandro. *Memoria del viento*. Córdoba: Babel, 2008.

Frondizim Arturo. *Mensajes presidenciales*. Vol. 1. Buenos Aires: Centro de Estudios Nacionales, 1978.

Gatica, Oscar. *Tiempos de liberación: Memorias de un militante de la JP, 1973–1976*. Buenos Aires: Pitanguá, 2008.

Germani, Gino, and Ruth Sautu. *Regularidad y origen social de los estudiantes universitarios*. Buenos Aires: Instituto de Sociología, 1965.

Guevara, Ernesto Che. "Socialism and Man in Cuba [1965]," in *Che Guevara Reader: Writings on Guerrilla Strategy, Politics, and Revolution*, edited by David Deutschmann, 197–214. Melbourne: Ocean Press, 1997.

Linhart, Robert. *De cadenas y de hombres*. Mexico City: Siglo XXI, 1979.

Llorens, José María. *Opción fuera de la ley*. Buenos Aires: Lumen, 2000.

Narzole, Cacho. *Nada a cambio: Una historia militante*. Buenos Aires: Imago Mundi, 2009.

Strasser, Carlos. *Las izquierdas en el proceso politico argentine*. Buenos Aires: Pallestra, 1959.

Taibo, Paco, II. *El regreso de la verdadera araña y otras historias que pasaron en algunas fábricas*. Mexico City: Joaquín Mortiz, 1988.

Periodicals

Análisis

Antropología 3er Mundo

Clarín

Cristianismo & Revolución

El descamisado

Envido

Estrella Roja
Gaceta de Filosofía y Letras
Gente
Nuevo Hombre
Panorama
Primera Plana
Semanario CGT
Siete Días
Vivir en familia

Archival Collections

Student Movement Collection, Centro de Investigación y Documentación de la Cultura de Izquierdas, Buenos Aires, Argentina.

DIPPBA (Dirección de Investigación de la Policía de la Provincia de Buenos Aires) Archive, Comisión Provincial por la Memoria, La Plata, Argentina.

Oral Archive, Memoria Abierta, Buenos Aires, Argentina.

Secondary Sources

Altamirano, Carlos. *Peronismo y cultura de izquierda.* Buenos Aires: Temas, 2001.

Barr-Melej, Patrick. *Psychedelic Chile: Youth, Counterculture, and Politics on the Road to Socialism and Dictatorship.* Chapel Hill: University of North Carolina Press, 2017.

Brennan, James. *The Labor Wars in Córdoba, 1955–1976: Ideology, Work, and Labor Politics in an Argentine Industrial City.* Cambridge, MA: Harvard University Press, 1994.

Campos, Esteban. *Cristianismo y revolución: El origen de Montoneros.* Buenos Aires: Edhasa, 2016.

Cano, Daniel. *La educación superior en la Argentina.* Buenos Aires: Grupo Editor Latinoamericano, 1985.

Carnovale, Vera. *Los combatientes: Historia del PRT-ERP.* Buenos Aires: Siglo XXI, 2009.

Chávez, Joaquín. *Poets and Prophets of the Resistance: Intellectuals and the Origins of Salvador's Civil War.* New York: Oxford University Press, 2017.

Davis, Belinda. "A Whole World Opening Up: Transcultural Contact, Difference, and the Politicization of New Left Activists," in *Changing the World, Changing Oneself: Political Protest and Collective Identities in West Germany and the US in the 1960s and 1970s*, edited by Belinda Davis et al., 255–73. New York: Berghahn, 2010.

De Riz, Liliana. *La política en suspenso, 1966–1976.* Buenos Aires: Paidós, 2000.

Eklof, Ben. *A Generation of Revolutionaries: Nikolai Charushin and Russian Populism from the Great Reforms to Perestroika.* Bloomington: Indiana University Press, 2017.

Gillespie, Richard. *Soldiers of Perón: Argentina's Montoneros.* Oxford: Clarendon, 1982.

Gordillo, Mónica. *Córdoba en los 60's: La experiencia del sindicalismo combative.* Córdoba: Universidad Nacional de Córdoba, 1996.

Gould, Jeff. "Solidarity under Siege: The Latin American Left, 1968." *American Historical Review* 112, no. 2 (2009): 348–75.

James, Daniel. *Resistance and Integration: Peronism and the Argentine Working Class, 1946–1976.* New York: Cambridge University Press, 1993.

Kublitshko, Doris. *El origen social de los estudiantes de la Universidad de Buenos Aires.* Washington, DC: PNUD–CEPAL, 1980.

Lumley, Robert. *States of Emergency: Cultures of Revolt in Italy, 1968–1978.* London: Verso, 1998.

Manzano, Valeria. *The Age of Youth in Argentina: Culture, Politics, and Sexuality from Perón to Videla.* Chapel Hill: University of North Carolina Press, 2014.

———. "La Reforna (no) ha caducado, 1968–1974," in *La Reforma Universitaria cuestionada*, edited by Alejandro Eujanian, 227–55. Rosario: Prohistoria, 2018.

Pensado, Jaime. *Rebel Mexico: Student Unrest and Authoritarian Political Culture during the Long Sixties.* Stanford, CA: Stanford University Press, 2013.

Pozzi, Pablo. *Por las sendas argentinas: El PRT-ERP, la guerrilla marxista.* Buenos Aires: EUdeBA, 2001.

Pucciareli, Alfredo, ed. *La primacía de la política: Lanusse, Perón y la Nueva Izquierda en tiempos del GAN.* Buenos Aires: EUdeBA, 1999.

Rancière, Jacques. "The Cause of the Other." *Parallax* 4, no. 2 (1998): 25–33.

Ross, Kristin. *May '68 and Its Afterlives.* Chicago: University of Chicago Press, 2002.

Rot, Gabriel. *Los orígenes perdidos de la guerrilla en la Argentina.* Buenos Aires: Waldhuter, 2010.

Rupar, Brenda. "El partido Vanguardia Comunista: Elementos para avanzar en una caracterización del maoísmo en la Argentina, 1965–1971." *Izquierdas*, no. 36 (2017): 105–25.

Sirinelli, Jean-François. "Éloge de la complexité." In *Pour une histoire culturelle*, edited by Jean-Pierre Rioux and Jean-François Sirinelli, 430–44. Paris: Pluriel, 1997.

Sorensen, Diana. *A Turbulent Decade Remembered: Scenes from the Latin American Sixties.* Stanford, CA: Stanford University Press, 2007.

Tarcus, Horacio. "El Mayo Argentino." *Observatorio Social de América Latina*, no. 24, October 2008, 161–80.

Tortti, María Cristina. *El viejo Partido Socialista y los orígenes de la Nueva Izquierda*. Buenos Aires: Prometeo, 2010.

Vrana, Heather. *The City Belongs to You: Student Activism in Guatemala, 1944–1996*. Oakland: University of California Press, 2017.

Zanca, José. "Más allá de la espada y el hisopo: Religión, política y sociedad durante el Onganiato." In *Política y cultura durante el Onganiato: Nuevas perspectivas para la investigación de la presidencia de Juan Carlos Onganía* (1966–1970), edited by Valeria Galván and Florencia Osuna, 45–65. Rosario: Prohistoria, 2014.

EIGHT

Protest Rock in the Soviet Bloc

Prague, Spring 1968

TIMOTHY W. RYBACK

In a closing scene to the Tom Stoppard play *Rock 'n' Roll*, Max, an aging and disillusioned professor, disparages the long-term effects of youth protests. When he is challenged with the question, "What about 1968?" Max responds with taunting cynicism, "What happened in 1968?" The response: "Revolution!" There follows a heated discussion about whether 1968 was really a political revolution or, as Max argues, just "street theater." He questions whether anyone at the time really thought they were going to overthrow the governments with protests and music and long hair. Max taunts, "We dressed up, so what?"[1]

Stoppard's *Rock 'n' Roll* traces the cultural and political travails of post-1968 Czechoslovakia, from the Prague Spring of 1968 to the Velvet Revolution of 1989, into the early 1990s, with a focus on the legendary Prague rock band the Plastic People of the Universe. At a more profound level it explores, as the dinner table debates suggest, fundamental questions of the nature of the social and political upheavals that occurred seemingly spontaneously and simultaneously in major cities across Europe, on both sides of the ideological divide—in London, Paris, Rome, Berlin, Warsaw, or Prague—and in the Americas, both North and South—San Francisco to Chicago to Washington, DC, to Mexico City to Rio de Janeiro to La Paz to Santiago. Some were contained and quickly crushed, like the student protests in Warsaw in February 1968, or in Mexico City in October of that year, in which scores of protesters were gunned down.[2] The student protests in France were embraced by millions of factory workers and laborers, with hints of social and economic utopianism, that resulted in strikes that paralyzed the country and came to include pitched battles in the streets with barricades and Molotov cocktails, not dissimilar to the "gilets jaunes" (yellow vests) protests that begin in France in October 2018 and continued in 2020 despite Covid-19 restrictions. Paris was transformed into a veritable war zone and, briefly, resulted in a counterprotest in which more than a million Parisians took to the streets in support of the government. Whether many of these protests were mere "street theater" or manifestations of transformative political change depended on the place and circumstances. While student protests were shaking the political establishment in West Germany, spawning political activism and terrorist violence that reached into the next decades, across the border in East Germany the "revolution" was barely a whimper that left its mark in muted cultural artifacts, such as the music of the East Berlin rock band the Puhdys and, as discussed in the chapter 6 by William Donahue, in the 1972 film *The Legend of Paul and Paula.*

Here I will aim demonstrate that the Prague Spring represented one of the most consequential and enduring revolutions of 1968, whose resonances, as the Stoppard play suggests, were sustained, in good part, by the underground rock scene. The Prague Spring was more than "street theater." It was a political and ideological revolution parading as cultural revolution that anticipated one of the most consequential revolutions in modern history, the protest movements that led to the collapse of the Soviet Bloc in the autumn of 1989, and with it an economic and political system that had dominated much of Eastern Europe for most of the twentieth century. The Prague Spring is also singular in another regard: the massive use of military force—a quarter million soldiers from five Warsaw Pact countries supported by 6,000 tanks—used to crush the movement. The heavy-handed response to this "cultural revolution" was intended to demonstrate the Kremlin's resolve in responding to reformist tendencies within the Soviet sphere of influence.

"When forces that are hostile to socialism try to turn the development of some socialist country towards capitalism," the Soviet premier Leonid Brezhnev declared in September 1968, the Kremlin would respond resolutely.[3] For the next twenty years, the "Brezhnev Doctrine" would define the limits of reform not only for the people of Czechoslovakia but for other communist-controlled countries in Eastern Europe—East Germany, Poland, Hungary, Romania, Bulgaria—and the fifteen "republics" of the Union of Soviet Socialist Republics.

The Soviets may have been successful in crushing the Prague Spring in 1968, but the seeds of revolt and anti-Soviet sentiment that pervaded the young revolutionaries at the time could not be eradicated and set, in a sense, the stage for the Velvet Revolution twenty-one years later. The year 1968 remained a pivotal moment in the Czech and Slovak consciousness, as demonstrated in August 1989 when the city of Prague was host to a rock concert intended to showcase solidarity between the young people of the Soviet Union and the Czechoslovak Socialist Republic. The televised event had been organized by Pragokoncert, the state concert booking agency, and staged in the Lucerna Hall, the city's largest concert venue. The concert featured a heavy metal band from Moscow. As the Soviet rockers prepared to perform to the packed concert hall, the Russian moderator took to the stage with her Czech cohost. Standing in the glare of stage lights and before live-broadcast television cameras, she asked, "Have you ever heard Russian heavy metal?" The Czech cohost's reply was quick and bitter, "Yes, on the streets of Prague in the summer of 1968."[4] The brazen public reference to the Warsaw Pact invasion should have been a career-ending affront, but the concert and broadcast continued. It was a sign of the times. Within months, the Velvet Revolution swept Czechoslovakia's Communist regime from power. By year's end, the Soviet Bloc was gone.

Politics, economics, and security were clearly central to developments within the Soviet Bloc, but rock music and its concomitant countercultural phenomena—drugs, antiestablishment sentiments, alternative lifestyles—played a role in shaping the attitudes and actions of the youth, which in turn carried with them significant ideological implications. Rock culture was frequently associated with anti-establishment activities in the West, ranging from anti-Vietnam protests in the United States to counterculture movements in the United Kingdom and Western Europe. However, its threat to the ideological orthodoxy of Marxist-Leninist doctrine meant that it came to play an inordinately important role in the policies and politics of the Communist-controlled governments. According to the Marxist-Leninist theory, there was a dialectical relationship between the "base"—the means of production—and the "superstructure," which represented the entire complex of social and cultural values that governed a society, such as religion, art, literature, music, and, increasingly during the 1960s, the emergence of Western rock culture.

LENINISM VERSUS LENNONISM

The influences of Western rock and pop culture in Soviet Bloc countries first assumed the proportions of a mass cultural phenomenon with the arrival of Beatlemania in the mid-1960s. The East German writer Erich Loest captured the spirit of the moment. "And then there were the Beatles," Loest wrote in his novel *Es Geht Seinen Gang*. "Suddenly they were everywhere and were in every hit parade. Everyone talked about them and every week they produced a fresh hit, it was like a fever, it grabbed us and shook us and threw us about and made us different from what we had once been."[5] Until then, Western rock had found its way into youth culture through jazz and pop music. Unlike a singer such as Elvis Presley, whose distinctive persona and music required specific qualities of voice and appearance, the Fab Four with their mop-top hair and collective vocal harmonies could be easily imitated and replicated. Every country had its Beatles band: the Crickets in Bulgaria, the Puhdys in East Germany, Olympic in Czechoslovakia, the Happy Fellows in the Soviet Union. The official government response to these "vocal instrumental ensembles"—the official euphemism for rock bands—was sporadic, inconsistent, oftentimes chaotic and contradictory. Kremlin officials issued denunciations of Western influences, but the Soviet Union's state-run record company, Melodiya, released in 1967 a recording of the Beatles' song "Girl" on a ten-inch vinyl of a compilation of popular songs.[6]

That same year, in the neighboring socialist country of Poland, the state concert booking agency, Pagart, invited a British "vocal instrumental ensemble" called the Rolling Stones to perform in the 3,000-seat Congressional Hall in Warsaw's landmark Stalinist-era Palace of Culture.[7] That April, as the band arrived to perform for a full house, an additional

8,000 young people massed outside the concert venue. When young people attempted to storm the concert hall, a riot ensued with thousands of young people rampaging through the streets of Warsaw throwing bricks, smashing windows and street lamps, and destroying the windshields of cars, until they were finally subdued by militia units using clubs and tear gas.

The mood inside the Palace of Culture was equally riotous. One reviewer compared the effect of the lead "wokalista," Mick Jagger, on the crowd to "dynamit." The 3,000 fans trashed the inside of the concert hall and were only brought under control by the intervention of militia units. The response by city officials was surprising. "The next time such a band comes, we should put them in the Gwardia Hall," it was noted. "The Gwardia Hall is larger and the temperamental youths could not cause as much damage there as they did in the beautiful Congressional Hall." The idea of banning did not seem to occur to them. The response by Communist Party officials was similarly surprising. Complaining of the danger of marginalization of "socialist ideology" by Western rock music, one Party official observed soberly that "the trumpets of the Beatles are not the trumpets of Jericho which will cause the walls of socialism to come tumbling down."[8]

The effects of rock music on East German youth was no less dramatic, but the official response was very different from neighboring Poland. In December 1965, the Central Committee of the East German Communist Party held its 11th Plenary Meeting in East Berlin to discuss the growing concern over the outbreaks of hooliganism and violence among the country's youth, all of which was blamed on their obsession with Western rock music.[9] The previous month, riot police, supported by a Panzer mounted with a water cannon, had been called into the city center of Leipzig to break up a demonstration by hundreds of young people protesting the disbanding of a local Beatles band, the Butlers. The brazen defiance of the youth who had ignored teachers' warnings against joining a protest, and assembled in defiance of laws governing the public order, had unsettled the highest levels of Communist leadership.

The Communist leaders expressed concern about the prevalence of Western music on radio programs, especially the youth program DT-64, which was "poisoning" the minds of East German youth. One official warned that "the enemy exploits this type of music to drive young people to excess through these exaggerated beat rhythms" and that the "pernicious influences of such music on the thoughts and actions of young people is being grossly underestimated." Another official gave an example of a fifteen-year-old East German who had dropped out of school in the fifth grade and could not even speak German properly "but sang popular songs in English evening after evening" in perfect English. "How did he do this? He listened to tapes forty times and learned by his own phonetic method to give off sounds that he perceived as being English. There is no doubt that with these methods, you could teach beat music to a parakeet." The aging Stalinist-era Party head Walter Ulbricht summarized the collective Central Committee sentiment when he proclaimed, "The endless monotony of this this 'yeah, yeah, yeah' is not just ridiculous, it is spiritually deadening."[10] Evidence of the success of the heavy-handed East German response can be found in the film *The Legend of Paul and Paula*, in which the two main characters dabble in hallucinogens and sexual promiscuity to a soundtrack by the Puhdys, which became the official sound of state-sponsored and state-regulated rock and roll for the next two decades.

Even as East Germans attempted to reinstate Marxist-Leninist orthodoxy, in neighboring Czechoslovakia the government was loosening the reins. There were public readings of the works of Alexander Solzhenitsyn. In 1965, the American poet Allen Ginsberg was invited to Charles University, where he found a youth culture indulging in excesses similar to those back home.[11] Young people overdosed on a locally produced stimulant Fenmetrazin, which could cause hallucination and addiction. They attended rock concerts, whose ecstatic excesses reminded Ginsberg of "secret rhythm of the belly in Orgasm." Ginsberg attended a concert by the Prague Beatles band Olympic in a venue beneath the Centrum department store. "The Olympics have descended / into the red velvet basement / theaters of Centrum," Ginsberg wrote, describing scenes of young people with "long hair" and "screams and screams."

By the mid-1960s, there were dozens of rock clubs across the city, the F-Club, the Olympik Klub, just two blocks from Wenceslas Square, and the Sluníčko Club in Národní Street, which held rock concerts every night except Sundays and Mondays, and featured bands such as the Matadors, performing covers of songs by the Kinks and The Who. Pragokoncert was regularly booking Western groups ranging from the British rock musician Manfred Mann to the Canadian pop musician Paul Anka. In

December 1967, the first national rock festival was organized in Lucerna Hall. It was a three-day music marathon attended by more than 12,000 people, featuring leading bands from across the country, including a new psychedelic rock band called the Primitives. They performed covers of songs by Jimi Hendrix, Frank Zappa, and the Fugs. The band members not only came to represent the extreme liberalization of the Prague Spring, but also played a leading role in the underground movement over the next two decades.

THE PRAGUE SPRING

The Prague Spring actually began in winter. On January 5, 1968, less than a month after Prague's first national rock festival, Alexander Dubček replaced Antonin Novotny as the first party secretary of the Czechoslovak Communist Party. Dubček had spent years in the Soviet Union and was considered a trustworthy official who had knowledge of Soviet sensitivities and contacts in the Kremlin, which would permit him to lead Czechoslovakia along a road to reform that would not unsettle the Soviet leadership. In March 1968, Dubček began purging the Party and government of Stalinist hardliners. In April, he unveiled his "27,000 Word Action Program"[12] for creating a "socialist democracy" in Czechoslovakia. Censorship was lifted in the press, radio, and television. Jails were cleared of political prisoners. It was a revolution from above in which the political establishment shared the same reformist spirit as the youth who were already driving change in the streets. It became known as "socialism with a human face." On June 27, Ludvík Vaculík, one of the more progressive members of the Communist Party, published an open letter in *Literárne Listy* titled "Two Thousand Words: A Manifesto for Prague," signed by a large group of writers and intellectuals, calling for more radical reforms of the Communist Party and socialist structures within the society.[13]

Dubček walked a fine line, driving reform within the country while engaging with his socialist and communist neighbors, especially the Soviet Union, to offer assurances that Czechoslovakia would remain firmly anchored within the Soviet Bloc. By late July, as the Dubček reforms advanced, there was growing unease among the other Communist leaders that the reformist impulse could destabilize their own societies, that this was more than a cultural revolution. In late July, Dubček met with Brezhnev in the town of Čierna nad Tisou, on the border between Czechoslovakia and the Soviet Union, to underscore his commitment to the Soviet Bloc despite the ongoing reforms in the country. Brezhnev demanded that Dubček bring dissenting media under control. Then two weeks later, Brezhnev phoned Dubček from Yalta, furious that the Czechoslovak press had continued to write critically about the Soviet system. Dubček assured Brezhnev that he was handling the matter, but emphasized that this would take more time. Brezhnev interpreted this as a stalling measure. "Your stubborn attitude towards the commitments we made at Čierna nad Tisou changes things completely," the Soviet leader told Dubček. "We must take issue with this and have no choice but to reassess the situation and take new, independent measures."[14] That these measures included invasion was not clear at that moment. It was the last conversation the two leaders had before Warsaw Pact troops invaded Czechoslovakia.

It is important to emphasize that Dubček was interested in reform, not revolution, and that the need for change was driven in good part by the country's economy. Dubček was seeking a "third way" between orthodox communism and unbridled Western capitalism. Nevertheless, Dubček's liberalizations aligned with the liberalizations that the country's young people had been advancing for several years. Unlike in most countries where revolutionary youth clashed with the establishment's political and economic structures, the first six months of the Prague Spring saw a coincidental but fortuitous alignment of the state and the street that seemed to be showing an alternative way into the future of the polarized world of Cold War power politics.[15]

On the night of Tuesday, August 20, 1968, while Czechoslovakia reveled in its seemingly endless political spring, Soviet military units seized Prague's two airports, while hundreds of thousands of Warsaw Pact troops from Poland, Hungary, and Bulgaria massed along the Czechoslovak border. East German troops did not participate in the operation out of concern for evoking memories of the Nazi invasion and occupation. In the early morning hours of August 21, the Warsaw Pact launched a massive military operation crossing onto the territory of Czechoslovakia. Two thousand Soviet tanks flooded the country, seizing bridges and occupying cities, towns, and villages. A half million soldiers poured over the border. The first outbreak of violence occurred at five o'clock that morning near the Central Committee building in Prague, when several hundred students confronted Soviet paratroopers. Two students who ran toward the building were cut down with machine gun fire. A third student was crushed by a tank. Two hours later, Soviet forces opened fire on a crowd of young people throwing rocks at Soviet tanks on Wenceslas Square.[16] Similar violence erupted in Bratislava. But the military incursion was mostly met with nonviolent opposition. Names of streets and towns were changed to confuse the military advance. Many were renamed "Dubček." In the narrow streets, young people swarmed around tanks and trucks to impede them.

Dubček was flown to Moscow for "consultation." He returned haggard but unbent. On Monday evening, August 26, five days after the invasion, he spoke to the nation on the radio. "The time is gone and far behind us," Dubček said. "And not only this party but this nation will not permit a return to pre-January conditions under any guise." A strange peace ensued. The Warsaw Pact tanks remained, but the Prague Spring continued. That autumn, the head of the communist youth league attended a "hippie congress" in the Moravian town of Lužná, and reiterated to hundreds of long-haired youth Dubček's assurance that the reforms would continue. He promised that the communist youth organization would support them in obtaining "exhibition rooms for their talented painters and facilities for their protest song writers and musicians." In December, Lucerna Hall was host to the country's second rock festival.

These were halcyon days for protest singers. Waldemar Matuška, who had performed with the rock band Mefisto, wrote the "Pied Piper" about a man who "radiates fear" for thousands of miles. "He sings words like 'we' and 'our country,' 'peace and honor' but he means you and your blood, war and a mailed fist." Marta Kubišová, a popular twenty-six-year-old vocalist with the band the Golden Kids, emerged as a symbol of the protest movement with her song "Prayer for Marta," which used lyrics from a seventeenth-century Moravian theologian: "May there be peace in this land. May anger, enmity, fear and conflict flee." The song became the signature for Czechoslovak television and the unofficial anthem of the resistance movement. Following one performance, the press ran a photograph of Dubček giving Kubišová a kiss and raising a glass in her honor.[17]

A twenty-eight-year-old singer, Karel Kryl, chronicled better than anyone the sense of betrayal, defiance, and despair that followed the Warsaw Pact incursion. In the early hours of August 21, when news came that the tanks had crossed the border, Kryl penned a song, "Close the Gate, Little Brother" ("Bratříčku zavírej vrátka"), about a young boy who is urged to close the door before "the wolf gets into the theater." Singing the song in a voice reminiscent of the plaintive tones of Bob Dylan, and with a simple guitar accompaniment, the song was picked up by the radio that same day. In the months that followed, Kryl toured the country. He performed two or three concerts a day, in student clubs, workers' clubs, factories, restaurants, concert halls, and outdoor theaters. He also held concerts in Germany and Norway. "In this spring, the leaves begin to yellow," he sang with foreboding in one song. "Snow falls upon the flowers."[18]

It was left to Jan Palach, however, to provide the iconic act of protest against the Warsaw Pact occupation. On January 16, 1969, the twenty-one-year-old philosophy student walked to Wenceslas Square, removed his coat, doused himself in kerosene, and set himself ablaze. With burns covering 85 percent of his body, he was rushed to the hospital, where he died three days later. In the pocket of his coat was a suicide note in which he demanded the "immediate abolition of censorship" and threatened "further torches will go up in flames." The note was titled "Torch 1." In the days that followed, four other young people committed acts of self-immolation.

NORMALIZATION

In April 1969, Dubček was replaced as first party secretary by Gustáv Husák, a former supporter of the Prague Spring reforms willing to realign his country with Kremlin dictates. Extending the metaphor of the Prague Spring, the cultural journal *Tribuna* declared that the government would not "permit all flowers to blossom." The paper declared, "We will cultivate, water and protect only one flower, the red rose of Marxism."[19] But the Prague Spring that began in the winter of 1968 continued into the summer of 1969. In June, the Beach Boys participated in a rock festival in Bratislava, where they were joined by leading Czechoslovak performers, including Waldemar Matuška and Karel Kryl. The Beach Boys also appeared in Prague at Lucerna Hall, where they paid a particular tribute to the Prague Spring. "We are happy to be here, all the way from the west coast of the United States of America," Mike Love said on stage. "We'll dedicate this next number, which is called 'Break Away' to Mr. Dubček, who is also here tonight."[20] The official press gave the concert middling reviews, and referred to the band, in Czech translation, as *Chlapci z pro-brezi* ("the boys from the seashore"), an ominous sign of the cultural purging that was to follow. In early 1970, many of Prague's leading rock venues were closed—Arena, *Sluníčko*, Olympik, F-Club, and others. Bands were forced to adopted Czech names. A popular band, Blue Effect, became Modrý Blue Efekt, then just Modrý Efekt, and finally M. Efekt. The third national rock festival was postponed until April 1971, but the only foreign bands allowed to perform were from Soviet Bloc countries.

Some bands, such as Olympic and M. Efekt, adapted to the censorship, but others simply withdrew from the official rock scene. "The establishment has no power to prevent those who reject all advantages that flow from being professional musicians from performing," Ivan Jirous, a leading figure in the alternative rock scene explained. "The establishment can only put pressure on those who want to be better off."[21] The spirit of 1968 moved from Prague into the Czechoslovak countryside, where towns such as Ledeč, Suchá, and Rudolfov became centers of a thriving rock scene. In 1974, the village of Rudolfov was host to the first Musical Festival of the Second Culture, which attracted hundreds of fans, and featured bands including DG-307, named after a medical designation for a psychological disorder, and the Plastic People of the Universe.[22] During the early 1970s, the government fought a series of pitched battles with rock fans, as militia moved in to break up or prevent rock concerts. Private residences used by musicians were confiscated. On one occasion a house was forcefully vacated then burned.

The government focused particular attention on the Plastic People of the Universe, whose members became leading figures in Czechoslovakia's alternative culture scene, attracting not only musicians but also poets, writers, and playwrights, including Václav Havel, who was an avid fan of Frank Zappa. In 1976, members of DG-307 and the Plastic People were indicted on obscenity charges that claimed their lyrics contained "extreme vulgarity with an anti-socialist and an anti-social impact, most of them extolling nihilism, decadence and clericalism."[23] The bands' members were denounced in television campaigns as long-haired drug addicts, perverts, and devil worshippers. The action drew condemnation from the international community, including from German Nobel laureate Heinrich Böll and American playwright Arthur Miller. International pressure caused the trial to be postponed four times, but eventually in September 1976, the band members were tried and sentenced to prison. "Not even the most tolerant person could call what they did art," a national newspaper wrote in defense of the verdict. "Modesty and the law prevent us from publishing examples of their lyrics. If we were to call them vulgar, it would be too weak a word. They are filthy, obscene." The paper went on to underscore the government's determination to "resist any moral filth and efforts to infect our youth with that which every decent person condemns."[24] The dissident Czech novelist Josef Škvorecký cautioned against the government crackdown. "If you make enemies of young people by suppressing their music," Škvorecký wrote, "they will hate you until their dying day."[25] The persecution and trial of the Plastic People of the Universe led to the creation of Charter 77, one of Eastern Europe's leading human rights movements.

The Husák regime's attempts to purge Czechoslovakia of the last vestiges of the reform spirit of the 1968 Prague Spring paralleled similar attempts to either crush or co-opt the popular music scene across the Soviet Bloc. However, the suppression simply spawned new forms of alternative music that echoed trends in the West—rap, punk, New Wave—always seeking to provoke and evade co-optation into the service of the state. The appointment of Mikhail Gorbachev as Soviet leader in March 1985 introduced not only the concepts of "glasnost" and "perestroika," which were, in fact, little more than an echo of the Dubček reforms of 1968, but also an embrace of Western rock and roll. In a public statement, Gorbachev admitted that he and his wife were fans of the late Beatle John Lennon.[26] The revolutions of 1989 that the Gorbachev reforms unleashed were led in many cases by rock musicians, including in Czechoslovakia, where the punk and heavy metal rock musician Michael Kocáb was elected to parliament.[27] A few months after the provocative reference to heavy metal in Lucerna Hall in August 1989, following the overthrow of the Husák regime, Kocáb was given the responsibility of overseeing the withdrawal of Soviet forces from the territory of Czechoslovakia. On assuming the assignment, Kocáb echoed the August 1989 Lucerna Hall double entendre, noting that he had devoted his life to one kind of heavy metal and was now turning to heavy metal of a different kind. In early 1990, shortly after becoming president, Václav Havel invited the American rock star Frank Zappa to Prague and appointed him as "special ambassador to the West on trade culture and tourism." Havel called Zappa one of the "gods of the

Czech underground."[28] A year and a half later, in June 1991, Zappa joined Kocáb on stage for a rock concert celebrating the departure of the last Soviet soldiers from Czechoslovakia. The event was billed "Adieu, Soviet Troops."[29]

What began in Prague in the mid-1960s as a collective mass cultural response to Western rock music, shared not only in Eastern Europe and the Soviet Union but also in many other regions of the world, gradually assumed characteristics unique to the tenor and dynamics of the reformist movement of the Prague Spring that became embedded and preserved in the underground rock culture during the subsequent years of "normalization," only to reemerge nearly two decades later in the reassertion of the spirit and defiance inherent in much of the original rock culture of the 1960s.

NOTES

1. Tom Stoppard, *Rock 'n' Roll* (London: Faber & Faber, 2006). The Prague premier of the play featured a live performance by the legendary underground band the Plastic People of the Universe.

2. For the Tlatelolco massacre in Mexico, see the National Security Archives, https://nsarchive2.gwu.edu/NSAEBB/NSAEBB10/intro.html.

3. On the Brezhnev Doctrine, see Sergei Kovalev, "The International Obligations of Socialist Countries," September, 26 1968, 4; cited in *Seventeen Moments in Soviet History: An Online Archive of Primary Sources*, http://soviethistory.msu.edu/1968-2/crisis-in-czechoslovakia/crisis-in-czechoslovakia-texts/brezhnev-doctrine/.

4. Timothy W. Ryback, unpublished notes from summer 1989 research tour of Eastern Bloc countries.

5. Erich Loest, *Es geht seinen Gang oder Mühen in unserer Ebene* (Munich: Deutscher Taschenbuch Verlag, 1998).

6. Official Beatles discography (USSR, Russia, and other former Soviet republics) from 1967 through 2017, http://beatlesvinyl.com.ua/ru/33D_20227.html.

7. For a video clip, see https://www.youtube.com/watch?v=qesnBkpUkjg.

8. Timothy W. Ryback, *Rock around the Bloc: A History of Rock Music in Eastern Europe and the Soviet Union* (Oxford: Oxford University Press, 1990), 93–95.

9. On the 11th Plenary, see Elimar Schubbe, ed., *Dokumente zur Kunst, Literatur- und Kulturpolitik der SED* (Stuttgart, 1972), 1076–1117.

10. Ryback, *Rock around the Bloc*, 88–90.

11. Ibid., 67–69. For more on Ginsburg and his visit to Czechoslovakia, also see Richard Kostelanetz, "Ginsburg Makes the World Scene," *New York Times*, July 11, 1965.

12. In Czech: Akční program KSČ, http://www.sds.cz/view.php?cislo-clanku=2008040901.

13. Ludvík Vaculík, "Dva tisíce slov, které patří dělníkům, zemědělcům, úředníkům, umělcům a všem" ("Two Thousand Words Belonging to Laborers, Farmers, Officials, Artists and Everyone"), also known as Ludvík Vaculík, "Two Thousand Words: A Manifesto for Prague." For an English version, see *Vertigo*, 3, no. 9 (Spring-Summer 2008), https://www.closeupfilmcentre.com/vertigo_magazine/volume-3-issue-9-spring-summer-2008/two-thousand-words-a-manifesto-for-prague/.

14. David Vaughn, "Dubček and Brezhnev: The Last Conversation," Radio Praha, August 10, 2003, https://www.radio.cz/en/section/curraffrs/dubcek-and-brezhnev-the-last-conversation.

15. For more detail on the position taken by the Soviets and the deliberations in Prague, see Jaromír Navrátil et al., *The Prague Spring '68* (Budapest: Central European University Press, 2006), based on documents uncovered by a group of researchers with help from the National Security Archive, an NGO, in Washington, DC.

16. The *New York Times* published a fiftieth anniversary retrospective of the 1968 events, which includes famous images taken by Czech photographer Josef Koudelka and smuggled out of Czechoslovakia at the time. See Marc Santora, "50 Years After Prague Spring, Lessons on Freedom (and a Broken Spirit)," August 20, 2018, https://www.nytimes.com/2018/08/20/world/europe/prague-spring-communism.html.

17. Ryback, *Rock around the Bloc*, 80–81.

18. Interview with Karel Kryl at Radio Free Europe in Munich, August 1986.

19. Ryback, *Rock around the Bloc*, 141. For more on the replacement of Dubček by Husák, see Jan Richter, "President Gustáv Husák, the Face of Czechoslovakia's 'Normalization,'" Radio Praha (January 10, 2012), https://www.radio.cz/en/section/czech-history/president-gustav-husak-the-face-of-czechoslovakias-normalisation.

20. Ryback, *Rock around the Bloc*, 84. See also Leslie Woodhead, *How the Beatles Rocked the Kremlin: The Untold Story of a Noisy Revolution* (London: Bloomsbury, 2013), 112. For a clip of the song, see https://brianwilson.websitetoolbox.com/post/the-beach-boys-in-czechoslovakia-in-1969-7741831.

21. *The Merry Ghetto*, booklet accompanying Egon Bondy's long-play album, *Lonely Hearts Club Banned* (Paris: Liberation, 1978).

22. For more on the festival and the Plastic People of the Universe, see Jonathan Bolton, *Worlds of Dissent: Charter 77, The Plastic People of the Universe, and Czech Culture under Communism* (Cambridge, MA: Harvard University Press, 2012).

23. H. Gordon Skilling, *Charter 77 and Human Rights in Czechoslovakia* (London: George Allen and Unwin, 1981), 11–12.

24. Ibid.

25. Josef Škvorecký, "The Unfinished End of the Jazz Section of the Czech Musicians' Union," in *A Besieged Culture: Ten Years after Helsinki*, ed. A. Heneka et al. (Stockholm and Vienna: Charta 77 Foundation, 1985), 146.

26. See interview with Yoko Ono in Woodhead, *How the Beatles Rocked the Kremlin*, 210.

27. For Kocáb's official government curriculum vitae, see https://www.vlada.cz/en/clenove-vlady/ministri-pri-uradu-vlady/michael-kocab/zivotopis/michael-kocab-52812/.

28. For more on Zappa and Havel, see Linda Maštalíř, "Frank Zappa's Connections to Prague," Radio Praha, May 23, 2006, https://www.radio.cz/en/section/curraffrs/frank-zappas-connections-to-prague.

29. "Prague Celebrates New Spring as Soviets Depart," *Washington Post*, June 25, 1991.

BIBLIOGRAPHY

Bischof, Günter, et al., eds. *The Prague Spring and the Warsaw Pact Invasion of Czechoslovakia in 1968*. Lanham, MD: Lexington Books, 2010.

Navrátil, Jaromír, et al. *The Prague Spring 1968: A National Security Archive Documents Reader*. Preface by Václav Havel and foreword by H. Gordon Skilling. New York: Central European University Press, 1998.

Ryback, Timothy W. *Rock around the Bloc: A History of Rock Music in Eastern Europe and the Soviet Union*. Oxford: Oxford University Press, 1990.

Skilling, H. Gordon. *Charter 77 and Human Rights in Czechoslovakia*. London: George Allen and Unwin, 1981.

———. *Czechoslovakia's Interrupted Revolution*. Princeton, NJ: Princeton University Press, 1976.

Troitsky, Artemy. *Back in the USSR: The True Story of Rock in Russia*. London: Faber & Faber, 1988.

Woodhead, Leslie. *How the Beatles Rocked the Kremlin: The Untold Story of a Noisy Revolution*. London: Bloomsbury, 2013.

NINE

University Reform in Tumultuous Times

The Uruguayan Student Movement before and after 1968

VANIA MARKARIAN

INTRODUCTION

In 1965, the Uruguayan student movement voiced its opposition to the launching of a "program to improve the teaching of sciences" run by the Organization of American States (OAS) at the Universidad de la República (UdelaR). With the support of a group of faculty, most of them at the School of Engineering, student representatives put together an articulate rationale to oppose this program because of its low academic standards and its alleged disagreement with the overall goals of the institution. As they pointed to the role of OAS in the subcontinent, anti-imperialism was a key part of their language, but emphasis was placed on the need to reconcile scientific policies and "national development" within the university.

Educational reform was of key importance in better-known episodes of global student protest in the 1960s, particularly at the outset of the May 1968 events in France. In the Latin American context, though, the influence of academic issues in the unfolding of the student movements of this decade has often been overshadowed by the rapid proliferation of discussions about revolutionary strategy, the adoption of violent methods, and the increasingly repressive response of the governments vis-à-vis all forms of popular mobilization. In this study of the Uruguayan case, I contend that the analysis of these developments (that is, the polarization of national politics) needs to take into account the dynamics of educational reform, because they were central to the evolving political and ideological definitions of the student movement and to its interactions with other university actors.

In the episode under consideration, the vocal positions and ensuing demonstrations of the students could not stop the OAS project in 1965, but their activities were instrumental in strengthening their alliance with faculty members focused on developing scientific research. They also facilitated both the appointment of Rector Oscar Maggiolo in 1966 and the drafting in 1967 of an ambitious program to advance science and technology in the university. These developments suggest that the contentious stance of the student movement in the mid-1960s was favorable for academic endeavors. However, the peak of unrest in 1968 was a decisive moment in these controversies. From then on, facing increasing repression and right-wing authoritarianism, most of the mobilized students set aside discussion of university reform and embraced radical political causes. Revolution replaced trust in higher education institutions as engines of social change. In the following pages, I analyze these changing positions with the aim of understanding the unfolding of increasingly violent instances of protest in the period leading up to the coup d'état of 1973, which took over the national university, cutting off this and other related debates.

THE OAS LANDS AT THE FIFTH FLOOR

In the 1960s in Uruguay, as in other Latin American countries suffering from economic crises and budgetary cuts, politicians and leaders of educational systems grew hungry for resources offered by foreign governments, foundations, and international organizations for the improvement of scientific activity and the consolidation of academic institutions, two key aspects of social development according to theories in vogue since World War II.

These funding sources flourished in the subcontinent after the Cuban Revolution, hand in hand with U.S. policies aimed at preventing revolutionary outbreaks through a diversity of assistance programs, such as the Alliance for Progress, launched in 1961. Although in previous decades academics and scientists had accepted this flow of money with the optimistic belief that it would have a positive effect on their societies, they soon began to question the explicit or implicit conditions associated with the sudden availability of money in a new, more confrontational political context.

When approaching these debates in the case of OAS funding for scientific programs in Uruguay, it is important to bear in mind that UdelaR had experienced in the past decade a twofold increase in its student population and also doubled its academic programs.[1] A new leadership, with substantial backing from the student movement, had achieved a progressive statute in 1958 that helped consolidate self-governing bodies with democratically elected representatives of students, faculty, and alumni. At the same time it enhanced the administrative, academic, and budgetary autonomy from the central government, and enlarged the scope of socially involved actions carried out by the institution. Debates about academic organization and the importance of scientific research lagged behind. Modeled after the French system from its foundation in the mid-nineteenth century, the university remained a federation of professional schools with few resources for science and technology. In addition, the institution suffered constant budgetary restrictions and delays in payments from the central government in a general climate of public spending cuts, currency devaluation, and financial crisis.[2] This complex situation helps explain why debates about accepting external funding in areas as diverse as mathematics, obstetrics, and sociology became a matter of public discussion and loomed high in national media headlines.

In fact, the initial offer to fund an educational center at the School of Engineering and Agrimensure (Facultad de Ingeniería y Agrimensura, FIA) in the framework of the Interamerican Program to Improve the Teaching of Sciences (Programa Interamericano para Mejorar la Enseñanza de las Ciencias, PIMEC) did not face many obstacles and was even hailed as a positive step for academic development in the country. After the Uruguayan delegate before OAS volunteered to host the program, the matter was discussed by the national Coordinating Commission of Education, where the university had a representative, and then approved by the main governing body of the institution (Consejo Directivo Central, CDC) in December 1964 without much debate. The student delegation abstained because the union they represented (Federación de Estudiantes Universitarios del Uruguay, FEUU) had not discussed the proposal.[3]

Six months later, in mid-1965, several members of the Student Center of Engineering and Agrimensure (Centro de Estudiantes de Ingeniería y Agrimensura, CEIA), part of FEUU, broke into the classrooms of the fifth floor of their school where classes in mathematics and chemistry imparted under the PIMEC were just starting. In harsh terms, they voiced their rejection of the initiative. This episode of student unruliness angered engineer Andrés Valeiras, the Argentine director of the OAS program in Uruguay, who sent exasperated letters of complaint to the dean of the school and the rector of the university, also addressing FEUU leaders. He argued, with all logic on his side, that the program had been discussed and timely approved according to the procedures set by the institution itself.[4]

Convened to explain their attitude before the CDC, the student delegates deployed a battery of questions and complaints. They presented a technical report (authored by a professor in their school) proving the low academic level of the syllabus for the mathematics class, insisted on the poor background of the teachers in charge of it, and questioned the criteria for selecting the students. Several other members of the CDC (professors, alumni, and deans from different schools) had to acknowledge that they lacked precise information on the courses already in progress. They did not know much about the general program either, other than that it was directed at improving the teaching of basic sciences in the subcontinent and that, according to the situation in the hosting country, the classes could be attended by individuals working in either tertiary or secondary education. The students were particularly incensed by this point. They feared that this lack of a clear standard would allow "mediocre people to perch" in Latin American universities. They employed similar arguments to attack the coordinators of PIMEC in Uruguay.[5]

In the next four months the CDC held nine meetings of about three hours each to discuss this matter. Student representatives such as Mario Wschebor and Rafael Guarga, from FIA, redoubled their assault against what they termed "a case of acritical reception" of foreign aid. Although it had not been able to reach a conclusion prior to the initial consideration of PIMEC, the student union had been paying attention to this issue for a while and the previous year had included it in the agenda of a seminar on university politics.[6] This was part of broader efforts to adapt to the challenges involved in the full participation of students in all the democratically elected governing bodies of the institution since the approval of the new statute in 1958. What many had decried as the inevitable bureaucratization of union activity did not translate into a decline in militancy.

On the contrary, in the early 1960s the Federation experienced booming activism and a marked shift in its ideological orientation. Until then, anarchist tendencies had been dominant and imposed a "third" (*tercerista*) position vis-à-vis the United States and the Soviet Union. Following this tradition, many leaders were initially wary before the triumph and early deeds of the Cuban Revolution. Instead, members of the Socialist Party applauded the Cuban experience and grew close to the Communists to form a new hegemonic coalition of Marxist leaning. From then on the FEUU, never detached from international matters, regularly expressed its open commitment to revolutionary movements all over the world, particularly those fighting U.S. intervention, and systematically opposed the national government for submitting to International Monetary Fund (IMF) guidelines. Uruguayan students were also active in extending their support to mobilized workers and participated in the process of creating a labor umbrella organization in 1966.[7]

When discussing the situation at FIA, FEUU delegates were faithful to this political reorientation of the student movement and offered a frankly negative evaluation of the goals and history of the OAS. They reminded other members of the CDC that the organization was instrumental to U.S. policies in the subcontinent, most recently through the expulsion of Cuba for not complying with the "imperial power." Fresh events in the Dominican Republic were also brought to the fore. In the same meeting where the students first voiced their anger with PIMEC, the CDC considered the possibility of inviting former Dominican president Juan Bosch, who less than two years previously had been thrown out of power by a coup supported by the United States.[8] Students were particularly concerned with exposing alleged linkages between these international developments and the proposal under consideration. They combined passionate rallying cries against OAS for trying to "penetrate" the university in order to "execute" U.S. policies, with straight analyses of the specific procedures of this and similar organizations inspired by soon to be fashionable "dependentist" literature.[9] Another ingredient of these debates was the exposure in Chile of "Project Camelot," a sociological study funded by the U.S. Army on the reasons for popular protest.[10]

However, the subtleties of academic evaluation and the technicalities of the specific program were never dodged in favor of pure anti-imperialist language. Student delegates spouted rallying cries and advanced often pompous declarations, but the focal center of their case was always that the university lacked any systematic reflection on how to improve its performance, and they had no blueprint addressing the urgent need to upgrade both scientific research and its curricula. Taking into account the ongoing financial crisis and budgetary cuts, the argument went, this made the institution extremely vulnerable in the face of overtures by international organizations and foreign governments. Nobody in academic circles could ignore this fact. As the CDC was discussing this particular program, several well-known professors, suffering from decreasing wages and a dearth of resources, were courting U.S. diplomats in Montevideo and asking for money for their projects.[11] According to frequent reports in national media on the "brain drain," many more were frantically applying for fellowships and internships in foreign universities.[12]

Members of the CDC and deans of different schools referred to this same situation as a reason to oppose the students' demand to suspend the agreement with OAS. They argued that it would help mitigate a situation of extreme need, and pointed out that none of their arguments seemed threatening enough to force them to violate the terms of the commitment already assumed by both the government and the university. Israel Wonsewer, dean of the School of Economics and Administration, presented an articulate rebuttal with references to the theses put forward by the UN Economic Commission for Latin America and the Caribbean (Comisión Económica para América Latina, CEPAL) on the role of higher education in national development, and the possibility of taking advantage of the contradictions between imperial and dependent countries to achieve a positive outcome for the latter. Héctor Fernández Guido, the dean of FIA, positioned himself to the right of this position with the aim of discrediting student protest as irrational and irrelevant before the prestigious OAS program.[13]

When answering these diverse takes, FEUU delegates kept repeating their initial rationale with documented depositions aimed at demonstrating the specific effects of PIMEC, while also insisting on their openness to proposals that would meet the needs of local scientific communities. With similar worries about pertinence and rationality, but much more vigilant about the credibility of the institution and its decision-making process before other national and international actors, university authorities led by rector Juan José Crottogini hoped for a compromise solution to the problem. As with other similar stalemate situations, debate at the CDC ended up with the creation of an ad hoc commission to reach a consensual solution.[14] It was a way of contemplating internal dissidence while avoiding the risk of wrecking the reputation of the university.

The only documentary evidence available on the work of this commission are minutes from a meeting between university leaders, including the rector, and OAS representatives ten days after its creation. On this occasion, Crottogini presented his own disagreement with the methods used to select the faculty involved in PIMEC and attacked the pragmatic rationale put forward by its administrators: that "efficiency" should never supersede "zeal" in university appointments. The mathematician Rafael Laguardia, a member of the commission and also the founder and director of the prestigious Institute of Mathematics and Statistics (Instituto de Matemática y Estadística, IME) of FIA, voiced his criticism of the poor quality of the courses and urged the OAS to be more in tune with the needs of scientific communities in each particular country. In the case of Uruguay, where mathematics had a relatively strong tradition and had gathered prestige in the region, Laguardia saw no need to impart this type of basic training and asked instead for help to develop systematic exchanges with first-rate scientific centers from abroad. OAS representatives thanked him for these "constructive opinions" and expressed a wish to continue collaborating with the university.[15]

THE RISE AND FALL OF THE REFORMIST AGENDA

In fact, this meeting did not lead to any decision to halt the PIMEC classes, which continued undisturbed on the fifth floor of FIA for several years. However, the debates of 1965 had a profound influence on university politics and were at least partly responsible for the consolidation of an alliance of students and faculty that was able to question the status quo within the university, promote alternative academic agendas, and even formulate a program for the structural reform of the institution in 1967. I contend that the critical impulse and contentious stance unfolded in these debates, particularly by the student movement, were key to these outcomes.

We can better illustrate this point by going back to what was happening in FIA in the mid-1960s, when the OAS proposal arrived. This school was then one of the few places in the university with solid scientific groups, such as the mathematicians working at IME. This institute was the rallying point for many FIA professors concerned about improving the teaching of basic sciences in UdelaR as the only means of radically challenging a system that still favored liberal studies to prepare graduates for professional roles. These academics had been slowly organizing to oppose the current authorities at FIA who clung to the liberal studies model and defended the place of applied technology in the curricula. Debates about foreign funding reignited these tensions since they questioned the modus operandi of this hegemonic group that had so far favored the quick approval of such proposals without discussing their effect on the general orientation of the institution.[16]

The group of challengers, whom we can term "reformist engineers," included people from diverse scientific areas and even more different politics. Among the more active were Óscar Maggiolo, a hydraulic engineer from the progressive sector of the traditional Colorado Party; Julio Ricaldoni, a structure specialist of similar political leanings; José Luis Massera, a world-renowned mathematician and main cadre of the Communist Party; and Rafael Laguardia, yet another mathematician with administrative skills and no definite political affiliation. They were united by their concern about boosting basic sciences in the curricula, their agreement on the need to achieve "national independence" in scientific matters, and their demand for more resources to accomplish these goals. In addition, all of them were full-time faculty at a time when such appointments were still rare.[17]

Whatever their academic prestige and articulate language, these "reformist engineers" had as of 1965 not been able to break the power of the leading faction in FIA, which was close to the conservative sector of the Blanco Party that dominated the national government.[18] This changed only when they forged an alliance with a growing sector of the student movement resisting this hegemonic group, mainly because it had forcefully refused to participate in the governing bodies of the institutions as sanctioned in the 1958 statute. Unlike faculty members, these youngsters were free and able to deploy a battery of forceful measures, including striking and occupying the school premises and defying the operating rules of the administration with behavior that was often termed "rude" by the elder authorities.[19] More importantly, they took advantage of their highly organized participation in the central governing bodies to present the situation in their school before the CDC, just as they had voiced their opposition to PIMEC. While this matter was still under consideration, members of CEIA went back to the fray and denounced the limits imposed on union activity within FIA, particularly regarding posting propaganda and using classrooms for their meetings. They also vented their discontent with academic policies, tenure review processes of professors who opposed the ruling group, and outdated curricula.[20] Some of these students were members of the Communist Youth, predominant within FEUU in the mid-1960s, while others had no clear political affiliation but admired the heroic politics of the Cuban Revolution, and were therefore close to a myriad of small radical groups challenging the Communist leadership. Ideological and political rifts notwithstanding, they came together as champions of (and spokesmen for) the faculty opposing the current state of affairs in FIA.[21]

Their alliance with these "reformist engineers" was key to achieving their shared goals. By late September 1966, the continuous exposure of increasingly turbulent conflicts within FIA forced the CDC to create yet another ad hoc commission to deal with the situation.[22] After two months, the commission issued a report that basically supported the students' claims and therefore bolstered the stand of the dissident faculty minority from FIA. The student delegation used the report to ask for intervention in the school by central university authorities. A majority of CDC members voted in favor of this proposal, arguing that rapprochement was no longer possible between the two quarreling factions.[23] The supervisory commission immediately set to work and the transformative process gained momentum.

In October 1966, together with the launching of this process and at the peak of influence of the alliance between FIA students and "reformist engineers," one of the latter, Óscar Maggiolo, was elected as rector of UdelaR with the backing of several faculty members and the majority of the student movement. His firm resolution and rigorous academic credentials were key to his swift formulation of a program for the structural reform of the university, known as "Plan Maggiolo," in mid-1967.[24] National politics were also favorable. The triumph of the Colorado candidate in the 1966 election for president seemed to open up a new era in the relationship between the university and the Executive Power. After a decade of Blanco governments that had cut the university's budget and often attacked its leaders, the new president, Óscar Gestido, visited the university and expressed his preference for dialogue.[25]

However, the impulse for "Plan Maggiolo" was related to a technical commission established under these Blanco governments to produce a general report on the social, political, economic, and cultural situation of the country. This initiative was in tune with the guidelines of the Alliance for Progress, which were directed toward providing aid for the Latin American countries that devised plans to improve their situation, with the overall goal of preempting popular mobilization and discouraging revolutionary activity. The work of the Uruguayan commission did not explicitly address this goal, but instead issued several volumes authored by a team of top specialists in each area and a series of recommendations for modernizing policymaking and public administration.[26] "Plan Maggiolo" responded to these recommendations because it was formulated as a budgetary program associating specific goals with each allocation of money, just as the commission had suggested.

This was an ironic coincidence, because Maggiolo himself had been critical of its proposals for the modernization of higher education.[27] His plan shared the aim of rationalizing the administration of university services and spending, but proposed a very different approach to the long-term role of the institution in the context of "national development."[28] This approach was rooted in the ideas of the "reformist engineers" and other similar groups in UdelaR and other public universities in the region. It was particularly consonant with the outlook of the anthropologist and former rector of the University of Brasilia, Darcy Ribeiro, who had been forced into exile in Montevideo after the 1964 coup in Brazil.[29] In 1967, he led a well-attended "Seminar on University Structures" where students, faculty, and alumni expressed their desire for change and general agreement with the reformist intention of the "Plan Maggiolo."[30]

Debate in the governing bodies was nonetheless contentious. Several deans and alumni delegates, for instance, resented the proposed system of central research institutes and horizontal coordination among services, since it risked their positions in the traditional power scheme of federated professional schools.[31] In addition, the student movement, so far instrumental to the ascension of Maggiolo and the promotion of his reformist agenda, began to show internal rifts even before the proposal was formally presented to the CDC. In March, when the new president, Óscar Gestido, visited the university, student delegates had hurried to express their doubts about the possibility of finding common ground with his conservative branch of the Colorado Party. In the following months, they staged a series of demonstrations against the Summit of the Americas celebrated in April at the upscale summer resort of Punta del Este with U.S. president Lyndon Johnson in attendance. This involved serious clashes with the police and heated declarations against the government.[32]

This climate of mobilization had not cooled when the student union began to officially discuss the "Plan Maggiolo." In May and June 1967, the Secretariat on University Matters of FEUU (Secretaría de Asuntos Universitarios, SAU) sent a couple of reports to the centers. The first one was authored by Luis Carriquiry, student of medicine, principal of SAU, and delegate before the CDC. It presented the plan without many adjectives and hurried to assure its readership that it did "not propose too innovative or imported ideas but departs instead from orientations that had been broadly conferred in our University."[33] Twenty days later, a second report exuded an even more self-justifying tone. It said that "far from being a luxury for the destitute, scientific development is today a political need for underdeveloped peoples." It also defended the proposal to "uniformize academic degrees" because it was not "an artificial import from foreign experiences," and it took pains to stress that FEUU had already put forward similar proposals.[34] Concurrent with this favorable position on academic reform, many student leaders were then taking part in the "Seminar on University Structures" led by Ribeiro.[35]

However, somewhat fragmentary evidence from discussions in the student centers shows that many activists opposed what they saw as an attempt by the leadership to reach an expeditious decision in favor of the plan. In July 1967, a booklet signed by four students from the schools of Economics, Medicine, Architecture, and the Institute for Secondary School Teachers rejected the "rosy" and "superficial" tone of the official reports because it blocked any "serious analysis." It also charged that in an attempt to deter the negative opinions, the plan itself had not been widely distributed.[36] A month later, another document authored by an unidentified student leader, most probably from FIA, called "hypocritical" and "inconsistent" those who blindly trusted the will of Maggiolo and his allies to really change the institution.[37]

Besides showing displeasure with conduct of the debate, these documents challenged the doctrinal foundations of the plan. From its very title, the aforementioned booklet said it was "a sellout proposal" and disputed the idea that it could be treated as a "mere formula" for "abstract pedagogic or scientific development."[38] The manuscript text by an anonymous leader was more explicit when it questioned why the budgetary request was calculated not according to "qualitative considerations" but as a percentage of GDP, which mirrored capitalist economic rules and arrangements. He also warned of the perils of "sowing false illusions" and falling into "a new fetishism of structures," thinking that university reform could solve the country's problems. Moreover, he warned against the danger of using "bourgeois culture from a critical point of view" and of possible "imperialist penetration," and advised against dealing with the "technocracy and the government."[39]

All these remarks were clearly aimed at denouncing the pro-economic development (*desarrollist*) underpinning they detected in the plan, which was depicted as the perfect reversal of any chance at real social change. This critique offered an overly simplified picture of a complex school of economic and social thought that was at the time in dispute and open to interpretation. These documents tended to identify this school with the work of the aforementioned commission launched under the umbrella of the Alliance for Progress programs. Their authors of course knew that the university leadership had an intense relationship with the work of this commission and its doctrinal bases: it had been mostly staffed with faculty from UdelaR, and its recommendations had influenced the administration of the institution, including the new rationale of the budgetary request as outlined in the "Plan Maggiolo." It was nonetheless ironic that the plan was attacked on this basis, since Maggiolo had been extremely critical of this commission because it put forward efficiency criteria for academic activity and stopped short of demanding national standards for science and technology according to global social needs and not market requirements.[40]

Without delving into these subtleties and different appropriations of "desarrollist" theories, the authors of the booklet were mainly concerned about denying "the possibility of University, research, and science development" prior to the "transformation of society and its fundamental structures." The unidentified leader followed a similar line when stating that "politics cannot be replaced" in any discussion on institutional reform.[41] Hints at the role of international foundations and U.S. cultural policies were at the heart of both these opinions, with frequent allusions to national and foreign cases of such interventions. At this point, though, they parted ways, since the anonymous writer contemplated the possibility of considering case by case according to university priorities, as the student representatives had done regarding PIMEC, while the booklet was quick to assimilate Maggiolo's proposals to "US cultural and economic domination," and then quote Che Guevara and Régis Debray in a call to take up arms and end "subordination to imperialism."[42]

These diverse critical stances affected the positions of student delegates in the CDC, but they did not lead the majority of the Federation, still controlled by the Communists, to turn against Maggiolo. They used to open their remarks by commending the reforming impulse, and then berating the rector for risking the participation of students, faculty, and alumni in the self-governing bodies of the institution, opening the way to foreign influences, and ignoring the real causes of the "national crisis." The student leaders ranked their priorities when pointing out that "the University we want will not be possible until there are profound changes" in the country's social structure.[43] For some sectors, the defense of concepts, such as "academic autonomy," that they had previously shared with other university actors, that had made possible the alliance that elected Maggiolo and helped design his plan, became contested ground or seemed no longer relevant.[44] This understanding of university politics forced them to take sides between what Marcos Lijstenstein, student at the School of Humanities and Sciences who reported on the "Seminar of University Structures" for the weekly *Marcha*, defined as the "two fidelities" of higher education: to the "needs of national development," now seemingly only achievable through revolutionary change, or to the "high international standards of knowledge," now allegedly incompatible with the former.[45]

It is clear that these opinions did not do much to advance the proposals of the "Plan Maggiolo." In late 1967, short of the legal deadline, the CDC set aside larger schemes and passed a general budgetary draft addressed to the government to continue working within current institutional frameworks.[46] The Executive Power assigned to the university half the money it had requested.[47] This suggests that, whatever the internal differences, the immediate reasons for the actual frustration of the plans for university reform lay outside the institution. A meeting with President Gestido to ask for more funding could not be held because he suddenly died in December. From the very onset of his tenure, his successor, Jorge Pacheco Areco, resorted to repressive measures and regressive economic policies. This authoritarian turn opened the door to a new cycle of protest led by the student and labor movements.

PROTEST MATTERS

What was the specific import of these developments in the university? As of 1968, debates about institutional reform, be it the "Plan Maggiolo" or any other proposal, were no longer the center of attention of the CDC or any other deliberative space within UdelaR. There were a few attempts at creating institutes that were included in the plan (i.e., the Computing Center and the Center for Latin American Studies), but instead of launching a new institutional arrangement they were integrated into the old federal system. In addition, the central governing bodies began to devote more and more time to more pressing matters, such as threats by the Executive Power to intervene in the university and reverse its democratic procedures and repeated assaults on its facilities by repressive forces searching for evidence of "subversive activity." They tended to blame the university for shielding the actions of the Tupamaros, a new, small, and still unseasoned guerrilla group.

Starting in June and for the rest of the year, the government resorted systematically to "prompt security measures," a limited form of a state of siege that allowed for the suspension of rights and control of the public space. This meant a qualitative change in the ways social movements organized and mobilized, with old structures and repertoires of protest often deemed no longer suitable for the new challenges and the escalating pace of repressive measures. The unions of high school students—new, unstable, and with a volatile membership—were the first to experience this transformation, but the older and steady FEUU soon followed. The painstaking construction of a bureaucratic apparatus to face the challenges of participating in the self-governing bodies, which had defined student activism in the previous decade, was overturned by these new developments. Groups of activists often launched spontaneous actions, sidestepping the decision-making mechanisms of both student centers and central bodies. In mid-1968, in response to the climate of permanent agitation, a mobilizations committee took on the responsibility of assisting the general secretary in making quick executive decisions regarding future actions and political matters. At least two of its members had been active in the conflicts of FIA in previous years and had also attended the "Seminar on University Structures" in 1967, one representing the Communist Youth and the other the new radical majority. This showed that concern about academic policy and reform was shared at the time by diverse tendencies within the movement, but also that the immediate mobilizing agenda was now the main priority of student leaders. In addition, for the first time in several years, Communist positions began to lose ground to the combined forces of the other groups, which, despite their many differences, agreed to support more confrontational methods of struggle.[48]

In August, police forces unprecedentedly entered the university by force. During the ensuing demonstrations, they killed a student agitating nearby at the School of Veterinary Medicine. It was the first of such events, followed in September by the assassination of two more young activists protesting in the streets of Montevideo. So far, the students had used disruptive and nonconventional methods, such as roadblocks and rock-throwing, often with a clear countercultural inspiration, mixing culture and politics in their rallies and festivals. However, there is no substantial evidence that they had systematically resorted to violent means or executed armed actions in this early period. Each escalation of repression, though, drove new contingents to challenge the police and brought about an increased interest in these confrontations, until then limited to rather small groups and usually restricted to the theoretical rather than practical details. This new penchant for confrontation cut across new and old groups, including the Communist Youth, which, consonant with its parent organization, the Communist Party, had favored a "peaceful" strategy and been very careful to emphasize that student actions should not supersede the role of the working class in the revolutionary process. By the end of the year, amidst these and related debates and through a spiral of confrontation with the increasingly diligent repressive forces, many of these young students, who had entered politics without a clear ideological allegiance or party affiliation, had committed to the different groups of the Left, including both the Communist Youth and the still small guerrilla units.[49]

The subtleties of university politics were often lost in this hardening of political stances. Many within the Left, particularly the Communists and their allies within the faculty, still defended the traditional importance of autonomy from political power more as a means of preserving a space for legal political action than as a way of achieving anything in academic terms.[50] For a significant minority with increasing influence within the student movement, the university was mainly a recruitment camp for their revolutionary projects. The equation had been turned around: trust in higher education institutions as engines of social change was abandoned in favor of the belief that only the radical transformation of society would alter the role of universities in reproducing social contradictions. This was in tune with the idea that it would only be possible to build a "true popular university" after profound social changes allowed for the disposal of the "old social scheme . . . which knowledge was the patrimony of an insignificant minority," according to Fidel Castro in March 1969.[51] For the Cuban leadership, very influential within the Latin American Left, these words meant a call to subordinate all intellectual activity to the requirements of revolutionary struggle.[52]

Let us go back to FIA to understand the full influence of these political drifts. In 1968 the agreement with OAS came to an end without much fuss, and the space on the fifth floor was taken by a state-of-the-art computer, the first of its kind in the country. Meanwhile, the centrally appointed supervisory commission had modified the curricula and paved the way for more academic innovations. In 1969, when its term ended, one of the "reformist engineers," Julio Ricaldoni, was elected as dean with a program for further reform. However, the general frame of mind had thoroughly changed since the onset of the transformative process in the mid-1960s. An example from 1970 will make this clear. On this occasion, Valeiras, the very same OAS representative, offered funds to bring foreign professors to collaborate with the IME, just as Laguardia had requested in the meeting they had about PIMEC in late 1965. The mathematicians did not hesitate and sent a letter to the rector requesting that he dismiss the proposal because it went beyond the "concrete sphere of scientific activity" to involve "doctrinary" matters. The letter then proceeded to point to OAS as the "Ministry of Colonies of the United States," describe some of its most recent actions, and condemn its "imperial policies." It also lambasted those within the university who thought they could accept this type of funding and still preserve their academic autonomy. When accepting such an offer, it argued, "the rest would come in due time": first, they would "get used to financial assistance," then "the creation of expectations would lead us to its orbit, which would allow for direct or indirect intervention in the design and execution of our tasks," and, at last, "it would influence the university's big political decisions." A unified improvement of scientific activities would not be possible, said the mathematicians, until the "social bases of our work change substantially." Among the twenty-four signers were Laguardia and several members of the student union who had been active in denouncing PIMEC, such as Mario Wschebor, and were now in faculty positions at IME.[53] In August 1970, the CDC unanimously approved a resolution that shared their arguments.[54]

The letter was drenched in dogmatic outrage and a sense of moral superiority openly at odds with the rationale—in terms of relevance and consistency of academic agendas—that had been present even in the most heated speeches by student delegates in 1965. They had then been concerned about showing they were not opposed to foreign aid per se, but had specific (and technical) reservations about this particular program. Anti-imperialism had been a substantial ingredient of their language back then also, but in the next five years it had become dominant within academic groups that had previously defended the autonomy of their field of action from direct political influence.[55] This erasure of the differences between the academic and the political fields is exactly what most literature refers to as the "radicalization" and "polarization" of social and political actors.

Despite all their efforts to keep up with his academic program, Maggiolo and his allies lost their power to set the agenda. At the end of his tenure as rector he was sharply aware of his failure.[56] In a climate of increasing confrontation, right-wing proposals such as creating new higher education institutions, erasing self-governing bodies, and limiting student registration grew stronger together with open attacks on UdelaR by the government.[57] A couple of years later, with the installation of an authoritarian regime and the violent takeover of the university, these sectors had the chance to put their dreams for higher education into practice. The ensuing twelve years of repressive rule and academic stagnation speak for themselves, but they are not part of this story.[58] The imprisonment of the dean of FIA, Julio Ricaldoni, for his alleged responsibility in the explosion of a bomb in the hands of a student related to one of the groups that had backed his tenure, may serve as a final sad note on the demise of the reformist coalition.[59]

FROM DEVELOPMENT TO REVOLUTION

The evolution of the reformist coalition within the Uruguayan university closely resembled what happened in intellectual milieus in other Latin American countries. In the late 1950s and early 1960s, discussions about the social role and structures of higher education institutions flourished in the region. Development and modernization theories were instrumental in thinking about knowledge and science as essential to social change. According to this logic, the promotion of these activities according to international standards was of primary importance to national development. Towards the end of the decade these ideas had lost their appeal. Right-wingers promoted the restructuring of higher education following short-term efficiency criteria defined by the marketplace, but many within public universities posited that only the radical transformation of their societies could lead to a change in the role of their institutions as guardians of the status quo.

Artists and writers followed a similar path from "commitment" to different political endeavors through the specific tools of their trade, to a paradoxical anti-intellectualism that subordinated their cultural skills to the needs of the revolutionary program. Much has been written about these radicalizing processes that took intellectuals and academics away from their traditional spaces and networks and led them to create new ones, often related to the Cuban leadership.[60] But much less is known about the role of these very same processes in the formulation of plans for university reform, which, drifting away from the optimistic perspective of development and modernizing projects, were nonetheless aimed at placing scientific research at the heart of their efforts and stressed the specific role of knowledge institutions in the promotion of social change.

My analysis of the developments at FIA emphasizes this somewhat counterintuitive effect of the politicization of intellectual endeavors in the university. It shows that in the early 1960s the anti-imperialist rationale behind student positions vis-à-vis foreign funding for academic projects combined well with the idea of the university as an engine for social change, to the extent that it was able to determine its own priorities. Although these postures may have had at times a paranoid and overzealous tone, they were also keenly into the study of the technicalities of each particular offer and had a strong influence over ongoing efforts to consolidate academic communities and institutional spaces for scientific research at the local level.[61] On the one hand, they questioned the legitimacy of the somewhat naïve association between scientific impulse and social development that had justified the uncritical acceptance of such funding in the past. On the other hand, these debates were relevant to the renewal of academic practices more firmly grounded on a reflection on the social role of science. In fewer words, I have tried to demonstrate that the very existence of these conflicts helped the different actors hone their approaches and learn how to work together. This, in turn, facilitated the alliance between students and faculty that was initially instrumental in the formulation of the "Plan Maggiolo," the boldest proposal for institutional reform so far.

The recognition of the importance of radicalization within university politics, that is, of the key contributions made by some of the most politicized actors to transform the institution, makes further developments more dramatic. Soon enough, a significant part of the student movement drifted away from the reformist alliance while most of the mobilized students set aside the discussion of university reform and scientific policy to embrace revolutionary projects. Their positions revealed the extent to which Cold War polarization had prompted resistance to the adoption of the academic progress paradigm set by world powers in the region. With the advance of repression and right-wing authoritarianism, the modernizing and proudly democratic impulse of the postwar period, which was at the inception of the golden era of reformism in the university, was discarded by many of its previous champions. However, let us not end with this somber note and remember that their contribution to imagining science in the small South American country survived the authoritarian period and was an inspiration for university politics in the transition back to democracy in the 1980s.

NOTES

1. Although there are no systematic studies before 1960, according to available data student population grew from 7,000 in the 1950s to 15,320 new students according to the 1960 census, and 18,610 in 1968. See Mario Otero, *El sistema educativo y la situación nacional* (Montevideo: Nuestra Tierra, 1969), 23;

and UdelaR, Dirección General de Planeamiento, *Datos básicos del VII censo de estudiantes universitarios de grado* (Montevideo: UdelaR, 2012).

2. For a general survey of UdelaR in this period, see M. Blanca París de Oddone, *La Universidad de la República: Desde la crisis a la intervención, 1958–1973* (Montevideo: Universidad de la República, 2010).

3. See Consejo Directivo Central (CDC), *Actas de Sesiones*, December 29 1964, in Archivo General de la Universidad de la República, Montevideo (hereafter AGU).

4. See CDC, *Actas de Sesiones*, June 21 and 28 and July 5 1965, in AGU.

5. See CDC, *Actas de Sesiones*, July 21 and 28, 1965, in AGU. See Centro de Estudiantes de Ingeniería y Agrimensura (CEIA), "Acerca del Centro Interamericano para Mejorar la Enseñanza de las Ciencias," n.d., and "Anotaciones acerca de los programas del instituto para profesores universitarios de matemáticas," July 26, 1965, Archivo Laguardia, Box 12, AGU.

6. See CDC, *Actas de Sesiones*, September 1, 1965, in AGU.

7. See Mark Van Aken, *Los militantes: Una historia del movimiento estudiantil universitario uruguayo desde sus orígenes hasta 1966* (Montevideo: FCU, 1990), and Vania Markarian, María Eugenia Jung, and Isabel Wschebor, *1958: El cogobierno autonómico*, and Markarian, Jung, and Wschebor, *1968: La insurgencia estudiantil* (Montevideo: AGU, 2008).

8. See CDC, *Actas de Sesiones*, June 21, 1965, in AGU.

9. See CDC, *Actas de Sesiones*, September 1, 1965, in AGU.

10. See CDC, *Actas de Sesiones*, August 2, 1965, in AGU; and "Proyecto Camelot: Contraespionaje universitario," *Marcha*, July 23, 1965.

11. See, for instance, "Memorandum of conversation," U.S. Embassy, Montevideo, August 7, 1965, National Archives and Records Administration (NARA), Washington, DC.

12. See, for instance, "La Universidad paralitica," *Marcha*, October 8, 1964.

13. See CDC, *Actas de Sesiones*, September 1, 1965, in AGU.

14. See CDC, *Actas de Sesiones*, September 1 and 15, 1965, in AGU.

15. See UdelaR, "Versión grabada de la reunión realizada el 24 de setiembre de 1965 por el Señor Rector y la comisión técnica respectiva designada por el CDC y los representantes de los cursos del Proyecto 212 de la OEA en la Facultad de Ingenieria y Agrimensura," Distribuido 740/65, Archivo Laguardia, Box 12, AGU.

16. In the previous decade, a proposal by the Armour Foundation had split the faculty at FIA along similar lines. See Vicente García, Óscar Maggiolo, and Julio Ricaldoni, "Consideraciones sobre la creación del Centro de Investigaciones Tecnológicas," 1956, Archivo Laguardia, Box 1, AGU. See also María

Laura Martínez, *75 primeros años en la formación de los ingenieros nacionales: Historia de la Facultad de Ingeniería, 1885–1960* (Montevideo: Facultad de Ingeniería de la Universidad de la República, 2014), 117–35.

17. For more information on them, see Vania Markarian, ed., *Un pensamiento libre: Cartas de José Luis Massera* (Montevideo: AGU, 2005); Markarian, ed., *Don Julio: Documentos del Archivo Ricaldoni* (Montevideo: AGU, 2007); and Markarian, ed., *Universidad, investigación y compromiso: Documentos del Archivo Maggiolo* (Montevideo: AGU, 2010); and Martha Inchausti, ed., *Una vida dedicada a la matemática: Documentos del Archivo Laguardia* (Montevideo: AGU, 2007).

18. See, for instance, "En la Facultad de Ingeniería: La persecusión ideológica de extremistas universitarios," *El Plata*, September 19, 1966.

19. See for instance CDC, *Actas de Sesiones*, June 21, 1965, in AGU.

20. See CDC, *Actas de Sesiones*, September 23, 1966, in AGU.

21. For tendencies within FEUU, see Van Aken, *Los militantes*, 197–216, and V. Markarian, *Uruguay, 1968: Student Activism from Global Counterculture to Molotov Cocktails* (Oakland: University of California Press, 2017), 74–89.

22. See CDC, *Actas de Sesiones*, September 23, 1966, in AGU.

23. See CDC, *Actas de Sesiones*, December 16 and 19, 1966, in AGU.

24. See Distribuido 396/67 ("Plan Maggiolo"), July 1967, AGU.

25. See Distribuido 27/67 ("Establecimiento de un plan nacional de relaciones entre el futuro gobierno nacional y la Universidad de la República"), January 18, 1967, AGU.

26. See Adolfo Garcé, *Ideas y competencia política en Uruguay, 1960–1973: Revisando el "fracaso" de la CIDE* (Montevideo: Trilce, 2002).

27. See Óscar Maggiolo, "Universidad y CIDE: Una tesis colonialista del desarrollo," *Marcha*, January 28, 1966.

28. See Distribuido 396/67 ("Plan Maggiolo"), July 1967, AGU. See, for instance, "Marcha: Cambio estructural de nuestra Universidad," July 1967, and "Exposición del Rector de la Universidad, Prof. Ing. Óscar J. Maggiolo, el 14 de septiembre de 1967 por cadena de televisión," Archivo Maggiolo, Box 11, AGU.

29. See Darcy Ribeiro, *La Universidad Latinoamericana* (Montevideo: Departamento de Publicaciones de la Universidad de la República, 1968). See also Haydée Ribeiro Coelho, "O Exilio de Darcy Ribeiro no Uruguay," *Aletria* (2002).

30. See *La estructura de la Universidad a la hora del cambio*, 2 vols. (Montevideo: Departamento de Publicaciones de la Universidad de la República, 1969–70).

31. See CDC, *Actas de Sesiones*, July 7, 12, 17, 24 and 31, 1967, AGU. See also París de Oddone, *La Universidad de la República de la crisis a la intervención*, 62–81, 107–19.

32. See *Boletín Informativo de la Gaceta de la Universidad*, March 1967, 5; and CDC, *Actas de Sesiones*, February 15, 1967, AGU.

33. See "Informe de la Secretaría de Asuntos Universitarios: Plan de desarrollo universitario, 1968–1973," Colección Trayectorias Universitarias (Donación Frevenza), AGU.

34. See "Informe de la Secretaría de Asuntos Universitarios: Plan de restructuración universitaria," Colección Trayectorias Universitarias (Donación Frevenza), AGU.

35. See Ribeiro, *La Universidad Latinoamericana*, 282.

36. See "Plan Maggiolo: ¿Una propuesta de entrega?," *Cuadernos del Militante* 1 (1967), 6–8, in Archivo Wschebor, AGU.

37. See handwritten texts from August 1967, Colección Trayectorias Universitarias (Donación Frevenza), AGU.

38. "Plan Maggiolo: ¿Una propuesta de entrega?," 5.

39. See handwritten texts from August 1967, Colección Trayectorias Universitarias (Donación Frevenza), AGU.

40. See, for instance, O. Maggiolo, "Universidad y CIDE: Una tesis colonialista del desarrollo," *Marcha*, January 28, 1966, 6–7 and 22.

41. "Plan Maggiolo: ¿Una propuesta de entrega?," 5, and handwritten texts from August 1967, Colección Trayectorias Universitarias (Donación Frevenza), AGU.

42. "Plan Maggiolo: ¿Una propuesta de entrega?," 12, 14, and 39.

43. See Consejo Central Universitario, *Actas de Sesiones*, July 17, 1967, AGU.

44. See, for instance, "Nuestra posición," in folder "Disidentes de FEUU" (Folder 3224), in Archivo de la Dirección Nacional de Información e Inteligencia (ADNII), quoted in Markarian, *El 68 uruguayo*, 76–77.

45. Marcos Lijstenstein, "La universidad en tela de juicio," *Marcha*, June 23, 1967.

46. See CDC, *Actas de Sesiones*, July 31, August 7, 14, and 28, September 11 and 19, and December 4 and 5, 1967, AGU.

47. Daniel Waksman, "Los planes y sus objetivos: Presupuesto universitario," *Marcha*, September 29, 1967.

48. See Markarian, *El 68 uruguayo*, 72–73.

49. See ibid., 89–101.

50. See V. Markarian, "Un intelectual comunista en tiempos de guerra fría: José Luis Massera, matemático uruguayo," *Políticas de la Memoria* 15 (2014–2015); see words by José Luis Massera, transcripted in S. Bagú et al., *Hacia una política cultural autónoma para América Latina*, 93–94.

51. Fidel Castro, "Universidad de ayer, Universidad de hoy," *Marcha*, April 18, 1969.

52. For the relationships between the revolutionary leadership and intellectual circles in Cuba and other Latin American countries, see, for instance, Claudia Gilman, *Entre la pluma y el fusil: Debates y dilemas del escritor revolucionario en América Latina* (Buenos Aires: Siglo XXI, 2003), and Kepa Artaraz, *Cuba and Western Intellectuals since 1959* (New York: Palgrave, 2009).

53. See UdelaR, "Nota sobre la OEA elevada por docentes del Instituto de Matemática y Estadística al Rector de la Universidad," Archivo Laguardia, Box 12, AGU.

54. See CDC, *Actas de Sesiones*, August 18, 1970, in AGU.

55. For another contemporary rejection of foreign funding, this time of the Ford Foundation by a group of historians, see "Problemas de la investigación," *Marcha*, March 13, 1970.

56. See, for instance, "Universidad, no pagan pero duplican los gastos: Guillermo Chifflet entrevista a Maggiolo," *Marcha*, September 24, 1971, and O. Maggiolo, "El gobierno y la Universidad," *Marcha*, November 26, 1971.

57. See María Eugenia Jung, "De la Universidad del Norte a la Universidad para el desarrollo, 1968–1970," *Contemporánea* 4 (2013).

58. See V. Markarian, "La Universidad intervenida: Cambios y permanencias de la educación superior uruguaya durante la última dictadura (1973–1984)," *Cuadernos Chilenos de Historia de la Educación* 4 (2015).

59. See Markarian, *Don Julio.*

60. See Oscar Terán, *Nuestros años sesentas* (Buenos Aires: Puntosur, 1991); Silvia Sigal, *Intelectuales y política en Argentina: La década del sesenta* (Buenos Aires: Siglo XXI, 2002); and C. Gilman, *Entre la pluma y el fusil.*

61. For a similar take on the social sciences, see Fernanda Beigel, ed., *The Politics of Academic Autonomy in Latin America* (Farnham: Ashgate, 2013).

BIBLIOGRAPHY

Beigel, Fernanda, ed. *The Politics of Academic Autonomy in Latin America.* Farnham: Ashgate, 2013.

Gilman, Claudia. *Entre la pluma y el fusil: Debates y dilemas del escritor revolucionario en América Latina.* Buenos Aires: Siglo XXI, 2003.

Markarian, Vania. *Uruguay, 1968: Student Activism from Global Counterculture to Molotov Cocktails.* Oakland: University of California Press, 2017.

París de Oddone, M. Blanca. *La Universidad de la República: Desde la crisis a la intervención, 1958–1973.* Montevideo: Universidad de la República, 2010.

Van Aken, Mark. *Los militantes: Una historia del movimiento estudiantil universitario uruguayo desde sus orígenes hasta 1966.* Montevideo: FCU, 1990.

TEN

What's in a Revolution?

'68 and Its Aftermath in West Germany

BELINDA DAVIS

The year 1968 in West Germany/West Berlin was—as in most venues—perceived by contemporary activists as being as much dystopian as it was utopian. It was a year marked by the highest hopes for "revolutionary" change, but also by the deepest despair, prompted by unrelenting and often physically dangerous attacks against "extraparliamentary" activists, and the attendant perceived dissipation and dissolution of a broad movement. By the end of 1968, West German activists found the verdict unassailably clear: the chance for any imminent "revolution" had passed. What was still unclear was whether there had ever actually been any chance for a rapid, apocalyptic realization of the change many had desired, however hazy their vision. Yet the profound disappointments surrounding the year and its outcome were not without their own great, even radical effects, many of them salutary. The April attempt on the life of prominent activist Rudi Dutschke, following the assassination of Martin Luther King Jr., following the fatal June 2, 1967, police attack on protestor Benno Ohnesorg;

the aftermath of the Paris May and the Prague Spring; the chasm between what activists sought and what transpired—altogether these contributed, paradoxically, to an ultimately productive rethinking of the timeline and of possible sites of change. This rethinking itself became part of "revolutionary" change of the period, including indeed a challenge to the concept of revolution itself, in its commonplace meaning in the modern political lexicon. Activists' work especially in the years following 1968, often far removed from the streets and squares of their erstwhile marches and sit-ins, their bold provocations, and their frequent bloody confrontations with police, may serve to alert us to some of the most significant manifestations of the era's popular political thought and experimentation—and some of its most important lessons, too often lost in the cultural memory of the period. This was a "cultural revolution" in the most positive sense.[1] It was also political.

We can see this in the many terrains on which activists pursued change. Prevailing circumstances in West Germany were, by the 1960s, at least, a world away from battles with military dictatorships and other authoritarian regimes in Colombia, Guatemala, Peru, and, soon, Chile, albeit West German activists sought out connections with Latin Americans. Yet these European activists too contended with state and social violence—psychological, economic, and physical.[2] This was at least in part motivation for these activists' particular strategies. Chased from the streets and other public venues, many West German activists pulled back by the end of 1968. They took time to rethink: to reconsider their understanding of politics and history, and their corresponding ability to enact desired change. Some concluded that their time scale had been off, that they needed to study further to properly read the signs for coming revolution. Others adopted a more voluntarist approach, moving into factories, for example, in efforts to actively foment radical change within the historic revolutionary class.

A great number looked for means of change closer to home, quite literally. "Living communities" (*Wohngemeinschaften*, WGs), or group houses, were by the late 1960s already long-standing products of necessity of the early postwar period and earlier still. The "cohabitation" of non-blood relatives had resurged as a practical measure during and just after the war, a necessity born of the catastrophic destruction of German housing stock, alongside the radical mobility spurred by the war.[3] As such, they had counterparts across Europe, and also beyond the European subcontinent, in practices of both legal and semilegal sharing of residences and of squatting. Yet these physical and conceptual structures burgeoned in this period also as one key site of experiments with the politics of everyday life. The "commune" movement also stretched beyond West Germany, to be sure; contemporary groupings from Czechoslovakia to Argentina drew on nineteenth-century inspiration to work toward utopian communities, prefigurative or otherwise.[4] Yet political WGs were nowhere more commonplace than they were in West Germany, relative to the larger population; scholars estimate there were at least tens of thousands of them from the early 1970s to the early 1980s.[5] They spread across West German cities (especially though not exclusively in poorer districts, and where buildings were often damaged or run down), but they existed too in small towns—and in the form of rural communes.[6]

Already from the mid-1960s, WGs were more than just a practical and affordable form of shelter: they were a response too to other "everyday needs." Spreading across West Germany by the early 1970s, these WGs created a fabric of communications and action of increasingly dense weave. Were such experiments a retreat to the personal only, as police chased activists off the streets, and as public and private employers alike exerted painful economic pressures on "radicals"? There was some of this, but these new experiments also offered fresh opportunities to rethink concepts of change: its sites, pace, depth, and scope.[7] WGs offered sites too for radical alternatives to the most intimate relationships, for activists seeking a total integration of life and "politics." They provided space for fresh forms of political process, allowing for transformed theoretical convictions and means of practice. Some questioned the practices as utopian self-ghettoization from mainstream society.[8] Paradoxical relations with state officials, and with the broader public, challenged just how insulated activists could be through the 1970s and into the 1980s, even insofar as they wanted to be.[9] WGs were moreover nodal points for the extraordinary efflorescence of the activism of the new social movements (antinuclear, environmental, feminist, gay, and, ultimately, peace), enabling entirely new forms of political organization. They were sources of "basis work," consisting of everything from novel modes of child-rearing and schooling to building semiautonomous economies, often around squatted cultural-political centers and workshops, clinics, and bookstores. They helped create entire "villages in the city." A premier lesson of these experiments was both a philosophical and practical one about the nature of change, a lesson radical in nature. That the personal was political is hardly a novel thesis. Yet, arguably, there is more still—also as relevant for today's politics—to be understood from this notion, including through the challenge to fundamental structures of modern politics.

In this chapter, I will use the biographies of young West German activists as a lens for a brief analysis of this phenomenon. I will focus particularly on the case of Hubert V., an activist from his early teenage years in Hannover.[10] Hannover was itself a liberal city of a half million in Lower Saxony, situated squarely between the more prominent bastions of popular, extraparliamentary politics, West Berlin and Frankfurt. Born in 1952, Hubert lived in Hannover for his entire activist life. Yet he left his family at a tender seventeen. Hubert plied his early politics through forms of experimental living space, first in a series of WGs, then in a squatted independent youth center (*Unabhängiges Jugendzentrum*, UJZ), one example of the offshoots to which WGs helped give rise.[11] Hubert's initial move at seventeen reflected paradoxes of the postwar era. Though Hubert grew up in a working-class neighborhood, his father insisted that Hubert take advantage of postwar social openings to attend *Gymnasium* (college preparatory school) starting at age eleven, where he found fellow pupils particularly interested in "politics." In his oral history, Hubert claimed to have felt alienated, "distant" from his parents as a child, and at the same time "too close" to them physically at home. As he came to think about sex, "which one certainly never addressed at home at all," he began to chafe at the "cramped living quarters" at home, which prohibited his "try[ing] out" sexual activity.[12]

This in itself sounds like a commonplace of modern puberty. Yet specifics of the period contributed to a particular politics. Those raised up in the postwar decades sought to live both more and less "alone." The postwar housing emergency meant that many young people grew up sleeping in a room with many brothers and sisters, and even with one or both parents and/or other adults.[13] This was in itself not necessarily a fundamental problem for youth who had not known any different, nor rare in many times and places. Yet the ambivalence toward and even the antipathy of many to family ties is of little surprise in a Federal Republic where relations in the family—nuclear and otherwise—could be so poisonous. The Nazi past and its ongoing effects, psychological and otherwise, were a piece of these poisonous relations, as it was of self-questioning among activists. Polls in the 1950s and '60s revealed that West Germans associated "family" ever less with notions of an "emotional homeland," of a "community of solidarity." On the contrary, West Germans of all ages felt far more able to depend on friends than on family in this period.[14] Officials and societal scions celebrated the virtues of the nuclear family, and yet, in the 1960s, large swaths of the West German population had lived recently or still lived in "family" constellations that reflected the great damage of World War II.

The experimental living Kommune 2, established in 1967, declared moreover that the nuclear family had indeed never been sufficient to the range of human needs.[15] More in postwar than in Nazi Germany, Kommune members saw family life as a site of "total control," contributing to a "growing emotional impoverishment," producing children unable to communicate or even understand their needs. Living collectives like their own were conversely to open up "a liberating social communication."[16] In the event, residents found WGs broadly could offer the "feeling of belonging and security," protection from "social isolation and loneliness."[17] As Susanne T. described her own first WG, "that *was* my family."[18] It was thus on philosophical, personal, and practical bases that, by the late 1960s, activists already sought out alternatives to nuclear-family living. Hundreds of thousands began to follow members of Kommune 2 and other radical living communities in viewing WGs not just as an affordable alternative to the nuclear family or to living alone, but also as a springboard "to revolutionize and politicize the everyday," linking politics with the most intimate spheres of life.[19] In another time and place Hubert might have just gritted his teeth until he was eighteen or nineteen, but at this moment, discussion at Hubert's new school evinced in him the sense that "everything was possible," even in the dismaying aftermath of 1968. So, when in 1969 a group of local students and others invited him to live in their WG, the seventeen-year-old jumped at the chance.

For some of the most engaged activists of the 1960s, however, such ideas were not welcomed from the start.[20] While attending West Berlin's Free University (FU), Klaus Hartung lived in a WG in 1964 with other members of the SDS (Sozialistischer Deutscher Studentenbund), the (West) German Socialist Student Union. The intent was both to hold down costs and to facilitate ongoing discussion of SDS political actions beyond formal assemblies. Yet the FU SDS board member found himself fully unprepared for the meeting of the political and the private when fellow activist Rainer Langhans moved into the WG for a time. The "rather neurotic" Langhans wanted to talk with his housemates about problems with his girlfriend and other personal concerns.[21] Hartung feared not only distraction from the group's more conventional political efforts. Langhans's practices were also prospectively embarrassing for these "rational functionaries of the SDS. This self-exposure bared us too. It brought us under suspicion: that completely personal motives underlay our political activity, that we went out in the street for Vietnam because we also were [sexually] frustrated."[22] When Rainer Langhans later joined Kommune 1, a political and living collective still more publicly challenging than Kommune 2, Langhans's "neurosis was out in public. It was the uprising of the aggrieved [*Geschädigten*, also damaged]," who "made public their plight." But, Hartung later acknowledged, he too came to understand this linkage between politics and the most intimate aspects of life as representing a new kind of revolution. This was not a distraction from but rather a "totalization of politics"—and not moreover as Nazis had viewed it, but in a voluntary form. "The intervention of Kommune I intensified once and for all the contradiction in dividing 'doing politics' and the everyday." This was central to constituting an "antiauthoritarian movement" that was both broad and enduring: he claimed at the moment of his reflections in 1989, "the shock waves could be felt still, now as earlier."[23] This was one piece of the radical change that both inspired and emerged with the widespread practice of these living and political communities.

The beginnings of this "revolutionary" politics of private life came coincident with and as a piece of the ravaging disappointments of 1968. As hundreds of thousands felt chased from the public expression of politics, sites such as WGs offered both an exciting and relatively protected locus of political thinking and experimentation. The potentially radical nature of these "personal politics" too was not entirely lost on less sympathetic West Germans. Hartung saw widespread public "hate" telegraphed across the "bourgeois press." In Frankfurt, the Social Democratic–affiliated newspaper *Kommunalzeitung* trumpeted in late 1968 that WGs were all secret dens of "pimping, orgies, and drug trade," a predictably lurid assortment of charges. "Behind it hid real if uncomprehending agitation."[24] Indeed, Hartung wrote in retrospect, "What they suspected and didn't comprehend was the revolutionary explosive power precisely in the collective expression of individual misery, that an amazing politically productive force lies in the transcendence of individual contradictions when it happens on the street."[25] Members of Kommune 2 also opined that officials and others understood "the collective form of living itself as a political act. . . . Because in their grotesque reaction to the communes, the violence of the system and its methods of repression were visible."[26] Regular, violent police raids particularly on squatted apartments and clinics, and the increasing official penetration of private space through the 1970s, took place under the guise of guilt by association for the small number of cases of activist violence. Nonetheless, overall these experiments transpired in relative peace—once groups could find landlords who would rent to them.[27]

Some contemporary activists perceived conversely that this sort of retreat to the interior was actually a sign of how little a threat of radical change activists posed, particularly after Kommune 1, Kommune 2, and other better-known such experiments folded by the dawn of the new decade. Yet the demise of the latter was not in itself a sign of failure: one of the critical lessons of this period was precisely the need for a constant renewal of effort, as one experiment had served its purpose, leading to the next, producing a critical new vision of what change looked like and how to produce it. WGs and other experiments combining politics and everyday life in the 1970s superseded these earlier undertakings in other ways, indeed demonstrating new notions of how to make change. That is, members of Kommune 1 and 2, for example, saw their "revolution of the bourgeois self" above all as a means to create of themselves a revolutionary vanguard, by which they would render themselves able to connect the more conventionally recognized political struggles of peoples in Southeast Asia and in Latin America to Europeans, acting as the agents of the former in Europe.[28] Conversely, members of WGs, and the larger "alternative" communities they built, came to see transformation of the self and of social, psychological, economic, and cultural relations with others as an increasingly meaningful end in itself. It related to larger visions of change within West Germany—as a piece of the continued close ties to those outside the country. But, as to developing themselves as a revolutionary vanguard, activists increasingly rejected such visions as caught up in modernist theory that had already demonstrated its bankruptcy as a means to understanding change in the present. This was no easy acceptance that one simply could not enact collective, widespread, and radical change. The move beyond the thinking of the Kommunes was itself a sign of change taking place at a deeper level still, concerning the episteme of modern political thought. This constituted an expressly political and cultural transformation; it argued against any easy differentiation between them.

Thus, though terrifying for many West Germans who looked on, the politicization of everyday life and the bringing of the everyday to politics were electrifying for others. So it was that, in 1969, the seventeen-year-old

Hubert entered his first WG with little clear idea except that of "pursu[ing] a *different* life, at all events." Pursuing difference, challenging expectations, norms, and the status quo was the starting point. Hubert's experience highlights how WGs functioned as laboratories for social relations. "The exciting thing was actually the everyday. So, that a person was all at once different from at home, where one [was] with one's parents or with one's brother. [There] were completely different people there, with respectively varied interests." It was not just new people. There were trade apprentices, and artists, living at the house for longer or shorter periods. Thus WG residents left the discomforts of home to find individuals (still) less like themselves, with whom they could work to form and develop "equitable and compassionate" bonds, in an "effort to revolutionize bourgeois individuality."[29] This was a critical means to "liberate everyday life" broadly, "living together without pressure to perform, frustration, and fear," through "counter models."[30] It became part of a larger project for Hubert, one of a broad fording of boundaries ("*Grenzüberschreitungen*"): boundaries among individuals, and those separating out discrete familial and societal roles; those dividing a day into "work," "free time," "home life," and, if at all, "politics." It was such boundaries that uncomfortably squeezed individuals into fractured identities, or those assumed by others: into memberships in one party, or demographic, or political belief or another.[31] It was out of these experiments in turn that contemporary activists came to challenge notions of a "productive society" (*Leistungsgesellschaft*), concerning jobs that, at the latest following the 1973–74 OPEC oil embargo—and bans on the hiring of "radicals"—seemed in any case few and far between. Thus, the 1978 "Tunix" (Do Nothin') festival and set of workshops in West Berlin, only the best known of such projects, drew a crowd of nearly 20,000.

How radical were WGs in practice? Reaching out beyond one's own family was, to be sure, a normal part of "bourgeois individuation" among young people. In the event, members of Hubert's WG and of many others found themselves reproducing timeworn roles and patterns in their new "families." Hubert himself really appreciated "how the people treated one another" in his own WG in 1969, especially "across age divisions. There were fifty-year-olds there, there were also really young people like me." At the same time, Hubert acknowledged, house members treated him tenderly, as the "baby" of the house. This was not only a question of age, but also because he represented the "working-class historical subject" in the eyes of some of his housemates, Hubert wryly conjectured. Like Hubert, Manfred D., born in 1956, played the "little brother" in the WG he himself joined in 1977.[32] This didn't mean that he participated any less in all household tasks: he prided himself on cooking as well as anyone in the group. He also demanded his share of input into decision-making, rendering a tense affair the regular house meetings (or "full assemblies," *Vollversammlungen*, as many WGs borrowed the term from the more formal political groupings of the 1960s). But not all his housemates found it easy to treat him as an equal member, because of his youth. At weekly meetings, "we discussed endlessly," and also "very fiercely, until bottles were thrown at people's heads, and knives were thrown on the spot, when one was really so completely furious."[33] Age, both relative and absolute, clearly played a role. The two older members of the WG "were a bit like the parents," harping on whether the bathroom had been cleaned well enough, or whether someone had left hair in the bathtub. It had "cost a lot of stress and a lot of energy" when he and other members finally decided they had to throw these "parents" out of the WG. This was not simply a facile rehearsal of childhood fantasies, Manfred argued, but rather a practical decision concerning the politics of the everyday—and, to the point, something indeed they could do more easily in a WG than in a traditional family. Of course, leaving the "parents" behind was as conventional as it got. Such descriptions challenge the charges of many older activists in the West German case that it was younger people—the "new generation" of activists after 1968—who adopted dogmatic stances, whether concerning historical materialism or standards of cleanliness.

More important, to point to the regular deep conflicts in WGs, even their regular reorganization and dissolution, as rehearsals of childhood fantasies—or as failed experiments—misunderstands the way change took place in WGs: as a process of a laborious working through, of discovering—and often remaking—meaning. How clean was important, and how should disparate views be reconciled? Did household order represent residual fetishes of fascism—or care for the WG community? This questioning itself was central to WG life and politics. WG life was not an event with a finite end, but rather a challenge to notions of radical change as coming necessarily through *événemental* politics. The very process of working through such issues, of questioning the most basic assumptions, was a central component of the larger experimentation, whether or not it worked within an individual WG for any length of time or, as in Manfred's case, did not. Members of Kommune 2 castigated the "old-fashioned [*altväterlich*, literally, "old-father-like"] notions of the former SDS authorities. The great expectations that were aroused above all in young comrades [*Genossen*] have certainly been miserably disappointed."[34] Yet by the time of Kommune 2's 1969 publication, the Kommune itself had already dissolved. It was from this very point, through the publication, that Kommune 2's experiment took on its greatest significance.

Like divisions across age, those across gender were another regular source of rancor in WGs—and a fillip for further questioning, debate, and transformation of practice at all levels.[35] Here again, this was personal, a "cultural" issue, and more, inseparable from "politics." In the film *Der subjektive Faktor*, activist filmmaker Helke Sander's protagonist Anni is pushed along with other women into the role of making coffee for the men holding a political meeting in the living room.[36] Together in the kitchen, the women make the coffee—and then come up with practical, politically significant solutions to the childcare problem—their own, immediate concern, and one preventing them from engaging politically. In contrast, Sander depicts the men in the living room as continuing on esoteric and ultimately unproductive discussion regarding how they could best represent Viet Cong interests in West Berlin, and best "make revolution in [their] own land." This too bespoke a transformation from "revolutionary vanguardism" to new forms of political efficacy.

In the context of gender all the more than of age, "housekeeping" broadly conceived constituted a thorny landscape of everyday politics in WGs. Notices to "please sit while peeing" decorated the walls of WGs across West Germany, as women signaled to men that splashing the toilet seat prospectively created both more cleaning work and an unpleasant experience for those who had to sit on the seat.[37] This was an issue of really trying to understand the perspective of others at the most fundamental level. But it could also be a matter of challenging conventional practices. Volker T. remembered the tissue of issues from the "other side," still smarting a little, it seemed: "One lived together, one ate, drank, cooked, tried to make it all happen. Of course there were permanent conflicts, yes, regarding cleaning, and who didn't clean the toilet again, who had to go shopping, and so on. . . . But it was a part of our . . . process of left socialization, yes, that one had to solve these problems too, and that one, that one, that there were something like solidarity and a feeling of responsibility and so on."[38]

Volker laughed humorlessly as he described the truly remarkable scene of a female housemate standing over him in the early 1970s, emphasizing that "it's not clean yet, you have to get back to it!" He made a direct comparison to his experience cleaning toilets during his military service, under a watchful officer's eye: "It was rather women in the WGs who set the standards, so to speak. Yes. So, how often cleaning took place and how clean it must be." He repeated this last three times, betraying the power the memory still held over him. "So, WGs tried to organize themselves so that each, regardless of whether woman or man. . . . We lived together, so we tried to scrape by making it work, and of course there were conflicts," Volker repeated. "That's certainly clear, so, about cleaning, and not making clean enough, not orderly, and so on, yes." "But," Volker concluded, "that is just part of the package," that was what being in a WG was about. How much of this actually transformed mores and relations? How much was rather a reversal of power roles?

On the whole, men seemed to find it transformed mores, notwithstanding the difficult process. Despite Volker's evidently enduring discomfort with the presumption of particular standards, many male activists spoke of learning to cook and clean in this way as a badge of honor: a mark of their own transformation through WGs, to both independence and interdependence, a hallmark of the "revolution of everyday life." Activist and later German foreign minister Joschka Fischer saw it explicitly as an important example of the everyday realization of the women's movement: "It was a real resocialization, a second socialization" for him, after growing up with his two sisters doing all the housework at home. "It was an unbelievably *painful* resocialization" that took years, he emphasized. But, it was "successful in the end."[39] It was also for him a key form of personal "liberation" across genders. "The transformation in gender relations thus played a very, very large role, retrospectively also a great gain for us men, because, when I think of my father, who," without his mother, "was completely incapable of surviving [*völlig lebensunfähig war*]," he trailed off. By contrast, Fischer "cooked myself, cleaned myself, did everything myself." Robert G. found it likewise an "emancipatory act": "one wanted to get away from these petite-bourgeois kitchen practices," such as only women cooking in the home.[40] Robert and a male housemate who had spent part of his life in Italy considered it their "calling" not only to take on the cooking in their WG, but also to introduce dishes to their housemates from around the world.

Many perceived the changes moreover as going further still. Robert further connected the preparation and then collective eating of food very directly to his own transformation in the period: "And this WG was then also a space, precisely concerning this food, in which one, I don't know how, now also had exchanged views a very, very lot, and, to be sure, on political questions," and also philosophical ones, during and then after these collective meals. So it was both in a broad and also "in a narrower sense even somehow emancipatory, as if it tapped a life world [*Lebenswelt*] in me that was previously completely unknown, that was completely new." It was nothing like the home he came from, where the evening often featured a lecture from his widowed father. The WG and women's movements were intimately entangled; WGs were a crucible for reworking gendered as well as other relations. Karl W. claimed to appreciate, at least in retrospect, that "the everyday life that ensued under the women's movement played a certain role in the whole question of the revolutionization of the everyday." He conceded that, in his WGs, "it was naturally a bit more conflict-ridden when in the '70s [the women] all joined the women's movement." But the "most intensive" conflicts he experienced were, he insisted, within an all-male WG, which he described retrospectively as "looking correspondingly chaotic and dirty."[41]

But that men began to cook and even clean was what advocates of the "bourgeois" women's movement and others have long claimed for the period, to be sure. The most powerful result of these intense interactions and struggles, played out over thousands of WGs and other households across West Germany, did not lie in men's learning to cook and clean, nor even in women's introspection concerning particular standards of cleanliness, where they came from, and what they meant. In West Germany, the more "radical" wing of the women's movement was associated with "difference feminism," often described as celebrating women's cultural and even biological differences with men.[42] In consequence of these living experiments, however, activists came overwhelmingly to reject generalities and essentialisms on the basis of gender, a perceived limiting case of "who one was." Activists came to see such generalizations as defying the purpose of these projects in the politics of everyday life: both prejudging others by one category or another, and failing to recognize the possibilities of individual change and growth. Sigrid T. saw cleaning as one locus through which to pursue "more justice and also another relationship between men and women": "that the men should also wash the steps." But she emphasized in her narration the individual nature of the "cleanliness" question: "I also threw a woman out once, because she never ever did housework here. . . . I thought, either we live together, and it also has to be taken care of together. But in principle I am 'for' neither man nor woman."[43] Conversely, between her boyfriend and her, there was "no problem. He could cook and also clean[ed]" more often than she did.

This challenge to identity politics questioned the presumptions of some contemporary feminists in other ways too. Women discovered that living only with other women did not preclude painful encounters. In an all-women WG in West Berlin in 1978, Wiebke S. recalled, "Naturally there were conflicts," often exceedingly painful ones, even if not usually over politics, nor over the fact that there were "singles and lesbians and heteros" living together. Rather, they were "more about order. . . . More about . . . soap, that was somehow lying wrong."[44] Of course, we may certainly ask, even if Wiebke didn't explicitly acknowledge it as part of the issue, what it meant that soap was lying "wrong." By the early 1980s, Andreas, of the Bahnhof Street WG in Bonn, expressed his annoyance at the "clichés" implied in his interviewer's query regarding the roles of "men" and "women" in WGs. He was not some "average" man, and did not care to be pigeonholed as such.[45] His own concern for the WG indeed was to see more "care" work in a broad sense: that all members take the WG itself seriously as a collective commitment, at the formal biweekly meeting and dinner, through the emotional as well as physical work of the WG, and through the development of relations with the others in the house.[46] This was about the development of the individual as a member of a community. He saw himself as such as a guardian of—as putting in the care work for—this tiny community.

Living together with women who were not blood relations was for the teenaged Hubert no prospect of contention in 1969, but rather an especial attraction of the WG. "Most interesting of all for me," Hubert recalled, "was girls. Yes, I really said that. Yes. That was very, that was important." These practices could bring about enormous change, despite, indeed arguably because of, their rootedness in attention to needs and desires. Hubert's first great love was with a WG housemate, "a university student, I was very proud of it, because she was simply much older than me, and so on." WGs provided and normalized the space he had sought while living in his parents' home to "try out" sex and couples relationships more broadly. Such partners often reflected WGs' trademark diversity. Eighteen-year-old Tulla R. found her own first "serious relationship" with a member of her WG in working-class West Berlin: a laborer and autodidact whose different political thinking was for her a source of constant stimulation.[47]

At the same time, the contemporary notion that communes and WGs were sites of "promiscuous" sex and group orgies were almost entirely the fantasies of fear (and otherwise) of those outside the broad movement. This applied even to the original "Horror Kommune," as Kommune I cofounder Dagmar Seehuber Przytulla noted drily.[48] This "'sexual liberation' was supposed to be 'a big rumor,'" one that Dieter Kunzelmann pushed members themselves to promote, precisely in order to challenge mainstream mores and provoke attention. Rainer Langhans remembered Kunzelmann demanding that he be allowed to sleep with Langhans's girlfriend. But in that early period of these processes, in the late 1960s, Przytulla observed that, in regard to sexuality at least, Kommune members all fundamentally wound up imitating their parents—despite the "psycho-terror sessions" they undertook together.[49] Members of Kommune 2 emphasized at the time that, despite exploitative media trolling for prurient stories, their own "attempts to revolutionize the bourgeois individual" had little to do with what they themselves deemed "petit-bourgeois utopias of group sex."[50]

Yet WGs did raise critical questions concerning conventional couples relationships and practices. Tulla loved her housemate qua boyfriend. Soon, however, their relationship pushed both partners to leave for other WGs. WGs first developed in part as a means to leave home without the pressure of developing one's own "narrow couples relationship" and then marrying.[51] In situations where couples did live together in WGs, all members virtually always had their own, individual bedroom/living space. Even so, Martin of the Bahnhof Street WG found it a problem, "when some couple only speaks in terms of 'we,' and the individual person seems to totally disappear." It was "very significant" how, in a WG he knew of that included a couple, when one member of the pair was out of town, the other claimed to be "'totally alone here'! Although he was still one among four."[52] In the event, couples relationships were discouraged in many WGs altogether. Karl W. quipped that there was an "incest taboo" in many WGs: none of the members could live in the same WG as their sexual partners. Such relations were often "deadly for the general climate."[53] When Karl's two housemates in one WG became romantically involved, "they created a common front against me," leaving relations a far cry from "equitable." WG residents often found living apart from their romantic interest better for them. Residing in separate WGs "helped the relation" with Karl's own partner: "The conflicts that normally arise in *Wohngemeinschaften*, or between men and women—why is the couch so dirty? or why haven't you washed the dishes yet?—because these conflicts existed within the WG, and they didn't necessarily exist within the relationship, [that] was very good for the relationship . . . of the couple, as well as bonds within the WG." This typical WG practice was more challenging to prevailing mores than Karl's facetious characterization might suggest. When feminist literary critic Eve Sedgwick wrote in the late 1980s about her experience living in an intimate and caring relationship with someone not her sexual partner, who lived elsewhere, it was considered a breakthrough in queer sexuality and life practices.[54] Such experiments were a mainstay of West German WG life by the 1970s. WGs challenged the nature of one's most intimate relations in many ways, not only dividing up these ties conventionally focused on a single other person, in a single cohabited space, but also "downgrading" the importance of the couple's relationship altogether. Members of Martin's WG agreed that it was important to be able to "come home" to talk about one's relationship—and everything else—with "many discussion partners." This could be good for romantic relationships themselves. But in many ways WG relations actually supplanted the latter. The WG was always Karin's first "emotional back-up. When something is going on," bad or good, "I always think first about the WG" to discuss, to find support, to celebrate. This was "very different" from "couples relationships." The latter often constituted a low priority among commitments for WG residents. Karin had no interest in marriage—or children—because of the "ten to fifteen years" of her life she had already spent caring for her younger siblings.[55] Even before moving into the Bahnhof WG, Karin had elected to sacrifice romantic relationships at various points, for example, in pursuit of the chance to live abroad for a period, although "everybody said, you're crazy, you can't do that to your boyfriend."

Moving to Bordeaux in 1979 "was the first thing I had really ever done just for myself." That set the example she followed into the future. Housemate Andreas was mildly resentful that his own girlfriend's work schedule was too inflexible for them to be able to spend much time together. But regarding time they both spent on and in their respective WGs, this latter seemed to take incontestable precedence.[56] He felt no need to develop any special bond with his busy girlfriend's child; she in turn seemed to depend on her WG and other adults to help her with parenting. Andreas's parents assumed the WG was just a "transitional phase" for him. Critically, "change" was the presumed norm in this politics of everyday life. Yet, of all possible futures, Andreas did not envision necessarily settling into a nuclear family at any point.

This experimentation, more and less explicit, in moving away from the heterosexual couple, the sexual couple, or the couple altogether as the core of the social and societal unit, drew on the same sources as the "sexual revolution," paradoxical as it may sound in the interest of "revolutionary" change. "Neurotic" SDS member and founding member of Kommune I Rainer Langhans proclaimed, along with many contemporary social scientists, that West Germans had a "sex hang-up," an "intercourse hang-up."[57] He saw the Kommune as responding to these "energies they held onto, that could not flow with life." He observed this among fellow activists. "We saw there how repressed they all were. . . . And then we said indeed, we don't want to live that way." So, Kommunards determined, "we'll go after all these hang-ups, so that life can be freer. That was our revolution that we wanted. The revolution of the everyday, [of] this whole hang-up." Langhans described his own relationship with Kommune cofounder Dieter Kunzelmann: "We were a fantastic 'married couple' [*Ehepaar*], a fantastic couple, which complemented itself in every respect, and was unbelievably effective." Langhans did not thereby reveal unknown sexual predilections or relations, or any kind of "exclusive" couple relations at all. Rather, he was thereby following contemporary transformations in disaggregating the relation between sexuality, eroticism, intimacy, and the single partner, exploding the package of conventional associations. He also offered insight into the very erotics of the WG, again, entirely aside from physical sexual acts. Langhans continued that it was the dominant boulevard newspaper *BILD* that turned such discussions "into the scandalous phrase 'whoever screws the same person twice belongs to the Establishment.'"

Initially, SDS members and other activists outside the Kommune were furious with this representation, which seemed to delegitimize their "politics," just as Klaus Hartung had feared. But, Kommunards responded, "'no, this is politics.'"[58] It was economics, too, Langhans averred, deeper than those of an imagined proletarian revolution. A transformation of the relations of production would only be "curing the symptoms," Langhans argued. It was rather the challenge to the foundational couples relationship that was the still deeper "revolutionary" act, Kommunards argued in the late 1960s. It was this that Klaus Hartung himself came to appreciate.

With the proliferation of WGs throughout the 1970s, WG members often lived apart from lovers. It was as such that such lovers contributed in fact to the connective tissue among WGs: they joined the "team" of "friends of the WG [*Hausfreunde-Riege*]."[59] Lovers and friends, political workmates from the range of settings, activities, and groupings, all helped join personal and political sites together explicitly in a way often unrecognized in the institutional organization of earlier times. It was through this means that all the WGs in Hannover were "networked," as Norbert T. described: drawn together via a dense web of relations that permitted steady contact and communications.[60] The regular change in housemates, and dissolution and reconstitution of WGs, only contributed to this phenomenon. Tulla recalled how, socially as otherwise, "one visited from one WG to the next. There were these famous parties, with cheap wine and noodle salad. Between WG and WG. Saturdays were always these big parties, where one stood around and talked." On principle, WGs tended to follow an "open-door" policy: those identifying generally with the broad movement were welcomed, for a meal and a discussion, for a short or even often a longer stay.[61] It was for such reasons that WGs often designated a room for guests who might visit, despite interest in keeping costs down. High schoolers such as Hubert, and Norbert, popped in after school, or for evening political meetings, and to expose themselves to "living differently" (although at the time Norbert was little tempted to join a WG full-time; this was yet another way of being part of this "scene" and the changes it engendered). Runaway youth spent days or weeks in a WG. This attitude challenged fixity, it kept things in flux, and, at the same time, it further developed connections among people and groupings. Everyone was in a sense "related"; despite constantly changing living circumstances, everyone who opted in to the broad community was "findable." This constituted yet another politico-cultural transformation, in the structures of modern political organization, along with political identities.

More than this: in these self-made living communities, these activists' embrace of difference, characteristic from the earliest days of the movement, played a prominent role.[62] In Tübingen, just as Tulla had described in West Berlin, Kerstin D.'s WG and women's center was "also an open house. Everyone could come. We had parties. . . . We could invite everybody, everyone could bring someone. One was really generous, everyone was invited to eat, and we always had something to drink, and so on."[63] But it was more than just a chance to come together, to "network," and to demonstrate that one was not "petit bourgeois." The experience allowed everyone to "grow" through their encounters. Hubert recalled his own excitement in his first WG, when political artists and literary figures came to visit, still more of a type he had never before encountered. "So there was always something happening, if you will, and indeed in spheres that I never even knew from home. That was the most important for me." Visitors frequently came too from abroad, in this way also generating ever broader and more diverse political networks and political ideas.[64] Hubert remembered:

> Then comrades from Spain came and then they were looking for a safe place to stay. Till one was practically at blows during discussion every evening, and I noted, I noted what kind of extraordinary perspectives were there in part. Because they had absolutely no understanding for this cultural departure, so it, so they were in the end very conservative in their personal attitudes. And for us that all seemed somehow rather confusing. Both in the, in relationships as well as in love relationships, then also the possibilities of, concerning readings, and also among political options.

We cannot judge the limits of "cultural departure" for the Spanish visitors. Radical cultural and political change was hardly limited to West Germany. But what is clear is that, as Hubert perceived it, he and those in his own community had undergone a radical shift in culture. In this way, the confrontation with difference played yet another role, opening Hubert up to a recognition of this transformation.

It was such visits that simultaneously consolidated the sense of a very broad movement linked under an expansive notion of a political Left and also that of what drew one most closely into concentric circles around oneself. These "comrades from Spain" "belonged," and yet their own views on "personal politics" rendered in relief the landscape these activists in West Germany created for themselves.[65] This was the case too among the many visitors who also came from outside Europe altogether, such as those from Latin America, who helped delineate differences—and also commonalities, in contrast with perceptions imagined by many West Germans, often expressed in terms of an undifferentiated continent of "backward" peasants.[66] Arguably a critical aspect of the broad "'68" movement in many if not all its geographic manifestations was a serious, personal engagement with those from elsewhere, at different levels. Many ethnic German activists in the movement were initially inspired by hanging out casually with foreigners (predominantly but not exclusively foreign students) whose concentrated, collective housing in dorms and even "villages" of non-Germans in turn gave Germans ideas about sites of living and acting politically.[67] Close work in West Berlin between renowned transplanted activists East German Rudi Dutschke and Chilean Gaston Salvatore represented only one among millions of points of transnational and transcontinental contact in the broader movement. But it offers an intriguing case in point, when in 1967 Salvatore responded to Dutschke's pleas to immediately translate Che Guevara's "Message to the Tricontinental" (famously concerning "Two, Three Vietnams," producing armed anti-imperialist resistance across Latin America, Africa, and Asia). The middle-class Salvatore recalled humorously his own confrontation with Dutschke's outwardly quite conventional living space, an apartment he shared with his new wife, American activist Gretchen Dutschke-Klotz. Inside, "unwashed dishes have piled up in the sink. Bits of food are stuck to them and are starting to turn green. The plates stink. I start to wash up," until Dutschke returned to the room with an ancient typewriter, urging Gaston to begin translating.[68] Dutschke and his wife may have already by that time transcended "bourgeois" concerns for cleanliness, but the scene was evidently a fillip to some kind of thought on Salvatore's own part.

On the whole, WGs were central sites of political and other forms of heterogeneity, across the range of the broad movement. The differences of political perspective made WG life "exciting," if also frequently frustrating.[69] Well-known figure in the "Paris May" Daniel Cohn-Bendit, arriving in Frankfurt after expulsion from France in 1968, quickly fell "in love" with "the [West] German movement" because of this yeasty admixture, in contrast with what he described as increasingly politically stratified French popular politics.[70] He thrived in the broad "political other" that developed out of an endless "multitude of subgroups" working in such proximity, which permitted him in turn to "define his [own] everyday life differently." Karl W. recalled an exemplary case: one of his WGs was "really great in atmosphere, even if there were many of these massive 'fractional' differences. There were people who were KPD, others who were in the Spartacus group"—that is, Maoists and those who adhered more closely to the GDR, normally considered the fiercest enemies. In that WG, they shared only a common political foe in the fiercely antiauthoritarian *Spontis*—which is how Karl himself identified, he recalled, laughing.[71] At home, these individuals talked, argued, and shared ideas with each other endlessly; Karl stayed in the apartment a full two years. Conversely, Hubert humorously described problems in an all-*Sponti* WG he moved into. "Group time" was always a chance affair in the WG: "Everyone was glad to see one another, when everyone was there. But it was precisely so anti-authoritarian that absolutely no group pressure developed." This made it difficult to plan for collective activities. Naturally, this was in itself a highly relevant topic of discussion: the relation of group pressure and other constraints on individual "freedom" to political efficacy, and the relation of WGs as a unit of political thinking and learning to action in or out of the group.

Karl's two years in his one WG was a long stretch in any single communal home—even if other house members had changed around him. The frequent adding or subtracting of a house member, the entire dissolution of a WG, was a part of movement life. Indeed, a defining characteristic of WGs was specifically their kaleidoscopic character, over time and also at a single moment, as a new perspective, an additional person, or ongoing discussions among members turned WGs around. This was a frequently painful aspect of the experience, but it was consistent with activists' initial approach to WGs: embracing difference, rather than seeking out the comfort of the familiar. The paradoxical comfort of impermanency in this most intimate of settings offered its own lessons, not least in terms of prefigurative politics more broadly. Each WG was an exciting new experiment to be carefully examined and cared for—until it was no longer workable. This changeability was one of the very ways in which alternative culture was to prefigure mainstream change.

This dynamism itself was transformative. This was an impetus to try out new living forms such as WGs in the first place. The very experience of living in WGs, which took away the crisis feel of near-constant change in the most intimate spheres, exponentially reinforced the sense that change was not only the norm, but something to seek at every level. Karin of Bahnhof Street noted, "I have no fixed picture of myself, of what I want to do. In my utopias," the plural emphasizing the very changing nature of her political vision, "I always swing between one way of life, like the one here, and something completely different." In turn, Karin's use of "utopias" alerts us to the most significant political lesson of the experiment with WGs. The plural, personalized, even ironic form bespeaks the challenge of WG experiences to dogmatism and to totalizing political visions altogether. It wasn't just that Karin had not yet found her perfect way of life, that Hubert had not yet identified the right WG, that Tulla still sought the correct political theory. It was whether there was any such thing, any "end of history." We have noted that contemporaries' experience, their disappointment, and their concomitant rethinking returned them to the belief that there was no "master plan," no necessary path forward, no "forward" in any grand sense. But if there was no "scientific socialism," neither should activists count on producing a "utopian socialism," in the sense of a timeless, hermetic living experiment. In a seminal collection of experiment reports concerning the "emancipation of everyday life," Frank Böckelmann wrote already in 1970 that "counter-models of living together and fulfilling needs . . . are no prognoses. . . . They don't purport that their realization is imperative and inevitable [*unumgänglich*], and they don't incorporate all the developing tendencies. They are to be provocations to think, and to recognize the paralyzing gravitational force of the status quo as arbitrary. They don't mean to distract, but rather to make one unsatisfied."[72]

In this extraordinary provocation, Böckelmann thus warned against putting too much faith in any single effort—and against seeking an "ultimate" transformation, an idea that was highly constraining instead of liberating. There was and would be no single right way that had simply eluded activists to date: it was about a new way of understanding—and acting on—change. Following the examples of Böckelmann, Kommune 2, and others, participants in WGs and other "life experiments" across West Germany took on the mantle of turning their experiences into demonstration projects, so that those across the broader movement could learn from the findings of one another. The answer was in the continual blossoming of the variety of experiments, simultaneous and serial, drawing on the last, but only as useful, through continued recounting and sharing of efforts. Contrary to seeking an end point, one should expect to always question, learn from others, and then still push for something that seems better. This arguably formed part of a radical epistemological change, a broad, on-site corollary to and expansion of some of the contemporary work and that was soon to come concerning postmodern understandings. *This* was a cultural revolution: a deep and lasting change that was a process of a convergence of widespread experience and attendant thought.[73] But it was very much also political—even if it did not and precisely in that it did not lead to some definitive end change. New strategies of pursuing change constituted new ways of understanding how change takes place—and arguably challenging the terms of modern politics altogether, versus, for example, notions of big change as reflected fundamentally by violent overthrow, or through adherence to binaries such as revolution and reform. It reflected a sense that individuals and groups were always actively making and remaking their societies, in fundamental ways.

Alternative living experiments played an increasingly significant political role throughout the 1970s, not exclusively but especially in West Germany: they were a powerful enactment precisely of the ever-greater challenge to more formalized political organization. They were also exemplary of the broader movement's character: comprising a self-identified "Left" in the widest sense; constituting "politics" too with the blurriest of borders. But what was the result of such work, not least in terms of formal political and economic structures? This intense work did not "ultimately" displace the role of hegemonic politics, though it contributed to bringing what were at least temporarily new kinds of party politics to the fore, in a form straddling parliamentary and movement activism.[74] The limits of change at these levels continues to serve as a source of disappointment for erstwhile activists. Yet I want to argue still for the truly radical forms of rethinking that emerged from experiments such as WGs that came especially in the wake of "'68." "Revolutionary" aspects of this thought—indeed, including the understanding of "revolution" within the modernist political model emerging from the French Revolution—continue to influence and reshape thought. Arguably the remarkable recent transformation of views of gender identity as essential and fixed is one notable result of the kind of work of rethinking that took place behind the doors of WGs and elsewhere. Yet there are also limits to how willing individuals have been to actively pursue such experimentation, such willingness to change. Joschka Fischer claimed in my 2007 interview with him that his self-transformation within the WG was "successful in the end." Klaus Hartung claimed in 1989 that "the shock waves could be felt still." But how much are they still now? Is there willingness—and ability—still to put in the enormous time and energy such experiments took, as part of political activism altogether? One lesson of these early activists was that "success" was always qualified, always limited. Change might be faster or slower at times; its radicality was often a discrete characteristic. But, activists at the time came to understand, the work toward change was never done—for good or ill. Their lessons might continue to serve us today.

NOTES

1. On the meanings of "revolution" to contemporary activists themselves, as it related to "politics," "culture," and otherwise, see Belinda Davis, *The Inner Life of Politics: Extraparliamentary Activism in West Germany, 1962–1983* (Cambridge: Cambridge University Press, forthcoming). Concerning specifically contemporary cultural revolution, see, e.g., Arthur Marwick, *The Sixties: Cultural Revolution in Britain, France, Italy and the United States, c.1958–c.1974* (Oxford: Oxford University Press, 1999); and Todd Gitlin, *The Sixties: Years of Hope, Days of Rage* (New York: Bantam, 1993), which specifically contrasts cultural and political revolution. See also A. James McAdams, *Vanguard of the Revolution: The Global Idea of the Communist Party* (Princeton, NJ: Princeton University Press, 2017). West Berlin was not part of the Federal Republic of Germany, but, in this piece, "West Germany" includes West Berlin, unless otherwise noted.

2. See Belinda Davis, "Jenseits von Terror und Rückzug: Die Suche nach politischem Raum und Verhandlungsstrategien in der BRD der 70er Jahre," in *Terrorismus in der Bundesrepublik: Medien, Staat und Subkulturen in den 1970er Jahren*, ed. H.-G. Haupt et al. (Frankfurt am Main: Campus, 2006), 154–86. On European–Latin American relations in this period, see, e.g., Massimo De Giuseppe's chapter 3 in this volume; also Quinn Slobodian, *Foreign Front: Third World Politics in Sixties West Germany* (Durham, NC: Duke University Press, 2012); cf. Jennifer Hosek, *Sun, Sex and Socialism: Cuba in the German Imaginary* (Toronto: University of Toronto Press, 2012).

3. On nonkin cohabitation in direct postwar Germany, see, e.g., Anonyma, *A Woman in Berlin* (New York: Picador, 2006); and the film *Germany, Year Zero*, dir. R. Rossellini (1948).

4. These experiments were highly variable, to be sure, even within West Germany, and certainly beyond. The United States particularly was also a site of such "intentional communities"; see, e.g., Timothy Miller, *The 60s Communes: Hippies and Beyond* (Syracuse, NY: Syracuse University Press, 1999); also Donald Pitzer, ed., *America's Communal Utopias* (Chapel Hill: University of North Carolina Press, 1997). For more recent examples of more and less similar experiments, see, e.g., George Ciccariello-Maher, *Building the Commune: Radical Democracy in Venezuela* (London: Verso, 2016). Naturally utopian communities and "communes" first emerged in the early nineteenth century. Thanks to Valeria Manzano for her observation that the more limited exercise of communal living in Argentina, for example, maintained a "highly romanticized view of love and heterosexual partnership" (email exchange with the author, August 28, 2018). See also on alternative cultures in Czechoslovakia in Timothy Ryback's chapter 8 in this volume.

5. See Herrad Schenk, *Wir leben zusammen nicht allein: Wohngemeinschaften heute* (Köln: Kiepenheuer und Witsch, 1984); also Sven Reichardt, *Authentizität und Gemeinschaft: Linksalternatives Leben in den siebziger und frühen achtziger Jahren* (Berlin: Suhrkamp, 2014). University students are most closely associated with the form in these years, but they were hardly the only population, and indeed those who were not yet and no longer students were certainly well represented—among others. See Davis, *Inner Life of Politics*.

6. Reichardt, *Authentizität und Gemeinschaft*.

7. See Vania Markarian's chapter 9 in this volume on the perceived need to broaden strategies and tactics beyond street demos, for example.

8. See Wolfgang Kraushaar, *Autonomie oder Getto?* (Frankfurt: Verlag Neue Kritik, 1978).

9. On ambivalent relations with authorities and public monies (*Staatsknete*), see, e.g., Sabine Jauer, "Autonome Frauenhäuser: Weiter ohne Staatsknete," *Die wöchentliche Courage* 9, no. 16 (1984): 5; Robert Stephens, *Germans on Drugs: The Complications of Modernization in Hamburg* (Ann Arbor: University of Michigan Press, 2007).

10. Interview with author, Hubert R., July 7, 2004. I am drawing on fifty-five oral histories I completed for Davis, *Inner Life of Politics*. Per the request of many I interviewed, I have given the lesser-known activists pseudonyms, such as Hubert R.

11. This youth center, one of the first in West Germany, which organized everything from auto and motorbike repair training, film screenings, personal

counseling, to explicitly political activities, is covered further in Davis, *Inner Life of Politics*; see also Heiko Geiling, *Das andere Hannover: Jugendkultur zwischen Rebellion und Integration in der Grossstadt* (Hannover: Offizin, 1996).

12. This reversion to the present tense was an interesting commonplace of many of my oral histories.

13. Compare Richard Birkefeld, et al., *"Mit 17 . . .": Jugendliche in Hannover 1900 bis heute* (Hannover: Historisches Museum, 1997), 113–14; also Willi Bucher et al., *Schock and Schöpfung: Jugendästhetik im 20. Jahrhundert* (Darmstadt: Luchterhand, 1986).

14. See Renate Köcher, "Lebensverhältnisse 1951–2001: Ein Rückblick mit Daten des Allensbacher Archivs," in *Fünfzig Jahre nach Weinheim: Empirische Markt- und Sozialforschung gestern, heute, morgen*, ed. Heins Sahner (Baden-Baden: Nomos Verlagsgesellschaft, 2002), 59–73, 62. In 1951, more West Germans believed indeed that a stranger was more likely to help them out than authorities, their doctor, or their preacher.

15. Kommune 2, *Versuch der Revolutionierung des bürgerlichen Individuums: Kollektives Leben mit politischer Arbeit verbinden* (Berlin: Oberbaumverlag, 1969), 17–18. From around the mid-1960s, young activists began looking to the work of political theorists such as Herbert Marcuse and psychologists such as Alexander Mitscherlich and Peter Brückner to understand themselves and their elders.

16. See Kommune 2, *Versuch*, 8; also Helmut Kentler, in *Pardon* 5 (May 1969): 43; cf. outside West Germany too, Gil Scott-Heron, "Home Is Where the Hatred Is," *Pieces of a Man* (1971), LP Flying Dutchman Records, on what "the revolution will not" be or do.

17. Schenk, *Wir leben zusammen nicht allein*, 17.

18. Interview with author, Susanne T.

19. Kommune 2, *Versuch*.

20. Schenk, *Wir leben zusammen nicht allein*, 10.

21. Klaus Hartung, "Küchenarbeit," in *CheShahShit*, ed. E. Siepmann et al. (Berlin: Elefanten, 1989), 103.

22. Ibid. Hartung seems to refer to the apocryphal story that Kommune 1 cofounder Dieter Kunzelmann had claimed that he *couldn't* worry about Vietnam when he was having trouble with his orgasm. Kunzelmann embraced the attribution after the fact, no doubt in order to reinforce its provocative character, but it also emphasizes the role of the personal in these histories and in this larger history.

23. Hartung, "Küchenarbeit."

24. Cited by "William Tell," in Daniel Cohn-Bendit, *Der große Basar* (Munich: Trikont, 1975), 112.

25. Hartung, "Küchenarbeit," 103.

26. Kommune 2, *Versuch*, 8.

27. See on the relation between "revolution" and violence, Eric Zolov's chapter 5 in this volume.

28. Ibid.; see also Valeria Manzano's chapter 7 (including concerning Che Guevara's "new man") and Patrick Barr-Melej's chapter 15 in this volume.

29. Schenk, *Wir leben zusammen nicht allein.*

30. Frank Böckelmann, *Befreiung des Alltags: Modelle eines Zusammenlebens ohne Leistungsdruck, Frustration und Angst* (Munich: Rogner & Bernhard, 1970), frontispiece.

31. Compare Manzano's chapter 7 and Michael Seidman's chapter 12 in this volume.

32. Interview with author, Manfred D., July 13, 2004.

33. Cf. Francesca Polletta, *Freedom Is an Endless Meeting: Democracy in American Social Movements* (Chicago: University of Chicago Press, 2004).

34. Kommune 2, *Versuch*, 23.

35. Cf. Timothy Brown, *West Germany and the Global Sixties: The Anti-Authoritarian Revolt, 1962–1978* (Cambridge: Cambridge University Press, 2015).

36. *Der subjective Faktor*, dir. Helke Sander (1981), based on her (re-) assessment of the early movement. On the concept of the "subjective factor," e.g., in psychology, compare the work of Frankfurt School theorists, including Theodor W. Adorno, *Negative Dialektik* (Frankfurt am Main: Suhrkamp, 1966), 171; also Peter Brückner, "Kritik an der Linken" (Cologne: RLV-Texte, 1972); and Klaus Horn, ed., *Gruppendynamik und der "subjektive Faktor": Repressive Entsublimierung oder politisierende Praxis* (Frankfurt am Main: Suhrkamp, 1972), among others.

37. See, e.g., the entire website devoted to this concept, http://im-sitzen-pinkeln.de/, one small manifestation of changes wrought in the era.

38. Interview with author, Volker T., June 28, 2004.

39. Interview with author, Joschka Fischer, October 26, 2006

40. Interview with author, Robert G., July 15, 2004.

41. Interview with author, Karl W., July 1, 2003.

42. See Kristin Schulz, *Der lange Atem der Provokation: Die Frauenbewegung in der Bundesrepublik und in Frankreich 1968–1976* (Frankfurt: Campus, 2002); also Ursula Nienhaus, "Feministisches Frauenbildungs- und Beratungszentrum, Berlin: Wie die Frauenbewegung zu *Courage* kam. Eine Chronologie," in *Als die Frauenbewegung noch Courage hatte: Die "Berliner Frauenzeitung Courage" und die autonomen Frauenbewegungen der 1970er und 1980er Jahre*, ed. Gisela Notz (Bonn: Friedrich-Ebert-Stiftung 2007), 7–22.

43. Interview with author, Sigrid T., July 28, 2005.

44. Interview with author, Wiebke S., July 18, 2005.

45. Schenk, *Wir leben zusammen nicht allein*, 46. In fact, Andreas saw specifically both of the two female house members as contributing too little, because of their "mainstream" work hours outside of the WG.

46. Ibid., 45.

47. Interview with author, Tulla R., July 19, 2005.

48. Dagmar Przytulla, "Niemand ahnte, dass wir in ziemlich verklemmter Haufen waren," in *Die 68erinnen: Porträt einer rebellischen Frauengeneration*, ed. Ute Kätzel (Berlin: Rowohlt, 2002), 201–18.

49. Przytulla, "Niemand ahnte," 206.

50. Kommune 2, *Versuch*; cf. Dieter Kunzelmann, *Leisten Sie keinen Widerstand* (Berlin: Transit, 1998).

51. Ibid., 10.

52. Ibid., 33.

53. Ibid., 48. Members of the Bahnhof WG agreed through their regular meetings to maintain their "couples" relationships outside the WG community. One of the housemates, Lisa, an ecotrophologist (specialist in nutrition, household management, and economics), had moved to Bahnhof Street in order to salvage her relationship with her boyfriend living in her old WG.

54. Eve Koslowsky Sedgwick, *Epistemology of the Closet* (Berkeley: University of California Press, 2008).

55. On West German "'68ers" as "parentified children" and other aspects of their earlier lives that predisposed them to these experiments, see Davis, *Inner Life of Politics*.

56. Schenk, *Wir Leben zusammen nicht allein*, 44–45.

57. Interview with author, Rainer Langhans, May 24, 2005.

58. Hartung, "Küchenarbeit."

59. Kommune 2, *Versuch*, 33.

60. Interview with author, Norbert T., July 14, 2005. Indeed, administrators at the University of Frankfurt tried to use such networks themselves to find and identify particular activists, even as activists attempted through their communications to shield their broader community from officials' arbitrary dragnets; Universitätsarchiv, Goethe-Universität-Frankfurt 413-05 Studenten-Demonstrationen.

61. Compare, inter alia, the infamous "guest towel" in *Taxi zum Klo*, dir. Frank Ripploh (1981).

62. See, e.g., Belinda Davis, "A Whole World Opening Up: Transcultural Contact, Difference, and the Politicization of 'New Left' Activists," in *Changing the World, Changing Oneself*, ed. Belinda Davis et al. (New York: Berghahn, 2010), 255–73.

63. Interview with Kerstin D., July 10, 2003.

64. Here too Kommune 1 formed a precedent, though hardly the only source. See, e.g., Hamburger Institut für Sozialforschung, File K1-03-03 Korrespondenz, Mäzenin, Spinner usw.

65. Compare also examples in *Unter dem Pflaster ist der Strand* (dir. Helma Sanders-Brahms), 1975.

66. See Slobodian, *Foreign Front*. Germans had robust long-term connections to Latin American countries, stepped up, for better or worse, in the direct aftermath of the war. Compare on these relations and how meaningful they were, Markarian, chapter 9 in this volume; also De Giuseppe's chapter 3 in this volume.

67. Davis, *Inner Life of Politics*.

68. Cited in Slobodian, *Foreign Front*, 75.

69. This embrace of "difference" had its limits, associated particularly with cadres of the East German–oriented German Communist Party (DKP) and the Maoist "K Groups," the Marxist-Leninist parties that sprang up from 1968, as one response to that year's perceived failures.

70. Cohn-Bendit, *Der große Basar*, 103, 105. Cohn-Bendit was born to German-Jewish parents who had fled Nazi Germany to France before the war. He grew up in both France and West Germany.

71. Activists, especially those interested in everyday-life politics, sometimes defined themselves as "Spontis" or "autonomists," often in contrast to others who self-defined as Maoist, or as DKP.

72. Böckelmann, *Befreiung*, frontispiece.

73. Compare here Valeria Manzano, chapter 7 in this volume and also Eric Drott's chapter 4 in this volume.

74. See, e.g., on the Alternative List, the Green List, and the Green Party, Silke Mende, *"Nicht rechts, nicht links, sondern vorn": Eine Geschichte der Gründungsgrünen* (Munich: Oldenbourg Wissenschaftsverlag, 2011); also Belinda Davis, "A Brief Cosmogeny of the Green Party," in "Creating Participatory Democracy: Green Politics in Germany since 1983," special issue of *German Politics and Society* (Winter 2015): 53–65.

PART THREE

Reactions to Change

ELEVEN

Chile 1960s

Intertwined Revolutions in Music and Politics

J. PATRICE McSHERRY

Was there a global cultural revolution in 1968 or in the "Long 1960s"? This chapter analyzes the case of the Chilean New Song movement, a new generation of musicians who, in the 1960s, began creating song that was beautiful, powerful, and socially conscious. The musicians drew from Chilean and Latin American folk roots but introduced multiple innovations and incorporated traditional indigenous instruments and rhythms from across the continent. They transformed, renewed, and modernized traditional folk music to invent new musical forms. At the same time, the musical movement was deeply engaged in mobilizations to structurally transform the entrenched social and political inequalities in the country.

The Chilean New Song movement was born of the popular struggles of the 1960s in Chile for land reform, university reform, control of resources, social inclusion, and deeper democratization. During this period, culture was democratized; masses of people became involved in new forms of popular music, dance, graphic and mural art, literature, and theater.

Artists and musicians were a vibrant and integral component of the social transformations taking place. With the election of democratic socialist Salvador Allende and his coalition Unidad Popular (Popular Unity, UP) in 1970, an intensified period of political and social change ensued. New Song transformed the musical culture of Chile at the same time as a peaceful political revolution swept the country.[1] Thus, Chile is a particularly rich case study of intertwined revolutions in music and politics.

Interest in popular music—music of the people—and similar folk revivals were appearing throughout the Americas, and in the world, in the 1960s, a time of significant global social, political, and economic transformation.[2] In the 1950s and '60s in the United States there was new interest in folk music that drew from the class-conscious songs of Woody Guthrie and other singers such as Pete Seeger, Joan Baez, and the early Bob Dylan. In Argentina, Atahualpa Yupanqui was a pioneer of socially conscious lyrics, and Mercedes Sosa and Armando Tejada Gómez, among others, were popular singers who founded *el Nuevo Cancionero* (the New Songbook) in 1963 with a specific political statement.[3] In Brazil, Chico Buarque created a wealth of socially conscious songs, and in Cuba, Pablo Milanés and Silvio Rodríguez, among others, emerged as central figures in *la Nueva Trova*. In Uruguay, Los Olimareños, Daniel Viglietti, and Alfredo Zitarrosa popularized Uruguayan folk music and wrote their own songs with social commentary. In Mexico, Amparo Ochoa sang stirring songs of the Mexican Revolution and popular ballads.

"New Song was really a continental phenomenon," said Eduardo Carrasco, musician and director of Quilapayún, a legendary New Song group in Chile.[4] "In Brazil, in Argentina, Ecuador, Cuba, later in Nicaragua, there were similar movements everywhere, a new culture of protest music, political music. It was part of a larger cultural movement that included the 'Latin American boom' in literature, Julio Cortázar, Mario Vargas Llosa, Gabriel García Márquez, magical realism, la Casa de las Américas. The movement became global; in fact, we had contacts with musicians in Europe, in the United States, such as Pete Seeger and many others. . . . Our roots were in Latin America as a whole."

In Chile, New Song music was enmeshed with the political activism and ideals of the time, both reflecting and contributing to the deep political and social change that marked the era. The musical movement became a key mobilizing force in politics in the 1960s and early '70s, inspiring, uniting, and motivating people in a common cause. New Song communicated a revolutionary and popular worldview, honoring the excluded and oppressed and the historic ability of masses of people to create social change. Even more important, the music communicated the vision of a different society of equality and social justice, making those dreams seem attainable and possible. Musicians such as Víctor Jara, Ángel and Isabel Parra, Patricio Manns, and groups Quilapayún and Inti-Illimani, to name a few, were a constant presence in demonstrations, marches, concerts large and small, and political acts for the UP.

This chapter briefly analyzes the complex interactions between changes in society and the explosion of creativity in this epoch. To understand the emergence of New Song one must analyze the political and cultural history of Chile, the interface between structural and individual transformations in the 1960s, and the complex interrelationships between global and national shifts and social and personal change. I argue that New Song expressed the aspirations of rising popular classes—workers, peasants, and *pobladores* (shantytown dwellers), students and intellectuals—and a counterhegemonic set of principles and values that challenged the elitist social order in Chile. The country changed dramatically from the decade of the '60s up until 1973, the year of the U.S.-backed military coup,[5] not only in terms of popular mobilization and progressive state policies but also in terms of transformed social relations and a surge of creativity in the arts. These historic changes in Chile's social, political, and cultural realms indeed constituted "a cultural revolution," in my view. New Song was an integral part of the popular movements that coalesced into a strong counterhegemonic force, reshaping the country. It was a time of optimism and joy, of discovery and experimentation, of social mobilization and public involvement, and of significant democratic advances in Chile.

THE EMERGENCE OF CHILEAN NEW SONG

The Chilean New Song movement was born in the midst of the political awakenings and social mobilizations of the '60s. Its roots lay in the folk music of decades past and in new cultural and political influences. New Song drew from popular musical traditions in Chile and Latin America that were passed down through the generations, and was shaped by the dramatic political events of the day. The young musicians created new departures and invented new musical, instrumental, and poetic forms. New Song revolutionized the musical culture of Chile and gradually became known worldwide. The origins of the New Song movement lay in the passion for the music among the youth of the '60s generation, their social consciousness and political commitment, and their fascination with discovering the rich heritage of Latin American music. Many of the young musicians were talented composers who produced a wealth of original music and song. Motivated by the spirit of the era, they were independent, socially and politically committed, and militant, and deeply connected to the social and political movements, fifty years in the making, which demanded political inclusion and social justice in Chile in the 1960s.

Jorge Coulon, a founder of Inti-Illimani, put it this way:

> The political and cultural environment of the 1960s was the result of a half century of democratizing struggles, which, over time, created and enlarged a cultural base that sustained, and explains, the appearance, among others, of the phenomenon of Chilean New Song. The 60s were the result of a process of growing cultural interaction [*coherencia cultural*] during fifty years. . . . Creative people and artists are part of, and a result of, social and cultural impulses. . . . The greatness of Chile in the 20th century was the encounter between organized workers and students, artists, and intellectuals. . . . That interaction gave us Chileans with the stature of Violeta Parra, Pablo Neruda, Gabriela Mistral.[6]

In Latin America, the role of the Chilean New Song musicians was particularly important and powerful because they were organically linked to political parties of the Left and popular movements deeply involved in these sociopolitical transformations. Many joined parties of the Left, especially the youth organization of the Partido Comunista Chileno (Communist Party of Chile, PC), known as Juventudes Comunistas, or La Jota (Young Communists). Chile's political system had, for various decades of the twentieth century, been relatively open to parties across the political spectrum, including Marxist parties. The PC—considered a threat by Washington during the Cold War years—had a long history of participation in electoral politics (even though it was proscribed several times by conservative governments) and had deep roots in the unionized working class and the cultural life of the country.[7] The PC was one of the oldest and largest communist parties in Latin America and had played an important role in unionization drives in the 1930s and '40s and, along with the Partido Socialista (Socialist Party), had pushed for progressive social policies during the Frente Popular (Popular Front) period from 1936 to 1941.

The PC supported the emergence of New Song with infrastructure and contacts at both national and international levels. But it is important to state that the movement came "from below," arising naturally and spontaneously from multiple cultural and artistic influences and popular roots. The New Song movement was not organized in any top-down way, nor was it led or directed by any one entity or political party, although the PC and La Jota provided important opportunities for the movement. I use the term "movement" to capture the sense of a decentralized mobilization of artists, without formal leadership or headquarters, but loosely united in a recognizable and common cultural effort and political cause. "There was a very deep cultural change," said Horacio Durán of Inti-Illimani Histórico, "and it never was an organized movement, not at all: it was an artistic movement, undefined politically, without an organization. New Song was a very spontaneous movement. It developed like those great rivers that begin with small streams and tributaries and become a powerful flow."[8]

How can New Song be defined? The musicians sang of the invisibilized workers and peasants of the region, *el pueblo*: their struggles and hopes, their trials and tragedies, their aspirations for social justice and change. In this sense the music expanded and resignified Chilean identity, which had been narrowly defined before.[9] The young musicians also rejected the influx of U.S. rock and pop music, which they saw as obliterating the music of Latin America. They sought to find their roots in authentic Latin American song, newly rediscovered instruments, and forgotten musical traditions. Two older singer-songwriters, the Argentine Atahualpa Yupanqui and the Chilean Violeta Parra,[10] pioneers of socially conscious songs that decried injustice, were especially influential for the young New Song musicians. New Song introduced new and exciting forms of music, using ancient instruments from across the region and adding modern touches, such as dissonant notes, new chord progressions, and innovative harmonies. The music honored the hardships of the excluded and popularized revolutionary ideas, and, most importantly, articulated the possibility of a different, socially just future. Víctor Jara, a legendary figure of the movement who authored many unforgettable songs and who was a PC militant, explained New Song this way:[11]

> What is New Song [*la Nueva Canción*]? A record by Violeta Parra appeared with songs where she speaks of the truth: the authentic, the real, of Chile. This made a huge impact in Chile. Forty years of her existence were spent collecting traditional music, singing songs of the people from all over Chile, passed down through generations. And a group of us, composers, felt this was the path we wanted to take, that we had to take in our country. We thought, enough of foreign music, of music that doesn't help us to live, that tells us nothing. . . . And we began to create these types of songs. Just in the moment when the workers in Chile began to unite, in what would become the *Unidad Popular* [UP]. . . . It was song that was born from the necessities of the country, the social movement of Chile. It wasn't song apart from that. Violeta marked the path and we have followed. Now New Song is essentially the language of the people, of the youth.

"You had to compose songs, write lyrics with political consciousness, this defined New Song," said singer-songwriter Ángel Parra, son of groundbreaking folk singer and composer Violeta Parra and a giant of the movement himself.[12] "It was the political situation that stimulated us to write songs, what was happening every day in those years, the situation itself nurtured our songs. . . . We were like reporters, some more like 'pamphleteers,' some more poetic, some more idealistic, but we were all reporters of a social reality. . . . We realized the dream of Simón Bolívar with our music: we sang Chilean music with instruments from many Latin American countries." The young musicians were also influenced by Pablo Neruda, the well-known Chilean poet and communist, especially his epic poem *Canto General*, by contemporary Argentine groups such as Los Trovadores and Los Fronterizos, and by the long Chilean tradition on the Left of blending political acts with cultural performances.[13]

Musicians such as Víctor Jara, Patricio Manns, Ángel Parra, Isabel Parra, Rolando Alarcón, Gitano Rodríguez, Quilapayún, Inti-Illimani, and Amerindios, among many others, became well-known and beloved figures of the new movement. Their striking appearance—many wore ponchos and projected a serious and committed presence—and their original songs captivated students, workers, and intellectuals in Santiago, and the movement quickly spread to other cities and towns in Chile. The new music demonstrated that evocative art/poetry and profound political/social content were not mutually exclusive.

THE CONSOLIDATION OF THE NEW SONG MOVEMENT

A key step in the development of New Song occurred when the children of Violeta Parra, Ángel and Isabel, returned from Paris in 1964 with songs written by Violeta for the Allende campaign.[14] The Parras also brought back from Paris new instruments from other Latin American countries—Paris was a magnet for various musicians in this period—that were completely unknown to urban Chileans: the Venezuelan *cuatro*, the Bolivian *charango*, the *quena* of Bolivia and Peru, and the Andean panpipes, known as *siku*, descended from the Inca empire. This music, later known as "Andean music," was a key component of New Song. The songs composed by Violeta Parra and brought back to Chile by her children included "Qué vivan los estudiantes" ("Long Live the Students," extolling the political leadership of the students), "Arauco tiene una pena" ("The Sorrow of Arauco [indigenous Mapuche territory]"), "La carta" ("The Letter," about the arrest of Violeta's brother and the injustice in Chile), and "Arriba quemando el sol" ("Above the Sun Is Burning," a lament about the women struggling to survive in the nitrate region of the Chilean north), among others. The PC considered the songs too political to use, but Ángel recorded them later that year. He noted that his mother's songs became "the basis for Chilean New Song."[15] Ángel Parra threw himself into Allende's campaign, as did other artists, such as his sister Isabel and Rolando Alarcón, who became an early New Song soloist. After the 1964 election, which Allende lost to Christian Democrat Eduardo Frei, Ángel and Isabel decided to open their house in central Santiago as a *peña*—a musical salon and popular gathering place—for progressive young people who were interested in the new currents of political music. Thus La Peña de los Parra was born in 1965. La Peña featured the new, socially conscious song that reflected the changing tides in Chile and the world. A stable group of musicians administered the *peña* and played their music there every weekend: Ángel and Isabel Parra,

Rolando Alarcon, Patricio Manns, and soon Víctor Jara. La Peña became the epicenter of New Song, and soon new *peñas* sprang up in universities, municipalities, union halls, factories, and other popular centers throughout Chile, organized by the musicians themselves along with students, workers, *campesinos*, and others. The Parras invited to La Peña other emerging groups and soloists who played Andean music and original songs with political messages. Some of the emblematic albums and songs of the 1960s that gave birth to the New Song movement included Patricio Manns's album *El Sueño Americano* (*The American Dream*), composed in 1965, and Ángel Parra's *Oratorio para el Pueblo* (*Oratory for the People*), also 1965. Both of these LPs had complete, unified sets of songs that told an epic story and communicated profound political and social content.

Manns's album related the history of the Americas, from the indigenous empires to Spanish colonization, slavery, independence, and twentieth-century interventions (he wrote the songs after the 1965 U.S. intervention in the Dominican Republic). Parra's album called for justice on earth and fused classical elements with folk music in an innovative departure. Víctor Jara composed many memorable songs also, including "Plegaria a un Labrador" ("Prayer to a Farmworker," 1969), a call for rural workers to unite and realize their strength, and "Preguntas por Puerto Montt" ("Questions about Puerto Montt," 1969), a song that denounced the massacre of landless families by a police riot control team. A song by Inti-Illimani that captured the vision of political change and hope embodied in Allende's 1969–70 campaign was the beloved "hymn" "Venceremos" ("We Will Win"), which became the UP's campaign song:[16]

From the deep forge of the homeland
Arises the popular clamor
The new dawn is already announced
All Chile begins to sing . . .

The epic cantata "Santa María de Iquique" sung by Quilapayún was an ensemble of songs released in 1970, telling the story of the massacre of protesting miners and their families in the north of Chile in 1907.[17] Many, many other songs could be named.

Another key development in the New Song movement occurred when La Jota, along with the musicians, created a new record label to record and distribute New Song, first called JotaJota, and later Discoteca del Cantar Popular (DICAP) (Discothèque of Popular Song). The label began producing records that commercial labels found too political. In a short time, DICAP became a hugely successful venture,[18] playing a decisive role in disseminating New Song music by building a parallel structure to bypass commercial record labels.

New Song was a harbinger of social change and a reflection of new political currents in Chile and in Latin America, a new country being born within the old. The cultural movement deepened people's awareness of belonging to an alternative, popular force and their commitment to the struggle for a new society, instilling a sense of people's power. The music animated, inspired, unified, and motivated masses of people and deepened their political consciousness. Moreover, a crucial factor in Allende's election was the unity of leftist and popular forces, and the New Song movement contributed to and cemented that unity. In Gramscian terms, a strong counterhegemony had arisen that defied existing power relations, and New Song was the music of that movement.

CULTURAL CHANGE IN CHILE: POWERFUL SOCIAL-POLITICAL MOVEMENTS

Before and during the UP government, increasing numbers of people in every social sector selflessly offered their talents and skills to improve living conditions for all and move the country forward. There was an explosion of popular participation linked to a new set of values. A new culture was emerging that was unselfish, dedicated, and committed to structural change in Chile. Young people and students, for example, formed the backbone of the massive "Voluntary Works" (Trabajos Voluntarios) movement. Up to 2 million Chileans participated in voluntary work projects to build housing and roads and dig water ditches in shantytowns, teach illiterate poor people to read and write, and bring cultural works and classes to poor neighborhoods.[19] The New Song musicians participated, singing songs during work breaks and sometimes joining work projects themselves. The Voluntary Works project was not simply the purview of the Left. Masses of people from the Christian Democrat Party and the Catholic Church participated. There was a fresh spirit of self-sacrifice, solidarity, anti-individualism, and a new sort of patriotism that motivated Chileans across the political spectrum.[20]

The university reform movement was another key example of social change in the 1960s and early '70s. This student-led movement emerged in the State Technical University (UTE) in 1961, demanding a voice in the governance of the university. The movement achieved important advances throughout the '60s, illustrating the growing political power of the students. In 1967 the Catholic University in Valparaíso was the site of a new movement for reform. The Federación de Estudiantes de la Universidad Católica (Student Federation of the Catholic University) organized a sit-in of the main administrative building of the university to demand changes in its elitist and authoritarian structures and commitment to the struggles of the poor. The right-wing newspaper *El Mercurio* published articles and editorials that portrayed the student movement as communist-inspired (even though most of the students were Christian Democrats) and falsely depicted acts of violence. The students, outraged, hung a huge sign on a campus building: "Chilean: *El Mercurio* lies!" In Chile, this was a startling act. The university was the most elite and conservative in Chile. The militancy of the students signified the rapid pace of political change taking place in the country.

The activism of the students resulted in the election of a progressive Christian Democrat, Fernando Castillo, as rector in 1967. He was the first rector of the Catholic University not named by religious authorities of the Church.[21] Castillo was instrumental in democratizing the university, opening channels for student input and participation. Like newly elected rector Enrique Kirberg of UTE, who opened that university to new ideas and reforms,[22] Castillo began to listen to, and consult with, professors and students. Under Kirberg, UTE broadened its access to the working classes: between 1968 and 1973, enrollments at UTE increased from about 9,000 to more than 32,000. Branches and institutes of the university grew from nine in 1968 to twenty-four in 1973, extending from the north to the south of Chile. The number of full-time professors increased from 500 in 1968 to 2,551 in 1973. New majors and programs were created, linked to developing the country economically and technically, and the university was opened to workers and their children.[23] By 1968 the reform movement had transformed all the major universities, including Universidad Federico Santa María, Universidad de Chile, and

Universidad de Concepción. Students had become politicized and engaged in the struggle for social change in Chile; they were a significant political actor.

By the 1960s, other movements were equally powerful and politically conscious: the organized workers; *campesinos* (peasants); and the *pobladores* (shantytown dwellers). A range of Chilean unions had banded together in 1953 to create the Central Única de Trabajadores (Unitary Workers' Central, CUT), which became a potent political actor. The organized workers' movement—composed largely of miners, construction and industrial workers—had been a protagonist in Chile since the early part of the twentieth century; it was closely linked to anarchist, communist, and socialist movements historically. Chilean organized workers were class-conscious and militant. The PC assumed a leading role in CUT in 1961 until the coup.[24]

The *campesinos* were a major force in the Agrarian Reform, initiated in a minimal way by conservative president Jorge Alessandri (1958–64), expanded by Frei (1964–70), and deepened by Allende (1970–73).[25] *Campesino* men and women took an active role in challenging the longstanding domination of the oligarchy in the countryside, the sector most hostile to any social change. *Campesinos* fought not only to redistribute land but also to contest the traditional political and social power wielded by the landowners. In the late '60s and especially under Allende they began to organize themselves into Peasant Councils. The *pobladores* were originally internal migrants from the countryside seeking work who settled in Santiago, in overcrowded tenements, urban slums, small rooms with family or friends, or in the squalid shantytowns that sprang up in surrounding urban areas. When political parties, notably the PC, began organizing these new communities, their political consciousness began to change. People began to see their precarious situations not as individual failures but as structural problems that required collective action to solve. The *pobladores* became politically self-aware, militant, and class-conscious, a result especially of the PC's "political heritage of decades of work in the popular culture and in the formation of a skilled generation of grassroots militants."[26] The *pobladores* organized a series of land takeovers beginning in 1957 to demand, and gradually achieve, recognized communities with stable housing, electricity, transportation, and running water.[27]

EXPLAINING THE INTERNATIONAL CONTEXT

A sense of change and possibility was sweeping across the world in the 1960s. Despite the sharp tensions and conflicts of the Cold War, there was a growing sense of popular power. The so-called Third World—former colonies in Asia and Africa and the increasingly anti-imperialist countries in Latin America—sought to free themselves from the political and economic control exercised by European countries and the United States. In 1961, countries in the less-developed world formed the Non-Aligned Movement (NAM), claiming the right to remain neutral in the Cold War/U.S.–Soviet conflict and focus on sovereignty, development, independence, and security.[28] The NAM condemned colonialism, racism, imperialism, and all big-power interference. Anticolonial and liberation struggles had erupted around the globe in the 1950s and continued into the '70s. In Latin America, which had gained independence in the early 1800s, there was growing awareness of the outflow of national resources and the situation of dependency in which many countries found themselves. For example, Chile's main export, copper, was controlled by several big U.S. multinational companies. Mass movements arose in the '60s demanding control of natural resources, deeper democracy, social equality, and political participation.[29] There was a sense that boundaries were falling and new potentials were emerging, and that ordinary people were becoming protagonists and seizing control of their own destinies.

The United States had emerged as a global capitalist power after World War II, opposed by the Soviet Union on the communist/socialist side, creating a bipolar world. Washington began to extend its political, economic, and military power worldwide in the late '40s, and began to intervene both overtly and covertly around the globe to undermine, or overturn, socialist, nationalist, or radical-democratic movements and governments that challenged its perceived interests.[30] The 1950s and 1960s were marked by the Cold War, by the rise of the Third World, by revolutions in Cuba and elsewhere, by the Bay of Pigs and the Cuban missile crisis, and by the Vietnam War, deeply politicizing many Chilean youths. Within the United States there was tumult in the '60s also. The powerful civil rights movement gained influence, John F. Kennedy, Malcolm X, Martin Luther King Jr., and Robert Kennedy were assassinated, and rioting occurred in major U.S. cities. Major demonstrations against the Vietnam War erupted, first led by students, and they gradually became massive. New ideas of freedom and equality for women, people of color, and gay people gained strength.

In 1964, the Brazilian military overthrew fiery progressive president João Goulart and established a repressive dictatorship, one of the first of the era in South America. In the region there were U.S. interventions in Guatemala (1954), Cuba (1961), the Dominican Republic (1965), and covert political interference in Chile (1964) and Brazil (1963–64).[31] The war in Vietnam increasingly outraged many of the generation that came of age in the '60s, including in the United States, who increasingly characterized the U.S. role in the world as imperialist.[32] The aggressive U.S. hostility toward popular movements for social change ignited an increasingly radical mood in Latin America in the 1960s. The rage against big-power domination targeting the poor and the weak was accompanied by a belief that change was possible if people mobilized. The era was characterized by a widespread sense of rebellion against injustice and domination paired with a sense of hope and possibility.

Chile in the 1950s and '60s was undergoing rapid change.[33] The country had functioned as an electoral democracy since the late 1800s, except for several unstable years in the 1920s. The government was elitist but relatively modern, with liberal democratic institutions. There had been advances in education and social welfare during the twentieth century, but these coexisted with extensive poverty, economic underdevelopment, and striking social inequalities. Until 1938 Chile was dominated by parties of the conservative upper and middle classes. In that year's election, a member of the secular and moderate Radical Party, Pedro Aguirre Cerda, representing the antifascist Popular Front, won the presidency. The Popular Front included the Communist and Socialist parties. Chile became the only Latin American country to incorporate Marxist parties in electoral politics, in a multiclass coalition that supported progressive social reforms.[34] After a period of conservative rule in the 1940s and '50s, the Socialist and Communist parties formed a new coalition along with smaller leftist parties: Frente de Acción Popular (Popular Action Front, FRAP). FRAP's candidate for the presidency in 1958 and again in 1964 was Salvador Allende, a medical doctor, Marxist senator of the Socialist Party, and strong supporter of Latin American independence, nationalism, and socialism.[35] He believed that Chile could achieve a nonviolent transition to socialism.

In the presidential campaign of 1964, both Christian Democrat Eduardo Frei and the FRAP supported a social welfare state. But Frei called for reform, not revolution, within the parameters of the Alliance for Progress. He proposed moderate measures, such as the "chilenization" (partial buy-back) of the copper industry from giant U.S. copper companies, while FRAP called for a transition from capitalism to socialism and for completely nationalizing copper. (The Allende government did just that in 1970, with the support of the congress.) Allende lost the 1964 election to Frei, partially as a consequence of covert U.S. funding of Frei's campaign and a major CIA-directed "black propaganda" offensive portraying Allende as an antidemocratic communist. Allende ran for president again in 1970, this time under the banner of an impressively broad coalition of left and center-left parties called the Unidad Popular.[36] Allende's election as president was seen as a triumph for the progressive movement in Chile, of which New Song was a key part, and for the idea of a constitutional path to socialism.

ANALYZING THE NEW SONG MOVEMENT

The New Song musicians were troubadours of the counterhegemonic movements in Chile. In previous work I have drawn from the ideas of Antonio Gramsci, the Italian theorist, to shed light on the ways in which cultural movements can become a counterhegemonic force. Gramsci noted that new cultural movements arose during periods of social and political change. He argued that the working classes needed their own organic intellectuals to challenge the hegemony of the dominant culture, which reflected the interests of the powerful and instilled the message that the status quo was normal, inevitable, and unchangeable. The cultural hegemony of the elites was a crucial pillar of class domination, contended Gramsci, because it limited what masses of people considered possible. In my view, the musicians were "organic intellectuals" in Gramsci's terms: artists with a counterhegemonic perspective from, or allied with, the popular social classes, who articulated their interests, empowered them, and transmitted the possibility of a different future. Gramsci thought that organic intellectuals were charged with demonstrating that the system did not benefit all, despite the dominant ideological paradigm, and that another system was possible. The musicians were organic intellectuals in the sense of translating the hopes and aspirations of millions of Chileans in their songs, denouncing social injustice and repression, and helping to make real the idea that a different society was possible.

New Song music empowered and unified people. The musicians sought to rediscover and express the invisible and suppressed music, values, and culture of majority populations of the region. Their music created consciousness and questioned existing relations of power. The musicians did not explicitly create their music to organize people, but their song helped to attract masses of people to the cause of social change. New Song helped to create, build, sustain, and mobilize communities of activists and militants. In short, major cultural change in Chile was inextricably intertwined with dramatic political change, and the musicians played a key role in convoking and stimulating both.

The musical presentations and concerts of New Song musicians, large and small, were a unique part of the political history of the era. They did not simply reflect or articulate the politics of the time; they helped to *create* the politics of the time, and embody it. John Street has argued that the Woodstock music festival not only reflected the times in the United States; Woodstock created history, it was a seminal political event in itself.[37] He also points out that politics and music are inseparably linked: music "forms and shapes the feelings and passions which animate political action."[38] As the New Song musicians created collective experiences and political unity through their music they became political as well as cultural actors. The music was a catalyst for social change and political action; it expressed new, counterhegemonic norms and values.

The New Song movement also played a role in reshaping social relations. The artists had a deeply democratic view: that all people were creative, that all had the potential to learn and practice music and the arts as means of self-expression and collective creativity. The music was embedded in new, egalitarian social relationships that were emerging in the 1960s. Everyone was seen as equal and valuable, in an altered environment of respect and social equity, a life-changing event for peasants and workers who had been invisible, marginalized, and excluded previously. The artists and musicians saw their social role in a new light. Popular musicians, artists, dancers, and theater groups began to rethink the purpose of their art. Many decided to dedicate their art to advancing the interests of *el pueblo* and representing their voices, to take their art beyond the individual and into the social domain, and most importantly, to engage and motivate people to participate in culture themselves, by learning an instrument, singing, painting, or acting in theater troupes. Artists and musicians saw themselves as intellectuals and activists and infused their art with social content and revolutionary commitment.[39] In the spirit of collective effort, and reflecting the socialist and radical-democratic values of anti-individualism and anti-consumerism, "people's artists" came together to bring their art to the people and create a popular culture that reshaped the identity of the nation. One of Allende's campaign slogans was "There is no revolution without song."

Mario Salazar of Amerindios explained the significance of New Song in the cultural-political transformation of Chile in these years:

> New Song is song that reflects the reality of those from below: those without land, those who work the land. It is a vindication of their right to dream, to the possibility of creating something new. . . . What terrified the Right was that New Song began to create a new common sense, a new reality, when humble workers who used to keep their eyes on the floor began to look at the boss directly, eye to eye, and call him '*compañero*' instead of 'sir'" . . . This change alarmed the oligarchy. It was a cultural change.[40]

Salazar's observations demonstrated that New Song contributed to changing political awareness in the popular consciousness in Gramscian terms, creating a new "common sense" and fostering more egalitarian social relationships. In the context of Chile this was a cultural revolution and a revolution in social relations.

GLOBAL ANALYSIS OF THE EMERGENCE OF NEW SONG

Why did these innovative political and cultural currents appear at this historical moment? In previous work, utilizing a Gramscian perspective, I have argued that as political and social structures in the world shifted, and popular social and political movements gained ascendancy, ordinary people were empowered. Through social and political movements people began to challenge ossified hierarchies and demand recognition and rights.

As ordinary people became active politically they began to express themselves artistically, and new artists arose from the movements. Gramsci noted that the rise of the opera and the novel occurred "with the appearance and expansion of national-popular democratic forces" in Europe in the eighteenth century.[41] Similarly, I argue that the rise of New Song was linked to the surge of popular power and participation in the 1960s.

As these counterhegemonic forces merged and became stronger, both the political and cultural arenas were significantly democratized. With deeper democratization and more freedom, formerly marginalized sectors involved themselves in cultural expression on a level never before seen in Chile. The result was an explosion of "people's culture," beginning in the second half of the 1960s and intensifying during the government of the UP. Through the medium of popular music the artists helped to build a powerful counterhegemonic movement in Chile that succeeded in changing the culture and politics of Chile, if only for a time. The musicians were inspired by, and participated in, the struggles in Chile for the expansion of popular power. They were also deeply connected to the quest of Latin America as a whole for development and social justice, influenced by the anti-imperialist and militant ethos of the 1960s. The movement dramatically changed the musical culture of the country, and played a key role in changing the political culture.

The social, political, and cultural movements of the 1960s in Chile arose during a time of systemic and state-level change, the result of political and technological shifts worldwide. From a historical-structural perspective, human agency interacted with fluctuating structural conditions as people moved to seize new political openings to push political and social demands. The New Song musicians, I have argued, defied the "rationality" of Chile's hegemonic system—as did other political actors such as political parties and social organizations—and large numbers of Chileans began to dream that equality and social justice were attainable. The New Song movement popularized democratic and socialist ideas that began to significantly erode the cultural and political hegemony of Chile's long-standing elites. Moreover, the artists were agents of cultural change who helped to create a new people's culture and a new sense of Chilean—and more broadly, Latin American—identity.

Cultural expression is closely linked to democracy and liberty, and in the 1960s fresh winds of freedom were blowing in Chile. Under the reformist government of Eduardo Frei Montalvo there were more openings for political participation and protest, unlike in nearby countries such as Argentina, Brazil, and Bolivia, where military coups and regimes marked the 1960s. Additionally, the '60s spirit of collaboration and collective effort, and the rejection of individualism identified with capitalist competition, stimulated the creative surge of the time. Political parties in Chile—especially the centrist Christian Democrats and the leftist Communist and Socialist parties—influenced and provided infrastructure and organizational resources to emerging social and political movements. As formerly excluded social sectors were freer to participate, to speak, to read, to communicate, to protest and organize, the creativity of ordinary people was unleashed. Workers, shantytown dwellers, peasants, and students demanded entry into the elitist political system and gradually gained a larger political voice. At the same time there was a burst of cultural and artistic innovation.

In short, there was a relationship between the political transformations of the 1950s and '60s and the appearance of new cultural forms, not only New Song but also experimental projects in theater, dance, poetry, literature, painting, and playwriting that reached large numbers of people. I have argued that the explosion of creativity in the 1960s and early 1970s in Chile was linked to the splintering of old social hierarchies and the rise of political actors "from below." These interrelated phenomena were the result of rapidly changing global and national political-economic structures, and new democratic openings pushed "from below" by people in many walks of life.

The New Song movement, fused with political parties and social movements, played a counterhegemonic role in Chile, albeit not intentionally. The musicians were organic intellectuals in the sense of translating the hopes and aspirations of millions of Chileans in their songs, denouncing social injustice and repression. The political vision of the music challenged the existing hegemonic sphere of music on radio and television, dominated by U.S. rock and roll, similar Chilean music (*Nueva Ola*, New Wave), and "typical" Chilean *huaso* music (the term refers to "horseman" music, the traditional folk songs of the landowners that reflected their hierarchical view of society). Moreover, the New Song musicians challenged the structure of power relations in Chile and Latin America that resulted in the immiseration of millions of people. New Song used its poetry to cry out for social justice, equality, self-determination, and structural change. That is, the New Song movement played a key role in challenging the hegemonic system of power relations through a popular medium, in ways anticipated by Gramsci.

Over time New Song filtered north, entrancing and inspiring people in Europe and the United States as political mobilization increased worldwide. It seemed as if the mass movements of people throughout the world for social justice, equality, power, and control over decisions affecting their lives—essentially, deeper democracy and egalitarianism—were becoming unstoppable. With Salvador Allende's election in Chile, the world witnessed the first effort to move toward socialism through democratic and constitutional processes. But a series of U.S.-backed military coups halted these movements for social change and regimes of state terrorism took power in the region in the 1970s, violently reversing the social reforms and collective values of the previous era.

ENDURING LEGACIES OF NEW SONG

After the bloody 1973 coup in Chile, New Song became the music of resistance worldwide, communicating the values and ideals of the Unidad Popular to people in many countries and helping to build a global solidarity movement for Chile. After the coup, many New Song musicians were detained, exiled, tortured, or killed. Víctor Jara was seized with hundreds of students and teachers in the Technical University, brought to the Chile Stadium, and tortured. Officers recognized Jara and singled him out, with a few others, for particularly harsh treatment. Finally he was shot repeatedly and his body thrown into a ditch. Thanks to the efforts of a committed public worker, Joan Jara was informed and managed to bury his body and then escape Chile with her two daughters. Ángel Parra was detained and brought to the National Stadium where thousands more UP supporters were held. He was tortured and then sent to a remote concentration camp in Chacabuco, in the northern desert of Chile. An international outcry succeeded in obtaining his release. Other musicians escaped through the good offices of various embassies. New Song musicians such as Patricio Manns, Gitano Rodríguez, and Isabel Parra managed to leave Chile in this way. Quilapayún and Inti-Illimani had been on tour when the coup occurred. The Pinochet dictatorship forbade their return for the next sixteen years. Owning New Song albums was sufficient cause for the military to detain and torture individuals. Even the indigenous instruments—the *charango*, the *quena*, the *bombo ligüero*—were outlawed by the regime, demonstrating its fear of the political power and symbolism of the music.

But Pinochet's repression and exiling of the New Song movement did not destroy it by any means. On the contrary, within Chile the music became a clandestine means of resisting, of connecting like-minded people in the underground, and of maintaining the spirit of the UP. Cassettes with New Song music were smuggled into Chile and passed among people who were struggling to survive in repressive conditions. Internationally, New Song music became a rallying cry and powerful call to remember the dreams, hopes, and struggles of the Chilean people and the ideals of the Allende administration. In many countries of the world the New Song musicians were honored guests, invited to sing in innumerable acts of solidarity and protests against the Pinochet regime.[42] The evocative and inspiring music drew together people across borders and across language barriers in protest of the repression in Chile.

New Song became a permanent part of Chile's cultural patrimony and heritage, and a source of strength and solidarity for Chileans both before and after the coup. Max Berrú, original member of Inti-Illimani, related a story of his return to Chile in 1988 at the close of Inti-Illimani's sixteen-year exile. Pinochet and the dictatorship were still in power, but the musicians had recently learned that the regime had removed them from its blacklist of those prohibited from returning. At the airport, thousands of people were waiting to greet them. They went to a park where thousands more Chileans had gathered spontaneously, and improvised a concert. Berrú explained:

> And the most important, what made such an impact on me, was that the people knew all the lyrics and sang along with us, including the most recent songs we'd done. What this said to me, and to my comrades, was that somehow they had heard the tapes, copied them clandestinely and passed them around to others. This was something so enormous, so important, that we'd entered the heart and soul of the people. It had fortified them to keep on struggling. And how many

> people have stopped me to say, thank you for this song. One woman came to me and told me that "Dolencias" ["suffering" or "affliction"] is the most beautiful for me because when I was tortured I thought of this song and I could bear it. Imagine. That something like this could happen—the result of work that was ethically correct.[43]

In short, New Song became globalized after the coup, even more powerful than before, and played a significant role in mobilizing opposition to the dictatorship. New Song inspired thousands of people worldwide to organize to assist Chilean exiles, oppose the Pinochet regime, lobby their governments to cut ties with Pinochet, and keep the spirit of solidarity and resistance alive in Chile.

CONCLUSION

Were these transformations in Chile a cultural revolution? I believe that they were. But the social and political changes and attitudes of the 1960s and early '70s were truncated by the violence of the 1973 coup. The Pinochet regime dedicated itself to reversing and erasing the profound changes in society, via harsh repression and state terror combined with neoliberal restructuring: essentially, a counterrevolution. Artists, unionists and workers, former UP supporters and officials, *pobladores*, intellectuals, peasant leaders, women, students, socially conscious priests and nuns: all were considered subversives and "internal enemies." Chilean society was terrorized, brutalized, and traumatized. Throughout Latin America there were fierce military coups that rolled back the social advances of the '60s and '70s and targeted these same social sectors for disappearance, torture, and death. Only in recent years have Chileans, especially young people, begun to overcome the legacy of fear and mobilize once again for rights: social equality, free public education, decent pensions, an end to impunity for the crimes committed by the military regimes, and recognition of the injustices committed again women, minorities, and gay people.

One difference today is that the enormous movements of peasants and workers of the past have not resurfaced. This is an issue that needs to be deeply analyzed. Clearly, there has been structural change worldwide wrought by global capitalism, which has weakened and atomized organized labor in many countries. In Chile, a key explanatory factor is that under the dictatorship's free market and anti-union policies many traditional industries collapsed and unemployment soared. Unions, workers' and peasant organizations, and political parties affiliated with them were primary targets of the military regime's repression. The Chilean dictatorship intervened or crushed all the institutions of democratic Chile: Congress, the judiciary, unions, universities, social organizations, the independent media. Chilean society still bears the scars of this period and is more disorganized, disarticulated, and splintered than before. Again quoting Jorge Coulon, original member of Inti-Illimani: "The current period is the result of thirty years of convalescence and recovery of a democracy destroyed, extending to its most basic expressions, by the dictatorship. To reconstruct the social and cultural fabric will take a lot of time."[44]

In sum, I contend that a cultural revolution did occur in Chile, but that it was systematically attacked and dismantled by the forces of the Right. Nevertheless, New Song and its socially committed music remain present in the hearts and minds of Chileans today. The movement wrote a new page in the political and cultural history of Chile and enriched the lives of hundreds of thousands of ordinary Chileans, who began to dream. The New Song movement was a product of the social and political movements of the time, and its creativity was linked to the deepening democratization of society.

Today, New Song is not solely a legacy of the past. Many of the musicians, such as Patricio Manns, Isabel Parra, Quilapayún, and Inti-Illimani, continue to create new music and perform to large crowds. The beloved musicians are honored as national figures and cultural icons, and many younger musicians name them as inspirations for their own work. In Chile, the marching song "El Pueblo Unido Jamas Será Vencido" ("The People United Will Never Be Defeated"), a popular "hymn" from 1973, still prompts audiences to rise to their feet and sing.

NOTES

1. For an analytical, book-length treatment of the New Song movement, see J. Patrice McSherry, *Chilean New Song: The Political Power of Music, 1960s–1973* (Philadelphia: Temple University Press, 2015). Many valuable articles,

chapters, and theses have explored New Song, including works by Jan Fairley and Nancy Morris. Most full-length books date from the 1970s–80s, often written by the musicians themselves or other participants. See, for example, Eduardo Carrasco, *Quilapayún: La revolución y las estrellas* (Santiago: Las Ediciones de Ornitorrinco, 1988); René Largo Farías, *La Nueva Canción chilena* (Mexico: Casa de Chile, 1970); Joan Jara, *Victor: An Unfinished Song* (London: Jonathan Cape, September 5, 1983); Osvaldo Rodríguez, *La Nueva Canción chilena: Continuidad y Reflejo* (Cuba: Ediciones Casa de las Américas, 1988); more recently, see Ángel Parra, *Mi Nuevo Canción chilena: Al pueblo lo que es del pueblo* (Santiago: Catalonia, 2016), and Horacio Salinas, *La canción en el sombrero: Historia de la música de Inti-Illimani* (Santiago: Editorial Catalonia, 2013).

2. See the introduction to this volume for an overview. See Ryback's chapter 8 herein for the role of protest rock in the Soviet Bloc; for an opposing view of the relevance of music in the case of France, see Drott's chapter 4 in this volume.

3. For the Manifesto that established this musical current, see "Manifiesto del Nuevo Cancionero," https://cancionero.net/manifiesto-del-nuevo-cancionero/. See also Oscar A. Chamosa, "The Latin American Imagination in the Argentine Folk Movement," paper prepared for delivery at the American Historical Association Annual Meeting, Atlanta, January 2016.

4. Author interview with Eduardo Carrasco, August 9, 2011, Santiago. See Alonso Cueto's chapter 17 in this volume for an analysis of changes in Latin American literature between the 1960s and the present day.

5. For evidence of U.S. covert involvement, see the Church Committee Reports of 1975, Hearings before the Senate Committee to Study Governmental Operations with Respect to Intelligence Activities (Church Commission Report), "Covert Action," December 4 and 5, 1975. https://data.ddosecrets.com/file/Major%20Investigations/Church%20Committee/Church%20Committee%20Volume%207%20-%20Hearings%20on%20Covert%20Action.pdf.

6. Interview with Jorge Coulon in *El Mostrador* (Chile), April 12, 2017; my free translation. Singer-songwriter Violeta Parra was the "mother" of New Song; Neruda and Mistral were Nobel laureates in Literature, and Neruda was a well-known communist.

7. For an academic analysis of the PC, see, among others, Rolando Álvarez, *Arriba los pobres del mundo: Cultura e identidad política del Partido Comunista de Chile entre democracia y dictadura, 1965–1990* (Santiago: Lom, 2011).

8. Author interview with Horacio Durán, June 13, 2011, Santiago.

9. Many works discuss this theme, which is too complex to enter into here. See J. Patrice McSherry, *Chilean New Song*, and Greg Walz-Chojnacki, "Canto al Huaso, Canto al Pueblo: La Música y el Discurso Político de la Identidad

Chilena durante los Años Sesenta y la Unidad Popular," ISP Collection, Paper 505, 2004; Juan Pablo González, Oscar Ohlsen, and Claudio Rolle, *Historia social de la música popular en Chile, 1950–1970* (Santiago: Ediciones Universidad Católica de Chile, 2009).

10. Useful sources include Isabel Parra, *El libro mayor de Violeta Parra*, 3rd ed. (Santiago: Editorial Cuarto Propio, 2011); Rodolfo Pino-Robles, "Music and Social Change in Argentina and Chile 1950–1980 and Beyond," *Ciencia Ergo Sum* 8, no. 2 (2001): 145–50; Ignacio Ramos Rodillo, *Políticas del Folklore: Representaciones de la tradición y lo popular. Militancia y política cultural en Violeta Parra y Atahualpa Yupanqui* (Master's thesis, University of Chile, 2012); Fernando Rios, "Andean Music, the Left, and Pan-Latin Americanism: The Early History," *Diagonal: Journal of the Center for Iberian and Latin American Music* 2 (2009): 1–13.

11. Interview with Víctor Jara on Panamericana Televisión, Perú, July 1973. He was tortured and murdered by the military, in Chile Stadium, shortly after the 1973 coup. See J. Patrice McSherry, "The Víctor Jara Case and the Long Struggle against Impunity in Chile," *Social Justice* 41, no. 4 (2015): 106–22. A key resource in English is Joan Jara, *Victor*.

12. Author interview with Ángel Parra, January 24, 2013, Santiago.

13. Luis Emilio Recabarren, a renowned labor leader and founder of the Chilean PC, began a tradition of writing plays for workers to perform in the 1910s and '20s and beyond, as a way of reaching workers and their families who could not read or write. He also started a number of regional newspapers for workers. The PC included cultural acts in its political rallies. Spanish Civil War songs and songs from the Mexican Revolution were well known in Chile.

14. Ángel Parra, *Mi Nuevo Canción chilena*, 90–95.

15. Ibid., 95.

16. A verse from the version by Inti-Illimani, 1970; my translation. This song was written by Claudio Iturra with music by Sergio Ortega. Alternate words for Allende's campaign were written by Víctor Jara.

17. The cantata was composed by classical musician Luis Advis for Quilapayún.

18. Author interviews with Juan Carvajal, former DICAP artistic director, August 15, 2012; and with Ricardo Valenzuela, former DICAP general director, August 21, 2012, Santiago; see also Gustavo Miranda Meza, "Cuando la cultura se escribe con la guitarra: El sello DICAP y la política de las Juventudes Comunistas, Chile 1968–1973," presentation in El Primer Congreso chileno de Estudios en la Música Popular, June 2011.

19. See, for example, Rolando Álvarez, "Trabajos voluntarios: El 'hombre nuevo' y la creación de una nueva cultura en Chile," in *Fiesta y drama: Nuevas*

historias de la Unidad Popular, ed. Julio Pinto Vallejos (Santiago: Lom, 2014): 173, 178. For a view of the minority and avowedly apolitical hippie movement at the same time in Chile, see Barr-Melej's chapter 15 in this volume.

20. Álvarez, "Trabajos voluntarios," 177, 182–83.

21. Gabriela García, "El Rey de La Reina," *El Mercurio revista*, August 2012, 83. See also Castillo's autobiography: Fernando Castillo Velasco, *Lecciones del tiempo vivido* (Santiago: Catalonia, 2008).

22. For more on Kirberg, see Luis Cifuentes Seves, *Kirberg: Testigo y actor del Siglo XXI* (Santiago: Editorial Usach, 1993).

23. Alejandro Yáñez B., "Allende y la reforma universitaria," in *Salvador Allende: Presencia en la ausencia*, ed. Miguel Lawner, Hernán Soto, and Jacobo Schatan (Santiago: LOM, 2008): 317–40, and http://www.g80.cl/documentos/docs/Allende_Reforma_U_en_la_UTE.pdf.

24. For more detail, see Franck Gaudichaud, "Construyendo 'Poder Popular': El movimiento sindical, la CUT y las luchas obreras en el período de la Unidad Popular," in Pinto Vallejos, ed., *Cuando Hicimos Historia*, 81–105. See Peter Winn for a case study of a textile factory where workers took over management and production during the UP, one of many that did so. Winn, *Weavers of Revolution: The Yarur Workers and Chile's Road to Socialism* (Oxford: Oxford University Press, 1994).

25. For an excellent, succinct analysis, see María Angélica Illanes y Flor Recabal, "Liberación y democracia en la tierra: Historia y memoria de la Reforma Agraria-Unidad Popular, Chile, 1971–2012," in Pinto Vallejos, ed., *Fiesta y Drama*, 17–50.

26. Cathy Lisa Schneider, *Shantytown Protest in Pinochet's Chile* (Philadelphia: Temple University Press, 1995), 9–11. This book is a detailed study of the interface between political parties, especially the PC, and the growing power of the *pobladores*, which also became the center of resistance to the Pinochet dictatorship.

27. All of these advances were violently overturned by the Pinochet dictatorship, which militarized, bulldozed, and repressed the shantytowns and forcibly moved the *pobladores* to areas far from the center of Santiago. See, for example, Francisca Allende and Scarlett Olave, *El despojo de la Villa San Luis de Las Condes* (Santiago: Editorial Ceibo, 2018). See also Mario Garcés, *Tomando su sitio: El movimiento de pobladores de Santiago, 1957–1970* (Santiago: Lom Ediciones, 2002); Mario Garcés, *El golpe en La Legua: Los caminos de la historia y la memoria* (Santiago: Lom, 2005); Garcés, "Construyendo 'las poblaciones': El movimiento de pobladores durante la Unidad Popular," in Pinto Vallejos, ed., *Cuando Hicimos Historia: La experiencia de la Unidad Popular* (Santiago: Lom, 2005), 57–79; and Garcés, "Los años de la Unidad Popular: cuando los pobladores recreaban las

ciudades chilenas," in Pinto Vallejos, ed., *Fiesta y drama: Nuevas historias de la Unidad Popular* (Santiago: Lom, 2014), 51–73.

28. For more on NAM, see Zolov's chapter 5 in this volume.

29. For the cases of Mexico, Argentina, and Uruguay, see chapters by Pensado, Manzano, and Markarian in this volume. For the effect of liberation theology in Italy, see De Giuseppe's chapter 3 in this volume.

30. An extensive literature documents this history. For an overview, see Jeffrey F. Taffet, "U.S.–Latin American Relations during the Cold War," *Oxford Bibliographies Online*, http://www.oxfordbibliographies.com/view/document/obo-9780199766581/obo-9780199766581-0104.xml. The Central Intelligence Agency, a key Cold War actor in Latin America, was created in 1947.

31. For an overview of the era of Latin American national security states, U.S. intervention, and the covert system Operation Condor, see J. Patrice McSherry, *Predatory States: Operation Condor and Covert War in Latin America* (Lanham, MD: Rowman and Littlefield, 2005).

32. See Melching's chapter 13 in this volume for a study of the transformation of international attitudes toward the United States in this era.

33. Space limits permit only an abbreviated and schematic history of Chile here.

34. Paul Drake, "Chile, 1930–58," in *Latin America since 1930: Spanish South America*, ed. Leslie Bethell (Cambridge: Cambridge University Press, 1991), 269–310, at https://ssandhbooks.files.wordpress.com/2015/04/the-cambridge-history-of-latin-america-vol-08-since-1930-spannish-south-america.pdf; Marcelo Casals Araya, *El alba de una revolución* (Santiago: Lom Ediciones, 2010).

35. Salvador Allende served as minister of health under Aguirre Cerda and sponsored measures to provide health insurance, establish an integrated public health system emphasizing basic nutrition and better standards of living, and initiate health services for mothers and children. The government also implemented literacy campaigns and reforms in public education, state investment in public enterprises, and other nationalist initiatives. See Mario Amorós, *Allende: La biografía* (Santiago: Ediciones B, S.A., 2013), chap. 4.

36. For more on the UP government, see Pinto Vallejos, ed., *Cuando Hicimos Historia*; Marco Álvarez Vergara, *Tati Allende: Una revolucionaria olvidada* (Santiago: Pehuén, 2017). For the program of the UP, see Luis Corvalán, *El gobierno de Salvador Allende* (Santiago: Lom Ediciones, 2003), 275.

37. John Street, *Music and Politics* (Malden, MA: Polity Press, 2012), 99.

38. John Street, "'Fight the Power': The Politics of Music and the Music of Politics," *Government and Opposition* (2003): 130.

39. Nelly Richard, "Lo político en el arte: Arte, política e instituciones," paper, Arcis University (Chile), n.d.

40. Author interview with Mario Salazar, August 23, 2012, Santiago.

41. Antonio Gramsci, "Popular Literature," in *Gramsci: Selections from Cultural Writings*, ed. David Forgacs and Geoffrey Nowell-Smith (Cambridge, MA: Harvard University Press, 1991), 378.

42. See J. Patrice McSherry, "The Political Impact of Chilean New Song in Exile," *Latin American Perspectives* 44, no. 5 (2017): 13–29.

43. Author interview with Max Berrú, June 14, 2011, Santiago.

44. *El Mostrador* interview, December 3, 2017.

BIBLIOGRAPHY

Álvarez, Rolando. *Arriba los pobres del mundo: Cultura e identidad política del Partido Comunista de Chile entre democracia y dictadura, 1965–1990.* Santiago: Lom, 2011.

Casals Araya, Marcelo. *El alba de una revolución.* Santiago: Lom Ediciones, 2010.

Forgacs, David, and Geoffrey Nowell-Smith, eds. *Gramsci: Selections from Cultural Writings.* Cambridge, MA: Harvard University Press, 1991.

Garcés, Mario. *El golpe en La Legua: Los caminos de la historia y la memoria.* Santiago: Lom, 2005.

———. *Tomando su sitio: El movimiento de pobladores de Santiago, 1957–1970.* Santiago: Lom Ediciones, 2002.

González, Juan Pablo, Oscar Ohlsen, and Claudio Rolle. *Historia social de la música popular en Chile, 1950–1970.* Santiago: Ediciones Universidad Católica de Chile, 2009.

Jara, Joan. *Victor: An Unfinished Song.* London: Jonathan Cape, September 5, 1983.

McSherry, J. Patrice. *Chilean New Song: The Political Power of Music, 1960s–1973.* Philadelphia: Temple University Press, 2015.

Pinto Vallejos, Julio, ed. *Cuando Hicimos Historia: La experiencia de la Unidad Popular.* Santiago: Lom, 2005.

———, ed. *Fiesta y drama: Nuevas historias de la Unidad Popular.* Santiago: Lom, 2014.

Schneider, Cathy Lisa. *Shantytown Protest in Pinochet's Chile.* Philadelphia: Temple University Press, 1995.

Street, John. *Music and Politics.* Malden, MA: Polity Press, 2012.

TWELVE

The French Sixties and the Refusal of Work

MICHAEL SEIDMAN

A new and radical critique of work emerged in the Long 1960s. It found its roots in the nineteenth-century industrial revolution when many workers regarded themselves as "wage slaves" and demanded liberation from wage labor. Luddites in the United Kingdom, Proudhonists in France, Free Soilers in the United States, and ordinary wage earners throughout the world desired to become independent farmers, shopkeepers, or artisans to escape the oppression of the lord, workshop, or factory. A century later, in the context of the 1960s when an industrial and urbanizing economy was rapidly eliminating the peasantry, this demand for independence transformed itself into a desire to avoid, as much as possible, working for wages or even, in many cases, becoming an individual entrepreneur. Breaking with a puritanical Left dominant throughout the world, some Sixties' revolutionaries imagined a cybernetic and hedonistic utopia where basic needs would be provided without much individual effort or sacrifice. The movements of the Sixties may have been the first time that antiwork sloganeering attracted a large, public, and transnational mass of followers, who included extreme leftists, beatniks, hippies, and some wage earners.[1] In the late Sixties, Italian workers voiced their demand, "We want it all." The refusal of work was radically antisocial and subversive, reflecting both a legitimacy crisis in Western societies and deepening a cultural revolution that promoted gender equality, sexual freedoms, and multiculturalism.[2]

Guy Debord, Henri Lefebvre, and Herbert Marcuse were among the most prominent who articulated antiwork attitudes. These intellectuals became popular because they seemed to be able to synthesize international Sixties' desires for simultaneous personal and social liberation.[3] Debord's and Lefebvre's appeal for a revolution in everyday life and Marcuse's endorsement of the "Great Refusal" of a consumerist and purportedly "repressive" capitalist society combined individual emancipation with a desire for profound social change. All three were radical secularists who rejected the curse of Adam and situated themselves in the Marxist tradition.[4] Debord and Marcuse believed that the bourgeoisie had developed the means of production to a level where it became possible to abolish work.[5] The advanced productive forces had the potential to render wage labor superfluous and promoted—at least among some—a vision of a prosperous utopia where machines would replace the labor of men and women. The critique of labor spread throughout the West. The American Students for a Democratic Society (SDS) asked, "Why meaningless work?"[6] In Berkeley, the defenders of People's Park identified "labor with oppression."[7] Radical Italian theorists went further and celebrated workers' struggles against work (absenteeism, lateness, faking illnesses, sabotage, theft, welfare and unemployment fraud) as the most significant and potentially emancipatory aspects of the class struggle.[8] In their eyes, many contemporary commodities or services served only to perpetuate irrationality. Those in more developed parts of the world articulated antiwork messages more than those in the global South.

Debord's Situationists critiqued the "spectacle" of goods and services that sustained a consumer society that constantly fabricated "false" needs. They envisaged the abolition of the commodity system and its replacement by a worldwide network of workers' councils. In the Situationist utopia, the overcoming of the commodity system implied the end of the need for work and its replacement by a new type of activity. In the councils the distinction between work and leisure would dissolve, and genuine desires that the spectacle had suppressed would return. The proletarian revolution promised to be a festival with play as its ultimate rationality: "To live without dead time and to enjoy [*jouir*] without inhibitions were its only rules."

STUDENTS

Social and economic factors help to explain why this critique of work emerged in the 1960s. Western societies were becoming more urbanized, and the service sector was growing rapidly. Thus, the connection between wage labor, production, and survival was less obvious than in any previous historical period. Much output came to be seen as senseless and environmentally destructive. At the same time, the weight of young people in the population, their increasing years of schooling, and their consequently delayed entry into full-time wage labor or individual entrepreneurship provided a large potential constituency for the spread of antiwork ideology. Of course, the traditional juvenile dislike of classroom discipline—often the training ground for future paid labor—continued. In addition, the expansion of education during the "thirty glorious years" (1945–75) of relatively full employment and unparalleled economic growth in postwar Europe and North America offered adolescents and young adults more opportunities to avoid working for wages. During the same period, commercialized leisure, such as rock concerts and mass tourism, spread to these young consumers.

In France the higher education policies of the Gaullist regime alienated the fast-growing body of university students. At the end of 1967, the government's plan to implement more selective standards for university admission galvanized students. President Charles de Gaulle realized that it would have been much easier to establish a more rigorous entry selection in 1962–63, when 280,000 were enrolled, than in 1967–68 with 600,000 students. The humanities and social sciences saw the fastest growth, and the regime persisted in its elitist university reforms. Although most students had bourgeois origins, they responded to government initiatives by copying the tactics of the workers' movement. They protested by striking, refusing to work or study, and intimidating "scabs," in this case students who wanted to attend classes and professors who wanted to offer them. The withdrawal of effort by students anticipated the giant work stoppages of May 1968.

Nanterre University, whose construction began in 1963, became a center of agitation. It enrolled 4,600 students in 1965, 8,500 in 1966, and 11,000 in 1967.[9] In 1968, the March 22 Movement (Mouvement du 22 mars) formed to protest against the "repressive" policies of the Gaullist government and the university administration. March 22 gained media attention when on that date dozens, then hundreds, of its supporters from various leftist organizations occupied the administrative tower of Nanterre University, thus creating an innovative and transgressive form of protest in France.[10] During this occupation, March 22 members engaged in petty vandalism and theft. Violations of property rights and destruction of property itself manifested a hatred of labor. Work, March 22 argued, was the central aspect of a repressive society. The French word (and those of many other Romance languages) for work, *travail*, came from the Latin *trepalium* (instrument of torture). Christianity, communism, and capitalism glorified work and lied about its nature so that workers would accept it. According to March 22, all these ideologies revealed their vileness by stressing the morality of labor. The future society must terminate the centrality of work and institute *autogestion* (workers' control), where the producer could become creative. After the revolution, work must become play. Nanterre pro-Situationist *Enragés* declared: "Work is a disgrace. . . . Its elimination is a prerequisite for the transcendence of the society of commodities."[11] The critique of labor—the *situs*' (Situationists) "Live without Dead Time" and "Never Work" remain among their most popular graffiti—continued a long tradition that harked back to Paul Lafargue, Max Stirner, Friedrich Nietzsche, the Surrealists, and even the libertines of the Old Regime.[12]

In April and early May, the student movement moved from the suburb of Nanterre into the heart of Paris. In the Latin Quarter students imitated the Nanterre model and occupied the Sorbonne, where they again damaged university property and blocked the normal functioning of the institution. On May 3 the chancellor called in police, whose repressive presence provoked much more student violence. Without student revolts, which continued throughout the spring of 1968, workers' strikes might have remained as isolated and localized as they were prior to their national strike wave of May. By challenging the state and, at the same time, inciting its constrained but dramatic brutality, students precipitated the enormous wave of work stoppages during the second half of May.[13]

Figure 12.1 "Never Work" (1953).

Students created an inclusive movement that was joined by the *trimards*, *blousons noirs*, *katangais*, *zonards*, *loulous*, all rough French equivalents to "vagabonds" or "lumpenproletariat."[14] These "marginals" were not averse to drinking, getting high, and, of course, living without wage or entrepreneurial labor.[15] *Trimards* expressed more regularly and radically the transient unconventional character and partying of student life, as reflected in the emancipatory hedonism in university dormitories during the Sixties.[16] Nor were they entirely innocent of acts of iconoclasm and vandalism.[17] Their example influenced a few middle-class students who organized robberies and combatted police.[18] "Revolutionary theft" politicized the common practice of shoplifting, which greatly contributed to the ruin of La Joie de Lire, the most important *tiers-mondiste* (Third Worldist) Parisian bookstore, which featured works by Latin American and other revolutionaries.[19] A variety of leftists, including radical Christian Democrats, broke down barriers and integrated *trimards* into the movement.[20] Indeed, the *trimards* triggered and supposedly justified police interventions in numerous provincial universities throughout France. Thus, they became major players in a national social drama. In some sense, this coalition between students and lumpen was an ephemeral Marcusian or Situationist moment that defied both religious and secular work ethics.[21] Skepticism about work led to new Sixties' movements that defended both prisoners and prostitutes, recognized enemies of productive labor.

WORKERS

The leaders of major trade unions agreed that the student challenges to the government, which had responded with unpopular repression, weakened it and thus offered an appropriate moment to call a one-day general strike for Monday, May 13. Even though downplayed by the state-monopolized television, the strike's success revealed a solidarity between young and old that contradicted the "generation gap" which many analysts presumed characterized the Sixties. Workers in 1968 continued various nineteenth-century traditions when wage earners took advantage of an upward economic cycle and nearly full employment to launch major strike waves, which often began in the spring and on Mondays (*Saint Lundi*) when workers spontaneously fashioned a long weekend.[22] Throughout the decade of the 1960s, Monday continued to be the day of greatest absenteeism.[23] Striking on Monday may have been an effective way of joining wage-earning men and women, since the latter—who composed, for example, about 20 percent of the work force in metallurgy—had especially high rates of absenteeism on the first workday of the week. Monday was the day when workers engaged in a general strike (May 13), stopped working in large numbers (May 20), and, as shall be seen, rejected the agreement among the government, unions, and employers (May 27). Despite the illegality of the strike (the five-day advance notice was ignored), the work stoppage was widespread. Nationally, by the end of Monday, May 20, more than 5 million workers had stopped laboring in a wide variety of branches—transportation, energy, post office, metallurgy, education, and banks.[24] Financial establishments began to limit withdrawals, and a black market for gasoline started to emerge.

In the industrial Parisian suburbs of Argenteuil and Bezons, the strike movement "developed massively" from May 20 onward.[25] On that Monday, strikers became more prone to illegality. A few workers ignored the CGT's (Confédération générale du travail) and the PCF's (Parti communiste français) condemnation of sequestrations or expelled management from factories.[26] Sabotage, however, seems to have been rare.[27] More commonly, strikers violated the "right to work of nonstrikers."[28] The occupations often contested management prerogatives and industrial hierarchy.[29] Employers complained bitterly of the collapse of state power and especially of the failure of the police to come to their aid.[30] Demonstrating an unexpected degree of tolerance, the Ministry of Interior ignored a petition from 1,200 Citroën employees who demanded that the state protect their right to work. Officials were not uniformly hostile to strikers. In fact, with the help of the Communist mayor of Levallois-Perret, police mediated between striking Citroën workers and strike-breaking foremen to arrange to pay workers in advance.[31] All these parties agreed that women—given their role as homemakers—would receive their advance before men. The police prefect's assertion that during the strike wave his men acted "as much as justices of the peace and mediators than as policemen" was only a partial mystification.[32]

On May 25, formal national negotiations among government, employers, and unions opened in Paris. On Monday, May 27, the major partners issued what became known as the Grenelle Accord, but, despite significant salary hikes, workers in large Parisian metallurgical firms rejected it and continued the work stoppage. The estimates of the total number of strikers at the height of the movement vary from 7 to 10 million.[33] Whatever the figure, it far outclassed the 1 million strikers of the previous great strike wave in the spring of 1936 during the Popular Front and demonstrated the strength of the working class in the French population in 1968.[34] Never in peacetime had France lost so much labor.

On May 29 a large CGT demonstration in Paris and de Gaulle's mysterious departure from the capital seemed to indicate a deep crisis in a regime no longer able to enforce a regular work routine. The following day, de Gaulle returned to Paris and addressed the nation on the radio, which recalled his Resistance leadership during World War II when he used the same medium from London. In his speech he promised to no longer tolerate those who "stop students from studying, teachers from teaching, and workers from working." His address was followed by a massive rightist demonstration that contested the leftist dominance of the streets of the capital. This huge Champs-Élysées gathering of May 30 in support of the Gaullist government called for an immediate return to work in the classroom and factory. One of its slogans was "Renault au boulot" ("Back to Work, Renault").[35] Marchers in provincial cities across the nation seconded the demand for the end of work stoppages.[36] Both Parisian and provincial pro-work demonstrators, who marched in fifty departments, paid homage to Republican order by placing its officials and deputies in the front ranks.[37] Demonstrators sang the "Marseillaise" and waved tricolor flags, which countered the radicals' "Internationale" and red flags. Patriotic displays symbolized the union of the nation and wage labor, an alliance as old as modern nationalism. Such pro-work sentiments were seconded by peasants who resented wage laborers' work stoppages and by wives who insisted that their husbands remain breadwinners.[38] This potent counterrevolutionary current brought together the entire Right, including its most prominent intellectual, Raymond Aron, who participated in the Parisian march and consistently challenged intellectuals and professors who supported the student and worker protests and strikes.[39] The demand for order also encouraged the granting of amnesty to the leaders of the failed and violent Organisation armée secrète (OAS), whose members—influential Gaullists believed—might be needed to supplement the pro-government Comités de Défense de la République in case of continuing strikes and an imagined Communist coup. On the day of de Gaulle's radio address, his minister of the interior ordered all prefects to take necessary measures to encourage a return to work: "It is your immediate duty to eliminate all obstacles to the right to work and to end the occupations in priority institutions."[40] At the end of May, the Right's coalition expanded as rapidly as the Left's had at the beginning of the month. The threat of revolutionary versus counterrevolutionary violence was elevated and sometimes consummated; however, in contrast to Eastern Europe and Latin America, both sides generally restrained their most murderous and destructive tendencies.[41]

In June, the government continued its offensive to guarantee "the right to work" and threatened recalcitrant strikers with reinforced state power. At Renault, CGT activists were aware of "important troop movements, notably armored cars and parachutists who are being called to Paris. In addition, a large number of OAS officers are being freed [from prison]."[42] At the beginning of the month, using minimum police and military force, the government was able to break the strike at the state-controlled media, the Office de radio et télévision française (ORTF).[43] On June 4–5, branches of the Postes, Télégraphes, Téléphones (PTT) and National Education voted to end their strikes. By June 6, the return was general in the PTT of the Paris region. Police ended the occupation of certain bureaus without noteworthy violence. In the first week of June, strikers in smaller firms returned to work, and gradually in the first half of that month, holdouts from the major enterprises negotiated firm-by-firm agreements, which ended work stoppages. At a press conference on Sunday evening, June 9, Prime Minister Georges Pompidou justified using force against strikers—such as at the Renault branch at Flins—by arguing that it was necessary to ensure the right to work.[44] The prime minister added, "The motto 'To Work' must be France's slogan at this moment." The following day police violence to enforce the "right to work" was responsible for the deaths of a seventeen-year-old Maoist militant at Flins and two young strikers at another major automobile firm, Peugeot at Sochaux. Under these circumstances, the work week of June 10–15 saw an end to the work stoppage by most remaining large metallurgical firms of the Paris region. Unlike in 1848 or 1871, authorities were able to fuel and feed the city and thus to prevent their adversaries from gaining the solid support of discontented housewives and homemakers.

Workers' actions could only with difficulty be seen as a "rupture" or, in the hyperbolic words of Pompidou and Minister of Culture André Malraux, "a crisis of civilization." Similarly, influential sociologists viewed wage earners as participating in a broader movement that challenged the social order.[45] They posited that salaried personnel desired *autogestion*, which demanded the end of separation between those who commanded and those who obeyed. *Autogestion* questioned the division of labor but not wage labor itself. According to these analysts and also recent historical accounts that have favored workers' control, wage laborers wanted to democratize their workplaces.[46] Other progressives sympathetic to the movement yearned so deeply to believe that workers wished to take over their factories that they invented the tale that the personnel of the CSF factory at Brest had initiated "democratic control" and were producing walkie-talkies.[47] The mythmakers—who included historians Alain Delale and Gilles Ragache, theorists Ernest Mandel and Serge Mallet, and the major newspapers *Le Monde* and *Témoignage chrétien*—proved as willing to take their desires for reality as any youthful *gauchiste*.[48]

As in the nineteenth and early twentieth centuries, strikers' demands remained materialist, and workplace democracy was seldom invoked by the workers themselves or their representatives.[49] Rather than reflecting worker sentiment, the call for *autogestion* may have served as a facile solution to the genuine and thorny problem of worker dissatisfaction with industrial discipline in particular and wage labor in general. The doctrines of self-management had little appeal to a mass of wage laborers for whom work remained *travail* and who were more enthusiastic about escaping the factory or enjoying the opportunities of consumption provided by the expanding economy. Despite the rhetoric of various unions and parties, including leftist *groupuscules*, workers never fully identified themselves as producers who wanted to take control of the means of production. The notion of workers' control in the 1960s recalled fin-de-siècle French revolutionary syndicalism, not Sixties' antiwork attitudes and actions. To a large degree, *autogestionnaire* militants and intellectuals demanded that the individual adapt to the productivist collectivity. In other words, *autogestion* was a slogan originating from the top down.[50] Workers inevitably questioned whether it was really advantageous for them to run the workplace.[51] Many concluded that it was not, since successful workers' control demanded a degree of professional and social commitment that they could not or would not provide.

Instead of *autogestion*, during the strikes of May/June the major CGT and even local Confédération française démocratique du travail (CFDT) affiliates recalled their agreement of January 1966, which pledged to struggle for a 35 percent increase in the minimum wage, higher salaries for skilled workers, job security, and a reduction of the working week. In metallurgy and other branches, the CGT and the CFDT demanded less work time—including a forty-hour work week and retirement at sixty for men or fifty-five for women—and more pay, particularly for the lowest-paid workers, who were often foreigners, women, or provincial youth.[52] This signaled the resolve of union activists (generally older French males) to reach out to other social groups who composed the majority of industrial workers.

Although militants occupied many factories—for example, thirty-one out of thirty-nine striking firms in the Parisian suburbs of Issy-les-Moulineaux and twenty out of forty in Boulogne-Billancourt—the occupations revealed that the rank and file had little desire to become actively involved. In other words, many wage earners possessed a working-class identity that actively avoided the factory. As one worker-intellectual put it, "occupying a factory is much more boring than working there."[53] Contrary to the assertions of the activists of the Union national des étudiants de France (UNEF) and other leftists, who adhered to the productivist legacy of Marxism and council communism, many forms of worker struggle did not imply "a total change of society."[54] In general, the number of workers actually engaged in the occupations remained a tiny percentage of the workforce. At Sud-Aviation, the pioneer plant of the occupation wave, the overwhelming majority of workers did not wish to participate in the sit-in but rather to spend time alone or with their families and friends. Their strike was more individualist than collective. Only 3,195 of 8,000 workers voted, and just 1,699 of them wanted to occupy the factory.[55] At Berliet in Vénissieux, fewer than half of 11,000 workers voted, and only 23 percent (2,550) wanted to continue the occupation of the factories.[56] Merely several hundred out of a workforce of 5,000 occupied the Renault factory at Cléon.[57] At Renault Flins, approximately 250 of 10,000 were occupiers. A few hundred of the 30,000 Renault workers at Boulogne-Billancourt remained inside the flagship plant. At Citroën, both strike meetings and the occupation revealed the passivity of the rank and file, who remained content to permit those union militants—usually mature males—who had initiated the strike to spend time at the workplace.[58] In the Citroën plant in the 15th arrondissement, usually no more than 100 occupiers out of a workforce of 20,000-plus were present. Leftists charged that the Citroën strike committee was more concerned with organizing ping-pong matches and card games than with educating workers politically. During the long weekend of Pentecost (June 1–3) when gasoline became readily available, only twelve remained in the factory. Throughout May and June, antagonists—strikers and non-strikers, students and police—generally respected the weekly rest and avoided confrontations during Saturday and Sunday. The occupations were the greatest wave in peacetime history, but the small number of occupiers suggested that the number of engaged militants was proportionally tiny.[59] In contrast to 1936, when masses of workers remained in the factories to prevent scabs from entering, in 1968—when full employment generally prevailed—the fear of scabbing was relatively weak, and workers felt less compelled to join sit-downs.

As the stoppages endured, mature breadwinners seemed more anxious to end the strikes than younger wage earners.[60] It was at the end of the strikes—not the beginning, as many have assumed—that a generation gap became relevant in the workplace. Occupations also disclosed gender divisions. Initially, women were excluded from certain sit-downs for "moral reasons," but in others they played important roles.[61] The 400 female workers at the Kréma chewing gum factory outnumbered the 200 males, but male domination of the strike provoked the resentment of women.[62] At a branch of the Compagnie des compteurs of Montrouge, women did participate in the occupation, yet only in their usual roles as cleaners and cooks. Men proved reluctant to allow them to spend the night at the factory in order "to avoid that bosses make an issue of morality."[63] Women rejected this argument and by the third night of the occupation were almost as numerous as men. Usually, the overwhelming majority of workers—female or male, foreign or French—preferred to stay away from the plant.[64]

Large numbers—whether male or female—displayed little commitment to the electoral process at the workplace, and participation in strike votes varied widely, from 40 to 75 percent.[65] The low level of attendance contrasts sharply with the late nineteenth century when meetings attracted 80 to 100 percent of strikers.[66] Union and nonunion strikers of some of the most important Parisian firms—Otis Elevators, Sud-Aviation, Nord-Aviation, Thomson-Houston, Rhône-Poulenc—reflected on striker passivity in a pamphlet written at the beginning of June. They contended that

> in order to win, a greater number of workers [must] get involved. While the strike forces everyone to make material sacrifices, many comrades rely on a minority and do not participate actively. This allows the government to divide workers by playing on the weariness of some and on the poor information of others. . . . There is only one response to these tactics of division: massive participation of all workers who have stayed away from the occupied factories.[67]

To encourage noncommitted or apathetic workers to join the movement, the pamphleteers recommended adopting the model of strike organization at Rhône-Poulenc (Vitry), where rank-and-file strikers elected strike committees that were easily revocable. Militants regarded the occupation of this firm as particularly impressive because 1,500 of a workforce of 3,500, or 43 percent, were actively involved.[68]

Even in this example of relatively high participation, approximately 57 percent of personnel avoided activism. Many stayed at home either to garden or to *bricoler*. Proposals from an interunion committee, action committees, and Nanterre students for a more innovative and participatory form of striking failed to interest wage earners. Committees recommended that workers engage in "freebie strikes" to rally opinion to their side and to direct public anger against the government. For example, garbage men should collect accumulated trash, transportation workers should permit free rides, and PTT employees should allow free postage and telephone calls.[69] However, sanitation, transport, and postal workers disappointed activists by making only customary bread-and-butter demands. The belief of the March 22 Movement that the occupations expressed the "unconscious yearning of the working class to take over the means of production" was wishful thinking.[70] The March 22 Movement's demand for the sabotage of the means of production in case of a police assault usually went unheeded.[71] Striking workers seldom damaged property, and when they did, their targets—telephone lines, vehicles, and such—were precise and limited. A certain respect for quality labor persisted.[72]

In the 1960s as in the 1930s, young people—who were relatively new to wage labor and unencumbered by familial responsibilities—were less accommodating to the daily grind of factory existence than their elders. The critique of work and the attack on accumulated labor that emerged from the revolt of the 1960s had, at least in part, demographic origins. The heavy bulge of youth in the workforce—workers fifteen to twenty-four constituted approximately a quarter of the working population—had the effect of prolonging the strike wave.[73] The stoppages made an important step towards the eventual reestablishment of the forty-hour work week, a major goal of organized labor throughout the nineteenth and twentieth centuries.[74] Almost all major trade union federations reaped the benefits of their successful demands for more pay and less work by an approximately 25 percent increase in membership.[75] The unions may have reached their zenith in the Sixties.

Many workers shared an ambivalent attitude towards salaried labor, which they considered not only wage "slavery" but also a part of their social identity. In other words, workers were both producers and refusers. Absenteeism, slowdowns, lateness, faking illness, turnover, sabotage, theft, and various forms of welfare cheating continued during "les années 68."[76] These revolts against work integrated various components of the class. Militants and rank and file, women and men, French and foreign, respectable and marginal could all participate in the everyday "guerrilla war" against wage labor. While avoiding work space and work time, wage earners used the same vocabulary that they had employed in the nineteenth century and labeled their enemies—whether scabs or cops—"lazy" (*fainéants*).

Following the strike wave, French management, assisted by a powerful state, quickly regained its dominance in the factory. Thus, the greatest wave of stoppages only marginally altered the authoritarian atmosphere that reigned on the shop floor and in the office.[77] The Gaullist government was much more effective in limiting resistance to work than its Popular Front counterpart in the 1930s or its contemporary Italian foil during the *maggio strisciante*. After 1968 in Italy—where both workers and employers shared a disdain for a weak and ineffective state—wage earners continued their struggles against wage labor.[78] In contrast, "the strong growth of [French] productivity after May was due in large part to profound restructuring within firms, accentuating worker mobility and intensifying work rhythms, the very processes under negotiation and challenge by the Italian unions."[79] In other words, French foremen once again became "wardens" who tried—relatively effectively—to increase production speed.[80] In comparison, Italian workers used established unions and *comitati* (independent grassroots organizations) to resist the authority of foremen, to hinder linking pay to productivity, and to avoid work time and space. According to a famous fictional character who represented northern Italy's unskilled proletariat of 1969, happiness meant working less for more pay.[81] In the years immediately following 1968, Italian employers could not lower wages nor dismiss unruly workers.[82]

A strong state proved as necessary to limit workers' refusal of wage labor in the late 1960s as it had during the Popular Front strike waves of the late 1930s. In contrast to 1936, when Prime Minister Léon Blum defied employers and endorsed the shortening of the work week from forty-eight to forty hours, Prime Minister Pompidou rejected workers' demands for a forty-hour week and negotiated a moderately progressive reduction of the work week—two hours for wage earners laboring more than forty-eight hours and one hour for those laboring between forty-five and forty-eight hours.[83] The Grenelle Accord's successor, the national agreement between employers and unions of December 13, 1968, decided in principle to return gradually to the forty-hour week without a reduction of buying power.[84]

Some analysts have neglected this coercive function of the state in favor of a focus on industrial relations in which the state mediates between organized labor and employers. Others, such as Herbert Marcuse, have dismissed labor entirely since they posited that consumer capitalism had integrated the working class. The 1968 stoppages did not support a Marcusian interpretation that workers were integrated into capitalist society since resistance to work, whether in the form of strikes, absenteeism, lateness, and such, had to be curbed by a strong state, which served, in workers' words, as a prison warden (*garde-chiourme*).[85] In contemporary consumer society the state's disciplinary role may have become even more important. In the nineteenth and early twentieth centuries, individual enterprises and the culture of the work ethic had partially subjugated labor, but by the late twentieth century the consumerist emphasis on immediate gratification had undermined the work ethic.[86] The challenges to the Protestant and Enlightenment work ethics rendered obsolete the project of workers' control, or *autogestion*, which was based on the identification of workers with the means of production. Simultaneously, it made the state's disciplinary task even more necessary. In 1968, especially in June, internalized work discipline proved inadequate to guarantee order and had to be supplemented by the repressive actions of the state. Late capitalism still needed the armed force of Leviathan to keep the workers in line.

In France, the everyday struggle against wage labor was reflected in the persistent popularity of *Reprise*. This late 1990s film, which was then made into a book on the thirtieth anniversary of May, shows the filmmaker, Hervé Le Roux, attempting to locate a woman who had been the subject of a nine-minute documentary movie, *La reprise du travail aux usines Wonder*, in 1968.[87] In June of that year, this female wage laborer, known only as Jocelyne, was captured on film as she defiantly refused to return to work when the strike at her metallurgical factory was being settled. The attractiveness in the Long '60s of antiwork ideologies quickly transformed the young woman into a rebellious heroine of the May revolt. Jocelyne's refusal to return to that "*taule*" ("prison")—in this case, a battery factory—transformed her into perhaps the most famous and certainly the most cinematic resister of wage labor during 1968 and in recent French memory. *La Reprise du travail aux usines Wonder* (1968) coincided with the more comical antiwork box-office hit, *Alexandre le bienheureux* of the same year, the sequel of *A Nous la Liberté* (1931).

Jocelyne's dramatic rejection of labor (*ne pas perdre sa vie à la gagner*, as the slogan went) pithily expressed the specific Sixties' synthesis of personal, social, and political concerns. Being both female and a worker further heightened her status as an icon of an ideology that had been articulated largely by male intellectuals. Her complete disappearance from the media spectacle enhanced her mystique.[88] Yet ultimately neither she nor any other individual or group could solve the problem of wage labor. Thus, ideologists of the Sixties proposed contradictory solutions that ranged from the abolition of work to its internalization in a democratic workplace.

Like Jocelyne, some young travelers from various social strata reflected the antiwork individualism of the 1960s by attempting to resolve the difficulty on their own. They avoided months and even years of wage labor by taking advantage of democratized and inexpensive air fares, road trips, and hitchhiking to explore different continents and civilizations. Mass consumption and prosperity promoted escape.[89] For a good number, drugs were part of the journey (after all, a "trip" applied to both kinds of voyages), and some never returned to a conventional salaried existence.[90] Like the ancient Cynics who proudly rejected paid labor, hippies and nomads engaged in multicultural begging, competing with natives even in Third World countries.[91] Their flight from work fulfilled a wish of the nineteenth-century workers' movement.[92] It also created itinerant friendships reminiscent of the *compagnons* of the craft guilds of the Old Regime: "This sociability of travel fused with the first types of workers' associations."[93]

NEW SOCIAL MOVEMENTS

The critique of work popularized in May planted the seeds of antiproductivism that would bloom after 1968. The Sixties democratized refusals of labor that had historically been the monopoly of the Old Regime aristocracy, bohemia, or unconventional intellectuals. The early twentieth century saw the expansion of the secularized work ethic to newly empowered communist and fascist elites, but the latter part of the century experienced the ephemeral rise of antiwork ideology. A focus on resistance to work refutes those who charged that 1960s' radicals embodied a rebirth of 1930s' fascism. It also helps to link the French movement to others around the world and to extend labor history to nonwage earners, such as vagabonds, beggars, prisoners, and prostitutes.[94]

In France and in other Western nations, a new type of labor history arose, and, for the first time, historians began to chronicle workers' everyday refusals of work.[95] During the 1970s, Michel Foucault and Michelle Perrot composed histories of the rejection of disciplinary techniques by workers, women, prisoners, and others.[96] This history from below resurrected the popular classes' search for autonomy and reflected a crisis of *militantisme*. As Foucault stated in the early 1970s, "The masses don't need him [the intellectual] to gain knowledge; they know perfectly well, without illusion; they know far better than he and they are certainly capable of expressing themselves."[97] Nonworker activists and militants (whom their detractors branded "political priests") had only minor roles to play when workers' autonomy and self-determination were the goals. Intellectuals could not lead the movement or provide it with revolutionary consciousness in the Leninist sense since, according to leftist critics of orthodox Marxism, the struggle itself—not well-meaning intellectuals—formed class consciousness.

Works of labor and social history by Perrot, Foucault, and others both reflected and sparked desires to revive libertarian traditions. Richard Gombin's key text reevaluated positively a leftism that Lenin had disdained as "infantile."[98] Indeed, anti-Leninist leftists dismissed direction by "revolutionary" political parties and supposedly representative trade unions in favor of wildcat strikes, factory occupations, and varieties of workers' control, which, they posited, prefigured the real socialism of the future. As the motto of the First International stated, "the liberation of the working class must be won by the working class itself." Gombin argued that the young Georg Lukács, Karl Korsch, and Anton Pannekoek agreed that a successful workers' revolution must rely ultimately only on the workers themselves.

Yet much like their Bolshevik opponents, these early twentieth-century councilists possessed a productivist notion of the revolution. They assumed that workers would efficiently manage the farms and factories that they controlled. The councilists' project contradicted the spirit of the antiwork advocates whose revitalized *ouvriérisme* (workerism) of the 1970s posited that "work is the curse of the class that drinks." Antiwork advocates believed that putting themselves at the service of the workers—as Maoists and Trotskyists proposed—continued the existence of both wage labor and wage workers. They rejected the sacrificial culture that other leftists developed.[99] The Situationist slogan—"Never Work"—exercised a powerful attraction among many of these young revolutionaries. The playful spirit of the Situationists rejected the transformation of artists into workers, as had occurred in communist states, in order to transmute workers into artists. The Situationists were undoubtedly provocative and clever, but it was questionable whether they or any other leftist group resolved the tension between workers' self-management and unavoidable social demands for production. In fact, *situs* tellingly mythologized as the apex of human achievement the collectives established by anarchists and Marxists during the Spanish Civil War.[100] Their understandable concern with the mesmerizing "spectacle" of consumption in the Long 1960s led them to ignore totally the refusals of work among the rank-and-file workers during the Spanish Revolution (1936–39). In other words, the post-1968 portrait of the working class as resisters of work was incompatible with the discipline and organization needed for the functioning of councils, soviets, and other types of productivist collectives.

Attacks on consumer society morphed into ecology that criticized the ravages of progress and production. New ecological concerns challenged hedonistic consumerism, which some blamed on the Sixties. In the 1970s, radical peasant movements began to raise doubts about industrial agriculture and its effects on the earth and the human body.[101] The decade-long fight from 1971 to 1981 to prevent the French military from occupying the plateau of Larzac gained local and national support and proved capable of conserving the plateau as a grazing area for sheep used to produce the archetypically French Roquefort cheese. Rural protests against the state and capitalist innovations, such as genetically altered crops and fast food (*la malbouffe*), were justified by ecological concerns rather than class struggle. Even among today's extreme Left, such as the Nouvel Parti Anticapitaliste, the negative slogan of "anticapitalism" has often replaced the celebration of socialism or communism.

The Lip watch company expressed this anticapitalism more than the *autogestion* for which it was famed.[102] The most famous self-management strike of the Long '60s began in the spring of 1973 when Lip workers cut production in half, then occupied the factory, and expropriated 30,000 finished watches. Participation in the struggle led some younger and a few older workers to denounce their work as unfulfilling, and—partially subscribing to "Never Work"—they distanced themselves from what they considered the self-exploitation of workers' control. Yet most workers knew that they could only seduce needed public support if they presented themselves as conscientious, even eager, producers. Influenced by progressive Catholicism, the local CFDT advocated "democratic" workers' control, which included daily assemblies—attended on average by only a third of the workers—and job changing within the factory. The latter had a particular appeal to unskilled female workers who felt imprisoned by their usual work routine. Production of watches was "more symbolic than . . . real" since only one of the four assembly lines operated in the summer of 1973. When workers took vacations in July, only fifteen or twenty workers assembled watches, which were nearly finished. Female workers enjoyed setting their own rotation and pace, but an important government mediator felt that Lip workers "had abandoned basic everyday work."

A niche market among politically progressive consumers developed for the timepieces, and "buyers wanted to believe they were purchasing watches which had been made" by self-management and were inaccurately assured by the local CFDT leaders "that this was the case." The conservative *Le Figaro* called the watch sales "the most successful advertising campaign of the year." Popularization of the struggle became more important than production. Lip wage earners maintained their preconflict pay with funds derived from the sale of confiscated watches and generous government unemployment benefits. Lip union leaders themselves spoke of "self-management of the struggle," rather than self-management of production. Thus Lip was "a representation of self-management," not the thing itself.

CONCLUSION

The end of the "thirty glorious years" in 1975 resulted in a growing scarcity of wage labor and encouraged French governments to reduce the work week and thus share available employment. In this context, the supposed revolutionary year 1968 was not exceptional and remained merely part of the gradual reduction of the French work week that began in 1962 (approximately 46 hours) and continued to the end of the century (generally 35–36 hours).[103] More competition for fewer jobs restrained turnover and discouraged labor indiscipline. As the relative weight of youth in the population diminished, their unemployment rates climbed. Growing unemployment undermined the popularity of antiwork theorists, movements, and *autogestion* while propelling counterrevolutionary forces, including the extreme Right. The questioning of wage labor diminishes when it becomes scarce, and, correspondingly, the push for individual effort increases. The hedonistic slogan of 1968 that had complained in an era of nearly full employment of an everyday life of "subway, work, and sleep" (*Métro, boulot, dodo*) disappeared in the face of popular demands for all three.[104] As has been seen, the revolution against work had immediately provoked an antiutopian counterrevolution.

The counteroffensive against refusal of labor endured well into the 1980s when the conservative neoliberals Ronald Reagan and Margaret Thatcher laid the basis for what some claim to be "illiberal" workfare that compelled the unemployed to labor.[105] In France during the 2007 presidential campaign, Nicolas Sarkozy repeated this attack from above on the Sixties' legacy when he blamed the "relativism" that he attributed to May 1968 for France's alleged moral, intellectual, and economic decline. Sarkozy's solution was to glorify work and workers and to defend, at least rhetorically, those who "se lève tôt" ("wake up early [for work]"). Like Sarkozy, others have exaggerated the importance of May as the starting point (*événement fondateur*) for individualism, hedonism, consumerism, cosmopolitanism, feminism, and gay liberation.[106] Marxists too have blamed May for individualism and hedonism, but, unlike conservatives, they have attributed these "capitalist" values to the failure of the 1968 collectivist workers' revolution.[107] Whereas leftists accuse "capitalist" egotism of negating the solidarity needed for a progressive future, conservative French intellectuals worry that unrestrained individualism subverts traditional France.

Yet the cultural counterrevolution never succeeded in completely eliminating the conquests of the Sixties in Western Europe and North America where gender equality, sexual freedoms, and multiculturalism promoted by that long decade have largely been accepted, even if constantly challenged. However, rejection of work remains intolerable and too subversive for any publicly proclaimed mass movement. As Herbert Marcuse, Henri Lefebvre, and Guy Debord argued, advanced capitalism can integrate many forms of protest, but the demand to abolish work is not among them.

NOTES

1. Nanni Balestrini, *Lo queremos todo*, trans. Herman Mario Cueva (Buenos Aires, 1974); Gianni Giovannelli, *Never Work: The Autobiography of Salvatore Messana*, trans. Bill Brown (New York, 2013); Jean-Pierre Le Goff, *La France d'hier: Récit d'un monde adolescent des années 1950 à Mai 68* (Paris, 2018), 237; Jacques Guigou and Jacques Wajnsztejn, *Mai 1968 et le Mai rampant Italien*

(Paris, 2008), 15; Serge Audier, *La pensée anti-68: Essai sur les origines d'une restauration intellectuelle* (Paris, 2009), 11. On Chile, see chapter 15 in this volume by Patrick Barr-Melej.

2. Arthur Marwick, *The Sixties: Cultural Revolution in Britain, France, Italy, and the United States, c. 1958–1974* (New York, 1998), 3–38; Bernard Brillant, *Les clercs de 68* (Paris, 2003), 319, 507–13; Boris Gobille, *Mai 68* (Paris, 2008), 6. See also the journal *Révoltes Logiques* (1975–1981).

3. Also one of the themes in chapter 6 by William Donahue in this volume.

4. For the importance of cultural Marxism in France, see chapter 4 by Eric Drott in this volume.

5. Herbert Marcuse, *An Essay on Liberation* (Boston, 1969), 5, 21; Anselm Jappe, *Guy Debord*, trans. Donald Nicholson-Smith (Berkeley, 1999), 151.

6. James Miller, *Democracy Is in the Streets: From Port Huron to the Siege of Chicago* (New York, 1987), 39.

7. Marwick, *Sixties*, 673.

8. Stephen Bouquin, ed., *Résistances au travail* (Paris, 2008), 30; Robert Lumley, *States of Emergency: Cultures of Revolt in Italy from 1968 to 1978* (London, 1990), 37–38.

9. Adrien Dansette, *Mai 1968* (Paris, 1971), 58; Pierre Grappin, *L'Ile aux peupliers* (Nancy, 1993), 241.

10. Jean-François Sirinelli, *Mai 68: L'événement Janus* (Paris, 2008), 62.

11. Partout, 19 March 1968, 1208W, art. 256, Archives départementales des Hauts-de-Seine, Nanterre.

12. For a partial musical return to the Old Regime, see chapter 16 in this volume by Carmen-Helena Téllez. The argument by minimalist composers that "less is more" would find advocates among antiwork activists.

13. Dogkyu Shin, "La CGT Berliet à Vénissieux en mai 1968: La réactivation de la mémoire locale et les enjeux de la contestation autour des conflits de 1967–1968," in *Mai–juin 1968: Huit semaines qui ébranlèrent la France*, ed. Xavier Vigna and Jean Vigreux (Dijon, 2010), 38–39; Louis Gruel, *La Rébellion de 1968: Une relecture sociologique* (Rennes, 2004), 41.

14. Claire Auzias, *Trimards: "Pègre" et mauvais garçons de Mai 68* (Lyon, 2017), 32; Brillant, *Les clercs*, 450.

15. Auzias, *Trimards*, 67, 154; Guigou, *Mai 1968*, 25; Mimmo Pucciarelli, *Claire l'enragée: Entretien avec Claire Auzias* (Lyon, 2006), 53.

16. Gruel, *La Rébellion*, 107, 117; Michael Seidman, "The Love Wars: Voices from France (1962–68)," *Modern and Contemporary France* 6 (May 2008): 125–41; Lilian Mathieu, "Le mai lyonnais," in Collectif de la Grande Côte, *Lyon en luttes dans les années 68: Lieux et trajectoires de la contestation* (Lyon, 2018), 21.

17. Auzias, *Trimards*, 120, 157. Cf. Ludivine Bantigny, *1968: De grands soirs en petits matins* (Paris, 2018), 58.

18. Mathieu, "Le mai lyonnais," 47–48.

19. Julien Hage, "Vie et mort d'une librairie militante: La Joie de Lire," in *68: Une histoire collective*, ed. Philippe Artières and Michelle Zancarini-Fournel (Paris, 2008), 536; Brillant, *Les clercs*, 98.

20. Auzias, *Trimards*, 146–47.

21. Audier, *La pensée anti-68*, 82.

22. Michelle Perrot, *Les ouvriers en grève: France 1871–1890* (Paris, 1974), 101, 109, 137, 722.

23. Absentéisme (1964), Archives Nationales [hereafter AN] 39AS 287.

24. *Les Échos*, May 21, 1968; Christian Charrière, *Le Printemps des enragés* (Paris, 1968), 232.

25. Groupement des industriels d'Argenteuil-Bezons et communes avoisinantes, "Enquête concernant les conflits sociaux," July–November 1968, Groupement des Industries Métallurgiques, Neuilly [hereafter GIM].

26. At Renault-Cléon, management was confined to its offices and held hostage to prevent a police raid. See *Notre arme c'est la grève* (Paris, 1968), 23; Jacques Baynac, *Mai retrouvé* (Paris, 1978), 139.

27. Patrick Rotman, *Mai 68 raconté à ceux qui ne l'ont pas vécu* (Paris, 2008), 86.

28. Situation sociale, May 27, 1968, GIM.

29. Centre national d'information pour la productivité des entreprises, *Les événements de mai-juin 1968 vus à travers cent entreprises* (Paris, 1968), 25; Daniel Singer, *Prelude to Revolution: France in May 1968* (New York, 1970), 234.

30. Crise de mai 1968, 22 May 1968, GIM; on the failure of Citroën management to get police to confront the occupiers, see Lucien Rioux and René Backmann, *L'Explosion de mai* (Paris, 1968), 438; Charrière, *Printemps*, 246; Mathias Bernard, "L'État en mai 68," in Vigna and Vigreux, eds., *Mai–juin 1968*, 141.

31. 24 May 1968, Fa 260, Archives de la Préfecture de Police.

32. Maurice Grimaud, *En mai, fais ce qu'il te plaît* (Paris, 1977), 218.

33. Bernard Pudal, "Les événements de mai et juin 1968: Bref récit chronologique," and Bernard Pudal and Jean-Noël Retière, "Les grèves ouvrières de 68, un mouvement social sans lendemain mémorial," in *Mai–Juin 68*, ed. Dominique Damamme (Paris, 2008), 192, 208; Antoine Prost, "Les grèves de mai-juin 1968," *L'Histoire*, no. 110 (April 1988): 36; Kristin Ross, *May '68 and Its Afterlives* (Chicago, 2002), 8, 184; Xavier Vigna, *L'Insubordination ouvrière dans les années 68* (Rennes, 2007), 37; Michelle Zancarini-Fournel, "L'épicentre," in Artières and Zancarini-Fournel, eds., *68*, 226; Michelle Zancarini-Fournel,

Le moment 68: Une histoire contestée (Paris, 2008), 46; Jacques Kergoat, "Sous la plage, la grève," in *La France des années 68*, ed. Antoine Artous, Didier Epsztajn, and Patrick Silberstein (Paris, 2008), 66; Xavier Vigna and Jean Vigreux, "Introduction," in Vigna and Vigreux, eds., *Mai–juin 1968*, 6.

34. Sirinelli, *Mai 68*, 68.

35. Bantigny, *1968*, 252.

36. Philippe Péchoux, "'Pas de Nanterre à Dijon' Construction de contradictions du mouvement étudiant dijonnais de mai–juin 1968: Entre réforme, révolution et réaction," and Lilian Mathieu, "Décalages et alignements des dynamiques contestataires: Mai–juin 1968 à Lyon," in Vigna and Vigreux, eds., *Mai–juin 1968*, 63, 179–83.

37. Bantigny, *1968*, 212.

38. Vincent Porhel, "Plozévet 68: La révolte au village?," in Vigna and Vigreux, eds., *Mai–juin 1968*, 123; Bantigny, *1968*, 63.

39. Brillant, *Les clercs*, 381.

40. 30 May 1968, AN 800273/61.

41. Charles Diaz, *Mémoires de Police dans la tourmente de Mai 68* (Paris, 2007), 96. For a contrast with police violence in Latin America and Eastern Europe, see chapters 14 and 8 in this volume by Jaime M. Pensado and Timothy W. Ryback, respectively.

42. Confédération Générale du Travail de la R.N.U.R. [Régie Nationale des Usines Renault], *33 jours 34 nuits* (Paris, n.d.), 12.

43. Jean-Pierre Filiu, "L'Intersyndicale durant le conflit," in *Mai 68 à l'ORTF* (Paris, 1987), 47; 4 June 1968, AN 820599/41.

44. *L'Aurore*, June 10, 1968.

45. Edgar Morin, Claude Lefort, and Cornelius Castoriadis, *Mai 68: La brèche* (Paris, 1988).

46. Gerd-Rainer Horn, *The Spirit of '68: Rebellion in Western Europe and North America, 1956–1976* (Oxford, 2007), 2; Richard Wolin, *The Wind from the East: French Intellectuals, the Cultural Revolution, and the Legacy of the 1960s* (Princeton, NJ, 2010), 98, 139, 192, 214.

47. Vincent Porhel, "L'autogestion à la CSF de Brest," in *Les Années 68: Le Temps de la contestation*, ed. Geneviève Dreyfus-Armand, Robert Frank, Marie-Françoise Lévy, and Michelle Zancarini-Fournel (Brussels: Éditions Complexe, 2000), 395; Vincent Porhel, *Ouvriers bretons: Conflits d'usines, conflits identitaires en Bretagne dans les années 1968* (Rennes, 2008), 76–104. See also Kergoat, "Sous la plage," 77–78, 83; Xavier Vigna and Jean Vigreux, "Conclusion," in Vigna and Vigreux, eds., *Mai–juin 1968*, 298.

48. Guigou, *Mai 1968*, 119.

49. Kergoat, "Sous la plage," 58; Perrot, *Les ouvriers*, 55, 83; Gobille, *Mai 68*, 45.

50. Frank Georgi, "Selbstverwaltung: Aufstieg und Niedergang einer politischen Utopie in Frankreich von den 1968er bis zu den 80er Jahren," in *1968 und die Arbeiter: Studien zum "proletarischen Mai" in Europa*, ed. Bernd Gehrke and Gerd-Rainer Horn (Hamburg, 2007), 260; Laure Fleury, Lilian Mathieu, and Vincent Porhel, "Vivement la révolution! Les dynamiques militantes de l'extrême gauche lyonnaise," in Collectif de la Grande Côte, *Lyon en luttes dans les années 68*, 85.

51. Sylvain Zegel, *Les idées de mai* (Paris, 1968), 43; Michel Pigenet, "Les mutations des mondes et du syndicalisme portuaires autour de 1968," in *1968 entre libération et libéralisation*, ed. Michel Margairaz and Danielle Tartakowsky (Rennes, 2010), 289–302; Rebecca Clifford, Juliane Fürst, Robert Gildea, James Mark, Piotr Oseka, and Chris Reynolds, "Spaces," in *Europe's 1968: Voices of Revolt*, ed. Robert Gildea, James Mark, and Anette Warring (Oxford, 2013), 167.

52. Situation sociale, période du 13 au 26 mai, GIM.

53. Daniel Mothé, "L'usine, l'amphi et l'association de quartier: Fermeture de trois espaces militants en mai 1968," *Esprit*, no. 344 (May 2008): 37.

54. UNEF militants quoted in Alain Schnapp and Pierre Vidal-Naquet, *Journal de la commune étudiante* (Paris, 1969), 302. This *gauchisant* orthodoxy is repeated in many other analyses.

55. Yannick Guin, *La commune de Nantes* (Paris, 1969), 17; Claude Poperen, *Renault: Regards de l'intérieur* (Paris, 1983), 167: "There was not always a rush to occupy the factory."

56. Shin, "La CGT," 51.

57. *Le Monde*, May 17, 1968; Philippe Labro, *Ce n'est qu'un début* (Paris, 1968), 71; Nicolas Hatzfeld and Cédric Lomba, "La grève de Rhodiaceta en 1967," in Vigna and Vigreux, *Mai–Juin 68*, 112. Cf. Ross, *May '68*, 68: "The workers [were] enclosed, for the most part, in occupied factories."

58. Patrick Hassenteufel, "Citroën-Paris en mai–juin 1968: Dualités de la grève" (Master's thesis, Université de Paris I, 1987), 49–101; Nicolas Hatzfeld, "Les morts de Flins et Sochaux: De la grève à la violence politique," in Artières and Zancarini-Fournel, eds., *68*, 325.

59. Sirinelli, *Mai 68*, 253–54. See also Jean-Pierre Duteuil, *Mai 68: Un mouvement politique* (La Bussière, 2008), 64, 123, 167.

60. Jean-Pierre Filiu, "Le gouvernement et la direction face à la crise," in *Mai 68 à l'ORTF*, 273; *Ouvriers face aux appareils: Une expérience de militantisme chez Hispano-Suiza* (Paris, 1970), 198; Fanny Callot, "La conflictualité à Renault Cléon en mai–juin 1968," in Vigna and Vigreux, eds., *Mai–juin 1968*, 29–31.

61. *Le Nouvel Observateur*, May 30, 1968; "CGT aux femmes," Tracts de mai 1968, Bibliothèque Nationale, Paris [hereafter BN].

62. *Le Nouvel Observateur*, May 30, 1968.

63. Ibid.

64. Gobille, *Mai 68*, 5.

65. Situation sociale, 6 June, GIM. Fifty-five percent of French industrial workers surveyed in 1969 declared that they had never participated in a union meeting. See Gérard Adam, Frédéric Bon, Jacques Capdevielle, and René Mouriaux, *L'Ouvrier français en 1970* (Paris, 1970), 21.

66. Perrot, *Les ouvriers*, 588–89.

67. "Défendons notre grève," Tracts de mai 1968, BN.

68. *Lutte Socialiste*, December 1968; Gilles Martinet, *La conquête des pouvoirs* (Paris, 1968), 69, which sees Rhône-Poulenc at Vitry as a model of "*tendances gestionnaires.*" Police reported that on June 12 only 300 out of a workforce of 3,700 favored a return to work. See 12 June 1968, AN 820599/41.

69. Groupes inter-syndicaux des salariés, Tracts de mai 1968, BN; Patrick Ravignant, *L'Odéon est ouvert* (Paris, 1968), 217; Schnapp, *Journal*, 311; Baynac, *Mai*, 176; Dansette, *Mai 1968*, 275.

70. Mouvement du 22 mars, *Ce n'est pas qu'un début, continuons le combat* (Paris, 1968), 99. Cf. also Lucio Magri, "Réflexions sur les événements de mai," *Les Temps modernes*, no. 277–78 (August–September 1969): 32: "Because of its spontaneous origin and the consequent occupation tactic, the workers' struggle profoundly upset the traditional relations between masses and leaders." Similar views are found in Alain Geismar, Serge July, and Erlyne Morane, *Vers la guerre civile* (Paris, 1969), 258.

71. Cohn-Bendit during June 1 press conference in Jean Bertolino, *Les Trublions* (Paris, 1969), 38.

72. Le Goff, *La France d'hier*, 49.

73. Roger Martelli, *Mai 68* (Paris, 1988), 54; Ronan Capitaine, "Dassault Saint-Cloud en mai–juin 1968" (Master's thesis, Paris I, 1990), 182; Henri Simon Oral History Project, interviews with workers, 1994, Paris.

74. Maurice Cohen, ed., *Le bilan social de l'année 1968* (Paris, 1969), 105–22, 387, 414. See also Accord du 13 décembre 1968, AN 860561; Xavier Vigna, "La CGT et les grèves ouvrières en mai-juin 1968: Une opératrice paradoxale de stabilisation," in Vigna and Vigreux, eds., *Mai–juin 1968*, 207–8.

75. Stéphane Paquelin, "Responsables syndicalistes face à l'événement et ses suites, le cas de mai–juin 1968," in Vigna and Vigreux, eds., *Mai–juin 1968*, 220.

76. Vigna, *L'Insubordination*; Isabelle Sommier, *La violence politique et son deuil: L'après 68 en France et en Italie* (Rennes, 1998), 13.

77. Henri Simon Oral History Project; Bernard, "L'État en mai 68," 144.

78. Lumley, *States of Emergency*, 10, 182–83, 250; Paul Ginsborg, *A History of Contemporary Italy: Society and Politics 1943–1988* (London, 1990), 314–19; Balestrini, *Queremos todo*, 76, 116, 126.

79. Michele Salvati, "May 1968 and the Hot Autumn of 1969: The Response of Two Ruling Classes," in *Organizing Interests in Western Europe*, ed. Suzanne Berger (New York, 1981), 351.

80. Nicolas Hatzfeld, "Les ouvriers de l'automobile: Des vitrines sociales à la condition des OS, le changement des regards," in *Les Années 68: Le Temps de la contestation*, ed. Geneviève Dreyfus-Armand, Robert Frank, Marie-Françoise Lévy, and Michelle Zancarini-Fournel (Brussels, 2000), 358–61.

81. Balestrini, *Queremos todo*, 165.

82. Martin Clark, *Modern Italy, 1871–1995* (London, 1996), 378; Lumley, *States of Emergency*, 251–52; Guigou, *Mai 1968*, 172.

83. Réunion tenue les 25–27 mai au Ministère des Affaires Sociales, AN 860561.

84. Cohen, *Le bilan social*, 105–22, 387, 414. See also Accord du 13 décembre 1968, AN 860561.

85. Michael Seidman, *The Imaginary Revolution: Parisian Students and Workers in 1968* (New York, 2004); Perrot, *Les ouvriers*, 44, 303.

86. Jonathyne Briggs, *Sounds French: Globalization, Cultural Communities, and Pop Music, 1958–1980* (New York, 2015), 16, 87.

87. Hervé Le Roux, *Reprise: Récit* (Paris, 1998); Ross, *May '68*, 139; Vigna, " La CGT," 206.

88. Antoine de Baecque, "*Reprise* d'Hervé Le Roux," in Artières and Zancarini-Fournel, eds., *68*, 275.

89. Axel Schildt, "Across the Border: West German Youth Travel to Western Europe," in *Between Marx and Coca-Cola: Youth Cultures in Changing European Societies, 1960–1980*, ed. Axel Schildt and Detlef Siegfried (New York, 2007), 151–53. See also chapters 8 and 6 by Timothy Ryback and William Donahue, respectively, in this volume.

90. Pucciarelli, *Claire*, 65, 91.

91. Patrick Cingolani, "Interminable Pérégrination: L'imaginaire de la route dans les années soixante," *Tumultes*, no. 5 (Novembre 1994): 116.

92. Ibid., 101; Laurent Chollet, "La route du Népal: La grande migration hippie," in Artières and Zancarini-Fournel, eds., *68*, 502–4.

93. Cingolani, "Interminable Pérégrination," 120.

94. Marcel van der Linden, *Transnational Labour History: Explorations* (Aldershot, 2003).

95. Antoine Prost, *La CGT à l'époque du front populaire: 1934–1939. Essai de description numérique,* (Paris, 1964); Rolande Trempé, *Les mineurs de Carmaux, 1848–1914* (Paris, 1971); Yves Lequin, *Les ouvriers de la région lyonnaise (1848–1914)* (Lyon, 1977). Certain histories continued to ignore refusals of work in favor of a traditional productivist approach. For example, Peter Winn, *Weavers of Revolution: The Yarur Workers and Chile's Road to Socialism* (New York, 1986), stresses workers' willingness to sacrifice for the revolution. However, the author is somewhat inconsistent: After seventeen months of worker control "without any significant drop in production" and Sunday "voluntary labor," he states that the military used authoritarian means to restore discipline and raise productivity in the Yarur firm. Winn bases his history essentially on testimony from militants belonging to parties and unions supporting the government of Popular Unity, which had initially promised them less work and more pay. Winn is more credible, but patronizing, when he writes, "Transitional problems, such as lax work discipline and uneven labor productivity, reflected unrealistic worker expectations of what 'liberation' would mean" (224). Perhaps, though, for many workers the revolution meant working less, if at all.

96. Perrot, *Les ouvriers*; Michel Foucault, *Discipline and Punish: The Birth of the Prison*, trans. Alan Sheridan (New York, 1977).

97. Foucault quoted in Wolin, *Wind*, 308; Michel Foucault, *Foucault Live (Interviews, 1961–1984)* (New York, 1996), 75.

98. Richard Gombin, *The Origins of Modern Leftism*, trans. Michael K. Perl (Harmondsworth, 1975).

99. Laure Fleury, "À la croisée du politique et de l'intime: La militantisme en couple dans les organisations maoïstes," in Collectif de la Grande Côte, *Lyon en luttes dans les années 68*, 305. On Maoist sacrificial culture in Argentina, see Valeria Manzano's chapter 7 in this volume.

100. For a recent analysis, see Alastair Hemmens, *The Critique of Work in Modern French Thought: From Charles Fourier to Guy Debord* (Cham, Switzerland, 2019), 158–61.

101. Jean-Philippe Martin, *Des "mai 68" dans les campagnes françaises? Les contestations paysannes dans les années 1968* (Paris, 2017), 30, 66–69, 133, 193.

102. The following paragraphs are based on Donald Reid, *Opening the Gates: The Lip Affair, 1968–1981* (London, 2018). See also Richard Vinen, *1968: Radical Protest and Its Enemies* (New York, 2018), 257–58.

103. Philippe Askenazy, Catherine Bloch-London, and Muriel Roger, "La réduction du temps de travail: 1997–2003," in *La France et le temps de travail (1814–2004)*, edited by Patrick Fridenson and Bénédicte Reynaud (Paris, 2004), 186.

104. Mothé, "L'usine," 43; Hemmens, *Critique of Work*, 169.

105. On this issue, see Desmond King, *In the Name of Liberalism: Illiberal Social Policy in the USA and Britain* (Oxford, 1999).

106. This was a major argument in the best seller by Éric Zemmour, *Le suicide français* (Paris, 2014).

107. Roland Holst, Willi Baer, and Karl-Heinz Dellwo, eds., *Paris Mai 68: Die Phantasie an die Macht* (Hamburg, 2011), 165.

BIBLIOGRAPHY

Archival Sources

Archives de la Préfecture de Police, Paris
Archives départementales des Hauts-de-Seine, Nanterre
Archives Nationales (AN), Paris
Groupement des Industries Métallurgiques (GIM), Neuilly
Henri Simon Oral History Project, Paris
Tracts de mai 1968, Bibliothèque Nationale (BN), Paris

Printed Primary Sources

L'Aurore
Le Monde
Le Nouvel Observateur
Les Échos
Lutte Socialiste
Schnapp, Alain, and Pierre Vidal-Naquet. *Journal de la commune étudiante*. Paris: Éditions du Seuil, 1969.

Secondary Sources

Adam, Gérard, Frédéric Bon, Jacques Capdevielle, and René Mouriaux. *L'Ouvrier français en 1970*. Paris: Armand Colin, 1970.

Artières, Philippe, and Michelle Zancarini-Fournel, eds. *68: Une histoire collective*. Paris: La Découverte, 2008.

Askenazy, Philippe, Catherine Bloch-London, and Muriel Roger. "La réduction du temps de travail: 1997–2003." In *La France et le temps de travail (1814–2004)*, ed. Patrick Fridenson and Bénédicte Reynaud, 157–86. Paris: Odile Jacob, 2004.

Audier, Serge. *La pensée anti-68: Essai sur les origines d'une restauration intellectuelle.* Paris: La Découverte, 2009.

Auzias, Claire. *Trimards: "Pègre" et mauvais garçons de Mai 68.* Lyon: Atelier de création libertaire, 2017.

Baecque, Antoine de. "*Reprise* d'Hervé Le Roux." In Artières and Zancarini-Fournel, eds., *68*, 275–79.

Balestrini, Nanni. *Lo queremos todo.* Translated by Herman Mario Cueva. Buenos Aires: Ediciones de la Flor, 1974.

Bantigny, Ludivine. *1968: De grands soirs en petits matins.* Paris: Éditiones du Seuil, 2018.

Baynac, Jacques. *Mai retrouvé.* Paris: R. Laffont, 1978.

Bernard, Mathias. "L'État en mai 68." In Vigna and Vigreux, eds. *Mai–juin 1968*, 131–44.

Bertolino, Jean. *Les Trublions.* Paris: R. Laffont, 1969.

Bouquin, Stephen, ed. *Résistances au travail.* Paris: Syllepse, 2008.

Briggs, Jonathyne. *Sounds French: Globalization, Cultural Communities, and Pop Music, 1958–1980.* New York: Oxford University Press, 2015.

Brillant, Bernard. *Les clercs de 68.* Paris: Presses universitaires de France, 2003.

Callot, Fanny. "La conflictualité à Renault Cléon en mai–juin 1968." In Vigna and Vigreux, eds., *Mai–juin 1968*, 23–35.

Capitaine, Ronan. "Dassault Saint-Cloud en mai–juin 1968. Master's thesis, Paris I, 1990.

Centre national d'information pour la productivité des entreprises. *Les événements de mai-juin 1968 vus à travers cent entreprises.* Paris: C.N.I.P.E., 1968.

Charrière, Christian. *Le Printemps des enragés.* Paris: Fayard, 1968.

Chollet, Laurent. "La route du Népal: La grande migration hippie." In Artières and Zancarini-Fournel, eds. *68*, 500–505.

Cingolani, Patrick. "Interminable Pérégrination: L'imaginaire de la route dans les années soixante." *Tumultes*, no. 5 (November 1994): 95–122.

Clark, Martin. *Modern Italy, 1871–1995.* London: Longman, 1996.

Clifford, Rebecca, Juliane Fürst, Robert Gildea, James Mark, Piotr Oseka, and Chris Reynolds. "Spaces." In *Europe's 1968: Voices of Revolt*, edited by Robert Gildea, James Mark, and Anette Warring, 164–92. Oxford: Oxford University Press, 2013.

Cohen, Maurice, ed. *Le bilan social de l'année 1968.* Paris: Revue pratique de droit social, 1969.

Collectif de la Grande Côte. *Lyon en luttes dans les années 68: Lieux et trajectoires de la contestation.* Lyon: Presses universitaires de Lyon, 2018.

Confédération Générale du Travail de la R.N.U.R. [Régie Nationale des Usines Renault]. *33 jours 34 Nuits.* Paris: Syndicat C.G.T. des travailleurs de la R.N.U.R., n.d.

Damamme, Dominique, ed. *Mai–Juin 68.* Paris: Les éditions de l'atelier, 2008.

Dansette, Adrien. *Mai 1968.* Paris: Plon, 1971.

Diaz, Charles. *Mémoires de Police dans la tourmente de Mai 68.* Paris: Textuel, 2007.

Duteuil, Jean-Pierre. *Mai 68: Un mouvement politique.* La Bussière: Acratie, 2008.

Filiu, Jean-Pierre. "Le gouvernement et la direction face à la crise." In *Mai 68 à l'ORTF*, 161–94.

———. "L'Intersyndicale durant le conflit." In *Mai 68 à l'ORTF*, 37–67.

Fleury, Laure. "À la croisée du politique et de l'intime: Le militantisme en couple dans les organisations maoïstes." In Collectif de la Grande Côte, *Lyon en luttes dans les années 68*, 301–20.

Fleury, Laure, Lilian Mathieu, and Vincent Porhel. "Vivement la révolution! Les dynamiques militantes de l'extrême gauche lyonnaise." In Collectif de la Grande Côte, *Lyon en luttes dans les années 68*, 49–96.

Foucault, Michel. *Discipline and Punish: The Birth of the Prison.* Translated by Alan Sheridan. New York: Pantheon Books, 1977.

———. *Foucault Live (Interviews, 1961–1984).* New York: Semiotext(e), 1996.

Geismar, Alain, Serge July, and Erlyne Morane. *Vers la guerre civile.* Paris: Éditions et publications premières, 1969.

Georgi, Frank. "Selbstverwaltung: Aufstieg und Niedergang einer politischen Utopie in Frankreich von den 1968er bis zu den 80er Jahren." In *1968 und die Arbeiter: Studien zum "proletarischen Mai" in Europa*, edited by Bernd Gehrke and Gerd-Rainer Horn, 252–75. Hamburg: VSA-Verlag, 2007.

Ginsborg, Paul. *A History of Contemporary Italy: Society and Politics, 1943–1988.* London: Penguin, 1990.

Giovannelli, Gianni. *Never Work: The Autobiography of Salvatore Messana.* Translated by Bill Brown. New York: Colossal Books, 2013.

Gobille, Boris. *Mai 68.* Paris: La Découverte, 2008.

Gombin, Richard. *The Origins of Modern Leftism.* Translated by Michael K. Perl. Harmondsworth: Penguin, 1975.

Grappin, Pierre. *L'Ile aux peupliers.* Nancy: Presses universitaires de Nancy, 1993.

Grimaud, Maurice. *En mai, fais ce qu'il te plaît.* Paris: Stock, 1977.

Gruel, Louis. *La Rébellion de 1968: Une relecture sociologique.* Rennes: Presses universitaires de Rennes, 2004.

Guigou, Jacques, and Jacques Wajnsztejn. *Mai 1968 et le Mai rampant Italien.* Paris: L'Harmattan, 2008.

Guin, Yannick. *La commune de Nantes.* Paris: F. Maspero, 1969.

Hage, Julien. "Vie et mort d'une librairie militante: La Joie de Lire." In Artières and Zancarini-Fournel, eds., *68*, 533–37.

Hassenteufel, Patrick. "Citroën-Paris en mai–juin 1968: Dualités de la grève." Master's thesis, Université de Paris I, 1987.

Hatzfeld, Nicolas. "Les morts de Flins et Sochaux: De la grève à la violence politique." In Artières and Zancarini-Fournel, eds., *68*, 322–26.

———. "Les ouvriers de l'automobile: Des vitrines sociales à la condition des OS, le changement des regards." In *Les Années 68: Le Temps de la contestation*, edited by Geneviève Dreyfus-Armand, Robert Frank, Marie-Françoise Lévy, and Michelle Zancarini-Fournel, 345–62. Brussels: Éditions Complexe, 2000.

Hatzfeld, Nicolas, and Cédric Lomba. "La grève de Rhodiaceta en 1967." In Damamme, ed., *Mai–Juin 68*, 102–13.

Hemmens, Alastair. *The Critique of Work in Modern French Thought: From Charles Fourier to Guy Debord.* Cham, Switzerland: Palgrave Macmillan, 2019.

Holst, Roland, Willi Baer, and Karl-Heinz Dellwo, eds. *Paris Mai 68: Die Phantasie an die Macht.* Hamburg: Laika Verlag, 2011.

Horn, Gerd-Rainer. *The Spirit of '68: Rebellion in Western Europe and North America, 1956–1976.* Oxford: Oxford University Press, 2007.

Jappe, Anselm. *Guy Debord.* Translated by Donald Nicholson-Smith. Berkeley: University of California Press, 1999.

Kergoat, Jacques. "Sous la plage, la grève." In *La France des années 68*, edited by Antoine Artous, Didier Epsztajn, and Patrick Silberstein, 58–83, Paris: Syllepse, 2008.

King, Desmond. *In the Name of Liberalism: Illiberal Social Policy in the USA and Britain.* Oxford: Oxford University Press, 1999.

Labro, Philippe, *Ce n'est qu'un début.* Paris: Éditions et publications premières, 1968.

Le Goff, Jean-Pierre. *La France d'hier: Récit d'un monde adolescent des années 1950 à Mai 68.* Paris: Stock, 2018.

Lequin, Yves. *Les ouvriers de la région lyonnaise (1848–1914).* Lyon: Presses universitaires de Lyon, 1977.

Le Roux, Hervé. *Reprise: Récit.* Paris: Ministère de l'emploi et de la solidarité, 1998.

Lumley, Robert. *States of Emergency: Cultures of Revolt in Italy from 1968 to 1978.* London: Verso, 1990.

Magri, Lucio. "Réflexions sur les événements de mai." *Les Temps modernes*, no. 277–78 (August–September 1969): 1–45.

Marcuse, Herbert. *An Essay on Liberation.* Boston: Beacon Press, 1969.

Martelli, Roger. *Mai 68.* Paris: Messidor, 1988.

Martin, Jean-Philippe. *Des "mai 68" dans les campagnes françaises? Les contestations paysannes dans les années 1968.* Paris: L'Harmattan, 2017.

Martinet, Gilles. *La conquête des pouvoirs.* Paris: Éditions du Seuil, 1968.

Marwick, Arthur, *The Sixties: Cultural Revolution in Britain, France, Italy, and the United States, c. 1958–1974.* New York: Oxford University Press, 1998.

Mathieu, Lilian. "Décalages et alignements des dynamiques contestataires: Mai–juin 1968 à Lyon." In Vigna and Vigreux, eds., *Mai–juin 1968,* 55–70.

———. "Le mai lyonnais." In Collectif de la Grande Côte, *Lyon en luttes dans les années 68,* 19–48.

Mai 68 à l'ORTF. Paris: La Doumentation française, 1987.

Miller, James. *Democracy Is in the Streets: From Port Huron to the Siege of Chicago.* New York: Simon and Schuster, 1987.

Morin, Edgar, Claude Lefort, and Cornelius Castoriadis. *Mai 68: La brèche.* Paris: Éditions Complexe, 1988.

Mothé, Daniel. "L'usine, l'amphi et l'association de quartier: Fermeture de trois espaces militants en mai 1968." *Esprit,* no. 344 (May 2008): 34–43.

Mouvement du 22 mars. *Ce n'est pas qu'un début, continuons le combat.* Paris: F. Maspero, 1968.

Notre arme c'est la grève. Paris: F. Maspero, 1968.

Ouvriers face aux appareils: Une expérience de militantisme chez Hispano-Suiza. Paris: F. Maspero, 1970.

Paquelin, Stéphane. "Responsables syndicalistes face à l'événement et ses suites, le cas de mai–juin 1968." In Vigna and Vigreux, eds., *Mai–juin 1968,* 215–28.

Péchoux, Philippe. "'Pas de Nanterre à Dijon' Construction de contradictions du mouvement étudiant dijonnais de mai–juin 1968: Entre réforme, révolution et réaction." In Vigna and Vigreux, eds., *Mai–juin 1968,* 169–83.

Perrot, Michelle. *Les ouvriers en grève: France 1871–1890.* Paris: Mouton, 1974.

Pigenet, Michel. "Les mutations des mondes et du syndicalisme portuaires autour de 1968." In *1968 entre libération et liberalisation,* edited by Michel Margairaz and Danielle Tartakowsky, 289–302. Rennes: Presses universitaires de Rennes, 2010.

Poperen, Claude. *Renault: Regards de l'intérieur.* Paris: Éditions sociales, 1983.

Porhel, Vincent. "L'autogestion à la CSF de Brest." In *Les Années 68: Le Temps de la contestation,* edited by Geneviève Dreyfus-Armand, Robert Frank, Marie-Françoise Lévy, and Michelle Zancarini-Fournel, 379–97. Brussels: Éditions Complexe, 2000.

———. *Ouvriers bretons: Conflits d'usines, conflits identitaires en Bretagne dans les années 1968.* Rennes: Presses universitaires de Rennes, 2008.

———. “Plozévet 68: La révolte au village?” In Vigna and Vigreux, eds., *Mai–juin 1968*, 111–28.

Prost, Antoine. *La CGT à l’époque du front populaire: 1934–1939. Essai de description numérique.* Paris: Colin, 1964.

———. “Les grèves de mai–juin 1968.” *L’Histoire*, no. 110 (April 1988): 34–46.

Pucciarelli, Mimmo. *Claire l’enragée: Entretien avec Claire Auzias*. Lyon: Atelier de création libertaire, 2006.

Pudal, Bernard. “Les événements de mai et juin 1968: Bref récit chronologique.” In Damamme, ed., *Mai–Juin 68*, 189–94.

Pudal, Bernard, and Jean-Noël Retière. “Les grèves ouvrières de 68, un mouvement social sans lendemain mémorial.” In Damamme, ed., *Mai–Juin 68*, 207–21.

Ravignant, Patrick. *L’Odéon est ouvert.* Paris: Stock, 1968.

Reid, Donald. *Opening the Gates: The Lip Affair, 1968–1981.* London: Verso, 2018.

Rioux, Lucien, and René Backmann. *L’Explosion de mai.* Paris: R. Laffont, 1968.

Ross, Kristin. *May ’68 and Its Afterlives.* Chicago: University of Chicago Press, 2002.

Rotman, Patrick. *Mai 68 raconté à ceux qui ne l’ont pas vécu.* Paris: Seuil, 2008.

Salvati, Michele. “May 1968 and the Hot Autumn of 1969: The Response of Two Ruling Classes.” In *Organizing Interests in Western Europe*, edited by Suzanne Berger, 331–66, New York, 1981.

Schildt, Axel. “Across the Border: West German Youth Travel to Western Europe.” In *Between Marx and Coca-Cola: Youth Cultures in Changing European Societies, 1960–1980*, edited by Axel Schildt and Detlef Siegfried, 149–60, New York: Berghahn Books, 2007.

Seidman, Michael. *The Imaginary Revolution: Parisian Students and Workers in 1968.* New York: Berghahn Books, 2004.

———. “The Love Wars: Voices from France (1962–68).” *Modern and Contemporary France* (May 2008): 125–41.

Shin, Dogkyu. “La CGT Berliet à Vénissieux en mai 1968: La réactivation de la mémoire locale et les enjeux de la contestation autour des conflits de 1967–1968.” In Vigna and Vigreux, eds., *Mai–juin 1968*, 37–51.

Singer, Daniel. *Prelude to Revolution: France in May 1968.* New York: Hill and Wang, 1970.

Sirinelli, Jean-François. *Mai 68: L’événement Janus.* Paris: Fayard, 2008.

Sommier, Isabelle. *La violence politique et son deuil: L’après 68 en France et en Italie.* Rennes: Presses universitaires de Rennes, 1998.

Trempé, Rolande. *Les mineurs de Carmaux, 1848–1914.* Paris: Les Éditions ouvrières, 1971.

van der Linden, Marcel. *Transnational Labour History: Explorations.* Aldershot: Ashgate, 2003.

Vigna, Xavier. "La CGT et les grèves ouvrières en mai–juin 1968: Une opératrice paradoxale de stabilisation." In Vigna and Vigreux, eds., *Mai–juin 1968*, 193–213.

———. *L'Insubordination ouvrière dans les années 68.* Rennes: Presses universitaires de Rennes, 2007.

Vigna, Xavier, and Jean Vigreux, eds. "Conclusion." In Vigna and Vigreux, eds., *Mai–juin 1968*, 291–300.

———. "Introduction." In Vigna and Vigreux, eds., *Mai–juin 1968*, 5–15.

———. *Mai–juin 1968: Huit semaines qui ébranlèrent la France.* Dijon: Éditions universitaires de Dijon, 2010.

Vinen, Richard. *1968: Radical Protest and Its Enemies.* New York: Harper, 2018.

Winn, Peter. *Weavers of Revolution: The Yarur Workers and Chile's Road to Socialism.* New York: Oxford University Press, 1986.

Wolin, Richard. *The Wind from the East: French Intellectuals, the Cultural Revolution, and the Legacy of the 1960s.* Princeton, NJ: Princeton University Press, 2010.

Zancarini-Fournel, Michelle. *Le moment 68: Une histoire contestée.* Paris: Éditions du Seuil, 2008.

———. "L'épicentre." In Artières and Zancarini-Fournel, eds., *68*, 210–69.

Zegel, Sylvain. *Les idées de mai.* Paris: Gallimard, 1968.

Zemmour, Éric. *Le suicide français.* Paris: Albin Michel, 2014.

THIRTEEN

Clash of the Icons

The Iconoclasm of the Image of the United States

WILLEM MELCHING

Questioning authority was at the heart of the cultural revolution of the Sixties. Children questioned the authority of their parents. Students questioned the authority of their professors. Women questioned the authority of paternalistic men. And everybody questioned the moral and political authority of the only democratic superpower: the Unites States. The image of the United States changed from that of the generous victor of World War II and trusted leader of the free world during the Cold War into that of an evil but at the same time vulnerable imperialist power. This swift change occurred between 1963 and 1972, and photography played a crucial part in this process. Photographs showing crimes or vulnerability seriously damaged the U.S. image as an exceptional moral superpower.

U.S. moral and political prestige were at their zenith with JFK's speech in Berlin in June 1963 and Martin Luther King Jr.'s March on Washington in August of the same year. The global mourning after Kennedy's death in November 1963 was the last time the world gathered around the United States in sympathy; after that, decline set in. The sharp contrast between the photographs of the crowded square in Berlin in 1963 and the many Vietnam demonstrations in all Western European capitals says it all. By 1972, U.S. credibility had sunk to almost zero. The publication of the "Napalm Girl" photo in that year concluded this process.

Since the United States was a NATO ally, the war in Vietnam became a *domestic* issue in all Western European member states. By criticizing the United States the protesters also criticized their own national governments as "accomplices" of the United States. The revolutionaries held their own governments responsible for U.S. behavior. From a friend the United States had turned into an enemy and a liability. Arthur Marwick concludes: "Since their own governments refused to condemn American involvement, it became yet another issue to add to their own more immediate grievances."[1] Vietnam became an integral part, if not a central focus, of the protest movements in Western Europe.

Most critiques of the United States were verbal and formulated in books, pamphlets, and speeches, but in my opinion the visual messages of iconic photographs played a pivotal role in demolishing U.S. prestige and moral standing in the Western world during the cultural revolution of the Sixties. During the Sixties visual media became more important and omnipresent. Because of the technical innovations, distribution of images was global and faster than ever before. The majority of many of these devastating visual messages came from the battlefield in Southeast Asia. But there were also iconic photographs from Europe and Latin America showing crimes the United States was held responsible for. Some became global icons. Others were iconic, but only on a national scale. Although the sources of these photographs were heterogeneous, they all pointed in the same direction: the United States.

I will shed light on the crucial role iconic photographs played in the cultural revolution of the Sixties. They were an actor in the political arena because of their visual rhetoric. I will try to establish the "eloquence" of these iconic photographs by analyzing this visual rhetoric. This is a relatively new approach in establishing the public and political influence of iconic photographs.

My analysis consists of three steps. First, I will define the concept of an iconic photograph. Second, I will go deeper into the theoretical concepts of visual rhetoric. I will explain which factors determine the rhetoric of an image and its effect in the public domain and political arena. Third, I will apply these concepts of visual rhetoric to two case studies: photographs showing the My Lai massacre, and the two martyrs who died as victims of U.S. imperialism: Benno Ohnesorg and Che Guevara.

In my conclusion I will formulate three theses on the importance of visual rhetoric for historians and other researchers.

ICONIC PHOTOGRAPHS—A DEFINITION

Various authors offer definitions of iconic photographs. These definitions can be easily combined into a practical and workable formula. We are dealing with *press* photographs produced to be published in printed or digital news media. These photographs are widely known and have an international or perhaps even global distribution. Their life span and message is prolonged because they are often reproduced in various media, win awards, and have an afterlife in (text)books, as stamps, works of art, statues, cartoons, or even other photographs. By then they are detached from their original context and have turned into symbols in their own right. Because of this "power of epic concentration" they become part of collective memory.[2] And most important of all: iconic photographs have a persuasive power because of their "moments of visual eloquence that acquire exceptional importance within public life."[3] As a rule, an icon urges the viewer to protest the conditions or situation depicted in the picture. Therefore icons play an important part in the political arena. Horst Bredekamp, a German art historian, sees a similarity with John Searle's speech act. Bredekamp says that images contain a *Bild-Akt*, an image act that appeals to us as citizens of democratic societies.[4] Iconic images play an important part in political discourse and stimulate us to action, protest, and emotions such as outrage, empathy, and joy. These unique combinations make photojournalism a "characteristically democratic art and the iconic photo is its signature work."[5]

VISUAL RHETORIC IN ICONIC PHOTOGRAPHS

Leading authors on iconic photographs, such as Robert Hariman and John Louis Lucaites, David D. Perlmutter, and the German pioneer in visual history Gerhard Paul, have established the importance of iconic photographs in the political arena, but they are not very explicit on the mechanism behind this "visual eloquence." What is it that gives these icons their eloquence? How and why do they appeal to the emotions of the audience? Why are they "a call to action" to their viewers? What induces viewers to raise their voice and demand that politicians or institutions undertake action?

In the field of rhetoric and argumentation theory there is a modest but vital current that tries to establish the visual rhetoric in editorial cartoons. By applying the principles of classical rhetoric to the visual argumentation in cartoons, the mechanism behind the persuasive power of images can be made explicit. In a pioneering and still relevant article,[6] Medhurst and Desousa have a convincing case that this is a fruitful way to analyze the rhetoric of images in a systematic way. Other authors, especially Schilperoord and Kjeldsen, have followed up on this and analyze both cartoons and photographs.[7] But I do think these lines of research can be developed further and applied more explicitly to iconic photographs.

Visual rhetoric is an instrument to describe how images communicate meaning. Just as oral or written messages do, visual rhetoric also uses classical rhetorical figures. Concepts from classical rhetoric can therefore be used to analyze the persuasive power of iconic photographs. Two genres are useful in analyzing photographs: deliberative and epideictic.[8]

Deliberative speech is "an attempt to convince a relevant audience of a claim about what we collectively should do or how we should act . . . providing good reasons for actions or evaluations."[9] To give just one example: the 1972 photo of the "Napalm Girl" was a call for the U.S. government to make an end to the suffering of the Vietnamese population.[10]

Epideictic speech was originally used on festive or ceremonious occasions and was used to "praise or blame."[11] This also applies to photographs, and especially to historical photographs because they have lost their urgency. The depicted situation cannot be altered anymore, the responsible politicians are probably not in office anymore. But the photographs still have rhetorical strength because now they appeal to more abstract and universal values. A classic example is the image of the gates of Auschwitz. The camp had been closed in 1945, but the photo is a reminder of the importance of upholding shared values and criticizing the violation of these values in general. Iconic photographs can evolve from a "deliberative" stage to a more universal "epideictic" meaning. The "Napalm Girl" is a typical example of this process. The photo dates from 1972 and is by now a global symbol for children as victims of war.

In order to analyze and explain the effect of visual messages we have to use another concept from classical rhetoric. The main instrument of persuasion in visual rhetoric is the use of a *topos*. In classical rhetoric, *topoi* are "ethical or political premises on which an argument can be built."[12] In visual rhetoric these *topoi* are images and stories already familiar to the viewer. The viewer then compares the iconic image with the images and stories he or she already knows. The differences and similarities made explicit by this comparison are the visual arguments that "trigger" the viewer. Religious art and biblical stories are a repository for strong and effective *topoi*. Kjeldsen points to the rhetorical appeal of "allusions to general pictorial themes or common places (*topoi*) evoking a cultural memory of shared narratives or myths,"[13] but he does not explore the topic any further.

Comparing the new image with the familiar one is the essence of visual rhetoric. In classical rhetoric this comparison is known as analogy: comparing the new image with familiar ones is making an argument. The viewer will interpret the new image according to the values and notions he or she has already bestowed on the familiar ones.

In this way the analogy is a visual way of making a complicated and abstract argument about the situation depicted in the photograph. One concrete example: photographs from Vietnam with soldiers stuck in the mud will be compared with familiar images from World War I *and* with the knowledge and sentiments the viewer has about that war, such as that it was senseless and unwinnable, without heroes and only victims.

In my opinion, the analogy is the essence and main source of the rhetorical power of these iconic photographs and many other news photographs. Analogy is more than a resemblance; it is about communicating abstract ideas and concepts.

Besides the *topoi* and analogies, certain presentational devices in iconic photographs do enhance the visual arguments and attract our attention immediately. To name just a few: the vulnerability of the naked body, mother and child, harmless children, and man versus machine. Photographers use effects such as contrasts in big/small and light/dark. Composition also enhances the argument. This does not mean that these icons have an unusual or extravagant composition. On the contrary: in most cases they are relatively conventional and have an effective but simple composition.

In my case studies I will go deeper into the use of *topoi* and analogies in analyzing iconic photographs. I will analyze the visual rhetoric of icons from the years 1967 and 1968. What they all have in common is a pivotal role in demolishing the prestige of the United States and questioning its moral standards and authority.

THE CASE STUDIES

My analysis is based on the role of *topoi* and *analogies* in these images. In this context, *topoi* are images and stories already familiar to the viewer. As I explained above, the main rhetorical instrument is the analogy. The photograph has an effect on the viewer because he or she will *compare* the photo with the familiar images and stories. These familiar images can be paintings, drawings, or even other photographs. The familiar stories can be religious, historical, or literary.

Icons are exemplary in quality and notoriety and therefore suitable as a case study, but this approach is also applicable to less well-known photographs. The "mechanism" behind the effect of photographs remains the same.

In my case studies I will first give a brief historical context and then focus on the analysis of the image in terms of visual rhetoric. Then I will deal with the afterlife of the photographs.

The first case study is from the Vietnam War, the second is from Germany and Latin America. The first case refers to the My Lai massacre, an example of what I describe as the *Holocaust-topos.*

The second case shows victims of U.S. imperialism. Both are based on the Crucifixion *topos.* The photographs from Germany and Latin America are analyzed together because they not only share their *topos*, but also because both dead persons were seen as *indirect* victims of U.S. foreign policy.

MY LAI: THE HOLOCAUST TOPOS

On March 16, 1968, the U.S. Army destroyed a few Vietnamese villages and killed at least 350 people, mostly civilians, among them many women and children. Initially the massacre was covered up, then an internal investigation was initiated. Investigative journalists Seymour Hersh and Wayne

Greenhaw made the story public on November 12, 1969. *The Plain Dealer*, a newspaper from Cleveland, published the story accompanied by explicit photographs of dead villagers. These shocking images that greatly enhanced the story were shot by Ron L. Haeberle, a U.S. Army photographer. He used his private camera, and therefore felt entitled to sell them to the press.

The story immediately attracted worldwide attention. My Lai was a truly global news event and soon became a synonym for U.S. misbehavior. Two weeks later some of the photographs were published in color in *Life* magazine, and the effect was devastating. In the Netherlands, for example, the news broke only days after the initial publication. The trial of the culprit, Lt. William Calley, in November 1970 was extensively covered not only in the United States but also in Europe.

There are two frequently used photographs. The first one shows a dirt road with at least a dozen corpses in civilian clothes. This picture was published on the front page of the *Plain Dealer*.[14] Often other news media reproduced the complete front page, which includes the photograph.[15] A second one shows a group of women and children, probably about to be shot (see fig. 13.1)

All these photographs have predecessors from World War II that serve as *topoi* here. There is a strong analogy with the numerous photographs from Nazi atrocities. After the Eichmann trial in 1961, the audience became interested in the Holocaust, and photographs from the Holocaust found their way to a wider audience through books and television documentaries. This included photos of the actions of the German *Einsatzgruppen* on the eastern front.

Even in the details there are parallels that must have been clear to the viewers when they saw the photographs of My Lai. The photo with the road and the pile of corpses has a strong resemblance with photographs from the liberation of Bergen-Belsen and other camps.[16] Those photographs had become symbols of Nazi atrocities. The same analogy applies to the photo of the group of women and children about to be shot. In German photographs we see people, very often terrified women, being chased to their death. The picture of a group of terrified Vietnamese women and children reveals one of them adjusting her clothes; it could very well be that she had just been raped. This is also a striking parallel with the victims of the Nazi SS—in many photographs we see naked or partially clad women, sometimes in the process of undressing. As we know

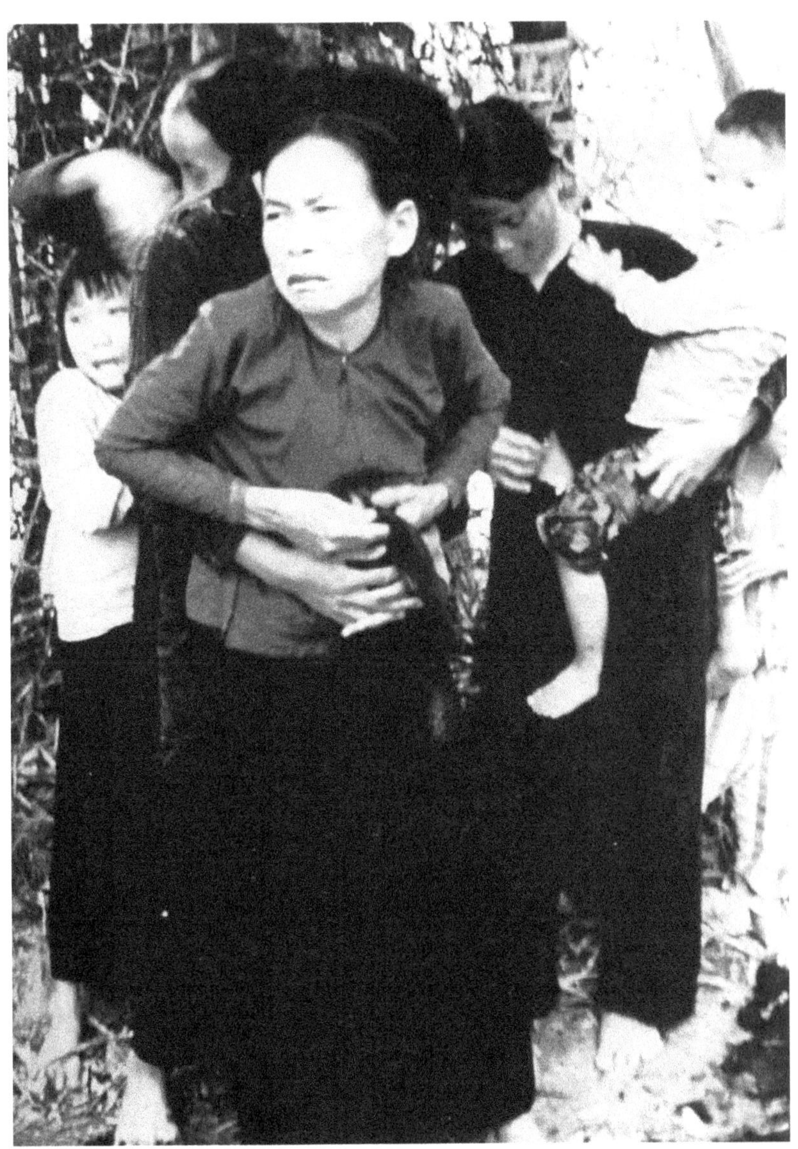

Figure 13.1 My Lai massacre.

Figure 13.2 Šíede, near Liepâja, Latvia.

from authors such as Barbie Zelizer, these photos, such as the group of women and children, belong to a special genre: images of people who are about to die.[17] We know that they will be dead minutes or seconds after the clicking of the shutter. Or in Susan Sontag's words: "To photograph people is to violate them, by seeing them as they never see themselves, by having knowledge of them that they can never have."[18] This knowledge gives these images a macabre attraction.

AFTERLIFE

The My Lai photographs became iconic immediately after their first publication on the front page of the *Plain Dealer* of November 20, 1969, showing the photograph of the road with dead civilians. *Life* magazine featured a long story on My Lai on December 5, 1969, including the color photos of the corpses on the road and the group of terrified women. Foreign newspapers and magazines, such as the German *Der Spiegel*, reproduced this front page as early as December 1, 1969. In those years Dutch newspapers were very reluctant to print explicit photographs of dead people. But in their articles the journalists all referred to the photographs.

My Lai became the symbol of what went wrong in Vietnam, and in retrospectives the newspaper front page and the photo of the group of terrified women and children are still widely used. There are also a few cartoons based on the My Lai photographs, all very critical of the U.S. government and its armed forces. One American cartoon shows "U.S. Conscience" lying in a ditch, and above this figure we see piles of corpses and people with banners expressing their support for Lieutenant Calley. The Dutch-German cartoonist Fritz Behrendt published a cartoon in which he placed My Lai in a long chain of massacres of innocent citizens. He compared My Lai with Nazi crimes and colonial warfare. In the Netherlands, My Lai became a symbol when it came to describing the crimes the Dutch army committed during the "police actions" in Indonesia in the years 1945–49. In an interesting development, journalists used the U.S. crime to break a taboo: the war crimes committed by the Dutch army. My Lai has by now become an international benchmark for violence against civilians and war crimes committed by regular armies.

The use of the Holocaust *topos* and the analogies with German war crimes was devastating for the U.S. reputation. Just like the Nazis, the Americans lost all respect for civilians in warfare and did not hesitate to rape and murder defenseless women and children. Comparing the photos from Vietnam with those of Nazi crimes is a very strong statement about the criminal nature of the Vietnam War in particular and war in general. By comparing the My Lai photos with their predecessors from the Holocaust, there was only one inevitable conclusion: the Americans are just as evil as the Nazis.

In many newspapers from 1969 and 1970, Telford Taylor, counsel for the prosecution at the Nuremberg Trials, made a direct comparison between the Nazis and the U.S. Army. From My Lai on it became customary to use the term "war crimes" to describe U.S. actions in Vietnam.[19] Many newspapers, including Dutch and German, compared My Lai in commentaries and cartoons with the slaughtering of the villages Oradour-sur-Glane in France and Lidice in Czechoslovakia. These were clear statements about the complete loss of moral authority of the U.S. government by their behavior in Vietnam.

MARTYRS OF IMPERIALISM: THE CRUCIFIXION TOPOS

The picture from West Berlin shows Benno Ohnesorg (see fig. 13.3). He was shot on June 2, 1967, by a policeman during the state visit to West Berlin by Mohammad Reza Pahlavi, Shah of Persia, and his wife. Students

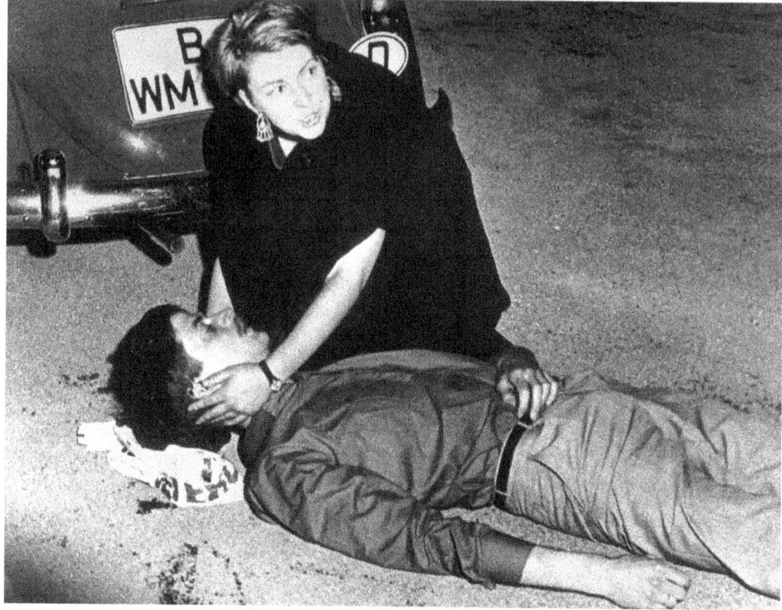

Figure 13.3 Death of a demonstrator, June 2, 1967.

and others organized a demonstration to protest against the Shah's dictatorship; as a faithful ally of the United States he was a symbol of a typical Third World dictator. The police had decided beforehand to give demonstrators a severe beating in order to end the unrest in the city. In this they were openly assisted by agents of the feared Persian secret police, the Savak. During a pursuit, Ohnesorg, a student and married father of a son, was shot in the back of the head by police officer Karl-Heinz Kurras. The policeman claimed to have acted in self-defense.

Che Guevara was a companion of Fidel Castro and one of the leading figures in the Cuban Revolution of 1959. Guevara had various posts in the revolutionary Cuban government. But he was not very successful as a politician and returned to guerilla warfare. His aim was to export the Cuban Revolution to other Third World countries. After fighting in Africa he joined the Bolivian resistance. He was betrayed and then captured in an ambush on October 7, 1967. Guevara was wounded, but not in mortal peril. The Bolivian authorities tried to interrogate him, but he refused to cooperate. Despite the fact that the Americans wanted to interrogate him in Panama, the Bolivian president ordered his execution. On October 8, he was shot several times, and the authorities made it look as if he had tried to escape. He was transported from La Higuera, where he was shot, to the mortuary in Vallegrande, where a series of pictures was taken by Freddy Alborta on October 9, 1967.[20] There were several slightly different variants, but in all we see Guevara's corpse lying on the table surrounded by a group of soldiers and some civilians.

Both photographs use the same *topos*: elements from the context of the Crucifixion. The biblical narrative and the apocryphal stories about the death of Christ are the basis for a number of strong and very widespread images. Classic is of course the *Pietà* an apocryphal story: Mary holds the corpse of her son. A most human and universal emotion: a mother mourning her dead son. Although not strictly biblical, it became one of the most frequently used themes in art. Michelangelo's famous statue had numerous mediaeval predecessors. Other images from the context of the Crucifixion are the mocking of the Christ by Roman soldiers and the Deposition, the body of Christ being taken down from the cross by his followers.

The Ohnesorg picture is a pietá. It shows a woman holding him in her arms in a desperate attempt to comfort him in his last moments. Of course, this person is not his mother, but she is evidently a tender and caring woman. The Guevara picture contains motifs from the Crucifixion and the Deposition. The scene on the table in the mortuary is a clear analogy with the Deposition, but with a twist: the soldiers are not his followers, but his enemies. This rouses associations with the mocking of Christ. While Jesus was dying on the cross, Roman guards were making fun of him and gambling for his garments. The analogy is almost perfect: the imperial occupier disrespecting the body of the Messiah. In the photograph we see how the allies of the U.S. imperialists are mocking the body of the deceased legendary guerilla fighter. Through these pictures Guevara immediately acquired cult status as the "Savior" of the Third World. No wonder German students carried signs with the slogan "Che lebt" (Che is alive). Ironically the magazine *Der Spiegel* called him "Che-sus" and "The Saviour from the Jungle."[21]

AFTERLIFE

In Germany, the Ohnesorg photograph is a supericon.[22] Newspapers and magazines published the photograph in articles on the riots.[23] In the *Der*

Spiegel Christmas issue of 1967, the Ohnesorg and Guevara photographs were united in a richly illustrated article looking back on a violent year.[24] Dutch newspapers did report on Ohnesorg's death, but did not use the photograph because of their policy not to publish images of corpses.

Since 1967, the image has been reproduced in practically all retrospectives, books, and documentaries about the Sixties in Germany. The death of Ohnesorg was seen as the spark that ignited radicalization of the student movement and was a landmark in the political consciousness of the younger generations. Many young Germans saw it as the beginning of their political awakening. For later terrorists it was the beginning of a process of radicalization. The photograph showed the workings of state violence and therefore legitimized their counterviolence.

On German television the famous journalist Ulrike Meinhof offered her stinging criticism of the authorities, and Gudrun Ensslin demanded the abdication of the Berlin mayor. Three years later both women were among the founding members of the Red Army Faction. One of their raids was dedicated to Ohnesorg. It is telling that the blockbuster movie *BMK* about the terrorist group Red Army Faction opens with a meticulous reconstruction of what happened that infamous day in June 1967.

The notoriety of the Ohnesorg picture is possibly surpassed by a photograph of the kidnapped Hanns Martin Schleyer from 1977. But in a bizarre way these two are connected: Schleyer was the victim of a terrorist group that wanted to avenge the death of Ohnesorg. They called themselves Bewegung 2. Juni (June 2 Movement). Together with the remnants of the Red Army Faction they kidnapped Schleyer in the dramatic "German autumn" of 1977, a last desperate terrorist offensive ten years after Ohnesorg's death.[25]

The Deposition photograph of Guevara is an icon. The leading left-wing weekly *Der Spiegel* reported about his death in semireligious terms as "Der bärtige Evangelist der Gewalt" (the bearded evangelist of violence), and his armed struggle was described as a "Crusade." Of course this article, and subsequent articles about his death, were accompanied with the picture from the Bolivian morgue.[26]

But the morgue photograph is outshined by another picture. After Guevara's death, the Italian left-wing publisher Giangiacomo Feltrinelli visited Cuba. There he spotted Albert Korda's portrait of Guevara. He took the photo back to Italy. It started appearing in magazines, but its traces were very vague. In 1967, the Irish artist Jim Fitzpatrick added the

Figure 13.4 *Che Guevara* (Albert Korda).

then-fashionable graphic effect and the photograph became the icon of the youth revolt. Soon it would adorn rooms around the globe, later to be followed by T-shirts and numerous artifacts. It is tempting to make a comparison with the biblical Veil of Veronica. A Dutch publisher who earned a fortune with the Guevara poster expressed himself a bit more profanely: he called Guevara "The Donald Duck of the Revolution." One could stick Che on anything and it would sell.[27]

Figure 13.5 Domenico Fetti, *The Veil of Veronica.*

The Crucifixion *topos* was very suitable when depicting victims of imperialism. Ohnesorg and Guevara were both seen by many as victims and martyrs of U.S. imperialism. Both were murdered by proxy. Although the West Berlin police and the Bolivian army pulled the triggers, the real murderers were the Americans. Ohnesorg died in a demonstration against the Shah of Persia, a faithful ally of the United States in the Gulf region. The conspicuous cooperation of West German authorities with the Persian secret service completed the picture: Ohnesorg was a victim of U.S. imperialism.

The case of Guevara is even more straightforward: he was killed by the right-wing regime of Bolivia that was allied with the United States. Historians stress that the United States did not want Guevara dead—clearly he was more an asset alive than dead. But these subtleties were then unknown. Public opinion concluded that Guevara was a victim of U.S. imperialism. It was the afterlife of his photographs that made him an immortal hero, the Messiah of the Third World.

VISUAL RHETORIC AND ICONIC PHOTOGRAPHS

I would like to conclude with three theses about the use of visual rhetoric by historians in analyzing iconic photographs.

1. Visual rhetoric is an essential instrument for historians. Photographs are often used as illustrations of the historical narrative. But not many historians use the photographs as an integral part of that narrative. The concept of "image act," as in speech act, is very useful. Images and especially iconic images are more than illustrations. Their eloquence makes the audience aware and induces them to criticize the responsible officials. Therefore they are active agents in the historical process, comparable with written sources such as pamphlets, books, and speeches.

2. Classical rhetoric offers useful tools to analyze the nature of the eloquence of photographs. Deliberative rhetoric has an effect on the audience and on politicians because it provides "good reasons for actions or evaluations."[28] This applies to photographs that call for an immediate action, or situations that need to be corrected as fast as possible. Epideictic speech was used to "praise or blame."[29] After some time photographs lose their urgency, but iconic photographs remain active in the public arena because they appeal to abstract and universal values and they find their way into collective memory. Some icons evolve from deliberative into epideictic and are a benchmark for common values and attitudes.

3. The concepts of "*topos*" and "analogy" are useful instruments for analyzing iconic photographs. A *topos* is an image or story that is well known to the viewer. The analogy between the familiar image and the new image makes the argument. By comparing the two, the viewer makes the argument by himself on the basis of similarities and differences. This argument incites the viewer to draw conclusions and undertake action. Because of

this effect on the viewer, the photographs are independent actors in the public arena and therefore important material for historians.

My case studies show the demise of the United States' reputation of a victorious nation of high moral standing. The United States did not notice that after the death of John F. Kennedy the world was changing. The U.S. government and military were convinced that they were fighting a just war against communism, both in Asia and Latin America. But they were fighting colonial wars in a postcolonial world and became an embarrassment to their allies. Many of these iconic photographs still haunt the United States because they evolved from a deliberative call to action, into an epideictic statement about the loss of moral standing the United States suffered and never recovered from.

During the Sixties the United States started realizing what it meant to be a superpower. No more glorious victories in a just war, no more grateful liberated civilian populations. The United States had to fight dirty wars under the scrutiny of the all-seeing eye of the camera. As Randy Newman sang in 1972: "It's lonely at the top."

NOTES

1. Arthur Marwick, *The Sixties. Cultural Revolution in Britain, France, Italy and the United States, c. 1958–c.1974* (Oxford: Oxford University Press, 1998), 543.

2. Rob Kroes, *Photographic Memories: Private Pictures, Public Images, and American History* (Hanover, NH: Dartmouth College Press, 2007), 13.

3. Robert Hariman and John Louis Lucaites, *No Caption Needed: Iconic Photographs, Public Culture, and Liberal Democracy* (Chicago: University of Chicago Press, 2007), 45.

4. Horst Bredekamp, *Theorie des Bildakts: Frankfurter Adorno-Vorlesungen 2007* (Berlin: Suhrkamp, 2010).

5. Hariman and Lucaites, *No Caption Needed*, 3.

6. Martin J. Medhurst and Michael A. Desousa, "Political Cartoons as Rhetorical Form: A Taxonomy of Graphic Discourse," *Communication Monographs* 48 (September 1981): 197–236.

7. Jens E. Kjeldsen, "The Rhetorical and Argumentative Potentials of Press Photography," in *Multimodal Argumentation and Rhetoric in Media Genres*, ed. Assimakis Tseronis and Charles Forceville (Amsterdam: John Benjamins, 2017), 51–79, and Joost Schilperoord, "Raising the Issue: A Mental-Space Ap-

proach to Iwo Jima-Inspired Editorial Cartoons," *Metaphor and Symbol* 28, no. 3 (2013): 185–212.

8. George A. Kennedy, *A New History of Classical Rhetoric* (Princeton, NJ: Princeton University Press, 1994), 4; Hariman and Lucaites, *No Caption Needed*, 298.

9. Kjeldsen, "The Rhetorical and Argumentative Potentials," 54.

10. Perlmutter, *Outrage*, *passim*, and Hariman and Lucaites, *No Caption Needed*, 173 and 364.

11. Kennedy, *Classical Rhetoric*, 4 and 58.

12. Ibid., 5.

13. Jens E. Kjeldsen, "Formulas of Prize-Winning Press Photos," in *Verbal and Visual Rhetoric in a Media World*, ed. Hilde van Belle et al. (Amsterdam: Leiden University Press, 2014), 465.

14. My Lai: http://media.cleveland.com/plain-dealer/photo/2017/09/23/my-lai-massacre-1968-30eb3662f31b6860.jpg.

15. E.g., *Der Spiegel*, December 1, 1969, and again on November 16, 1970.

16. Bergen-Belsen: https://1.bp.blogspot.com/-_SyErxWH1PE/VrJD1GbFzzI/AAAAAAACE9k/qXorTx66RUQ/s1600/Bergen-Belsen%2BConcentration%2BCamp%252C%2B1945%2B1.jpeg.

17. Barbie Zelizer, *About to Die: How News Images Move the Public* (New York: Oxford University Press, 2010).

18. Susan Sontag, *On Photography* (London: Allan Lane, 1978), 14.

19. *Der Spiegel*, December 7, 1970.

20. Death of Che: http://historyisfun1111.blogspot.com/2016/02/the-death-of-che-guevara.html.

21. Cover of *Der Spiegel*, July 29, 1968.

22. Marion G. Müller, "Der Tod des Benno Ohnesorg: Ein Foto als Initialzündung einer politischen Bewegung," in *Das Jahrhundert der Bilder 1949 bis heute*, ed. Gerhard Paul (Göttingen: Vandenhoeck & Ruprecht 2008), 338–45.

23. *Der Spiegel*, June 12, 1969.

24. *Der Spiegel*, December 25, 1967.

25. The death of Ohnesorg was a source of inspiration for a novel by the famous German novelist Uwe Timm, who was befriended by Ohnesorg. In 2005, he published *Der Freund und der Fremde: Eine Erzählung* (*The Friend and the Stranger: A Story*).

26. *Der Spiegel*, October 16, 1967.

27. Interview with Engel Verkerke (in Dutch), https://www.vpro.nl/speel~POMS_VPRO_478539~portret-engel-verkerke-2~.html.

28. Kjeldsen, "The Rhetorical and Argumentative Potentials," 54.

29. Kennedy, *Classical Rhetoric*, 4 and 58.

BIBLIOGRAPHY

Bredekamp, Horst. *Theorie des Bildakts: Frankfurter Adorno-Vorlesungen 2007*. Berlin: Suhrkamp, 2010.

Hariman, Robert, and John Louis Lucaites. *No Caption Needed: Iconic Photographs, Public Culture, and Liberal Democracy*. Chicago: University of Chicago Press, 2007.

Huebner, Andrew J. *The Warrior Image: Soldiers in American Culture from the Second World War to the Vietnam Era*. Chapel Hill: University of North Carolina Press, 2008.

Kennedy, George A. *A New History of Classical Rhetoric*. Princeton, NJ: Princeton University Press, 1994.

Kjeldsen, Jens E. "Formulas of Prize-Winning Press Photos." In *Verbal and Visual Rhetoric in a Media World*, edited by Hilde van Belle et al., 461–85. Amsterdam: Leiden University Press, 2014.

________. "The Rhetorical and Argumentative Potentials of Press Photography." In *Multimodal Argumentation and Rhetoric in Media Genres*, edited by Assimakis Tseronis and Charles Forceville, 51–79. Amsterdam: John Benjamins, 2017.

Kroes, Rob. *Photographic Memories: Private Pictures, Public Images, and American History*. Hanover, NH: Dartmouth College Press, 2007.

Marwick, Arthur. *The Sixties: Cultural Revolution in Britain, France, Italy and the United States, c. 1958–c. 1974*. Oxford: Oxford University Press, 1998.

Medhurst, Martin J., and Michael A. Desousa. "Political Cartoons as Rhetorical Form: A Taxonomy of Graphic Discourse." *Communication Monographs* 48 (September 1981): 197–236.

Müller, Marion G. "Der Tod des Benno Ohnesorg: Ein Foto als Initialzündung einer politischen Bewegung." In *Das Jahrhundert der Bilder 1949 bis heute*, edited by Gerhard Paul, 338–45. Göttingen: Vandenhoeck & Ruprecht, 2008.

Paul, Gerhard. *BilderMACHT: Studien zur Visual History des 20. und 21. Jahrhunderts*. Göttingen: Wallstein, 2013.

———. *Das visuelle Zeitalter: Punkt und Pixel*. Göttingen: Wallstein, 2016.

Perlmutter, David D. *Photojournalism and Foreign Policy: Icons of Outrage in International Crises*. Westport, CT: Praeger, 1998.

Schilperoord, Joost. "Raising the Issue: A Mental-Space Approach to Iwo Jima-Inspired Editorial Cartoons." *Metaphor and Symbol* 28, no. 3 (2013): 185–212.

Sontag, Susan. *On Photography*. London: Allan Lane, 1978.

Zelizer, Barbie. *About to Die: How News Images Move the Public*. New York: Oxford University Press, 2010.

FOURTEEN

The Anonymous Dead of 1968 Mexico

A Comparative Study of Counterrevolutionary Violence and Protest with Uruguay and Brazil

JAIME M. PENSADO

"Libertad de Expresión" ("Freedom of Expression") has become one of the most recognized images of the 1968 student movement in Mexico. Yet, this iconic poster has a much longer history. Originally designed in 1954 by Adolfo Mexiac, "Libertad" was a response to two specific events: the CIA-sponsored coup in Guatemala and the firing of Mexico's general director of the National Institute of Fine Arts, Andrés Iduarte.[1]

Like his contemporaries at the Taller de Gráfica Popular (Popular Graphic Art Workshop, TGP), the artist used the 1954 image as a medium of political protest. At the time of its creation, Mexiac was living in San Cristobal de las Casas, Chiapas, where, according to his own recollections, he saw the North American airplanes flying over southern Mexico that were used to launch a war against the reformist administration of Jacobo Arbenz. That same year, painter Frida Kahlo committed suicide after grueling years of physical pain. Her longtime friend Andrés Iduarte paid

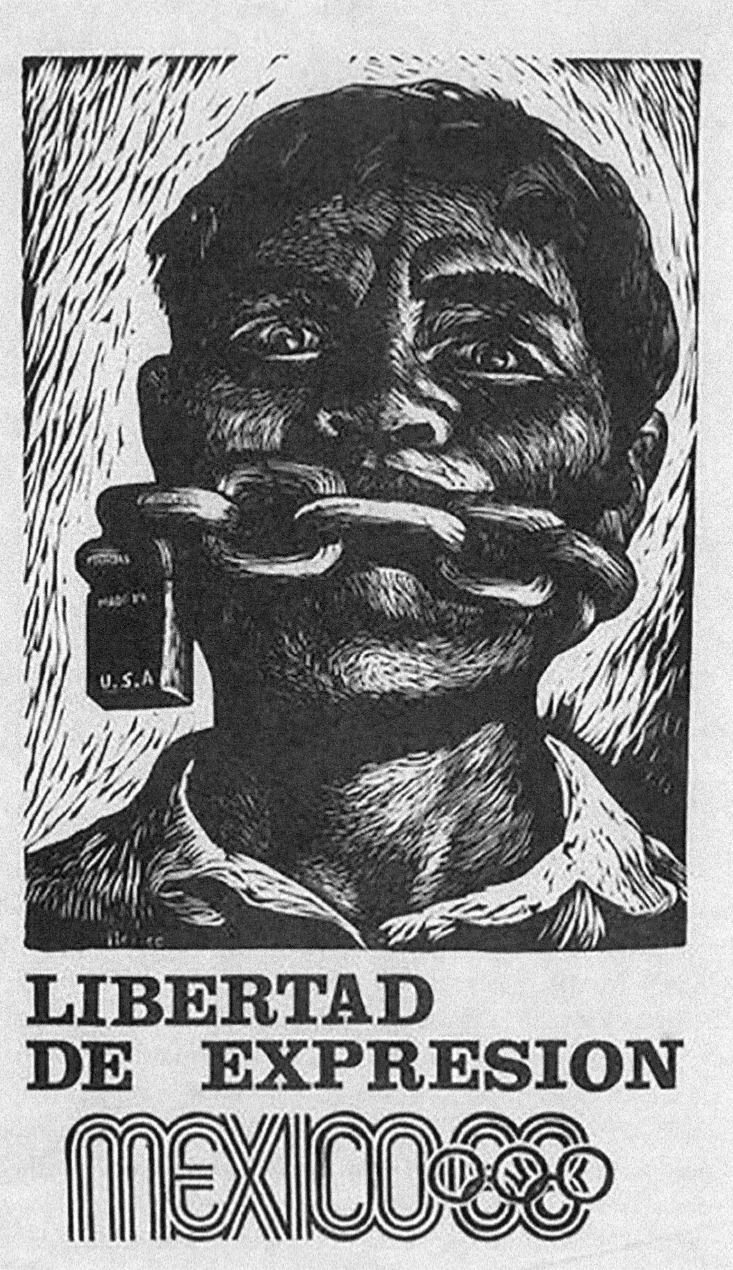

Figure 14.1 Adolfo Mexiac, *Libertad de Expresión* (1954/1968).

homage to the artist and, respecting her death wishes, placed her coffin in the lobby of the Fine Arts Palace draped with the red banner of the Communist Party. Pointing to the hammer and sickle as evidence that Iduarte was a "Soviet sympathizer," as broadly reported in the press, the Mexican government forced him to resign from his position as leading representative of the National Institute of Fine Arts. The renowned muralist David Alfaro Siqueiros was outraged and publicly denounced government officials as "petty agents" of the United States, and, agreeing with Mexiac, he saw the lack of freedom of expression as one of "the most brutal act[s] of despotism that has been registered in Mexico in recent times."[2]

An unidentified indigenous young man from a Tzotzil community in Chiapas served as the model for Mexiac's image. In its original linocut, the harsh cuts in woodcut style depicted those who would be tortured and disappeared in Latin America throughout the Cold War period (ca. 1954–80s). The "MADE IN U.S.A" padlock locking the same chain that gagged the protestor left little room for ambiguity and clearly pointed to the "imperialist North" as the main actor involved in the repression of dissidents during these years.[3]

Not many people were exposed to "Libertad de Expresión" in the 1950s. But the image lived on and acquired new meanings. In July 1959, the Soviet Union organized its Seventh World Youth Festival in Vienna, Austria, where the triumph of the Cuban Revolution became one of the hottest topics of discussion and an inspiration for the rising New Left. Organized for the very first time outside a communist country, the central goal of the conference was to encourage European youth to forge stronger ties with the Third World. Representing the Mexican team was Mexiac. Sympathetic to the efforts of solidarity promoted by the conference and seeing the 1954 image as a representative example of the colonized world, he gave a copy of his iconic art piece to a young French woman. Nine years later, the image reappeared during the May student uprisings in Paris. A few months later, Mexican students reappropriated it, and with the guidance of sympathetic artists, including Mexiac, they reproduced it massively to protest against the authoritarian and anticommunist government of Gustavo Díaz Ordaz (1964–70). Drawing from the visual wit that also characterized the silk screen posters of the movement in France, the Mexican students added the state-sponsored logo of "Mexico 68" to draw attention to a sardonic connection between the rings of the Olympic Games, which were scheduled to begin on October 12, and those interlocking rings that made up the violent chain of repression (see fig. 14.1).[4] But in the broader context of Latin America, the revamped image also captured the atmosphere of suffocation and the sense of despair that thousands of young men and women felt across the continent in 1968.

In this chapter, I examine state repression in Mexico with particular attention to those students killed during the 1968 movement *prior to* the October 2 massacre at the Plaza of Tlatelolco. I frame the long history of 1968 in the broader context of the Cold War era by drawing partial and selected comparisons to the Uruguayan and Brazilian student movements.[5] As historians of the region have argued, and as De Giuseppe, Zolov, McSherry, and Markarian examine in their respective chapters (3, 5, 11, 9) in this volume, in Latin America such a period "was rarely cold." Those in power used the language and rationale of the Cold War "to wage a war against their citizens."[6] The year 1968 was one of these brutal episodes. Unlike the student movement in Western Europe, where the United States played a less significant role, the student protests in Mexico, Uruguay, and Brazil distinguished themselves with the brutal killing of dozens of young people.[7] Yet, responses to these killings differed significantly in these three Latin American countries and so did the repertoires of counterrevolutionary repression and the actors who came in support of the students.

In contrast to Uruguay and Brazil, where the deaths of young activists were transformed into powerful rallying calls for the movements, the Mexican students did not identify their martyrs by name, and in failing to do so missed an opportunity to force the state to acknowledge its brutal use of force. These victims were anonymous and would remain nameless in the aftermath of 1968. Moreover, unlike the 1968 uprisings in Uruguay and Brazil, in Mexico there were no massive vigils to recognize those who were killed during the movement. On the contrary, relying on the almost total complicity of the Mexican press and a sophisticated use of propaganda, the administration of Díaz Ordaz organized a slander campaign that effectively erased the names of those who died in 1968 and silenced those who attempted to bring attention to the victims. The lack of freedom of expression in Mexico, which Mexiac so vividly captured in his image, made it difficult for students to contest a biased press and a conservative Catholic Church that overwhelmingly sided with the state. By comparison, in Uruguay and Brazil the massive vigils that students organized to commemorate those who were killed in 1968 not only created an opportunity for collective mourning but also provided the movements with broader support from various sectors of society, including a significant number of activists from the working class, in the case of Uruguay, and a progressive wing of the Catholic Church, in the case of Brazil. In Mexico, the strong corporatist control of the labor sector at the hands of government unions and the overwhelming silence of a conservative and anticommunist Church that had aligned itself with the state since the 1940s prevented this from happening. Instead, popular support in 1968 Mexico was overwhelmingly limited to artists, intellectuals, and university professors, who decried the violation of the autonomy of the university and protested loudly and massively against the authoritarianism of the Partido Revolucionario Institucional (Institutional Revolutionary Party, PRI), but saw no need to provide the names of those killed during the movement.

PRI authorities tried to portray Mexico as an exceptional country, one that successfully avoided becoming a military dictatorship. In this effort, and unlike in Uruguay and Brazil, government authorities in Mexico preferred the use of illegal mechanisms of control to contain the student movement. In particular, they relied on the systematic use of agents provocateurs and thugs-for-hire to negotiate with and repress student activists. When these efforts proved ineffective, they then relied on harsher repertoires of repression that included the use of paramilitary gangs and military forces. Paradoxically, in "democratic" Mexico these forces of repression left more students dead in 1968 than in Uruguay and Brazil, combined. Yet, like the dark-skinned indigenous young man in Mexiac's drawing, these martyrs at the hands of PRI authorities remained anonymous. In multiple posters students drew attention to the mourning mothers of 1968; yet the names of their sons and daughters were not included in these visual forms of protest. Rather, they became "myths" that were repeatedly discredited in the press and ignored by the leading figures of the Catholic Church. Here, I provide some of their names, but their stories have yet to be examined at length. Moreover, the exact number of those killed and disappeared on October 2 at the Plaza of Tlatelolco has yet to be determined.

REPERTOIRES OF STATE REPRESSION, THE DEAD, AND COLLECTIVE MOURNING IN MEXICO AND URUGUAY

The publication of two manuals on "Civilian Disturbance Control" by the Police Department of Montevideo provides a detailed and informative glimpse into the logic of state repression in Uruguay in the 1960s. Coronel Edison Alonso Rodríguez of the Professional Training Institute of the Police published the first of these documents in 1964. It stated that the civil riots on the streets of the capital, which were becoming ever-more violent, required new security forces and preventative control measures. In particular, the textbook recommended that police forces become acquainted with different types of disturbances, both political and social. It explained the psychology and mental state of the masses and detailed different mechanisms of control that had been used in different parts of the world since World War II.

The preferred means of repression, according to the 1964 manual, included tear gas, water cannons, bludgeons, and rifles with bayonets, the latter to be used to incapacitate, rather than to kill, indicated the document. Show of force "should be firm, moderate and not provocative." Water cannons and tear gas were described as "the most reasonable means to repressing riots since they allowed for crowds to be attacked from a distance of 70 to 100 [yards] . . . and although the immediate effects of tear gas could be severe, exposure to air or, in the more extreme cases, washing the eyes with some water would eliminate all effects in a matter of minutes." Use of bayonets was to be avoided, and, if needed, the rifles were used only to produce shots into the air in an effort to intimidate; any lethal use of these weapons could be counterproductive. Hurting students could radicalize the movement and create martyrs, which was to be avoided when possible. When tear gas and water cannons failed, the manual explained, "bulletproof forces and the cavalry" could be deployed, since these were effective in "bringing street barricades down and psychologically affecting" the rioters.[8]

The second "Civilian Disturbance Control" manual of the Professional Training Institute was published in 1968. Unfortunately, it did not make a detailed list of the new means of control and repression adopted by the military and police forces. Nevertheless, the manual stands out because it differentiates between the three types of strife that security forces presumably faced during the Cold War: the classic (invasions, war declarations against other countries, etc.); the nuclear (that became a serious threat again after the missile crisis in Cuba); and the subversive.

Subversive strife—or "revolutionary," as the manual also called it—was the most worrying and relevant type of violence on the streets of Montevideo in 1968. It included strikes, insurrections, boycotts, terrorist acts, and civil resistance, but it also manifested itself in guerrillas, communist organizations, and self-defense groups. The first and most important step to combating all of these different types of resistance consisted in "understanding them" and, for these purposes, the document presented a detailed report on the political, social, and psychological tactics used by subversive leaders in their attacks on the repressive state forces and in their efforts to recruit popular-sector adherents to their respective movements. "Subversion," the document read, "encompasses any premeditated act, designed with the purpose of toppling the government or the legal authority of a nation through the use of force, violence or any other illegal means." Its first stage is illegal, and if it does not lead to its destruction, it grows into an "open war," which forces the state into using force and justifying its use.[9]

The student movement of 1968 in Montevideo, like its Mexico City counterpart, was seen by the authorities not as a spontaneous explosion, but as a subversive act, open and massive, the magnitude of which required new and more effective mechanisms of control. Both movements were violently repressed, but in different ways and with different results. In Mexico, the government tried to avoid the use of military force. From the movement's very beginning in July, precisely in response to the brutality of the force displayed by the ill-trained *granaderos* (riot police), Díaz Ordaz's administration relied on the use of shock brigades composed of pseudo-students, or *porros*, which had been very effective in previous years, not only to selectively repress student insurrections, but also to divide the Left and sow confusion among the students, since the press did not distinguish between *porro* and student violence and between self-defense or legitimate protest acts. However, when the use of instigators as a means of control failed to yield the expected results in 1968 and after witnessing the dramatic defeat of agents provocateurs and the riot police in schools and streets across Mexico City, the government started to increasingly rely on military and paramilitary forces. At the end of September, when the most influential newspapers and magazines in Europe and Latin America started spreading word of the repressive character of the Mexican government, the Díaz Ordaz administration had already reached the decision to put an end to the student movement.

State repression reached a boiling point in September. On the 18th, the executive ordered the Mexican army to "protect" the National Autonomous University of Mexico (UNAM) facilities with more than 10,000 troops. The unprecedented decision to occupy the university buildings with war tanks and soldiers armed with bayonets was taken "to reestablish normality" and to defend the actual students from "activities foreign to the academic process" and "openly antisocial . . . delinquent . . . and criminal acts," according to a telegram sent to all Mexican embassies on September 19. The telegram paradoxically insisted that the purpose was to "guarantee the autonomy of the university."[10] A week later, the government ordered that the facilities of the National Polytechnic Institute (IPN) be occupied. Unlike the UNAM students, the IPN students clashed violently with the repressive forces, producing injuries and casualties on both sides. The repression reached its most violent day on October 2, when hundreds of people were shot down on Plaza de Tlatelolco, and dozens lost their lives. Later on, the main leaders of the National Strike Council (CNH) were arrested and, once the Olympics were over, they decided to put an end to the movement.

The main demands of the students were first recorded in August, including the following:

1. Freedom for political prisoners;
2. Discharge of the police chiefs Luis Cueto Ramírez, Mendiolea Cerecero, and Alfonso Frias;
3. Dissolution of the riot police and commitment to not creating a new one;
4. Repeal of articles 145 and 146 bis of the Federal Criminal Code, which integrated the "law of social dissolution" [that served as a legal recourse for the aggression inflicted on the students];
5. Compensations to the families of those injured and killed from July 26 on;
6. An outline of responsibility and sanctions for those functionaries found responsible [for the bloody events].[11]

Faced with these six demands, the administration of Díaz Ordaz never showed any will to negotiate with the students and never admitted to any culpability. The chiefs of police mentioned on the list were not dismissed from their positions, and those responsible for the repression, including the chief of staff, Luis Echeverría Álvarez, continued climbing the government apparatus of the PRI. In 1970, Echeverría was elected president of Mexico, and throughout his six-year tenure engaged in his own repression. In his fifth presidential report of September 1, 1969, Díaz Ordaz reasserted the authority of his government and his own responsibility as the patriarchal head of the nation. Years later, during a news program in 1977, he gave a televised interview in which he again denied that the events had produced "hundreds of dead" and reiterated how "proud" he felt of the fact that he had had the chance to save the country in 1968.[12]

In Montevideo, the repressive police forces (primarily the Metropolitan and Republican Guards) had been present from the very birth of the student movement in March when the students rejected an increase in the price of the student bus ticket. During these first days, the vast majority of the activists in Uruguay were represented by high school students and, even though the police did wield guns and rifles, state repression against the movement was limited to shots fired into the air designed to intimidate (just like the 1964 manual on "Civilian Disturbance Control" recommended). The army stayed away from the streets. However, starting in June, its influence was ever-more present, and the clashes with students and workers became extreme. In particular, the students radicalized in response to the "Prompt Security Measures," adopted on June 13 via a decree by President Pacheco Areco, who vehemently condemned the Latin American Organization for Solidarity (OLAS), which had been promoted from Cuban soil since August 1967. Pressed upon Pacheco Areco (1967–72) by the U.S. government, the measures went hand in hand with the outlawing of leftist parties and organizations (towards the end of 1967), including newspapers and weeklies, resulted in a reduction of individual rights, and declared martial law. From June on, numerous cases of injured students were reported, and instigators financed by the state started playing an important role infiltrating the movement. State authorities insisted that extremist agents led the movement and many rejected it as youthful restlessness, but the number of the injured kept growing over July and August. In addition, under the Security Measures, student and trade union leaders were incarcerated, barred from making statements to the press, and systematically repressed at school or in their factories. Popular discontent rose when the state froze salaries, outlawed strikes and trade unions, militarized public employees, and infringed upon university autonomy in August under the pretext of containing the supposed threat of the incipient urban guerrillas of the Tupamaros.[13]

Unlike the events that had unfolded in the preceding years, the demonstrations organized by university students were subjected to open fire by the Metropolitan and Republican Guards, who were no longer limited to water cannons and tear gas. Since the students declared their solidarity with the workers and the public employees (who were imprisoned and humiliated with head shavings and military exercises each time they demanded wage increases), the repressive forces were able to freely shoot to kill. The shots were no longer meant to intimidate, remembers a student, "they aimed directly . . . at our bodies." In a fashion similar to the one adopted by Díaz Ordaz in Mexico, President Pacheco Areco, who had recently received a shipment of "anti-riot rifles" from the United States, justified the repression in the following way: "If a society is assaulted, it must meet the aggression with aggression."[14]

Mid-August marked a critical juncture in the history of the Uruguayan student movement, as Líber Arce, a dentistry student and militant in the Union of Communist Youth (UJC), died of a gunshot wound in the groin. The wake, which first started at the university and culminated with the participation of more than 200,000 people on the way to the Buceo cemetery, transformed the movement not only into a genuine social conflict reflective of the discontent of an Uruguayan society "not ready for [or used to] such sacrifices," as historian Vania Markarian has argued, but also into a powerful symbol that would henceforth be celebrated annually on August 14 to commemorate all "student martyrs."[15]

The massive wake that took place in August, which included the participation of diverse sectors of society, made it difficult for the press to ignore the death of Líber Arce. However, at this stage, the government could "no longer be bothered to explain [its actions]" and, once the wake had taken place, the repression continued. According to a student journal, the repressive forces "proceeded unrestrained with all the brutality typical of dictatorships." The only alternative available to the movement was to "intensify its fight" and, "just like [Líber Arce] did," commit to "keep their heads high." "A mate murdered in the fight," another manifesto insisted, "means a lot to us. That's why the pain of his militant sacrifice won't silence our protest. On the contrary, it will strengthen our commitment to the fight, the fight of our fallen mate. . . . We, the students, prefer to die fighting to living in repression."[16]

Following the killing of Líber Arce, the movement acquired more political overtones. Student demands were no longer limited to school-related issues, such as the immediate cancellation of university debt, subsidies for student transportation, cafeteria installations in schools, and a broader scholarship system. Moreover, ever since the infringement on university autonomy in August, massive marches, general strikes, and occupations of schools and factories took place in addition to street barricades, and students demanded salary adjustment, the repeal of the Prompt Security Measures, observance of Uruguay's constitution, and the liberation of political and trade union prisoners. Workers joined them to demand an end to the militarization process, the repeal of all limitations on individual rights, the rehiring of all workers fired during the protests, a freezing of external debt, and a break-up with the International Monetary Fund (IMF) (rightfully accused of the repeal of industrial protection and cuts in public spending), agricultural reform, and bank and trade nationalization. As an activist eloquently put it, during these times "each student became a rabble-rouser."[17]

Many Uruguayan students thought that the fight was becoming increasingly violent and, just like their Mexican peers, they took measures to bring their strategies up to date. They started throwing Molotov cocktails, burned tires, and carried out lightning attacks against police forces in addition to their traditional tactics of barricades, traffic interruptions, and school occupations. Students stopped police horses with pepper, attacked dogs and police officers with slingshots, and soaked their handkerchiefs in ammoniac and lemon juice to reduce the effects of tear gas. They rioted on banks, U.S. corporations, and government offices.[18] The clashes, increasingly violent, continued until September, when Pacheco took more drastic measures to combat student activism.

Unfortunately, Líber Arce was not the only student who died in a hail of police bullets. The counterrevolution yielded two more deaths in mid-September, Hugo de los Santos and Susana Pintos. Unlike previous clashes between the students and the repressive forces of the state, this time the victims suffered from injuries related to the use of fragmented projectiles and pellet rifles.[19] The Executive Committee of the Medical Syndicate of Uruguay prepared a detailed report on the events that led to the killings of these students, which shows both the excessive violence used by the authorities and their basic failure at providing even minimal aid to the victims. According to the September 20 report, the Metropolitan Police, armed with patrol cars, shields, and "long-range and large-caliber guns, machine guns, and double-barrel rifles," shot "gas grenades at the march that fell behind the nearest barricades." The repression added at least forty injured to the fifty that the events of September 18 had produced. The students organized "an emergency unit" to attend to all injuries and ordered a call for ambulances. However, "after a while the latter called to inform that they could not go to the University because the police were not allowing them to go through."[20] Left without ambulance service, medical students took charge of tending to the injuries, used classroom doors as improvised gurneys, and waved white flags in an effort to get to those most gravely hurt. Police officers still shot at them and killed twenty-year-old economics student Hugo de los Santos and twenty-seven-year-old student Susana Pintos.[21]

To commemorate the three killed students, the leaders proposed a new, more aggressive fight on "three fronts: propaganda, agitation and organization."[22] Specifically, they recommended strengthening their alliance with the workers, who, with student support, continued occupying factories and fighting against police forces. Together, students and workers organized a general strike on September 24, commemorated the three casualties and, again, put the Pacheco government in a tight spot. However, the media launched their own propaganda attack, blaming communists for the violence and university authorities for corrupting and agitating the youth.[23]

The Pacheco government responded in a way similar to that of Díaz Ordaz, that is, by committing to "protecting" the country and "safeguarding" university autonomy. On September 22, he signed a decree that closed high schools and universities until October 15. He then ordered that the repressive forces block academic centers, arrest those partaking in the general strike of September 24, and close the offices of the National Workers' Convention (CNT) and the Bankers' Association. In an effort to demonstrate the foreign influence on the movement, the Pacheco government then expelled three diplomats from the Soviet Union on the night of September 24.[24]

The students remained willing to continue fighting, but found it difficult to maintain the massive phase of the movement in the face of schools closed and guarded by state forces, and a society increasingly anxious for order to be reestablished. By the beginning of November, with many of them exhausted, beaten, arrested, and injured, and with three deaths, they were forced to reexamine their participation in the movement. Just like in Mexico (and Brazil), many of them continued fighting. Some did it in a clandestine way within the different resistance cells that sprang up in the

New Left. Others clashed head-on with the state, joined the ranks of the disappeared, left the movement, or went into exile.[25]

THE KILLINGS OF STUDENTS IN MEXICO

Mexico also reported student deaths throughout July, August, and September (see table 14.1), but unlike in Uruguay, these undetermined killings did not give rise to mass wakes.[26] General references to the deaths were mentioned at demonstrations and marches. They were honored with massive protests and mentioned in multiple posters, but those killed were never named or given a public vigil. Instead, photographs of the movement demonstrate public burials in which the students mockingly carried coffins of the 1917 Constitution, the status quo, and the autonomy of the university. For their part, the government and the media deliberately played down and questioned the lethal repression and disappearances of students. The silence of the Catholic Church, as we will see later in this chapter, played a similar role in minimizing the significance of those who were killed during the movement.

One of the first student victims of the excessive use of force by the army was Federico de la O. García, a twenty-year-old business administration student at UNAM, who died after receiving a blow to the head the night of July 29, when a group of soldiers broke down the historic gate of the Preparatoria de San Ildelfonso. A report published by an anarchist magazine several weeks later claimed that three other students—José Richard Fuentes, Arturo Quiroz, and Pedro Colin Morín—had also lost their lives that day.[27] The Mexican press only mentioned Federico and, in an insolent fashion characteristic of these years, claimed that he had died of poisoning after eating a sandwich at a cafeteria. Others claimed that he had died of "cerebral hemorrhage caused by a firearm injury [received] a year before" in a fight with another student.[28]

By the end of September, the French magazine *L'Express* had claimed that at least fifteen people had been killed since the eruption of the student movement in late July. Documents from the U.S. embassy in Mexico made similar claims but explained that it was difficult to determine the exact number of deaths mainly because the national media and government officials had launched a campaign to discredit all of the student allegations. These tensions became evident as early as the first week of August.

TABLE 14.1 Estimate of people killed and/or disappeared in Mexico City during the 1968 student movement, July to September

Dates	*Killed/Disappeared* *(c) = confirmed in multiple sources* *(a) = alleged, but not confirmed in multiple sources.*	*Occupation/Further Details* *N/A = Unknown, further details not available*
July 26–29.	Federico de la O. García; killed (c).	Twenty-year-old business administration student at UNAM and native from Guerrero
July 26–29.	Joel Richard Fuentes; killed (c).	Student at the National Preparatory School #3
July 26–30.	Joel's brother; disappeared (a).	N/A
July 26–29.	Arturo Quiroz; disappeared (a).	Student
July 26–29.	Arturo Colin Morín; killed (c).	Student at the Technological School #4
July 26–29.	Pedro Colin Morín; killed (a).	N/A
July 26–30.	José L. Gómez Pedraza; disappeared (a).	Student, N/A
July 26–30.	Pina Palacio (a).	First name: N/A. Allegedly killed after bazooka was fired at the Preparatory School
July 26–August 11.	Miguel Rodríguez Hernández; disappeared (a).	Student at the National Preparatory School # 4
July 26–August 11.	Samuel Fuentes (a).	Father of a student. He allegedly died of a heart attack after learning of his son's fatal wounds.

TABLE 14.1 Estimate of people killed and/or disappeared in Mexico City during the 1968 student movement, July to September (*cont.*)

Dates	*Killed/Disappeared* *(c) = confirmed in multiple sources* *(a) = alleged, but not confirmed in multiple sources*	*Occupation/Further Details* *N/A = Unknown, further details not available*
July 26–August 11.	Juan Othón Rodríguez; disappeared (a).	N/A
July 26–August 11.	Jorge Casillas; disappeared (a).	Student at the Vocational School # 5
July 26–August 11.	Ricardo Dávila Zavala; disappeared (a).	Student at the Technological School # 1
July 26–August 11.	J. José Velasco Méndez; disappeared (a).	Student at the Dental School
July 26–August 11.	Osiris Rodríguez Elgar; disappeared (a).	Female student at the School of Medicine
July 26–August 11.	Gregorio Rosales Meteta; disappeared (a).	Student at the Law School
Sept 21–24.	Luis Lorenzo Rios Ojeda; killed (c).	N/A
Sept 21–24.	Lorenzo Hernández Reséndiz (c).	N/A
Sept 21–24.	Víctor Manuel Hernández Linares (c).	N/A
Sept 21–24.	Angel Santiago Luna (c).	N/A
Sept 21–24.	Angel Martínez Velásquez; killed (a).	A bystander, also referred to as Angel Valdez Velasco
Sept 21–24.	Three *granaderos*; killed (a).	Three *granaderos* were allegedly killed in flames when students fired what was described as a homemade bazooka from a school.
TOTAL	**Confirmed people killed: 7** **Allegedly killed and/or disappeared: 17**	

At UNAM, the School of Arts canceled its academic activities on the 4th in mourning for the infringement of university autonomy and "the murdered students." Four days later a group of IPN students threatened that they would encourage the boycott of the Olympics unless the government provided information regarding the students killed. They claimed that the government had disposed of bodies and had cremated them at the Military Hospital. In response, a committee of IPN professors took upon itself the task of investigating the killings and disappearances of the students. Government officials denied the accusations and noted on August 8 that "to date not one specific parent had filed a protest or had complained about a student killed or unaccounted for as a result of the recent riots." Five days later, the CNH responded to the government by providing the list of twenty people who had been killed, wounded, and disappeared during the movement since July 26. Yet again government officials created a reproving counternarrative by claiming that the names of the people on the lists were "fictitious, were not bona fide students, or had simply moved or died of natural causes." The press followed suit. Journalists sympathetic to the government claimed that the names of students included in the CNH list were false and encouraged parents of those killed and/or disappeared to provide concrete evidence to the press.[29]

The Secretary of the Interior Luis Echeverría Alvarez and the mayor of Mexico City Alfonso Corona del Rosal continued to publicly deny the deaths of students throughout the months of August and September. Yet, in hundreds of placards and manifestos students called Díaz Ordaz an "assassin" and demanded immediate indemnification to all those who had been brutally killed by his government. Similarly, in multiple posters, students emphasized the pain of the mourning mothers and adamantly claimed that Mexico could no longer be described as a democratic nation.

Rather, Mexico was transforming into a military state. Holding the same bayonet that had killed the students, one of these iconic posters explicitly suggested, Gustavo Díaz Ordaz had morphed into a "gorilla" who was personally responsible for slaying the peaceful movement of 1968. The image of the mourning mother appeared in multiple posters, particularly in the aftermath of the violent clashes between students of the IPN and the police authorities at the end of September. The massive reproduction of these visuals provided a powerful protest claiming that more students had been killed during these clashes. But yet again, the government and the media denied the accusations. In response, more than 1,500 women dressed in black organized a massive protest marching from the Monument to Mexican Mothers to the Chambers of Deputies. At the government building, the mother of Luis Rios Ojeda spoke with a microphone pledging that she would continue to fight to defend the memory of her son, killed during the September clashes at the Polytechnic Institute. A little girl also grabbed the microphone and claimed that her mother had died of a heart attack following the news that her brother had been killed during a violent clash with the police. A manifesto signed by more than 300 mothers on behalf of the National Union of Women demanded liberty to all political prisoners and indemnification to the mothers of those who had been killed since July. An extensive article published in *La Prensa* attempted to discredit the protesters by suggesting that the mothers dressed in black were not mourning but were rather having a good time celebrating a day off from their domestic obligations. The reporter claimed to have interviewed several women who, under pressure, allegedly admitted that their sons had never been killed. Rather, they were part of the number of "*acarreados*," or the hauled masses bused to protests by politicians interested in publicly defying the authority of the government.[30]

The media campaign against the students started in August and took a more condemnatory tone in September. As journalist Jacinto Rodríguez Munguía discovered in government reports, following the massive marches of late August, Díaz Ordaz gave direct orders to the press, including to all of the major newspapers, not to employ the terms "student" or "student movement/conflict" in their coverage. Rather, journalists were encouraged to use the following adjectives to describe the protesters: "adjured, terrorist, guerrillero, agitator, anarchist, unpatriotic, mercenary, traitor, foreigner," and "villainous." Euphemism, Rodríguez Munguía fittingly concludes in his analysis of 1968, served as an effective mechanism of propaganda. The manipulation of language, in short, served as a powerful "weapon [of the state]."[31]

A cover-up of the October 2 massacre took place immediately after the brutal events unfolded at the Plaza of Tlatelolco. However, the presence of an international media in Mexico City covering the Olympics made this a much more difficult task. Nonetheless, it is yet to be determined the exact number of people who were killed in 1968 in the nation's capital on that horrifying day.

In reference to the dead, most historians cite the numbers given in the first book published on the 1968 movement by Octavio Paz, *Posdata* (1970), where the famous intellectual wrote a potent critique of the authoritarianism of the PRI and noted that 325 people had been killed. The sources that he used came from articles published in the British newspaper *The Guardian*, by John Rodda where the journalist initially argued that more than 500 had been killed and then claimed that the numbers were closer to 267 people. These figures were vastly different from those given by the Mexican government and published in the national press, which ranged from 7 to 44. In a 1977 televised interview, Gustavo Díaz Ordaz denied that more than 100 people had been killed, alleged that the numbers instead ranged between 30 and 40, and encouraged civil society to make public a list detailing the names of the dead. Years later, after consulting numerous sources, the senior analyst of U.S. policy in Latin America at the National Security Archive, Kate Doyle, published a list of forty-four names who had been killed on October 2. Many scholars have recently pointed out that the people who were killed in Tlatelolco were probably more in the range of 44 to 100 (see table 14.2).[32] Yet, as Doyle fittingly lamented, "by guessing at numbers without linking them to names, we confiscate the very identities of the victims of Tlatelolco: their faces, their families, their lives before they were lost."[33]

More than five decades after 1968, Mexico has yet to provide a trustworthy human rights report on the Tlatelolco massacre.[34] What is clear today, moreover, is that the overwhelming emphasis in the literature on October 2 has overshadowed the killings of those killed from July to September. Also without a doubt, which historians have tended to neglect, is the vast support Díaz Ordaz received from various sectors of the nation's conservative society and influential political figures, including powerful labor and religious leaders.

THE REPRESSION OF STUDENTS IN MEXICO

One of the Mexican government's most influential allies in its fight against the student movement was Fidel Velázquez, whose career at the head of trade union corporativism had started in the 1930s. A decade later, when the PRI was founded (in 1946), the government took a turn to the

TABLE 14.2 People killed on October 2, 1968, as differently reported in sources frequently cited in the scholarship.

Date/Year Published	*Source*	*Number of people allegedly killed*
October 2, 1968.	Fernando Gutiérrez Barrios, director of the Federal Security Directorate (DFS).	26
October 2, 1968.	Directorate of Political and Social Investigation (IPS).	31
October 2–5, 1968.	National Strike Council (CNH).	40–150
October 3, 1968.	Fernando M. Garza, press spokesman of Gustavo Díaz Ordaz.	7
October 4, 1968.	John Rodda, *The Guardian.*	500+
October 3–5, 1968.	Mexico's most influential newspapers.	23–40
December, 1969.	National Strike Council (CNH).	150
1970.	Octavio Paz, *Posdata.*	325
1970 and 1977.	Gustavo Díaz Ordaz, televised interviews.	30–40
August 18, 1972.	John Rodda, *The Guardian.*	267
1978.	Sergio Zermeño, *México: Una democracia utópica.*	200
1993.	Plaque erected at the Plaza of Tlatelolco .	30+
2006.	Kate Doyle and Susana Zavala Orozco, "The Dead of Tlatelolco," *The National Security Archive.*	44

right, and communism became the enemy of the "revolution." Velázquez, at the head of the Confederation of Mexican Workers (CTM, the country's most important union), played a decisive role in liquidating the independent trade union movement. In 1958, "Don Fidel," as he came to be known both in the trade unions and after several reelections in the Senate, faced his greatest challenge when great swaths of the country were shaken by a strike of railroad workers that quickly spread to electrical and telegraph workers, rural teachers, and students. However, because of a combination of brutal repression, the imprisonment of the strike's leaders, and the compensation that Velázquez's corporate apparatus dispensed to those workers and trade unions who continued supporting the government, the railroad workers' movement died out just as the other Fidel was announcing the revolution's triumph in Cuba. Velázquez remained in charge of the Mexican trade unions throughout the 1960s, and his slogan of a "classless society" continued working against the "communist" threat of an independent trade union. The CTM leader was equally important in 1968, when he defended the Díaz Ordaz government and pressured his trade unions and workers into not supporting the students.

The students had taken measures to legitimize their discontent with state repression in general and political prisoners in particular since the inception of the 1968 movement. One of their first banners explicitly demanded Demetrio Vallejo's freedom, who had been held prisoner since the 1958 railroad workers' movement. Because of that, the reaction of Fidel Velázquez received widespread attention. Just like the government, he employed an increasingly violent and reactionary tone in his comments. Initially, the trade union leader recognized "the student's right to voice their demands . . . provided that s/he did it through the appropriate channels." However, days later he argued that the movement lacked "a noble cause" and, following "foreign slogans," it only purported to "disrupt public order and undermine the government's authority." In August, these critiques gave way to threats, first to the workers who lent their support to the students, such as the teachers who were threatened with contract termination, and later to the students, who were warned that if they did not stop insulting the nation and the president, they would incur the wrath of the trade unions. For example, Demetrio Vallejo declared his support of the student movement and identified President Díaz Ordaz as "the only one responsible for his torture" from prison at the end of August. In an indirect response, Velázquez declared that "any measure of repression by the government against the movement would be completely justified." Later on, when he saw that a small but growing number of workers sympathized with the movement, he declared that the CTM was taking measures to integrate "a committee of defense against subversive acts that would count on shock brigades." Its mission would consist in defending the country against "foreigners and bad Mexicans" and reestablish "order and truth."[35]

Existing published chronicles on the movement do not establish if such brigades were ever created. However, students did clash with paramilitary groups. Before 1968, school and government authorities had frequently used instigators (*porros*) to infiltrate student groups and spy on them. Grouped in task forces, these individuals played an important role in splitting up the student Left and/or negotiating with its leaders. They were also employed to beat up activists in gatherings, school occupations, and elections. The state used these pseudo-students as agents of negotiation and repression without having to directly infringe upon university autonomy. Even though provocation had always been part and parcel of the movement, *porrismo* (the use of *porros*) did not yield the expected results as a mechanism of control. On the contrary, the groups allied to the state and the extreme Right, such as the National Federation of Technical Students (FNET) and the University Movement of Renewed Orientation (MURO), respectively, lost their hegemony in the schools. Two main reasons explain this loss. Both the massive nature of the student movement and the self-defense brigades and fighting committees, organized by the students to protect the occupied schools and the marches, served to overshadow the shock brigades. The second reason had to do with the democratic nature of the CNH and the instigation brigades. Historically, the government could and did frequently co-opt the main leaders, but found it impossible to control or buy off the numerous school representatives who in 1968 used to change often.

Faced with a crisis of *porrismo* and frequent riot police defeats, the repressive repertoire widened to include paramilitary groups that violently attacked selected occupied schools and street demonstrations. Unlike the *porro* groups, the paramilitaries' repression quickly escalated to lethality since they used machine guns, rather than pellet guns. This type of attack was first used in August and primarily targeted vocational schools and high schools. Its modus operandi varied little: a group of thugs would arrive at the school by car and open machine-gun fire. The shots would break the building's windows, and a group of armed individuals would descend, break the barricades with chains and sticks, and beat the students. The media would report the attacks as "terrorist" acts or acts committed by the extreme Right or the militant Left, without ever mentioning the government.

The Mexican state used propaganda in conjunction with repression from the very beginning of the student movement and this further intensified in late August. The media and the parties affiliated with the government—such as the Popular Socialist Party (PPS in its Spanish acronym) of the old Marxist Vicente Lombardo Toledano—insisted that foreigners (who ranged from CIA to Cuba in their allegiance) had infiltrated the student movement. Only law and order could save the country. In August, the paramilitary attacks were used as evidence of the student problem, and, months later, a plethora of apocryphal books, pseudo manifestos, and fictitious declarations were published and distributed. *¡El Móndrigo! Bitácora del Consejo Nacional de Huelga* (1969) is the best example of this type of book. The apocryphal book was published by the Federal Security Directorate (DFS) with the support of the minister of interior and was supposedly authored by a leader of the 1968 movement. It tells the story of an "enraged" and "agitated" Trotskyite who allows the "hard" wing of the movement to manipulate him and, in exchange for his errors, dies riddled with bullets in the Plaza of Tlatelolco at the hands of a group of snipers anxious to overthrow Díaz Ordaz's government. *¡El Móndrigo!* began circulating after the October 2 student massacre and, not unlike other false texts from the period, combined real names and true pieces of information with completely false or vastly exaggerated information in an effort to smear the movement leaders' reputations, slander the left-leaning intellectuals who sympathized with the students, and justify the state's use of violence.[36]

The school assemblies and the street brigades played a crucial role in refuting government propaganda and creating self-defense groups. According to one of the main leaders of the movement, 1968 was characterized by the relationship between four different organs or horizontal forms of expression. Main among them was the National Strike Council (CNH). Formed by representatives of each school committee, this organ functioned as the "brain" of the student movement and the main decision-making body (with decisions relating to the demand sheet, the demand for public dialogue, and the marches taken there). The second consisted of the "massive demonstrations" that were organized throughout August and September. The latter functioned as "the muscle system" of the movement and gathered between 200,000 and 400,000 people. The third consisted of the "*asambleas*" that made decisions on the day-to-day routine of the movement after long debates and discussions, which went on until a collective agreement was reached. Working independently of student political parties, the latter symbolized the "nervous system of the student movement. Finally, the brigades represented the "circulatory system."[37]

The brigades were composed of small groups that represented thousands of students from different high schools and universities. They had a triple, much more creative, spontaneous, and frequently independent (of the CNH) function. The brigades formed protection guards to prevent *porro* attacks during the night. During the day, they were "in charge of the establishment and functioning of the cafeterias where all participants in the movement gathered to eat."[38] The fundamental role of the brigades had to do with propaganda: promoting support for the movement among all social sectors and condemning the fake news and the physical repression used by the government. The participants—who frequently also included teachers, artists, and representatives of the student sections of political parties—first discussed, edited, and printed leaflets and then got out of the schools to distribute the propaganda on the streets, in the markets, movie theaters, on the buses, in the neighborhoods, restaurants, city plazas, theaters, factories, and small businesses. The brigades took advantage of their presence in these places (and in the occupied schools) to agitate, organizing lightning rallies, graffiti paintings, happenings, and improvising polemic dialogues among themselves and with the people who engaged with them.[39] Finally, and very successfully, the brigades also took advantage of these opportunities to interact with different social classes to collect money necessary for the food served at the occupied schools and for the production of the movement's propaganda. These dialogues and interactions served as the engines behind the movement's horizontal mobilization, the springboard of direct action, and the forums where broader popular support was sought.

The sheer variety of projects—ranging from Catholic messages (that have received little historical attention) to more left-wing messages—presented by the brigades reflected the spontaneous and heterogeneous character of *brigadismo.* In general, the vast majority of the brigades represented two principal discourses: one defending constitutional rights and another one condemning state repression (both physical and in terms of propaganda). Some social sectors had a favorable view of student activism. However, despite its democratic and moderate tone, the movement frequently experienced the resistance of ordinary people on the streets. In the factories, the brigades were often seen in a negative light because of the aforementioned reasons, and the students frequently had to deal with the workers' indifference despite their emphasis on political prisoners and their condemnation of the unions' antidemocratic nature. The media often took advantage of the heterogeneity of the brigades and frequently highlighted (and, in many cases, invented) the "violent character" of the brigadiers. They were eventually also targeted by the state's repressive apparatus, especially from August onward when paramilitary groups replaced the thugs-for-hire. When some students assumed a more violent attitude, the riot police and the army intensified their aggression.[40]

Instigators also existed in Uruguay. However, the systematic use of clash forces that characterized the Mexican case was never institutionalized as a mechanism of control and repression there. The Pacheco government and the military juntas that followed opted for using its repressive forces unashamedly. Uruguay ranked first in political prisoners per capita in the mid-1970s when the country was under the control of its military. The war against the "subversives" in general and against the militant youth in particular would continue not only in Uruguay, but also throughout neighboring countries, including Brazil where youth were arrested, tortured, and disappeared, and where the dirty war grew into a continental project of unprecedented military collaboration.

THE CATHOLIC CHURCH AND THE 1968 STUDENT MOVEMENTS IN MEXICO AND BRAZIL

More than one hundred Catholic student federations met on July 20, 1964, at Georgetown University for the XXVI Inter-Federal Assembly of Pax Romana. The central theme of the conference was "Christianity in an Age of Transition," and the keynote speaker was U.S. attorney general Robert F. Kennedy. In his remarks, Kennedy noted, "The ambitions, the sensitivity, and the responsibility of university students in every country today will soon shape the success or failure, war or peace, prosperity or misery of your countries and our world tomorrow." Specifically, in response to the progressive, even radical, language that emerged with Vatican II and the rise of communism that spread across the continent in the aftermath of the Cuban Revolution, Kennedy argued that young Catholics could no longer afford to sit on the sidelines and patiently wait for change. They had to assume the role of the vanguard in facing the world's most pressing threats, including exploitation, extreme poverty, tyranny, hunger, nuclear armament, and communism. Kennedy continued:

> These are not problems to be mulled over, they must be solved in a single generation . . . you as men and women of learning and faith have a responsibility to choose . . . to become world citizens who can make tolerant and educated judgments concerning problems not only of our lives and lands, but of men everywhere. . . . All of us have to participate. All of us are needed. The question is whether to be a critic or a participant. The question is whether to bring a candle to the barricade or to curse the darkness. At this assembly, devoted to social responsibility, I think the choice must be for light.[41]

More than seventy countries attended the meeting in Washington, DC. With dozens of leaders, representing multiple and divergent Catholic organizations, Latin America sent some of the largest delegations of students. Of these delegates, the most radical and influential were those led by Brazilian students, who had begun to see themselves as important agents of continental change since the mid-1950s. In particular, they became critical of the nationalism, reformism, and Eurocentric language of an earlier era, and instead began to see themselves as "Latin Americans" with shared problems, histories, and challenges. Drawing from the writing of Jacques Maritain and the encyclicals *Mater et magistra* (1961) and *Pacem in terris* (1963), they rejected the anticommunist rhetoric of Pax Romana and called for the creation of grassroots bases (with Christian principles) capable of liberating the continent from capitalism and imperialism.[42] The most radical of these voices questioned the political and economic institutions responsible for the exploitation of the masses. Embracing a growing Third World sentiment, moreover, they championed a "theology of commitment" and called on their peers to abandon a paternalistic relationship with the poor and instead become more politically engaged with them by building a "mystic sense of community." The university Catholic community, they concluded, could no longer afford to side with the status quo. It needed to be transformed into a hub of radical change.[43]

For this, Brazilian Catholic students advocated the "See, Judge, Act" method, as originally articulated by Belgian cardinal Joseph Cardjin in the 1930s, and as reevaluated in the aftermath of both the Cuban Revolution and the adoption of Freire's pedagogical concept of "*concientización*." For them, the humanist goals of the Cuban regime and the focus of achieving an in-depth understanding of the structural forces that caused the injustices of the world coincided with the progressive turn that started to take place with *aggiornamento* within the Church; also discussed in the chapters by Manzano (7), Barr-Melej (15), Walker (18), and especially De Giuseppe (3) in this volume. Radically, the method asked university Catholic students to step outside their ivory tower and "see" the life conditions of the majority of Brazilians; "judge" that situation by providing a critical analysis of that reality and a close reading of the Bible and the tools of sociology (including those written by Marxists); and, upon reflection, engage (or "act") in a dynamic response that was compatible with Christian ideals of justice and solidarity. Through this method of *Revisión de Vida* ("Revision of Life"), as it was known at the time, university Catholic students across Brazil learned the important role they could play to change the world around them. But their role as leaders was not confined to the national reality. For this, they complemented their readings of Maritain and Freire with those from Herbert Marcuse and leading voices of Latin America's dependency theory, and others. Moreover, in rejecting collaboration with U.S. institutions, they reached out for support to progressive figures within the hierarchy of the Latin American Church and the Latin American Episcopal Council (CELAM), including Dom Hélder Câmara, Carlos McGrath, and Gustavo Gutiérrez, who by 1968 had become critical voices of the excesses of capitalism and imperialism, sharp critics of armed struggle, and rising advocates of liberation theology.

The progressive turn to the Left within the Latin American Church, overwhelmingly influenced by Brazilian figures, reached a defining moment in 1968 during the Conference of Latin American Bishops meeting in Medellín, Colombia. There, the method of *Revisión de Vida* was embraced to shift the Church's emphasis towards the poor majority and, with repeated citations from *Populorum progressio* (1967), the leaders of the conference urged Latin American youth to join forces in the defense of human rights and endorse a commitment to political change. The goal was to create an "authentic liberation" of the continent.[44] Catholic youth across Latin America responded by engaging in a variety of protests that ranged from the occupation of churches to hunger strikes and marches (see, for example, chapter 15 on Chile by Barr-Melej in this volume). In Brazil, where the military crackdown on dissent coincided with the timing of the Medellín Conference, the involvement of progressive Catholic figures was also evident in the defining role they played during the 1968 student movement.

The 1968 student movement in Brazil first emerged as a small series of four-year protests aimed at democratizing higher education. In late March, the movement erupted on a massive scale after the police stormed into a local restaurant where students were protesting against the poor quality of the cafeteria food, and shot and killed Édson Luís de Lima Souto, a young high school student at the Federal University of Rio de Janeiro. Students responded by taking the corpse of the teenager to the State Legislative Assembly where they conducted fiery speeches throughout the day and night. As historian Victoria Langland has documented, more than 20,000 people participated in a collective mourning by accompanying the body of Édson in a funeral procession, which began at the State Assembly building and concluded with a solemn burial at the cemetery.[45] The police made efforts to prevent the funeral, but with the intervention of Bishop Dom José de Castro Pinto and a group of priests, the vigil continued. A riot then erupted after the police proceeded to throw tear gas at the cathedral and beat up a group of students. The repressive police action killed another student while the activists responded by reorganizing the National Union of Students (UNE), which had been outlawed since the fall of Goulard in 1964. During the following months, with myriad banners reproducing the face of Édson Luís, the movement had transformed into a massive denunciation of the atrocities of the military dictatorship and a piercing call for the return to democracy. Violent student riots followed. In June, the movement had spread into the streets and into various regions of Brazil.

On June 21, more than twenty students were killed in violent clashes between the students and the police in what came to be known as "Bloody Friday."[46] Five days later, students, intellectuals, artists, lawyers, teachers, journalists, and leading Catholic figures participated in the "March of the Hundred Thousand" demanding justice for the students who had been killed during the movement. Progressive and influential members of the clergy, including Hélder Cámara, but also Candido Padim, Castro Pinto, Antonio Batista Fragoso, and José Medeiros Delgado, not only sympathized with the student movement but also took advantage of its massive nature to draw attention to all of the victims of exclusion, oppression, and torture that had fallen victim to the military forces since the 1964 coup. In June, Dom Candido Padim read a critical document to the Brazilian Episcopate on the "Doctrine of National Security" where the bishop drew a comparison between the methods of repression and annihilation by Nazi Germany and those employed by the Brazilian authorities. Both of these fascist regimes, he argued, threatened to eliminate the Church and had launched a brutal war against their citizens. That same month, a group of more than one hundred priests formed a human chain to prevent a further violent class between students and the police.[47]

The military state responded to both the student movement and the radical Catholic organizations that emerged in the context of the Medellín Conference by issuing the Institutional Act No. 5 (AI-5) in December 1968. Initially, the new law provided the local police and the armed forces with the power of detaining civilians without charges. Yet, like Uruguay's Prompt Security Measures, AI-5 was soon broadened to give unprecedented powers to the repressive apparatus of the military state as it censored the press, banned political opposition, suspended the activities of Congress, closed all schools, and outlawed political meetings and strikes.[48] A new and bigger wave of arrests soon followed, including the imprisonment of eighteen priests and fifty-seven Catholic leaders who came in support of the movement and a total of more than 700 students, and so did a growing list of people tortured and disappeared.[49] The repression only escalated further in February 1969 following Decree 477, which brought an end to the student movement, but, like in Uruguay, pushed many activists underground to continue fighting for democracy. Specifically, the decree ordered:

> the expulsion from the university and the permanent exclusion from any other educational institutions of any student or professor that "directs or participates in, prepares, prints, stores, or distributes subversive material of whatever nature" or "participates in acts associated with the organization of subversive movements, parades, marches, or unauthorized events."[50]

Catholic students and clergy joined forces with artists and intellectuals to launch more campaigns to denounce state repression. They collected statements of those tortured, provided the names of activists who were killed and disappeared, documented the abuse of political prisoners, identified the right-wing groups responsible for attacks against the schools, and sought international support, making it increasingly more difficult for the U.S. government to continue to justify in public its unconditional support of the military dictatorships in the Southern Cone. The denunciations against repression continued during the following years. Between 1969 and 1972, the progressive wing of the Church played a key role in protecting dissident organizations, calling for a nonviolent liberationist movement, and promoting human rights.[51]

THE CATHOLIC CHURCH IN 1968 MEXICO

From the perspective of student activists in Mexico and further evident in the vast literature on the 1968 movement, the Catholic Church represented an archaic institution, blinded in superstition and anticommunism, and hegemonic in its rejection of the new social, cultural, and religious movements of the era. Voiced throughout the movement, this sentiment was ultimately ratified on October 2, when an undetermined number of people were killed at the Plaza of the Three Cultures in Tlatelolco. As students ran for their lives following the shootings, many pounded their fists on the doors of the Church of Santiago located at the heart of the Plaza, but the doors were never opened. For many, such refusal pointed to a Church that had failed to protect the students from the bullets, in particular, and from a repressive state throughout the movement, in general. Years later, however, it was revealed that the Church had been taken over by the same paramilitary group that played a determining role in the student massacre, the Batallón Olimpia (Olympic Battalion). As remembered by a person who was inside the church on October 2 during a wedding ceremony and well documented in the literature, the members of the Batallón were wearing civilian clothes that day, but also a white glove on one of their hands as a distinctive sign. These agents of repression were part of the Presidential Guard responsible for carrying out the student massacre, and to date there is no longer any doubt that the president of

Mexico, who received economic, political, and intelligence support from the U.S. government during (and before and after) the movement, was ultimately responsible for the deaths. The leading forces in charge of the operation also used the roof of the church to place the snipers responsible for the shooting that ignited the massacre, and they kept the doors of the building shut to prevent students from entering.[52] The ecclesiastical authorities neglected to make a statement in the aftermath of the massacre to explain why some of the shooting had taken place from the church, which many interpreted as their complicity with the state. This is essentially true, but it is also worth noting that isolated voices did break from a long history of silence and expressed support of the student movement. But these voices paled in comparison to their Brazilian counterparts.

One of the first influential documents of the Mexican Church alluding to youth activism was released in March 1968. Written by a group of bishops in response to the first anniversary of *Populorum progressio* as a "Pastoral Letter on the Development and Integration of the Country," part of the document described youth activism not as an irrational consequence of the manipulation of international forces, as many within the hierarchy had insisted in the past, but rather as a response to the rising economic crisis and the infringement of constitutional rights. The Mexican Revolution had improved the lives of many Mexicans, but, the bishops argued in the document, the country was still marked by drastic inequalities. This sentiment was repeated during the first official report published on September 10, 1968, in direct response to the student movement. Signed by thirty-seven priests and supported by the president of Mexico's Social Secretariat, Pedro Velázquez, the report demanded "a respectful dialogue" between state authorities and the students. It rejected the official narrative of the state, which inequitably insisted that international communist forces were leading the student uprising, and instead referred to the movement as a generational conflict that demanded freedom and justice. In addition, the priests condemned what they saw as a dirty war launched against the students composed of a psychological campaign of moral panic based on rumors and lies, on the one hand, and the illegal use of provocateurs, on the other. Yet in their strong condemnation of political violence, the letter said nothing in response to the student deaths. This silence was partially and unsatisfactorily broken on October 9 when the archbishop of Oaxaca, Ernesto Corripio Ahuma, published a pastoral letter on behalf of the Episcopate Committee. The letter condemned all forms of violence, including acts of vandalism committed by the students, and without making references to the state or to political prisoners; it incomprehensibly noted that "we were all responsible" for the massacre in the Plaza of Tlatelolco. Similar statements were made by other influential figures of the Church, including the president of the Episcopate Octaviano Márquez and the bishops of Mexico City, Guadalajara, and Zamora, Miguel Dario Miranda, José Garibi, and José Salazar, respectively.[53]

The support that the Catholic Church gave to the administration of Díaz Ordaz was overwhelming. Yet there were some isolated voices that took a more critical view of the state, mainly the Jesuit priest, Enrique Maza, and the "Red Bishop" of Cuernavaca, Sergio Méndez Arceo. Both came from conservative backgrounds but welcomed and participated in the progressive turn of the Church, which in Mexico began in 1966, but was first noticed publicly with the 1968 pastoral letter. For Maza, the year 1968 coincided with the time when he was named director of the influential journal *Christus*, a tenure that lasted until 1973, when the Jesuits asked Maza to resign and replaced him with the more conservative Xavier Cuenca. Under Maza's leadership, *Christus* took a distinctive turn to the Left. It published articles by some of Latin America's most influential figures and sympathizers of liberation theology: Marcos McGrath, Segundo Galilea, Hélder Cámara, and the Mexican leaders Luis del Valle, Jesús García, Martín de la Rosa, Sergio Méndez Arceo, and Samuel Ruiz. The themes covered by these figures in their articles and pastoral letters varied. Many specifically touched on the concept of youth and described at length the role university students should assume in providing a better future for the nation. In this tone, Enrique Maza published one of the most cogent articles related to the 1968 student movement in which he provided a strong condemnation of state violence and a poignant critique of those who came in support of the government, including a national Church that refused to listen to the students. In his chronology of the movement, the Jesuit priest mentioned the students killed in July and September and suggested that at least one hundred people had died during the October 2 massacre, but he admitted that it was difficult to determine the exact number. Maza called for a detailed investigation, but lamented that the media had only created greater confusion by failing to make a responsible distinction between the truth and apocryphal news sponsored by the state.

For this, he provided a list of government-sponsored myths associated with the movement in which students were overwhelmingly described as dupes of various political forces and foreign institutions from both the militant Left and the reactionary Right. Rather, he described the movement as a genuine protest that successfully exposed the limitations of the economic miracle and the nation's lack of true democracy. He admitted that students made mistakes but argued that they had successfully challenged the "dictatorial" powers of the state. In agreement with the students, he argued that Mexico lacked a judicial system and a responsible press. The corrupt governing elite relied too often on illegal and repressive mechanisms of control and was the first to violate the constitution. "The PRI," he concluded without obscurity, "had suffocated the student movement." But in the optimistic tone that Maza used in his article, he simultaneously argued that students "had awakened our consciousness, opened a space for reflection, and [demanded from us to adopt] a new and more politicized mentality." In short, the movement as seen by Maza represented a "socio-political-cultural revolution" that was violently repressed, smeared with government-sponsored lies, and for the same reason was poorly understood. For its part, the Church in general, and unreceptive Catholics in particular, were also to be blamed. Their silence had made them complicit. In ignoring the teachings of Vatican II and *Populorum progressio*, they had failed to see the democratic nature of the movement and its commitment to social justice. Students were imprisoned. They fought and many lost their lives, he indignantly lamented, but the key leaders of the Church had remained absent and thus culpable for the repression.[54]

A second and more influential Catholic figure who came in support of the movement escaped Maza's condemnation, and also provided harsh criticisms of the Catholic hierarchy and the government, was Sergio Méndez Arceo, bishop of Cuernavaca, a position he had held in the Zapatista state of Morelos since 1952. Present at the Christians for Socialism Conference in Chile (1972), the ecumenical Méndez Arceo had emerged in the 1960s as the *enfant terrible* of the Mexican Church. With sympathetic priests, he oversaw the crafting of the pastoral letter of 1968. With peasants and the unemployed, he defended squatters who took possession of unused private lands. With Catholic students devoted to the "See, Judge, Act" method, he participated in small Bible-reading groups. With workers, he defended their rights to create independent labor unions. With the Belgian monk Gregorio Lemercier, he welcomed the introduction of psychoanalysis into the monastery. With the controversial Austrian priest Iván Illich, he transformed the Intercultural Documentation Center (CIDOC) into an influential hub of countercultural, political, and religious figures that made up Latin America's New Left. And with the international community, he became an outspoken critic of the war in Vietnam and a frequent sympathizer of both the Cuban Revolution and Camilo Torres, but he ultimately called for active nonviolence.[55]

In 1968, the bishop of Cuernavaca faced a "mute Church" that had turned its back on the student movement. In homilies and interviews, published and conducted between 1968 and 1971, Méndez Arceo echoed many of the sentiments that were simultaneously expressed by Maza, mainly by describing the student movement as a legitimate democratic uprising that had successfully exposed the brutality of the state. But it was his acts of solidarity with political prisoners that most people remember. On December 10, 1969, a group of political prisoners organized a hunger strike to protest judicial impunity. Two days later, Méndez Arceo dedicated his homily to the strike and told his followers that they could no longer afford to ignore the lives of more than ninety activists who had remained behind bars in the aftermath of the movement. Two months later, on Christmas night, he then spoke about his visit to the activists at the infamous prison of Lecumberri: "We have been tolerating too many injustices in the name of order and peace for far too long." A year later, Méndez Arceo elaborated his critique of the government in a homily he read at the Basilica of Guadalupe in Mexico City in which he urged his followers to take a more proactive approach in the name of justice: "A true believer is one who is committed." He is "a rebel who rejects all forms of injustices . . . one who is committed with a *permanent* and not an *institutionalized* revolution."[56]

In sum, the leading figures of the Latin American Church who welcomed the radical language of the era that culminated at the Medellín Conference agreed with Robert Kennedy and also argued that in this "age of transition" Catholics could no longer afford to sit on the sidelines. Yet, they did not embrace Kennedy's anticommunist rhetoric, and with good reason and no exaggeration saw the U.S. government as largely responsible for the military brutality that swept the Latin American continent during some of the most turbulent years of the Cold War period. The conservative Church was also to be blamed, where in the case of Mexico it overwhelmingly sided with the state.

CONCLUSION

In late September 1968, the writers and university professors Rubén Bonifaz Nuño and Miguel León-Portilla found a passed-out, dying woman in the eighth-floor restroom of the Humanities building of UNAM. Upon examining her, one of them shouted, "She's alive!" On her way to the medical unit, the woman was identified as Alcira Soust Scaffo. She was an Uruguayan writer who had arrived in Mexico in the 1950s on a UNESCO scholarship; a rural teacher and known among friends as a bohemian poet, trade union artist, translator of children's short stories, and "a foolish and transparent legend" of '68, as she was described by one of her most beloved friends and key intellectual leader of the student movement, José Revueltas. According to some, Alcira had gone to the restroom in an effort to hide from the soldiers who invaded the university on September 18, as part of the Díaz Ordaz government's "Operation Clean-up"—the same name given by the Brazilian authorities, "Operaçao Limpeza," in reference to the purging of the country's alleged "subversives." According to the myth that several years later another one of her friends, Roberto Bolaño, immortalized in his novels, Alcira, though very weak, had survived twelve days of military occupations by drinking water from the toilets. She later explained to one of her friends that she "got on top of the toilets and locked the door so that, when they entered, the soldiers could not see anyone."[57] Others maintained that the Uruguayan artist had played León Felipe's disk "Voz Viva" on the speakers of the Humanities radio in the Philosophy building to protest the soldiers' presence. Still others insisted that Alcira herself shouted out the poems. Apart from the legend surrounding these events, what appears to be clear and explains Alcira's fear is that through the restroom window, she witnessed Mexican students being beaten and arrested at gunpoint. Like many of the detained, Roberto Bolaño tells Alcira's story in Auxilio Lacouture's voice: "I knew what my duty was. . . . I knew that I had to resist. I sat on top of the toilet and took advantage of the last hours of the day to read three poems by Pedro Garfias. Then, I closed the book, shut my eyes closed and said to myself . . . citizen of Uruguay, Latin American, poet and traveler, [you must] resist."[58]

In another poem written in French that Alcira gave to her friend José Revueltas in December 1967, she described these years:

Le Bonheur sera pour tous
Dans un monde si enivrant
Où n'y aura lieu por la faim . . .

Le Bonheur sera pour tous
Quand l'amour tourner la terre.[59]

The myth of Alcira symbolizes the peculiar character of 1968 in Latin America. On the one hand, her poem's emotion and the love that her friends professed for her hint at the optimism and activism of the period. On the other hand, the surrealist nightmare that Alcira lived in the Humanities tower represents the terror and the trauma that many youths went through as a result of the repressive violence that also characterized the period. "Everything had stuck together in [her] soul," José Revueltas remembers upon seeing Alcira in the hospital. "The Vietnam war, the repression of blacks, the emptiness, the pain of being alive."[60] As Diana Sorensen has rightly contended, and as several contributors to this volume have argued, in Latin America, unlike Europe and the United States, the "spirit of liberation" that characterized this period was marked by its "intensity." The 1960s, a decade that started with the Cuban Revolution and ended with the U.S.-backed coup in Chile in 1973, stands out with its "twin rhythms of euphoria and despair."[61] This rhythm reached one of its most intense moments in 1968.

In Mexico, Uruguay, and Brazil, where three of the most massive student movements across the world took place, the revolutionary euphoria of the 1960s was manifested in barricades, sit-ins, occupations, assemblies, demonstrations, and brigades that rejected state repression. As the long history of Mexiac's "Libertad de Expresión" reminds us, this repression needs to be understood in the broader context of the Latin American Cold War in which the United States played a defining role. The desperation of the period was lived in the spaces of protest created in 1968 and was intensified by the excessive and brutal state repression that, in the Mexican case, hid under the façade of a tolerant and supposedly democratic country but, as in South America, also opted for furiously repressing its youth. In Uruguay, 1968 represented a true watershed in the history of its democratic regime. Pacheco's Prompt Security Measures gave rise to a wave of military violence that lasted until the 1980s. In Brazil, the repression started in 1964, but further intensified in 1968 with the emergence of new and more vindictive laws of repression. In Mexico, it is difficult to distinguish between a "before" and an "after." The PRI took a left turn in the 1970s, as it had done before, but continued repressing dissidents with illegal and harsh mechanisms of control. In all of the three places examined here, the governments took steps to "modernize" their security apparatuses and, in justifying the repression, they infringed upon university autonomy and identified the student youth as "the enemy."[62]

The student movements of 1968 in Mexico, Uruguay, and Brazil shared parallel histories: all witnessed the emergence of "youth power," which aimed at creating a fairer and more democratic world. Through their movements, the students demanded respect for constitutional rights. Engulfed in their logic of repression, the authorities declared these demands antinational acts. In all three, state repression radicalized the student movements and propelled hundreds of youths into the most activist wings of the New Left. Some even took up arms. However, despite these similarities, the three movements are also characterized by key differences. In Uruguay, where independent trade unionism had a longer history, 1968 produced a coalition between students and workers that never really materialized in Mexico. In Brazil, this support came from a progressive wing of the Catholic Church that enjoyed a much more reduced space in Mexico. The Mexican 1968 movement questioned authoritarian trade unionism and used *porrismo* as a control mechanism in the crisis, but the apparatus of the PRI remained strong and so did the support it continued to receive from a conservative Church and a sympathetic neighbor in the North. The trade unions under Fidel Velázquez, a loyal ecclesiastical elite, and a media in charge of spreading apocryphal news in defense of the government all played crucial roles in delegitimizing the student movement and justifying counterrevolutionary violence. The many different currents within the Left affected the student movement. However, on the subject of armed strife, they split anew after the Tlatelolco student massacre. Its most militant wings were repressed and, later, co-opted during the Luis Echeverría administration (1970–76). In contrast, state repression in the Southern Cone managed to bring together the sundry factions of the Left. In Uruguay, this took place under the front of the Frente Amplio. In Brazil, a group of progressive leaders extended this support to the Church. In the 1970s, many of the activists of these movements created their own list of martyrs. In Mexico, the victims of state repression in the 1970s were never named. Students demanded a more democratic nation, and through the use of brigades and new grassroots movements engaged in innovative and more horizontal forms of participation. Yet, as before, these brigades did not see the need to provide the names of those killed in 1968, from July to October. Worse yet, Tlatelolco is still remembered today, but we know very little about its victims.

NOTES

1. Oscar Méndez, *Libertad de Expresión: Adolfo Mexiac* (Ediciones Pentagrama, 2009), DVD.

2. David Alfaro Siqueiros, "Homenaje Postumo a Frida Kahlo," *Arte Público*, November 1954, 3.

3. It is worth remembering that a twenty-six-year-old Ernesto Guevara was present in Guatemala in 1954. After witnessing the CIA-sponsored coup, the rising leader of the New Left came to the conclusion that armed struggle would be necessary to launch a revolution capable of defending Latin America from further threats by the "Imperialist North."

4. Margaret Timmers, *A Century of Olympic Posters* (London: V & A Publishing, 2008), 77.

5. For a different version of this chapter, see Jaime M. Pensado, "Entre perdigones, provocadores y noticias apócrifas: Un caso comparativo a la represión estatal durante el movimiento estudiantil del '68 en México y Uruguay," in *Movimientos estudiantiles del siglo XX en América Latina*, ed. Vania Markarian (Rosario, Argentina: Facultad de Humanidades y Artes, 2018), 109–47. See also Jeffrey L. Gould, "Solidarity under Siege: The Latin American Left, 1968," *The American Historical Review* 114, no. 2 (2009): 348–75.

6. Gilbert M. Joseph, "What We Now Know and Should Know: Bringing Latin America More Meaningfully into Cold War Studies," in *In from the Cold: Latin America's New Encounter with the Cold War*, ed. Gilbert M. Joseph and Daniela Spenser (Durham, NC: Duke University Press, 2008), 3.

7. Arthur Marwick, *The Sixties: Cultural Revolution in Britain, France, Italy, and the United States, c. 1958–1974* (London: Bloomsbury, 1998).

8. Coronel Edison Alonso Rodríguez de la Jefatura de Policía de Montevideo, Instituto de Enseñanza Profesional, "Control de disturbios civiles," 1964, in "Uruguayan Political Ephemera Collection," Department of Special Collections, Hesburgh Libraries of Notre Dame (hereafter, UPEC-DSP-HLND).

9. Jefatura de Policía de Montevideo, Instituto de Enseñanza Profesional, "Control de disturbios civiles," 1968, in UPEC-DSP-HLND.

10. Exp. III 664 (12) 34490, no. 52051, September 19, 1968, in Archivo Histórico Genaro Estrada, Dirección General de Asuntos Diplomáticos (hereafter, AHGE-DGA).

11. Ramón Ramírez, *El movimiento estudiantil de México: Julio–diciembre de 1968*, Tomo II, *Documentos* (Mexico City: Ediciones Era, 1969), 123.

12. "Entrevistas a Gustavo Díaz Ordaz en 1970 y 1977," https://www.youtube.com/watch?v=a4P_L-QVfMA.

13. *Boletín de la FEUU*, August 12, 1968, in UPEC-DSP-HLND; and Vania Markarian, *Uruguay, 1968: Student Activism from Global Counterculture to Molotov Cocktails* (Los Angeles: University of California Press, 2017).

14. Jorge Landinelli, *La revuelta estudiantil de 1968* (Montevideo: FHCE, 1988), 34, 44; and Clara Aldrighi, *El caso Mitrione: La intervención de Estados Unidos en Uruguay, 1965–1973* (Montevideo: Trilce, 2007), 392.

15. Markarian, Vania, *El 68 uruguayo: El movimiento estudiantil entre molotovs y música beat* (Buenos Aires: Universidad de Quilmes, Bernal, 2012), 104.

16. Gremial de Profesores, "Dos meses de medidas," *Boletín Extraordinario*, August 1968; "La escalada fascista en Enseñanza Secundaria," August 14, 1968; and *Órgano de la FEUU*, August 22, 1968, all in UPEC-DSP-HLND.

17. "Carta abierta," August, 1968; Manifiestos del Centro de Estudiantes de Odontología, FEUU/CNT, "El Pueblo debe de saber"; and "Defensa de las libertades y la soberanía," September 1968, all in UPEC-DSP-HLND.

18. Carlos Bañales and Enrique Jara, *La rebelión estudiantil* (Montevideo: Editorial Arca, 1968), 97; and "Defensa de las libertades y la soberanía," September 1968, in UPEC-DSP-HLND.

19. "Nuevas armas de fuego," September 20, 1968; "Ayer la policía asesinó a dos jóvenes," 20 de septiembre, 1968; "Asesinaros a dos compañeros," *CU-Boletín Informativo*, no. 9, September 23, 1968; and "Declaración del Sindicato Médico del Uruguay," September 24, 1968, all in UPEC-DSP-HLND.

20. "A la opinión pública: Los hechos registrados frente a la Universidad," September 21, 1968, in UPEC-DSP-HLND.

21. Ibid.; and "Asesinaros a dos compañeros," in UPEC-DSP-HLND.

22. "Asesinaros a dos compañeros," in UPEC-DSP-HLND.

23. "Comunicado del Sindicato Médico de Uruguay," September, 1968; and "Asesinaros a dos compañeros," both in UPEC-DSP-HLND.

24. Landinelli, *La revuelta estudiantil de 1968*, 130.

25. Eduardo Rey Tristán, "Movilización estudiantil e izquierda revolucionaria en el Uruguay (1968–1973)," *Revista Complutense de Historia de América* 28 (2002): 185–209; Gould, "Solidarity under Siege"; and Jaime M. Pensado and Enrique C. Ochoa, eds., *México beyond 1968: Revolutionaries, Radicals, and Re-*

pression during the Global Sixties and Subversive Seventies (Tucson: University of Arizona Press, 2018).

26. My conclusion regarding this argument is based on my archival research on reading some of the most detailed chronologies and collection of primary documents of the movement. This includes research at the Archivo Histórico del Politécnico; the Archivo de la Nación, Fondo Dirección Federal de Seguridad; and the Archivo Histórico de la UNAM, México 1968, http://www.ahunam.unam.mx/68/index.html. The main chronologies include Ramírez, *El movimiento estudiantil de México*; Elena Poniatowska, *Massacre in Mexico*, trans. Helen R. Lane (Columbia: University of Missouri Press, 1991); Daniel Cazés Menache, *Este día en 1968*, crónica en audio, 12 vols. (Mexico City: Radio UNAM, 2003); and Raúl Jardón, *1968, el fuego de la esperanza* (Mexico City: Siglo XXI, 1998).

27. *Tierra y Libertad*, no. 308, September 1968; and Carlos Monsiváis, *Días de Guardar* (Mexico City: Ediciones Era, 1970), 22.

28. Jardón, *1968, el fuego de la esperanza*, 32.

29. Ramírez, *El movimiento estudiantil*, 189; and Ortega, "Hechos," *Revista de América*, August 17, 1968. U.S. government reports are available in Kate Doyle, "Tlatelolco Massacre: Declassified U.S. Documents on Mexico and the Events of 1968," in National Security Archive Electronic Briefing Book No. 10, October 2, 1998, https://nsarchive2.gwu.edu/NSAEBB/NSAEBB10/intro.htm.

30. "Más de 1500 madres ante los diputados," *La Prensa*, October 1, 1968.

31. Jacinto Rodríguez Munguía, *La otra guerra secreta: Los archivos prohibidos de la prensa y el poder* (Mexico City: Debate, 2007), 69. A similar argument was made by one of the most influential leaders of the movement in Raúl Alvarez Garín and Raúl Álvarez Garín, *La Estela de Tlatelolco* (Mexico City: Grijalbo, 1998), 255–58.

32. See a similar list published in Sergio Aguayo Quezada, *1968: Los archivos de la violencia* (Mexico City: Grijalbo, 1998), 251.

33. Kate Doyle, "The Dead of Tlatelolco," The National Security Archive, October 1, 2006, https://nsarchive2.gwu.edu/NSAEBB/NSAEBB201/.

34. Efforts have been made to provide a detailed human rights report, but these have lacked a rigorous methodology. They have reproduced extensive details based on government intelligence sources, but have failed to include reliable and conclusive analyses. See, for example, FEMOSPP, *Informe histórico presentado a la sociedad Mexicana* (Mexico City: Comité 68 Pro Libertades Democráticas, A.C., 2008).

35. Cazés Menache, *Este día en 1968*; and Ramírez, *El movimiento estudiantil.*

36. On *porrismo* and the use of apocryphal propaganda, see Jaime M. Pensado, *Rebel Mexico: Student Unrest and Authoritarian Political Culture during the Long Sixties* (Stanford, CA: Stanford University Press, 2013).

37. Marcelino Parelló in Nicolás Echeverría, *El Memorial del 68* (Mexico City: TVU, Centro Cultural Universitario, 2008), DVD.

38. Jardón, *1968, el fuego de la esperanza*, 47.

39. José Revueltas, *México 68: Juventud y revolución* (Mexico City: Ediciones Era, 1978), 179–84; and Gilberto Guevara Niebla, "Antecedentes y desarrollo del movimiento de 1968," *Cuadernos Políticos*, no. 17 (July-September 1978): 6–33.

40. Guevara Niebla, "Antecedentes y desarrollo." On the different reactions to the brigades, see the visual depictions in Leobardo López Aretche, *El Grito* (Mexico City: CUEC, 1968), DVD.

41. "Welcoming Remarks by Attorney General Robert F. Kennedy to the Opening Session of the Inter-federal Assembly of Pax Romana, Georgetown University, Washington, DC, Monday, July 20, 1964, 3 pm," in *Speeches of Attorney General Robert F. Kennedy*, https://www.justice.gov/ag/speeches-25.

42. In *Mater et magistra* (*Mother and Teacher*), John XXIII called for social justice and aid to underdeveloped countries. In *Pacem in terris* (*Peace on Earth*) he addressed the broader theme of nuclear nonproliferation and called for the dignity of all individuals.

43. Jaime M. Pensado, "El Movimiento Estudiantil Profesional (MEP): Una mirada a la radicalización de la juventud católica mexicana durante la Guerra Fría," *Mexican Studies/Estudios Mexicanos* 31, no. 1 (2015): 156–92; Michael Löwy, "El cristianismo de la liberación y la izquierda en Brasil," *Anuario IEHS*, no. 24 (2009): 465–76; and Joseph Holbrook, "Catholic Student Movements in Latin America: Cuba and Brazil, 1920s to 1960s" (PhD diss., Florida International University, 2013). For a European perspective, see Gerd-Rainer Horn, *The Spirit of Vatican II: Western European Progressive Catholicism in the Long Sixties* (Oxford: Oxford University Press, 2014).

44. In *Populorum progression* (*On Development of Peoples*) (March 26, 1967), Paul VI called for the importance of human dignity, dialogue, and solidarity.

45. Victoria Langland, *Speaking of Flowers: Student Movements and the Making and Remembering of 1968 in Military Brazil* (Durham, NC: Duke University Press, 2013). See also James N. Green, *We Cannot Remain Silent: Opposition to the Brazilian Military Dictatorship in the United States* (Durham, NC: Duke University Press, 2010); and Christopher Dunn, *Contracultura: Alternative Arts and Social Transformation in Authoritarian Brazil* (Chapel Hill: University of North Carolina Press, 2016).

46. State sources put the number of students killed at three, but hospitals reported as many as twenty-eight protesters dead. See R. S. Rose, *The Unpast: Elite Violence and Social Control in Brazil, 1954–2000* (Athens: Ohio University Press, 2005), 156–57.

47. Dom Candido Padim, "A Doutrina da Segurança Nacional a luz da Doutrina de Igreja," *SEDOC* (September 1968): 432–44.

48. The repression that came to symbolize AI-5 should be read in the broader context of the post-1964 period. Following the coup, Congress passed the so-called Suplicy Law, which set control on student activities. In 1967, the government amended the law by "abolishing all student organizations at national and state levels." As further noted in a CIA report, the law also banned "student strikes and involvement in outside political activity, and further declare[d] illegal all secondary school organizations except athletic, civic, cultural, and social groups." See "Brazil Restless Students," *Weekly Summary Special Report*, CIA, No. 44, August 30, 1968, https://www.cia.gov/library/readingroom/docs/CIA-RDP79-00927A006600050003-4.pdf.

49. "Reflexo de uma situaçao de opressao (1968–1979)," *SEDOC* (May 1979): 1170–83.

50. Michael Lowy, "Students and Class Struggle in Brazil," *Latin American Perspectives* 6, no. 4 (1979): 102.

51. The year 1972 marked a defining moment in the Catholic '60s across Latin America when the Colombian Adolfo López Trujillo was elected general secretary of CELAM (until 1984) and began a counteroffensive against liberation theology.

52. Mireya Cuellar, "Una boda teñida de sangre," *La Jornada*, October 2, 2001. On the role of the United States during 1968, see Jefferson Morley, *Our Man in Mexico: Winston Scott and the Hidden History of the CIA* (Lawrence: University Press of Kansas, 2008); and María del Carmen Collado Herrera, "La guerra fría, el movimiento estudiantil de 1968 y el gobierno de Gustavo Díaz Ordaz, La mirada de las agencias de seguridad de Estados Unidos," *Secuencia*, no. 98 (May-August 2017): 158–203.

53. "Carta Pastoral sobre integración y desarrollo del país," March 26, 1968; "Al pueblo mexicano," September 10, 1968; and Ernesto Corripio Ahumada, "Mensaje Pastoral," October 9, 1968, all in Archivo Histórico de la Archidiosesis de México (hereafter AHAM).

54. Enrique Maza, SJ, "El movimiento estudiantil y sus repercusiones para la Iglesia," *Christus*, no. 397, December 1, 1968, 1234–67. Other people affiliated with the Church who also expressed positive views of the student movement included, among others, the director of CENCOS, José Alvarez Icaza; the

Dominican and leading figure of the Parroquia Universitaria, Alex Morelli; and leading representatives of the Juventud Obrera Católica (JOC) and the Movimiento Estudiantil Profesional (MEP).

55. See the long file of Sergio Méndez Arceo at the Directorate of Federal Security (DFS) Archives, "Versiones Públicas." See also Lya Gutiérrez Quintanilla, *Los volcanes de Cuernavaca: Sergio Méndez Arceo, Gregorio Lemercier, Iván Illich* (Mexico City: La Jornada Ediciones, 2007); and Todd Hartch, *The Prophet of Cuernavaca: Iván Illich and the Crisis of the West* (Oxford: Oxford University Press, 2015).

56. "Homilía en la Basílica de Guadalupe," IPN—Sergio Méndez Arceo, public version, 1971, 5–26 (emphasis is mine).

57. Elisa Villa Román, "La joven que se ocultó del ejército en los baños de la UNAM," in *El Universal*, January 8, 2017.

58. Roberto Bolaño, *Amuleto* (Barcelona: Editorial Anagrama, 1999), 34–35.

59. "Joy will be for all of us / In this intoxicated world / In a place with no room for hunger . . . / Joy will be for all of us / When love returns to earth"; Revueltas, *México 68*, 77–78.

60. Ibid., 78.

61. Diana Sorensen, *A Turbulent Decade Remembered: Scenes from the Latin American Sixties* (Stanford, CA: Stanford University Press, 2007), 1–14. See also Gould, "Solidarity under Siege."

62. Pensado and Ochoa, *México beyond 1968*.

BIBLIOGRAPHY

Gould, Jeffrey L. "Solidarity under Siege: The Latin American Left, 1968." *The American Historical Review* 114, no. 2 (2009): 348–75.

Horn, Gerd-Rainer. *The Spirit of Vatican II: Western European Progressive Catholicism in the Long Sixties*. Oxford: Oxford University Press, 2014.

Langland, Victoria. *Speaking of Flowers: Student Movements and the Making and Remembering of 1968 in Military Brazil*. Durham, NC: Duke University Press, 2013.

Markarian, Vania. *Uruguay, 1968: Student Activism from Global Counterculture to Molotov Cocktails*. Los Angeles: University of California Press, 2017.

Pensado, Jaime M. *Rebel Mexico: Student Unrest and Authoritarian Political Culture during the Long Sixties*. Stanford, CA: Stanford University Press, 2013.

Poniatowska, Elena. *Massacre in Mexico*. Translated by Helen R. Lane. Columbia: University of Missouri Press, 1991.

PART FOUR

Then and Now

FIFTEEN

A '68 Chileno?

Politics, Culture, and the Zeitgeist of '68

PATRICK BARR-MELEJ

In his book on the events of 1968 in Paris, Prague, and Mexico City and their lasting impressions and implications, the late Mexican novelist and essayist Carlos Fuentes describes that year as "one of those constellation-years in which events, movements, and personalities that were unexpected and separated by space coincided without an immediately explicable reason." Capturing a sense of exceptionalism that frames many popular and academic reflections on 1968, Fuentes assesses student movements in those cities in particular, noting their similar political and cultural imperatives and some shared contextual elements in which they operated.[1] It is certain that 1968 was a landmark year, as Fuentes reminds us, and the confluence of happenings that made it so, though perhaps not immediately explicable, became the subject of much scholarly research and popular interest. Recently, a new historiography on the "global Sixties" has emerged—some of it to mark the fiftieth anniversary of the "global '68"—that has taught us much about transnational and local revolutionary gestures, including cultural and countercultural ones, and wars of position that were at hand across the Americas, Europe, and elsewhere in 1968. Occurrences and circumstances in and around 1968, interconnected and situated within the long and broad flows of political, cultural, and socioeconomic change during the Cold War, speak to what we might call the "zeitgeist of '68," an equivocal and thus useful conceptualization that simultaneously privileges and decenters the momentous year, helping to further conceptualize the ruptures, continuities, spectacles, banalities, and emotions that shaped the "spirit" of the 1960s.[2]

The sweeping context for both 1968 and the zeitgeist of '68—with the latter preceding and outliving the former—included such factors as disaffection wrought by the Cold War's deadlock (darkened further by the threat of nuclear destruction and the war in Vietnam) and a concomitant and grinding sense of impasse; the rise of New Left alternatives to party-driven (Old Left) radicalism; the standoffish dispositions of governments, including authoritarian ones with democratic guises; the apparent inability of global capitalism to solve the era's pressing problems; significant postwar demographic shifts and intergenerational dissonance; changes in cultural values, including sexual mores and practices; technological change and the amplification of the culture industry; unrest in the streets, on university campuses, and among workers; and a palpable sense shared by many of hope, determination, and faith that the world could change for the better in short order. In turn, arising or further evolving in the 1960s were responses, with multifarious characteristics and magnitudes, to prevailing political, social, cultural, and economic structures and conditions, challenging dominant systems and practices. These included radical movements, not the least of which were university-student movements, which were organized and often voluntarist, with degrees of ideological and functional coherence and workability. In a great many cases in Latin America and Europe, police or militaries (or both) ferociously repressed such movements on campuses and in the streets. Also in play were consequential cultural developments that were transnational, largely ad hoc, imbued with immediacy and unpredictability, and loosely congealed by way of some shared complaints, claims, desires, and patterns of consumption. In particular, counterculture became a widely evident and influential manifestation of the cultural-revolutionary agency of young people during the long 1960s. With strongly emancipatory, antisystemic, and generational qualities that drew from and fed the zeitgeist of '68, counterculture was the subject of intense criticism (and repression, at times) as defenders of "mainstream" culture rushed to stir moral panic and blunt the trend's cultural-revolutionary potential.

The political, social, and cultural history of Chile during Latin America's long 1960s (1959–73), bookended by the Cuban Revolution and the military coup that ended Marxist president Salvador Allende's "Chilean road to socialism" (*vía chilena al socialismo*), provides an insightful point of access into the zeitgeist of '68 and the '68 phenomenon generally. Whereas certain actors and events in Chile evinced the reach of and contributed to the zeitgeist of '68, many of the essential factors of what transformed 1968 into '68 transnationally in collective memory and in the relevant historiography were played out differently there, were of a lesser magnitude, or simply did not unfold. By way of illustration, a university reform movement in 1967–68 realized its immediate goals under a centrist government touting a "Revolution in Liberty"—circumstances that were quite alien to student protesters in Mexico City or Paris. And although 1968 saw bouts of unrest and conflict in the streets of Santiago, often with radical youths pitted against police, such eruptions were small and brief, did not significantly impede the rhythms of life in the capital (much less the country), and principally were outcroppings of political clashes between political parties and blocs.

A vital factor shaping Chile's experience was the absence of a profound and perilous (or promising, depending on one's position) sense of impasse—a consideration that spans many of the contributing factors leading to 1968's explosiveness in other contexts—in its politics and culture during the late 1960s, notwithstanding deep frustration voiced by workers, various student and youth groups, and other constituencies, especially on the more radical (and radicalizing) Left, with regard to systemic elements of the country's political culture and socioeconomic architecture.[3] Furthermore, with democratic and pluralistic qualities buttressing an electoral environment in which leftist political parties participated earnestly for many decades, Chile's pre-1973 political culture afforded space (albeit highly contested) for the rise and development of radical politics, including that of young people. Since the 1920s, political democratization, interrupted in a few instances by countervailing moments, such as the banning of the Communist Party between 1948 and 1958, essentially provided a mechanism—a pressure valve, let's say—that allowed for the steady outlet for and channeling of postwar revolutionary energies into mainstream politics.

The victory of Allende, a Socialist physician, and his Socialist- and Communist-led coalition, Popular Unity, in the presidential election of September 1970 is a telling indication of Chile's state of affairs during the long 1960s. Far from the product of a voluntarist vanguard, Allende's win was the crowning moment of a long slog on the part of leftist parties through electoral politics since the 1930s, with many of the same leaders present throughout. The original infrastructure and ongoing leadership of Popular Unity largely were those of an Old Left that had participated in the Popular Front of the late 1930s and early 1940s and had propelled Allende's four presidential bids between 1952 and 1970. Meanwhile, spurred on by the triumph of the Cuban Revolution, *guevarismo* and guerilla warfare, and Cold War confrontations around the world, there emerged New Lefts in Chile and elsewhere in the Americas (and the world) during the long 1960s, driven largely by young and energetic radicals wedded to revolutionary vanguardism and with little patience for the Old Left's democratic incrementalism.[4] With a tradition of persistent sociopolitical mobilization and party politics, and in the face of New Left alternatives, Chile's Old Left came to power in 1970 with the world's eyes upon it, a far from monolithic composition, and, generally speaking, with a certain orthodoxy vis-à-vis what revolutionary behavior, liberation, and culture should entail.

Working in and through political parties, party-affiliated organizations, unions, and other groups tied to Allende and Popular Unity, radicals young and older asserted revolutionary ideas, labored to build a socialist society, and contributed prominently to the coalition's *revolutionary culture*, that is to say, its assemblage of values and beliefs, creative substance, and language, which were part and parcel of its ideological commitments and revolutionary goals. But did Popular Unity engender a '60s- or '68-like *cultural revolution*, which I see as a far more expansive undertaking grounded in the imperative to upend and replace a broad and deep system of cultural values and orthodoxies? In many ways, Popular Unity reflected and reinforced the emancipatory and democratizing principles, hopes, and even utopian propositions that precipitated and shaped the zeitgeist of '68 and events explored in this volume. Concurrently, however, the coalition's leading voices often pilloried modes of cultural heterodoxy and new values—aspects central to a transnational cultural revolution in the making—that many young people elaborated during the global Sixties and in '68s around the world. Thus, though some have been tempted to reckon that a Chilean '68 came to fruition in 1970 with Allende's momentous victory, I submit that Allende's "revolution from above" did not propose to negate and substitute some fundamental underpinnings of mainstream Chilean culture, therefore limiting substantially its cultural-revolutionary profile.[5] In fact, the coalition's leaders and constituents often emphasized just how culturally mainstream and "Chilean" Popular Unity was, declaring that it sought to protect the traditional family, morality, and both private and public spheres from emergent trends, movements, and heterodox ways of life that were conspicuous transnationally during the era. The case at hand, then, provides us more nuanced understandings of Chilean circumstances during the long 1960s and sheds further light on the broader story of '68 in the West. Getting at such nuance, and bearing in mind the important roles played by young people in '68s that unfolded in Latin America and Europe, I approach Chile's relationship with the zeitgeist of '68 through the lens of youth-driven politics and youth culture. Although the history of 1968 and its zeitgeist must not be reduced to a history of youth, the individual (and individualist) and collective (and collectivist) interventions of young people together constitute a distinguishing element of the global Sixties and of the '68 phenomenon, particularly in relation to this volume's thematic cornerstone: the question of cultural revolution.

With an eye on broader political-cultural considerations, what follows begins with a brief survey of Chile's university-reform movement of the mid-1960s. Like university students elsewhere in or around 1968, the reformers demonstrated the agency of young people and the coalescing might of a generational identity, but they saw an outcome quite unlike those experienced by student activists in such places as Mexico, Argentina, Uruguay, Brazil, and France, as other contributions in this volume describe them. I then take stock of episodes of unrest in Santiago in 1968 amid global and regional occurrences of which Chileans were well aware. Our discussion subsequently addresses the coming and unfolding drama of Allende's project and what for the Left and others was the alarming appearance of a cultural-revolutionary gesture in their country: counterculture, a phenomenon with a culturally emancipatory vibe that contributed to the transnational zeitgeist of '68. Counterculture offered reimagined and apostatical sensibilities in regard to human relationships. It was, as Robert Vincent Daniels puts it, the "life-style component of the many-sided revolutionary experience" of the long 1960s.[6] In Chile, a culturally conservative society and with heightened social and political tension leading up to and after Allende's election, a cross section of the younger generation discovered and partook in a counterculture that they adopted and adapted as their own.[7] Theirs was a heterodox revolutionary gesture in most every respect: it was unorganized, undisciplined, lacked an ideological foundation, and exploded normative conceptualizations of what "liberation" and "revolution" were, could be, and meant. Meanwhile, ardent defenders of mainstream cultural values and outlooks, including leading voices of the Left, were stirred into (re)action.

REFORM AND UNREST IN THE LATTER SIXTIES

Youthful agency has deep roots in Chile's modern history. By the 1920s, for instance, university students, including some anarchists, were pronounced actors in the streets and on campuses as capitalist modernization's booms and busts changed their society dramatically.[8] By the middle third of the century, most every political party had a youth faction. The Communist Youth formed in 1932, and the Socialist Youth, established in 1935, included a twenty-something Allende. The Right also had vibrant youth groups, as did reformist sectors. Such party-affiliated groups and associations shared the milieu with many important student organizations, including federations of students at Santiago's two top universities: the Pontifical Catholic University and the University of Chile. By the 1960s, elections within these federations were closely watched by the media and politicians as weather vanes for public opinion and national electoral trends, demonstrating the degree to which such organizations were taken seriously in the body politic.

The student-led university-reform movement, which arose most forcefully in 1967 and spilled into 1968 (but with roots reaching to the beginning of the decade and to as early as 1918), evinced focus, discipline, and an agenda with specific policy pursuits. Its methods, which included the occupation of university buildings, were similar to those employed by student movements elsewhere in Latin America and in Europe during the era, but the experiences of Chile's university-reform movement differed from those other instances in important ways. With beginnings at the Catholic University of Valparaíso in June 1967, the reform movement quickly spread to the Pontifical Catholic University (PUC) in Santiago. Led by its Federation of Students (Federación de Estudiantes de la Universidad Católica, FEUC) and with the support of many young faculty members, student protesters at the PUC, like those in Valparaíso, demanded the empowerment of students in the selection of the institution's leadership, a call that drew the stiff resistance of administrators, the Church, many Catholic reformers, conservative politicians, and right-wing students. As tensions mounted, and upon the reform movement's seizure of the PUC's main campus in central Santiago in August 1967, the Church agreed to sack the university's rector and adopt a democratic system for the selection of top administrators, thus affecting nearly every aspect of the institution. Emboldened by events at the PUC, similar activism rocked Chile's other major universities over subsequent months. The reform process continued until the 1973 coup, when the military seized the country's universities and began obliterating and rebuilding a higher education system it deemed a hotbed of subversion.

The university-reform movement occurred under the government of Eduardo Frei (1964–70) of the Christian Democratic Party (Partido Demócrata Cristiano, PDC), which pledged to apply communitarian principles in Chilean society through its "Revolution in Liberty," a considerably reformist agenda that included initiatives in education, landholding, state ownership of industry, and other areas, all with an approving wink and funding from the United States in the spirit of President Kennedy's Alliance for Progress. Critics on the Left argued that Frei's reforms did not fundamentally undo capitalism and its destructive effects, and right-wing voices, who had supported Frei's 1964 campaign against Allende (the latter making his third bid for the presidency at that time), soon soured on the "Revolution in Liberty," claiming it was overly revolutionary and trampled the liberties of the middle and upper classes. The university-reform campaign put Frei in a difficult position and evinced the line he and the PDC walked between the forces of revolution and reaction.

Key leaders of the FEUC and of the PUC's occupation were from the president's own party and were members of the Christian Democratic

Youth (Juventud Demócrata Cristiana, JDC).[9] JDC activists, such as FEUC president Miguel Ángel Solar, essentially were young, bourgeois reformers whose actions were "revolutionary" in the PUC's hallways and in Chilean higher education in general, but their broader claims and goals were far more moderate than those of Marxist youths. The reform movement's seizure of the university's principal building on August 11 left Frei with the task of finding a solution without condoning the defiant behavior of many of his own young supporters, who, moreover, had the open support of leftist youth groups, including the Communist Youth. Complicating matters further for Frei was the Right's widely circulated and untruthful assertion—propagated by the country's largest newspaper, *El Mercurio*—that the university-reform movement was a Marxist plot, a claim that the movement's leaders, including Solar, refuted forcefully. Also from the Right there emerged the Movimiento Gremial (Guild Movement), which was formed by PUC law students who opposed the FEUC's leaders and university reform. (The university's Guild Movement included Jaime Guzmán Errázuriz, who became an ideological guru of the Right and was a close confidant of Gen. Augusto Pinochet after the 1973 coup.) What is more, Frei had a measure of moral authority to wield during the occupation but little direct power over the private, pontifical university's response despite his party's Catholic identity. In the end, it took Frei until the August 11 occupation to assume a more active role: he asked the Vatican to allow the archbishop of Santiago, Cardinal Raúl Silva Henríquez, to directly negotiate a solution. Within days, Silva and the students forged the agreement that overhauled the university's governance.[10]

JDC activists were aggravated by Frei's initial hesitation to intervene on behalf of the university-reform movement, which many students had understood implicitly to be in step with the administration's "Revolution in Liberty." Already miffed by the PDC's sluggishness, and then disappointed by the party leadership's refusal in 1969 to join the leftist Popular Action Front (Frente de Acción Popular, FRAP), which soon morphed into Popular Unity, a faction of younger Christian Democrats, including Solar, bolted to form the Unitary Popular Action Movement (Movimiento de Acción Popular Unitaria, MAPU) and enlisted in Allende's Popular Unity. Thus, not only were political and cultural leaders during the Frei years ultimately willing to bend to the stipulations of student protesters, but also when some of the reform's young leaders became disaffected, they had something to do about it (form a splinter party, in 1969) and had somewhere to go (Popular Unity) to continue their political work, all within the flow of the country's mainstream political culture.

SANTIAGO, 1968

Aside from its structural effects, the university-reform movement provided a huge morale boost to many young Chileans on the eve of student protests around the world in 1968. Indeed, by the end of 1968, and owing considerably to such press services as Reuters and the Associated Press, a significant portion of Chilean higher-education students could relate, at least superficially, with student protesters in, say, Mexico City, but the former's experiences and context differed substantially from the latter's. In addition to publishing news of the profoundly influential student and worker demonstrations and strikes in Paris (a subject to which we will return), the Chilean press also brought attention to student unrest in Italy, Japan, Poland, Portugal, West Germany, Yugoslavia, New York, and elsewhere in the global North. Coverage of happenings closer to home included articles on the repression of students in Brazil, Argentina, and Uruguay, and the Mexican state's massacre of hundreds of students at Tlatelolco in Mexico City in October 1968 prompted especially large headlines.[11] Chile's conservative daily newspaper *El Mercurio* expressed little sympathy toward the Mexican students, while the Movement of the Revolutionary Left (Movimiento de Izquierda Revolucionaria, MIR), a New Left and voluntarist Marxist movement that largely operated outside the mainstream Left (the FRAP and, later, Popular Unity), called the butchery a "traumatic scar," arguing that Mexico's ruling Institutional Revolutionary Party (Partido Revolucionario Institucional, PRI) showed "its internal crisis, its sclerosis, and the incapacity to absorb and accept the petitions of young people."[12]

Appearing alongside such accounts from abroad in 1968 were reports of unrest in Santiago. In August, leftist students at the University of Chile's Pedagogical Institute threw rocks at police and erected barricades during a demonstration in support of a dramatic strike of rural workers at a well-known agricultural estate in the country's Central Valley. *Carabineros* (national police) responded to the Santiago demonstrators with water cannons and tear gas and by arresting sixteen students. The Frei government and the conservative media roundly condemned the young activists involved, with *El Mercurio* making sure to note that students sullied the walls of the institute with posters of Argentine revolutionary Ernesto Che Guevara and the flag of North Vietnam.[13] In October, university and high school students demonstrated in the downtown area in response to what happened at Tlatelolco, political strife in Peru, and a crackdown on civil liberties in Uruguay. Such "grave disorder," according to *El Mercurio*, involved hundreds of young people, many of whom associated with the University of Chile's Federation of Students, who tossed stones through the windows of businesses and the nearby U.S. and Uruguayan embassies. *Carabineros* intervened, arresting dozens and injuring a handful. The Frei administration did not hesitate to criticize the demonstrators, with Minister of the Interior Edmundo Pérez Zujovic declaring, "The government respects all manifestations of opinion that the citizenry wishes to express as long as they are done legally, but it cannot tolerate or condone any manifestations of violence." Moreover, Minister of Foreign Relations Gabriel Valdés Subercaseaux noted, "It is evident that those who supposedly act to show their support for democratic institutions adopt measures that are incompatible with their stated objectives."[14] *El Mercurio* added, "There exists clamor among citizens for the state's protection against delinquency."[15] In early December, hundreds of mostly university students built barricades in front of the city's principal rail terminal, bringing traffic on the capital's main boulevard to a standstill. This time, the young demonstrators were calling for a larger budget for the State Technical University. The crowd dispersed after some scuffling occurred between the protesters and *carabineros*.[16] The broader significance of such episodes and others did not escape their critics, who understood that a generational component was at work in the period's conflicts. "The signs of inquietude among young people are global," *El Mercurio* observed.[17]

Conservative media outlets such as *El Mercurio* were also quite peeved to learn that strife, imbued with a generational vibe, had also emerged within the Church. On the heels of the incidences at the Pedagogical Institute in August 1968, and exactly one year after the university-reform movement took over the PUC's main building, a group called the Young Church (Iglesia Joven, IJ) occupied the Metropolitan Cathedral in Santiago for about a day. Composed of clergy from working-class neighborhoods and also laypeople, including university-reform leader and MAPU member Miguel Ángel Solar, the IJ's ideas reflected the imprints of liberation theology and Vatican II, which had significant influence in Latin America and Europe (as Massimo De Giuseppe's chapter 3 in this volume describes) during the long 1960s and beyond. The IJ announced its opposition to the Church's lack of social action, arguing that it should be involved in the furthering of social revolution in Chile and around the globe. The group also criticized the Church's traditional position on contraception, which more progressive elements of the clergy had questioned as early as 1964, owing to the country's high and rising abortion rate.[18]

The cathedral's occupiers sang, conducted Mass, and expressed reverence for revolutionary figures, including the dead Colombian guerilla-priest Camilo Torres and Che Guevara. A spokesman for the group explained, "We are hand-in-hand with our Marxist brothers, on the barricades of the people against capitalism, following the example of Camilo Torres. We are members of the Young Church."[19] The papacy's reaction was uncomplicated. The Vatican condemned the IJ's occupation of the cathedral and identified the 200 or so activists involved as "arrogant and profane," and Cardinal Silva, who had played a key role ending the standoff at the PUC a year earlier, assured the faithful (and the papacy) that the IJ's young priests and their followers "do not represent, in any way, what the Church in Santiago thinks." He stated, "This small group, which seeks radical and sudden change, should know that their methods shall not be successful."[20] After his initial criticism of the occupiers, Silva soon adopted a less confrontational tone. He visited the occupied cathedral and later explained that the IJ's declarations would be taken seriously as part of ongoing discussions within the Church. It is worth noting that Silva also became more amenable to radical politics after Allende's win in 1970, noting, "The basic reforms contained in the program of Popular Unity are supported by the Chilean Church. We look upon this with intense sympathy."[21]

If one considers such cases as the Santiago demonstrations of late 1968, the IJ's emergence and its occupation of Santiago's cathedral in August 1968, and the university-reform movement sweeping through institutions of higher learning, it may seem that a '68 was unfolding in Chile in 1967–68. These episodes—each with young people at the very center of the goings-on—and others in Chile's long 1960s were well within, and were in dialogue with, transnational currents of agency that reflected and contributed to a zeitgeist of '68. Yet, although the protesters in Santiago made very '68-like radical declarations, Chile's Marxist political parties, their youth organizations, and their allies were making the very same claims (and had for a long time), and there was much expectation among leftists, including young ones, that the electoral system would in fact see them to victory in the March 1969 congressional elections (the PDC went on to lose its congressional majority and the Left showed laudable gains) and in the presidential election of 1970. The disturbances of 1968 also were far from massive, even along Chilean lines. Not only did they not propel an enormous upwelling of direct action, but also incidences like those at the Pedagogical Institute in August 1968 even paled in comparison to clashes in downtown Santiago in 1920 that involved radical university students (including many anarchists), right-wing students, and police, for example.[22] In regard to the IJ, its actions were relatively isolated and the group's general propositions were, in a short period of time, absorbed and co-opted by the Church, which, as Cardinal Silva expressed, had some sympathy for Popular Unity's agenda after Allende's victory and often praised the country's democratic political culture. Lastly, the university-reform movement of 1967–68 saw some tense moments, but, as we noted above, it realized its basic goals in a relatively short period of time. It spread further in Chilean higher education, and its principles essentially became the stuff of policy under Allende, again indicating the possibility and promise of substantial change in the country's institutions, as Popular Unity greatly deepened and accelerated a process of social change already evident in the latter 1960s. That process came to a crashing halt in September 1973, but not before demonstrating the capacity of Chilean political culture—and especially that of reformers and the mainstream Left—to absorb and channel the energies of change-minded and radical young people.

Young people elsewhere were faced with rather different situations. In 2008, Alain Geismar, one of the leaders of the 1968 uprising in Paris, noted that the May demonstration of students and workers succeeded as "a social revolution, not as a political one." That is to say, the Parisian spring did not revolutionize the structures and nature of the state and its political-economic architecture. The French government of Charles de Gaulle successfully repressed the upwelling—after being paralyzed by it for a short time—and reasserted its legitimacy after winning new elections that de Gaulle called in the wake of the disturbances. No Sixth Republic emerged. Geismar observed that however unsuccessful the demonstrators were in seeing through a political revolution, they had thrown France into a bout of sociocultural introspection with lasting effects. French society and culture began to change as, over time, 1968's critical psyche and democratizing impulse cracked the country's conservative sociocultural edifice. A telling indication of such change, Geismar observed, is that, as a divorced man, French president Nicholas Sarkozy (2007–12) "couldn't have been invited to dinner at the Élysée Palace, let alone be elected president of France" if 1968 had not transpired.[23] Across the Atlantic, in Mexico City, tens of thousands of students from the National Autonomous University and other campuses took to the capital's public spaces in the autumn of 1968 with demands for democratization and economic reforms that, generally speaking, were not unlike those of the French students and workers. At heart, the Mexican demonstrators sought the ear of President Gustavo Díaz Ordaz, who, on many occasions, including on the eve of the Mexico City Olympics, responded by repressing the movement violently and successfully, as Eric Zolov's chapter 5 herein reminds us. Yet, a rebellious youth culture—with a creative and energetic countercultural component—endured. It challenged cultural normativity and created new cultural spaces in the face of the PRI-dominated state's intransigence.[24]

THE AMBIGUITIES OF "REVOLUTION"

Two years after the Mexican government killed hundreds of student protesters in October 1968 at Tlatelolco, the eyes of the world were focused on Chile, when a Marxist and his coalition won a free and fair national election. In November 1970, at his inaugural address at the capital's National Stadium, Allende restated Popular Unity's prerogative of revolutionary change through an incrementalist and constitutional path to socialism. The middle-class Marxist, who three times had run unsuccessfully for the presidency (1952, 1958, and 1964), also spoke directly to his nation's young people in generational terms, explaining to them their responsibilities and their collective revolutionary promise. Referring to himself as a once-rebellious student, Allende told young people, "I will not criticize [youthful] impatience, but it is my duty to ask you to think calmly." He explained, "Thousands upon thousands of young people have demanded a place in the social struggle. The time has come for all young people to participate in that action."[25] Allende's appeal reflected his understanding that young people had consequential revolutionary potential, and such energy was best channeled and exercised through the parties of Popular Unity and his government—and most radical young people went along with that. Their participation deepened and expanded during the Allende years in all areas of Popular Unity's agenda, including its cultural initiatives, again evincing youthful radicalism and enthusiasm that were emblematic of the zeitgeist of '68.

Allende often indicated that existing institutions and the country's constitution provided avenues to enact a revolutionary project, and the commitment of his Socialist Party to electoral politics since the 1930s reflected that posture. Whether or not Allende intended to instate a new political order upon realizing a socialist society is a question worth debating, but clearly evident is that Allende focused on changing Chilean society by incrementally upending capitalism and U.S. economic power rather than through pursuing extensive alterations to the electoral system or constitutional arrangements. Moreover, the Chilean road to socialism was to be a top-down affair, and thus it strained Allende's relationship with New Left alternatives, including the MIR, which pursued vanguardist and grassroots revolutionary projects and remained outside Popular Unity.[26] The MIR emerged as a splinter group of the Socialist Party in the mid-1960s. By 1967, it was in the hands of a group of young radicals from the University of Concepción in the country's south, and it rose to challenge Popular Unity by promoting the immediate seizure of the means of production, including land, which Allende saw as a dangerous, extralegal path. *Mirista* ideas reflected a blend of Marxism-Leninism and the Guevarist and Castroist image of the heroic guerrilla that some others, such as the Socialist Youth, also found attractive. In particular, the MIR's rallying of rural workers, peasants, and urban squatters to engage in *tomas* (property takeovers), in defiance of Allende's call for a legalistic road to socialism, speaks to the group's New Left credentials, youthful voluntarism, and '68-ish energy.

As it pursued its revolution from above, Popular Unity's cultural profile was considerable, as Allende, his coalition, and their constituency continued to mold a revolutionary culture with footings established during the first third of the century. The Left's cultural project located the "common" Chilean at its core, and when principal voices of Popular Unity spoke of revolutionizing culture, they usually were alluding to pedagogical, intellectual, literary, and related projects to "lift the culture" of the masses. Allende, for instance, contended that his unconventional Marxist revolution would ensure "the right for all people to obtain proper education and culture" and the "right to health, well-being, and culture." It would relieve the shared predicament of those who "have practically no access to culture."[27] The Left's cultural outreach to the masses and Popular Unity's cultural politics furthered cultural democratization and growth in the areas Allende underscored, and radical youths were vital participants in the coalition's cultural affairs and those of the nation. In terms of artistic-aesthetic and creative dimensions of Popular Unity's revolutionary culture, the Communist Youth was widely known for its colorful and striking murals in support of the Chilean road to socialism, and, as Patrice McSherry's chapter 11 herein demonstrates, the *Nueva Canción* (New Song), with many young performers, furthered Allende's project and provided the Marxist movement its soundtrack, helped in no small way by the Communist Youth record label Discoteca del Cantar Popular (DICAP).[28] Yet, Popular Unity's cultural politics, revolutionary culture, and social-revolutionary project fell short of constituting a Sixties-ish cultural revolution. In pursuing cultural democratization, the Old Left did not fundamentally question many cultural values that were mainstream and against which many '68 movements ran afoul. Instead, it conveyed certain mainstream and bourgeois cultural outlooks as it defended "family values" and the nuclear family, wielding what amounted to a conservative cultural discourse in conjunction with an otherwise antibourgeois, anticapitalist, and anti-imperialist project. The coalescence of Chile's *criollo* (homegrown) counterculture and the reaction it engendered exposed this cultural-political position plainly.[29] Against the backdrop of youths mobilizing politically and culturally for Popular Unity (and its opponents), a portion of the younger generation chose not to engage directly in parties or other political organizations. They sought other experiences and embraced heterodox values and cultural practices that opened up new possibilities regarding what revolution and liberation could mean during the long 1960s.

Upon Chilean counterculture's emergence at the end of the 1960s, much of the Left joined moderate and conservative sectors in stoking moral panic as forces mobilized to protect the country's "values." Meanwhile, as those groups fought it out in the trenches of politics and often in the streets, their criticism of counterculture also served immediate political needs, as opponents in the electoral arena blamed each other for threats they claimed counterculture posed to morality, the family, and the nation. For Chile's Marxists (and older ones in particular), counterculture's emphasis on the self and personal freedom negated the imperative of social consciousness (notwithstanding counterculture's communalist inclinations), ignored the reality of class struggle, and evinced the egoism of capitalism. Concurrently, culturally heterodox young people offended the Right because counterculture disregarded traditional forms of authority and because its emphasis on freedom did not center on the imperative of private property. The Right's posture, then, was consistent with its capitalist credentials, elitist pedigree, and some measure of Church influence, while moderate Catholics, with more progressive political and cultural inclinations, saw in the counterculture many of the same general threats and disruptions that ardent conservatives did.

The question of counterculture and the global '68 is complex, especially in light of the encounters and disencounters between counterculture and the New Left during the Sixties in France, Mexico, the United States, and elsewhere.[30] Counterculture, which included but was not limited to hippie counterculture, contributed to the zeitgeist by further disputing—through an array of sensibilities and ad hoc practices rather than ideological propositions—dominant sociocultural values, including those related to sexuality and the liberation of the self, which New Lefts also took up as critical issues. In Mexico, for instance, as Mexican sociologist Roger Bartra observed, counterculture and Molotov cocktails were congruent, inspiring many young people influenced by counterculture to actively pursue social, economic, cultural, and political change by way of radical vanguardism and voluntarism. Bartra explained, "Marijuana was linked with Marxism, unconventional forms of eroticism went along with [support for the] guerrillas. In my house, beatniks and aspiring revolutionaries would get together; those searching for artificial paradises along with those who wanted to destroy systems of oppression."[31] Some intermingling between counterculture and the Left happened in Chile, especially among some younger Communists, but the views of Popular Unity's Old Left in regard to counterculture dominated the Left's discourse on the matter.

For most Chileans, counterculture was something far off, odd, and vague for much of the long 1960s—until a certain "happening" happened.

Over a long weekend in October 1970, a few thousand hippies, with many dressed in the typical counterculture attire of the era, gathered on a patch of land in the municipality of Las Condes, now an affluent sector of the Santiago metroplex. Some say the Piedra Roja ("Red Rock") festival—Chile's version of Woodstock—drew 40,000 people and perhaps upwards to 50,000, but estimates of 5,000 are more realistic. Regardless of its size, what is clear is that many young people gathered to join in a collective and countercultural experience the likes of which Chile had not seen, coalescing around shared affinities for rock music and marijuana and indicative of a generationally informed rebelliousness. Counterculture and a slew of issues related to it, some signs of which had reached the Chilean press in the late 1960s, crashed onto the local scene most spectacularly when reports about and photos of Piedra Roja flooded the local media. After an initial explosion of attention paid to hippies and the like during the weeks following the festival, investigations and scrutiny of counterculture persisted during the early 1970s, as concerns about sexual liberation, the consumption of marijuana, the length of men's hair, and the purported prevalence of many lazy, lawless, and otherwise lost young people (to mention only some complaints) were substantial and were instrumentalized politically in a range of discourses.

In greater Santiago, two main sites of countercultural sociability emerged by 1970, each with many young people who made their ways to Piedra Roja: Providencia, a well-to-do municipality, and Parque Forestal (Forest Park), a wooded space that transects the capital's downtown. Providencia was the cradle of the "moneyed counterculture," and it was common to see hippies—mingling, smoking, chatting, stoned—on sidewalks along its main thoroughfare during the Allende years. Upscale Providencia was the epicenter of much of the *criollo* counterculture, but the phenomenon crossed class lines in a country where class divisions were unmistakable and contested. Hippies of lesser social standing and from working-class sectors of Santiago, in addition to many bohemians, gathered regularly at Parque Forestal, which was known as a hive of marijuana consumption and where tents dotted the landscape in the Allende years. Together, the poor and wealthier who were attracted to counterculture and who gathered at Piedra Roja caught a great many Chileans off guard; in particular, many were stunned not by the festival's size but, rather, for what the event meant—or what they believed it meant. Piedra Roja was small, certainly when compared to other rock gatherings in Latin America during the early 1970s, such as Mexico's Avándaro festival of 1971, but it signaled to all that Chile was not isolated from a global countercultural wave in the 1960s and early 1970s that the country's conservatives, moderates, and leftists found abhorrent and cringeworthy. It also occurred at a critical and unique moment in Chile's and Latin America's social and political history.

To many well-positioned and influential Marxists, Piedra Roja, which was organized by a band of intrepid and mostly middle-class teenagers, and its countercultural expressions were clear indications of bourgeois depravity: they were self-centered, lacked a (properly) radical social conscience or solidarity with the working masses, and they undeniably were imported from the imperialist power to the north. Writers for the Communist Party's newspaper *El Siglo* lashed out against hippies for Piedra Roja's "imported and imitative character," arguing that it straightforwardly copied the music, aesthetics, and general conduct of Woodstock and attracted "young people with a good standard of living and bourgeois parents." One editorial concluded that Piedra Roja was "not a manifestation of youthful vitality but rather a manifestation of the mentality of colonialism." It was "Made in the USA."[32] Spoiled and indolent brats of the bourgeoisie, leftist commentators also asserted, were "indifferent toward our national problems, they show an absolute lack of dedication toward the destiny of the people, and, in all reality, are accomplices of reactionary politics." The pro-Allende press reasoned, "It is true that these young people really haven't rebelled against anything" and merely demonstrate "their class's loss of values." What is more, there were no more obvious signs that Piedra Roja was the epiphenomenal tragedy of capitalism than the complicity of the Andina Coca-Cola Bottling Company, which sold Coke and Sprite on the festival's grounds, and the fact that *carabineros* (still under the Frei administration) failed to head off Piedra Roja because it took place on private property: a parcel of land owned by the father of a friend of the festival's chief organizer. Marxists seized on the latter circumstance to make the case that the sanctity of private landownership had trumped the greater sociocultural good and that the Chilean road to socialism would fix that.[33]

Though often the topics of debate within Popular Unity, especially within the Socialist Party and between Socialists and Communists, the meanings of "revolution" and "liberation" essentially had prescribed contours in Allende's Chile. Marxist leaders typically found nothing revolutionary or liberating in counterculture. Indeed, those on the Left who ascribed an absence of social consciousness and a "lack of values" to Piedra Roja often assumed conservative positions vis-à-vis emergent and counterhegemonic cultural values of the long 1960s, especially in regard to sexual liberation, which were thrown into greater relief by '68s. As we see in numerous contributions to this volume, the unfolding cultural revolution of the Sixties and '68s positioned sexual freedom as an avatar for and in the liberation of the self and society. Having long-held mainstream views on family, gender, and sexuality, Chile's old-guard leftists denounced sexual liberation (that of women, mostly), and they tied such freedom to other alleged maladies, such as marijuana and rock music, with Piedra Roja serving as rich fodder. For example, alarmed that a "majority of the young girls" at the festival had brought with them contraceptive pills, the pro-Allende press offered suspicions that many births would happen nine months after the event, bemoaned a likelihood that many young women had lost their virginity there, and complained that Piedra Roja's pernicious rock music and marijuana inspired couples to make love openly and unapologetically amid the crowd.[34] Such lamentations were mainstream and part of a broader discourse that stressed the importance of proper sexuality (marital and heterosexual) and the nuclear family, and the role of women in both.[35]

The conservative press also had plenty to say in the matter of counterculture, especially in the week or so after Piedra Roja, and often focused on moral problems that rightists attributed to Popular Unity. *El Mercurio*, the leading defender of the conservative National Party's interests in the daily press, chastised cultural decay in "developed societies." In one instance, it picked on U.S. popular culture, best exemplified, or so the newspaper described, by the documentary film *Woodstock: Three Days of Peace and Music*. Appearing in Santiago cinemas in September 1970, the film "seems to have been behind the decision among some Chilean adolescents to put on a similar event," an editorial complained. "It is evident that our youth, just like those around the world, act without inhibition. . . . They skirt their educational responsibilities, they show pride in the way they treat their parents, and they adopt habits like smoking marijuana."[36] *El Mercurio* thus deduced, "All of this speaks to the effects of a type of moral denationalization [*desnacionalización*], of a crisis of family values, and young peoples' loss of the sense of themselves due to certain circles of youths who fortunately only represent a minority seeking publicity," and that "without a doubt, tolerance [of counterculture] is a grave error."[37] Moreover, in a September 1971 editorial, conservatives blamed the Allende government for failing to adequately protect the nation's morality and "proper manners."[38]

Elected officials also had their say. "In the end, the only thing coming to light from this orgy," explained Carlos Gana, a Socialist and Las Condes municipal councilman, "is that there were groups of young people, in the minority, who did what they did out of imitation, who consumed drugs and alcohol and, with impunity, humiliated the public morality."[39] In addition, Luis Pareto González, a Christian Democrat and prominent member of the Chamber of Deputies, was among many politicians in the National Congress who railed against Piedra Roja, hippies, and marijuana within hours of the festival's conclusion.[40] As a result, the Chamber of Deputies voted on October 13 (in the final days of the Frei administration) to investigate the use of marijuana and other drugs among young Chileans "in light of what happened last week [in Las Condes]." Deputies reasoned that "the spectacle put on by *criollo* hippies constitutes a grave threat not only for the sector of our youth who participated [in the festival] but also for the future of the country, and it is necessary to take energetic measures to keep 'festivals' like that from happening."[41] Furthermore, the government-operated newspaper *La Nación*, which was in the hands of Christian Democrats until Allende's inauguration, announced a police investigation involving "the consumption of drugs, erotic excesses, robberies, and the disappearances of minors at that orgy of long hair." *La Nación* also lambasted the "*criollo* hippie festival" for its putative immorality.[42]

Interestingly, there was some crossover of countercultural outlooks among younger Marxists, in particular among members of the Communist Youth, who did not appreciate the unambiguous distinction made by their elders between properly revolutionary behavior and aspects of "liberation" that countercultural young people pursued. In short, some young Communists grew their hair and explored their sexualities despite the "family-values," mainstream, and moralistic cultural discourse emanating from Popular Unity's leadership. But far from arguing for a very different sort of revolution than Popular Unity's, such young radicals instead located some countercultural elements under the rubric of political-revolutionary praxis. This was common in the pages of *Ramona*, a youth-focused magazine produced by the Communist Youth between 1971 and 1973, which repeatedly challenged the patience of the Old Left's leadership (and especially that of the Communist Party) by publishing articles that threw into question mainstream cultural positions on sexuality, long hair on young men, and other issues.[43] The *miristas*, however, were largely critical of counterculture for its lack of an authentically revolutionary ethos in the pursuit of social, political, and economic change, but MIR men often grew their hair and sported beards.[44] Counterculture, one *mirista* wrote in mid-1971, questioned cultural and social values and was creating new ones, and capitalism, so flexible and adaptive, had generated a "hippie industry" featuring clothes and such. That power, she argued, must be combated by a "Chilean vanguard" with its own intense and dynamic project of cultural change, and Popular Unity was not up to the challenge. "In Chile, where there has not been a social revolution but instead a process of change rooted in bourgeois legality, the tendency for the durability of institutions and values of a reactionary fashion is very strong, and they can only be counteracted if they truly become the objects of attention and become central concerns in the operation of the most revolutionary sectors," the writer explains.[45]

Allende understood that young people collectively had significant revolutionary potential, and he communicated to radical youths in particular that they had a place in Popular Unity's national project. Many occupied that place, while others, such as the *miristas*, remained outside the coalition as they pursued revolutionary goals through different means. In the context of a democratic and pluralistic political culture in which radicalism had a legitimate and rather consequential position, Allende, the bulk of his supporters, and a great many teens and twentysomethings were convinced that party politics was the ideal conduit for their anti-imperialism, critiques of capitalism, and vitality, hopes, and dreams that were characteristic of the transnational zeitgeist of '68. At the same time, Popular Unity placed clear limits on what acceptable revolutionary agency and "liberation" should look like for young people, figuratively and literally, mostly shunning the vanguardism and voluntarism of New Lefts and types of bottom-up sociopolitical mobilization seen in France, Mexico, and beyond in the late 1960s. And although Popular Unity had a revolutionary agenda with cultural elements, it did not create or further a broader cultural revolution, the likes of which is commonly associated with the global Sixties and with 1968, largely because of the coalition's imperatives, outlooks, and its overall fidelity to identifiably mainstream cultural positions.

IMPRESSIONS

At the dawning of the Age of Aquarius, new and inventive movements and trends emerged around the world in response to ideas, structures, and practices they comprehended to be at odds with justice, freedom, and happiness. Their protagonists were essential contributors in the elaboration of a zeitgeist with significant reach, complexity, and, for the historian, analytic value, whether those movements and trends realized their goals fully, partially, or not at all. Amid worrisome global, regional, and local conditions, and running up against governments whose responses ranged from acquiescence to belligerence, those activists, protesters, and sympathizers were spurred on by emotion, hopefulness, and, at times, spontaneity, in addition to any ideological commitments and practical considerations. As one former Chilean hippie recalled of her teenage years in the late 1960s, "There was a lot of searching in Chile—a lot of searching for the magical."[46] In that vein, many young Chileans had taken to the streets, seized university buildings, and engaged in other forms of individual and collective action, through or outside political parties and associated groups, before Allende and his coalition embarked on the road to socialism. As he took the presidential sash, Allende assured young people sympathetic with Popular Unity that the coalition had a place for them in it, but that place entailed certain expectations for proper revolutionary behavior in a revolution "from above." Overall, the examination of the long 1960s in Chile evinces '68-ish sensibilities, such as youthful activism and hope for radical change, but the country's political culture and telling characteristics of its Left made for circumstances unlike those seen in other theaters in which '68s happened.

It has not been my purpose to necessarily undermine the importance of 1968 as "one of those constellation-years," as Fuentes put it, or a "year that rocked the world," as Mark Kurlansky describes it, but rather to situate, in general ways, Chilean political, social, and cultural circumstances vis-à-vis the global Sixties and in relation to the zeitgeist of '68.[47] Also, I have not attempted to specifically periodize the zeitgeist of '68, thus avoiding the trap of conflating it with the long 1960s, even though that period has been our focus. In that vein, and at the risk of watering down its usefulness, one might venture to argue that, in some ways, the spirit of 1968 persisted for a very long time, and perhaps still does. To wit, events in Chile four decades after 1968 seemingly recaptured that zeitgeist, but under very different local circumstances and in a rather different world. The striking mobilization of many tens of thousands of high school students beginning in 2006 brought hundreds of schools to a standstill and led to a national strike involving 600,000 students. Frustrated by the center-left governing coalition's inactivity in regard to reversing neoliberal educational policies established by the dictatorship, the students' demands included the deprivatization and democratization of primary and secondary education, free university-entrance exams, and passes for public transit. The Penguin Movement (Movimiento Pingüino) or Penguin Revolution (Revolución de Pingüinos), as it came to be known, saw the largest mass demonstrations since the country's return to democracy in 1990.

The *pingüinos* (the term comes from the local practice of calling young people "penguins," derived from the color scheme of secondary-school uniforms) expressed sensibilities not unlike those that emerged among student movements in the 1960s, and their methods—among them, taking to the streets instead of working through the political process and party politics (although young party members were present and very active)—was very much in tune with '68's vibe. As in the case of the university-reform movement in 1967–68, the demonstrators largely saw their demands met. In 2011, moreover, another round of student protests arose, in that instance also involving university students and federations, which called for further democratization, increased government spending on education, and an end to for-profit higher education. The demonstrations included hunger strikes, kiss-ins, and dances. One protester explained, "The whole country is watching this movement. The generation of our parents is watching us with hope, with faith that we have the strength to change this education system and make history."[48] Among those looking on was Miguel Ángel Solar, who became a physician after his eventful education at the PUC. "The most notable thing is that these kids, who have been fighting for quality education, have studied the Constitution, have analyzed laws, [and] have researched ministerial documents, all things that we never did," noted Solar in 2012, in his late sixties at the time. "All of these protests have been like an intensive course in civic education, and that's marvelous because we're going to have a generation of citizens of superior quality."[49] Of course, time will tell.

NOTES

1. Carlos Fuentes, *Los 68: París-Praga-México* (Mexico City: Debate-Random House Mondadori, 2005), 11.

2. I borrow "zeitgeist" (spirit) from Gerd Rainer-Horn, *The Spirit of '68: Rebellion in Western Europe and North America, 1956–1976* (Oxford: Oxford University Press, 2007).

3. A fine synthesis on the working-class movement during the long Sixties is Luis Theilemann, "La rudeza pagana: Sobre la radicalización del movimiento obrero en los largos sesenta. Chile, 1957–1970," *Izquierdas* 44 (June 2018): 114–33.

4. On the Old Left/New Left relationship, see Vania Markarian, "Sobre viejas y nuevas izquierdas: Los jóvenes comunistas uruguayos y el movimiento estudiantil de 1968," *Secuencia* 81 (September-December 2011): 161–86, and Eric Zolov, "Expanding Our Conceptual Horizons: The Shift from an Old to a New Left in Latin America," *A Contracorriente* 5, no. 2 (2008): 47–73.

5. See, for instance, Yanko González, "'Sumar y no ser sumado': Culturas juveniles revolucionarias. Mayo de 1968 y diversificación identitaria en Chile," *Alpha* 30 (July 2010): 111–28; Adalberto Santana, "1968 en la memoria de América Latina y el mundo," *Revista Mexicana de Ciencias Políticas y Sociales* 63, no. 234 (2018): 177–99; and Carlos Salazar, "Cristina Hurtado: 'La utopía de Mayo del 68 pudo ser algo increíble en Chile de no ser por los milicos,'" *The Clinic* (Santiago), May 6, 2018.

6. Robert Vincent Daniels, *Year of the Heroic Guerrilla: World Revolution and Counterrevolution in 1968* (Cambridge, MA: Harvard University Press, 1996), 59.

7. One methodological issue that arises when addressing "generation" is that it does not disaggregate gender, class, and race. Yet, the concept was consequential in terms of individual and collective identities and mobilization during the Sixties.

8. Consult Raymond Craib, *The Cry of the Renegade: Politics and Poetry in Interwar Chile* (New York: Oxford University Press, 2016), and Patrick Barr-Melej, *Reforming Chile: Cultural Politics, Nationalism, and the Rise of the Middle Class* (Chapel Hill: University of North Carolina Press, 2001).

9. The PDC, like other mainstay political parties, has a history of organizing and rallying youths. It did so on a massive scale in 1964 in support of Frei's presidential campaign. In what was billed as the March of the Young Fatherland (Marcha de la Patria Joven), tens of thousands of PDC youths across the country began treks that ended in a large Santiago park and with a rallying speech by Frei. See Frei, "Discurso de la Patria Joven," in *Eduardo Frei M.: Obras escogidas,*

1931–1982, ed. Oscar Pinochet de la Barra (Santiago: Ediciones del Centro de Estudios Políticos Latinoamericanos Simón Bolívar, 1993), 292–96.

10. Consult Manuel Antonio Garretón, *Universidades chilenas: Historia, reforma e intervención* (Santiago: Editores Sur, 1987); Garretón, "Universidad y política en los procesos de transformación en Chile, 1967–1973," *Pensamiento Universitario* 14, no. 14 (2011): 71–90; and Luis Cifuentes Seves, *La reforma universitaria en Chile, 1968–1973* (Santiago: Editorial Universidad de Santiago, 1997). Also see a collection of reflections from a seminar that marked the fiftieth anniversary of the 1967 events: *A 50 años de la reforma universitaria en la UC: Seminario 1967–2017*, ed. Patricio Bernedo (Santiago: Ediciones Universidad Católica de Chile, 2017).

11. For stories on unrest in Europe and the United States, see the *El Mercurio* (Santiago) editions of March 3, 15–17, 21, and 24; April 13–14; June 1–12 and 25; July 7; October 8; and December 9, 1968. For events in Brazil, consult, for example, *El Mercurio*, April 3–5, June 22, and October 23, 1968. Also see Victoria Langland, "Il est Interdit d'Interdire: The Transnational Experience of 1968 in Brazil," *Estudios Interdisciplinarios de América Latina y el Caribe* 17, no. 1 (2006): 61–81. For Argentina, see *El Mercurio*, June 16, 1968, and for Uruguay, *El Mercurio*, June 23 and August 10–12, 1968.

12. *Punto Final* (Santiago), April 13, 1971.

13. *El Mercurio*, August 2, 1968, and *La Nación*, August 1–2, 1968.

14. *El Mercurio*, October 5, 1968.

15. Ibid., October 11, 1968. For a more sympathetic treatment of the protests, see the Communist Party's *El Siglo*, October 5–10, 1968.

16. *El Mercurio*, December 7, 1968. Also see the December 4 and 9 issues.

17. Ibid., June 5, 1968.

18. James R. Whelan, *Out of the Ashes: Life, Death, and Transfiguration of Democracy in Chile* (Washington, DC: Regnery Gateway, 1989), 717–18.

19. Quoted in ibid., 719.

20. *El Mercurio*, August 14, 1968.

21. Whelan, *Out of the Ashes*, 720–21.

22. Consult Craib, *The Cry of the Renegade*, and Barr-Melej, *Reforming Chile*, chap. 6.

23. *New York Times*, April 29, 2008. On some links between May 1968 in France and the development of a generational identity among youths in Chile, especially among the organized Left, see Yanko González, "'Sumar y no ser sumado,'" 111–28.

24. Eric Zolov, *Refried Elvis: The Rise of the Mexican Counterculture* (Berkeley: University of California Press, 1999), chaps. 4–6.

25. Salvador Allende, "Inaugural Address in the National Stadium," in *The Salvador Allende Reader*, ed. James Cockcroft (Melbourne: Ocean Press, 2000), 58.

26. Consult Marian Schlotterbeck, *Beyond the Vanguard: Everyday Revolutionaries in Allende's Chile* (Berkeley: University of California Press, 2018).

27. Cockcroft, ed., *The Salvador Allende Reader*, 264, 38, 214. Also see Martín Bowen Silva, "El proyecto sociocultural de la izquierda chilena durante la Unidad Popular," *Nuevo Mundo Mundos Nuevos*, January 21, http://journals.openedition.org/nuevomundo/13732.

28. Also see J. Patrice McSherry, *Chilean New Song: The Political Power of Music, 1960s–1973* (Philadelphia: Temple University Press, 2015), and Patrick Barr-Melej, "Manipulando 'el alma del pueblo': Cultura y prácticas políticas en Chile contemporáneo," in *Historia política de Chile, 1810–2010: Historia de las prácticas políticas*, ed. Juan Luis Ossa and Iván Jaksic (Santiago: Fondo de Cultura Económica, 2017), 301–30.

29. Studies on Latin American counterculture include Patrick Barr-Melej, *Psychedelic Chile: Youth, Counterculture, and Politics on the Road to Socialism and Dictatorship* (Chapel Hill: University of North Carolina Press, 2017); Christopher Dunn, *Contracultura: Alternative Arts and Social Transformation in Authoritarian Brazil* (Chapel Hill: University of North Carolina Press, 2016), and Dunn, *Tropicália and the Emergence of a Brazilian Counterculture* (Chapel Hill: University of North Carolina Press, 2001); Vania Markarian, *El 68 uruguayo: El movimiento estudiantil entre molotovs y música beat* (Quilmes, Argentina: Editorial de la Universidad Nacional de Quilmes, 2012); and Zolov, *Refried Elvis.*

30. Consult Zolov, "Expanding our Conceptual Horizons"; Doug Rossinow, "The New Left in the Counterculture: Hypotheses and Evidence," *Radical History Review* 67 (1997): 79–120; and Van Gosse, *Rethinking the New Left: An Interpretative History* (New York: Palgrave, 2005).

31. Quoted in Zolov, "Expanding our Conceptual Horizons," 47.

32. *El Siglo* (Santiago), October 13, 1970.

33. Ibid., October 14, 1970. Piedra Roja's principal organizers indeed were from the more affluent sectors of the capital, but by no means was the festival limited to bourgeois partakers. Only rarely did the pro-Allende press concede that working-class young people also were drawn to counterculture, essentially building a distinction between morally suspect well-to-do Chileans and good Chileans. Just after Piedra Roja, a leftist publication noted, "In Chile, all of this started in the summer of 1968–69. That period marks the beginning of widespread marijuana use among adolescents from families with abundant economic resources. But soon it expanded to people with lower incomes and budgets" (*Puro Chile*, October 14, 1970).

34. *El Siglo*, October 14, 1970; *Clarín* (Santiago), October 13, 1970; "El festival de droga y sexo," *Vea*, October 16, 1970, 6–7.

35. See Barr-Melej, *Psychedelic Chile*, chap. 3.

36. *El Mercurio*, October 12, 1970.

37. Ibid., October 16, 1970.

38. Ibid., September 28, 1971.

39. Ibid., October 15, 1970.

40. *Clarín*, October 14, 1970.

41. Ibid., October 14, 1970.

42. *La Nación* (Santiago), October 12, 1970.

43. See the insightful Alfonso Salgado, "'A Small Revolution': Family, Sex, and the Communist Youth of Chile during the Allende Years (1970–1973)," *Twentieth Century Communism* 8 (Spring 2015): 62–88.

44. Such aesthetic and ideological issues are taken up in Florencia Mallon, "*Barbudos*, Warriors, and *Rotos:* The MIR, Masculinity, and Power in the Chilean Agrarian Reform, 1965–74," in *Changing Men and Masculinities in Latin America*, ed. Matthew Gutmann (Durham, NC: Duke University Press, 2003), 179–215.

45. Vania Bambirra, "La mujer chilena en la transición al socialismo," *Punto Final*, June 22, 1971, 7–8.

46. María Ester Lezaeta, interview by the author, Santiago, May 2006.

47. See Mark Kurlansky, *1968: The Year That Rocked the World* (New York: Ballantine, 2004).

48. *New York Times*, August 4, 2011.

49. Vicente Parrini, "Miguel Ángel Solar: El regreso del líder perdido," *Revista Paula*, October 27, 2012, https://www.latercera.com/paula/miguel-angel-solar-el-regreso-del-lider-perdido/.

BIBLIOGRAPHY

Barr-Melej, Patrick. "Manipulando 'el alma del pueblo': Cultura y prácticas políticas en Chile contemporáneo." In *Historia política de Chile, 1810–2010: Historia de las prácticas políticas*, edited by Juan Luis Ossa and Iván Jaksic, 201–30. Santiago: Fondo de Cultura Económica, 2017.

———. *Psychedelic Chile: Youth, Counterculture, and Politics on the Road to Socialism and Dictatorship*. Chapel Hill: University of North Carolina Press, 2017.

———. *Reforming Chile: Cultural Politics, Nationalism, and the Rise of the Middle Class.* Chapel Hill: University of North Carolina Press, 2001.

Berman, Paul. *A Tale of Two Utopias: The Political Journey of the Generation of 1968*. New York: W. W. Norton, 1996.

Cifuentes Seves, Luis. *La reforma universitaria en Chile, 1968–1973*. Santiago: Editorial Universidad de Santiago, 1997.

Cockcroft, James, ed. *The Salvador Allende Reader*. Melbourne: Ocean Press, 2000.

Craib, Raymond. *The Cry of the Renegade: Politics and Poetry in Interwar Chile*. New York: Oxford University Press, 2016.

De la Barra, Oscar, ed. *Eduardo Frei M.: Obras escogidas, 1931–1982*. Santiago: Ediciones del Centro de Estudios Políticos Latinoamericanos Simón Bolívar, 1993.

Dunn, Christopher. *Contracultura: Alternative Arts and Social Transformation in Authoritarian Brazil.* Chapel Hill: University of North Carolina Press, 2016.

———. *Tropicália and the Emergence of a Brazilian Counterculture*. Chapel Hill: University of North Carolina Press, 2001.

Farber, David, ed. *The Sixties: From Memory to History*. Chapel Hill: University of North Carolina Press, 1994.

Fuentes, Carlos. *Los 68: París-Praga-México.* Mexico City: Debate-Random House Mondadori, 2005.

Garretón, Manuel Antonio. *Universidades chilenas: Historia, reforma e intervención*. Santiago: Editores Sur, 1987.

———. "Universidad y política en los procesos de transformación en Chile, 1967–1973." *Pensamiento Universitario* 14, no. 14 (2011): 71–90.

González, Yanko. "'Sumar y no ser sumado': Culturas juveniles revolucionarias. Mayo de 1968 y diversificación identitaria en Chile." *Alpha* 30 (July 2010): 111–28.

Gosse, Van. *Rethinking the New Left: An Interpretative History*. New York: Palgrave, 2005.

Grandin, Greg, and Gil Joseph, eds. *A Century of Revolution: Insurgent and Counterinsurgent Violence during Latin America's Long Cold War*. Durham, NC: Duke University Press, 2010.

Gutmann, Matthew, ed. *Changing Men and Masculinities in Latin America*. Durham, NC: Duke University Press, 2003.

Jian, Chen, Martin Klimke, Marsha Kirasirova, Mary Nolan, Marilyn Young, and Joanna Waley-Cohen, eds. *The Routledge Handbook of the Global Sixties: Between Protest and Nation-Building*. New York: Routledge, 2018.

Katsiaficas, George. *The Imagination of the New Left: A Global Analysis of 1968*. Boston: South End Press, 1987.

Kurlansky, Mark. *1968: The Year That Rocked the World.* New York: Ballantine, 2004.

Langland, Victoria. *Speaking of Flowers: Student Movements and the Making and Remembering of 1968 in Military Brazil.* Durham, NC: Duke University Press, 2013.

Lipset, Seymour Martin, ed. *Students in Revolt.* Boston: Houghton Mifflin, 1969.

Markarian, Vania. *El 68 uruguayo: El movimiento estudiantil entre molotovs y música beat.* Quilmes, Argentina: Editorial de la Universidad Nacional de Quilmes, 2012.

———. "Sobre viejas y nuevas izquierdas: Los jóvenes comunistas uruguayos y el movimiento estudiantil de 1968." *Secuencia* 81 (2011): 161–86.

McSherry, J. Patrice. *Chilean New Song: The Political Power of Music, 1960s–1973.* Philadelphia: Temple University Press, 2015.

Pensado, Jaime M. *Rebel Mexico: Student Unrest and Authoritarian Political Culture during the Long Sixties.* Stanford, CA: Stanford University Press, 2013.

Rainer-Horn, Gerd. *The Spirit of '68: Rebellion in Western Europe and North America, 1956–1976.* Oxford: Oxford University Press, 2007.

Rojas Hernández, Jorge. *Sociedad bloqueada: Movimiento estudiantil, desigualdad y despertar de la sociedad chilena.* Santiago: RIL, 2012.

Rossinow, Doug. "The New Left in the Counterculture: Hypotheses and Evidence." *Radical History Review* 67 (1997): 79–120.

Salgado, Alfonso. "'A Small Revolution': Family, Sex, and the Communist Youth of Chile during the Allende Years (1970–1973)." *Twentieth Century Communism* 8 (Spring 2015): 62–88.

Scheuzger, Stephan. "La historia contemporánea de México y la historia global: Reflexiones acerca los 'sesenta globales.'" *Historia Mexicana* 68, no. 1 (2018): 313–58.

Schlotterbeck, Marian. *Beyond the Vanguard: Everyday Revolutionaries in Allende's Chile.* Berkeley: University of California Press, 2018.

Suri, Jeremi. *The Global Revolutions of 1968: A Norton Casebook in History.* New York: W. W. Norton, 2007.

———. *Power and Protest. Global Revolution in the Age of Détente.* Cambridge, MA: Harvard University Press, 2003.

———. "The Rise and Fall of International Counterculture." *American Historical Review* 114, no. 1 (2019): 45–68.

Whelan, James R. *Out of the Ashes: Life, Death, and Transfiguration of Democracy in Chile.* Washington, DC: Regnery Gateway, 1989.

Zolov, Eric. "Expanding Our Conceptual Horizons: The Shift from an Old to a New Left in Latin America." *A Contracorriente* 5, no. 2 (2008): 47–73.

———. "Introduction: Latin America in the Global Sixties." *The Americas* 70, no. 3 (2014): 349–62.

———. *Refried Elvis: The Rise of the Mexican Counterculture*. Berkeley: University of California Press, 1999.

SIXTEEN

Arvo Pärt

The Unexpected Profile of a Musical Revolutionary

CARMEN-HELENA TÉLLEZ

The 1960s and the year 1968, in particular, witnessed several controversial innovations in both popular and classical music that, in hindsight, have been tagged as part of the revolutions that swept through all cultural strata, as noted throughout this book. Since then, classical music composers, and living composers in particular, arguably have lost the position of cultural preeminence they once had in Western society,[1] but the case of Estonian composer Arvo Pärt, known to classical music lovers as an artist who transitioned successfully from a Soviet republic to the West to become the most performed living composer of our time,[2] poses interesting questions about the difference between revolutionary acts and long-term revolutionary influence. The year 1968 marked the start of a drastic reorientation in Pärt's compositional style that would prove to be extremely consequential. That year, after a thorough training but limited success in a Soviet-accepted style of musical modernism, Pärt presented his work *Credo* for piano, chorus, and orchestra in Talinn. The religious implication

Figure 16.1 Arvo Pärt, by Rene Jakobson. Permission of the Arvo Pärt Centre.

in the composition created a scandal that brought irreversible consequences for Pärt's career. The upheaval forced him into a period of seclusion and ultimate exile, out of which he emerged completely transformed as an artist, with a thoroughly original grammar and style of musical composition. *Credo* was the beginning of an existential revolution for Pärt, with consequences that eventually connected with unexpected professional strands, responding to cultural factors not yet fully examined in Western European contemporary concert music. Pärt's personal journey may have had a revolutionary effect on Western classical music, as yet unacknowledged but still ongoing fifty years later.

ARVO PÄRT INSIDE THE CONFLICT BETWEEN SOVIET SOCIALIST REALISM AND THE EUROPEAN AVANT-GARDE

Arvo Pärt was born in Estonia, in the city of Paide, on September 11, 1935. He was raised in Ratvere, to the north of the country. Born after the Estonian declaration of independence in 1918, and growing up during a period of autocratic rule, he was barely ten years old during the subsequent Soviet annexation of Estonia after World War II. As a consequence, Pärt's formative years witnessed the tension between the memory of nationalistic pride and the reality of Soviet domination.[3] This tension would eventually progress into another kind of opposition, between the artistic style sanctioned by the Soviet establishment, often labeled "socialist realism," and the increasingly radical innovations of Western Europe's musical avant-garde, considered decadent by the Soviet regime.[4] Pärt pursued composition studies under Heino Eller (1887–1979), founder of the Tartu School of Composition, and Veljo Tormis (1930–2017), a figure who in the last years of the twentieth century attained his own considerable prestige in the West. Tormis, who was trained at the Moscow State Conservatory, tried to maintain a delicate balance between the rules of the Soviet-sanctioned styles and nationalistic languages that preserved a sense of Estonian identity.[5] He aimed to offer his students as broad a perspective as possible, but he and his students still had to operate under the supervision of the director of the Estonian Conservatory, Eugen Kapp (1908–96), who had been a favored Stalinist composer, a member of the Communist Party, and the chairman of the Composers' Union.[6] In time, as Pärt matured as a professional, Kapp and the Union engaged in sporadic censorship and ostracism of his music, compounding the circumstances that promoted Pärt's eventual exile to Berlin in 1980.

The Soviet regime sought to promote the communist way of life through the arts, and specifically acknowledged the power of music to affect the sense of identity and affective well-being of an audience. The specifics of the acceptable socialist realist style remained unclear, but among composers, the works had to meet two central tenets: the composition's message had to advance Soviet revolutionary ideals and narratives, and the style had to remain populist, in a way that would be easily understood by the proletariat.[7] The argument for Soviet realism included attacks on the musical styles of the West for their selfish promotion of useless artistic innovation and decadent formalism without a clear social benefit.

There is no denying that, by the late 60s, art music in Western Europe had come to a point where innovation became the central objective. The term "avant-garde," derived from military strategy, referred to a heterogeneous and rhizome-like movement attacking the traditional musical systems seen to stand for the old regime destroyed by World War II.[8] The preeminent laboratory for European musical experimentation resided in Paris around the figure of the *enfant terrible* of French music, Pierre Boulez (1925–2016), who would eventually establish the Institut de Recherche et Coordination Acoustique/Musique (IRCAM) in 1970, with support from the French government. Boulez dominated European contemporary music alongside his brother-in-arms Karlheinz Stockhausen (1928–2007) in Darmstadt, Germany. Composers from all over Europe and the world came to IRCAM and Darmstadt to be counted among the elite of avant-garde music. Those welcomed to participate in these activities constituted the crème de la crème of contemporary music in their respective countries. Similar laboratories aspiring to advanced research and innovation of materials, structures, and lexicons of both acoustic and electroacoustic music sprouted in the world's developed countries. Their composers' stance remained revolutionary with a strong utopian streak. Much has been written about how the cataclysms of the two world wars and the Holocaust destroyed the European sense of self, and how composers in Western Europe rejected the mirages of nationalism and fascism stoked by popular culture and propaganda. The capacity of music to stir the emotions became immediately suspect among composers of the French and German avant-garde. From this epicenter, they influenced contemporary composition all over Europe and the Americas. Abandoning the goal of persuasion through the emotions, they focused on uncompromising exploration of musical structures and sounds with a scientific perspective and zeal.[9] Like in other cultural manifestations in the 1960s, the composers of the Western European avant-garde engaged in a constant breakdown of preexisting structures, continuous renewal of musical techniques, and, in short, an ongoing revolution whose goal was revolution itself.

By contrast, the Soviet institutions formulating the style of socialist realism, even as it purportedly represented its own decades-old revolution, sought to control and codify artistic expression, albeit with ambivalent and nonspecific tenets, distributed through official agencies through all the Soviet republics. Musical life in Pärt's Estonia mirrored these artistic positions and decisions emerging from the Soviet Union. They were handed down by key appointees to the Estonian Conservatory and the Composers' Union, and great composers labored under these constraints imposed by the state. Pärt was not the only composer in Estonia or in the Soviet Union who met with a range of disapproving gestures by the Soviet establishment. In fact, many biographies of Soviet composers tell the tale of a game of influences between the establishment and artists who would be left to rot in indifference, derision, ignominy, and even prison or exile. This became particularly grievous during the Stalinist regime.

It is interesting to observe how the communist experiment of the Soviet Union generated many echoes and controversies within avant-garde intellectual and artistic circles in the West. It now appears baffling that not a small number of artists and intellectuals, especially in Europe and Latin America, defended the Soviet and Cuban revolutions as the point of reference to fuel their own diatribes against the equally suffocating power of the United States.[10] Still, the Soviet Union sternly continued to oppose the artistic styles adopted by the avant-garde artists in the West, notwithstanding their political sympathies towards communism. These artistic polarizations perhaps represent a minor plot in the larger geopolitical drama playing out during the 1960s, but they lie at the core of the struggles in Pärt's early professional life, as he navigated the artistic risks embedded in both acceptance and rejection by the Soviet state.

Pärt came into his early career after Stalin's death, at the onset of the Nikita Khrushchev era starting in 1953. The establishment's demands for the Soviet realist style relaxed slightly, but there remained other subtle impediments to the free development of a creative personality. Soviet musical authorities continued their regular criticism of Western "formalism" and its arrogant preference for purely technical and aesthetic goals. When presented in conferences of the Estonian Composers' Union, Pärt's first efforts at composition were always met with ambivalence. For example, his first *Sonatina* of 1958 was criticized for following a "formalist" neoclassical style, including "deficiencies in the ideological and creative development . . . undervaluing the national-folkloric music."[11] Indeed, the apparent relaxation of the Soviet aesthetic guidelines after the death of Stalin hid another type of pressure from the central decision-makers. First of all, the Cold War imposed a terrible isolation on composers inside the Soviet republics. Very little musical information or scores would enter from the West. In spite of this, composers enjoyed a relatively privileged career, partaking in a network fully controlled by either the Soviet establishment, the Composers' Union, or each republic's state concert agency, peppered with official commissions, premieres, recordings, grants, and traveling to Soviet conferences and festivals. It follows that a lack of approval from the establishment would result in these privileges being withdrawn. Given that all musical activity depended on the state, any criticism from the top meant that the disgraced composer's music would not be performed anywhere, and the name would disappear from the circuit.

It should come as no surprise that, under this politicized system of rewards and punishment, Pärt's early career was marred by alternating waves of tepid tolerance and open disapproval. The periods of criticism had direct consequences on his ability to make a living, and the recurrent stress eventually resulted in damage to his health. Pärt had also observed over the years that other artists were ostracized in irreversible ways, or sent into exile from which they never returned. As Pärt's career progressed, his *Nekrolog* for orchestra (1960) received even more aggressive criticism than his *Sonatina* (1959) for exploring the decadent technique of dodecaphony,[12] even though other composers were also testing the waters with this style. Pärt was blacklisted. To supplement his income during the period of ostracism, Pärt engaged in more pragmatic professional pursuits, some of which would be considered second-class employment for a composer. Significantly, Pärt became a sound engineer (*toonmeister*) for Estonian Radio. This activity would prove to be a game changer for Pärt and for the development of his individual style in two respects. First, the station had access to many recordings that would not circulate freely elsewhere, of both historical music written before the eighteenth century and recent compositions from the West brought in by the occasional traveler. Second, Pärt's aural sensibility became extremely attuned to the nature of recorded sound, and to the potential technological manipulations thereof, a skill that would prove important later for the development of the new style that would make him famous.[13] Indeed, later on, Pärt acknowledged *Nekrolog* as the beginning of a life-changing spiritual quest.[14]

AN INNER REVOLUTION

More than the polarity between Soviet and Western styles, Pärt's early work manifests a tension between the requirement to meet the sanctioned Soviet realist style and the desire to satisfy an internal drive for communicating something personal and original. Compared with Pärt's post-Soviet style after his crisis of 1968, one could sense in the pre-1968 works a struggle for authenticity and, at the same time, the lack of a distinctive compositional voice. Looking backwards, a scholar can carve out the seeds of the mature Pärt in these early works, because in the end Pärt's struggle transcended the simple duality between Soviet realism and Western so-called formalism though a totally original language. Behind it all, there was a deeper quest for spiritual fulfillment. By 1968, Pärt was part of a growing musical movement in the Soviet republics rejecting atheist materialism to return to religion and religious musical genres.[15] Pärt's second wife, Nora, who is ethnically Jewish, had converted to the Eastern Orthodox Church. A woman of unquestionable clarity of judgment, she often expresses Pärt's musical and religious positions with uncanny power and poetry. Her narrative of how Pärt came to a belief in Jesus Christ suggests a slow awakening over several years. The premiere of *Credo* for piano, chorus, and orchestra in 1968 was both a gradual culmination and an explosion after a long process.

In September 1968, Pärt agreed to talk on a radio program, and it became clear how spiritually focused he had become. His answer to a question about how he understood progress in art was revealing: "Art has to deal with eternal questions, not just sorting out the issues of today. . . . Art is in fact nothing else than pouring your thoughts or spiritual values into a most suitable artistic form or expressing them in artistic ways." He added that wisdom resides in reduction, throwing out what is redundant. He spoke about "the correct solution to all fractions, epochs, and lives." Ivalo Randalu, the interviewer, did not air one part of the interview with Pärt because it contained material that would guarantee a ban. He hid the tape with the edited-out section, but the full recording eventually became available. It contained the following exchange. Randalu asked about Pärt's most important paragons: "Of course, Christ," answered Pärt without hesitation and continued: "Because he solved his fraction perfectly, godly."[16]

Pärt's pivotal work, *Credo*, was premiered in Talinn on November 16, 1968, soon after the aforementioned radio interview, by the Estonian Radio Chorus and Symphony Orchestra conducted by Neeme Järvi. Written for piano, chorus, and orchestra, it opened with the statement by the chorus, "I believe in Jesus Christ." The text, not a canonic Credo, still reveals the tone of his revolutionary intent:

> *Credo in Jesum Christum. Audivistis dictum: oculum pro oculo, dentem pro dente.*
>
> *Autem ego vobis dico: non esse resistendum injuriae. Credo!*

> I believe in Jesus Christ. You have heard it said: an eye for an eye, a tooth for a tooth.
>
> But I say to you: do not resist evil. I believe!

The musical materials in *Credo* were overtly and unapologetically based on Johann Sebastian Bach's Prelude no. 1 from *The Well-Tempered Clavier* (BWV 846), an iconic work of the eighteenth century easily recognizable by musicians and nonmusicians alike. It may be opportune to remember that early music was equally disavowed by the Soviet regime, but furthermore, conductor Neeme Järvi did not request permission from the authorities to perform the piece. Musicologist Ivana Medic also adds that "since *Credo* was written in the second half of the year . . . it is plausible that Pärt's piece was at least partially inspired by the 1968 invasion of Czechoslovakia."[17]

The negative reaction against *Credo* was immediate. There are many reasons why in the context of Estonian music this work created a stir. Beyond any possible protest against the invasion of Czechoslovakia, *Credo* had an ostensible religious reference, in itself illegal in the Soviet Union. In terms of its external features, *Credo* was a work imbued with polystylism, meaning that the composer had overtly juxtaposed at least two contrasting and ostensibly incongruent musical styles. Summarily speaking, the opening of the work deliberately references J. S. Bach, projecting nostalgia for the music of the past. This contrasts with later sections written in the complex and dissonant Western technique of serialism. The complete sixteen-minute work persists in this polarization, with no reconciliation of opposites. Even more, the consistency of the assignment of Bach's style to the piano establishes a conflict between the pianist's music and the massive orchestra. Although this opposition is typical of piano concertos as a whole, in this case it was exacerbated by the difference in style between the two performance actors. The chorus commented as a witness in the struggle, projecting the composition as a de facto drama that may have mirrored Pärt's internal quest.[18]

Clearly Pärt used polystylism as a transitional experiment in his search for a personal language. Polystylism had emerged in the Soviet republics as an innovation away from the stale tenets of Soviet realism, but avoiding the consistently atonal Western serialism that would have resulted in retaliation. In spite of the coalescence of disparate styles and discourses in a single piece, polystylism maintained an appeal to the audience through familiar tonal elements and connections with well-known genres, both classical and popular. It became one of the favored styles among composers seeking to revive religious musical genres. The Russian composer Alfred Schnittke (1934–98), a good friend of Pärt, is widely recognized as the pioneer and exemplary representative of Soviet polystylism. A few years after Pärt's *Credo*, Schnittke wrote a requiem in 1975, a work with a peculiar religious format in that it also included a Credo, which requiem masses typically do not include. Schnittke, of mixed Jewish and German ethnicity, imbued his requiem's Credo with the strands of rock 'n' roll, another forbidden musical style. The whole piece shows both a passionate searching ethos and a dispassionate irony. It can be considered a pioneer of the postmodern styles that are still current in art music in the twenty-first century.

Schnittke stayed loyal to polystylism until his death, but for Pärt, the polystylism of his 1968 *Credo* represented a transition through which he crossed to a new state of artistic being. He used it to represent himself as an artist seeking the spiritual clarity of J. S. Bach, a believer, whose Baroque music still retained in the twentieth century a power against the cacophony of modern life. At the same time, the polystylism in *Credo*, by itself, did not constitute the focus of the criticism by the Soviet musical establishment, but the religious content did. It turned out that Jesus Christ constituted a bigger enemy of the state than the inclusion of Western serialism within a taunting polystylistic piece.[19]

It was clear to the Soviet authorities that Pärt had become disobedient to the regime in the worst possible way. His music was banned from all concerts and radio transmissions. Even though he was not expelled definitively from the Composers' Union, Pärt suffered a psychological and physical crisis. He became a recluse. He composed two other concert works in eight years, Symphony no. 3 and the cantata "Soul to the Beloved" (*Laul armastatule*), later deleted from the catalogue. He also created music for short films and commercials, but, essentially, he entered a hiatus as a composer of concert music. He dedicated his time to studying Gregorian chant and the polyphony of Guillaume de Machaut (1300–1377) and Josquin Desprez (1455–1521). Then, one morning in 1976, he penned a short piano piece of utter simplicity, in a completely new style. He called it *Für Alina.*

Pärt continued to compose in the new manner, receiving the appreciation of a close circle of friends. In January 1980, he acted on the suggestion from a colleague to immigrate to Israel, on account of his wife's Jewish ethnicity. They left just before the doors for emigration closed. Some of the pieces in Pärt's new style (notably *Tabula Rasa* and *Missa Syllabica*) had leaked to the West, and had found success in nonconformist music festivals, with the happy result that Alfred Schlee, editor of the prestigious Universal Editions, promised to help him, meeting him in Vienna with open arms. Pärt never went to Israel, but proceeded on to Berlin, where he stayed with his family until the collapse of the Soviet Union. He returned to Estonia in 1992.[20]

TINTINNABULI AS A THIRD WAY FOR EUROPEAN ART MUSIC

When Pärt came out of his seclusion in 1976 with the piano work *Für Alina*, he had conceptualized a new style of utter simplicity and contemplation. It displayed a radical opposition to both the increasing complexity and constant innovation of the West, and the redundancy of the socialist realist epic narratives of the Soviet Union. After a long study of Gregorian chant and music from the Middle Ages and the Renaissance, Pärt decided to produce his own language, and it showed the influence of music before 1600. The historical repertoires had been unknown to him as a student. The Soviet music education system avoided early music, on the one hand partaking of the progressivist opinion that music before the late eighteenth century was primitive and inferior compared to the technical achievements of the nineteenth and twentieth centuries, but more importantly, because early music most frequently used the sacred texts of liturgical and devotional rituals. The sacred content was antipodal to the Soviet communist experiment. At the same time, Pärt did not "react" to early music. Instead, he proactively sought a solution to an obsessive question, specifically, how a musical content can remain essential and transcend its time, style, and performance medium over centuries. He sought utter distillation of the elements of music. In short, he went in the opposite direction of everyone else working among the elites of music composition in the 1960s and 70s.

At first, Pärt focused on studying and then emulating dozens of melodic designs in Gregorian chant. He sought to discover the potency of the combination of two or three notes. He then moved to the polyphonic works of Machaut, Desprez, and Victoria in order to understand how a voice could interact with another in the most compelling way.[21] He constructed thousands of exercises, composing melodies in the manner of Gregorian chant or reproducing in a melody the simplest design for birds, clouds, and other objects.[22] All the while, he embraced the aesthetics of sacred art in the Eastern Orthodox Church, which indicates that music must not act as the vehicle of human self-expression, but as a window for God to appear again to us.[23] Within such extraordinary constraints, Pärt came to the development of a technique that was both efficient and utterly symbolic of his aims. The technique was rigorous and responsive. Inspired by the concept of bells, whereby the clapper clashes with the rim, he termed the technique *tintinnabuli.*

Tintinnabuli is an evocative name for a rigorous compositional process. As the name suggests, one musical element must clash and "tintinnabulate" with another. In Pärt's original model, a linear scale of tones interacts with a triad of tones. As the pitches of the scale and the melodies coalesce by compositional design around different positions of the pitches of triad, they clash with them, like the clapper with the lip of the bell, creating alternations of consonances and dissonances. The scale has been defined as the archetypal unit of music, a set of contiguous pitches out of which the composer creates melodies. All cultures of the world have characteristic scales. In Western classical music we identify major, minor, modal, whole-tone, octatonic, and composer-designed scales, all carved out of intervallic relationships between the twelve possible chromatic pitches we all can try at the piano. A triad is another archetypal unit, specifically of Western tonality, formed by three discontinuous notes of the scale, delineating a major, minor, diminished, or augmented chord. Pärt has confessed his fascination with the purity of the triad. He also has labeled it as a symbol of the Trinity. Pärt goes on further to explain why *tintinnabuli* satisfied his quest for a sacred music language. The scale represents human life, it is who we are; and the triad symbolizes God, who is taking care of us and is embracing us. Once more, Nora Pärt describes the process with precision, by stating that the scale and triad for each new work by Arvo are conceptualized together as a unit, and can be defined by the formula 1 + 1 = 1.[24]

By pursuing this methodology, Pärt rejected the idea that complexity is the mark of great music. He has declared that he seeks something achieved by choice and distillation, in order to avoid redundancies, to get to what is deemed indispensable to bring into the world. This stood in direct contrast to the quest for radical rational innovation and increasing complexity among composers affiliated with the avant-garde in the West. Pärt rejected the idea that music exists to express the personal preoccupations of a single composer. He considered the quest for self-expression an act of vanity and pride. The composer instead must emulate the painter of icons of the Orthodox Church, who must be humble, follow rigorous rules, and, instead of expressing erratic human emotions, give us a glimpse of the Trinity, the Holy Mother, and the saints in eternity. Pärt also dismissed the idea that there is progress in music and that further technical discoveries would lead to richer and better expression. Instead, music exists between the notes, and not in the notes themselves. This was the secret that Pärt sought in his strenuous study of Gregorian chant during his period of seclusion after 1968.

One can find aspects of Pärt's earlier Soviet-Estonian practice remaining with him after the crisis of 1968 that led to his conceptualization of the *tintinnabuli* style in 1976. Some elements relate to the attitude, if not the specifics, of serialism. His treatment of the relationship between text and music demonstrates this most clearly, if not exclusively. This relationship is rarely rhetorical in the manner of Western music after the Renaissance; it does not include "text painting" and the emulation of visual images through musical design, or the reproduction of emotional gestures (such as sighing or rage) into visual and aural musical motifs. Instead, Pärt creates a "series" of rules for the usage of intervals, dynamics, and musical punctuations according to numerical patterns embedded in the text. For example, if a word had four syllables, its setting would use four subsequent pitches in his chosen scale, which in turn would "tintinnabulate" against his chosen triad. We see this very overtly in his *Missa Syllabica* (1977), *De Profundis* (1980), and other early works after the 1968–76 hiatus. In this respect, Pärt adopts the compositional principle that the choice of a process ahead of starting the composition determines its development. Rotation, permutations, inversions, retrogrades, and other techniques used in serialism can apply in a distilled fashion to the scales and the triads of *tintinnabuli*. This preexistent DNA determines the flow of the composition's morphology and discourse. This approach places much weight on the period of reflection and planning before starting to write the work, as Pärt does not relinquish control of the result by embracing just a process.[25]

Composition by a predetermined process has existed in Western music at least since the onset of liturgical polyphony around the tenth century. Strict rules were followed then. Process composition existed in the Renaissance and in the Baroque, as canons, fugues, and variations all follow procedural rules. Process composition lies at the foundation of serialism, since a scale is designed using all twelve chromatic notes of the Western system, without repeating one, and then possibilities of transposition, inversion, retrogression, and retrograde inversion apply more or less systematically throughout. American minimalist composers such as Steve Reich and Terry Riley have also followed stringent processes involving canons. In this respect, Pärt is not unique in adopting the restrictions of a preestablished process, but he did invent a new one in *tintinnabuli*.

The use of process and the attitude of intellectual rigor may be common to all these styles, but the motivation in Pärt does not equate to intellectual self-aggrandizement. The process emulates the painter of icons, who, through strict procedural rules and a period of intense meditation and reflection, reaches precisely the visual gesture that will elicit in the viewer a distancing from the struggles of the world, and an attitude of contemplation of the divine mysteries. Pärt's motivation is religious, concurring with the assertion that the indispensable factor in sacred music is a sincere belief in God.[26]

The third recurrent element in Pärt's style, besides *tintinnabuli* and serialized text-music relationships, is the structural use of silence. Silence is a constant presence in his music, for both musical and theological reasons. It relates to the Orthodox aesthetic in that silence establishes an equivalence with stillness. Silence stands in the same hierarchy of actual sound as a compositional element in Pärt's music. This equivalence subverts the expectations of Western musical narrative, and projects the alternative goals of Pärt's asceticism.[27]

There exists a paradox in the fact that Pärt wrote music for texts in Latin and German, used in the Catholic and Lutheran Churches, as much or more than texts in the Orthodox Church's Slavonic. This took place naturally as he moved to the West and he began to receive commissions for sacred music from different patrons. He also did not see himself in direct line with the liturgical music of the Orthodox Church, namely, the Byzantine chant. As the primary music of the Orthodox Church, the performance of Byzantine chant requires specialized training within a more restricted circle than classical music in general. Given Pärt's life experience as a classical music composer in atheist Estonia and then in the West, he made the choice of extending his sensibility about the role of sacred music to texts from all Christian traditions.[28]

PÄRT'S STYLE AMID THE PREVAILING ART MUSIC TRENDS IN 1968

When one compares the consequences of Pärt's existential jolt in 1968, namely, his achievement of the *tintinnabuli* technique, to the styles dominating the contemporary music establishment in Western Europe and the Soviet Union, Pärt's music stands in stark contrast to both of them, as a unique and original third way that may appear reactionary to some. In Western Europe's musical avant-garde, the fetish of constant innovation came with a sense of superiority based on a belief in continuous learning and globalized progress. This stance had long roots in European society, even before the Enlightenment. An elite of intellectuals, wise men with sophisticated education, developed pinnacles of philosophy, science, and art to guide the rest of society towards a better world, with results aimed to withstand continuous scrutiny. As Europe recovered from World War II, and in spite of the collapse of traditional beliefs and structures, the governments of different European countries continued to support classical and contemporary art music for the benefit of society. Radio stations established resident professional choirs and orchestras, and sound engineers joined forces with experimental composers to create a whole network unto itself, prosperous and full of imagination. Universities in the United States founded music departments ready to educate optimistic generations of baby-boom composers, taught to create newly complex musical languages, each one aspiring to be original, and each one seeking to be different from the rest. The already mentioned revolutionary sympathies and social concerns of these composers did not require "relinquishing an abiding preoccupation with technical advance and conceptual innovation."[29] They continued in this manner, even as they were contested by others who catalogued the European avant-garde among the tools of white imperialism over non-Western European art, including African American and Latin American art music.[30]

In spite of their lofty creative ideals, most works of living art music composers have not been embraced by the public at large in Western societies, as the music field grows increasingly atomized. After World War I, music became split into specific streams, each with a goal, an audience, and acceptable professional outlets. By the 1960s, the enjoyment and cultivation of pre-1900 classical music was thoroughly separated from its originating social contexts. In the United States, it took sometimes a luxury-brand glow for the upper classes,[31] and gained an aspirational value for the middle classes, especially for immigrant families moving up the socioeconomic ladder while wishing to consort with the elites. At the same time, sacred music originally conceived for actual liturgies before the nineteenth century moved over to the concert hall strictly on the artistic merits of its composers, even as the Church lost the social and economic standing to support the high arts.[32] The idea of music as art, as an intellectual pursuit of the highest possible complexity, became entrenched as the worthier practice, in contrast to the commercial urban popular styles designed to entertain the masses. Art music became the purview strictly of professionals. Only choral music remained an activity widely practiced by amateur singers, in churches and choral societies, especially in economically prosperous countries. As the century progressed, the composers of the French and German avant-garde composed choral music only for the professional choruses affiliated with the European radio stations, as the only ones with the capacity to perform their extremely complex textures. Based on the observation of programming practices of choral ensembles over the years, the conjecture arises that the increasing separation between the avant-garde composers and a wide audience in the 1960s came in part as a result of their lack of production of choral works for intermediate-level musicians. After all, these choral singers also tend to go to classical music concerts of all kinds.

It would be a serious error to suppose that no great musical works arose among the radical avant-garde simply because of its alienation from the regular listener. On the contrary, many compositions created under this aegis will endure the test of time, beyond today's controversies, but it is demonstrable that, so far, they have been embraced mostly by a small circle of devotees. Nevertheless, sometimes affiliation with other art forms—especially film and dance—could expand the public for avant-garde composers. Befriending the French and German avant-garde in the 1960s was a group of composers who had been able to develop original languages in Poland and Hungary, even within the Soviet sphere. Inspired by electronic music, they experimented with acoustic sonorities in such a way that they secured credibility as musical innovators, while at the same time igniting the curiosity of both publishers and regular concertgoers. Witold Lutoslawski (1913–94), Krzysztof Penderecki (b1933), and György Ligeti (1923–2006) had discovered the potential of sonority for its immanent expressive quality, separated from melody, harmony, and rhythm, while liberating sound from the traditional elements of a musical composition. Their soundscapes had such intrinsic interest in their materiality that they were absorbed often into film culture for their potential to express the horrors of recent wars and revolutions, or simple psychological unease. This gave them an unlikely foothold in broader culture. Consider, for example, the presence of Ligeti's music in Stanley Kubrick's 1968 film *2001: A Space Odyssey.* In fact, the relative success of these composers had tempted Pärt into exploring the techniques of sonority composition before 1968. As with his attempts with neoclassicism, polystylism, and serialism, these experiments proved briefly fruitful but were ultimately rejected.

Beyond the prestige of academia and new music institutes, in the broadest cultural sense, there ensued the perception that the connection between the avant-garde composer with the wide audience was lost. Or perhaps, the connection with the ideal of a large audience was lost, as composers felt the high-mindedness of their efforts constituted sufficient validation. Was there ever a large audience for art music before World War I? Before the nineteenth century, composers created for their own audience, circumscribed by their service to the aristocracy or to the Church. How many people were there in these circles? In the twentieth century, the patronage of the aristocracy all but disappeared, but in compensation, the rise of musicology in academia, and the marketing campaigns of record labels promoting the aristocratic culture of classical music have disseminated the masterpieces of composers from the past to a point where audiences for classical music now emerge from any social class and any country. Symphony orchestras and opera houses have become the sign that a city has achieved the proper urban dignity. After the extensive academic analysis of their merits, the composers of the past stand lionized and canonized in the culture. Living composers have pursued inclusion among them, but even as the audience for classical music today is arguably the largest it has ever been, the composers of the past also have become the competition of the composers of the present. The situation has grown complicated by the constant availability of content produced by mass media. The American phenomenon of commercial popular music, emulated throughout the world and accessible through dance halls, radio, recordings, television, movies, and all media, gradually has taken hold of the private listening time of most people. In a world flooded by information, cultural choices, immigrant displacement, job stress, and now social media, urban popular music has continued to be the easy companion of life, while art music, and especially that of the avant-garde, requires concentration and effort.[33]

As these cultural categories have settled, the art music composer has become the focus of niche groups. The more radical and bizarre his or her artistic language, the more prestige could be potentially gained among the supporters. A group of acolytes could enjoy the glowing certitude of consorting with a rare and unique musical experience, inaccessible to the uninitiated. Conversely, popularity with the masses could imply the loss of prestige for a composer, the selling out to commercial forces, and the renunciation of the discipline of intellectual discourse for vulgar popular success. It is in the midst of these polarizations that Pärt's new style, honed after his crisis in 1968, suddenly erupted in the late 1970s and early '80s as a third stream that confounded many in both the Soviet and Western establishments. The nature of his revolution consisted of breaking down the expected rules that paralyzed art music composers for decades, proposing that good music consisted of something else altogether.

PÄRT'S CULTURAL INFLUENCE AND ENSUING CONTROVERSIES

How can we judge if the events and the consequences in Pärt's life in 1968 had any long-standing cultural influence? Let us look at the context: in classical music, historians look back to clear transitions when the reiterated elements that conformed the accepted style and its respective artistic goals definitely changed. There have been style shifts in music that responded immediately and abruptly to major social and political convulsions, such as the Reformation, the French Revolution, and World War I, but there have been also gradual style shifts over long processes, such as the Industrial Revolution. Since much of the repertoire that we now call classical music was part of the fabric of religious and courtly life, it changed whenever the affected social classes changed. We can track the developments of classical music inside the higher social classes that wrote and kept records (the aristocracy, the clergy, and the artists and intellectuals who served them). Traditional folk styles preserved ethnic bonding in a comparatively immutable manner until the Industrial Revolution and the world wars provoked the migrations of large groups of people, gradually bringing many of these styles into the fold of the emerging urban popular genres.

By the time Pärt experienced the ostracism caused by his *Credo* of 1968, the separation seemed complete between the worlds of contemporary classical music and urban popular styles. During the student protests in Europe and Latin America in 1968, protest songs based on folk genres became the emblems of political discourse. Not so with contemporary classical music. Art music composers embraced the political diatribes through their compositions' titles, text choices, and musical narratives. After all, most of them espoused many left-leaning causes, worker and peasant rights, and even full-fledged communism. Furthermore, political causes seemed essential to artistic credibility at the time, to the point that composers originally from socialist countries, such as Krzysztof Penderecki, from Poland and a Catholic, would focus on the atomic bomb and the general cruelty of man, while having to remain circumspect about the communist domination of his country. Art music composers such as the Greek Iannis Xenakis (1922–2001) and the Italian Luigi Nono (1924–90) protested political repression, but their message stayed generally circumscribed to their audience of other intellectuals and artists, while support came from state institutions, not the audience. Their language continued to be uncompromisingly atonal and radical, alien to the taste of most regular concertgoers. Their music never exerted a national cohesive role such as Giuseppe Verdi achieved with the Italians during the *Risorgimento* in the nineteenth century. The great avant-garde German composer Hans Werner Henze (1926–2012), who collaborated many times with film and theater auteur Volker Schlöndorff (also a contributor to this volume), is quoted as saying that the composer had come "to depend for everything on what the system has to offer." The increasing awareness of this problem demanded that novel approaches to musical language and technology should include some form of genuine political engagement.[34]

It seemed inevitable that after the 1980s, with the dissolution of the Soviet Union, the clamor in the West in favor of socialism would seem anachronistic. Radical modernism gradually evolved into a postmodern irony, represented by the Argentinian Mauricio Kagel (1931–2008), the Brazilian Gilberto Mendes (1922–2016), and others. Art music composers turned their intellectual sword unto themselves, mocking their own system, seeking a recombination of the elements into surreal or multidiscursive edifices, while provoking wistful self-criticism. Composers in the Soviet Union continued to test polystylism, as Alfred Schnittke had done. The continuous pressure for Soviet musical realism relented somewhat in the early 1980s, when Pärt's contemporaries, such as the Tatar-Russian Sofia Gubaidulina (b. 1931) and the Georgian Giya Kancheli (b. 1935), enjoyed some tolerance in their explorations of a transcendent spirituality with elongated tempi and unusual tunings. After the dissolution of the Soviet Union in 1991, there ensued an inkling of alternative compositional solutions among post-Soviet composers, but they continued to use relatively grand symphonic and epic formats, a legacy of the Soviet era. At the same time, Western urban popular music began a process of refinement, adopting even classical music gestures (such as in the Beatles' *Sgt. Pepper's Lonely Hearts Club Band* LP of 1967),[35] iconic folk music practices, and increasingly better poetry. In short, commercial urban popular music started to aspire to be art.

Compared to these polarizations, the stylistic choices by Pärt appear truly radical. He did not turn towards any of the salient directions of the West or the ex-Soviet republics. He simply separated himself completely from the fray by going towards the deep past. Surprisingly, as a consequence of these choices, he upended many conventional relationships in the classical music profession, including those between creator and performer, between the live concert and the recorded album, and between the position of the artist as a high priest of culture above the corruptions served out by the marketing and branding of popular music. This happened in more than one fashion.

Pärt's search of compositional solutions in medieval and Renaissance music constituted only one facet of his relationship with this historic repertoire. His co-creative exchanges with eminent conductors who specialized in the performance practices of such repertoires emerged as an equally critical development, especially his rapport with Andres Mustonen, music director of the Estonian ensemble Hortus Musicus, and then, after migrating to Berlin, with the British conductor Paul Hillier, director of the Hilliard Ensemble. The success of his vocal music in live concerts eventually would depend on the approach to choral technique used for early music. This relationship between Pärt's contemporary music and pre-1600 performance practices turned out to be revelatory and influential. Although avant-garde composers in the West maintained ongoing relationships with instrumental and vocal virtuosos, their time arrow was "going forward" towards new and experimental performance techniques. Pärt benefited instead from the exquisite refinement of tuning, the vocal production without vibrato, and a nonemotional delivery appropriate for the sacred styles of Renaissance polyphony. The record suggests that Pärt remained uncertain of the quality of his choral music, including his breakout masterpiece, *Passio Domini Nostri Jesu Christi secundum Joannem* (1982), until Paul Hillier and the Hilliard Ensemble premiered and recorded it in 1988.[36] This recording secured Pärt's fame and prestige definitively. He also said, referring to another work, "without the Hilliard Ensemble, there would be no *Miserere*." This reveals that the perception of the quality of Pärt's vocal music in a live performance feels tied inextricably to the discipline of the historical performance practice of vocal music written before 1600. This aspect of Pärt's evolution must stand as an essential component of his outlier profile.

Contrary to standing twentieth-century practice, Pärt also designed the musical content of his compositions to remain viable through variable instrumentations. Pärt has reiterated the transcendence of polyphony over timbre by transcribing many of his pieces (such as *Fratres* and *Spiegel im Spiegel*) for diverse instrumental combinations, in opposition to what had been the practice of Western music since late Romanticism, whereby a piece of music ideally remained tied to its original instrument. With the rise of the mid-twentieth century's avant-garde, transcriptions of all kinds were deemed worthless musical exercises lacking in the necessary originality. Pärt ignored this pretension and integrated the art of transcription into his methodology.

Pärt also engaged in deep and co-creative relationships with other artists, especially with the record producer Manfred Eicher, who has led the label ECM (Edition of Contemporary Music) as an artist in his own right. This has to be viewed in the context of a professional culture that values the primacy of the author above all other persons involved in the generation of a new composition. Pärt's years as a sound engineer in Estonian Radio gave him the sensibility to compose his music with a view to recordings down the line. He would say that he counted Eicher and his team as his coauthors and among his blessings.[37] This suggests that his music's authentic point of perception can occur through the recording and not only through the live performance. This stands in many ways as a thoroughly radical concept. Pärt has accepted recordings as an alternative but equally valid mode of experiencing music, rather than a substitute in the absence of live performance. Although this may appear obvious to all of us who enjoy music regularly through a recorded medium, it is not clear that art music composers have accepted yet the recording as an end in itself, equivalent to live performance. Consider this fact with a view to the enormous difficulty that Pärt's pristine music poses to performers in a live concert. Apparently simple on the score, its success depends on impeccable delivery. The aesthetics of Pärt's sound owe a lot to record producer Eicher. Understanding the already discussed relationship between Pärt's music to the performance discipline of the virtuoso early music ensemble (as proven by conductor Paul Hillier), Eicher carefully designed Pärt's recorded sound, and matched it with beautifully designed packages and gorgeous photographs of austere landscapes imbued with spiritual longing, for a vivid interdisciplinary experience. In short, Eicher co-created the Arvo Pärt "brand" with the composer himself. Their association has changed the balance of artistic validity between the act of live performance and the creation of a recording as an artistic sound object, but also stoked controversies about Pärt's position as a genuine artist versus a commercial product.

These choices matched Pärt's own motivations and interartistic leanings as someone with a sensibility for the visual image, and who understood design as one of the foundations for his music. These interactions with star conductors and record producers fluidly merged with the marketing of Pärt's image, both by ECM and Universal Editions. There seemed to exist no friction between Pärt's own lifestyle as a devout Orthodox Christian, his public statements, and the brand created about him as an ascetic artist projecting the image of the composer as a prophet or a theologian equal to an Orthodox icon painter. He became, after all, the winner of the Ratzinger Prize for theological achievements in 2017. This brand has remained inviolable over thirty-five years because it is authentic. It also represents a successful application of what has been operational in popular music for decades. In short, Pärt did not reject a central aspect of modern celebrity culture. He has accepted it as a matter of contemporary life, and has not espoused the notion that this mode of branding is intrinsically corrupt.[38]

Another interesting interartistic phenomenon has taken place between Pärt's music and film. Without him being responsible for the dedicated soundtrack, oftentimes the austerity of his music becomes the perfect foil for harrowing images of human desolation and cruelty, as with Michael

Moore's 2004 film *Fahrenheit 9/11*. The film director acknowledges that Pärt's music had nothing to do directly with the content of his film. Nonetheless, his choice to use Pärt's music affords the viewer the ability to view the film, as it offers the balm necessary to endure the viewing, or a subtext of understanding of human frailty and folly in this world. The emotional austerity of the music allows it to be co-opted, legally or illegally, into countless videos and films online and on social media.[39] This case of conceptual blending has now become ubiquitous in film and video culture, also with other composers of a minimalist aesthetic.[40]

By the mid-1980s, Pärt began to be grouped among other composers labeled colloquially as "Holy Minimalists." This development attests to the growing awareness of his influence on contemporary music culture. The other composers typically named in this group include the Brit John Tavener (1944–2013), and the Pole Henryk Górecki (1933–2010). Neither of them used the *tintinnabuli* technique, but their mature styles developed out of examinations of austere aspects of sacred music, and their public personas had associations with a religion; John Tavener had converted to the Eastern Orthodox Church, and Górecki was a devout Catholic. They also cultivated musical languages that relied on slow tempi, incantatory repetition, and disciplined musical processes, even though these processes differed substantially from Pärt's. They both made a splash in popular culture, respectively with *The Song for Athene* performed during the funeral of Princess Diana, and the *Symphony of Sorrowful Songs*, that topped the British classical charts and sold more than a million copies. The term "Holy Minimalist" defined the concern with the sacred in all these composers, and separated them from the American Minimalists—Philip Glass (b. 1937), Steve Reich (b. 1936), and Terry Riley (b. 1935)—who came to develop musical processes with minimal materials, out of a study of Eastern music and Buddhism. It also both contrasts and parallels the work of other famous composers in the West who created works before 1970, also imbued with religious fervor but with different, nonminimalistic profiles, including Igor Stravinsky, Francis Poulenc, Maurice Duruflé, and Olivier Messiaen.

The label of "Holy Minimalist" belies an initial derision by critics, academics, and other composers alike, accusing the style of rejecting the heritage of Western music, which is assumed to be narrative, complex, and dialectic. The criticism implies, without stating it, a lack of diligence. Scottish composer James Macmillan (b. 1959), also a devout Catholic with a truly important oeuvre of sacred compositions, critiques Pärt's stylistic choices (and by extension Tavener's and Gorecki's) for their static discourse as a metaphor for eternity. He considers that the Western mind's need for dialectic argument represents the reality of worldly conflict and violence that can be resolved in the musical discourse.[41] The eminent theologian of the arts Jeremy Begbie also says: "The music of Pärt offers a cool sonic cathedral in a hot, rushed and overcrowded culture, and this is the reason for its popularity." He protests that this represents the assumption that the more we reach out to God, the more we separate from the world and its dynamics. "This goes against what Christ actually did, meaning, He engaged with the world to the point of Crucifixion." Pärt has not addressed directly these objections, but he has been clear about the theology of his music, one of representation of the serenity of God's countenance, as espoused in Eastern Christianity.[42] All other labels and explanations must contend with this declaration by the composer.

CONCLUDING NOTES

Time alone will give the measure of Pärt's revolutionary effect on Western art music after 1968. However, it is now clear that his personal choices, as delineated above, are seeping through the career paths of composers of the following generation. His influence on the culture of contemporary choral music seems certain. A tremendous rise in the composition of new music for chorus has taken place, especially in the ecstatic, serene, and nonnarrative style that generally describes Pärt's work. Estonian composers and other composers of the Baltic region are expected now to offer new choral repertoire to satisfy a thirst for sacred choral music with Pärt's stylistic profile. In many respects, choral ensembles and choral repertoire have become one of the most reliable professional outlets for contemporary art music composers, as an echo of Pärt's tremendous success with this genre. This reverses the trend of the mid-twentieth century, when popular choral repertoires remained circumscribed to pre-1940 styles, while cutting-edge stylistic debates were relegated to niche professional groups. The artistic merits of the followers of Pärt's influence remain very variable, perhaps because not all the composers aspire to the strict discipline that Pärt adopts with his own music.[43] Now that Pärt's success is undeniable, responses to his meditative style prosper both in Europe and North America. Latin America still has to react to his influence.

The reception of Pärt's music within orchestras is still evolving. The orchestral practice builds around the coalescence of extraordinary virtuosos. The performance of Pärt's slow lines and transparent atmospheres appears on the surface to neglect the orchestral player's capacity for extremely complex emotional narratives and high technical achievement. In other words, the challenges of performing a score by Pärt do not show ostensibly to the spectator. Perhaps the self-denying sacredness of the language seems alien to the symphonic concert hall, which emerged in the nineteenth century as Europe celebrated virtuosic individualism in composers and conductors. Still, in 2009 Pärt premiered his first symphony in forty years, titled *Los Angeles*, with the Los Angeles Philharmonic, led by their former music director Esa-Pekka Salonen. It could be argued that, because Salonen stands as the poster child of conductors and composers trained by the European avant-garde, this commission and première acknowledged that Pärt has joined the list of great composers of the twenty-first century. In a way, Pärt has come full circle.[44]

As Pärt enters the ninth decade of his life, conflicting forces still play in the musical establishments of both Western European and the former Soviet republics. We still find radical avant-garde composers. American minimalism is pervasive everywhere, especially in film music, and these previously rejected minimalist composers from both sides of the Atlantic have met with reluctant recognition in academia. Pärt's influence did not consist in superimposing his style above all others. In a career spanning fifty years after his crisis and self-transformation in 1968, Pärt has represented an exit from the polarizations in classical music that risked the connection with the audience and their concerns. This exit would be considered an individually chosen seclusion, apart from any discussions of a revolutionary cultural influence, should he have remained unknown and separate from the world. On the contrary, his success has posed important reevaluations in art music's professional culture. It proposes provocatively that a composer may be both rigorous and accessible; the path to a new style may lie in early music rather than in constant innovation; your performer can stand as your co-creator and not your servant; there are new artistic pathways embedded in the recording technologies; the career practices of popular music may still hold lessons for the art music composer; and more importantly, that music can be a sacrament, a connection to the divine, not always through narratives of human experience, but as a locus for timelessness and serenity. In so many ways, Pärt's crisis of 1968 led him on a quest for answers in the deep past of the European musical experience. He succeeded in finding something that he interpreted as sacred and essential, resurrecting it for generations to come. In so doing, he effected an unexpected revolutionary influence on the culture of Western art music.

NOTES

1. Articles and analyses about the decline of classical music are plentiful. The distinguished critic of the *Washington Post*, Anne Midgette, summarized the vagaries of this discussion in Midgette, "Classical Music: Dead or Alive," *Washington Post*, January 30, 2014, https://www.washingtonpost.com/news/style/wp/2014/01/30/classical-music-dead-or-alive/?utm_term=.c0b83f06d717.

2. Silver Tambur, "Arvo Pärt Is the Most Performed Living Composer Seventh Year Running," *Estonian World*, http://estonianworld.com/culture/arvo-part-worlds-performed-living-composer-seventh-year-running/.

3. Immo Mikhelson, "A Narrow Path to the Truth: Arvo Pärt and the 1960s and 70s in Soviet Estonia," in *The Cambridge Companion to Arvo Pärt*, ed. Andrew Shenton (Cambridge: Cambridge University Press, 2012), 11.

4. Ivana Medic, "I Believe . . . in What? Arvo Pärt's and Alfred Schnittke's Polystylistic Credos," *Slavonica* 16, no. 2 (2010): 96–111. Medic indicates that besides avant-garde music, the Soviet Union also officially condemned religious music, early music, and improvised music, not to mention Western rock, pop, and jazz.

5. Mikhelson, "A Narrow Path," 12.

6. The Estonian Music Information Center indicates that Kapp was a member of the Central Committee of the Estonian Communist Party (1951–61), ambassador of the Estonian Soviet's Supreme Council (1947–55), and the Soviet Union's Supreme Council (1954–62). He was also the chairman of the Estonian Composers' Union (1944–66), and rector of the conservatory (1949–57 and 1964–66), http://www.emic.ee/?sisu=heliloojad&mid=58&id=28&lang=eng&action=view&method=biograafia.

7. Mikhelson, "A Narrow Path," 17.

8. Hugh F. van den Berg addressed the avant-garde in van den Berg, "Some Introductory Notes on The Politics of a Label," in *Sound Commitments: Avant-Garde Music and the Sixties*, ed. Robert Adlington (New York: Oxford University Press, 2009), 21. He points out that the term "avant-garde" became pervasive as a synonym for "modern art" during the boom in culture after World

War II. The concept achieved a kind of hegemony in the period from about 1940 to about 1970. At this time, all artists (and composers with them) were aware of their radical stance vis-à-vis the rest of culture, cultivating a specialized critical discourse. For composers, this radical stance declined by 1980, but the term "avant-garde" remained an all-inclusive umbrella for all artistic "modernism," and hence, a shorthand for the values of innovation associated with it.

9. A perceptive and entertaining account of the achievements and fissures of contemporary art music, summarized in the next few paragraphs, can be found in Alex Ross, *The Rest Is Noise: Listening to the 20th Century* (New York: Picador, 2007).

10. The interactions between European and Latin American composers with the developments in either or both the Soviet Union and Cuba stand as too complex to discuss here, but they have garnered attention from scholars for their power in defining the actual artistic work and the dynamics between the individual composer and the surrounding audience and establishment. The reader can continue to investigate in Adlington, ed., *Sound Commitments*, and Ana Maria Alonso-Minutti, Eduardo Herrera, and Alejandro Madrid, eds., *Experimentalisms in Practice: Music Perspectives from Latin America* (Oxford: Oxford University Press, 2018).

11. Mikhelson, "A Narrow Path," 17.

12. Arnold Schoenberg (1874–1951) developed the technique of dodecaphony (also known as twelve-tone serialism, or twelve-tone technique) in 1921 to organize musical discourse after he abandoned functional tonality, the ruling system in Western music. Contrary to tonality, which determines the structural and perceptual preeminence of one note, the tonic, dodecaphony requires the composer to create a "series" using all twelve chromatic notes, manipulating them through procedures of transposition, inversion, retrograde motion, and retrograde inversion, so as to avoid giving any single note the rank of a tonic. The resulting harmonic environment is deemed to be atonal.

13. Mikhelson, "A Narrow Path," 14–15.

14. Paul Hillier, *Arvo Pärt* (New York: Oxford University Press, 1997), 36. Pärt recognized *Nekrolog* as his first mature work. Although ostensibly an obituary for the victims of fascism, he indicated that he saw it as an obituary for the living. In spite of the general criticism, the Estonian establishment acknowledged the seriousness of Pärt's compositional character and his high aims.

15. Medic, "I Believe . . . in What?," 97. She explains that "numerous Soviet composers, especially those belonging to the generation born in the 1930s and commonly referred to as non-conformist, 'avant-garde' or 'unofficial,' such as . . . Sofia Gubaidulina (b. 1931), Alfred Schnittke (1934–1998), Arvo Pärt (b. 1935), Alemdar Karamanov (b. 1935), and Valentin Silvestrov (b. 1937), renounced dialectical materialism, embarked upon a search for spiritual values, and devel-

oped a fascination with the powerful taboo that was religion" (97). These composers resorted to polystylistic languages to express these ideas. Pärt did the same, but only briefly.

16. Arvo Pärt, interview for *Creation and Time*, a radio program hosted by Ivalo Randalu, September 11, 1968, Estonian Public Broadcasting Sound Archives, ASCDR1716.

17. Medic, "I Believe . . . in What?" 96.

18. Ibid., 101.

19. Mikhelson, "A Narrow Path," 27.

20. Ibid., 36–37.

21. It may be perceived as incongruous, but it could be asserted that Pärt returned to the serene religious styles of the past seeking the comforting and the familiar at a time of personal crisis. In chapter 4 in this volume, Eric Drott considers that revolutionary genres tend to be characterized by a return to the familiar, to learned repertoires of political and artistic action. Pärt did not write revolutionary songs, of course, and none of the religious styles were "familiar" to him as someone who grew up in Soviet Estonia, but these styles may have been missed in the West, after the musical disruptions of Vatican II. Witness the popularity of early music ensembles around the same time.

22. Mikhelson, "A Narrow Path," 36.

23. Ivan Moody, "Music as a Sacred Art," *Contemporary Music Review* 12, no. 2 (1995): 23–34.

24. For a comprehensive and detailed overview of *tintinnabuli*, the reader can refer to Paul Hillier, *Arvo Pärt*, and Paul Hillier and Tõnu Tormis, *On Pärt* (Copenhagen: Theatre of Voices Edition, 2005).

25. For a detailed review of Pärt's serialist techniques explained here, refer to Thomas Robinson, "Analyzing Pärt," in Shenton, ed., *The Cambridge Companion to Arvo Pärt*, 75–110.

26. John Tavener, "The Sacred in Art," *Contemporary Music Review* 12, no. 2 (1995): 49–54.

27. Leo Normet, "The Beginning of Silence," *Teater. Muusika. Kino* 7 (1988): 37–47.

28. Andrew Shenton, "In His Own Words," in Shenton, ed., *The Cambridge Companion to Arvo Pärt*, 112.

29. Robert Adlington, "Introduction," in Adlington, ed., *Sound Commitments*, 4–6. Indeed, there was a widespread conviction that aesthetic experiment and social progressiveness made natural bedfellows. At the same time, this stance inevitably threw up some sharp dilemmas. And although some avant-garde musicians were content simply to graft a political element onto their existing musical preoccupations in a manner that could be viewed as essentially self-congratulatory and condescending—"radical chic" was the term coined by the

writer Tom Wolfe—others felt compelled to question the very principles of their creative practice.

30. Benjamin Piekut, "Demolish Serious Culture," in Adlington, ed., *Sound Commitments*, 38–51.

31. The concert programs of many major symphony orchestras in the United States provide a ready demonstration of donor tiers, tied to privileges of exclusive interaction with conductors and performers.

32. Paul Hillier, the brilliant conductor who helped establish Pärt in the West, also commented in direct conversations with me that "the sounds of early music—timbre, articulation, and particularly vocal sonority—have provided a new range of expressive potential which quite a number of contemporary composers seem to find beneficial for their own music." I contend that early music sounds related to music created for the Church have now become an aesthetic choice available to composers besides the experimentations of the avant-garde.

33. Indeed, Michael Seidman in chapter 12 of this volume says that "the weight of young people in the population, their increasing years of schooling, and their consequently delayed entry into full-time wage labor or individual entrepreneurship provided a large potential constituency for the spread of anti-work ideology." Alongside these social and economic realities, it was commercial urban popular music that came to occupy the preeminent space of companionship to daily life, especially among the unoccupied youth, and not the old folk genres or the works of the avant-garde composer.

34. Beate Kutsche, "Aesthetic Theories and Revolutionary Practice," in Adlington, ed., *Sound Commitments*, 90–91.

35. Steve Marinucci, "Why The Beatles' 'Sgt. Pepper's Lonely Hearts Club Band' Should Be Considered Classical Music," *Variety*, http://variety.com/2017/music/news/beatles-sgt-peppers-anniversary-classical-music-1202450173/.

36. Enzo Restagno, *Arvo Pärt Peeglis, Arvo Pärt peeglis: Vestlused, esseed ja artiklid*, trans. Maarja Kangro et al. (Tallinn: Eesti Entsüklopeediakirjastus, 2005), 77.

37. Steve Lake and Paul Griffiths, *Horizons Touched: The Music of ECM* (London: Granta, 2007), 381.

38. "100 Estonian Brands," http://www.estonianbrands.com/arvo-part.

39. Laura Dolp, "Arvo Pärt in the Marketplace," in Shenton, ed., *The Cambridge Companion to Arvo Pärt*, 177.

40. The film by C. T. Dreyer, *The Passion of Joan of Arc*, proves to be a fascinating parallel case, demonstrating the emergence of a possible trend, as its painful story can be seen now accompanied by the soothing oratorio *Voices of Light* of American composer Richard Einhorn.

41. Andrew Shenton, "The Essential and Phenomenal Arvo Pärt," in Shenton, ed., *The Cambridge Companion to Arvo Pärt*, 8.

42. Ibid.

43. "Chorally Fixated on Arvo Pärt and Eric Whitacre," in *The New Canon*, a radio program, https://www.wqxr.org/story/204796-chorally-fixated-on-arvo-part-and-eric-whitacre/.

44. Review of Los Angeles Philharmonic, http://www.latimes.com/entertainment/arts/la-et-cm-la-phil-part-review-20160523-snap-story.html.

BIBLIOGRAPHY

Adlington, Robert, ed. *Sound Commitments: Avant-Garde Music and the Sixties.* New York: Oxford University Press, 2009.

Begbie, Jeremy, and Steven R. Guthrie, eds. *Resonant Witness: Conversations between Music and Theology.* Grand Rapids, MI: Wm. B. Eerdmans, 2011.

Bouteneff, Peter. *Arvo Pärt: Out of Silence.* Yonkers, NY: St. Vladimir's Seminary Press, 2015.

Griffith, Paul. *Modern Music and After.* New York: Oxford University Press, 2010.

Harley, Maria Anna. "To Be God with God: Catholic Composers and the Mystical Experience." *Contemporary Music Review* 12, no. 2 (1995): 25–45.

Hillier, Paul. *Arvo Pärt.* Oxford: Oxford University Press, 1997.

Hillier, Paul, and Tõnu Tormis. *On Pärt.* Copenhagen: Theatre of Voices Edition, 2005.

McCarthy, Jamie. "An Interview with Arvo Pärt." *Contemporary Music Review* 12, no. 2 (1995): 55–64.

Medic, Ivana. "I Believe . . . in What? Arvo Pärt's and Alfred Schnittke's Polystylistic Credos." *Slavonica* 16, no. 2 (2010): 96–111.

Moody, Ivan. "Music as a Sacred Art." *Contemporary Music Review* 12, no. 2 (1995): 23–34.

Pärt, Arvo. *Credo.* Vienna: Universal Editions, 1968.

———. *Für Alina.* Vienna: Universal Editions, 1976.

———. *Miserere.* Vienna: Universal Editions, 1989/1992.

———. *Passio domini nostri Jesu Christi secundum Johannem.* Vienna: Universal Editions, 1982.

———. *Symphony No. 4 "Los Angeles."* Vienna: Universal Editions, 2009.

Ross, Alex. *The Rest Is Noise: Listening to the 20th Century.* New York: Picador, 2007.

Shenton, Andrew. "The Essential and Phenomenal Arvo Pärt." In *The Cambridge Companion to Arvo Pärt*, edited by Andrew Shenton, 1–9. Cambridge: Cambridge University Press. Kindle edition.

SEVENTEEN

Words as Acts

A Literary Rebellion

ALONSO CUETO

There was a time when Peruvian authors really thought they could make a change by writing novels. The 1960s offered a suitable environment for this illusion. I seek to show that the faith that fueled these authors has not been completely lost, at the very least not in the case of one of them.

The idea of literature as a weapon of revolution and social utopia took hold among Peruvian and Latin American intellectuals and writers during the 1960s. This understanding had to do with two key factors: migration and the Cuban Revolution. In the middle of the twentieth century, Latin America was waking up to a new awareness of its social problems. The region was an ensemble of societies in movement. A great migration from villages to cities had already taken place, with metropolises such as Mexico D.F., Buenos Aires, and Bogota each harboring several million inhabitants. Alfredo Lattes indicates that the increase in urbanization in Latin America between 1950 and 1975 affected between 41.4 and 61.2 percent of the total population.[1] In Lima, the migration that had started in the 1920s grew in strength in the 1940s and saw the population increase eightfold in the course of forty years. According to the National Statistical Institute of Peru, the capital's population grew from 600,000 people in 1940 to 1,900,000 in 1960 and to 4,800,000 inhabitants in 1980.[2] Migration turned Lima into a city of immense proportions that slipped out of the control of inefficient and inert governments. The arrival of Andean immigrants to the outer rims of the city heightened both the racism and discrimination of the traditional society and the awareness, prevalent among intellectual and university circles, of an unjust social reality in need of a change.

Peruvian fiction soon reflected these changes. The novels and short stories of the 1950s presented the capital as a chaotic and crowded center plagued by violence and poverty. Enrique Congrains's *Lima Hora Zero* (1954) (Lima, Zero Hour), Julio Ramón Ribeyro's *Los Gallinazos sin Plumas* (1955) (The Gallinazos without Feathers), and Sebastián Salazar Bondy's *Náufragos y sobrevivientes* (1954) (Shipwrecked and Survivors) all portray Lima as an extended megapolis, a no-man's-land subject to the law of the strongest. Lima is a city marked by a mosaic of races and ethnicities. Mario Vargas Llosa creates a similar image in his first novel, *The Time of the Hero* (1963). Its setting is the military boarding school called Leoncio Prado in the La Punta neighborhood of Callao, which brings together students from different races and points of origin within the country. The mountain-dweller Cava, the Black Vallano, and the Caucasian Alberto from Lima form a small society that reflects the diversity of a multicultural and multiethnic country, very much like the one Lima had acquired as a result of the migrations.[3] This novel presents settings and characters that represent the cultural and racial variety of the Peruvian society, as do his two subsequent works—*The Green House* (1967) and *Conversation in the Cathedral* (1969). The plot of the former takes place in the Peruvian jungle and the coastal desert-like region of Piura. The latter unfolds during General Odría's government (1948–56). Both weave together characters from different races and regions of origin in a single panoramic picture reflective of the racial and ethnic diversity of the Peruvian society.

The influence of the movements for political change and, in particular, the Cuban Revolution, also define the climate of this decade. The Cuban Revolution provided a concrete example to those calling for a revolution to deal with social injustice. Fidel Castro's struggle convinced many of the worthiness of fighting for a social utopia. The evidence in support of this idea was that the latter had come to fruition in the Caribbean country. As far as the means of achieving such a goal were concerned, there was a certainty that any sacrifice was worth it. The ideals of social utopia and rebellion found many followers in Mexico, Argentina, Peru, and the rest of the continent under the slogan "The end justifies the means." Indeed, in the introduction to his last book, *La llamada de la tribu* (2018) (*The Call of the Tribe*), Vargas Llosa remembers his first affiliation with the Cuban Revolution: "Just like me, many perceived Fidel's feat not just as the heroic and generous adventure of idealist fighters who wanted to put an end to Batista's corrupt dictatorship, but also as a non-sectarian socialism that would allow for criticism, diversity and even dissidence. Many of us believed this and it was this perception that made it possible for the Cuban Revolution to garner such massive support from all over the world during its first years."[4]

These factors—the movement from villages to cities and the advent of the Cuban Revolution—created a setting favorable to the idea of the novel as an instrument of strife. If Vargas Llosa had not matured as a writer in the 1960s, if he had not absorbed the spirit of an era marked by an impetus for change and a spirit of rebelliousness, he would most likely not have become the writer he is. The 1960s deeply affected his conceptualization of rebellion and freedom as history's driving forces, and his understanding of utopia and of the power that words and novels wield.

Jean-Paul Sartre is crucial in the relationship that Vargas Llosa develops with the decade in which he produced his first novels. This influence is rooted in the author's experience in Paris, where he spent several years as a young man from 1959 onward. The French tradition of the intellectual enthralls Vargas Llosa. The intellectual, as conceptualized by Emile Zola on the occasion of the Dreyfus affair, is not only a creator but also a thinker and a moral conscience that influences the march of his or her society. This French tradition of perceiving an author as a moral conscience of the collective had also been adopted by Victor Hugo, another one of the writers greatly admired by Vargas Llosa, and this is firmly rooted in the Peruvian novelist's understanding of what it means to be an author. Other intellectuals, such as Malraux with his passionate discourses as a minister in de Gaulle's cabinet, also fascinate him. But Sartre remains his greatest influence. Upon reading *What Is Literature?* for the first time, Vargas Llosa was captivated by Sartre's definition of a writer: "Thus, the prose-writer is a man who has chosen a certain method of secondary action which we may call action by disclosure. It is therefore permissible to ask him this second question: 'What aspect of the world do you want to disclose? What change do you want to bring into the world by this disclosure?' The 'engaged' writer knows that words are action. He knows that to reveal is to change and that one can reveal only by planning to change."[5]

Sartre claims that words are actions, actions of disclosure and creation of a new awareness. Thus, they are agents of change. Authoring a novel that stirs up social consciousness is thus a form of subversion. According to Sartre, each word is an irrevocable act, a trace that marks an author's passage through the world, and the simple action of writing, delving into reality beyond the appearances supplied by the established system, contains a moral message and produces a real effect. To write is to disclose and, thus, to rebel. To write is to fight against the lies and the justifications advanced by the system. Sartre perceives fiction as the most suitable instrument in an engaged artist's toolkit precisely because it is the best way to make sense of reality and to call attention to its injustices. This is why he insists that novelists are "directors of being": "But, if we know that we are directors of being, we also know that we are not its producers. If we turn away from this landscape, it will sink back into its dark permanence."[6]

The fact that no novel had ever been written in defense of dictatorships, oppressors, or their immorality seemed to convincingly demonstrate novels' moral value to Sartre in *What Is Literature?* According to him, even though authors could espouse a fascist ideology, their novels could not. In his personal memoir *A Writer's Reality* (1991), Vargas Llosa refers to Sartre's influence on his own work:

> I liked Sartre's idea that literature is not and cannot be gratuitous, that it is unacceptable for literature to be pure entertainment, that literature is serious because a writer, through his books, can be a voice in society, can change things in life. I knew by heart the presentation of *Le Temps Modernes*, a literary magazine Sartre published in France in the late forties, in which he said that words are acts that can produce social change, historical change, and that if a writer has this power he has the moral obligation to use it to fight for the victims of society, denouncing all the mystifications, all the wrong doings of his time.[7]

This idea that words are acts and that a novel can contribute in a meaningful way to social strife and social change decisively marks Vargas Llosa's works of the 1960s, throughout the course of which he follows

Sartre's instructions to be an intellectual activist. He writes a chronicle of the Cuban Revolution during the missile crisis, pays homage to Javier Heraud, the Peruvian poet who lost his life in a guerrilla adventure in 1963, and defends the guerrilla insurgency during Fernando Belaúnde's first government in Peru.

All of these are clear traces of the context in which Vargas Llosa writes his novels in the 1960s. The premise of *The Time of the Hero* (1963), *The Green House* (1966), and *Conversation in the Cathedral* (1969) supposes that the system is responsible for the moral degradation of those who make it up, as Efraín Kristal has wisely observed.[8] However, little by little Vargas Llosa's idea of freedom becomes incompatible with the idea of political engagement. Another Peruvian writer, José María Arguedas, author of *Deep Rivers* (first published in Spanish in 1958), writes a letter to him and singles him out as his successor in social and political strife. Sebastián Salazar Bondy, author of *Lima la Horrible* (1965) (Lima, the Horrible), does the same. They believe that Vargas Llosa's work contributes to the awakening of a new conscience and, thus, to the revolution.[9] This idea of a panoramic representation of reality was key to their conception of the novel as an instrument of change. As Sartre had proposed, only the novels that portrayed societies with their injustices and deficiencies could bring about a real change. Vargas Llosa refers to this idea in his famous acceptance speech of the Rómulo Gallegos prize—"Literature Is Fire"—in 1967.[10] His understanding of literature as an act of rebellion is admirably described in this speech, and serves as a point of reference for the works of all the writers of his generation:

> This idea of utopia, which can be traced back to a phrase uttered in May 1968 ("Let's be realist. Let's demand the impossible."), is reflected in different ways in the works of Vargas Llosa, García Márquez, Carlos Fuentes, and Julio Cortázar. Rebellion and utopia are two concepts that interrelate and feed off of one another. These authors seek and hope for a change, and this motif is intimately related to the period they work in.[11]

The first significant disagreement between Vargas Llosa and Sartre takes place on the occasion of a statement that the French philosopher makes in an interview with Madeleine Chapsal published by *Le Monde.* Sartre believes that, when faced with a choice between writing and playing a political role, any writer should stop writing and take a political stand in his or her society. In his 1964 article "Los otros contra Sartre" ("The Others against Sartre"), Vargas Llosa rejects this claim "with disappointment and bitterness"[12] and insists that literature plays an important social and historical role that is neither immediate nor direct. In the same paragraph, Vargas Llosa cites Claude Simon's ironic response to Sartre: If writers were to give up writing in order to teach African children how to read and write, these readers would only have translations of Sartre's work available. "How could I—a native of an underdeveloped country who is trying to write novels in Paris—fail to support Claude Simon on this issue?" asks Vargas Llosa.[13]

Later on, he comments on Sartre's statement, "I have seen children starving to death. In the face of a dying child, *Nausea* does not stand the comparison." In response, Vargas Llosa once more cites Claude Simon: "When did we start using the same scale to compare corpses and literature?" Nevertheless, he proceeds to agree with Sartre's key ideas about the engaged writer. "What does it mean to be engaged? . . . that by writing we did not only realize a vocation, something through which we brought our dreams to fruition. We realized a state of mind, a state of spirit . . . and we somehow participated in the marvelous and exciting enterprise of solving problems and making the world better."[14]

This relationship between Vargas Llosa and Sartre illustrates a crucial aspect of what being an intellectual and a writer means in Latin America. Sartre believes that a writer should be a political activist, someone who promotes ideas, participates in rebellions, and makes public declarations. But he should also be an important actor in his country's social and political strife. This is the dilemma that the protagonist of *Conversation in the Cathedral* faces, particularly from chapter 4 onward. Santiago Zavala wants to make the transition from thinking to acting. He wants to act but, deep down in his mind, he doubts the Marxist ideology that he espouses. Vargas Llosa, just like Sartre, believes that the intellectual and the writer express a moral voice. They represent the conscience of their society and should direct its strife in search of a clear objective.

In the 1970s, Vargas Llosa's distancing from Sartre and subsequent affiliation with Camus's (1981) ideas become especially marked.[15] Camus's idealist skepticism is much more aligned with the Vargas Llosa of the

1970s who has forsaken the revolutionary ideals of the previous decade. Vargas Llosa abandons his admiration of Sartre and instead admires the work and ideals of Camus. Camus does not represent an artist committed to a cause or an ideology; he is committed to his own individual and moral conscience. Doubt, not certainty, defines him.

This change coincides with a shift in the protagonists of his novels from the 1970s. From *Captain Pantoja and the Special Service* (1973) onward, his characters are portrayed as individuals whose commitments are nuanced by doubt and humor. As Efraín Kristal indicates, the novels written in the 1980s portray rebels as crazy or enlightened individuals who oppose the natural march of their societies.[16] The rebel is no longer a moral hero who seeks the truth, but a saboteur who wants to subject reality to his or her whims. This is the defining feature of El Conselheiro in *The War of the End of the World* (1981), and Mayta in *The Real Life of Alejandro Mayta* (1984). If his characters of the 1960s had moral conscience on their side, the rebels in his novels of the 1980s are dangerous individuals capable of making reality shake and sway. This shift coincides with Vargas Llosa's rejection of Marxism in favor of liberalism.

Nevertheless, the same ideas of Sartre's that had influenced Vargas Llosa throughout the 1960s made an unexpected comeback in the latter's novels published since the 1990s. In his most recent works, Vargas Llosa no longer blames social ills on the system—like he did in *The Time of the Hero*. Nor does he characterize rebels as delirious individuals—like he did in *The War of the End of the World* and *The Real Life of Alejandro Mayta*. Instead, he praises the hero's commitment to rebelling.

It is legitimate to argue that his most recent novels are marked by multiple traces of his original understanding of literature as praise of rebels and a document of social influence. In a paragraph in *Conversaciones en Princeton*, he states:

> If good novels teach us to see reality in a more complex way, great novels show us that appearances do not say it all, that they are but a deceitful surface, and that, to truly understand the world, one must thoroughly investigate in order to discover the mechanisms behind behaviors and facts. Literature generates pleasure, makes us enjoy it, shows us the immense possibilities of language, but it also makes us

> more skeptical of reality. It encourages us to go beyond appearances to see what is behind a social, political or personal event. This is a function not of literature in particular, but of art in general.[17]

If the migration to the cities (and Lima in particular) and the Cuban Revolution exerted a decisive influence on Vargas Llosa's attitude in the 1960s, his return to his old ideas is marked by two contemporary phenomena, namely, globalization and the widespread protests in favor of women's rights, the legalization of drugs, and the rights of the LGBTQ community. These events have characterized the new century and have left their mark on his ideas and his new heroes.[18] A series of testimonies has demonstrated Vargas Llosa's awareness of the fight for gender equality and a free expression of sexual identities. Globalization, in turn, has led him to defend travelers and migrants.[19]

Not only have these topics been the focus of numerous articles, they have also become the central motifs of *The Way to Paradise* (2003), *The Bad Girl* (2006), *The Dream of the Celt* (2010), *The Discreet Hero* (2013), and *The Neighborhood* (2016). In these novels, Vargas Llosa once more portrays the world as a setting plagued by corruption and violence that could, nevertheless, be saved by a hero. Social utopia and paradise are illusions, not tangible realities. However, the stories collected in these novels mark a revival of social rebellion, this time from the perspective of individual behavior. In *The Way to Paradise*, Flora Tristan's rebellion against established social norms (through her fight for women's rights and gender equality, among others) serves as a parallel to the revolution in the arts exemplified by Gauguin's works. *The Bad Girl* marks the first time a woman has been one of the protagonists and has played the decisive role in a Vargas Llosa novel's plot. *The Dream of the Celt* praises Roger Casement, the homosexual character who fights for the rights of the indigenous people in Putumayo and the rebels in Ireland. He is a rebel both on the social and political scene—and in his sexuality. *The Discreet Hero* tells the story of a man who resists extortion and finds out that his son is the man behind the scheme. *The Neighborhood* describes a heroic journalist's rebellion against the system of Fujimori[20] and Montesinos.

The main characters in these novels are marginals who overcome their own social position in order to realize personal and social feats: a homosexual, three women, an artist, a family man. Their feats could be crowned by success or they could fail, but Vargas Llosa is unconditionally on their side. His characters are lucid, conscious, and resolute. His novels once more praise rebels, but these rebels from the new century do not always seek to transform the entire political system. In contrast to Sartre's heroes, they do not profess a Marxist ideology. They are heroes of liberalism. Their morals are personal.

Throughout his life as a writer, Vargas Llosa never forsook the idea learned in the 1960s that literature is not a gratuitous pleasure but a form of engagement that a writer has with him- or herself and those around him. In this sense, a recent declaration applies both to his body of work and to his life: "This is the great idea at the root of existentialism that marked me and marked a whole generation. Sartre demonstrated that literature is not a gratuitous pleasure, but an instrument that helps the reader understand reality, because it opens up an ethical, moral vision before him/her. This is why literature in particular and culture in general are indispensable."[21]

This is why, in a broad sense, the spirit of the 1960s lives on in his works. His novels continue to extol his idea of the purest human: the transgressor, the rebel, the hero with moral principles. A romantic author, he carries on firmly on the side of Prometheus's race, even at eighty-two and after having published dozens of novels, essays, and plays.

NOTES

1. Alfredo Lattes, "Población urbana y urbanización en la America Latina," in *II Jornadas Iberoamericanas de Urbanismo sobre las Nuevas Tendencias de la Urbanización en América Latina* (Quito: BiblioFlacosoandes, 2000), 49–76.

2. Instituto Nacional de Estadística e Informática, "Lima Metropolitana Perfil Socio-Demográfico," August 12, 2007; see Eduardo Arroyo, *El Centro de Lima: Uso social del espacio* (Lima: Fundación Friedrich Ebert, 1994).

3. Vargas Llosa: "The idea I had of my country was a very short, very brief idea"; Sergio Vilela Galván, *El Cadete Vargas Llosa: La historia oculta tras "La ciudad y los perros"* (Lima: Planeta, 2003), 24.

4. Mario Vargas Llosa, *La llamada de la tribu* (Barcelona: Alfaguara, 2018), 13.

5. Jean Paul Sartre, *What Is Literature and Other Essays*. Introduction by Steven Ungar (Cambridge, MA: Harvard University Press, 1988), 37.

6. Ibid.

7. Mario Vargas Llosa, *A Writer's Reality* (Syracuse, NY: Syracuse University Press, 1991), 49.

8. Efraín Kristal, *Tentación de la Palabra: Arte literario y convicción político en las novelas de Mario Vargas Llosa* (Lima: Fondo de Cultura Económica, 2018).

9. Ibid.

10. Speech delivered on August 4, 1967, in Caracas, Venezuela.

11. See Mario Vargas Llosa, "Literature Is Fire," speech, Caracas, Venezuela, August 4, 1967.

12. Mario Vargas Llosa, *Entre Sartre y Camus* (Río Piedras, Puerto Rico: Ediciones Huracán, 1981), 45.

13. Ibid., 47.

14. Ibid. All information about Vargas Llosa's debate with Sartre and his rapprochement with Camus can be consulted in José Miguel Oviedo, "Entre Sartre y Camus," in *Specular Narratives: Critical Perspectives on Carlos Fuentes, Juan Goytisolo, Mario Vargas Llosa*, edited by Roy Boland and Inger Enkvist (Melbourne: La Trobe University, 1997), 183–93.

15. The change in the nature of Vargas Llosa's novels coincides with the changes in Spanish American literature more broadly. The following generation of writers follows a new paradigm, alien to the awareness of social strife. See Oviedo, "Entre Sartre y Camus."

16. Kristal, *Tentación de la palabra*.

17. Mario Vargas Llosa, *Conversación en Princeton con Rubén Gallo* (Barcelona: Alfaguara, 2017).

18. Winston Manrique Sabogal, "Legalizar la droga es la única solución para acabar con el narcotráfico" [Legalizing drugs is the only way to end drug trafficking], *El País*, September 18, 2012; "Apoyo a campaña Déjala decidir" [I support the "Let Her Decide" campaign], *América Noticias*, April 2, 2014; "Mario Vargas Llosa encabeza movimiento a favor de la 'Unión Civil' gay en Perú" [Mario Vargas Llosa heads the movement in favor of Civil Union for homosexual couples], *La Républica*, September 30, 2013.

19. On several occasions, Vargas Llosa has used his own mother, a migrant to the United States, as an example; see Mario Vargas Llosa, "Los inmigrantes," *El País*, August 24, 1996.

20. President of Peru from 1990 to 2000.

21. Vargas Llosa, *Conversación en Princeton con Rubén Gallo*, 112.

BIBLIOGRAPHY

"Apoyo a campaña Déjala decidir" [I support the "Let Her Decide" campaign]. *América Noticias*, April 2, 2014.

Arguedas, José María. *Los ríos profundos*. Buenos Aires: Losada, 1958.

Arroyo, Eduardo. *El Centro de Lima: Uso social del espacio*. Lima: Fundación Friedrich Ebert, 1994.

Congrains Martín, Enrique. *Lima, Hora Cero*. Lima: Populibros Peruanos, 1954.

Instituto Nacional de Estadística e Informática. "Lima Metropolitana Perfil Socio-Demográfico." August 12, 2007.

Kristal, Efraín. *Tentación de la Palabra: Arte literario y convicción político en las novelas de Mario Vargas Llosa*. Lima: Fondo de Cultura Económica, 2018.

Lattes, Alfredo. "Población urbana y urbanización en la America Latina." In *II Jornadas Iberoamericanas de Urbanismo sobre las Nuevas Tendencias de la Urbanización en América Latina*, 49–76. Quito: BiblioFlacosoandes, 2000. https://biblio.flacsoandes.edu.ec/catalog/resGet.php?resId=19146.

"Mario Vargas Llosa encabeza movimiento a favor de la 'Unión Civil' gay en Perú" [Mario Vargas Llosa heads the movement in favor of civil union for homosexual couples]. *La Républica*, September 30, 2013.

Oviedo, José Miguel. "Entre Sartre y Camus." In *Specular Narratives: Critical Perspectives on Carlos Fuentes, Juan Goytisolo, Mario Vargas Llosa*, edited by Roy Boland and Inger Enkvist, 183–93. Melbourne: La Trobe University, 1987.

Ramón Ribeyro, Julio. *Los Gallinazos sin Plumas*. Lima: Fond de Cultura Económica, 1955.

Sabogal, Winston Manrique. "Legalizar la droga es la única solución para acabar con el narcotráfico" [Legalizing drugs is the only way to end drug trafficking]. *El País*, September 18, 2012.

Salazar Bondy, Sebastián. *Lima la Horrible*. Lima: Populibros Peruanos, 1965.

———. *Náufragos y sobrevivientes: Cuentos*. Lima: Club del Libro Peruano, 1954.

Sartre, Jean-Paul. *What Is Literature?* Translated by Bernard Frechtman. London: Methuen, 1950.

Vargas Llosa, Mario. *A Writer's Reality*. Syracuse, NY: Syracuse University Press, 1991.

———. *Cinco esquinas*. Miami, FL: Alfaguara, 2016.

———. *Conversación en la Catedral*. Barcelona: Seix Barral, 1969.

———. *Conversación en Princeton con Rubén Gallo*. Barcelona: Alfaguara: Penguin Random House Grupo Editorial, 2017.

———. *El héroe discreto*. Doral, FL: Alfaguara, 2013.

———. *El paraíso en la otra esquina*. Madrid: Alfaguara, 2003.

———. *El sueño del celta*. Doral, FL: Alfaguara/Santillana, 2010.

———. *Entre Sartre y Camus*. Río Piedras, Puerto Rico: Ediciones Huracán, 1981.

———. *Historia de Mayta*. 658. Barcelona: Seix Barral, 1984.

———. *La casa verde*. Barcelona: Seix Barral, 1983.

———. *La ciudad y los perros.* Barcelona: Editorial Seix Barral, 1963.

———. *La llamada de la tribu.* Barcelona: Alfaguara, 2018.

———. "Literature Is Fire." Speech, Caracas, Venezuela, August 4, 1967.

———. "Los inmigrantes." *El País*, August 24, 1996.

———. *Pantaleón y Las Visitadoras.* Barcelona: Editorial Seix Barral, 1973.

———. *Travesuras de la niña mala.* Mexico: Alfaguara, 2006.

Vilela Galván, Sergio. *El Cadete Vargas Llosa: La historia oculta tras "La ciudad y los perros."* Lima: Planeta, 2003.

EIGHTEEN

Reform or Revolution

Latin America's Dilemma in the "Long '68"

IGNACIO WALKER

I was seventeen at the time of the military coup on September 11, 1973, in Chile (our 9/11). I belong to that generation. We were a generation that was shaped by both the lofty aspirations for meaningful social and economic change that had emerged in the 1960s, encapsulated by the year 1968, and the battle between reform-minded and revolutionary politicians over how these changes were to be implemented. Coming out of this context, our lives would never be the same following the traumatic 1973 coup, which was itself a manifestation of the broader process of democratic breakdown and authoritarianism that took place in Latin America in the late 1960s and the early 1970s (the "Long '68").[1]

At the time of the coup I was a high school senior about to graduate from Saint George's College, a Catholic school in Santiago run by the Congregation of Holy Cross. My school was founded in the 1940s as an English school for boys and ended up being, by the early 1970s, a true example of a "liberating education." This concept had been coined by the

Latin American bishops in their Medellín (Colombia) Conference of 1968 (yes, 1968!). Saint George's had gone through a radical process of transformation since this meeting—to which I shall refer in greater detail later in this chapter—and our education was heavily influenced by Vatican II and its far-reaching implications in the life of the Church in Chile, in Latin America, and worldwide. Coeducation, self-discipline, and social and economic integration in a school that was aimed at the formation of future elites were some of the central aspects of this educational reform, which took place within the context of deep social, political, and cultural transformations that were being undertaken in Chile and in Latin America.[2]

Following the coup, the military junta notably intervened in only one private school in Chile, Saint George's College. Its priests were accused of being "Marxists"—in fact they were simply committed to social justice—and they were all expelled from the school, and some of them from the country. A commander of the air force was appointed as the principal of Saint George's. From September to December 1973, in the year of our graduation (in Chile the academic year finishes in December), Saint George's was surrounded by military soldiers who were transported in a bus from the nearby Escuela Militar Bernardo O'Higgins, a military school only a few blocks away. Their presence had the clear purpose of intimidating the academic community, including the students. Every day at 8 a.m. we sang the national anthem, including the second paragraph that had been reintroduced by the military following the coup: "vuestros nombres valientes soldados" ("your names brave soldiers"). Some of us remained silent as this second paragraph was being sung. It was my first (silent) protest against the military regime. Later on, at the age of twenty-three, this experience would lead me to become a human rights lawyer at the Vicariate of Solidarity of the Catholic Church of Santiago, under the leadership of Cardinal Raúl Silva Henríquez, who defined the Church as "the voice of the voiceless."[3]

We took our final exams with a military conscript (who must have been seventeen or eighteen years old, just about our age) holding a machine gun inside the classroom, all of which made a strong impression on us (at least on me). I had been elected as the representative of the students in the Consejo Superior, a collective, representative body of all the different components of the educational community, including the workers and the administrative staff. These were times of deep structural transformations in Chilean and Latin American societies, and Saint George's was no exception.

I can only say that my experience at Saint George's—and that of my generation overall—and the profound changes that took place within the Church, was transformative. There was a distinct generational component to it that extended over the years to come.

My personal engagement as part of this generation had begun much earlier, in the middle of the 1960s. I was eight years old when I attended the final rally of the Marcha de la Patria Joven (The March of the Young Fatherland) in the Parque Cousiño in Santiago in 1964, as the culmination of the electoral campaign that led Eduardo Frei Montalva, the candidate from the Christian Democratic Party (PDC), to the presidency of the Republic (1964–70). Under the banner of "The Revolution in Freedom," Frei's administration represented an attempt to undertake deep structural changes, including agrarian reform; peasant unionization; partial nationalization of the copper industry; "Promoción Popular" (referring to the creation and strengthening of a vast network of social and community organizations or "intermediate bodies," as they were referred to by the social doctrine of the Catholic Church); educational and tax reform; and massive programs of social housing for the poor, among other initiatives.

The speech delivered by President Frei at that rally was—and still is, when I hear it again—electrifying. It is considered one of the great pieces of rhetoric in contemporary Latin America, an encapsulation of a non-populist, modernizing strategy, seeking social justice for the poor and the marginalized sectors of society. It is rightfully compared with the significance of the speech delivered by President Salvador Allende on September 11, 1973, through a radio broadcast from La Monega palace on the day of the military coup.

I attended that rally with my mother, who was elected by the PDC as *regidora* (municipal councillor) for the years 1963–71, exactly coinciding with the Revolution in Freedom of President Frei. Thus, from very early in my life I felt I was a close witness of the unprecedented process of deep social and cultural transformations that took place in Chile.

In my childhood, living in Pirque, a rural place close to Santiago, I was fully aware of the characteristics of the *ancien régime*, which consisted of premodern and semifeudal social structures that had been in place for 300 years. These structures were exemplified by the *latifundio* or *hacienda* (large, generally nonproductive, landholdings) and the *inquilinos* (the peasants, living in conditions close to servitude). I witnessed at a very young age conditions in which the poor children of the *campesinos* attended school, wearing no shoes, in a rotten infrastructure of dark rooms, clay floors, and fragile desks (*pupitres*). These conditions existed despite the various attempts throughout the history of Chile at providing access to public education and also to private schools, attempts that were very much colored by the role of the Catholic Church.

I was fourteen when Salvador Allende was elected president of the Republic in 1970. As a member of the Christian Democratic Party, I had already been influenced by the social doctrine of the Church, in opposition to Allende's Popular Unity government (1970–73). However, a Marxist president within a coalition of Marxist parties that were democratically elected tells us something about the representativeness and inclusiveness of Chilean democracy at the time, and the possibilities that were open to political parties and ideologies from a variety of backgrounds.

Nonetheless, this inclusiveness was also taking place within the context of a deep polarization that was emerging in Chile and in Latin America in those years. I was relatively young at the time of Allende's election, but old enough to recognize the deep contradictions that were already present between the political forces that were seeking social justice through reform and those that were advocating revolution, both in Chile and in Latin America generally. The Revolution in Freedom under the leadership of Eduardo Frei, which received strong and active support and inspiration from the Catholic Church, had made the case for reform. It represented a serious attempt at bringing about social change within the broader process of modernization and development that was taking place within Third World, underdeveloped countries in the late 1960s, including Latin America. If Frei Montalva represented the political forces of reform, Allende and his experiment[4] with the Vía Chilena al Socialismo (Chilean Road to Socialism) in "democracy, pluralism and freedom," as he defined it in 1970, represented the political forces of revolution. Following the Revolution in Freedom, this second revolution in less than a decade led to a deepening of some of the social reforms that were launched by President Frei.

The changes under Allende included agrarian reform and the introduction of even more radical steps, such as the full nationalization of copper and the creation of a "Social Property Area," which led to the nationalization of more than 500 firms in a variety of fields, including banking, financial, and industrial businesses.

In these respects, Frei and Allende, a Christian Democrat and a Socialist, represented two contrasting approaches to similar goals. They shared a commitment to social justice but had radical disagreements over the means to achieving that goal. As I shall suggest momentarily, their differences were aggravated by a political climate that was heavily influenced by the Cuban Revolution in the midst of the Cold War. These circumstances led to irreconcilable positions between the developmentalist forces of reform, which were exemplified by Christian Democracy, and the revolutionary forces of the Left, such as the Popular Unity government. Adding to these tensions, a third group represented by the traditionalist, conservative forces remained very much on the defensive, standing in favor of preserving the status quo.

If we consider the military coups that took place in Brazil (1964), Uruguay (1973), and Argentina (1976), the coming tragedy of Chile was also the tragedy of the countries of the Southern Cone. In their preauthoritarian settings, these countries' leaders all had in common the desire to effect social change. But they advocated different and contradictory paths towards this goal.

The split between Frei and Allende and its outcome, the democratic breakdown leading to the military coup, was only one example of the split between the forces of reform and of revolution throughout Latin America, notwithstanding these regimes' similar aims and programmatic blueprints. In addition to the coups and the advent of right-wing authoritarian regimes in the Southern Cone, we also have to take into account the leftist military coups that took place in the same time period, always around this dilemma between reform or revolution. This was the case, for example, of the "Revolutionary Government of the Armed Forces," which came to power following the military coup in Perú in 1968, led by Gen. Juan Francisco Velasco Alvarado. The revolutionary government advocated agrarian reform, the nationalization of basic industries, and a mix of revolutionary and reformist policies, both in terms of its rhetoric and policies, under an authoritarian form. Something similar happened in Panama, also in 1968, following the military coup led by Col. Omar Efraín Torrijos Herrera. Omar Torrijos was a nationalist and populist military leader, similar in many ways to Velasco Alvarado in terms of his revolutionary, antioligarchical rhetoric. These leftist coups help us to appreciate the different patterns that were present in the region around the issue of social change, whether under a democratic or authoritarian political form, within the broader perspective of modernization and development.

The tensions that emerged between the forces of reform and the forces of revolution were not entirely new to Latin America. They were also reflected in the "nationalist" (a term that was abused by some of its critics as synonymous with "communist") and reformist movements in Guatemala in the mid-1950s and the Dominican Republic in the mid-1960s, to the emergence of bureaucratic-authoritarianism[5] in the Southern Cone (Brazil, Uruguay, Chile, and Argentina) in the late 1960s and early 1970s, and the "leftist" (this term was also abused by its own advocates) experiences of Velasco Alvarado in Perú and Torrijos in Panama. Whether they are understood in terms of nationalism or populism, of developmentalist or dependency theories and strategies around "structural reforms," or of reform or revolution, all of these movements shared the desire to overcome traditional, oligarchical social structures. Later, they all shared the fate of democratic breakdown and authoritarianism. In these respects, the "spirit of 1968" in Latin America may have begun with a few signs of hope but it also ended up with multiple, ugly faces.

At the core of the confrontation between the forces of reform and revolution was "ideological escalation," a concept the economist Albert Hirschman underscored as one of the key components in explaining democratic breakdown in the region.[6] The concept of inflation in the 1960s and 1970s, according to Hirschman, should not only be understood in economic terms but also in terms of ideological escalation. This escalation gave birth to utopian remedies that ended up in failed experiments. In contrast to the features of ideological escalation, a Hirschmanian approach to social change—one he viewed favorably—would have had different components: a recognition of the necessity of moving away from "general laws," "historical laws," and "structural determinants" in the field of social sciences; an appreciation of the concepts of possibilism, gradualism, and incremental change; and the recognition that there is a broad divide between revolution and reaction.

High ideologization leading to political polarization was one of the key aspects of the cultural atmosphere in the "Long '68," especially at the level of the political and intellectual elites. This was certainly the case in

Latin America, in Europe, and in the United States. Whether the authoritarian outcome came from external intervention, as in the cases of Guatemala and the Dominican Republic in the mid-1950s and mid-1960s, or from the Right (Brazil, Uruguay, Chile, and Argentina), or from the Left (Peru and Panama), it is also important to recognize that there was eventually a positive outcome to these developments. The lessons drawn from those experiences and the learning process associated with it were at the core of the third wave of democratization starting in the late 1970s.

In the 1970s, only Colombia, Venezuela, and Costa Rica had remained as democracies in Latin America (if we also include among authoritarian regimes, following the definition by Mario Vargas Llosa, the "perfect dictatorship" that existed in Mexico, which was anything but a democratic regime). The forces of reform and revolution were on the offensive, trying to advance their programmatic blueprints in favor of social change within a context of increasing polarization, but democracies remained fragile.

Despite these enormous challenges, however, the good news is that by the end of the 1970s, democracy began its slow return throughout Latin America. Fortunately, with a few but important contemporary exceptions (mainly Cuba and Venezuela, and increasingly so Nicaragua) and in spite of myriad problems (crime and corruption, poverty and inequality), we are still in the third wave of democratization today, forty years after it first returned to the Dominican Republic in 1978.[7] This success story is unique in the history of Latin America.

THE INTERNATIONAL CONTEXT OF THE "SPIRIT OF '68" IN LATIN AMERICA

I have argued elsewhere that the process leading to democratic breakdown has more to do with internal rather than external forces, and political rather than economic forces.[8] Still, it is impossible to avoid referring to the international context when it comes to explaining the "Long '68" and the cultural transformations that it brought about.

Arguably, the most important factor in this respect was the East–West confrontation that took place during the 1960s and 1970s. This context played a central role in exacerbating the confrontation between the forces of reform and revolution from one country to another, countries attempting through different means to overcome the traditional structures of the *ancien régime* in favor of development and modernization.

The Cold War became internalized—and thus the politics of "containment" that was at the core of the foreign policy of the United States was seriously challenged—with the Cuban Revolution in 1959. Cuba came to be seen as a "beachhead" for revolutionary forces in the region, resulting in further radicalization and confrontation.

It is hard to exaggerate the influence of the Cuban Revolution when it comes to explaining Latin American politics and the cultural atmosphere in the 1960s. The leaders of the Sierra Maestra created the impression that paradise (with the *hombre nuevo* of Ernesto Che Guevara) was around the corner, and that the political forces of the Left did not have to wait for the different stages of capitalist development to unfold. This created heated debates within the Left itself as the Cuban Revolution challenged the *etapismo* (leapfrogging) and the orthodoxy defended by the Communist Party, the idea of moving towards socialism through the different stages of capitalist development as it had been foreseen by the classics of Marxism (e.g., Engels and Marx).

In different countries of the region, communist parties had denounced the "ultra-leftist" forces that were present throughout Latin America, including different expressions of guerrilla warfare—*foquismo*, *guevarismo*, and the like. Some of those expressions corresponded to the same sectors of the (ultra) Left that had denounced reformism as treason to socialism ("El reformismo, traición al socialismo").[9]

In particular, the Cold War and the Cuban Revolution contributed to the deepening of the ideological and political confrontation between the forces of reform and revolution in Chile. This was expressed in a dramatic way in the conflict between Frei and Allende. Although they had been lifelong friends and fellow senators, they could not escape this radical confrontation.

The effect of this hemispheric conflict, within the broader context of the Cold War, was expressed in the confrontation between the Alliance for Progress under the Kennedy and Johnson administrations, with its reformist orientation, and the Cuban experiment, with its increasing revolutionary appeal. Almost no country in the region escaped from this confrontation.

In order to fully grasp and capture the spirit of '68 in Latin America, we must also recognize a second international element that is especially important for understanding the true meaning of these dilemmas and cultural transformations. This was the deep and profound change that occurred within the Catholic Church following Vatican II. The process of *aggiornamento* that took place within the Church—an institution that had been regarded as being part of the traditional and oligarchic forces of conservatism, and its social and economic structures—can be seen from a variety of perspectives. Unfortunately, not all of them are positive. One was the way it contributed to further ideologization and polarization between the forces of reform or revolution, in spite of the commitment of all three forces (the revolutionary Left, the reformist center, and the Church itself) to deep, structural transformations in the social and economic realms.

One major example of the Church's attempt to scrutinize the "signs of the times" and the "lights and shadows" of the modern world was the seminal meeting in 1968 in Medellín, Colombia, of the regional council of Catholic bishops known as CELAM (Conferencia Episcopal Latino Americana). The document resulting from this meeting, "La Iglesia en la actual transformación de América Latina a la luz del Concilio," had a tremendous influence in the region, one which fully expressed the spirit of 1968 and its cultural significance.[10]

The meeting was inaugurated by Pope Paul VI himself. It was the first time that a pope had visited Latin America. In the background was the recent encyclical *Populorum progressio* (1967), which referred to development as "a new name for peace," in clear contrast to the premodern, underdeveloped, social, and economic structures of Latin America. The encyclical also meant a clear endorsement, on the part of the Church and the pope himself, of the deep transformations that were taking place in the region. It opposed the "signs of the times" that were at the core of Vatican II and its many documents, with the "tragic sign of underdevelopment" that appeared as a dominant feature of the traditional structures of Latin America. Open references were made to the concepts of liberation, justice, solidarity, integral promotion of man and the communities, all along the lines of a clear denunciation of the structures of oppression and the different forms of exploitation that were related to those structures.

CELAM explicitly endorsed the social reforms that were being undertaken in Latin America in terms of liberation and emancipation from servitude and social injustice, and denounced imperialism under any ideology. A special mention was directed to the key concept of the "preferential option for the poor" (no. 475), which was developed some years later at the meeting of the Latin American bishops in Puebla (1979) as a central aspect of the pastoral commitments of the Church in Latin America.

Another key concept, that of "social sin," referred to the collective and social responsibilities behind the widespread reality of poverty and inequality in the region. There was not only the reality of individual sin, but of social sin. The Medellín document argued that justice was a condition of peace, but denounced "institutionalized violence" as a result of structures of injustice, which, in turn, constituted a violation of fundamental rights (no. 175).

It is easy to understand the significance of these pronouncements. Since they came from the hierarchy of the Church, including the pope himself, the local churches, and the national conference of bishops, they underscored the "prophetic" role of the Church in proclaiming the kingdom of God and its commitment to social justice, while denouncing any currents that went against these principles.

An example of the implications of all these changes for the internal life of the Church were the first writings, documents, and books on "teología de la liberación" (liberation theology), which were very much influenced by Medellín. I perfectly remember having read, in 1972 at the age of sixteen at Saint George's College, the book on liberation theology by Gustavo Gutiérrez, the Peruvian theologian and a professor at the University of Notre Dame for many years.[11]

Our lives were profoundly shaped by these events and the political processes and intellectual effervescence of the late 1960s. These influences reinforced our awareness of the "social question," which had been at the core of social and political struggles from the early twentieth century. They were also at the core of the social doctrine of the Church, which was directed at social justice while critical of both Marxism and of liberal capitalism.

The Church's focus on the questioning, and eventually the transformation, of the social structures took the form of a denunciation of "social sins" and "institutionalized violence," along with the advocacy of a "preferential option for the poor." These concepts had profound implications for the social and political forces that were committed to social change, whether under reformist or revolutionary means.

One must also take into account that these kinds of statements and the intellectual, political, social, and even theological fervor that was present in Latin America in the late 1960s and the early 1970s did not come forth in a political vacuum. They were not abstract formulations. In fact, they were full of deep contradictions with reality itself, and especially with the repressive nature of many existing structures. An example of these political contradictions was the massacre of Plaza Tlatelolco in Mexico City in October 1968. In the same year that CELAM was received as a sign of hope, the repression and the killing of hundreds of students and civilians on October 2 was a further demonstration of the very deep tensions that still existed in Latin America.

From a global perspective, it is noteworthy that the Tlatelolco massacre took place in the same year as the suppression of Alexander Dubček's Prague Spring; this event too was characterized by the widespread repression of dissidents, but under a different form of authoritarianism. In this way, what happened in both Latin America and Eastern Europe corresponded to the "shadows"—following the language of Vatican II and the "theology of the signs of the times"—of the contradictory processes of social and cultural changes that were unleashed in the "Long '68."

Yet, the killing of students and civilians by military and police forces in Tlatelolco not only meant government repression of the political opposition. On the positive side, the students' protests represented a major challenge to the one-party system (or dominant-party system) represented by the PRI (Partido Revolucionario Institucional/Institutional Revolutionary Party) and forced the regime to gradually open itself to society and democracy. The movement that led this challenge, much as in the case of other student movements with similar aims in Latin America, Europe, and the United States during roughly the same time period, paved the way for an eventual democratic transition in Mexico.

The change was slow in coming. In terms of the transition in power, it would take thirty-two more years to come to fruition through the election of Vicente Fox, the leader of the Partido de Acción Nacional (PAN), in 2000. In the intervening years, political repression continued to be a key factor in the policies of the PRI regime, under the administration of Gustavo Díaz Ordaz, with Luis Echeverría as secretario de gobernación. In 1971, three years after the Tlatelolco massacre, another wave of political repression took place under the new Luis Echeverría administration with the "Corpus Christi" massacre, also in Mexico City.

These atrocities represented the dark side ("the shadows") of political developments. Although new signs of hope were emerging in the region, represented by the Medellín Conference and its documents, the massacres of Tlatelolco and Corpus Christi only demonstrated that the advances in favor of social change took place in a continuing political context full of contradictions, of advances and setbacks, with both internal and external causes.

MODERNIZATION AND DEVELOPMENT

At this point, allow me to turn to the arguments of two social scientists, Samuel Huntington and Albert Hirschman, who can provide us with theoretical insight into the deep and contradictory processes of social and political change of this time. Both authors emphasized the importance of interpreting the period against the backdrop of modernization and development. Whether these events took place under democratic or authoritarian political forms, under reformist or revolutionary rhetoric and strategies, Huntington and Hirschman argued that these regimes' search for modernization and development was a response to the crisis of oligarchic rule that had emerged in the first decades of the twentieth century.

The year 1968 saw the publication of Huntington's seminal book in the field of social science that had much to do with the processes we are addressing in this chapter: *Political Order in Changing Societies.*[12] It is not a coincidence that Huntington's book about the subject of political order was published in 1968. It appeared in the middle of the struggles of the civil rights movement, the Vietnam War, the May 1968 events in Paris and other cities in Europe, all at a time when the dilemma between reform and revolution was at the core of the struggles in favor of social change in Latin America.

In very significant ways Huntington's book was a reaction, a response, and a questioning of the social scientific theories that were dominant in the social sciences, especially in the United States in the 1950s. These theories shared a kind of widespread optimism that was present not only in the thinking of social scientists, but was also to be found in concrete policies of economic and political development that prevailed during the postwar period, in spite of the tensions arising from the Cold War. To summarize their main arguments, many of these theories proposed that economic development would lead to both political stability and democracy. This was the case, for example, with the "optimist equation" expressed in Seymour Martin Lipset's classic book, *Political Man: The Social Bases of Politics*, which had appeared in 1960.[13]

By the mid-1960s and early 1970s, however, the validity of this approach was subject to radical questioning, first as a result of the facts themselves and later by intense intellectual and academic debate about how to interpret these facts. In *Political Order in Changing Societies*, Huntington argued that, far from leading to political stability, modernization was in itself disruptive and destabilizing. He wrote, "It is not the absence of modernity, but rather the efforts to achieve it, that produce political disorder," adding that "modernity breeds stability, but modernization breeds instability."[14] In particular, Huntington asserted that in the case of Latin America, this instability was reflected in the successful coups that had already occurred in seventeen of the twenty countries in the region.

Additionally, Huntington argued that the high levels of social mobilization and the expansion of political participation associated with modernization, especially when they occurred under low levels of political institutionalization, had led to a decline in the political order during the postwar period, undermining the authority, effectiveness, and legitimacy of these governments. In his view, the subsequent destabilization of the political order could be explained by the existence of a gap between economic development, social mobilization, and political participation, on the one hand, and political institutions, on the other. Huntington argued that it was the existence of strong political institutions that made the difference between political development and underdevelopment. Thus, *modernity*, which is brought about when political participation is combined with adequate institutions, is synonymous with stability, while *modernization* is synonymous with instability. The relation between the levels of political participation and institutionalization determines the existence of political stability or instability. When institutions cannot fulfill their proper role, social processes surpass them (leading, in an extreme form, to "mass praetorianism"). In some cases, weak institutions can lead to military intervention or even to revolution, both understood as agents of modernization.

I find Huntington's work quite illuminating as a way of addressing social mobilization, not as a pathology—as has been the case in the works of a variety of authors and schools within the social sciences, especially in the United States—but as inherent to the process of modernization. *Political Order in Changing Societies* not only focuses on the disruptive effects of modernization but also on the vital role of institutions in dealing with social change with the aim of maintaining political order. In these respects, Huntington's book made a significant contribution to the emergence in the upcoming years and decades of the "new institutionalist school" within the social sciences, including economics and political science.

Huntington is usually depicted as a conservative intellectual, especially because of his bias in favor of "political order" and his support for U.S. foreign policy in the 1960s. Yet his focus on the crucial role of strong institutions in maintaining order raises an important question. Does the adoption of "institutionalist" approaches preclude the need for or the possibility of advocating or introducing far-reaching change, including structural reforms, within the social and economic realm?

This topic was at the core of the question of political order in developing societies in the 1960s. This is where Hirschman returns to our conversation with his insightful approach to the question of social change, not only in Latin America but in all Third World, underdeveloped countries. In numerous works, Hirschman set out to provide a comprehensive comparative perspective on development, in accord with an eclectic, multidisciplinary approach, what he called "essays in trespassing"[15] that covered fields ranging from economics to philosophy, from sociology to political science and beyond.

Hirschman had lived in Colombia in the 1950s—the best years of his life, "providing an environment to reinvent himself," according to Jeremy Adelman.[16] As a result of this experience, he took a close look at the transformations that were undertaken in the 1960s around the questions of modernization and development, and at those involving the confrontation between the forces of reform and revolution. In questioning traditional theories on both modernization and development, Hirschman looked at these issues without theoretical preconceptions, providing a point of view that was in many ways at odds with the orthodoxies forged in U.S. universities. According to Adelman, he was also skeptical of all ideological formulas that were based on abstract theories.[17]

Focusing on theories of economic development, while criticizing abstract model-building, Hirschman made the case in the late 1950s and early 1960s in favor of "reform as the first rays of revolution shone out from the horizon."[18] In line with his unorthodox, reformist approach, he found fault with the "simplistic optimism" of such initiatives as the Alliance for Progress. At the same time, he was strongly critical of the Cuban Revolution and the ideological and political influence it exercised among the intellectual elites in Latin America, especially on the Left. In these ways, Hirschman seems to have anticipated that the clash between the forces of reform and revolution could end up risking the sustainability of social change, leading to unforeseen outcomes.

Hirschman was definitely on the side of social change, including "structural reforms." However, along with his criticisms of "ideological escalation," especially at the level of the political and intellectual elites, he also underscored the need to move away from "general laws," "historical laws," or "structural determinants" that were so pervasive in the field of social sciences. Those approaches had failed to acknowledge the complexities of social and political reality, and the sustainability of the processes of social change. He advocated a clear position in favor of reform, along the lines of a more gradual, incremental approach to social change, which was well expressed in his central concept of "possibilism." The idea that there is a broad space for reform between revolution and reaction is one of the central aspects of his thought.

This approach corresponds to what Javier Santiso refers to, within a Hirschmanian framework, as the "political economy of the possible." It is the opposite of both the "political economy of the impossible" that characterized Latin America in the age of utopias and global planning (*planificaciones globales*) in the 1960s, and the "political economy of impatience" that characterizes populist regimes in general.[19]

In an early book, *Journeys toward Progress: Studies of Economic Policy-Making in Latin America*, published in 1963, Hirschman explicitly stated that his purpose was "to break down the rigid dichotomy between reform and revolution and to show that the changes that occur in the real world are often something wholly outside these two stereotypes."[20] He also questioned the theories in the fields of social science that pointed to the "requisites," "prerequisites," "conditions," or "preconditions" to achieving democracy and development. All of these approaches, in his view, ended up undermining the prospects of development and modernization, both intellectually and politically.

A typical example of this way of thinking, according to Hirschman, was dependency theory, especially in its early versions, which he labeled a "structuralist fallacy." This theoretical orientation, he argued, had much to do with the role and the influence of intellectual elites in the 1960s in leading to ideological escalation, polarization, and democratic breakdown.

In the context of this more recent (and long) third wave of democratization, I would like to suggest that, fifty years after 1968, we may be going through a kind of "Hirschmanian moment" in Latin America—especially in terms of the learning process and the lessons that can be drawn from the related experiences of democratic breakdown and authoritarianism. This moment may allow for an approach to social change through reform and gradual, incremental policymaking that will take place along the lines of a political economy of the possible. It is a moment of moving away from the extremes, away from the ideological escalation and the utopian thought that were at the core of the "Long '68" and that contributed to the erosion of democracy.

In making this point, I am not arguing or even implying that democratic breakdown was inevitable. One of the lessons I have learned throughout my political life is that nothing is "irreversible" or "inevitable" within the realm of politics. One of the consequences of a Hirschmanian approach to politics consists precisely in moving away from "deterministic" views of any kind, and abstract formulas.

Today, Latin American countries are not condemned to choose between revolution or right-wing authoritarianism. That is a dilemma of the past. There is a broad space in between along the lines of a middle-of-the-road, reform-oriented way of thinking and undertaking social and political change in a sustainable way.

This Hirschmanian moment in today's Latin America may lack the epic character or the heroic features that were present in the events of 1968, but perhaps this new wave of democratization in the forty years since 1978 is a further demonstration that when it comes to introducing social change in a sustainable way, Hirschman's approach will prove more promising than the kind of utopian and highly ideological atmosphere of the 1960s.

This is especially the case when we consider what I have labeled the "new social question"[21] in Latin America, referring to the reality of middle-income countries characterized by the rise of new (aspirational and emerging) middle sectors of society, half way toward development, seeking to achieve both democracy and modernity. Within this context and understanding the image—and the reality—of Third World, underdeveloped countries, as in the 1960s and early 1970s, corresponds more to the past than to the present.

This Hirschmanian moment may be at odds with the image and the slogans of 1968 in Paris ("be realistic and ask for the impossible," "decree the permanent state of happiness") or the appeal for the *hombre nuevo* of Che Guevara, as in Cuba and Latin America in the 1960s. But at least one may be assured (or reasonably expect) that gradual change, as a central aspect of possibilism, will create new possibilities for advancing social change in the pursuit of social justice in a sustainable way, without any traumatic breakdowns. This is especially the case under the premise that there are no shortcuts on the path toward development, and that there always exists the possibility of authoritarian regression.

Just as 1968 was the time of "voice," these may not be necessarily the times for "exit,"[22] but perhaps a time for a more eclectic approach to social change, both in the fields of politics and of the social sciences. Perhaps a new understanding of "loyalty" along the lines of an "ethics of responsibility," within a Hirschmanian and Weberian understanding of the concepts, is emerging in Latin America fifty years after the events of 1968 and forty years after the new wave of democratization that started in the Dominican Republic in 1978.

The outline of this "Hirschmanian moment" in Latin America shows up in one of Hirschman's essays, "Political Economics and Possibilism," in which he provided an alternative way of thinking to the political attitudes of revolutionaries and conservatives.[23] Perhaps there is nothing more distant or detached from the heroic features of the revolutionary spirit of 1968 than "possibilism" and the commitment to gradual and incremental social change. But, I believe this approach will help us to overcome the confrontation, polarization, and ideologization of that era, while at the same time achieving a more sustainable process of social transformation.

The title of Hirschman's book *A Bias for Hope* may end up being not only a posthumous homage to his work but to all the victims (unfortunately this is not a metaphor) of the tragic political outcome of the radical confrontations between the forces of reform and revolution that took place in Latin America in the 1960s and 1970s. It has yet to be seen where contemporary trends may lead in the post-Bolivarian revolution of the "socialism of the 21st century" and to what extent we have learned from the experiences of that past.

1968: A CULTURAL REVOLUTION?

Did Latin America experience a cultural revolution in 1968?

In the case of my generation, I can only say that we have had to wrestle with the significance of this question for a long time. I was seventeen at the time of the military coup and thirty-four at the time of the recovery of democracy in 1990, which means that we spent half of our lifetime under a dictatorship—we have learned the hard way. Our idea of "Nunca Más" (Never Again) is not a slogan or an abstract formula, or something that we have learned in the textbooks or in the social sciences literature, but something very real and concrete that has to do with the lives and the dreams of our generation and the generations to come. After all, the memories of polarization that led to democratic breakdown and authoritarianism are still fresh. Thus, questions of "historical memory" and "the process of learning from the past" are the most promising intellectual avenues in postauthoritarian Latin America.

This brings me back to where I began this chapter. My experiences at Saint George's College, under the influence of Vatican II and the documents of CELAM, in contrast to the new wave of authoritarianism that started with the military coup in Brazil in 1964, were formative. In my case, they somehow anticipated the "lights" and the "shadows" of the struggles of the peoples of Latin America and the role of the intellectual and political elites. They all reflected the dilemmas, lessons, and learning process surrounding the deep changes that were undertaken in Latin America.

My generation and I, we are not renegades of the spirit of '68, of the zeitgeist of '68, or the "Long '68." We are even less inclined to adopt the position of Daniel Cohn-Bendit as was expressed in the title of his recent book *Forget 68*, written fifty years after the events and the cultural transformations 1968 brought about.[24] We can extract the best of that spirit and still advance our ideals and values with the methods of democracy. By all means, they should be reformist methods, however boring they may be in practice.

The term "zeitgeist" is generally used to refer to a time of significant changes in the ideas and beliefs of a society. It also has strong intellectual and moral connotations. My own understanding is that my generation and I can live with this conception, not as renegades of '68 but as bearers of the new spirit of 2018, having to do with both the lights and shadows of our times, especially in terms of the new generations that are trying to find their "place under the sun." We can offer them our own experience, our own lessons, and our own dreams, including those of the zeitgeist of '68. This can be done without abandoning this new spirit in an era in which the storms that appear on the horizon (climate change, national populism, the violation of basic human rights) may be as threatening and challenging as the ones we saw emerging in the "Long '68," whether they came from the Right or the Left.

So, did Latin America experience a cultural revolution in 1968?

In response to this question, I prefer the answer by the philosopher, psychologist, and anthropologist Edgar Morin, in his own portrait of '68: "more than a protest, but less than a revolution."[25] This definition does not deprive the spirit of '68 of any true meaning. The truth of the matter is that "1968" is not a closed chapter of contemporary history but still an open page for my generation and the generations to come.

1968 has died, long live 1968!

NOTES

1. See Richard Vinen, *The Long '68: Radical Protest and Its Enemies* (London: Allen Lane, 2018); and "Born to Be Wild; A Radical Year," *The Economist*, April 7, 2018, 71.

2. The film *Machuca* by Andrés Wood, a former student at Saint George's, which directly referred to 1973, captures much better than these words the mood, the atmosphere, the possibilities, the limitations, and the contradictions of that educational reform in Saint George's.

3. Following the military coup of 1973 it could be said that only two institutions remained in place in Chile: the Armed Forces and the Catholic Church. Most of the other political and social institutions, such as Parliament, political parties and unions, and social organizations, were either outlawed or repressed. In many ways it could be said that, at least until 1978, the Armed Forces led by Augusto Pinochet and the Catholic Church led by Cardinal Silva took the place of government and the opposition, respectively, around the issue of human rights.

4. I refer to the "experiments" of both Frei and Allende because there was a kind of social engineering in their actions, along with a certain utopian orientation, that is well captured in the book by the Chilean historian, Mario Gón-

gora. Góngora coined the term "planificaciones globales" (ideological experiments) referring to the all-encompassing and highly ideological social programs that were undertaken in the three revolutions under different political parties that took place successively under Frei, Allende, and Pinochet. In this respect, Góngora's breaking point in the contemporary history of Chile is not before and after 1973 (the year of the military coup) but before and after 1964, the year in which Frei came to power. See Mario Góngora, *Ensayo histórico sobre la noción de Estado en Chile en los siglos XIX y XX* (Santiago: Ed. La Ciudad, 1981).

5. See Guillermo A. O'Donnell, *Modernization and Bureaucratic-Authoritarianism: Studies in South American Politics*, Politics of Modernization Series 9 (Berkeley: Institute of International Studies, University of California, 1979).

6. See Albert Hirschman, "The Turn to Authoritarianism in Latin America and the Search for Its Economic Determinants," in *The New Authoritarianism in Latin America*, ed. David Collier (Princeton, NJ: Princeton University Press, 1979), 81.

7. This was the topic of "IV Foro Internacional de Santo Domingo: 'El Estado de la democracia en América Latina: 40 Años desde la tercera ola de la democracia,'" Santo Domingo, Dominican Republic, 2018.

8. See Ignacio Walker, *Democracy in Latin America: Between Hope and Despair*, trans. Krystin Krause, Holly Bird, and Scott Mainwaring (Notre Dame, IN: University of Notre Dame Press, 2013).

9. Camilo Escalona, leader and many times president of the Socialist Party of Chile, refers to this accusation in the following terms: "The slogan 'Reformism, treason to socialism' demonstrated a lack of awareness of what was really at stake; it was not only a national dilemma, but one of broad international dimensions. The United States was moving away from the support of democracy in the region, backing coup plotters and dictators. The ultra Left never understood this"; Camilo Escalona, *De Allende a Bachelet: Una vida política*, 1st ed. (Santiago de Chile: Aguilar, 2012); my translation.

10. General Conference of the Latin American Episcopate. "La Iglesia en la actual transformación de América Latina a la luz del Concilio" (Medellin, Colombia, 1968).

11. Gustavo Gutiérrez, *Teología de la liberación: Perspectivas* (Lima: CEP, 1971).

12. Samuel P. Huntington, *Political Order in Changing Societies* (New Haven, CT: Yale University Press, 1968).

13. Seymour Martin Lipset, *Political Man: The Social Bases of Politics*, expanded ed. (Baltimore: Johns Hopkins University Press, 1981).

14. Huntington, *Political Order in Changing Societies*, 41, 43.

15. See Albert O. Hirschman, *Essays in Trespassing: Economics to Politics and Beyond* (Cambridge: Cambridge University Press, 1981).

16. See Jeremy Adelman, *Worldly Philosopher: The Odyssey of Albert O. Hirschman* (Princeton, NJ: Princeton University Press, 2013).

17. Ibid.

18. Ibid., 350.

19. See Javier Santiso, *Latin America's Political Economy of the Possible: Beyond Good Revolutionaries and Free-Marketeers* (Cambridge, MA: MIT Press, 2006).

20. Cited in Jeremy Adelman, *Worldly Philosopher: The Odyssey of Albert O. Hirschman* (Princeton, NJ: Princeton University Press, 2013), 379.

21. I develop this concept in Walker, *Democracy in Latin America*, chap. 7.

22. See Albert O. Hirschman, *Exit, Voice, and Loyalty: Responses to Decline in Firms, Organizations, and States* (Cambridge, MA: Harvard University Press, 1970).

23. See Albert O. Hirschman, *A Bias for Hope: Essays on Development and Latin America* (New Haven, CT: Yale University Press, 1971), chap. 1.

24. Daniel Cohn-Bendit, *Forget 68* (De l'Aube, 2018).

25. Quoted in Fernando Fuentes, "A Cinco Décadas de 1968, El Año Que Marcó al Mundo," *La Tercera*, April 2, 2018.

BIBLIOGRAPHY

Adelman, Jeremy. *Worldly Philosopher: The Odyssey of Albert O. Hirschman*. Princeton, NJ: Princeton University Press, 2013.

"Born to Be Wild; A Radical Year." *The Economist*, April 7, 2018.

Cohn-Bendit, Daniel. *Forget 68*. De l'Aube, 2018.

Escalona, Camilo. *De Allende a Bachelet: Una vida política*. 1st ed. Santiago de Chile: Aguilar, 2012.

Fuentes, Fernando. "A Cinco Décadas de 1968, El Año Que Marcó al Mundo." *La Tercera*, April 2, 2018.

Góngora, Mario. *Ensayo histórico sobre la noción de Estado en Chile en los siglos XIX y XX*. Santiago: Ed. La Ciudad, 1981.

Gutiérrez, Gustavo. *Teología de la liberación: Perspectivas*. Lima: CEP, 1971.

Hirschman, Albert O. *A Bias for Hope: Essays on Development and Latin America*. New Haven, CT: Yale University Press, 1971.

———. *Essays in Trespassing: Economics to Politics and Beyond*. Cambridge and New York: Cambridge University Press, 1981.

———. *Exit, Voice, and Loyalty: Responses to Decline in Firms, Organizations, and States*. Cambridge, MA: Harvard University Press, 1970.

———. "The Turn to Authoritarianism in Latin America and the Search for Its Economic Determinants." In *The New Authoritarianism in Latin America*, edited by David Collier, 61–98. Princeton, NJ: Princeton University Press, 1979.

Huntington, Samuel P. *Political Order in Changing Societies*. New Haven, CT: Yale University Press, 1968.

"IV Foro Internacional de Santo Domingo: 'El Estado de la democracia en América Latina: 40 Años desde la tercera ola de la democracia.'" Santo Domingo, Dominican Republic, 2018.

Lipset, Seymour Martin. *Political Man: The Social Bases of Politics*. Expanded ed. Baltimore: Johns Hopkins University Press, 1981.

O'Donnell, Guillermo A. *Modernization and Bureaucratic-Authoritarianism: Studies in South American Politics*. Politics of Modernization Series 9. Berkeley: Institute of International Studies, University of California, 1979.

Santiso, Javier. *Latin America's Political Economy of the Possible: Beyond Good Revolutionaries and Free-Marketeers*. Cambridge, MA: MIT Press, 2006.

Vinen, Richard. *The Long '68: Radical Protest and Its Enemies*. London: Allen Lane, 2018.

Walker, Ignacio. *Democracy in Latin America: Between Hope and Despair*. Translated by Krystin Krause, Holly Bird, and Scott Mainwaring. Notre Dame, IN: University of Notre Dame Press, 2013.

LIST OF CONTRIBUTORS

PATRICK BARR-MELEJ is professor of history at Ohio University in Athens, Ohio. He received his PhD in Latin American history at the University of California at Berkeley. Barr-Melej specializes in the political, cultural, and intellectual history of modern Latin America, with a focus on twentieth-century Chile, and is the author of *Psychedelic Chile: Youth, Counterculture, and Politics on the Road to Socialism and Dictatorship* (University of North Carolina Press, 2017), and *Reforming Chile: Cultural Politics, Nationalism, and the Rise of the Middle Class* (University of North Carolina Press, 2001). He has published numerous articles and essays and has been a visiting professor at Chile's Pontifical Catholic University and University of Concepción.

ALONSO CUETO has published seventeen books (novels, short story collections, and essays). His novel *The Blue Hour* won the Premio Herralde for best novel in 2005. Another one of his novels, *El Susurro de la Mujer Ballena*, was a runner-up for the 2007 Planeta Casa América prize. His works have been translated into sixteen languages. His English translator, Frank Wynne, won the Valle Inclán prize for his translation of *The Blue Hour*. The Editorial House of the Republic of China singled the latter out as the best Spanish-language novel of 2004–2005. Three of his novels have been adapted into movies by directors Francisco Lombardi and Salvador del Solar. Cueto has received the German Anna Seghers prize for his body of work, the Guggenheim Foundation fellowship, and the Inca Garcilaso medal. The Peruvian state recognized him as an honorary personality of culture. He is a member of the Peruvian Academy of Language and a professor in the Department of Humanities at the Catholic University of Peru.

BELINDA DAVIS is professor of history at Rutgers University and director of the Rutgers Center for European Studies. She is author or coeditor of four books, including *Changing the World, Changing Oneself: Political Protest and*

Transnational Identities in 1960s/70s, West Germany and the U.S. (Berghahn, 2010) (coedited with M. Klimke, C. MacDougall, and W. Mausbach); and *The Internal Life of Politics: Extraparliamentary Opposition in West Germany, 1962–1983* (Cambridge University Press, forthcoming).

MASSIMO DE GIUSEPPE obtained his doctorate in history (peoples, cultures, and religious professions) at the Catholic University of Milan. He taught history of relations between Europe and Latin America at the University of Bologna, and now teaches contemporary history at the International University of Languages and Media, Università IULM, in Milan. His main research interests include the study of social, religious, and political movements, transnational networks and the effect of conflicts in Latin America and Italy during the twentieth century. He is a member of the editorial staff of the scientific magazines *Contemporanea* and *Modernism*, and he is a member of the scientific committee of Historia de las mentalidades and Annali di Storia dell'educazione. He has published articles in various international journals, such as *Historia Mexicana*, *Italia Contemporanea*, *Ricerche di Storia politica*, and *Mitteilungsblatt des Instituts fur Soziale Bewengungen*, and he wrote entries for the *Dictionnaire historique de la théologie de la libération*. He has participated in many international conferences, in Europe (Italy, Spain, Germany, France, UK, Holland) and the Americas (United States, Mexico, El Salvador, Chile, Argentina). Among his volumes are *Giorgio La Pira: Un sindaco e le vie della pace* (Milan, 2001); *Oscar Romero: Storia, memoria attualità* (Bologna, 2005); *Messico 1900–1930: Stato, Chiesa, popoli indigeni* (Brescia, 2007) (winner of the 2008 Pirovano prize of the Rome Luigi Sturzo Institute for the best research in religious history); *Romero Giustizia e pace come pedagogia pastorale* (Brescia, 2011); with Guido Formigoni he edited *Primo Mazzolari: Scritti sulla pace e sulla guerra* (Bologna, 2010); with Isabel Campos, *La cruz de maiz: Política, religión y identidad en México entre crisis de la colonia y crisis de la modernidad* (México, 2011); and with Hilda Iparraguirre and Ana María González, *Otras miradas de las revoluciones mexicanas* (México, 2015). His last book is *L'altra America: I cattolici italiani e l'America latina. Da Medellin a Francesco* (Brescia, 2017), and currently he's working on a research project about Italian Third Worldism.

WILLIAM COLLINS DONAHUE is the Cavanaugh Professor of the Humanities, professor of German studies, and concurrent professor in the Department of Film, Television and Theatre in the College of Arts and Letters at the University of Notre Dame. He also serves as director of the Initiative for Global Europe and professor of European Studies in the Keough School of Global Affairs at Notre Dame. His *The End of Modernism: Elias Canetti's Auto-da-Fé*, awarded the Modern Language Association's 2002 Aldo and Jeanne Scaglione Prize for Studies in Germanic Languages and Literatures, was recently republished in paperback with a new preface by the author (2020). With Martin Kagel, he edited *Die große Mischkalkulation: Institutions, Social Import, and Market Forces in the German Literary Field* (Paderborn: Wilhelm Fink Verlag, 2021). Donahue and Kagel co-direct the annual German Literary Institutions: The Berlin Seminar (formerly the Notre Dame Berlin Seminar), which brings scholars of German literary and cultural studies together with experts, practitioners, and leading figures in Germany's *Literaturbetrieb*.

ERIC DROTT received his PhD from Yale University in 2001 and now is associate professor of music at the University of Texas at Austin. His research focuses on contemporary music cultures, music and protest, genre theory, avant-garde movements in music, French cultural politics, and the sociology of music. His *Music and the Elusive Revolution* (University of California Press, 2011) examines music and politics in France after May '68, in particular how different music communities responded to the upheavals of the period. He is also a recipient of a research fellowship from the National Endowment for the Humanities.

VALERIA MANZANO is researcher at the Consejo Nacional de Investigaciones Científicas y Técnicas (Argentina) and associate professor of history at the Instituto de Altos Estudios Sociales, where she co-coordinates the Program on Recent History. She is the author of *The Age of Youth in Argentina: Culture, Politics, and Sexuality from Perón to Videla* (University of North Carolina Press, 2014), and coeditor of *Los sesenta de otra manera* (Buenos Aires: Prometeo, 2010), and has published two dozen articles in *Journal of Latin American Studies*, *Hispanic American Historical Review*, *The Americas*, *Journal of Social History*, and *Journal of the History of Sexuality*, among others. She is now completing a book manuscript on the history of youth, sexuality, and politics in twentieth-century Argentina. She has been visiting professor at many institutions, including the University of Geneva and the University of Chicago.

VANIA MARKARIAN received her bachelor's degree from the Universidad de la República (Uruguay) in 1996 and her PhD from Columbia University in 2003. Afterward, she was a postdoctoral fellow at New York University and taught at the City University of New York. In 2008, she spent a semester as visiting professor at Princeton University, and in 2013 she was the Tinker Visiting Professor at the Institute for Latin American Studies at Columbia University. She has several publications on Latin American contemporary history, among them *Left in Transformation: Uruguayan Exiles and the Latin American Human Rights Networks, 1967–1984* (2005), also published in Spanish in 2006. Her latest book is *El 68 uruguayo: El movimiento estudiantil entre molotovs y música beat* (2012), published in English as *Uruguay, 1968: Student Activism from Global Counterculture to Molotov Cocktails* (2017). She currently works at the Universidad de la República.

A. JAMES McADAMS is the William M. Scholl Professor of International Affairs at the University of Notre Dame. For sixteen years he was director of the Nanovic Institute for European Studies. He has also served as chair of the Political Science Department. McAdams has written widely on European affairs, especially on Central Europe. His books include *East Germany and Détente: Building Authority after the Wall*; *Germany Divided: From the Wall to Reunification*; *Judging the Past in Unified Germany*; and *The Crisis of Modern Times*. His latest book, *Vanguard of the Revolution: The Global Idea of the Communist Party* (Princeton University Press, 2017), examines the political history of communist parties from the 1840s to the present and covers their panoply from Germany to Russia, China, Poland, North Korea, Cuba, and many others, making it the first comprehensive international history of communist parties.

J. PATRICE McSHERRY, PhD in political science from the Graduate School of the City University of New York, specializes in comparative politics, particularly Latin American politics. She is professor of political science emerita at Long Island University (LIU) and a researcher in collaboration with the Institute of Advanced Studies (IDEA) of the University of Santiago, Chile. An internationally known expert on Operation Condor, she has lectured on this repressive system on several continents. She is a three-time Fulbright grant recipient and winner of many other academic grants and honors. McSherry's books are *Chilean New Song: The Political Power of Music, 1960s–1973* (Philadelphia: Temple University Press, 2015) (winner of the 2015 Cecil B. Currey Book Award from the Association of Third World Studies); *Predatory States: Operation Condor and Covert War in Latin America* (Rowman & Littlefield, 2005) (winner of a Choice Award for Outstanding Academic Title of 2006); *Incomplete Transition: Military Power and Democracy in Argentina* (St. Martin's Press, 1997, reissued in 2008, iUniverse, Inc.); and coeditor of *The Iraq Papers* (Oxford University Press, 2010).

WILLEM MELCHING is senior lecturer in modern history at the University of Amsterdam, Netherlands. His main teaching and research interests are modern German history, international relations, and visual history. He has written numerous monographs and articles, some of which have been translated into English.

ANTHONY MONTA is the associate director of the Nanovic Institute for European Studies at the University of Notre Dame. He earned a PhD in English (2001) from the University of Wisconsin-Madison, and taught English literature at Louisiana State University before being hired to help coordinate academic affairs at the Louisiana Board of Regents, the governing authority for all postsecondary institutions of education. He has been assisting the development of the Nanovic Institute at Notre Dame since 2007.

JAIME M. PENSADO is associate professor of history at the University of Notre Dame. A specialist in modern Mexican history, Pensado earned his PhD at the University of Chicago in 2008. He taught at Lehigh University before coming to Notre Dame. Pensado's main interests include modern Mexican history with a particular emphasis in student politics, youth culture, and the Cold War. His book-length publications include *México Beyond 1968: Revolutionaries, Radicals, and Repression during the Global Sixties and Subversive Seventies*, which he coedited with Enrique C. Ochoa (University of Arizona Press, 2018). He is the author of *Rebel Mexico: Student Unrest and Authoritarian Political Culture during the Long Sixties* (Stanford University Press, 2013).

TIMOTHY W. RYBACK is author of *Rock around the Bloc: A History of Rock Music in Eastern Europe and the Soviet Union*. He is director of the Institute for Historical Justice and Reconciliation, in The Hague, and former deputy director general of the Académie Diplomatique Internationale in Paris. He also served as vice president and resident director at the Salzburg Global Seminar. He earned his PhD at Harvard University, where he taught in the concentration of history and literature and has written extensively on the intersection of culture and politics.

VOLKER SCHLÖNDORFF is an internationally renowned film director. Recognized as one of the founders of the movement known as New German Cinema, he began his career working with such luminaries as Louis Malle, Alain Renais, and Jean-Pierre Melville. Schlöndorff's early films, *Young Törless* and the television production *Baal*, won critical acclaim for their unflinching statements about the German legacy of authoritarianism and violence. His later film, *The Lost Honor of Katharina Blum*, which he codirected with Margarethe von Trotta, is a searing indictment of police and media injustice when Germany was under attack by the terroristic Red Army Faction. In 1979, Schlöndorff's most celebrated film, *The Tin Drum*, won both the Palme d'Or at the Cannes Film Festival and the Academy Award for Best Foreign Language Film. Subsequently, Schlöndorff has directed numerous successful films, including *Swann in Love*, *Death of a Salesman*, *The Handmaid's Tale*, *Homo Faber/Voyager*, *The Ninth Day*, *Diplomacy*, and *Return to Montauk*.

MICHAEL SEIDMAN is professor of history at the University of North Carolina-Wilmington, having studied at the University of Amsterdam, University of California-Berkeley, and Swarthmore College. His first book, *Workers against Work: Labor in Barcelona and Paris during the Popular Fronts, 1936–38* (1991), has been translated into six languages. Other publications include *Republic of Egos: A Social History of the Spanish Civil War* (2002, Spanish translation, 2003); *The Imaginary Revolution: Parisian Students and Workers in 1968* (2004, Spanish translation and partial French translation, 2018); and *The Victorious Counterrevolution: The Nationalist Effort in the Spanish Civil War* (2011, Spanish translation, 2012). His most recent book is *Transatlantic Antifascisms from the Spanish Civil War to the End of World War II* (Cambridge University Press, 2017, Spanish translation, 2017).

CARMEN-HELENA TÉLLEZ balances activities as a creative artist, conductor, scholar, producer, and administrator as professor of conducting at the University of Notre Dame. Previously, Téllez was director of Graduate Choral Studies and the director of the Latin American Music Center at the Jacobs School of Music of Indiana University, where she directed their Contemporary Vocal Ensemble. She is also the artistic codirector of Aguavá New Music Studio, an artists' group, with which she records and tours internationally. In addition to many other positions, she has been the resident conductor of the Chicago Contemporary Chamber Players (Contempo), the music director of the National Chorus of Spain, and a visiting professor at Dartmouth College.

IGNACIO WALKER has been senator of the Republic of Chile (2010–18), president of the Christian Democratic Party (2010–15), minister of foreign affairs (2004–2006), and a lawyer (University of Chile). He holds a PhD in politics from Princeton University. He wrote *Democracy in Latin America: Between Hope and Despair* (University of Notre Dame Press, 2013).

ERIC ZOLOV is professor of history and the former director of Latin American and Caribbean studies at Stony Brook University. He is the former senior editor of *The Americas* and author of *The Last Good Neighbor: Mexico in the Global Sixties* (2020), and *Refried Elvis: The Rise of the Mexican Counterculture* (1999), in addition to several edited collections. He has published widely on popular culture, twentieth-century Mexico, and U.S.–Latin American relations.

INDEX

Page numbers in *italics* indicate illustrations or tables.

CPSIA information can be obtained
at www.ICGtesting.com
Printed in the USA
LVHW011805030621
689285LV00013B/534